A Reading/Language Arts Program

Program Authors

Dr. Donald R. Bear
University of Nevada, Reno
Reno, Nevada

Dr. Janice A. Dole
University of Utah
Salt Lake City, Utah

Dr. Jana Echevarria
California State University, Long Beach
Long Beach, California

Dr. Douglas Fisher
San Diego State University
San Diego, California

Dr. Vicki Gibson
Longmire Learning Center, Inc.
College Station, Texas

Dr. Jan E. Hasbrouck
Educational Consultant - J.H. Consulting
Seattle, Washington

Dr. Scott G. Paris
University of Michigan
Ann Arbor, Michigan

Dr. Timothy Shanahan
University of Illinois at Chicago
Chicago, Illinois

Dr. Josefina V. Tinajero
University of Texas at El Paso
El Paso, Texas

Macmillan/McGraw-Hill

Contributors

Time Magazine, Accelerated Reader

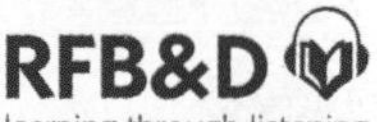

Students with print disabilities may be eligible to obtain an accessible, audio version of the pupil edition of this textbook. Please call Recording for the Blind & Dyslexic at 1-800-221-4792 for complete information.

A

The McGraw·Hill Companies

Published by Macmillan/McGraw-Hill, of McGraw-Hill Education, a division of The McGraw-Hill Companies, Inc., Two Penn Plaza, New York, New York 10121.

Printed in the United States of America

2 3 4 5 6 7 8 9 006/043 11 10 09 08 07

Program Authors

Dr. Donald R. Bear

University of Nevada, Reno
- Author of *Words Their Way* and *Words Their Way with English Learners*
- Director, E.L. Cord Foundation Center for Learning and Literacy

Dr. Douglas Fisher

San Diego State University
- Co-Director, Center for the Advancement of Reading, California State University
- Author of *Language Arts Workshop: Purposeful Reading and Writing Instruction* and *Reading for Information in Elementary School*

Dr. Scott G. Paris

University of Michigan, Ann Arbor
- Chair, Graduate Program in Psychology, University of Michigan
- Principal Investigator, CIERA, 1997–2004

Dr. Janice A. Dole

University of Utah
- Investigator, IES Study on Reading Interventions
- National Academy of Sciences, Committee Member: Teacher Preparation Programs, 2005–2007

Dr. Vicki Gibson

- Owner and Director, Longmire Learning Center, Inc.
  College Station, Texas
- Author of *Differentiating Instruction: Grouping for Success*

Dr. Timothy Shanahan

University of Illinois at Chicago
- Member, National Reading Panel
- President, International Reading Association, 2006
- Chair, National Literacy Panel and National Early Literacy Panel

Dr. Jana Echevarria

California State University, Long Beach
- Author of *Making Content Comprehensible for English Learners: The SIOP Model*
- Principal Researcher, Center for Research on the Educational Achievement and Teaching of English Language Learners

Dr. Jan E. Hasbrouck

Educational Consultant
- Developed oral reading fluency norms for Grades 1–8
- Author of *The Reading Coach: A How-to Manual for Success*

Dr. Josefina V. Tinajero

University of Texas at El Paso
- Past President, NABE and TABE
- Co-Editor of *Teaching All the Children: Strategies for Developing Literacy in an Urban Setting* and *Literacy Assessment of Second Language Learners*

Contributing Authors

Dr. Adria F. Klein
Professor Emeritus,
California State University,
San Bernardino

- **President, California Reading Association, 1995**
- **Co-author of *Interactive Writing* and *Interactive Editing***

Dr. Doris Walker-Dalhouse
Minnesota State University,
Moorhead

- **Author of articles on multicultural literature and reading instruction in urban schools**
- **Co-chair of the Ethnicity, Race, and Multilingualism Committee, NRC**

Dolores B. Malcolm
St. Louis Public Schools
St. Louis, MO

- **Past President, International Reading Association**
- **Member, IRA Urban Diversity Initiatives Commission**
- **Member, RIF Advisory Board**

In memory of our esteemed colleague and friend, Dr. Steven A. Stahl

Program Consultants

Dr. Stephanie Al Otaiba
Assistant Professor,
College of Education
Florida State University

Dr. Susan M. Brookhart
Brookhart Enterprises LLC – Helena, MT
Coordinator of Assessment and Evaluation
Duquesne University, Pittsburgh, PA

Kathy R. Bumgardner
Language Arts Instructional Specialist
Gaston County Schools, NC

Dr. Connie R. Hebert
National Literacy Consultant
Lesley University
The ReadWrite Place
West Springfield, MA

Dr. Sharon F. O'Neal
Associate Professor,
College of Education
Texas State University – San Marcos

Dinah Zike
Dinah-Might Adventures, L.P.
San Antonio, TX

Florida Program Reviewers

Holly Bagwell
Reading Resource Specialist, K–5
Horizon Elementary
Broward County
Sunrise, FL

Janice Choice
Principal
Pinelock Elementary
Orange County
Orlando, FL

Dr. Lillian Cooper
Principal on Special Assignment
LA/Reading K–5
Miami-Dade County
Miami Springs, FL

Stacey Councill
Teacher, Grade 2
Manatee Elementary
Brevard County
Viera, FL

Michelle D'Intino
Academic Intervention
Specialist
Just Elementary
Hillsborough County
Tampa, FL

DeeAnna Durden
Teacher, Grade 2
Hogan-Spring Glen Elementary
Duval County
Jacksonville, FL

Mary Fischer
Reading Resource Specialist
K–5
Nob Hill Elementary
Broward County
Sunrise FL

Sherri Goodwin
Reading Resource Teacher
Morgan Woods Elementary
Hillsborough County
Tampa, FL

Elaine Grohol
Elementary Instructional
Specialist
Osceola County
Kissimmee, FL

Deborah Jackson
Teacher, Grade 1
Citrus Elementary
Orange County
Ocoee, FL

Katy Kearson
Reading First Coach, Grades
K–3
Duval County
Jacksonville, FL

Pam LaRiviere
Reading/Curriculum Specialist
Grades K–5
Lehigh Elementary
Lee County
Lehigh Acres, FL

Robin Matthes
Principal
Hillcrest Elementary
Orange County
Orlando, FL

Lois Mautte
AP Schwarzkopf Elementary
Hillsborough County
Lutz, FL

Mary Mickel
Principal
Sabal Palm Elementary
Duval County
Jacksonville, FL

Joy Milner
Reading Specialist
Wesley Chapel Elementary
Pasco County
Wesley Chapel, FL

Carla Mosley
Reading First Coach, Grades
K–3
Broward County
Fort Lauderdale, FL

Beth Nichols
Teacher, Kindergarten and First
Grade
Wesley Chapel Elementary
Pasco County
Wesley Chapel, FL

Melinda Ossorio
Reading Resource Specialist, K–5
Watkins Elementary
Broward County
Miramar, FL

Tara Taylor
Assistant Principal
Port Malabar Elementary
Brevard County
Palm Bay, FL

Blanca Villalobos
Teacher, Grade 5
Christina Eve Elementary
Miami-Dade County
Miami, FL

Harriet Waas
Teacher, Grade 4
Pineview Elementary School
Leon County
Tallahassee, FL

Robin White
Reading First Instructional
Specialist
Fulton Holland Educational
Center
Palm Beach County
West Palm Beach, FL

Deborah Wood
Reading Facilitator
Elementary Programs
Brevard County
Viera, FL

Why It Matters

Comprehension

Janice A. Dole

Comprehension strategies are routines or procedures that teachers can use to improve students' reading comprehension. The goal of strategy instruction is to assist students in becoming independent, active, and engaged readers that use multiple strategies as they read.

There are a number of strategies that have been shown to improve reading comprehension. Some of these strategies include analyzing story structure or text structure, making mental images (visualizing), asking questions, summarizing, and using graphic organizers.

Best Practices

Effective comprehension instruction

- explains the purpose of the strategy and when to use it
- models for students how to use the strategy while reading
- offers guided practice in using the strategy
- provides opportunities for students to demonstrate use of the strategy
- teaches students how to be flexible in the use of their strategies

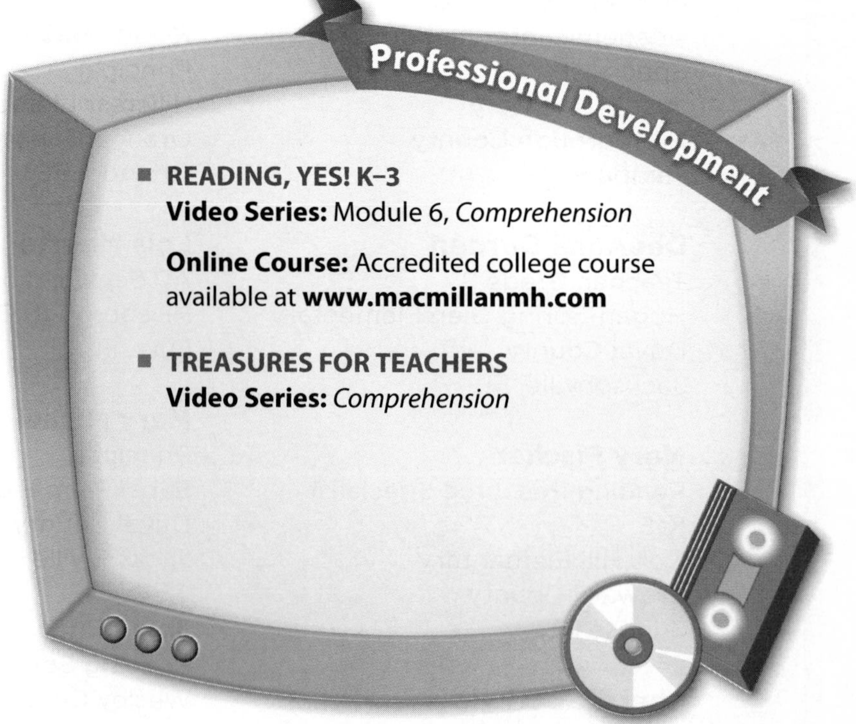

- **READING, YES! K–3**
  Video Series: Module 6, *Comprehension*

  Online Course: Accredited college course available at **www.macmillanmh.com**
- **TREASURES FOR TEACHERS**
  Video Series: *Comprehension*

References

- Dole, J. A., Duffy, G., Roehler, L. R., & Pearson, P. D. P. (1991). Moving from the old to the new: Research on reading comprehension instruction. *Review of Educational Research*, 61, 239–264.
- Pressley, M., Alamsi, J., Schuder, T., Bergman, J., & Kurita, J. A. (1994). Transactional instruction of comprehension strategies: The Montgomery County, MD, SAIL Program. *Reading & Writing Quarterly: Overcoming Learning Difficulties*, 10(1), 5–19.
- *Report of the National Reading Panel*, National Institute of Child Health and Human Development (NICHD), 2000.
- Rosenshine, B., & Meister, C. (1994). Reciprocal teaching: A review of the research. *Review of Educational Research*, 64 (4), 475–530.

Theme: Determination

Planning the Unit

Using the Student Book

Wrapping Up the Unit

Additional Lessons and Resources

Main Selections

Unit Assessment

Unit 4 Contents

Theme: Determination

pages 10J–45V

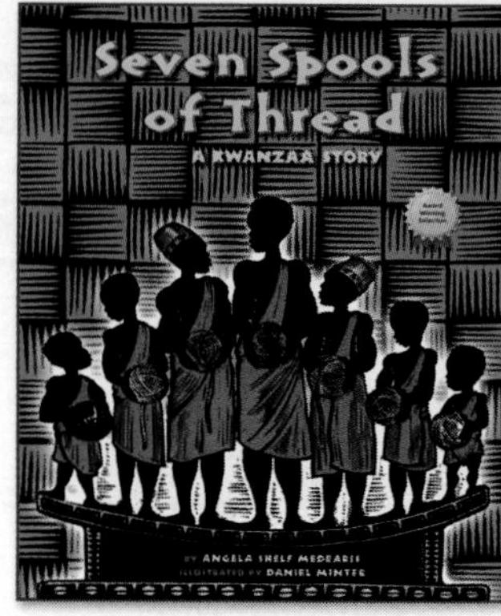

pages 46A–77V

	WEEK 1	WEEK 2
ORAL LANGUAGE • **Listening, Speaking, Viewing**	**Theme** What's Cooking? **Build Background**	**Theme** Getting Along **Build Background**
WORD STUDY • **Vocabulary**	**Vocabulary** FCAT *magnificent, masterpiece, ingredient, recipes, tasty* FCAT Dictionary: Idioms	**Vocabulary** FCAT *beamed, argued, possessions, fabric, purchased, quarreling* FCAT Dictionary: Multiple-Meaning Words
• **Phonics/Decoding**	**Phonics** Words with /ô/	**Phonics** Words with /ou/
READING • **Comprehension**	**Comprehension** Strategy: Make Inferences and Analyze FCAT Skill: Compare Characters, Settings, Events	**Comprehension** Strategy: Make Inferences and Analyze FCAT Skill: Plot Development
• **Fluency**	**Fluency** Repeated Reading	**Fluency** Repeated Reading
• **Leveled Readers/ELL Readers**	APPROACHING *Measurement* ON LEVEL *Measurement* BEYOND *Measurement* ENGLISH LANGUAGE LEARNERS *Measure Up*	APPROACHING *Androcles and the Lion* ON LEVEL *A True Hero* BEYOND *The Lost Brocade* ENGLISH LANGUAGE LEARNERS *The Diamond*
LANGUAGE ARTS • **Writing**	**Writing** Narrative	**Writing** Poster
• **Grammar**	**Grammar** Verbs *be, do,* and *have*	**Grammar** Linking Verbs
• **Spelling**	**Spelling** Words with /ô/	**Spelling** Words with /ou/

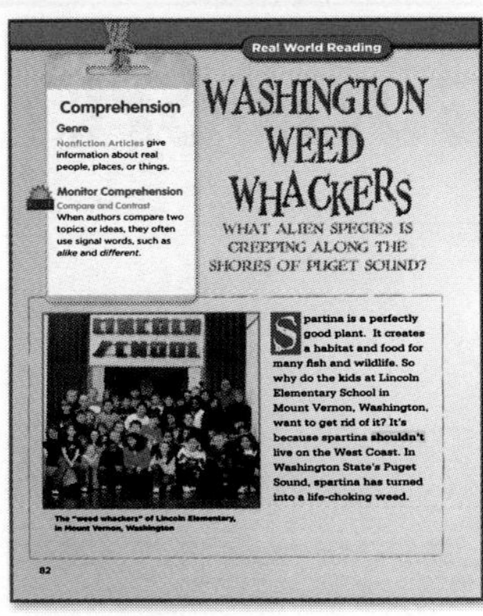

pages 78A–89V

pages 90A–111V

pages 112A–145V

Review and Assess

WEEK 3

Theme
Protecting Our Natural Resources

Build Background

Vocabulary
FCAT *native, shouldn't, research, sprout, clumps*

FCAT Word Parts: Contractions

Phonics
Words with Soft *c* and *g*

Comprehension
Strategy: Monitor Comprehension
FCAT Skill: Compare and Contrast

Fluency
Repeated Reading

APPROACHING
Resources All Around Us

ON LEVEL
Resources All Around Us

BEYOND
Resources All Around Us

ENGLISH LANGUAGE LEARNERS
Resources

Writing
Personal Narrative

Grammar
Main and Helping Verbs

Spelling
Words with Soft *c* and *g*

WEEK 4

Theme
Getting Involved

Build Background

Vocabulary
FCAT *tour, volunteers, community, thrilled, slogan, grownups, deserve, interviewed*

FCAT Context Clues: Example

Phonics
Homophones

Comprehension
Strategy: Monitor Comprehension
FCAT Skill: Author's Purpose

Fluency
Repeated Reading

APPROACHING
Patching a Playground

ON LEVEL
Patching a Playground

BEYOND
Patching a Playground

ENGLISH LANGUAGE LEARNERS
Kids Make a Difference

Writing
Expository

Grammar
Irregular Verbs

Spelling
Homophones

WEEK 5

Theme
A Place of My Own

Build Background

Vocabulary
FCAT *separate, determination, storage, crate, exact, ruined, luckiest*

FCAT Word Parts: Endings *-er, -est*

Phonics
Plurals

Comprehension
Strategy: Monitor Comprehension
FCAT Skill: Plot Development

Fluency
Repeated Reading

APPROACHING
The Slightly Tipping Tree House

ON LEVEL
A Winter Adventure

BEYOND
The Science Fair

ENGLISH LANGUAGE LEARNERS
Safe in the Storm

Writing
Expository

Grammar
Contractions with *not*

Spelling
Plurals

WEEK 6

FCAT **Spiral Review**
Draw Conclusions
Compare and Contrast
Author's Purpose
Context Clues
Multiple-Meaning Words
Time Line

FCAT **Writing Workshop**
Expository

Unit 4 Assessment, 111–144

Comprehension
Compare Characters, Settings, Events; Plot Development; Compare and Contrast; Author's Purpose

Vocabulary Strategies
Dictionary: Idioms, Multiple-Meaning Words; Context Clues: Examples; Word Parts: Contractions, Endings *-er, -est*

Text Features/Literary Elements/Study Skills
Diagram; Rules; Using Computer Search Engines; Rhyme Scheme, Refrain, Repetition; Features of an Encyclopedia Article

Grammar
Verbs

Writing
Expository

Fluency Assessment

Diagnose and Prescribe
Interpret Assessment Results

Literature

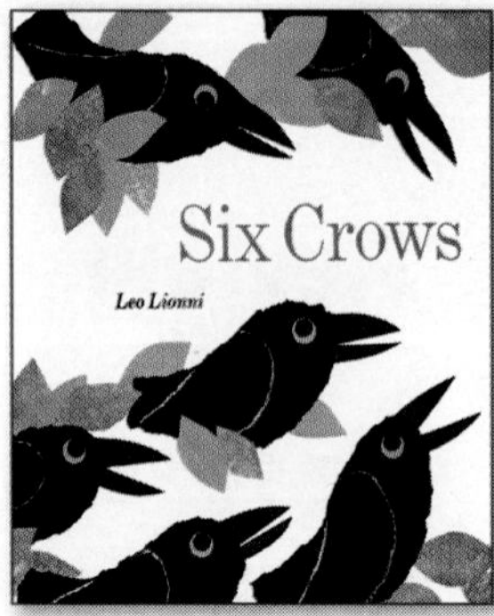

Read Big Book to Introduce Unit Theme

Student Edition

Read-Aloud Anthology Includes Plays for Readers' Theater

Intervention Anthology

Leveled Readers

ELL Reader

Classroom Library Trade Books

Teaching Support

Teacher's Edition

Transparencies

ELL Teacher's Guide

Teacher's Resource Book

Dinah Zike Foldables™

Vocabulary Cards

Class Management Tools

Small Group How-To Guide

Weekly Contracts

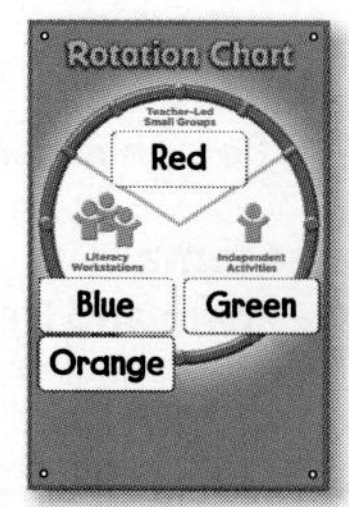

Rotation Chart

Student Practice

Approaching Level | On Level | Beyond Level | English Language Learners

Leveled Practice

Phonics/Spelling Practice Book

Grammar Practice Book

Home-School Connection
- Take-Home Stories
- Homework Activities

Literacy Workstation Activities

FCAT Success!

Time for Kids FCAT Edition with Teacher's Manual

Time for Kids Articles on Transparencies

FCAT Test Prep and Practice

Questions in FCAT Format

Technology

AUDIO CD
- Listening Library
- Fluency Solutions

CD-ROM
- New Adventures with Buggles and Beezy
- Vocabulary PuzzleMaker
- Handwriting
- Instructional Navigator Interactive Lesson Planner
- Student Navigator
- Accelerated Reader Quizzes

LOG ON www.macmillanmh.com
- Author/Illustrator Information
- Research and Inquiry Activities
- Vocabulary and Spelling Activities
- Oral Language Activities
- Computer Literacy
- Leveled Reader Database
- Florida Anchor Papers and Constructed Response Sample Responses

READING, YES!
- Videos
- Online Course

TREASURES FOR TEACHERS
- Videos

READING **Triumphs**

AN INTERVENTION PROGRAM

Treasure Chest

FOR ENGLISH LANGUAGE LEARNERS

Screening, Diagnostic, and Placement Assessments

Screening

Use your state or district screener to identify students at risk. See pages 5–12 in our **Screening, Diagnostic, Placement Assessment** book for information on using DIBELS and TPRI as screeners.

Diagnostic Tools for Instructional Placement

For individually-administered Diagnostics, use TPRI or your state or district diagnostic assessment. See pages 13–20 for diagnostic information, and the Informal Reading Inventory passages on pages 96–103 in our **Screening, Diagnostic, Placement Assessment** book.

For a group-administered Placement Test, see pages 199–208 in our **Screening, Diagnostic, Placement Assessment** book.

Use the results from these assessments to determine the instructional levels of your students for differentiated instruction grouping.

Monitoring Progress

Ongoing Informal Assessments

- Daily Quick Check Observations
- Weekly Comprehension Check
- Weekly Fluency Practice Passages

Formal Assessments

- **Weekly Assessment**
- **Fluency Assessment**
- **Running Records**
- **Unit Assessment**
- **Benchmark Assessment**
- **ELL Practice and Assessment**

  Weekly Tests

  Unit Progress Test

Managing and Reporting

Assessment Online

Instructional Navigator Interactive Lesson Planner

- All Teacher Edition pages
- Student Blackline Masters
- Electronic Lesson Planner

FCAT

Test Alignment

GRADE 3 UNIT 4 ASSESSED SKILLS	FCAT	DIBELS*	TPRI
COMPREHENSION STRATEGIES AND SKILLS			
• Strategies: Make Inferences and Analyze, Monitor Comprehension	◆	◆	◆
• Skills: Compare Characters, Settings, Events; Plot Development; Compare and Contrast; Author's Purpose	◆	◆	◆
VOCABULARY STRATEGIES			
• Dictionary: Multiple-Meaning Words	◆		◆
• Word parts	◆	◆	◆
• Context clues	◆		◆
TEXT FEATURES AND STUDY SKILLS			
• Diagrams	◆		
• Using computer search engines in the media center			
• Guide words, headings, and captions (encyclopedia articles)	◆		
GRAMMAR, MECHANICS, USAGE			
• Linking, helping, and irregular verbs	◆		
• Contractions with *not*	◆		
• End punctuation and complete sentences	◆		
• Quotation marks in dialogue	◆		
• Subject-verb agreement	◆		
• Correct verb forms	◆		
WRITING			
• Expository	◆		

*Data from DIBELS serve as indicators of overall reading comprehension performance, not specific skills.

KEY

FCAT	Florida Comprehension Achievement Test	TPRI	Texas Primary Reading Inventory
DIBELS*	Dynamic Indicators of Basic Early Literacy Skills		

*Data from DIBELS serve as indicators of overall reading comprehension performance, not specific skills.

Theme Project

LA.3.6.2.1 Determine information needed for a search

Build Background Write this theme statement on the board: Persevere to meet your goals. Explain that to *persevere* means "to keep on going, even when you get discouraged." Ask:

- What goals do you have?
- What challenges do you face in meeting your goals?
- What helps you persevere when you get discouraged?

Research and Inquiry

LA.3.6.2 Use a systematic research process for the collection, processing, and presentation of information.

Self-Selected Theme Project

LA.3.6.2.1 Determine information needed by identifying key words
LA.3.3.1.1 Generate ideas from multiple sources

Step 1 **State the Problem and Identify Needed Information** Tell students to think about a goal they want to accomplish when they get older. It can be a career goal, a sports goal, or any other goal they have thought about. They are going to research information that could help them meet their goal. Help students choose two areas of interest and brainstorm ideas and key words for their research.

LA.3.6.1.1 Read and organize informational text for purpose of conducting interviews
LA.3.6.2.2 Select multiple representations of information to gather information

Step 2 **Identify Resources for Finding Information** Tell students to think of sources that probably have information about the goal they would like to meet or people who have accomplished it. You might suggest interviews, encyclopedias, autobiographies and biographies, diaries and letters, and personal essays. Remind students to respect the age, gender, position, and culture of anyone they interview.

RESEARCH STRATEGIES

Take Notes

- Write your information in an organized way, so that you will understand it later.
- You can use your sources to write an outline or to make a list of steps in a process (such as reaching a goal).
- Write events in time order.
- Write steps from first to last.
- List all resources.

LA.3.6.2.3 Communicate information in format that includes main ideas and relevant details;
LA.3.4.2.2 Record information related to a topic

LA.3.6.2.2 Select reference materials

Step 3 **Find the Information** Have students find information in at least three of the sources they identified. They can also use the library or media center.

LA.3.6.1.1 Organize information for purpose of making a report

Step 4 **Organize the Information** Have students take sequenced, organized notes using key words for the purpose of making a report.

See the Unit Closer on pages 149K–149L for **Step 5: Create the Presentation** and **Step 6: Review and Evaluate.**

Cross-Curricular Projects

Art Activity

LA.3.6.4.2 Use digital tools to present and publish; LA.3.6.3 Develop and demonstrate an understanding of media literacy

GET THE MESSAGE

Point out that determination is presented in different media including cartoons or comic strips.

- Have students find a cartoon or comic strip in which someone shows tremendous determination—for better or worse.
- Have students create their own cartoon that expresses their own point of view about determination. Remind students they can use digital tools, such as multimedia, to help with their cartoons. Have students share their cartoons and the ideas.

Science Activity

LA.3.6.1.1 Read and organize information for purpose of making a report; LA.3.5.2 Apply listening and speaking strategies; LA.3.6.2.3 Communicate information in an informational report

SC.H.3.2.1.3.1 Contribution of scientists; SC.H.3.2.1.3.2 Reference materials related to science concepts

AGAINST THE ODDS

Have students do library research to learn how a scientist's discoveries helped him or her overcome obstacles to meet a goal.

- You may wish to assign a scientist, such as George Washington Carver or Barbara McClintock (who earned a Nobel Prize in Physiology, or Medicine).
- Have students present their findings in a written report in which they tell about the scientist and discuss concepts related to his or her discoveries.
- Encourage students to ask questions and contribute to discussions.

CHARACTER BUILDING—RESPONSIBILITY

While students are researching scientists who showed determination, discuss the relationship between determination and responsibility. Explain that responsibility means to do your best—and to keep on trying. Ask students to describe additional ways of being responsible to themselves and to others.

DISCUSSION AND CONVERSATION GUIDELINES

Working in Groups

When working in groups remind students to:

- Respectfully ask questions to obtain or clarify information.
- Work together to solve problems and understand tasks.
- Share their information with others in an appropriate way, using formal and informal language.

LA.3.5.2 Apply listening and speaking strategies

For Technology research and presentation strategies, see the Computer Literacy Lessons on pages 149I–149J.

LA.3.6.4.1 Use appropriate available technologies

Student Book Selections

Weekly Theme: What's Cooking?

Week At A Glance

Whole Group

VOCABULARY
ingredient, magnificent, masterpiece, recipes, tasty

FCAT Dictionary/Idioms

COMPREHENSION
Strategy: Make Inferences and Analyze
FCAT **Skill:** Compare Characters

WRITING
FCAT Narrative/Paragraph

FCAT **Science**
The Nature of Matter

Small Group Options

Differentiated Instruction for Tested Skills

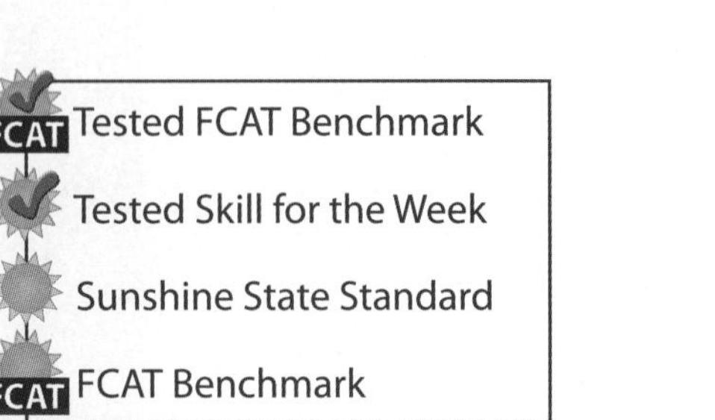

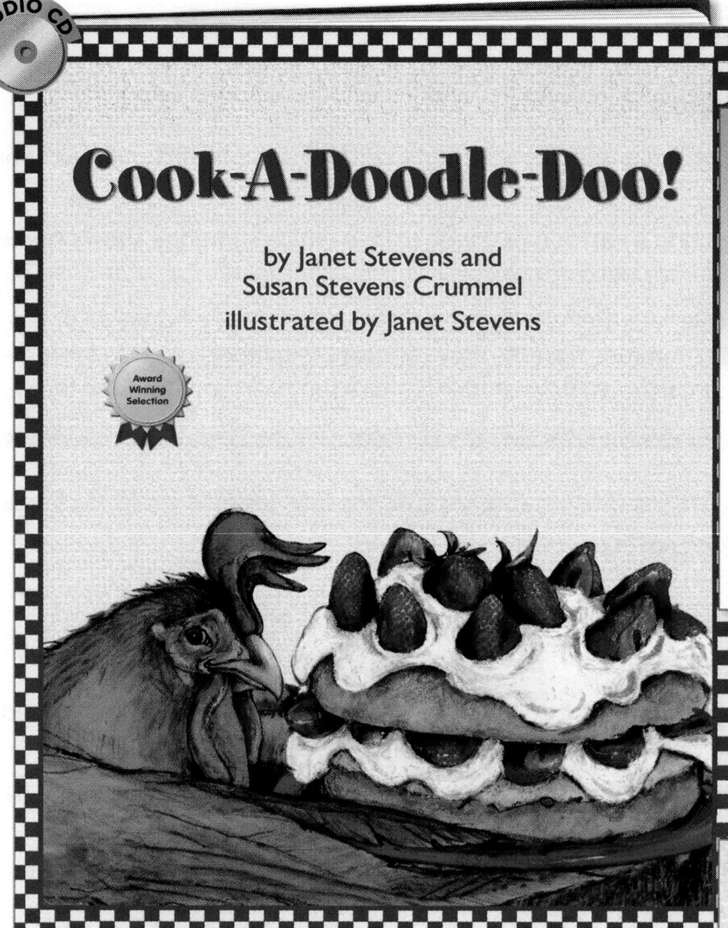

AUDIO CD
Cook-A-Doodle-Doo!
by Janet Stevens and
Susan Stevens Crummel
illustrated by Janet Stevens
Award Winning Selection

Main Selection

Genre Humorous Fiction

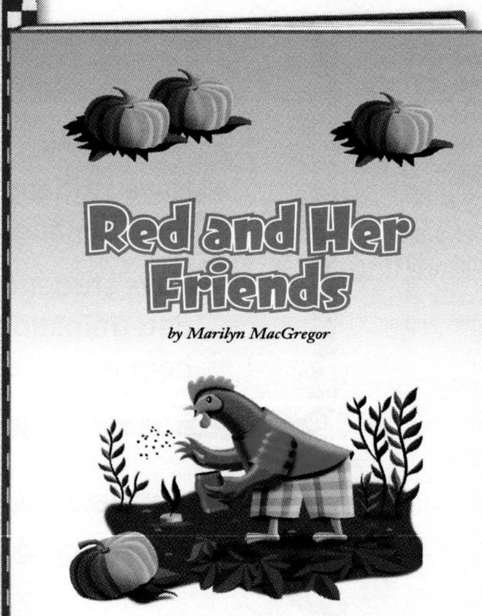

Vocabulary/ Comprehension

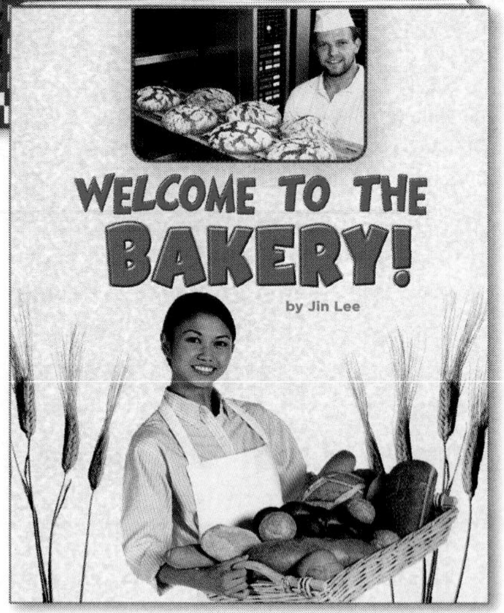

Science Link

Genre Nonfiction Article

Read-Aloud Anthology
- Listening Comprehension
- Readers' Theater

Resources for Differentiated Instruction

FCAT LEVELED READERS: Science

GR Levels M–Q

Genre Informational Nonfiction

- Same Theme
- Same Vocabulary
- Same Comprehension Skills

Approaching Level

On Level

Beyond Level

English Language Leveled Reader

Sheltered Readers for English Language Learners

ELL Teacher's Guide also available

LEVELED PRACTICE

Approaching

On Level

Beyond

ELL

INTERVENTION PROGRAM

- Phonics and Decoding
- Comprehension
- Vocabulary

Also available, *Reading Triumphs*, Intervention Program

CLASSROOM LIBRARY

Genre Informational Nonfiction

Approaching

On Level

Beyond

Trade books to apply Comprehension Skills

FCAT Success!

- FCAT Edition
- Content Area Reading

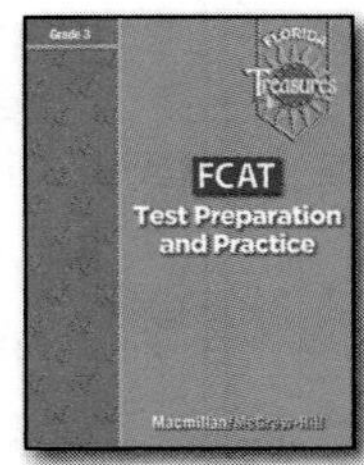

FCAT Test Preparation and Practice

FCAT Benchmark Assessments

FCAT Unit and Weekly Assessments

HOME-SCHOOL CONNECTION

- Family letters in English, Spanish, and Haitian Creole
- Take-Home Stories

FLORIDA Suggested Lesson Plan

Cook-A-Doodle-Doo! 14–37

Integrated ELL Support Every Day

Whole Group	Day 1	Day 2
ORAL LANGUAGE • Listening • Speaking • Viewing	**Listening/Speaking/Viewing** Focus Question What snack or meal do you know how to make. Tell how you make it. Build Background, 10 **Read Aloud:** "When the Rain Came Up from China," 11 LA.3.2.1	**Listening/Speaking** Focus Question Who will help Rooster bake a strawberry shortcake? LA.3.5.2
WORD STUDY • Vocabulary • Phonics/Decoding	**Vocabulary** LA.3.1.6.1 *magnificent, masterpiece, ingredient, recipes, tasty,* 12 Practice Book A-O-B, 112 FCAT **Strategy:** Dictionary: Idioms, 13 LA.3.1.6.10	**Vocabulary** LA.3.1.6.1 Review Vocabulary Words, 14 **Phonics** LA.3.1.4.1 Decode Words with /ô/, 45E Practice Book A-O-B, 118
READING • Develop Comprehension • Fluency	**Read** "Red and Her Friends," 12–13 LA.3.1.6.1 Student Book **Comprehension,** 13A–13B **Strategy:** Make Inferences and Analyze FCAT **Skill:** Compare Characters LA.3.2.1 Practice Book A-O-B, 113 **Fluency** Partner Reading, 10R LA.3.1.5 Model Fluency, 11	**Read** *Cook-A-Doodle-Doo,* 14–37 LA.3.2.1 Student Book **Comprehension,** 14–37 **Strategy:** Make Inferences and Analyze FCAT **Skill:** Compare Characters LA.3.2.1 Practice Book A-O-B, 114 **Fluency** Partner Reading, 10R LA.3.1.5.2 Echo-Reading, 23
LANGUAGE ARTS • Writing • Grammar • Spelling	FCAT **Writing** Daily Writing: Write a step-by-step recipe for a food you know how to cook. Narrative, 44–45B LA.3.4.1.1 **Grammar** Daily Language Activities, 45I Verbs *Be, Do,* and *Have,* 45I LA.3.3.4.4 Grammar Practice Book, 97 **Spelling** Pretest, 45G LA.3.3.4.1 Spelling Practice Book, 97–98	FCAT **Writing** Daily Writing: Write a menu for a dinner you would like a chef to cook for you. Include your favorite foods. Narrative, 44–45B LA.3.4.1.1 **Grammar** Daily Language Activities, 45I Verbs *Be, Do,* and *Have,* 45I LA.3.3.4.4 Grammar Practice Book, 98 **Spelling** Words with /ô/, 45G LA.3.1.4 Spelling Practice Book, 99
ASSESSMENT • Informal/Formal	Quick Check **Vocabulary,** 12 **Comprehension,** 13B	Quick Check **Comprehension,** 25, 37 **Phonics,** 45E
Turn the Page for Small Group Lesson Plan	Differentiated Instruction 45M–45V	Differentiated Instruction 45M–45V

FCAT Benchmarks

Vocabulary	Comprehension	Writing	Science
Vocabulary Words **Dictionary/Idioms** **LA.3.1.6.10** Determine meanings using a dictionary	**Strategy: Make Inferences and Analyze** **Skill: Compare Characters** **LA.3.2.1.2** Identify plot, character, and setting	**Narrative** **LA.3.4.1.1** Write narratives	**The Nature of Matter** **SC.A.1.2.1.3.1** Measurement

Turn the Page for **Small Group Options**

Day 3

Listening/Speaking

Focus Question How is "Red and Her Friends" similar to *Cook-A-Doodle-Doo!*? How are the two stories different?

Summarize, 39 LA.3.1.7.8

Vocabulary LA.3.1.6.3

Review Words in Context, 45C

FCAT **Strategy:** Dictionary: Idioms, 45D LA.3.2.1.5

Practice Book A-O-B, 117

Phonics

Decode Multisyllable Words, 45E LA.3.1.4.3

Read *Cook-A-Doodle-Doo!*, 14–37 LA.3.2.1

Student Book

Comprehension

FCAT Comprehension Check, 39

Skill: Author's Purpose, 39B LA.3.1.7.2

Fluency Partner Reading, 10R

Repeated Reading, 39A

Practice Book A-O-B, 115 LA.3.1.5.2

FCAT Writing

Daily Writing: Suppose that you are one of Rooster's friends who shared the strawberry shortcake. Describe how the shortcake tasted and how you felt while eating it.

Writer's Craft: Vary Sentences, 45A LA.3.3.3.2

Narrative, 44–45B LA.3.4.1.1

Grammar Daily Language Activities, 45I

Subject-Verb Agreement, 45J LA.3.3.4.5

Grammar Practice Book, 99

Spelling Words with /ô/, 45H LA.3.1.6

Spelling Practice Book, 100

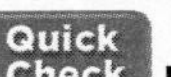
Quick Check **Fluency,** 39A

Differentiated Instruction 45M–45V

Day 4

Listening/Speaking

Focus Question How is making bread like making a strawberry shortcake?

Expand Vocabulary: Cooking Tools, 45F LA.3.1.6.4

Vocabulary LA.3.1.6.1

Content Vocabulary: *measurements, temperature, thermometer,* 40

Homophones, 45F LA.3.1.6.8

Apply Vocabulary to Writing, 45F

Phonics LA.3.1.6

Rhyming Riddles, 45E

Read "Welcome to the Bakery!" 40–43

Student Book

Comprehension

Science: Nonfiction Article LA.3.2.2

FCAT **Text Feature:** Diagrams, 40

Practice Book A-O-B, 116

Fluency Partner Reading, 10R LA.3.1.5

FCAT Writing

Daily Writing: Write a description of the best meal you ever tasted. Explain why it was so good.

Writing Trait: Ideas and Content, 45B LA.3.3.3.3

Narrative, 44–45B LA.3.4.1.1

Grammar Daily Language Activities, 45I

Verbs *Be, Do,* and *Have,* 45J LA.3.3.4.4

Grammar Practice Book, 100

Spelling Words with /ô/, 45H LA.3.3.4.1

Spelling Practice Book, 101

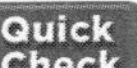
Quick Check **Vocabulary,** 45D

Differentiated Instruction 45M–45V

Day 5 Review and Assess

Listening/Speaking

Focus Question Compare Red's friends to Rooster's friends. Are Red's friends as helpful as Rooster's friends? Explain.

Speaking and Listening Strategies, 45A

Vocabulary LA.3.1.6

Spiral Review: Vocabulary Concentration Game, 45F

Read Self-Selected Reading, 10R

Student Book

FCAT Comprehension

Connect and Compare, 43 LA.3.1.7.3

Fluency Partner Reading, 10R LA.3.1.5

Practice, 39A

FCAT Writing

Daily Writing: Who is your favorite character in *Cook-A-Doodle-Doo!*? Write about what makes this character your favorite.

Narrative, 44–45B LA.3.4.1.1

Grammar Daily Language Activities, 45I

Verbs *Be, Do,* and *Have,* 45J LA.3.3.4.5

Grammar Practice Book, 101–102

Spelling Posttest, 45H LA.3.1.6

Spelling Practice Book, 102

FCAT **Weekly Assessment, 189–200**

Differentiated Instruction 45M–45V

Differentiated Instruction

What do I do in small groups?

Focus on Skills

Use your Quick Check observations to guide additional instruction and practice.

Phonics
Decode Words with /ô/

Vocabulary
Words: magnificent, masterpiece, ingredients, recipes, tasty
FCAT **Strategy:** Dictionary/Idioms

Comprehension
Strategy: Make Inferences and Analyze

FCAT **Skill:** Compare Characters, Settings, Events

FCAT **Fluency**

Suggested Lesson Plan

	Day 1	Day 2
Approaching Level • **Additional Instruction/Practice** • **Tier 2 Instruction**	Fluency, 45N Vocabulary, 45N Comprehension, 45O 	Phonics, 45M Vocabulary, 45O Leveled Reader Lesson, 45P • Vocabulary • Comprehension 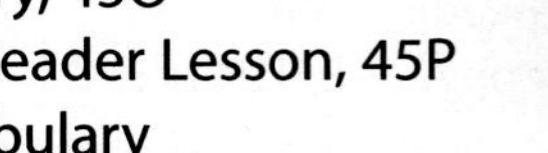
On Level • **Practice**	Vocabulary, 45Q Leveled Reader Lesson, 45R • Comprehension  ELL Leveled Reader, 45U–45V 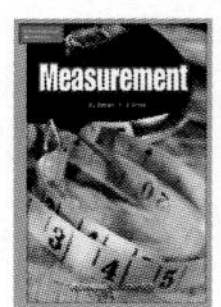	Phonics, 45M Leveled Reader Lesson, 45R • Comprehension • Vocabulary 
Beyond Level • **Extend**	Vocabulary, 45S Leveled Reader Lesson, 45T • Comprehension 	Leveled Reader Lesson, 45T • Comprehension • Vocabulary 

For intensive intervention see READING Triumphs

Small Group Options

Focus on Leveled Readers

Levels M–Q

Apply FCAT skills and strategies while reading appropriate leveled books.

Approaching

On Level

Beyond

N
Measure Up
ELL

Additional Leveled Reader Resources

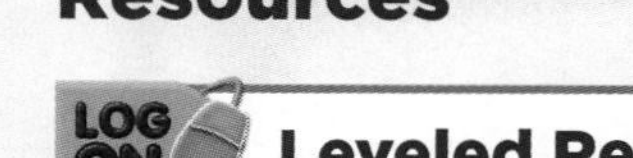

Leveled Reader Database
Go to www.macmillanmh.com

Search by

- Comprehension Skill
- Content Area
- Genre
- Text Feature
- Guided Reading Level
- Reading Recovery Level
- Lexile Score
- Benchmark Level

Subscription also available.

Focus on Science

Teacher's Annotated Edition
The Nature of Matter
SC.A.1.2.1.3.1 Measurement

Additional Leveled Readers
Oops! Food Surprises
Follow the Pizza Trail

Day 3

Phonics, 45M
Fluency, 45N
Vocabulary, 45O
Leveled Reader Lesson, 45P
- Comprehension

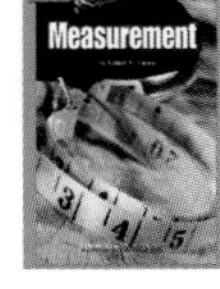

Fluency, 45Q
Vocabulary, 45Q
Leveled Reader Lesson, 45R
- Comprehension

Fluency, 45S
Vocabulary, 45S
Leveled Reader Lesson, 45T
- Comprehension

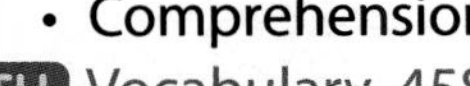
ELL Vocabulary, 45S

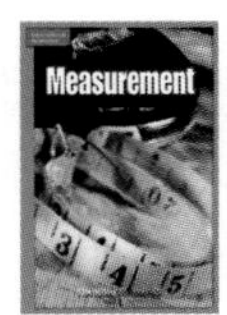

Day 4

Phonics, 45M
Leveled Reader Lesson, 45P
- Comprehension
- ELL Skill: Compare Characters, Settings, Events

Leveled Reader Lesson, 45R
- Comprehension

Text Feature, 45S
Leveled Reader Lesson, 45T
- Comprehension

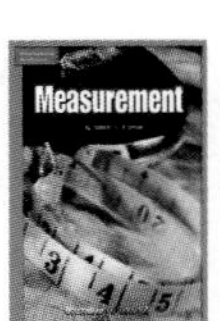

Day 5

Fluency, 45N
Leveled Reader Lesson, 45P
- Make Connections Across Texts

Fluency, 45Q
Leveled Reader Lesson, 45R
- Make Connections Across Texts

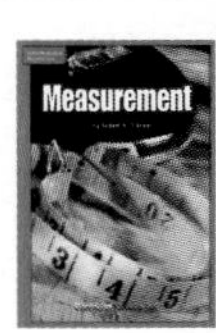

Fluency, 45S
Self-Selected Reading, 45T

Managing the Class

What do I do with the rest of my class?

Class Management Tools

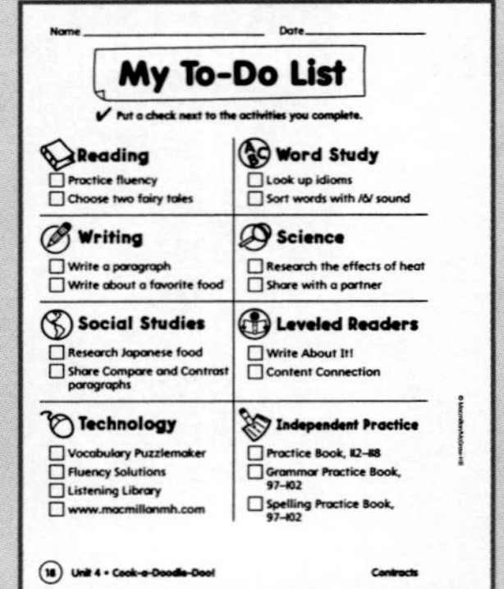

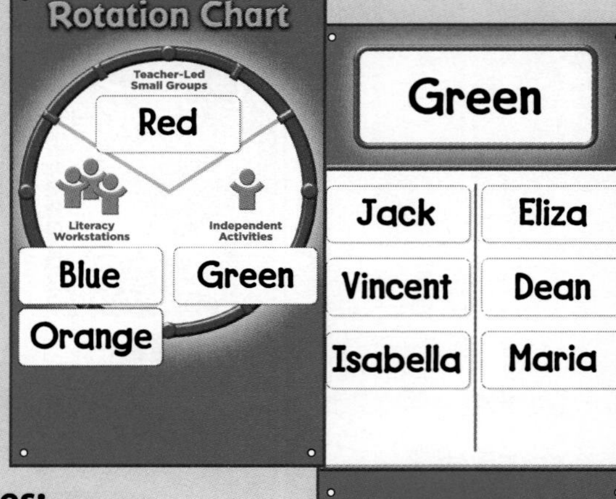

Includes:

- How-to Guide
- Rotation Chart
- Weekly Contracts

FOLDABLES™

Hands-on activities for reinforcing weekly skills

Three-Pocket Foldable

Standing Cube Foldable

Independent Activities

Reinforcing Weekly Skills

LEVELED READERS: Science

For Repeated Readings and Literacy Activities

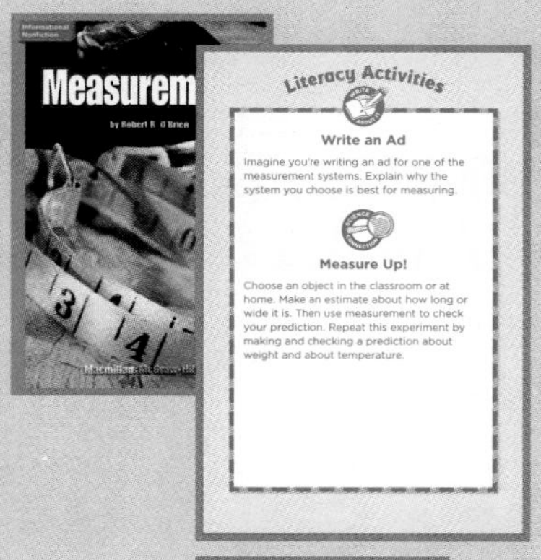

Approaching

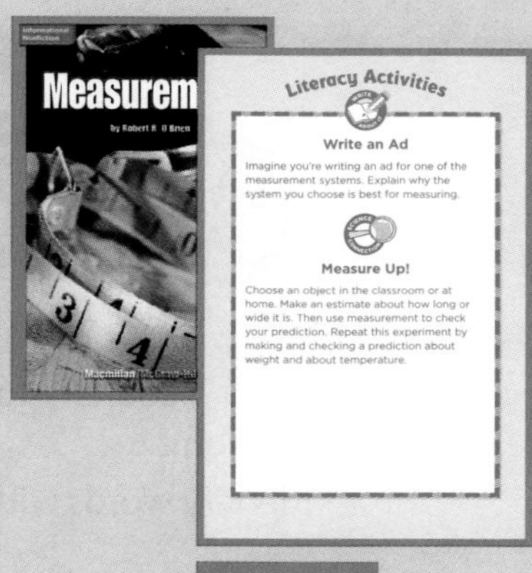

On Level

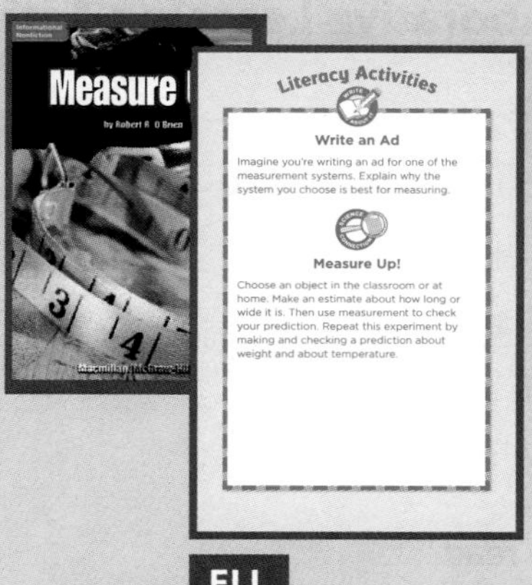

ELL

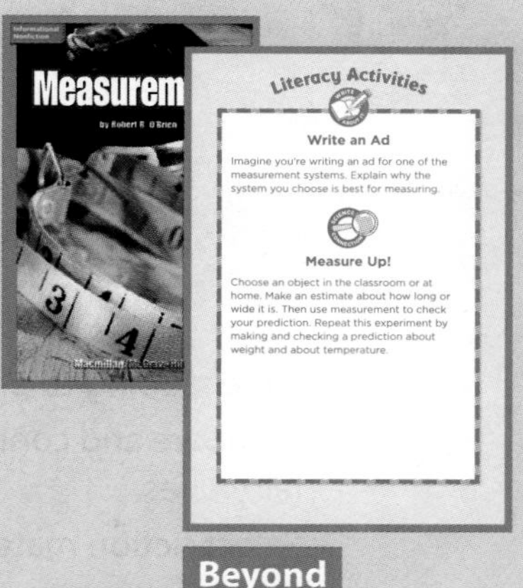

Beyond

LEVELED PRACTICE

Skills: Phonics, Vocabulary, Compare Characters, Fluency, Idioms, Diagrams

Approaching

On Level

Beyond

ELL

Technology

LOG ON

ONLINE INSTRUCTION www.macmillanmh.com

- Meet the Author/Illustrator

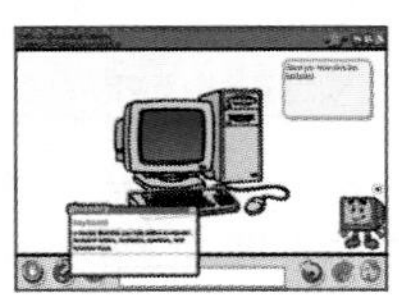

- Computer Literacy Lessons

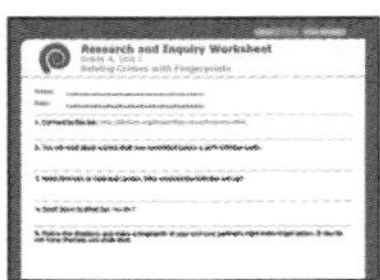

- Research and Inquiry Activities

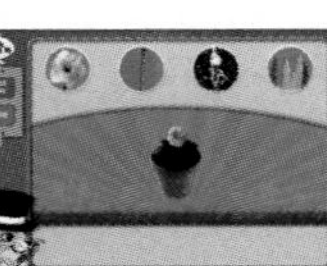

- Oral Language Activities

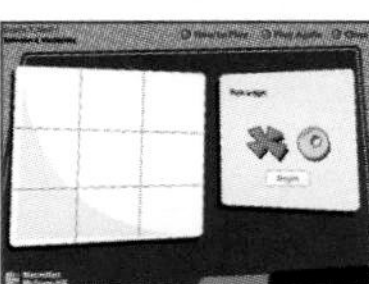

- Vocabulary and Spelling Activities

- Leveled Reader Database

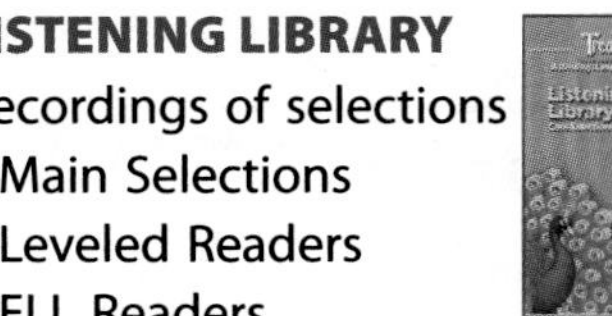

LISTENING LIBRARY

Recordings of selections
- Main Selections
- Leveled Readers
- ELL Readers
- Intervention Anthology

FLUENCY SOLUTIONS

Recorded passages for modeling and practicing fluency

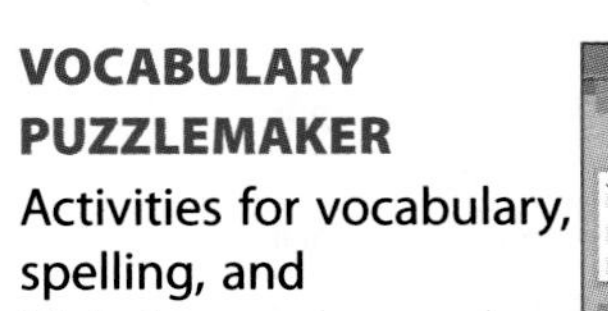

VOCABULARY PUZZLEMAKER

Activities for vocabulary, spelling, and high-frequency words

NEW ADVENTURES WITH BUGGLES AND BEEZY

Phonemic awareness and phonics practice

Turn the page for Literacy Workstations.

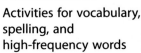

Literacy Activities

Collaborative Learning Activities

Reading

Objectives

- Time reading to practice fluency
- Compare and contrast characters in fairy tales
- Select fiction materials to read

Word Study

Objectives

- Use a dictionary to find the meaning of idioms
- Identify words with /ô/

LA.3.1.5 Demonstrate the ability to read text orally with expression

Reading — **Fluency** — 20 Minutes

- Choose a reading buddy. Take turns reading aloud page 115 of your Practice Book.
- Read the dialogue the way the character would say it. Keep in mind how reading dialogue is different reading narration.

Extension

- Read aloud page 115 of your Practice Book again. This time, do not use different voices for the characters.
- Discuss differences between reading narration and reading dialogue.
- **Time Your Reading:** Listen to the Audio CD.

Things you need:
- Practice Book

Fluency Solutions
Listening Library

31

LA.3.1.6.10 Determine meanings using a dictionary

Word Study — **Dictionary** — 20 Minutes

- An idiom is a saying that means something different from the everyday meaning of the words. People in the same region often share the same idioms.
- Use a dictionary. Learn what the underlined idiom means. Look up key words: *His team missed the goal, but he did not lose heart.*

Extension

- When you do not know the meaning of an idiom, the sentence may seem silly. Draw a picture to show the silly meaning of *lose heart*.

Things you need:
- pencil and paper
- crayons or colored markers

For additional vocabulary and spelling games, go to www.macmillanmh.com

Vocabulary PuzzleMaker

31

LA.3.1.7.7 Compare and contrast characters

Reading — **Independent Reading** — 20 Minutes

- Choose two fairy tales or fables from different countries. They may be versions of the same story or different stories.
- Compare and contrast the main characters in the two stories. Make and fill in a Compare and Contrast Chart.

Compare	Contrast

Extension

- In your response journal, write a list of your favorite fairy tales. Tell why you like them.

Things you need:
- two stories
- paper and pencil
- journal

For more book titles about What's Cooking, go to the Author/Illustrator section of www.macmillanmh.com

32

LA.3.1.4 Demonstrate knowledge of alphabetic principle

Word Study — **Words with /ô/** — 20 Minutes

- Make a chart with three columns. Write these spelling patterns at the top of the columns: *aw, au,* and *al.*
- Then write each of these words in the correct column: *lawn, salt, hauls, bawls, taught, squawk, halls, hawks, yawn.*

Extension

- Choose a partner. Take turns using these words in spoken sentences: *crawled, paused, drawing, caused.*

Things you need:
- pencil and paper

For additional vocabulary and spelling games, go to www.macmillanmh.com

New Adventures with Buggles and Beezy

32

Literacy Workstations

Writing

Objectives

- Write a paragraph explaining how to make a snack
- Write a descriptive paragraph about food
- Write with enthusiasm

Content Literacy

Objectives

- Write a compare-and-contrast paragraph
- Research the effect temperature has on liquids and solids

LA.3.4.2.1 Write in expository forms

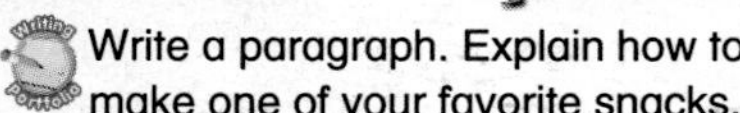

Writing — **Explanatory Writing** — 20 Minutes

- Write a paragraph. Explain how to make one of your favorite snacks.
- Include lots of details in your paragraph. Be sure to write each step in the correct order. Use time-order words, such as *first, then,* or *next.*
- You may also choose a different activity to write about in your paragraph.

Extension

- Draw a picture to illustrate your paragraph.

Things you need:

- pencil and paper
- crayons or colored markers

31

LA.3.6.2.2 Select reference materials; LA.3.4.2.1 Write in expository forms

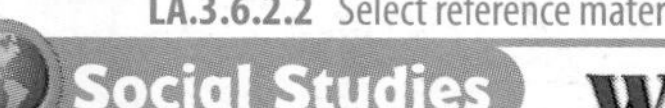

Social Studies — **What's Cooking in Japan?** — 20 Minutes

- Use an encyclopedia, a book about Japan, or the Internet. Research foods that people in Japan like to eat.
- Write a Compare and Contrast paragraph. Compare one of the foods you like to eat for lunch with one of the foods people in Japan like to eat for lunch.

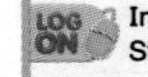

Extension

- Read your paragraph to a partner. Ask your partner to read his or her paragraph to you.

Things you need:

- encyclopedia, book about Japan, or computer
- pencil and paper

LOG ON Internet Research and Inquiry Activity
Students can find more facts at www.macmillanmh.com

31

LA.3.4.1 Develop and demonstrate creative writing

Writing — **YOUR FAVORITE FOOD** — 20 Minutes

- Write a paragraph. Describe your favorite food.
- Include lots of details in your paragraph. Tell how this food looks, smells, and tastes.

Extension

- Read your paragraph to a partner.
- Has your partner ever tried this food? Does he or she agree with your description?
- Maybe your partner has never tried this food. Did your description make your partner want to try it?

Things you need:

- pencil and paper

32

LA.3.6.1.1 Read informational text to be informed; LA.3.6.1.1 Organize information for purpose of performing a task

Science — **Heat and Energy** — 20 Minutes

- Heat is one kind of energy. We use heat to cook our food.
- Use an encyclopedia, science book, or the Internet. Learn about the effect temperature has on liquids and solids. Take notes.

Extension

- Tell a partner what you learned.

Things you need:

- encyclopedia, science book, or computer
- pencil and paper

32

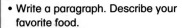

Prepare

ORAL LANGUAGE
- Build Background
- Read Aloud
- Expand Vocabulary

VOCABULARY
- Teach Words in Context
- Dictionary: Idioms

COMPREHENSION
- **Strategy:** Make Inferences and Analyze
- **Skill:** Compare Characters

SMALL GROUP OPTIONS
- Differentiated Instruction, pp. 45M–45V

Oral Language

Build Background

ACCESS PRIOR KNOWLEDGE

Share the following information:

Today many young people are learning to cook. They use cookbooks to make tacos, chili, and hamburgers, and other tasty treats.

TALK ABOUT WHAT'S COOKING?

Discuss the weekly theme.

- What dishes would you like to learn how to cook? Why?

FOCUS QUESTION Ask a volunteer to read "Talk About It" on **Student Book** page 11 and describe the photograph.

- How do you think the girl feels? How can you tell?

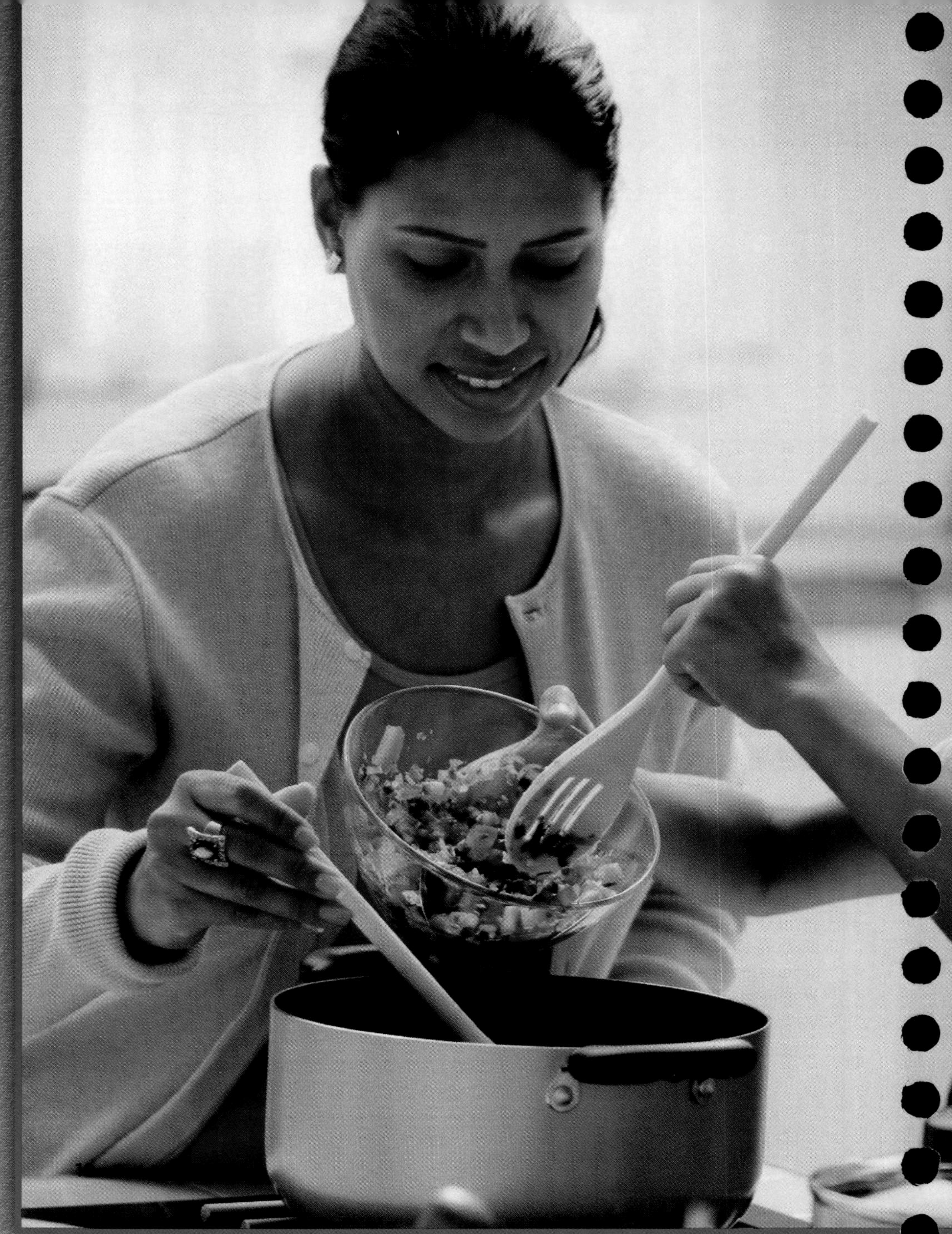

ENGLISH LANGUAGE LEARNERS Access for All

Beginning **Activate Background Knowledge** Have students say what they can about the photograph. Help them identify new vocabulary. Say: *Do you help in the kitchen? What do you know how to do?* Use gestures to demonstrate cooking verbs like *stir*, *cut*, and *chop*.

Intermediate **Use Descriptive Words** Have students talk about the photograph. Draw on students' experiences by asking whether or not they help out in the kitchen and what they know how to make. Encourage students to give descriptive details.

Advanced **Sequence Events** Do the Intermediate task. Then ask students to describe to partners the steps to prepare one thing to eat. Encourage students to use signal words.

Talk About It

What snack or meal do you know how to make? Tell how you make it.

LOG ON Find out more about cooking at **www.macmillanmh.com**

What's Cooking?

11

Picture Prompt

Look at the photograph. Write about what the girl is doing. You can write a poem, a story, a description, or use any other type of writing you like.

Technology

For an extended lesson plan, Web site activities, additional Read Alouds, for **oral language** and **vocabulary development**, go to **www.macmillanmh.com**

LA.3.2.1 Identify elements of literary text

Read Aloud

Read "When the Rain Came Up From China"

GENRE: Tall Tale Explain that a tall tale is often about characters on the American frontier, has a larger-than-life main character who solves a problem in a funny way.

Read Aloud pages 71–74

LA.3.1.6.2 Listen and discuss familiar text

LA.3.2.1 Analyze elements of fiction

LISTENING FOR A PURPOSE

Ask students to listen for the way the writer exaggerates in "When the Rain Came Up From China" in the **Read-Aloud Anthology**. Choose from among the teaching suggestions.

Fluency Ask students to listen carefully as you read aloud. Tell students to listen to your phrasing, expression, and tone of voice.

LA.3.2.1 Apply knowledge of elements of literary text

RESPOND TO THE TALL TALE

Ask students: What exaggerations did you notice? Was the tone funny or serious?

LA.3.1.6.4 Categorize key vocabulary

Expand Vocabulary

Ask students to listen carefully to the story and find three or more words from the selection that go with the theme of What's Cooking? For example, *kettle*, *soup*, *dinner*, *menu*, *salt*, *pepper*, *kitchen*, *meal*, and *stove*. Have students list the words, give meanings, and use each in a sentence.

Use the routine card to teach Expand Vocabulary words in Read Aloud lesson.

Vocabulary

FCAT

TEACH WORDS IN CONTEXT

Use the following routine: LA.3.1.6.1 Use new vocabulary taught directly

Routine

Define: Something that is very beautiful or wonderful is **magnificent**.
Example: I saw a magnificent sunset at the seashore.
Ask: What is a magnificent thing that you have seen? EXAMPLE

- A **masterpiece** is a great work or a very good example of something. The painting is a masterpiece. What else can be a masterpiece? EXAMPLE
- An **ingredient** is any one of the parts of a mixture. Flour is one ingredient used to make bread. What is another ingredient used to make bread? EXAMPLE
- Access for All **Recipes** are lists of ingredients and directions for making food. Grandma gave me some of her favorite recipes. Where else can you find recipes? PRIOR EXPERIENCE
- If something is **tasty**, it has a good flavor. We ate a tasty meal. What other word means almost the same thing as *tasty*? *(delicious)* SYNONYM

LA.3.1.6.8 Use knowledge of synonyms

Vocabulary
magnificent **recipes**
masterpiece **tasty**
ingredient

Dictionary
FCAT An **idiom** is a phrase with a meaning that is different from the meaning of each word in it.

see eye to eye = agree

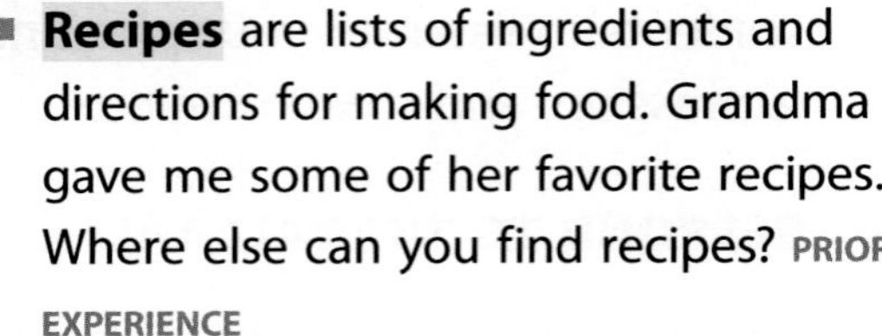

Red and Her Friends

by Marilyn MacGregor

A hen named Red lived in a city. Red and her pals did everything together. One day, Red and her feline friend Fiona went shopping. As they passed a trash-filled, weed-covered lot, Red smiled. "Wouldn't that lot be a **magnificent** spot for a garden?" she asked.

Fiona didn't see eye to eye with Red. "This place is a mess. It's a disaster!"

"We'd have to clean it up, of course," said Red. She called Ricardo over and asked for help.

"Sorry. I have a dentist appointment," Ricardo barked and walked away wagging his tail.

Red was disappointed. Fiona hissed angrily.

"I'll help you," said Fiona.

12

Quick Check **Do students understand word meanings?**

During **Small Group Instruction**

If No → **Approaching Level** Vocabulary, p. 45N

If Yes → **On Level** Options, pp. 45Q–45R

Beyond Level Options, pp. 45S–45T

ELL Access for All

Act Out Write on the board a recipe for a simple, familiar food, such as pancakes. Say: *I'm going to make [pancakes]. Here is my recipe. Here are my ingredients. How many ingredients are there? Pancakes are tasty for breakfast. What other foods are tasty for breakfast?* Have students answer the questions in full sentences.

Red and Fiona cleaned the lot. Then it was time to plant seeds.

"I wish I could help," said Ricardo, "But I have bones to dig up."

"I'll help," said Fiona, shaking her head at the dog.

Red and Fiona planted beans, carrots, pumpkins, and squash. Soon the seeds grew and made the garden beautiful. It looked like a **masterpiece**! Red asked her friends to help weed and water. Only Fiona had time to help. When it was time to pick the vegetables, only Red and Fiona did the work.

"I'll make dinner," said Red. "Each vegetable will be an **ingredient** in my **recipes** for cooking vegetable stew and pumpkin pie." Red licked her lips. "Those are **tasty** dishes."

Ricardo happened to walk by just then.

"I'd be happy to come to dinner," he said.

"You didn't help clean, weed, water, or pick. What makes you think you're invited?" asked Fiona. Red nodded firmly.

Of course, Fiona was invited, and everything was delicious.

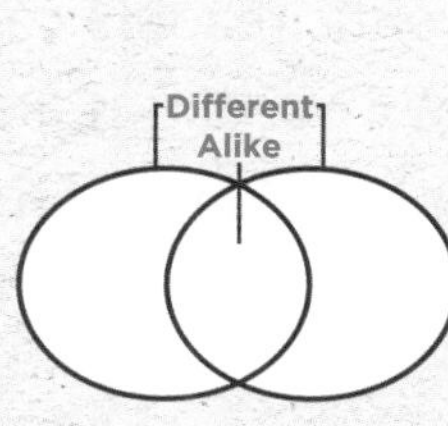

Reread for Comprehension

FCAT **Make Inferences and Analyze**

Compare Characters To compare and contrast characters you need to make inferences about how the characters are **alike** and **different**. As you read, think about each character's actions, traits, and feelings. Then ask yourself how they are alike and different. A Venn Diagram can help you compare characters. Reread the selection to compare Fiona with Ricardo.

Different
Alike

13

Vocabulary

LA.3.1.4 Demonstrate knowledge of alphabetic principle

Using the Strategies To figure out unfamiliar words, students can

LA.3.1.6.7 Use meaning of base words, affixes to determine meanings

LA.3.1.6.3 Use context clues to determine meanings

- decode words using knowledge of the alphabet and phonics principles,
- look for base words and word parts, such as prefixes and suffixes,
- look for context clues, or
- use a dictionary.

FCAT **STRATEGY**
USE A DICTIONARY

LA.3.1.6.10 Determine meanings using a dictionary and digital tools

LA.3.1.7.8 Clarify by checking other resources

Idioms Explain that an idiom is a group of words that has a special meaning. The meaning cannot be understood from the definition of each separate word. For example, *to pull one's leg* is an idiom. When readers look up *leg* in a student dictionary, they find the idiom and its meaning, "to trick or tease." Explain that not all idioms are listed in dictionaries. When an idiom is not listed, students can ask an adult, such as a teacher or a librarian, for help.

Point to the words *eye to eye* on **Student Book** page 12. Explain that it is an idiom. Help students see that it means "agreed about something."

LA.3.1.6.3 Use context clues to determine meanings

Read "Red and Her Friends"

As students read "Red and Her Friends," ask them to identify clues that reveal the meanings of the highlighted words. Tell students they will read these words again in *Cook-A-Doodle-Doo!*

FCAT **Success!**

Test Prep and Practice with vocabulary, pages 6–31

On Level Practice Book O, page 112

A. Write the vocabulary word that best completes each of the sentences below.

recipes	magnificent	ingredient
tasty	masterpiece	

1. José read many __recipes__ until he found the best one for chocolate cake.
2. He planned to bake the most __magnificent__ cake ever for his grandmother's birthday.
3. The only missing __ingredient__ was the chocolate!
4. Chocolate would make the cake very __tasty__.
5. José put the finished cake on the counter. It looked like a __masterpiece__.

B. Write the definitions for two of the vocabulary words. Possible responses below.

7. magnificent—very beautiful and grand
8. ingredient—any one of the parts that go into a mixture

Approaching Practice Book A, page 112

Beyond Practice Book B, page 112

Vocabulary

Review last week's vocabulary words: **instance**, **illustrate**, **style**, **textures**, **sketches**, and **suggestions**.

Objectives

- Make inferences and analyze
- Use academic language: *compare, contrast*
- Identify similarities and differences among events, characters, settings

Materials

- Comprehension Transparencies 16a and 16b
- Graphic Organizer Transparency 16
- Leveled Practice Books, p. 113

FCAT Skills Trace

Compare Characters	
Introduce	U2: 181A–B
Practice / Apply	U2: 182–203; Leveled Practice, 46–47
Reteach / Review	U3: 307B; U4: 13A–B, 14–37, 45M–T; Leveled Practice, 114–115
Assess	Weekly Tests; Unit 2, 3, 4 Tests; Benchmark Tests A, B
Maintain	U4: 139B; U6: 353A

ELL Access for All

Clarify Say: *When I compare two things, I ask, How are they the same?* Show a pen and a pencil. *How are a pen and pencil the same?* List ideas. Say: *When I contrast two things, I ask, How are they different? How are a pen and pencil different?* List ideas.

Reread for Comprehension

LA.3.1.7.3 Determine implied inference

STRATEGY

MAKE INFERENCES AND ANALYZE

Authors don't always tell a reader every detail in a story. Readers often have to look carefully at the information in the story and then **make inferences** about it. To make inferences, good readers use what they know, as well as clues in the story, to figure out what is missing. Readers can make inferences to identify similarities and differences among characters, settings, and events.

LA.3.1.7.8 Use strategies to repair comprehension

SKILL

COMPARE CHARACTERS, SETTINGS, EVENTS

EXPLAIN

LA.3.2.1.2 Identify plot, character/character development, and setting

Access for All

To identify **similarities** and **differences** in characters, settings, and events, readers can **compare** and **contrast** them. To compare, tell how two things are alike. To contrast them, tell how they are different. Making inferences can help readers compare and contrast ideas, characters, and events in a story.

Transparency 16a

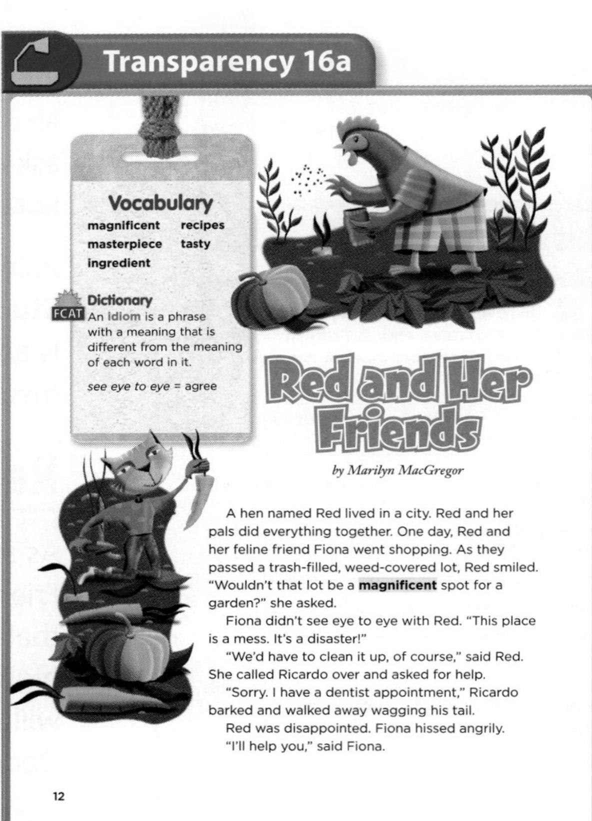

Vocabulary

magnificent **recipes** **masterpiece** **tasty** **ingredient**

Dictionary

An idiom is a phrase with a meaning that is different from the meaning of each word in it.

see eye to eye = agree

Red and Her Friends

by Marilyn MacGregor

A hen named Red lived in a city. Red and her pals did everything together. One day, Red and her feline friend Fiona went shopping. As they passed a trash-filled, weed-covered lot, Red smiled. "Wouldn't that lot be a **magnificent** spot for a garden?" she asked.

Fiona didn't see eye to eye with Red. "This place is a mess. It's a disaster!"

"We'd have to clean it up, of course," said Red. She called Ricardo over and asked for help.

"Sorry. I have a dentist appointment," Ricardo barked and walked away wagging his tail.

Red was disappointed. Fiona hissed angrily.

"I'll help you," said Fiona.

12

Transparency 16b

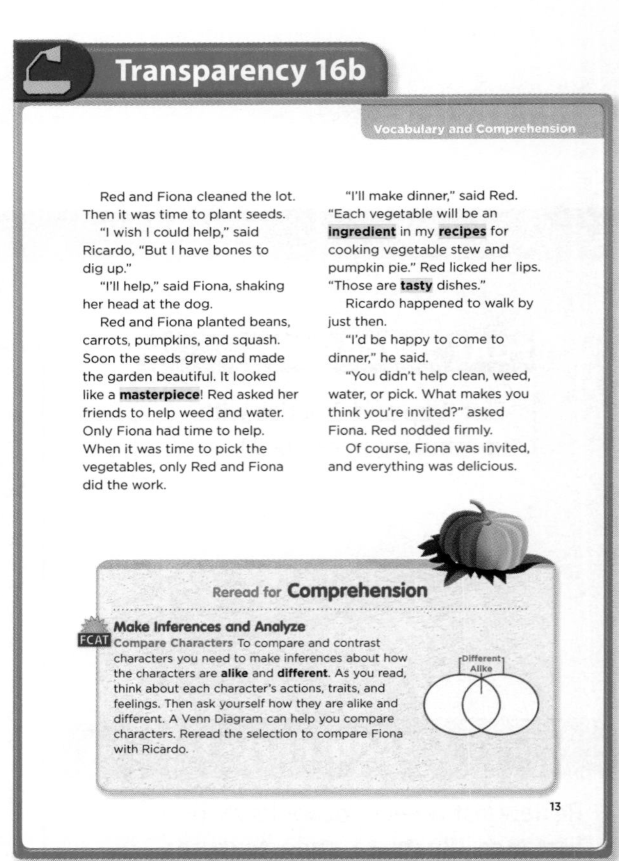

Vocabulary and Comprehension

Red and Fiona cleaned the lot. Then it was time to plant seeds.

"I wish I could help," said Ricardo, "But I have bones to dig up."

"I'll help," said Fiona, shaking her head at the dog.

Red and Fiona planted beans, carrots, pumpkins, and squash. Soon the seeds grew and made the garden beautiful. It looked like a **masterpiece**! Red asked her friends to help weed and water. Only Fiona had time to help. When it was time to pick the vegetables, only Red and Fiona did the work.

"I'll make dinner," said Red. "Each vegetable will be an **ingredient** in my **recipes** for cooking vegetable stew and pumpkin pie." Red licked her lips. "Those are **tasty** dishes."

Ricardo happened to walk by just then.

"I'd be happy to come to dinner," he said.

"You didn't help clean, weed, water, or pick. What makes you think you're invited?" asked Fiona. Red nodded firmly.

Of course, Fiona was invited, and everything was delicious.

Reread for **Comprehension**

Make Inferences and Analyze

Compare Characters To compare and contrast characters you need to make inferences about how the characters are **alike** and **different**. As you read, think about each character's actions, traits, and feelings. Then ask yourself how they are alike and different. A Venn Diagram can help you compare characters. Reread the selection to compare Fiona with Ricardo.

13

Student Book pages 12–13 available on Comprehension Transparencies 16a and 16b

MODEL

Read aloud the first page of "Red and Her Friends" on **Student Book** page 12.

LA.3.2.1.2 Explain character/character development

Think Aloud I want to think about how Fiona and Ricardo are alike and how they are different. I know they are alike because they are both animals. They are also both friends of Red, so that is something else they have in common. They are different because one is a cat and the other is a dog. Comparing and contrasting these characters help me to understand them better.

LA.3.2.1 Analyze elements of literary text

GUIDED PRACTICE

Display the Venn Diagram on **Transparency 16**.

- Point out the labels on the Venn Diagram. The left oval is for Fiona, and the right oval is for Ricardo. Under the Fiona label write *cat*, and under the Ricardo label write *dog*.
- Help students identify other ways Fiona and Ricardo are different, and write these details in the Venn Diagram under their names. (Fiona helps Red with the garden. Ricardo doesn't help Red with the garden.)
- Work with students to place what Fiona and Ricardo have in common in the middle of the Venn Diagram where the ovals intersect. (They are both friends with Red.)

LA.3.2.1 Apply knowledge of elements of literary text

APPLY

Have students reread the second page of "Red and Her Friends." Help them think about who Red invites to her special dinner. Then have students complete the Venn Diagram with this information. (Fiona is invited to Red's dinner. Ricardo is not invited to Red's dinner.)

Quick Check **Can students make inferences to compare and contrast characters?**

During **Small Group Instruction**

If No → **Approaching Level** Comprehension, p. 45O

If Yes → **On Level** Options, pp. 45Q–45R

Beyond Level Options, pp. 45S–45T

Transparency 16

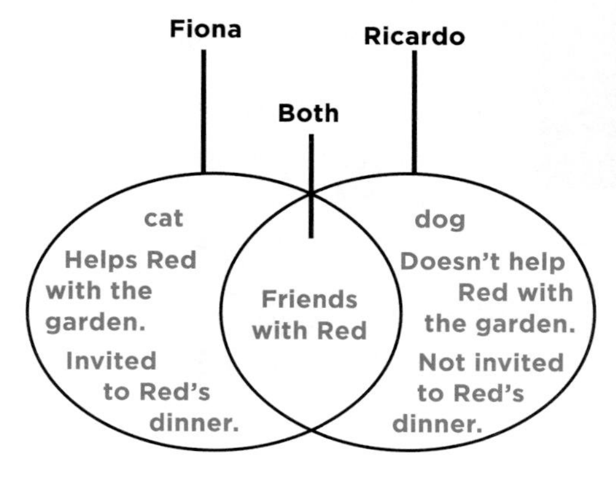

Graphic Organizer Transparency 16

FCAT Success!

Test Prep and Practice with compare characters, settings, and events, pages 125–152

On Level Practice Book O, page 113

When you **compare and contrast** things, you look at the characteristics of each and point out how they are alike and how they are different.

Read the following paragraph and answer the questions below. Possible responses provided.

George the rooster and Stu the chicken have been friends for many years. They both loved being in the kitchen, but George liked to bake cookies and Stu liked to bake pies. Stu made his pies with different types of fruit, and George made his cookies with different nuts and chips. Both the cookies and pies were very tasty. Because everyone liked their cookies and pies, George and Stu decided to open a bakery so everyone could try them. George sells his cookies by the pound, and Stu sells his pies one at a time. Both of them sold everything on their first day.

1. Compare the similarities between George and Stu.
Both George and Stu like to be in the kitchen and they both like to bake. They both sell their food in a bakery, and they both sold everything on their first day.

2. Contrast what you read about George and Stu.
George liked to bake cookies, and Stu liked to bake pies. George used nuts and chips in his cookies, and Stu used fruit in his pies. George sells his cookies by the pound, and Stu sells his pies one at a time.

Approaching Practice Book A, page 113

Beyond Practice Book B, page 113

Read

MAIN SELECTION
- *Cook-A-Doodle-Doo!*
- **Skill:** Compare Characters, Settings, Events

PAIRED SELECTION
- "Welcome to the Bakery!"
- **Text Feature:** Diagrams

SMALL GROUP OPTIONS
- Differentiated Instruction, pp. 45M–45V

Comprehension

LA.3.2.1 Identify elements of fiction

GENRE: HUMOROUS FICTION

Have a student read the definition of Humorous Fiction on **Student Book** page 14. Students should look for clever language, funny characters, unexpected events, and funny illustrations.

STRATEGY
MAKE INFERENCES AND ANALYZE

LA.3.2.1 Analyze elements of fiction

LA.3.1.7.3 Determine implied inference

Good readers use their own experiences and clues in the story to figure out information the author has not included. This strategy is called **making inferences**. It helps readers better understand what they read.

SKILL
COMPARE CHARACTERS, SETTING, EVENTS

LA.3.2.1 Apply knowledge of elements of literary text

To **compare** characters, settings, or events, a reader tells how they are alike. To **contrast,** a reader tells how they are different.

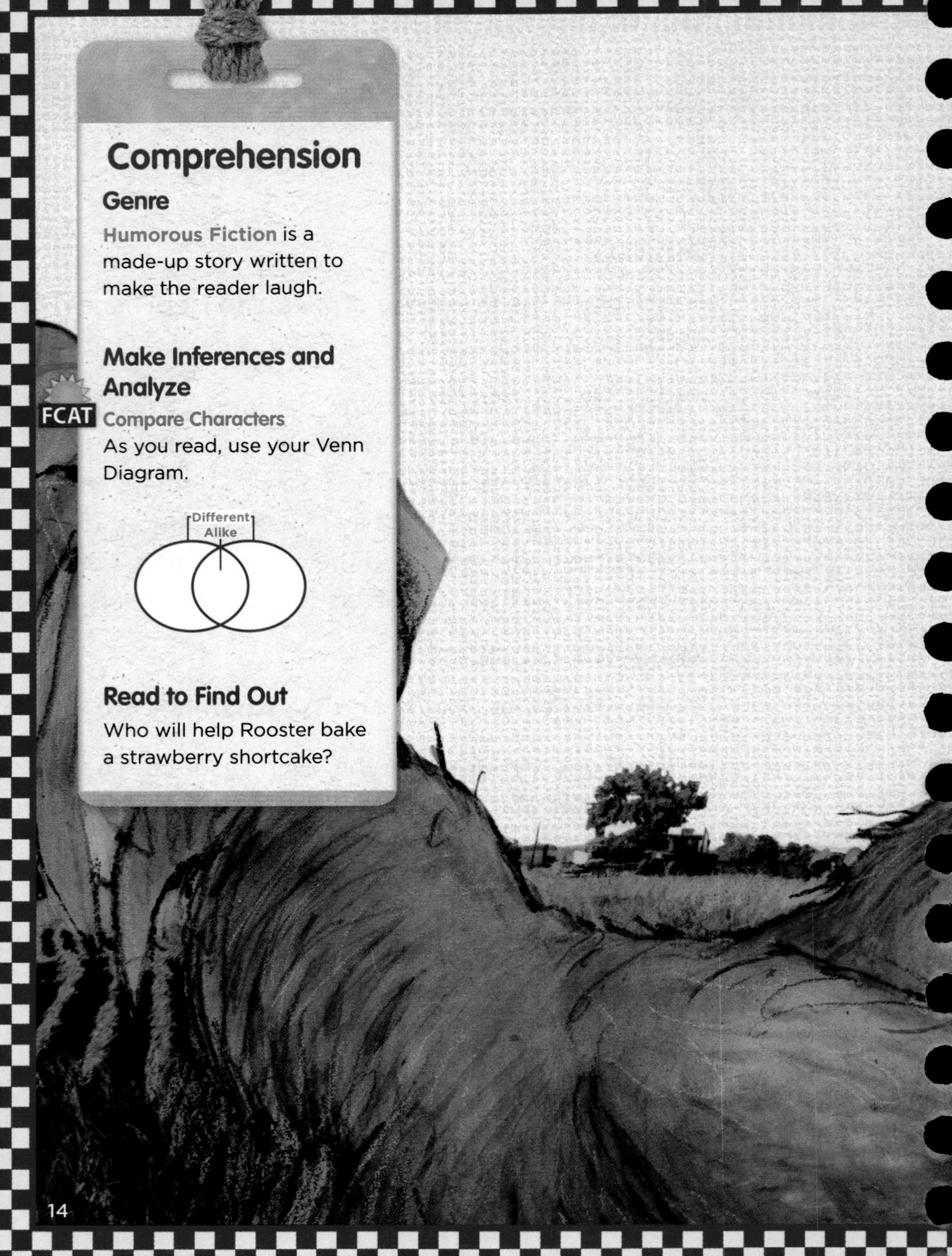

Comprehension
Genre
Humorous Fiction is a made-up story written to make the reader laugh.
Make Inferences and Analyze
FCAT
Compare Characters
As you read, use your Venn Diagram.
Different
Alike
Read to Find Out
Who will help Rooster bake a strawberry shortcake?
14

FCAT Vocabulary

Vocabulary Words Review the tested vocabulary words: **magnificent**, **masterpiece**, **ingredient**, **recipes**, and **tasty**.

Story Words Students may find these words difficult. Pronounce the words and present the meanings as necessary.

potbellied (p. 20): having a big round stomach or belly, like some types of pigs

degrees (p. 21): units used to measure temperature

LA.3.1.6.1 Use new vocabulary taught directly

Main Selection

by Janet Stevens and
Susan Stevens Crummel
illustrated by Janet Stevens

Read Together	Read Independently
If your students need support to read the Main Selection, use the prompts to guide comprehension and model how to complete the graphic organizer.	If your students can read the Main Selection independently, have them read and complete the graphic organizer. Suggest that students set purposes, adjust reading rate, and choose reading strategies based on the purpose.

If your students need an alternate selection, choose the **Leveled Readers** that match their instructional levels.

LA.3.1.5.2 Adjust reading rate based on purpose

Technology

Story available on **Listening Library Audio CD**

Preview and Predict

LA.3.1.7.1 Use text features to make predictions

Ask students to read the title, preview the illustrations, and note questions and predictions about the story. Do they think this story is serious or funny? Is it realistic fiction or fantasy? Have students write their predictions.

Set Purposes

LA.3.1.7.1 Use text features to establish purpose for reading

FOCUS QUESTION Discuss the "Read to Find Out" question and how students can look for the answer as they read.

Point out the Venn Diagram in the **Student Book** and on **Leveled Practice Book** page 114. Explain that students will fill it in as they read.

Read *Cook-A-Doodle-Doo!*

LA.3.1.6.2 Read text

Use the questions and Think Alouds for additional instruction to support the comprehension strategy and skill.

On Level Practice Book O, page 114

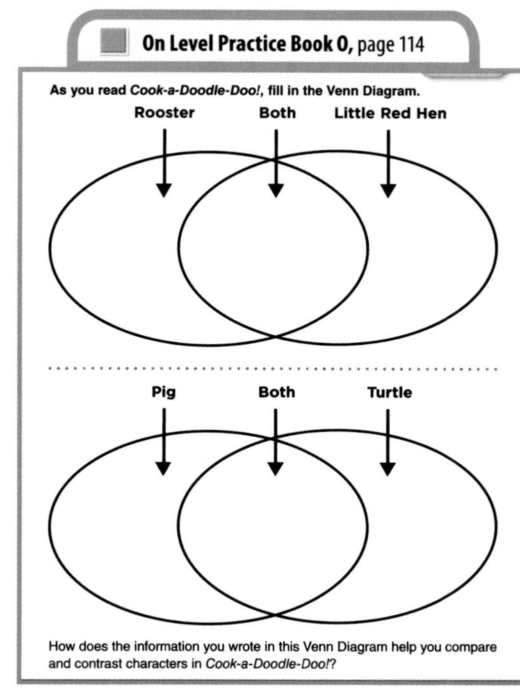
As you read *Cook-a-Doodle-Doo!*, fill in the Venn Diagram.

Rooster | Both | Little Red Hen

Pig | Both | Turtle

How does the information you wrote in this Venn Diagram help you compare and contrast characters in *Cook-a-Doodle-Doo!*?

Approaching Practice Book A, page 114

Beyond Practice Book B, page 114

Develop Comprehension

1 EVALUATE

LA.3.1.7.7 Compare and contrast texts

Why is it important to know the story *Little Red Hen* when you read *Cook-A-Doodle-Doo*? (*Little Red Hen* is a famous story about a hen who decides to bake some bread. The character Little Red Hen is Rooster's great-grandmother. Knowing what happened in the story of the Little Red Hen will help me understand this story.)

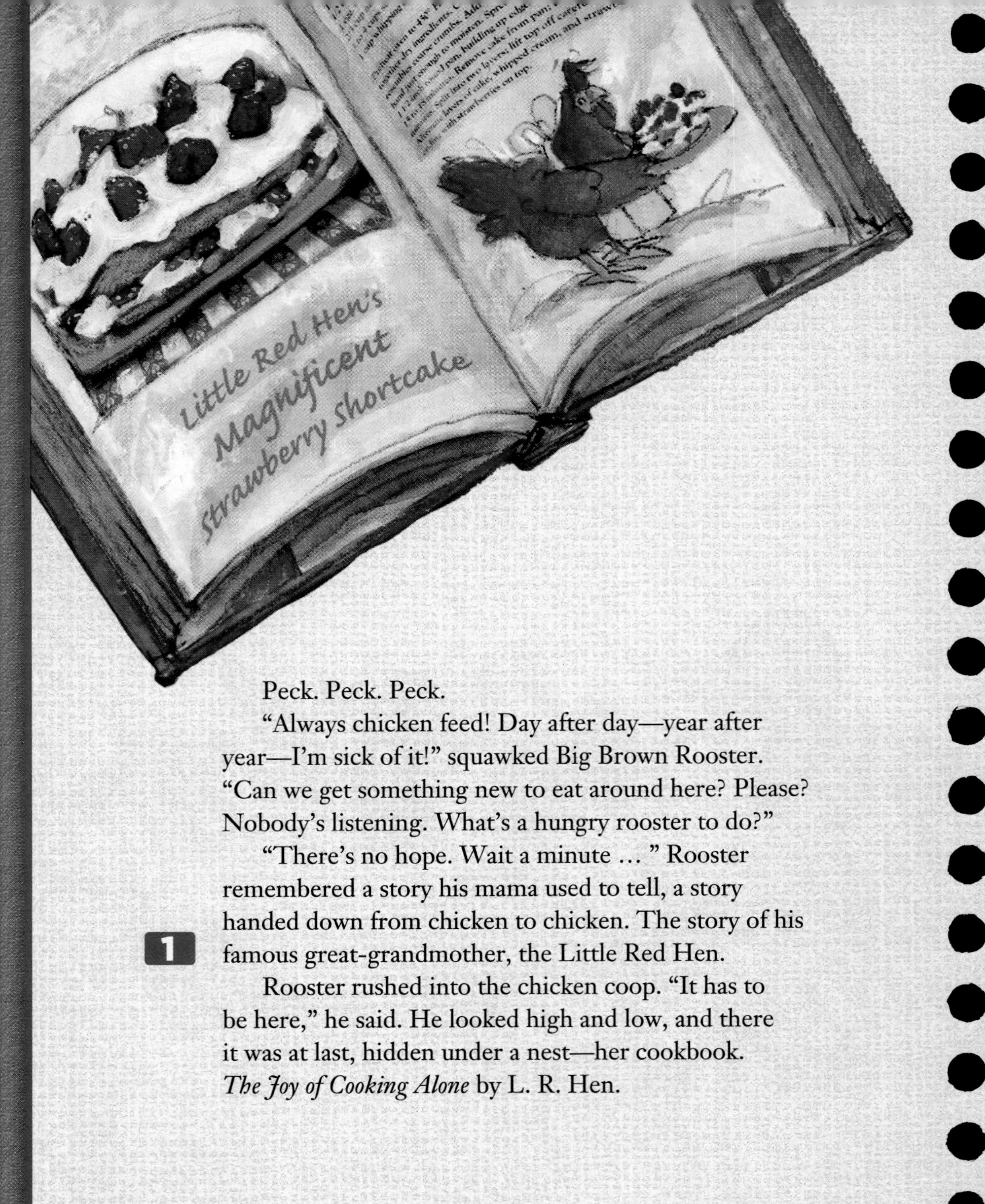

Peck. Peck. Peck.

"Always chicken feed! Day after day—year after year—I'm sick of it!" squawked Big Brown Rooster. "Can we get something new to eat around here? Please? Nobody's listening. What's a hungry rooster to do?"

"There's no hope. Wait a minute ... " Rooster remembered a story his mama used to tell, a story handed down from chicken to chicken. The story of his
1 famous great-grandmother, the Little Red Hen.

Rooster rushed into the chicken coop. "It has to be here," he said. He looked high and low, and there it was at last, hidden under a nest—her cookbook. *The Joy of Cooking Alone* by L. R. Hen.

16

Comprehension

Fractured Fairy Tales

Explain A fractured fairy tale is a humorous variation of a traditional fairy tale in which elements have been changed. Sometimes the tale is told from another character's point of view, set in another time or place, or has a different ending. The purpose is always to make the reader laugh.

Discuss Review the plot of the original Little Red Hen tale: The Little Red Hen grows wheat, grinds it into flour, and makes bread from it without anyone's help. Discuss with students how *Cook-A-Doodle-Doo!* is a funny variation on this tale.

Apply Have students choose another fairy tale, such as *The Three Little Pigs* or *Cinderella*, in a print or video version and also find a "fractured" version to read or view. Have students compare the two versions. Then they can form literature circles, discuss how the tales are different, and tell which one they like better.

LA.3.2.1 Identify elements of literary text; **LA.3.1.6.2** Read familiar text; **LA.3.1.7.7** Compare and contrast texts

Rooster carefully turned the pages. "So many **recipes**—and I thought she just baked bread! Look at the strawberry shortcake!"

"That's it! I'll make the most wonderful, **magnificent** strawberry shortcake in the whole wide world. No more chicken feed for me!"

"Yes sirree—just like Great-Granny, I'll be a cook! COOK-A-DOODLE-DO-O-O!" crowed Rooster as he pranced toward the big farmhouse. **2**

FCAT **Compare Characters**
How is Rooster like Great-Granny? How is he different?

17

ELL Access for All

STRATEGIES FOR EXTRA SUPPORT

Question 2 COMPARE CHARACTERS
Explain that Great-Granny is the mother of Rooster's grandmother. Her name was Little Red Hen. Ask: *What do you know about Great-Granny? What do you know about Rooster?* Ask questions to help them compare the information. *Are they both chickens? Are they from the same family? Are they both good cooks? Are they both roosters?*

Develop Comprehension

2 COMPARE CHARACTERS

FCAT LA.3.1.7.3 Determine implied inference

How is Rooster like Great-Granny? How is he different? You may need to make inferences about these characters to compare them. Record this information in your Venn Diagram. (The characters are alike in several ways: Both are chickens; Little Red Hen is Rooster's great-grandmother, so they are from the same family; both of them are interested in cooking. The characters are also different from one another: One is a rooster and the other was a hen; Little Red Hen was a great cook, but Rooster doesn't know how to cook.)

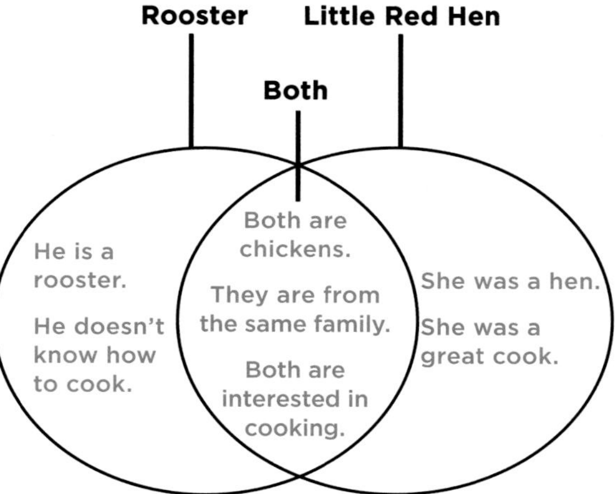
Rooster
Little Red Hen
Both
He is a rooster.
He doesn't know how to cook.
Both are chickens.
They are from the same family.
Both are interested in cooking.
She was a hen.
She was a great cook.

Vocabulary

Read the sentence on page 17 with the vocabulary word **magnificent**. What word means nearly the opposite of *magnificent*? (*awful, terrible, bad*)

LA.3.1.6.8 Use knowledge of antonyms

Develop Comprehension

3 STRATEGY
USE A DICTIONARY

FCAT

LA.3.2.1.5 Explain author's use of idiomatic language

LA.3.1.6.10 Determine meanings using a dictionary and digital tools

On page 19 Rooster says "cooking is in my blood." How can you find out what the **idiom** "in my blood" means? (Rooster also says that cooking is "a family tradition," so "in my blood" probably means something similar. "In my blood" must mean a talent or skill that people in the same family have. To confirm my prediction, I can look the idiom up in a dictionary under the key word *blood*.)

"*Cook*-a-doodle-doo?" said Dog.
"Have you lost your marbles, Rooster?" asked Cat.
"You've never cooked anything before!" said Goose.
"That doesn't matter," replied Rooster. "Cooking is in my blood—it's a family tradition. Now, who will help me?" **3**
"Not I," said Dog.
"Not I," said Cat.
"Not I," said Goose.
And away they went.
Rooster pushed open the kitchen door. "It looks like I'm on my own … just like Great-Granny." He sighed and put on his apron. **4**

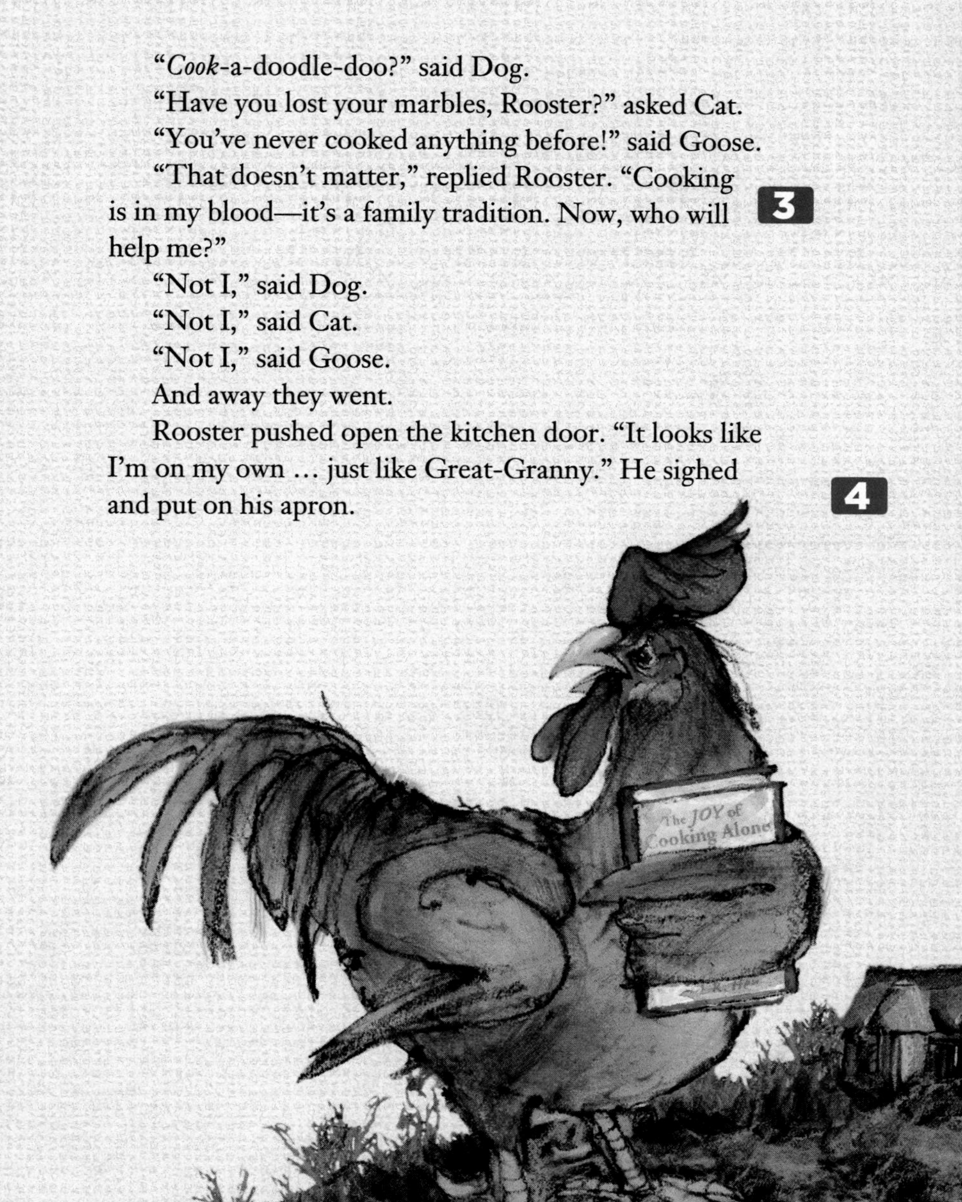

FCAT Comprehension

Compare Characters, Settings, Events

Explain When readers **compare**, they tell how things are alike. When readers **contrast**, they tell how things are different.

Discuss Ask: *On page 19, what do you learn about Rooster?* (He wants to bake a cake. He wants help.) *What do you learn about Dog, Cat, and Goose?* (They don't want to help.) *How are Rooster and his friends alike?* (They are all animals. They live on the same farm.) *How are they different?* (Rooster thinks he can learn how to cook, but his friends don't. Rooster thinks baking a cake is a good idea, but his friends don't.)

Apply Have students compare and contrast Rooster and his friends in a Venn Diagram.

LA.3.1.7.5 Identify text structure; **LA.3.2.1.2** Identify and explain character/character development

Develop Comprehension

4 COMPARE CHARACTERS

FCAT **LA.3.1.7.3** Determine explicit ideas and information in grade level text

How is Rooster's feeling about cooking different from the feelings of his friends, Dog, Cat, and Goose? (Rooster thinks he can learn to cook. He also thinks cooking is a good idea. Rooster's friends don't think that he will be able to cook. They think he is crazy.)

Develop Comprehension

5 STRATEGY
MAKE INFERENCES AND ANALYZE

LA.3.1.7.3 Determine implied inference

Teacher Think Aloud I know that authors don't always tell me everything in a story. To better understand the story and the characters' actions, I can make inferences using story clues and my own experience to figure out details that are left out. In this story, Cat, Dog, and Goose won't help Rooster bake the strawberry shortcake, but Turtle, Iguana, and Potbellied Pig want to help. By comparing the actions of the two groups, I can figure out which animals are really Rooster's good friends, even though the authors don't directly tell me this. I know that good friends are always ready to help, and this is what Turtle, Iguana, and Pig offer to do. So I can make an inference about them. They are good friends to Rooster, while the other animals are not. By making inferences about the characters' actions, I now better understand what is happening in the story.

"We'll help you."

Rooster turned, and there stood Turtle, Iguana, and Potbellied Pig.

"Do you three know anything about cooking?" Rooster asked.

"I can read recipes!" said Turtle.

"I can get stuff!" said Iguana.

"I can taste!" said Pig. "I'm an expert at tasting."

5

20

"Then we're a team," declared Rooster. "Let's get ready and start cooking!"

Turtle read the cookbook. "Heat oven to 450 degrees." **6**

"I can do that!" said Iguana. "Look, I'll turn the knob. 150, 250, 350, 450. Hey, cooking is easy!"

Rooster put a big bowl on the table. "What's our first **ingredient**?" he asked.

"The recipe says we need flour," said Turtle.

"I can do that!" said Iguana. He dashed outside and picked a petunia. "How's this flower?" **7**

Little Red Hen's Magnificent Strawberry Shortcake

A cookbook gives directions for making many different things to eat. Each type of food has its own recipe—a list of everything that goes into it and step-by-step directions on how to make it.

One of the oven knobs controls the temperature of the oven. The higher the number on the knob, the hotter the oven. Temperature is measured in degrees Fahrenheit (°F) or degrees Celsius (°C). On a very hot day the temperature outside can be over 100°F (38°C). Can you imagine what 450°F (232°C) feels like?

Ingredients are the different things that go into a recipe. Each ingredient may not taste good by itself, but if you put them all together in the right way, the result tastes delicious.

21

ELL Access for All

Clarify Write the words *flour* and *flower* on the board. Say the words with students. Ask: *Do the words sound the same? Do they mean the same thing?* Draw a flower on the board. Ask: *Which word is this? Spell the word.* Draw a line from the word *flower* to its drawing. Ask: *What does Turtle need for his recipe? Spell the word.*

Develop Comprehension

6 STRATEGY
MONITOR AND CLARIFY: READ AHEAD

LA.3.1.7.8 Use strategies to repair comprehension

How can you figure out what "heat the oven to 450 degrees" means? (I can read ahead and look through the information in the box at the bottom of the page to figure out the meaning. I see that it means how hot to make the oven.) Remember to use other self-monitoring and self-correction strategies as you read.

7 GENRE: HUMOROUS FICTION

LA.3.2.1 Analyze elements of fiction

Why is it funny when Iguana goes outside and brings back a petunia? (Turtle asked for flour, but Iguana misunderstood. He thought Turtle asked for a flower. It's funny when Iguana brings back a petunia because this action surprises the reader.)

Develop Comprehension

8 COMPARE CHARACTERS

FCAT

LA.3.2.1.2 Identify and explain character/ character development

Think about Pig and Turtle. How are these characters alike? How are they different? You may need to make inferences about the characters to compare them. Record this information in a new Venn Diagram. (Pig and Turtle are both animals, but one is a pig and one is a turtle. Both are friends with Rooster. They also live on the same farm. Pig likes to taste things. Turtle likes to read recipes.)

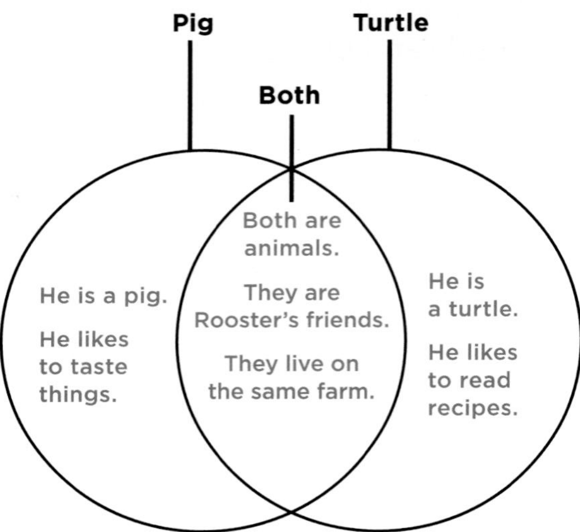
Pig
Turtle
Both
Both are animals.
They are Rooster's friends.
They live on the same farm.
He is a pig.
He likes to taste things.
He is a turtle.
He likes to read recipes.

"No, no, no," said Rooster. "Not *that* kind of flower. We need flour for *cooking*. You know, the fluffy white stuff that's made from wheat."

"Can I taste the flour?" asked Pig.

8 "Not yet, Pig," said Turtle. "The recipe says to sift it first."

"What does *sift* mean?" asked Iguana.

"Hmmm," said Turtle. "I think *sift* means 'to search through' . . . "

9

Make sure you use a big bowl that will hold all of the ingredients. It's best to set out everything before you start cooking, so you don't have to go looking for your ingredients one-by-one like Iguana!

Flour is made from wheat grains that are finely ground. Long ago, the grinding was done by hand; now it is done by machines. Rooster's Great-Granny had to grind the grain into flour by hand, but you and Rooster can buy flour at the grocery store.

You will find many different kinds of flour at the store—including all-purpose flour, whole-wheat flour, cake flour, and high-altitude flour. Rooster's recipe calls for all-purpose flour.

Sifting adds air to the flour so it can be measured accurately. Some sifters have cranks, some have spring-action handles, and some are battery powered.

Make sure you put waxed paper on the counter before you start sifting. It will make cleanup a lot easier!

22

ELL Access for All

STRATEGIES FOR EXTRA SUPPORT

Question 8 COMPARE CHARACTERS

Ask students: *What do we know about Pig? What do we know about Turtle? Let's make a list for each character and then compare and contrast the information. This will help us know where to put the information on our Venn Diagram.* Ask: *What do we know about Pig? Who is his friend? What does he like to do? Where does he live?* Repeat the questions for Turtle.

"You mean like when I sift through the garbage looking for lunch?" asked Pig.

"I can do that!" said Iguana. And he dived into the flour, throwing it everywhere!

"No, no, no," said Rooster. "Don't sift the flour like that. Put it through this sifter." Rooster turned the crank and sifted the flour into a big pile.

"Can I taste the pile?" asked Pig.

"Not yet, Pig," said Turtle. "Now we measure the flour."

23

Develop Comprehension

9 AUTHOR'S PURPOSE

LA.3.1.7.2 Identify the author's purpose

Why do you think the authors include information in the boxes at the bottom of pages 21 and 22? What is the authors' purpose? (The box on page 21 gives facts and information about a cookbook, the oven, and ingredients. The box on page 22 has details about flour and sifting. The authors give important information about cooking in the boxes. This information will also help the reader understand what happens in the story. The authors' purpose is to inform.)

Fluency

Echo-Reading

Explain Tell students that good readers pay special attention to the difference in intonation when reading dialogue and reading narration. They also listen for the differences between the characters' voices.

Model Read lines 4–7 on **Student Book** page 22, which is also available on **Fluency Transparency 16**. Model how to give each of the characters distinct voices. For example, Pig should sound excited or anxious, Turtle's comments are more responsible, and Iguana is asking a question.

Apply Have students read the passage with partners and give each character a distinct voice. One partner should read the dialogue for Pig and Iguana; the other partner should read for Turtle and Rooster. Partners can offer corrective feedback.

LA.3.1.5 Demonstrate the ability to read text orally with expression

Develop Comprehension

10 PLOT DEVELOPMENT

LA.3.2.1.2
Identify plot

Which friend is most helpful to Rooster? How do you know? (Turtle is the most helpful. He reads the cookbook and measures the ingredients carefully. Pig and Iguana aren't as helpful. All Pig wants to do is taste, and Iguana doesn't understand the instructions.)

"I can do that!" said Iguana. He grabbed a ruler. "The flour is four inches tall."

"No, no, no," said Rooster. "We don't want to know how *tall* it is. We want to know how *much* there is. We measure the flour with this metal measuring cup."

"We need two cups," added Turtle. "So fill it twice."

10 Rooster dumped the two cups of flour into the bowl.

24

“Can I taste it *now*?” asked Pig.

“Not yet, Pig,” said Turtle. “Next we add two tablespoons of sugar, one tablespoon of baking powder, and one-half teaspoon of salt.”

Compare Characters How is Pig different from Rooster?

11

Measuring cups for dry ingredients are made of metal or plastic and usually come in sets of four—1 cup, 1/2 cup, 1/3 cup, and 1/4 cup. Pick the measuring cup that holds the amount you need, then dip it into the dry ingredient, getting a heaping amount. Level it off with the straight edge of a knife and let the extra fall back into the container (although Pig would be very happy if just a little fell on the floor!).

Dry ingredients can be measured in cups or grams.

1 cup = 227 grams

2 cups = 454 grams

Some ingredients are included for flavor, but not baking powder. Even Pig thinks it tastes terrible! When baking powder is added to the shortcake, bubbles of gas form and get bigger while the cake bakes, which makes it rise.

Dry ingredients are all sifted together so they will be evenly mixed.

25

Extra Support

FCAT

Compare Characters

Guide students in recognizing how the characters are different. Ask: *What does Pig always want to do?* (Pig always wants to taste things.) *What does Rooster want to do?* (He wants to bake a shortcake.) *Which animal works hard? Which doesn't?* (Rooster works hard; Pig doesn't work hard.)

If students have difficulty, review what it means to compare and contrast. Have students put the information about Pig and Rooster on a Venn Diagram so they can see the ways they are alike and different.

LA.3.1.7.8 Use strategies to repair comprehension

Develop Comprehension

11 COMPARE CHARACTERS

LA.3.2.1.2 Identify and explain character/ character development

LA.3.1.7.3 Determine implied inference

How is Pig different from Rooster? You may need to make inferences about these characters to compare them. (Pig and Rooster are very different. One is a pig and one is a rooster. Rooster wants to cook the food. All Pig wants to do is taste it. He does not think about being helpful, and he does not work hard. Rooster doesn't try to taste the food before it is ready. He works hard and tries to get the job done.)

LA.3.1.7.1 Use text features to confirm predictions

Have students respond to the story by confirming or revising their predictions. Encourage students to revise or write additional questions they have about the story.

Quick Check **Can students compare characters as they read? If not, see the Extra Support on this page.**

Stop here if you wish to read this selection over two days.

Develop Comprehension

12 SUMMARIZE

LA.3.1.7.8 Summarize to repair comprehension

What has happened in the story so far? Remind students to focus on main events when they summarize. (Rooster wants to cook, just like his great-grandmother, Little Red Hen. He uses the recipe for strawberry shortcake in Great-Granny's cookbook. Turtle, Iguana, and Pig help him. Turtle reads the recipe, Iguana gets the ingredients, and Pig wants to taste everything. Even though Rooster gets frustrated with his friends, they work together to mix the ingredients.)

12

"I can do that!" said Iguana. He looked under the table. "But where are the tablespoons?" He looked in the teapot. "No teaspoons in here!"

"No, no, no," said Rooster. "Don't look in the teapot or under the table! These spoons are for measuring. Each holds a certain amount." Rooster measured the sugar, baking powder, and salt, poured them into the big bowl, then sifted all the dry ingredients together.

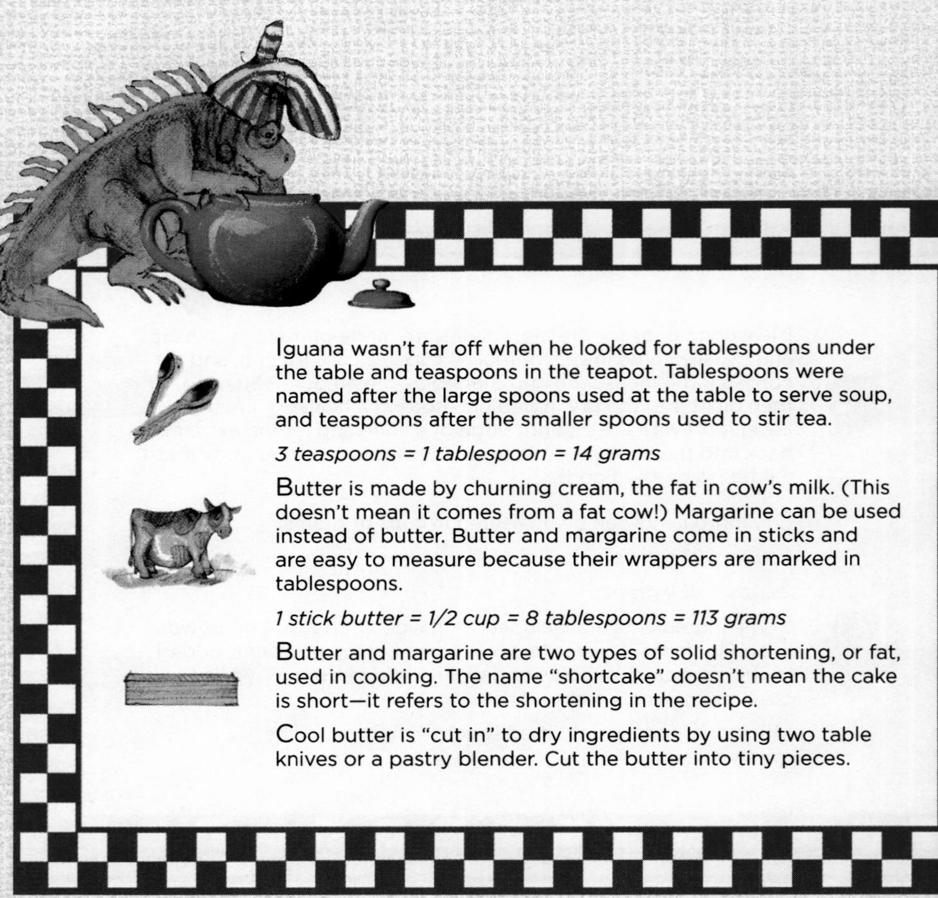

Iguana wasn't far off when he looked for tablespoons under the table and teaspoons in the teapot. Tablespoons were named after the large spoons used at the table to serve soup, and teaspoons after the smaller spoons used to stir tea.

3 teaspoons = 1 tablespoon = 14 grams

Butter is made by churning cream, the fat in cow's milk. (This doesn't mean it comes from a fat cow!) Margarine can be used instead of butter. Butter and margarine come in sticks and are easy to measure because their wrappers are marked in tablespoons.

1 stick butter = 1/2 cup = 8 tablespoons = 113 grams

Butter and margarine are two types of solid shortening, or fat, used in cooking. The name "shortcake" doesn't mean the cake is short—it refers to the shortening in the recipe.

Cool butter is "cut in" to dry ingredients by using two table knives or a pastry blender. Cut the butter into tiny pieces.

26

FCAT Comprehension

Author's Purpose

Explain The reason why an author writes something is called **author's purpose**. There are three main purposes: to inform, to entertain, or to persuade. The purpose of most nonfiction is to inform. The purpose of all advertisements is to persuade. The purpose of most fiction is to entertain.

Discuss Read the first page of *Cook-A-Doodle-Doo!* Help students understand that the authors' purpose is to entertain. Help them identify what is enjoyable and funny about the story. (an interesting character, funny details, and lively language)

Apply Have students look at the box on page 26. Ask: *How is this section different from the rest of the story?* (It has information.) *What do you think the purpose of this section is? Why?* (The purpose is to inform. The section is nonfiction, so it gives facts and information.)

LA.3.1.7.2 Identify the author's purpose

"Looks awfully white in there," said Pig. "I better taste it."

"Not yet, Pig," said Turtle. "Now we add butter. We need one stick."

"I can do that!" cried Iguana. He raced outside and broke off a branch. "How's this stick?"

"No, no, no," said Rooster. "Not *that* kind of stick. A stick of *butter*." Rooster unwrapped the butter and dropped it into the bowl. 13

"That butter is just sitting there like a log," said Pig. "Maybe I need to taste it."

27

Develop Comprehension

13 MULTIPLE-MEANING WORDS

FCAT

LA.3.1.6.9 Determine correct meaning of words with multiple meanings in context

What kind of stick does Iguana bring back? Why? (Iguana brings back a stick from a tree, but the kind of stick Turtle asked for was a stick of butter, not a tree branch. Iguana was confused because the word *stick* has more than one meaning.)

Develop Comprehension

14 STRATEGY
MAKE INFERENCES AND ANALYZE

LA.3.1.7.3 Determine implied inference

Teacher Think Aloud An author may leave information out of a story. Good readers make inferences using story clues and their own experiences to figure out this missing information. What story clues and personal experiences can you use to answer this question: How does Rooster feel when his friends make so many mistakes?

(Encourage students to apply the strategy in a Think Aloud.)

Student Think Aloud To answer this question, first I'll look at what Rooster says and does. He has to stop Iguana from putting the wrong ingredients into the bowl. He has to keep Pig from eating the ingredients. Most people would get mad and yell, but Rooster doesn't really do that. He is very patient. I think he likes having his friends help him, even though they make mistakes. When I looked at the details in the story and thought about my own experiences, I was able to make an inference about how Rooster might feel.

"Not yet, Pig," said Turtle. "Next we cut in the butter."

"I can do that!" said Iguana. "Uh-oh. Scissors don't cut butter very well."

"No, no, no," said Rooster. "Don't cut the butter with scissors. Use these two table knives, like this."

Rooster cut in the butter until the mixture was crumbly.

"Looks mighty dry in there," said Pig. "Perhaps I should taste it."

"Not yet, Pig," said Turtle. "Now the recipe says to beat one egg."

14

28

"I can do that!" cried Iguana.

"No, no, no," said Rooster. "Don't beat an egg with a baseball bat! We use an eggbeater." Rooster carefully broke the egg into a dish, beat it with the eggbeater, and poured it into the big bowl.

"That looks tasty," said Pig. "Please let me taste it."

"Not yet, Pig," said Turtle. "Now add milk. We need two-thirds of a cup."

15

Break an egg by hitting the shell gently on the edge of a countertop or bowl to make a small crack. Place both thumbs in the crack and pull the shell apart. Always crack an egg into a small bowl before you add it to the other ingredients in case the egg is bad or shell pieces fall in. Eggs add color and flavor and help hold the cake together.

You can beat eggs with a fork, a hand beater (like Rooster's), or an electric mixer. If you use an electric mixer, make sure to put the eggs in a big bowl and start off on a low speed. If you start with the mixer on high, you'll get egg on your face!

Liquid measuring cups are made of glass or plastic. Each measuring cup has a spout for pouring and extra room below the rim so you don't have to fill it to the top and worry about spilling. Always put the cup on a flat surface and measure at eye level.

Grease the pan with a solid shortening so the cake will not stick.

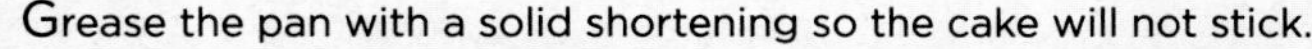

Rooster is mixing the batter by hand, which means to stir with a spoon instead of a mixer. (How would Iguana mix by hand?)

29

Develop Comprehension

15 CHRONOLOGICAL ORDER

FCAT

LA.3.1.7.3 Determine chronological order of events

In what order do Rooster and his friends add the ingredients on pages 28 and 29? (First they cut in the butter, next they beat an egg and pour it in, then they get two-thirds of a cup of milk.)

FCAT Ways to Confirm Meaning

Semantic/Syntactic Clues

Explain/Model Tell students that good readers sometimes use what they know about context clues and grammar to help them understand a difficult word. They usually begin by sounding out the word. Read the word *spout* in the bottom box in context.

Think Aloud I've never seen the word *spout* before, but I know it is a noun and something on the measuring cup because the text says "each measuring cup has a spout." I also know the spout is "for pouring." When I put these clues together, I think a spout is a part of the cup that helps you to pour.

Apply Tell students to use decoding, context clues, clues from the story, phonics knowledge, and their background knowledge to help them with other difficult words or phrases.

LA.3.1.6.3 Use context clues to determine meanings of unfamiliar words; **LA.3.1.6** Use multiple strategies to develop grade-appropriate vocabulary

Develop Comprehension

16 PLOT DEVELOPMENT

Why does Pig suggest that they fill the measuring cup to the top with milk and then let him "drink down a third"? (Pig is trying to help Rooster measure the ingredients for the shortcake, but he also likes to eat and drink. He wants to taste all the ingredients in the shortcake.)

LA.3.2.1.2 Identify and explain plot

"I can do that!" said Iguana. "Here, hold that glass measuring cup and I'll saw off a third. We'll use the other two-thirds to measure the milk."

16 "Wait," said Pig. "Why don't we fill the measuring cup to the top and I'll drink down a third?"

"No, no, no," said Rooster. "The cup has marks on it—1/3—2/3—1 cup. We'll fill it to the 2/3 mark." Rooster poured the milk into the bowl.

"It surely needs tasting now!" said Pig.

"Not yet, Pig," said Turtle. "Now we mix the dough and put it in a greased baking pan." Rooster stirred and spread as Turtle read, "Bake in the oven for fifteen to eighteen minutes."

30

Music

Cross-Curricular Connection

FOOD, GLORIOUS FOOD

Ask students if they know any songs about food. Tell them that there is a song called "Food, Glorious Food" from the musical play *Oliver!* Ask if they have heard of the musical play or seen the movie. In this song, boys who live in an orphanage sing about their favorite foods.

Define the word *glorious*, and play the song for the class. Have students find other words in the song that describe food, including unfamiliar dishes. Ask them to name other songs about food, such as "On Top of Spaghetti." Challenge students to write their own songs about food, using rhythm and rhyme. They may wish to use figurative language, too.

LA.3.4.1.2 Write a variety of expressive forms; **LA.3.4.1.2** Employ figurative language

"I can do that!" cried Iguana.

Iguana shoved the pan into the oven. "Let's see, fifteen minutes equals nine hundred seconds. I'll count them. One, two, three, four—"

"No, no, no," said Rooster, and he set the timer so that Iguana would stop counting the seconds. Pig burned his tongue on the oven door trying to taste the shortcake. Turtle studied the cookbook to see what to do next.

"Let's cut up the strawberries and whip the cream," said Turtle.

17

Make sure you stay nearby, so you can hear the timer when your cake is ready! Cooking times are given in hours, minutes, or seconds.
1 hour = 60 minutes
1 minute = 60 seconds

Wash the strawberries first and cut off their tops. Use a cutting board and cut each strawberry in half, then cut each half in half. (How many pieces do you have now?) Watch out for your fingers!

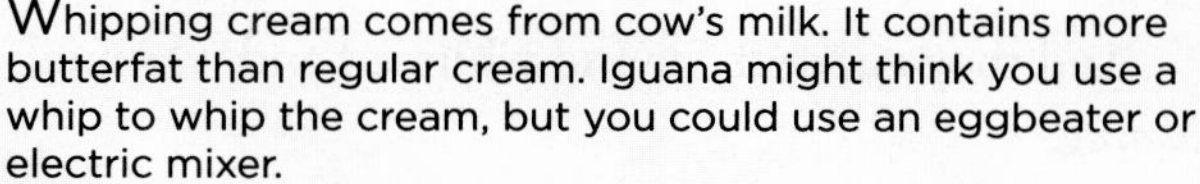

Whipping cream comes from cow's milk. It contains more butterfat than regular cream. Iguana might think you use a whip to whip the cream, but you could use an eggbeater or electric mixer.

When you take something out of a hot oven, make sure you use a pot holder or oven mitt.

A trick to tell if your shortcake is done: Stick a toothpick or knife in the center of the cake. If it comes out clean, without any cake sticking to it, the shortcake is ready.

Don't forget to turn off the oven when you're finished!

31

Develop Comprehension

17 **STRATEGY**
MONITOR AND CLARIFY: ADJUST READING RATE

LA.3.1.5.2 Adjust reading rate based on purpose, text difficulty, form, style

How will you adjust your reading rate when you read the information in the box at the bottom of page 31? Why? Explain your thinking. (I will slow down. Reading the information in these boxes is different from reading the main story. The main story is fiction, and it moves along quickly. When I get to the box, I am reading nonfiction. It includes a lot of details and information. I need to read this more slowly so I can understand everything.)

Develop Comprehension

18 MAKE INFERENCES

LA.3.1.7.3 Determine implied inference

What does "ding!" mean? How do you know? (The oven timer has just rung. This means that the shortcake is ready. I know this because Rooster grabs the mitt from Iguana's head and takes the shortcake out of the oven. I have also heard a timer ring when something has finished cooking.)

And they cut and cut and whipped and whipped, until 18 ... *ding!*

Rooster grabbed the oven mitt off Iguana's head and took the shortcake carefully out of the oven.

"Oh, it's beautiful, and it smells *sooo* good," said Pig. "I know I have to taste it now."

"Not yet, Pig," said Turtle. "We need to let it cool."

Soon the shortcake was ready to cut. Rooster sliced it in half.

32

They stacked one layer of cake, one layer of whipped cream, one layer of strawberries.

Then again—cake, cream, berries.

It looked just like the picture of the strawberry shortcake in the cookbook.

"This is the most wonderful, magnificent strawberry shortcake in the whole wide world," said Rooster. "If Great-Granny could see me now! Let's take it to the table." **19**

"I can do that!" cried Iguana.

33

Develop Comprehension

19 PROBLEM AND SOLUTION

FCAT

LA.3.2.1.2 Identify and explain problem/resolution

In the beginning of the story, some of Rooster's friends don't think he will be able to cook a strawberry shortcake. How was he able to do it? (Rooster followed the directions in the cookbook very carefully. Even though it took a lot of time and hard work, he never quit. Rooster also got a lot of help from his friends Pig, Turtle, and Iguana.)

Comprehension

Exaggeration

Explain/Discuss An **exaggeration** describes something as larger, greater, or more important than it is. A more literary term for exaggeration is **hyperbole**. Authors often use exaggeration or hyperbole in tall tales and other tales to add humor. Ask students how Rooster uses exaggeration on this page. (He says it is the most wonderful, magnificent strawberry shortcake in the whole wide world.)

Apply Ask students to look for other examples of exaggeration, such as "it was our masterpiece" on page 34, as they read the story. Then have students write their own examples of exaggeration.

LA.3.4.1.2 Employ figurative language; **LA.3.2.1.5** Examine how language describes objects

Develop Comprehension

20 FICTION TEXT FEATURES

LA.3.1.7.1 Identify a text's features

Why is the word *splat* in large, colored type? How does it help you understand what is happening in the story? (When I see the word *splat* in large, colored type, I know that the shortcake fell on the floor and made a loud sound. The special type treatment helps me understand that this is an important event in the story.)

21 AUTHOR'S PURPOSE

LA.3.1.7.2 Identify the author's purpose

What do you think the authors' main purpose is in writing this story? How do you know? (The authors' main purpose is to entertain. They use a lot of humorous scenes and language throughout the story. The characters do and say a lot of funny things while they work together. The story makes the reader laugh and feel happy.)

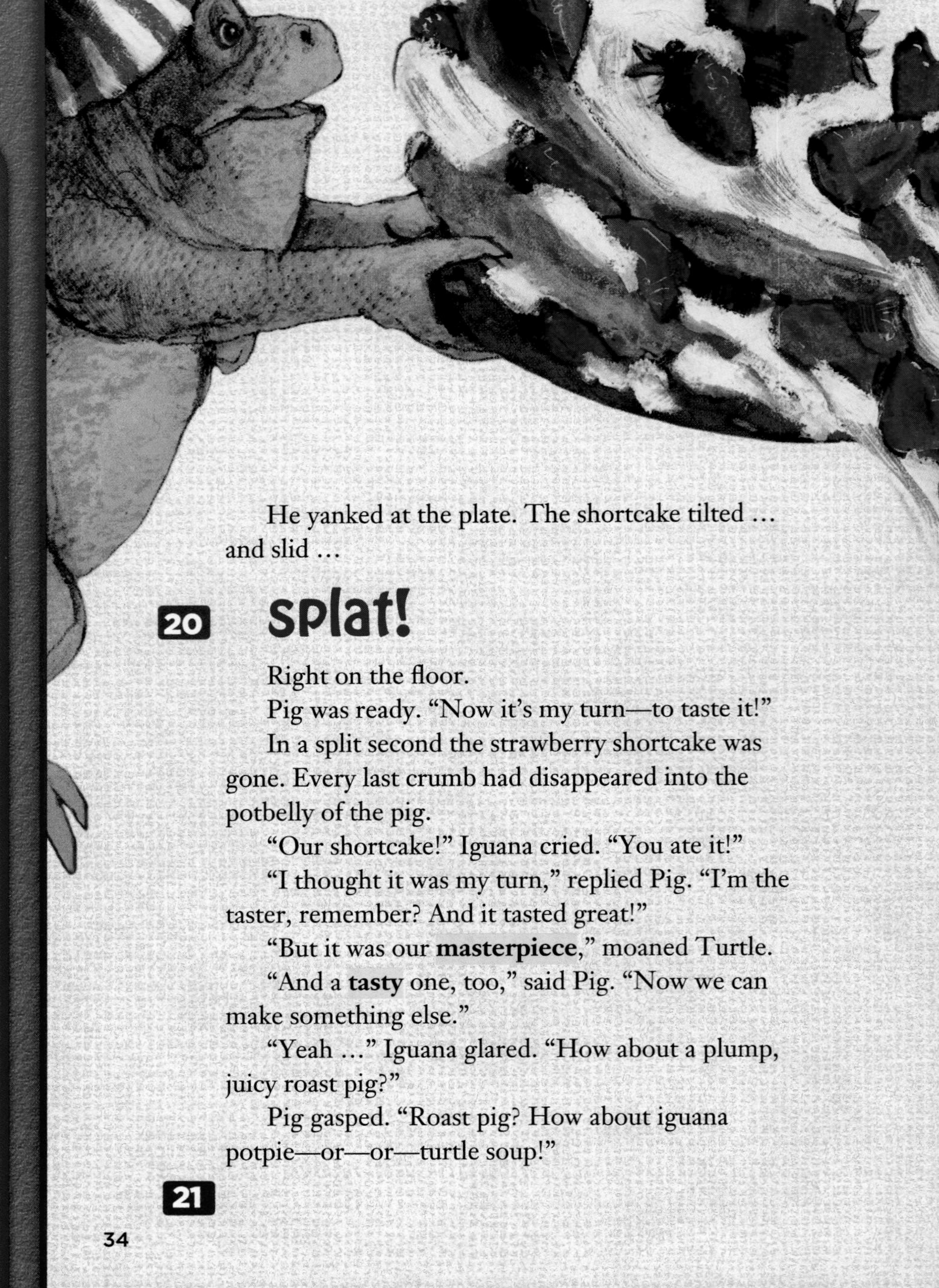

He yanked at the plate. The shortcake tilted … and slid …

20 **splat!**

Right on the floor.

Pig was ready. "Now it's my turn—to taste it!"

In a split second the strawberry shortcake was gone. Every last crumb had disappeared into the potbelly of the pig.

"Our shortcake!" Iguana cried. "You ate it!"

"I thought it was my turn," replied Pig. "I'm the taster, remember? And it tasted great!"

"But it was our **masterpiece**," moaned Turtle.

"And a **tasty** one, too," said Pig. "Now we can make something else."

"Yeah …" Iguana glared. "How about a plump, juicy roast pig?"

Pig gasped. "Roast pig? How about iguana potpie—or—or—turtle soup!"

21

34

Vocabulary

Read the sentence with the vocabulary word **tasty**. What is another word that means the same as *tasty*? (*delicious, yummy*)

LA.3.1.6.8 Use knowledge of synonyms

"No, no, no!" cried Rooster. "Listen to me! We made this shortcake as a team, and teams work together." 22

"But Pig ate it!" whined Turtle.

"Iguana dropped it," pouted Pig.

"Turtle should have caught it," grumbled Iguana.

"It doesn't matter," said Rooster. "The first shortcake was just for practice. It won't be as hard to make the second time!"

"Well," added Turtle, "we don't have to worry about messing up the kitchen. It's already a mess."

"So, who will help me make it again?" asked Rooster.

Pig, Turtle, and Iguana looked at each other.

35

Develop Comprehension

22 STRATEGY

MAKE INFERENCES AND ANALYZE

LA.3.1.7.3 Determine implied inference

How can making inferences help you better understand what kind of character Rooster is? Explain your thinking in a Think Aloud.

Student Think Aloud The authors don't tell me what kind of character Rooster is, but I can use his actions and words and my own experiences to figure this out. In this part of the story, Rooster decides to bake another shortcake with his friends because Pig ate the first one. Most people would give up after ruining the first cake. I also see that Rooster isn't mad at his friends, even though they made a mess of the first cake. Most people would have been angry. Using these clues and my own experience with people, I see that Rooster is the kind of character that does not give up. He is also a good friend because he wants his friends to help him one more time. By making inferences, I understand exactly what kind of character Rooster is.

Develop Comprehension

23 COMPARE EVENTS

LA.3.1.7.3 Determine explicit information

How is the second cake different from the first one? How is it like the first one? (The first cake took a lot of hard work. Rooster and his friends made a lot of mistakes. The second cake is easier and faster to make because all the animals know what the right ingredients are and how to measure them. Both cakes have the same ingredients and follow the same recipe. The first cake fell on the floor, but the second cake is wonderful and magnificent.)

24 ESSENTIAL MESSAGE

LA.3.1.7.3 Determine explicit information

What is the author's message in this story? How do you know? (The author's message is that teamwork and friendshop are the most important things needed to finish a project. I know this because the animals work together to bake the best shortcake in the world, even thought they have to do it twice.

"I will!" said Pig.
"I will!" said Turtle.
"I will!" said Iguana.
"Cook-a-doodle-dooooo!" crowed Rooster. "Let's get cooking again!"

36

Together they made the second most wonderful, magnificent strawberry shortcake in the whole wide world. And it was a lot easier than the first time! 23 24

37

Develop Comprehension

LA.3.1.7.1 Use text features to confirm predictions

RETURN TO PREDICTIONS AND PURPOSES

Review students' predictions and purposes. Were they correct? Could they make inferences about characters and events? Were they able to compare and contrast characters and events? Have students think of other questions about the story that they might like to have answered. What strategies can they use to answer the questions?

LA.3.1.7 Use strategies to comprehend text

REVIEW READING STRATEGIES

How did comparing and contrasting characters and events help students to understand the story?

Journal

LA.3.2.1.6 Write a book report.

LA.3.2.1.7 Respond to literary selections

PERSONAL RESPONSE

Have students write a book report about *Cook-A-Doodle-Doo*. They should identify the main characters, and summarize the plot including the problem, solution and important events in order. Have students include a recommendation to read or not to read and then share their reports with partners.

Quick Check **Can students compare characters and their actions as they read?**

During **Small Group Instruction**

If No → **Approaching Level** Leveled Reader Lesson, p. 45P

If Yes → **On Level** Options, pp. 45Q–45R

Beyond Level Options, pp. 45S–45T

Author and Illustrator

WHAT'S COOKIN' WITH JANET AND SUSAN?

Have students read the biographies of the authors and the illustrator.

DISCUSS

LA.3.1.7.2 Identify how author's perspective influences text
LA.3.2.2.1 Identify and explain the purpose of text features

- How do you think Janet and Susan came up with the idea for this story?
- How do Janet Stevens's illustrations help make the story humorous?

LA.3.2.1.8 Select fiction to read
LA.3.2.2.5 Select nonfiction to read

For fiction and nonfiction books related to the weekly theme, recommend that students read books from the Theme Bibliography on page T18.

WRITE ABOUT IT

LA.3.4.2.4 Write thank-you notes

Ask students to write a thank-you note to Rooster, from the point of view of Pig, Turtle, or Iguana, thanking him for teaching them how to cook and make the "second most wonderful, magnificent strawberry shortcake in the world." Students can share their notes.

FCAT Author's Purpose

Help students to use the humorous scenes in the story to figure out the authors' purpose. The authors wrote a funny story. It does not include information about a nonfiction topic. Help students to conclude that the authors' purpose is to entertain.

LA.3.1.7.2 Identify the author's purpose

LOG ON Technology

Tell students they can find more information about Janet Stevens and Susan Stevens Crummel at **www.macmillanmh.com**

LA.3.6.4.1 Use appropriate available technologies

What's Cookin' With Janet and Susan?

Janet Stevens and Susan Stevens Crummel

Authors Janet Stevens and Susan Stevens Crummel were not very close when they were growing up, but now they have as much fun working together as the animals in their story did.

They are sisters who both like animals. Janet's favorite books as a child were about animals. She still reads animal stories today. Janet likes telling old tales in new ways, just as she did in this story. The sisters wrote this book together. Then Janet created the illustrations. She's been drawing ever since she was a child.

Other books by Janet Stevens and Susan Stevens Crummel: *Jackalope* and *And the Dish Ran Away with the Spoon*

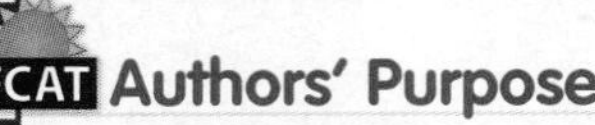

FCAT Authors' Purpose

What was the authors' purpose for writing *Cook-a-Doodle-Doo!*? Did they want to explain or entertain? How did they meet their goal?

LOG ON Find out more about Janet Stevens and Susan Stevens Crummel at **www.macmillanmh.com**

38

FCAT Author's Craft

Word Play

The authors of *Cook-A-Doodle-Doo!* add humor to the story by having characters confuse the meanings of **homophones** and **multiple-meaning words**.

- When Iguana mistakes one word for another, it causes mix-ups that make the reader laugh. For example: *"The recipe says we need flour," said Turtle. "I can do that!" said Iguana. He dashed outside and picked a petunia. "How's this flower?"* (p. 21)

Iguana does not realize that *flour* is different from *flower*. Discuss how Iguana's mistake adds humor to the story. Ask students to find other examples of humorous word play on pages 22 and 23 (*sift*), page 26 (*teaspoon* and *tablespoon*), page 27 (*stick*), and pages 28 and 29 (*beat*).

LA.3.1.6.8 Use knowledge of homophones
LA.3.1.6.9 Determine correct meaning of words with multiple meanings

FCAT Comprehension Check

Summarize

Summarize *Cook-a-Doodle-Doo!* Use the Venn Diagram to help you compare Pig and Rooster. Compare and contrast the main characters. Use descriptions of their personalities and events in the story.

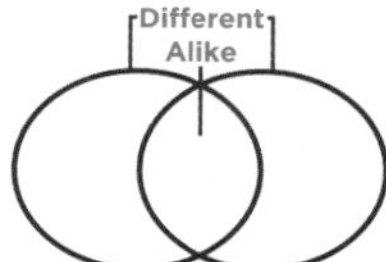

Think and Compare

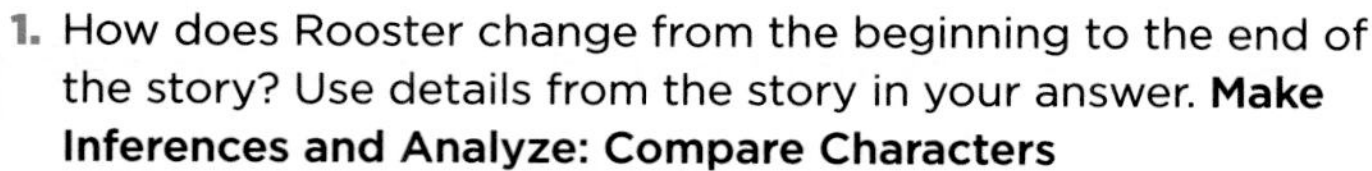

1. How does Rooster change from the beginning to the end of the story? Use details from the story in your answer. **Make Inferences and Analyze: Compare Characters**

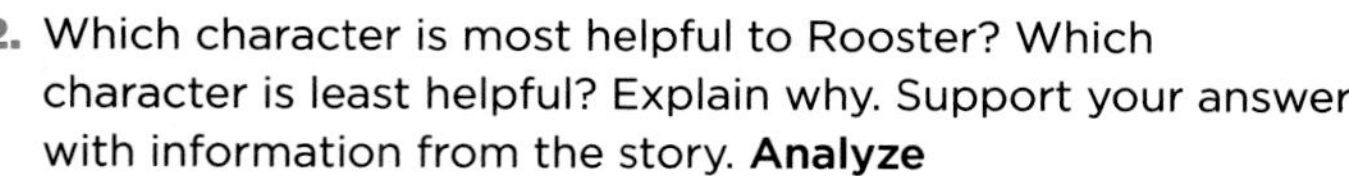

2. Which character is most helpful to Rooster? Which character is least helpful? Explain why. Support your answer with information from the story. **Analyze**
3. Suppose you wanted to bake a cake. Which of the characters in the story would you ask to help you? Why? **Apply**
4. Why is it important to follow directions in **recipes**? Explain your answer. **Evaluate**
5. Read "Red and Her Friends" on pages 12–13. How is it similar to *Cook-a-Doodle-Doo!*? How are the two stories different? Use details from both stories in your answer. **Reading/Writing Across Texts**

39

Strategies for Answering Questions

On My Own

Model the On My Own strategy with question 3. Students will not find the answers to On My Own questions in the story. Sometimes they will form an opinion based on what they have read. Other times they will use information they already know.

Question 3 Think Aloud: I won't find the answer in the story. I will use what I know about the characters to form an opinion. Pig didn't really help, Iguana made a lot of mistakes, but Turtle did a good job reading the directions, so I would choose Turtle. Using what I learned about the characters helped me to form an opinion and answer this question.

LA.3.1.7 Use a variety of strategies to comprehend grade level text

Comprehension Check

SUMMARIZE

LA.3.1.7.8 Summarize to repair comprehension

Have partners summarize *Cook-A-Doodle-Doo!* Remind students that their Venn Diagrams can help them organize their ideas.

THINK AND COMPARE

Sample answers are given.

LA.3.2.1.2 Identify and explain character/character development

1. **Compare Characters:** In the beginning of the story, Rooster wants to cook his own way. At the end he just enjoys making the most wonderful strawberry shortcake in the world with friends.

LA.3.1.7.3 Determine explicit information

2. **Analyze:** Turtle is most helpful because he reads the recipe and tells Rooster and Pig what to do. Pig is the least helpful because all he wants to do is taste ingredients.

LA.3.2.1.7 Connect text to self

3. **Text-to-Self:** Students may say they would ask Turtle to help bake because he was the most helpful with reading directions. USE ON MY OWN

LA.3.2.1.7 Connect text to world

4. **Text-to-World:** Students may say it is important to follow recipe directions in order for the cooking to be successful and taste good.

FOCUS QUESTION

LA.3.2.1.7 Connect text to text

LA.3.1.7.7 Compare and contrast settings, characters and problems

5. **Text-to-Text:** Both stories are about animals that work together. The main character in both stories is a chicken. In "Red and Her Friends," they plant vegetables, and the masterpiece is a garden. In *Cook-A-Doodle-Doo!* they bake, and the masterpiece is a shortcake. Red has only one friend helping, and Rooster has three.

Objectives

- Read accurately with proper phrasing
- Rate: 82–102 WCPM

Materials

- Fluency Transparency 16
- Fluency Solutions Audio CD
- Leveled Practice Books, p. 115

ELL Access for All

Read with Expression
Review the meaning of the passage first. Then echo-read the passage with students. Encourage students to mimic your expressiveness. Have students role-play the dialogue in groups of four. Students may also listen to the Audio CD.

AUDIO CD

On Level Practice Book O, page 115

As I read, I will pay attention to punctuation.

Even kids can be inventors. Frank Epperson was eleven
9 years old when he proved it! One night he mixed powdered
20 fruit flavor in a cup of soda water. He stirred it with a stick.
34 That's how people made fruit drinks in 1905. But after a
44 sip or two, Frank left his drink on the back porch.
55 The night grew very cold. By morning, Frank had a
65 magnificent surprise. His fruit soda had frozen to the stick.
75 Frank showed it to his friends. At first everyone thought
85 Frank had lost his marbles. They thought he was crazy.
95 But after one lick, everyone cheered. Frank's invention was
104 a masterpiece. A work of art! Frank called it an Epsicle.
115 Frank decided to sell the icy treats. 122

Comprehension Check

1. How was a fruit drink made in 1905? **Main Idea and Details**
   Powdered fruit flavor was mixed with soda water.
2. How did Frank Epperson discover popsicles? **Main Idea and Details**
   Frank left his drink on the back porch, and it froze during the night, creating an Epsicle.

	Words Read	–	Number of Errors	=	Words Correct Score
First Read		–		=	
Second Read		–		=	

Approaching Practice Book A, page 115

Beyond Practice Book B, page 115

Fluency

Repeated Reading: Intonation and Pausing

LA.3.1.5 Demonstrate the ability to read text orally with accuracy

EXPLAIN/MODEL It is important for readers to have good prosody to show they understand what they have read. Good readers learn to read groups of words together in phrases. Explain that the text on **Transparency 16** has been marked with slashes that indicate pauses and stops. A single slash indicates a pause. A double slash indicates a full stop. Read the passage while students listen carefully.

Transparency 16

"Can I taste the flour?"/ asked Pig. //

"Not yet,/ Pig,"/ said Turtle.// "The recipe says to sift it first."//

"What does *sift* mean?"/ asked Iguana.//

"Hmmm,"/ said Turtle.// "I think *sift* means 'to search through' . . ."//

"You mean like when I sift through the garbage looking for lunch?"/ asked Pig.//

"I can do that!"/ said Iguana.// And he dived into the flour,/ throwing it everywhere!//

"No, no, no,"/ said Rooster.// "Don't sift the flour like that.// Put it through this sifter."//

Fluency Transparency 16
from *Cook-A-Doodle Doo!* pages 22–23

LA.3.1.5 Demonstrate the ability to read text orally with expression

AUDIO CD

Access for All

PRACTICE/APPLY Reread the first two sentences of the passage with students. Have them keep in mind the differences in intonation between the dialogue and the narration. Then divide them into two groups. Have groups read chorally as they alternate reading sentences. For additional practice, have students use **Leveled Practice Book** page 115 or the **Fluency Solutions Audio CD.**

Quick Check **Can students read accurately with proper phrasing?**

During **Small Group Instruction**

If No → Approaching Level Fluency, p. 45N

If Yes → On Level Options, pp. 45Q–45R

Beyond Level Options, pp. 45S–45T

Comprehension

FCAT REVIEW SKILL
AUTHOR'S PURPOSE

LA.3.1.7.2 Identify the author's purpose

EXPLAIN/MODEL

An **author's purpose** is the reason an author writes a story, an article, or a book. Authors write to entertain, inform, or explain. Knowing an author's purpose can help a reader evaluate and understand what he or she reads.

- An author who tries to make the reader laugh and enjoy a story is writing to **entertain**.
- An author who gives a lot of information or facts about a topic is writing to **inform**.
- An author who wants to show how to do something or why someone should do something writes to **explain**.

Model how to identify the author's purpose in "Red and Her Friends" on pages 12–13. Point out that this is a made-up story. It's about how a hen and her friend make a garden in an old lot. It does not present facts about a nonfiction topic or explain how to do something. It is a fun story to read. Using these clues, a reader can figure out that the author's purpose is to entertain the readers with a story about how a hen and her cat friend created a masterpiece.

Cooperative Learning

PRACTICE/APPLY

Ask a student to lead a discussion to answer the questions below about *Cook-A-Doodle-Doo!* For comprehension practice, use graphic organizers on pages 99–112 in the **Teacher's Resource Book**.

LA.3.2.1 Identify and analyze elements of fiction

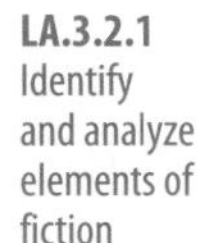

- What kind of story is *Cook-A-Doodle-Doo*? (It is a humorous story based on a familiar fairy tale.)
- How do readers feel when they read the story? Why do they feel this way? (Readers feel amused because the story is funny.)
- What is the authors' purpose? Use story clues to help you figure it out. (The story tells how Rooster, the Little Red Hen's great-grandson, bakes a cake, and it is very funny. The authors' purpose is to write an entertaining version of *The Little Red Hen* with different characters.)

LA.3.2.1.8 Select fiction materials to read

Have groups of students read and discuss another fairy tale about animals. Ask them to identify the author's purpose and share with other groups.

Objective

- Identify author's purpose in text
- Use academic language: *author's purpose, entertain, inform, explain*

FCAT **Skills Trace**

Author's Purpose	
Introduce	U1: 33B
Practice / Apply	U1: 66, 111B; U2: 259A–B; Leveled Practice, 67–68,
Reteach / Review	U2: 2770–P, R, T; U4: 94–102, 1100–P, R, T; Leveled Practice, 134–135
Assess	Weekly Tests; Unit 1, 2, 4, 6 Tests; Benchmark Tests A, B
Maintain	U1: 111B; U2: 259A-B; U4: 39B, 93A-B; U6: 361A-B

Informational Text: Science

LA.3.2.2 Identify elements of informational texts

GENRE: NONFICTION ARTICLES

Have students read the bookmark on **Student Book** page 40. Explain that a nonfiction article

- gives information about a topic;
- often contains diagrams to make information easy to understand;
- often has photographs that show how something is done;
- usually has headings that tell the topic of the text that follows.

Text Feature: Diagrams

LA.3.2.2.1 Identify and explain the purpose of text features

EXPLAIN Point out the diagram on page 42. Explain that this diagram shows how bread is made step by step.

- A **diagram** is a special picture that shows how something works or how it is put together.
- Some diagrams explain steps in a process. Arrows show the path to the next step. Labels name each step These kinds of diagrams often appear in science and social studies books.

APPLY Have students identify the title of the diagram and what is shows. (How Bread Is Made; the steps in making bread)

LA.3.2.2.1 Explain purpose of text features

Have students find examples of diagrams in their science and social studies books and explain what the diagrams show and why they are useful to the reader.

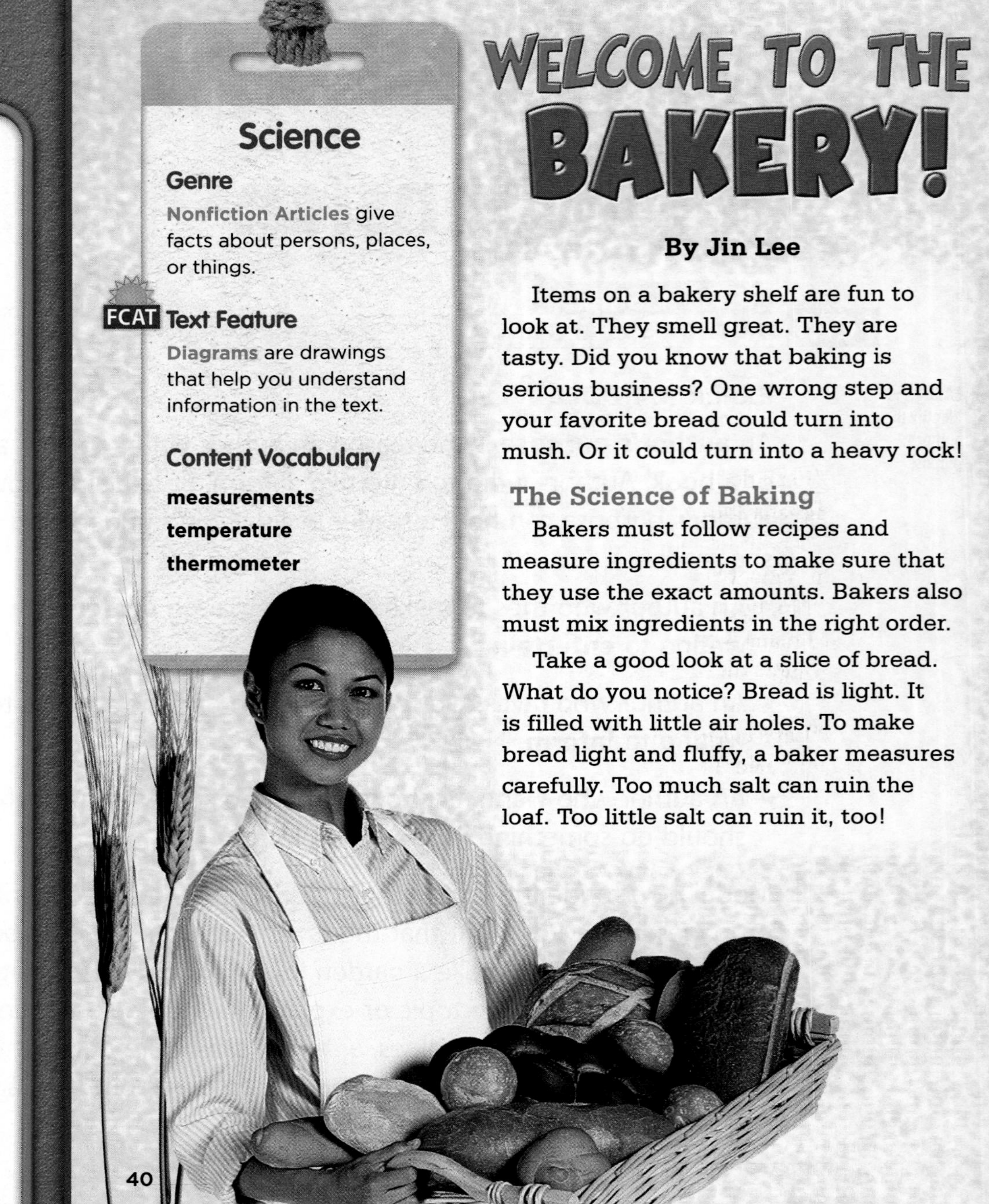

Science
Genre
Nonfiction Articles give facts about persons, places, or things.
FCAT Text Feature
Diagrams are drawings that help you understand information in the text.
Content Vocabulary
measurements
temperature
thermometer
WELCOME TO THE BAKERY!
By Jin Lee
Items on a bakery shelf are fun to look at. They smell great. They are tasty. Did you know that baking is serious business? One wrong step and your favorite bread could turn into mush. Or it could turn into a heavy rock!
The Science of Baking
Bakers must follow recipes and measure ingredients to make sure that they use the exact amounts. Bakers also must mix ingredients in the right order.
Take a good look at a slice of bread. What do you notice? Bread is light. It is filled with little air holes. To make bread light and fluffy, a baker measures carefully. Too much salt can ruin the loaf. Too little salt can ruin it, too!
40

Content Vocabulary

LA.3.1.6.1 Use new vocabulary that is introduced and taught directly

Review the spelling and meaning of each content vocabulary word for "Welcome to the Bakery!"

- **Measurements** are the size, volume, area, mass, weight, or temperature of an object. What measurements can you use to find the distance from your head to your toes?
- **Temperature** is how hot or cold something is. What is your favorite temperature when you are outside?
- A **thermometer** is an instrument used to measure temperature. When would you use a thermometer?

Cups and Spoons

To make bread, the baker mixes milk, sugar, salt, shortening, flour, and yeast. Yeast is the ingredient that makes the bread rise. Special cups and spoons with just the right space for each ingredient are used. Spoons and cups can be used to measure the dry ingredients. Spoon **measurements** can be as small as 1/8 of a teaspoon or as large as a tablespoon. **1**

Another measuring tool a baker uses is a cup—but not the cup you drink from! There are special containers that hold cup measurements, such as 1/4 cup and 2 cups. Only exact measurements will do when baking.

Hot and Cold

The **temperature** of the water used to dissolve the yeast must also be measured. To measure water temperature, a baker uses a **thermometer**. The temperature of a bread mixture will change as new ingredients are added. If the ingredients are too hot or too cold, the bread will not bake properly. **2**

The baker must take the bread out of the oven at exactly the right time.

Informational Text

Read "Welcome to the Bakery!"

Access for All
LA.3.1.6.3 Use context clues

As students read, remind them to apply what they have learned about reading a diagram and identify clues to the meanings of the highlighted words.

1 RELEVANT DETAILS

LA.3.2.2.2 Answer questions related to relevant details

What measuring tools do bakers use to bake bread? (They use measuring spoons and cups for dry ingredients and special cups for liquid.)

2 MAIN IDEA AND DETAILS

LA.3.1.7.3 Determine implied inference
LA.3.1.7.3 Determine main idea

What is the unstated main idea of the section under the heading "Hot and Cold"? How do you know? (Temperature is an important measurement in baking bread. Water temperature is important for dissolving yeast; if bread temperature is too hot or cold, it will not raise properly.)

ENGLISH LANGUAGE LEARNERS

Access for All

Beginning Use Visuals Have students say what they can about the pictures and the title. Talk through the process the baker is working through using sequence words. Use gestures to show the actions and have students repeat the gestures.

Intermediate Retell Have students complete the Beginning task. Ask how the photo is useful in understanding the process of baking. Help students retell in sequence what they can about a baker's day. Encourage students to use gestures.

Advanced Compare and Contrast Complete the Intermediate task. Have students compare and contrast the baking process with another food-making process.

Comprehension Paying attention to diagrams and illustrations improves students' comprehension of texts as well as their recall of important parts of a selection. Diagrams and illustrations seem to enhance both the quantity and quality of what students remember from text.

Janice A. Dole

Log on to **www.macmillanmh.com**

Informational Text

3 TEXT FEATURE: DIAGRAMS

FCAT

LA.3.1.7.1 Identify a text's features

How many steps are shown in the diagram? What do they show? (The diagram shows seven steps needed to make bread.. .)

4 TEXT FEATURE: DIAGRAMS

FCAT

What happens right after the dough is sized and cut into pieces? (The dough is kneaded, or pressed and stretched.)

5 TEXT FEATURE: CHART

FCAT

LA.3.1.7.1 Identify a text's features

What information can you find on the chart? Why is it useful for bakers?(The chart shows measurements for measurements for volume of fluids and weight. The information is useful, because it will help bakers know exactly how much of each ingredient to use.)

LA.3.6.4.1 Use appropriate available technologies

Encourage students to use digital tools, such as Web sites and electronic encyclopedias to find more information about running a bakery.

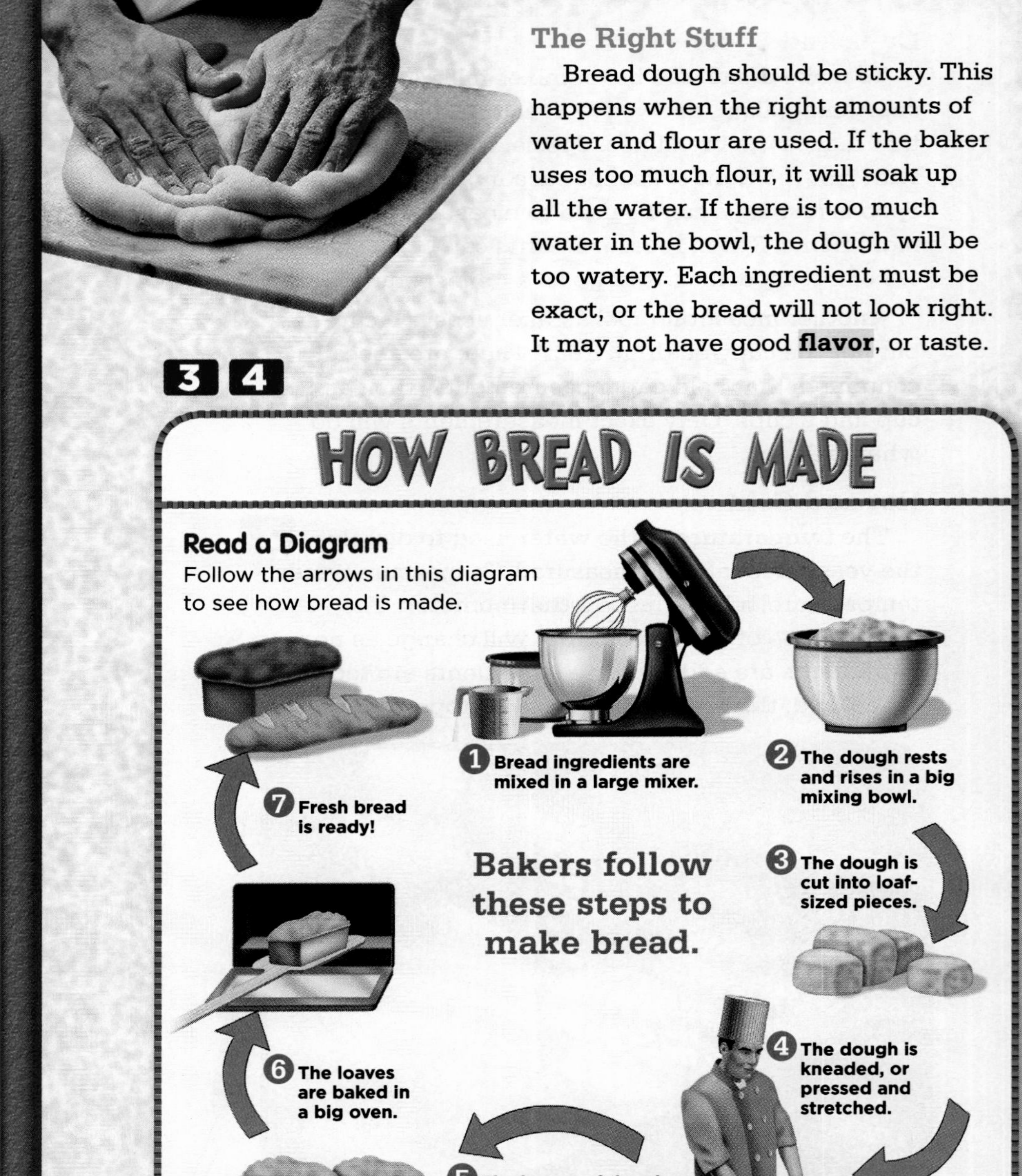

The Right Stuff

Bread dough should be sticky. This happens when the right amounts of water and flour are used. If the baker uses too much flour, it will soak up all the water. If there is too much water in the bowl, the dough will be too watery. Each ingredient must be exact, or the bread will not look right. It may not have good **flavor**, or taste.

3 4

HOW BREAD IS MADE

Read a Diagram

Follow the arrows in this diagram to see how bread is made.

1 Bread ingredients are mixed in a large mixer.
2 The dough rests and rises in a big mixing bowl.
3 The dough is cut into loaf-sized pieces.
4 The dough is kneaded, or pressed and stretched.
5 The loaves of dough rest and rise again.
6 The loaves are baked in a big oven.
7 Fresh bread is ready!
Bakers follow these steps to make bread.

42

On Level Practice Book O, page 116

A **diagram** is a drawing that explains information. Some information is easier to understand by looking at a diagram than by reading about it.

All the food that you eat needs to be digested. Look at the diagram that shows how food is digested. Use these words to help you answer the questions.

mouth esophagus stomach pancreas liver intestine

esophagus
mouth
liver
stomach
intestine
pancreas

1. What would be a good title for this diagram? The Digestive System
2. On the correct line in the diagram, label the body part you use to chew food. mouth
3. On the correct line in the diagram, label the body part that leads to the stomach. esophagus
4. The pancreas makes juices that help you digest food. Which body part is nearest the pancreas? stomach

 **Approaching Practice Book A,** page 116

◆ **Beyond Practice Book B,** page 116

If you have a favorite recipe, make sure you follow it exactly. Measure each ingredient carefully. The baker knows how important correct measurement is. Remember to think like a baker next time you follow a recipe.

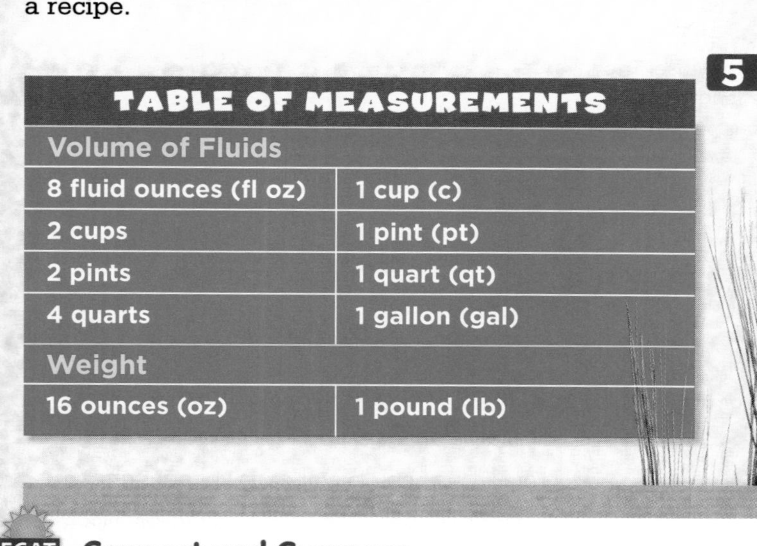

5

TABLE OF MEASUREMENTS	
Volume of Fluids	
8 fluid ounces (fl oz)	1 cup (c)
2 cups	1 pint (pt)
2 pints	1 quart (qt)
4 quarts	1 gallon (gal)
Weight	
16 ounces (oz)	1 pound (lb)

FCAT **Connect and Compare**

1. Look at the diagram called How Bread Is Made. What happens first? What happens last? **Reading a Diagram**
2. Why is it so important to measure carefully when making bread? **Explain**
3. How is making bread like making a strawberry shortcake in *Cook-A-Doodle-Do*? **Reading/Writing Across Texts**

Science Activity

Find a recipe for something you like to eat. Draw a diagram that shows the steps you take to make it.

LOG ON Find out more about baking at **www.macmillanmh.com**

43

LOG ON Technology

Internet Research and Inquiry Activity Students can find more facts at **www.macmillanmh.com**

Informational Text

Connect and Compare

FCAT LA.3.1.7.3 Determine explicit information LA.3.1.7.3 Determine relevant supporting details

SUGGESTED ANSWERS

1. First, the ingredients for the bread are mixed in a large mixer. The loaves come out fresh from the oven last. READING A DIAGRAM
2. If the ingredients are not measured correctly, the bread will not bake properly or taste right. ANALYZE

FOCUS QUESTION

LA.3.2.1.7 Connect text to text

3. Both are made by following steps in a similar process. Also each ingredient is measured with special cups and spoons. Bread and strawberry shortcake should be baked at certain temperatures. READING/WRITING ACROSS TEXTS

RESEARCH INQUIRY

Science Activity

Remind students that they should check measurements of ingredients and order of steps to create their diagram. Have students present their diagrams to the class.

SC.A.1.2.1.3.1 Properties of materials can be compared and measured; **LA.3.5.2.2** Give an oral presentation; **LA.3.5.2.1** Interpret information presented orally; **LA.3.3.2.2** Organize information into logical sequence

Connect Language Arts

FCAT WRITING
- Narrative
- Writer's Craft: Vary Sentences

FCAT WORD STUDY
- Words in Context
- Idioms
- **Phonics:** Words with /ô/
- Vocabulary Building

SPELLING/GRAMMAR
- Words with /ô/
- Verbs *be, do,* and *have*

SMALL GROUP OPTIONS
- Differentiated Instruction, pp. 45M–45V

Writing

FCAT Vary Sentences

LA.3.3.3.2 Create clarity by using a combination of sentence structures

READ THE STUDENT MODEL

Read the bookmark about varying sentences. Explain that good writers use both simple and compound sentences and a variety of sentence types. Different kinds of sentences make writing more interesting to read.

Have students reread the third paragraph on page 12. Point out and discuss the simple and compound sentences.

LA.3.4.1.1 Write narratives based on real events

Then have the class read Marcus G.'s personal narrative and the callouts. Tell students that they will write their own stories about making something with their families. They will also learn to use a variety of sentence types to improve their writing.

Write About a Family Meal

Writer's Craft

FCAT Vary Sentences

Good writers **vary** the types of **sentences** they use. They also vary the lengths of their sentences.

Breakfast Surprise

by Marcus G.

I began my story with a question and an exclamation.

What tasty treat is shaped like an animal? Pancakes! Last weekend Dad taught us how to make animal pancakes for breakfast. First we helped him mix the ingredients in a bowl. I was in charge of the salt and sugar. My brothers were in charge of the flour. They made a big mess! "We must clean as we go along," Dad warned. Dad poured the mixture onto the hot griddle and asked us to name our favorite animals. Before we knew it, we had animal pancakes!

I used long and short sentences to give my writing variety.

My brother asked, "Can I have a walrus?" Dad tried to make one, but it looked like a rabbit to me! It was the best breakfast. Pancakes are now my favorite food!

44

Features of a Personal Narrative

A personal narrative tells a true story about an experience the writer had. The writing is presented in an appropriate format.

- The writer uses the first-person point of view, and pronouns such as *I, me, we,* and *our.*
- The narrative includes vivid details to describe what the writer did, saw, heard, thought, and felt. It may include dialogue.
- Most personal narratives tell about events in time order, and use time-order words like *last week, before, first, then, next, soon,* and *finally.*

LA.3.4.1.1 Write narratives that include logical sequence of events; **LA.3.4.1.2** Employ appropriate format; **LA.3.4.1.2** Employ dialogue; **LA.3.3.2.2** Organize information through use of time-order words; **LA.3.3.3.3** Create interest by adding supporting details; **LA.3.3.3.1** Evaluate draft for use of point of view

Writing Prompt

Families sometimes like to make things together.

Think of something you have made with your family.

Now write a story about what you made with your family.

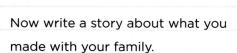

FCAT Writer's Checklist

- ☑ **Focus:** I have a clear topic.
- ☑ **Organization:** I tell the story in the order in which it happened.
- ☑ **Support:** I include specific details that support my main idea.
- ☐ **Conventions:** I use the verbs *be, do,* and *have* correctly. I **vary** my **sentences**. All my words are spelled correctly.

Transparency 61: **Sequence Chart**
Transparency 62: **Draft**
Transparency 63: **Revision**

Transparency 61

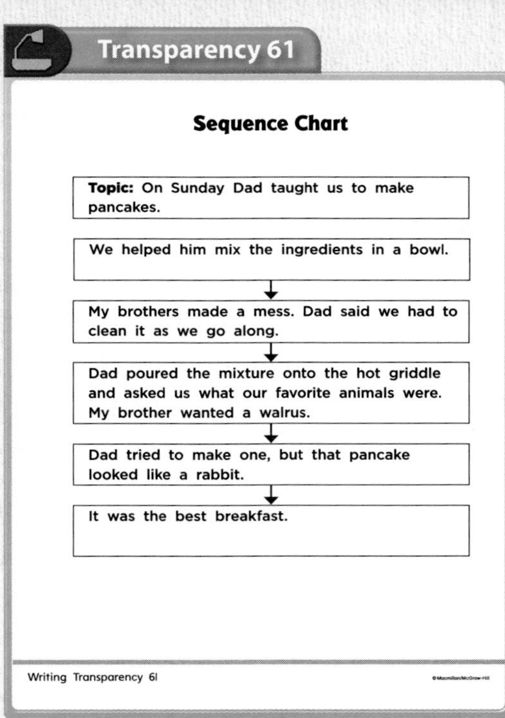

Sequence Chart

Topic: On Sunday Dad taught us to make pancakes.

We helped him mix the ingredients in a bowl.

My brothers made a mess. Dad said we had to clean it as we go along.

Dad poured the mixture onto the hot griddle and asked us what our favorite animals were. My brother wanted a walrus.

Dad tried to make one, but that pancake looked like a rabbit.

It was the best breakfast.

Writing Transparency 61

Writing Transparency 61

Connect

Writing Student pages 44–45

PREWRITE

LA.3.3.1.1 Generate ideas from multiple sources
LA.3.3.1.2 Determine purpose and intended audience of a writing piece

Discuss the writing prompt on page 45. Students can work independently or with partners or use their writer's notebooks or portfolios to brainstorm ideas. Have them identify the purpose (to entertain) and audience (teacher and classmates).

LA.3.3.1.3 Use organizational strategies to make a plan for writing

Display **Transparency 61**. Discuss how Marcus used a Sequence Chart to plan his writing. Have students create Sequence Charts about what their families do together. Have them add ovals for more details as needed.

DRAFT

LA.3.3.2.2 Organize information through use of time-order words; LA.3.4.1.1 Write narratives that include logical sequence of events

Display **Transparency 62**. Discuss how Marcus used details from his chart to write a draft. Discuss how he could improve the draft. Then have students use their Sequence Charts to write their narratives in logical sequence using time-order words.

REVISE

LA.3.3.3 Revise draft
LA.3.3.3.2 Create clarity by using a combination of sentence structures
LA.3.3.3.3 Create interest by adding supporting details
LA.3.3.3.4 Apply appropriate tools or strategies to refine draft
LA.3.3.4 Edit and correct draft for standard language conventions

Display **Transparency 63**. Discuss how the changes improved the narrative. Students can revise their drafts or place them in writing portfolios to work on later. Before students revise, present the **Vary Sentences** lesson on page 45A and the minilessons **Create a Strong Lead** and **Writing Trait: Vivid Details** on page 45B. If they choose to revise, have them work in pairs, using peer review and the Writer's Checklist on page 45. Then have students **proofread/edit** their writing. For lessons on grammar and spelling, see page 45B and **5 Day Spelling** and **Grammar** on pages 45G–45J.

For **Publishing Options**, see page 45A.

Writer's Craft

LA.3.3.5.1 Prepare writing in format appropriate to audience and purpose; LA.3.3.5.2 Add graphics where appropriate

Publishing Options

Students can read aloud their personal narratives to the class. See Speaking and Listening tips below. They can also use their best cursive to write their paragraphs. (See **Teacher's Resource Book** pages 216–221 for cursive models and practice.) Have students make cartoon strips to illustrate events in their personal narratives. Suggest that they use thought bubbles to show what people in the narrative said and thought.

Speaking and Listening

SPEAKING STRATEGIES

- Speak with expression, and pause before you start each new sentence.
- Make eye contact with your audience.

LISTENING STRATEGIES

- Listen for details that describe people, events, and the setting.
- After the speaker has finished, ask questions about the narrative and discuss it..

LA.3.5.2.2 Use appropriate voice and eye for presentation ; LA.3.5.2.1 Recall information presented orally

6-Point Scoring Rubric

Use the rubric on page 149G to score published writing.

Writing Process

For a complete lesson, see Unit Writing on pages 149A–149F.

SUPPORT Vary Sentences

LA.3.3.3.2 Create clarity by using a combination of sentence structures

EXPLAIN/MODEL

Good writers use a variety of sentences to make their writing flow smoothly. Review types of sentences—statements, questions, commands, exclamations, and simple and compound sentences. Display **Transparency 64**. Have volunteers read the first two paragraphs.

Think Aloud In the first paragraph, all the sentences are short statements. There is no variety in the sentences, and, as a result, the paragraph is not very interesting. In the second paragraph, the writer has used a variety of sentences—a question, an exclamation, a compound sentence, and a statement. When I read this paragraph, the sentences flow nicely and the writing is more interesting. Using different kinds of sentences improves writing.

Transparency 64

Vary Sentences

No Sentence Variety

People eat oatmeal with fruit. It tastes good. I make it on weekends. My whole family eats it. Everyone should eat oatmeal with raisins for breakfast.

Sentence Variety

Have you ever eaten oatmeal with fruit? It tastes fantastic! I make it on weekends, and the whole family gobbles it up. Everyone should eat oatmeal with raisins for breakfast.

People like fruit. It is a great food. It tastes good. It is healthful.

(Why should people eat fruit? It is a great food! It tastes good, and it is healthful.)

Writing Transparency 64

LA.3.3.4.5 Edit for correct use of subject/verb agreement in simple and compound sentences

PRACTICE/APPLY

Have a volunteer read the last paragraph. Then work with students to revise it using a variety of sentences, such as a question, an exclamation, a statement, and a compound or complex sentence. Write the revision on the board, read it aloud, and compare it to the original. Discuss how sentence variety improved the writing.

As students revise and proofread/edit, they should use a variety of sentence types and lengths. Explain that mixture of sentences will make help the writing flow smoothly. Remind them to check for subject/verb agreement in simple and compound sentences.

Writer's Toolbox

LA.3.3.3.3 Create interest by adding supporting details; LA.3.4.1.2 Employ dialogue

SUPPORT

Writing Trait: Ideas and Content

Explain/Model **Vivid details** can make writing come to life. One way to add details to a personal narrative is to add **dialogue**. Work with students to identify an example of dialogue in the first paragraph on page 44. Discuss how the dialogue gives readers more information about Dad, and helps readers to picture events in the story.

Practice/Apply Have students identify dialogue in the second paragraph of the story and how it adds information. As students revise their writing, have them add dialogue that contains important details about the characters or the events.

CONVENTIONS

Verbs *Be*, *Do*, and *Have*

Explain/Model Explain that *be*, *do*, and *have* are verbs that are often used in writing. Discuss the present- and past-tense forms of these verbs and subject-verb agreement.

Practice/Apply Have students identify the verb in the sixth sentence on page 44. Help them determine that *were* is the past tense of *be* and that the subject, *brothers*, is plural. For a complete lesson on *be*, *do*, and *have* and subject-verb agreement, see pages 45I–45J.

LA.3.3.4.4 Edit for correct use of present and past verb tense; LA.3.3.4.5 Edit for correct use of subject/verb agreement
LA.3.6.4 Develop essential technology skills ;LA.3.6.4.2 Use digital tools;

Technology

Remind students that if they make a change they don't like as they write or revise, they can use the Undo function to go back to what they had before the change.

LA.3.3.3 Refine draft for clarity and effectiveness

SUPPORT

Create a Strong Lead

Explain/Model The opening sentence, or lead, of a story should grab the reader's attention. Writers can use a question, a quote, or a vivid description to begin their writing. Have students look at the opening sentence on page 44. Point out that the question catches the reader's attention and introduces the topic of the story—making pancakes with the family.

Practice/Apply Have students think of other strong leads, or opening sentences, for Marcus's story. Record them on the board and discuss why they are effective. As students revise their personal narratives, have them evaluate their opening leads and think of ways that they might improve them by using a question, quote, or vivid description.

CONVENTIONS

Spelling Words with /ô/

Have students find the word *taught* in the third sentence on page 44. Explain that the sound /ô/ in *taught* is spelled *augh*. It can also be spelled *au* as in *cause*, *aw* as in *lawn*, or *ough* as in *bought*. Ask students to pay attention when they spell words with the /ô/ sound. Remind students that they can use a print or digital dictionary to check spelling as they proofread/edit. For a complete lesson on spelling words with /ô/, see pages 45G–45H.

LA.3.3.4.1 Edit for correct use of spelling; LA.3.3.4.1 Edit using a dictionary or other resources

FCAT Success!

Test Prep and Practice with Writing+, pages 180–230

Word Study

Objectives

- Apply knowledge of word meanings and context clues
- Use strategies to determine the meaning of idioms

Materials

- Vocabulary Transparency 31
- Vocabulary Strategy Transparency 32
- Leveled Practice Books, p. 117
- dictionary
- thesaurus

Vocabulary

magnificent (p. 17) wonderful; very beautiful

masterpiece (p. 34) a great work; a very good example of something

ingredient (p. 21) one of the parts of a mixture

recipes (p. 17) lists of ingredients and directions for making food

tasty (p. 34) having a good flavor

ELL — Access for All

Make Associations
Say: *pizza*. Students respond with the vocabulary word that best matches and explain why. Accept any reasonable explanation.

Review Vocabulary

Words in Context

LA.3.1.6.3 Use context clues to determine meaning

EXPLAIN/MODEL

Review the meanings of the vocabulary words. Display **Transparency 31**. Model how to use word meanings and context clues to fill in the first missing word.

Transparency 31

masterpiece magnificent
ingredient tasty recipes

The cook wanted to make a (1) magnificent dish for the banquet. It had to be wonderful.

She carefully read all of her favorite (2) recipes to find the perfect food. The directions for cooking were easy to follow.

She listed each (3) ingredient for the dish. One item was hard to find. "How will we get this?" her helper shouted.

"I'll find it," the cook said. And she did. The dish she cooked was a (4) masterpiece. It was a great example of her skill.

Everyone loved the food's delicious flavor. It was very (5) tasty.

Vocabulary Transparency 31

LA.3.1.6.8 Use knowledge of synonyms

Think Aloud I see that the chef wants to make a dish that is wonderful. I know that another word for *wonderful* is *magnificent*. When I try *magnificent* in the sentence, it makes sense.

PRACTICE/APPLY

LA.3.1.6 Use multiple strategies to develop grade-appropriate vocabulary

Access for All

Have students use context clues to write missing words for items 2–5 on separate pieces of paper. Students can exchange papers, check answers, and explain the context clues they used.

LA.3.1.6.8 Use knowledge of antonyms

LA.3.1.6.6 Identify "shades of meaning" in related words

Antonym Scale Have student pairs write antonym scales for *masterpiece*, *magnificent*, *tasty*, or another word from the story. Have them use a thesaurus to help them arrange the words by shades of meaning from the most to the least. For example, for the word *hot* they might write *red-hot*, *boiling*, *hot*, *warm*, *cool*, *cold*, *freezing*, *subzero* or for the word *magnificent* they might write *gorgeous*, *beautiful*, *plain*, *ugly*, *hideous*. Then have them present their scales to the class and discuss them.

STRATEGY
DICTIONARY: IDIOMS

LA.3.2.1.5 Explain author's use of idiomatic language

LA.3.1.6.10 Determine meanings using a dictionary

LA.3.1.6.3 Use context clues

EXPLAIN/MODEL

- An **idiom** is an expression whose meaning is different from the meaning of each separate word. Many idioms are listed in the dictionary. For example, the idiom *to hit it off* is listed under the entry word *hit* and means "to get along well." Sometimes students can use context clues to help them figure out an idiom, too.

Read the idioms on **Transparency 32**. Model how to complete item 1 by identifying the context clue (very happy) and then write the idiom that goes with it on the blank line.

Transparency 32

Idioms

on cloud nine	eat his words
drive me bananas	piece of cake

1. Allison was very happy when she won first place. She was ______. (very happy; on cloud nine)
2. It was easy for Sara to do her homework. It was a ______. (easy; piece of cake)
3. In an interview before the game, the player said he was sure his team was the best. If he loses, he will have to take that back, or ______. (take that back; eat his words)
3. The puppies were making me crazy by darting through the house and hiding my socks under the couch. If they continue, they are sure to ______. (making me crazy; drive me bananas)

Vocabulary Strategy Transparency 32

LA.3.1.6 Use multiple strategies to develop grade-appropriate vocabulary

LA.3.1.6.1 Use new vocabulary

PRACTICE/APPLY

Access for All

Have students complete items 2–4. Then have them each write a sentence using one of the idioms and read it aloud. Have students look up the idiom *to pull one's leg* in the dictionary under the entry for *leg* and write sentences using it.

Quick Check **Can students use context clues to figure out word meanings and use a dictionary to find the meaning of an idiom?**

During **Small Group Instruction**

If No → **Approaching Level** Vocabulary, pp. 45N–45O

If Yes → **On Level** Options, pp. 45Q–45R

Beyond Level Options, pp. 45S–45T

ELL Access for All

Use Idioms Write on the board: *I would be on cloud nine if* ______. Complete the sentence and create other examples. Discuss them with students and then have students write their own. Use this technique with other idioms.

Vocabulary

Review last week's vocabulary words. Give students this idiom and meaning: *Cramp my style* means "keep me from enjoying myself." Example: *Don't cramp my style. Let me sing by myself.* Challenge students to use the idiom in their own sentences.

FCAT Success!

Test Prep and Practice with vocabulary, pages 6–31

On Level Practice Book O, page 117

An **idiom** is a phrase with a meaning that is different from the meaning of each word in it.

Authors use **idioms,** or special words or phrases, to make their language more colorful. To figure out the meaning of an idiom, read the sentence carefully to understand how it is used.

A. Circle the idiom in each sentence below. Write the meaning of the idiom on the next line. Possible responses provided.

1. Both Dad and Mom work hard (to bring home the bacon).
to bring home money or a paycheck
2. Hitting a home run was (a piece of cake) for our best batter.
easy to do
3. She had (to use her noodle) to figure out how to fix the bike.
to think about something, use your brain
4. Sam is (the big cheese) because he was elected president.
the boss or head person
5. That's the recipe (in a nutshell).
explained in a few words

B. Write a sentence using one idiom from above. Possible response provided.

6. Baking a pie was a piece of cake for the baker.

 **Approaching Practice Book A,** page 117

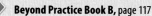

Beyond Practice Book B, page 117

Word Study

Objectives

- Segment and blend words with /ô/
- Decode words with /ô/

Materials

- Leveled Practice Books, p. 118
- Teacher's Resource Book, pp. 87–90

ELL — Access for All

Letter-Sound Correspondence Write the words *paw, fault,* and *mall*. Discuss their meanings. Say the words, emphasizing the /ô/ sound. Have students repeat after you. Underline the letters that make the /ô/ sound. Pronouncing the /ô/ sound may be difficult for Spanish and Korean speakers.

On Level Practice Book O, page 118

The letters *aw* that you hear in *draw* may also be spelled *al* as in *walks*, or *au* as in *haul* and stand for the /ô/ sound.

A. Read the words in each row. Circle the words that have the /ô/ vowel sound you hear in the word *lawn*.

1.	math	(false)	brake
2.	cash	snout	(sauce)
3.	(talk)	salmon	sail
4.	frown	(fawn)	fruit
5.	tour	take	(taught)
6.	route	(salt)	rate
7.	(launch)	land	month
8.	year	hare	(yawn)
9.	(caught)	catch	lost
10.	heal	(hawk)	hope

B. Write rhyming words for each word below that has the /ô/ vowel sound in *lawn*. Possible responses provided.

11. fall call, mall, tall
12. law draw, paw, raw
13. chalk talk, walk
14. yawn fawn, lawn, pawn

Approaching Practice Book A, page 118
Beyond Practice Book B, page 118

Phonics

Decode Words with /ô/

EXPLAIN/MODEL

LA.3.1.4 Demonstrate knowledge of alphabetic principle

- The letters *aw* as in *paw*, *au* as in *fault*, and *a* as in *tall* stand for the /ô/ sound.
- Recognizing the letters that stand for /ô/ can help readers figure out an unfamiliar word.

Write the word *launch*.

LA.3.1.4.1 Use knowledge of pronunciation to decode words

Think Aloud I know the letter *l* has the /l/ sound. The letters *au* often stand for the /ô/ sound. The letter *n* has the /n/ sound. The letters *ch* stand for the /ch/ sound. The sounds are /l/ /ô/ /n/ /ch/. I'll blend these sounds together: /lllôôônnnch/. The word is *launch.*

PRACTICE/APPLY

Display these words: *vault, lawn, small, straw, caught*. Have volunteers underline the letters that stand for the /ô/ sound in each word. Have them segment and blend the sounds and read the words aloud.

LA.3.1.4.3 Decode multi-syllabic words in isolation and in context

Decode Multisyllabic Words Have students use their knowledge of phonics patterns, compound words, and word parts to decode long words. Write these words on the board: *August, tallest, faucet, jigsaw, awesome, strawberry, audience*. Model how to decode *August*, focusing on the /ô/ sound. Then work with students to decode the other words with /ô/ and read them aloud. For more practice in decoding multisyllabic words, see decodable passages on pages 87–90 of the **Teacher's Resource Book**.

LA.3.1.6 Use multiple strategies to develop vocabulary

Rhyming Riddles Have partners choose rhyming pairs of /ô/ words, such as *gnaw* and *claw,* and write riddles. For example, *What rhymes with* gnaw *and is a cat's sharp nail?* (claw)

Quick Check **Can students decode words with /ô/?**

During **Small Group Instruction**

If No → Approaching Level Phonics, p. 45M

If Yes → On Level Options, pp. 45Q–45R

Beyond Level Options, pp. 45S–45T

Vocabulary Building

LA.3.1.6 Use multiple strategies to develop vocabulary
LA.3.6.4.1 Use appropriate available technologies
LA.3.6.4 Develop essential technology skills

LA.3.1.6.4 Categorize key vocabulary

Oral Language

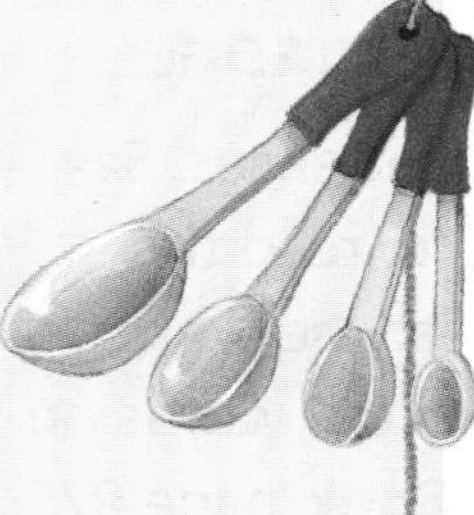

Expand Vocabulary Work with students to brainstorm words about tools that people use to cook and write the words in a semantic web like the one below.

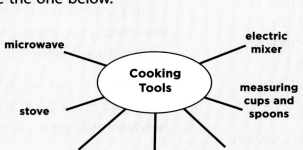

Cooking Tools
- microwave
- electric mixer
- measuring cups and spoons
- pots and pans
- bowls
- recipes
- stove

LA.3.1.6.1 Use new vocabulary

Apply Vocabulary

Write a Paragraph Have each student use the vocabulary words *magnificent*, *masterpiece*, *ingredient*, *recipes*, and *tasty* in a paragraph about cooking, or have them self-select a topic. Students can read their paragraphs aloud.

Vocabulary Building

Homophones Homophones are words that sound the same but have different spellings. *Flower* and *flour* appear in *Cook-A-Doodle-Doo!* Have students use a dictionary to find the meanings of the following homophones: *ad/add*, *hear/here*, *night/knight*, *weak/week*. Then have them write context sentences for each pair of homophones.

Review last week's vocabulary words. Challenge students to find homophones for *instance* and *style*. (*instants*, *stile*)

LA.3.1.6.8 Use knowledge of homophones

Spiral Review

Vocabulary Concentration

Use the **Vocabulary Cards** for *depart*, *aisles*, *ingredient*, *illustrate*, *recipes*, *sketches*, *textures*, and *wrapping*. On separate index cards write the definitions. Shuffle all the cards and place them facedown in a 7 x 7 array. Divide the class into two teams.

- Team 1 turns over two cards. If the two cards are a word and its definition, the team keeps the cards. If not, the two cards are placed facedown again. A Team 2 player turns over two cards, using the same process.
- Play continues until all the words and definitions are matched. The team with the most cards wins.

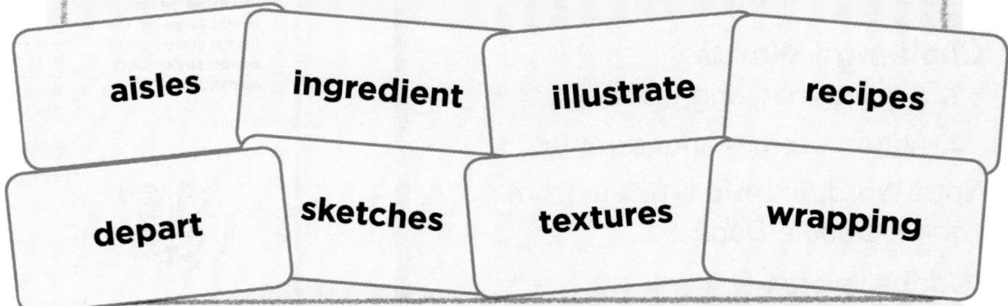

aisles
ingredient
illustrate
recipes
depart
sketches
textures
wrapping

LA.3.1.6.1 Use new vocabulary that is introduced and taught directly

Technology

Vocabulary PuzzleMaker

For additional vocabulary and spelling games, go to www.macmillanmh.com

5 Day Spelling

Spelling Words

yawn	hauls	drawing
taught*	hawks	caused
salt	squawk	paused
lawn	bought*	crawled
halls	bawls	coughing*

Review joyful, coins, spoiled

Challenge walrus, autumn

Dictation Sentences

1. The sleepy boy began to yawn.
2. Who taught you how to cook?
3. The soup needs **salt** and pepper.
4. Who will mow the lawn?
5. The halls at school are long.
6. The man hauls heavy boxes.
7. Hawks have strong claws.
8. I can hear the bird **squawk**.
9. I bought a new book.
10. The baby bawls loudly.
11. This drawing shows a cat.
12. The heavy rain caused a flood.
13. We paused for five minutes.
14. The baby crawled on the floor.
15. The daughter was coughing.

Review Words

1. Her birthday was a joyful time.
2. Tom has coins in his pocket.
3. The rain spoiled our picnic.

Challenge Words

1. A walrus has long tusks.
2. Autumn comes after summer.

Note: Words in **bold** type are from *Cook-A-Doodle-Doo!*

*Oddball words

Display the Spelling Words throughout the week.

LA.3.3.4.1 Correctly use spelling; LA.3.1.4 Demonstrate knowledge of alphabetic principle

Words with /ô/

Day 1 Pretest

ASSESS PRIOR KNOWLEDGE

Use the Dictation Sentences. Say the underlined word, read the sentence, and repeat the word. Have students write the words on **Spelling Practice Book** page 97. For a modified list, use the first 12 Spelling Words and the 3 Review Words. For a more challenging list, use Spelling Words 3–15 and the Challenge Words. Have students correct their own tests.

Have students cut apart the Spelling Word Cards BLM on **Teacher's Resource Book** page 129 and figure out a way to sort them. Have them save the cards for use throughout the week.

Students can use Spelling Practice Book page 98 for further practice.

For leveled Spelling word lists, go to **www.macmillanmh.com**

Spelling Practice Book, pages 97–98

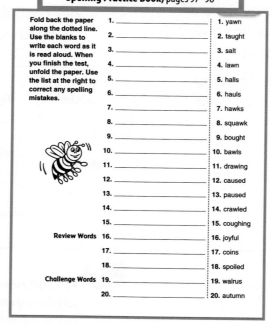

Fold back the paper along the dotted line. Use the blanks to write each word as it is read aloud. When you finish the test, unfold the paper. Use the list at the right to correct any spelling mistakes.

1. ______ 1. yawn
2. ______ 2. taught
3. ______ 3. salt
4. ______ 4. lawn
5. ______ 5. halls
6. ______ 6. hauls
7. ______ 7. hawks
8. ______ 8. squawk
9. ______ 9. bought
10. ______ 10. bawls
11. ______ 11. drawing
12. ______ 12. caused
13. ______ 13. paused
14. ______ 14. crawled
15. ______ 15. coughing

Review Words 16. ______ 16. joyful
17. ______ 17. coins
18. ______ 18. spoiled

Challenge Words 19. ______ 19. walrus
20. ______ 20. autumn

Day 2 Word Sorts

TEACHER AND STUDENT SORTS

- Review the Spelling Words, point out the /ô/ spellings, and discuss meanings. Point out the oddball spellings of *bought* and *coughing.*
- Use the cards on the Spelling Word Cards BLM. Attach the key words *paw, cause, mall,* and *oddball* to a bulletin board.
- Model how to sort words with letters that spell /ô/, and place the cards beneath the correct key words.
- Have students take turns choosing cards, sorting them, and explaining how they sorted them.
- Then have students use their own Spelling Word Cards. After placing the key words on their desks, they can sort the Spelling Words several times. Have students write their last sort on Spelling Practice Book page 99.

Spelling Practice Book, page 99

yawn	lawn	hawks	bawls	paused
taught	halls	squawk	drawing	crawled
salt	hauls	bought	caused	coughing

Pattern Power!

Write the spelling words that have these patterns.

/ô/ spelled *au*
1. hauls 2. caused 3. paused

/ô/ spelled *aw*
4. squawk 5. yawn 6. lawn 7. drawing 8. hawks 9. bawls 10. crawled

/ô/ spelled *a*
11. halls 12. salt

/ô/ spelled *augh*
13. taught

/ô/ spelled *ough*
14. bought 15. coughing

LA.3.3.4.1 Edit for correct use of spelling; LA.3.1.6 Develop grade-appropriate vocabulary

Day 3 Word Meanings

WORD CLUES

Display the word clues below. Have students write the clues and the Spelling Words that go with them in their word study notebooks.

1. large birds (hawks)
2. carries (hauls)
3. cries (bawls)
4. picture (drawing)
5. food flavoring (salt)

Challenge students to come up with clues for other Spelling Words.

Have partners identify two rhyming words with the same spelling pattern and two with a different spelling pattern, then write sentences for each, leaving blanks where the words should go. Then have them trade papers and write the missing words.

Day 4 Review and Proofread

SPIRAL REVIEW

Review words with /oi/. Write *joyful*, *coins*, and *spoiled*. Have students find letters that spell /oi/.

PROOFREAD/EDIT

Display the sentence below. Have students proofread/edit to correct the errors.

> The artist tawght painting and drauing. (taught, drawing)

Remind students to check spelling of words with /ô/ as they proofread/edit during the week.

BLIND SORT

Partners use their Spelling Word Cards and write key words *paw*, *cause*, *mall*, and *oddball* on paper. Then they take turns. One draws cards, says the words; the other writes. After both have finished, they can check their work.

Day 5 Assess and Reteach

POSTTEST

Use the Dictation Sentences on page 45G for the Posttest.

If students have difficulty with any of the words in the lesson, have them place them on a list called "Spelling Words I Want to Remember" in their word study notebooks.

WORD STUDY NOTEBOOK

Challenge students to search for other words with /ô/ in their reading for the week and write them in their word study notebooks under the heading "Other Words That Sound Like *Law*, *Fault*, and *Tall*."

Spelling Practice Book, page 100

yawn	lawn	hawks	bawls	paused
taught	halls	squawk	drawing	crawled
salt	hauls	bought	caused	coughing

What's the Word?

Complete each sentence with a spelling word.

1. The chef __taught__ us how to bake cookies.
2. She __bought__ a loaf of bread at the bakery.
3. There was too much __salt__ in the soup.
4. Watch out! Those large __hawks__ are trying to eat our picnic food!
5. My mother __bawls__ when she loses her favorite recipe book.
6. We set up a lemonade stand on the front __lawn__.
7. Margaret is __drawing__ a picture of a strawberry shortcake.
8. She __hauls__ the burnt cookies to the trash.
9. The smell of pepper made us start sneezing and __coughing__.
10. After he finished dinner, Bob let out a big __yawn__ and fell asleep.
11. You could smell the cookies all the way down our __halls__.
12. The smell __caused__ me to smile.

Synonym Alert!

For each word below, write the spelling word that has the same meaning.

13. creeped __crawled__
14. squeal __squawk__
15. stopped __paused__

Spelling Practice Book, page 101

Proofreading

There are four spelling mistakes in this paragraph. Circle the misspelled words. Write the words correctly on the lines below.

Steps for making a salad:

1. Always wash your hands with soap and water before you start cooking.
2. Make sure you (baught) everything you need.
3. Get out the things you will need for the dressing, such as oil, vinegar, and (sawlt).
4. Toss together the lettuce and the other vegetables.
5. If you have a garden next to your (lown), you can add fresh vegetables to your salad.
6. Remember what you were (tought) for the next time you make a salad.

1. __bought__ 3. __lawn__
2. __salt__ 4. __taught__

Writing Activity

Write the steps for another activity you like to do. Use at least three spelling words in your paragraph.

Spelling Practice Book, page 102

Look at the words in each set below. One word in each set is spelled correctly. Look at Sample A. The letter next to the correctly spelled word in Sample A has been shaded in. Do Sample B yourself. Shade the letter of the word that is spelled correctly. When you are sure you know what to do, go on with the rest of the page.

Sample A: Ⓐ sawlt Ⓑ sealt ● salt Ⓓ sault

Sample B: Ⓔ fawl ● fall Ⓖ faul Ⓗ faol

1. Ⓐ yaun Ⓑ yonn ● yawn Ⓓ yann
2. ● taught Ⓕ tawt Ⓖ tawght Ⓗ tauht
3. Ⓐ sault Ⓑ sawlt Ⓒ selt ● salt
4. ● lawn Ⓕ laun Ⓖ laugn Ⓗ lohn
5. Ⓐ hawls Ⓑ haughls ● halls Ⓓ haulls
6. Ⓔ haughls Ⓕ hals Ⓖ hawls ● hauls
7. Ⓐ hauks ● hawks Ⓒ haks Ⓓ haulks
8. Ⓔ squauk ● squawk Ⓖ sqwack Ⓗ squock
9. Ⓔ baught Ⓕ bawt ● bought Ⓗ baght
10. Ⓐ boughls Ⓑ bals Ⓒ bauls ● bawls
11. ● drawing Ⓕ drauing Ⓖ drauwing Ⓗ draughing
12. Ⓐ cawsed Ⓑ cassed ● caused Ⓓ coused
13. Ⓐ pased Ⓑ poused Ⓒ pawsed ● paused
14. Ⓔ crowled Ⓕ crauled ● crawled Ⓗ craled
15. Ⓐ caughing ● coughing Ⓒ cawfing Ⓓ coghing

Daily Language Activities

Use these activities to introduce each day's lesson. Write the day's activities on the board or use **Transparency 16**.

DAY 1
1. Sue are a chef. **2.** Joe do like helping in the kitchen **3.** The brothers has two muffin. (1: is; 2: does; kitchen.; 3: have; muffins)

DAY 2
1. The cook is busy yesterday. **2.** He do chop the vegetables last week. **3.** I have a sandwich for lunch an our ago. (1: was; 2: did; 3: had; hour)

DAY 3
1. Tim and Sue is happy now **2.** Last night Tim and Sue was hungry. **3.** Tim do the dishes after lonch every day. (1: are; now.; 2: were; 3: does; lunch)

DAY 4
1. Rob and Dan was at Sues house last night. **2.** sue did the cooking **3.** They all has a good time. (1: were; Sue's; 2: Sue; cooking.; 3: had)

DAY 5
1. Grandma are in the kitchen.
2. What time do we eat yesterday.
3. Joey had the napkins now.
(1: is; 2: did; yesterday?; 3: has)

ELL **Access for All**

Generate Sentences Write all the pronouns on the board. Write an example sentence using a pronoun and the verb *be*: *I am happy.* Ask students to supply similar sentences for the other pronouns. Go through the same process with the verbs *do* and *have*.

LA.3.3.4.4 Edit for correct use of present and past verb tense;

Verbs *Be, Do,* and *Have*

Day 1 Introduce the Concept

INTRODUCE PRESENT-TENSE FORMS OF VERBS *BE, DO, HAVE*

Present the following:

- *Am, is,* and *are* are present-tense forms of the verb *be.*
- *Do* and *does* are present-tense forms of the verb *do.*
- *Have* and *has* are present-tense forms of the verb *have.*

Examples:

I am	a boy is	boys are
I do	a boy does	boys do
I have	a boy has	boys have

See Grammar Transparency 76 for modeling and guided practice.

Grammar Practice Book, page 97

- The verbs *be, do,* and *have* all have special forms in the present tense. The chart shows which form to use with a sentence subject.

SUBJECT	BE	DO	HAVE
I	am	do	have
he, she, it	is	does	has
we, you, they	are	do	have

Write the correct present-tense form of *be* to finish each sentence.

1. She __is__ our favorite baker.
2. We __are__ big fans of her strawberry pie.
3. They __are__ the best pies in the world.
4. I __am__ certain you will like them.
5. You __are__ never hungry when you leave this bakery.

Write the correct present-tense form of *do* to finish each sentence.

6. It __does__ take a lot of work to pick strawberries.
7. We __do__ think the effort is worth it.
8. He __does__ not like strawberries.
9. I can tell that you __do__ like them.
10. I __do__ think I could eat strawberries every day.

Write the correct present-tense form of *have* to finish each sentence.

11. We __have__ many strawberry plants in our garden.
12. You __have__ to help me pick the strawberries tomorrow.
13. It __has__ to be finished by noon.
14. I __have__ a feeling you will like our strawberries.
15. They __have__ the most delicious flavor.

Day 2 Teach the Concept

REVIEW PRESENT-TENSE FORMS OF VERBS *BE, DO, HAVE*

Review with students the present-tense forms of *be, do,* and *have.*

INTRODUCE PAST-TENSE FORMS OF VERBS *BE, DO, HAVE*

Explain the following:

- *Was* and *were* are past-tense forms of the verb *be.*
- *Did* is the past-tense form of the verb *do.*
- *Had* is the past-tense form of the verb *have.*

Examples:

I was	a girl was	girls were
I did	a girl did	girls did
I had	a girl had	girls had

See Grammar Transparency 77 for modeling and guided practice.

Grammar Practice Book, page 98

- The verbs *be, do,* and *have* all have special forms in the past tense. The chart shows which form to use with a sentence subject.

SUBJECT	BE	DO	HAVE
I, he, she, it	was	did	had
we, you, they	were	did	had

Write the correct past-tense form of *be* to finish each sentence.

1. She __was__ young when she opened the bakery.
2. We __were__ her first customers.
3. I __was__ happy her pies were so good.
4. They __were__ a big success.
5. You __were__ not living here at the time.

Write the correct past-tense form of *do* to finish each sentence.

6. Last week we __did__ a report on strawberry farming.
7. It __did__ make me hungry to talk about my favorite fruit.
8. Fortunately, I __did__ bring some strawberries to class.
9. You __did__ not eat any.
10. We __did__ think you would like them.

Write the correct past-tense form of *have* to finish each sentence.

11. Yesterday we __had__ to water the plants in our garden.
12. I __had__ a lot of work to do.
13. You __had__ to study for your test.
14. My brother and sister said they __had__ something else to do.
15. They __had__ to clean their rooms so I watered the garden myself.

LA.3.3.4.4 Edit for correct use of noun-verb agreement and of present and past verb tense;
LA.3.3.4.5 Edit for correct use of subject/verb agreement

Day 3 Review and Practice

REVIEW PAST-TENSE FORMS OF VERBS *BE, DO, HAVE*

Review with students the present- and past-tense forms of *be*, *do*, and *have*.

MECHANICS AND USAGE: SUBJECT-VERB AGREEMENT

- The present-tense forms of *be*, *do*, and *have* must agree with their subjects.

I am	Tim is	The girls are
I do	Tim does	The girls do
I have	Tim has	The girls have

- The past-tense forms of *be* must agree with their subjects.

I was	Tim was	The girls were

See Grammar Transparency 78 for modeling and guided practice.

Grammar Practice Book, page 99

- Remember that the verbs *be*, *do*, and *have* have special forms. The present-tense forms of *be*, *do*, and *have* must agree with their subjects. The past-tense form of *be* must agree with its subjects.

Write the correct form of the given verb to finish each sentence.

1. have "I ___have___ the same food all the time," thought Rooster.
2. have Suddenly, Rooster ___had___ a great idea.
3. have "Grandmother ___has___ a great strawberry shortcake recipe in her book," Rooster said.
4. be "I ___am___ going to make that cake!" announced Rooster.
5. be Rooster ___is, was___ very excited about his plan.
6. be Turtle, Iguana, and Pig ___are, were___ eager to help Rooster.
7. be "We ___are___ a team!" said Rooster.
8. do "I'll ___do___ the reading," said Turtle.
9. do Iguana ___does, did___ not know what kind of flour to put in a cake.
10. do Now the recipe ___does___ not seem as easy as it looked.
11. have "We ___have___ to read the recipe carefully," Turtle said.
12. be Pig ___is___ a good mixer.

Day 4 Review and Proofread

REVIEW VERBS *BE, DO, HAVE*

Review with students the past- and present-tense forms of the verbs *be*, *do*, and *have*.

PROOFREAD

Have students write the sentences below and then proofread/edit to correct errors.

1. Jane am a cook. (is)
2. The girls is happy. (are)
3. Yesterday Jan and I have fruit for a snack. (had)
4. I is going to a picnic today. (am)
5. Today he have a cooking class. (has)

Remind students to check for subject-verb agreement as they proofread/edit their writing.

See Grammar Transparency 79 for modeling and guided practice.

Grammar Practice Book, page 100

- Remember that the verbs *have*, *do*, and *be* have special forms.

Proofread the passage. Circle any incorrect uses of *have*, *do*, or *be*.

I (is) learning to bake. Grandma (are) teaching me. We (was) at her house today. She asked if I knew how to bake a strawberry shortcake. I told her I did not. I (does) like strawberries, though! Grandma agreed to let me help her.
After we baked the cakes we served it to the family.
"I (is) very impressed," declared Mom.
"It (be) a fantastic strawberry shortcake!" said Dad.
"You (does) a great job!" said Grandma.
"We (was) a good team," I said.

Writing Activity

Rewrite the passage. Use the correct forms of *have*, *do*, or *be*.

I am learning to bake. Grandma is teaching me. We were at her house today. She asked if I knew how to bake a strawberry shortcake. I told her I did not. I do like strawberries, though! Grandma agreed to let me help her.
After we baked the cakes we served it to the family.
"I am very impressed," declared Mom.
"It is a fantastic strawberry shortcake!" said Dad.
"You did a great job!" said Grandma.
"We are a good team," I said.

Day 5 Assess and Reteach

ASSESS

Use the Daily Language Activity and page 101 of the **Grammar Practice Book** for assessment.

RETEACH

Write the following on index cards: *do, does, did, am, is, are, was, were, have, has, had*. Repeat with *I, a cat, dogs, a boy, a girl, Now*, and *Yesterday*. Place the cards in three piles: subjects, verbs, and time. Have students form sentences by selecting a card from each pile and adding extra words. Example: *Yesterday I was hot.* Have students create a Word Wall with their sentences.

Use page 102 of the Grammar Practice Book for additional reteaching.

See Grammar Transparency 80 for modeling and guided practice.

Grammar Practice Book, pages 101–102

Choose the correct word to complete each sentence.

1. This story ______ about a rooster who bakes.
   a. are (b.) is c. have d. am
2. Rooster ______ tired of his regular food.
   a. were (b.) was c. am d. have
3. He ______ a recipe for strawberry shortcake.
   a. am b. is (c.) had d. have
4. His friends ______ asked to help.
   a. has b. are c. is (d.) were
5. They ______ no experience baking!
   a. were b. are c. has (d.) had
6. They ______ not know what to do in the kitchen.
   a. am (b.) did c. had d. have
7. The story ______ very entertaining.
   (a.) is b. are c. be d. has
8. The animals ______ funny things on every page.
   a. was b. were (c.) do d. does

Administer the Test

Weekly Reading Assessment, pages 189–200

ASSESSED SKILLS

- Compare Characters, Settings, Events
- Vocabulary Words
- Dictionary/Idioms
- Words with /ô/
- Verbs *Be*, *Do*, and *Have*

Administer the **Weekly Assessment** from the CD-ROM or online.

Weekly Assessment, 189–200

Fluency

Assess fluency for one group of students per week. Use the Oral Fluency Record Sheet to track the number of words read correctly. Fluency goal for all students: **82–102 words correct per minute (WCPM).**

Approaching Level	Weeks 1, 3, 5
On Level	Weeks 2, 4
Beyond Level	Week 6

Fluency Assessment

- **ELL Assessment**, pages 110–111

ELL Assessment, 110–111

Diagnose		Prescribe
	IF . . .	**THEN . . .**
VOCABULARY WORDS **VOCABULARY STRATEGY** Dictionary/Idioms Items 1, 2, 3	0–1 items correct . . .	Reteach skills using the **Additional Lessons**, page T5. LOG ON Reteach skills: Log on to **www.macmillanmh.com** CD ROM Vocabulary PuzzleMaker Evaluate for Intervention.
COMPREHENSION Skill: Compare Characters, Settings, Events Items 4, 5, 6	0–1 items correct . . .	Reteach skills using the **Additional Lessons**, page T1. Evaluate for Intervention.
GRAMMAR Verbs *Be*, *Do*, and *Have* Items 7, 8, 9	0–1 items correct . . .	Reteach skills: **Grammar Practice Book**, page 102.
SPELLING Words with /ô/ Items 10, 11, 12	0–1 items correct . . .	LOG ON Reteach skills: Log on to **www.macmillanmh.com**
FLUENCY	73–81 WCPM 0–72 WCPM	AUDIO CD Fluency Solutions Evaluate for Intervention.

READING
Triumphs
AN INTERVENTION PROGRAM

Also Available

To place students in the Intervention Program, use the **Diagnostic Assessment** in the Intervention Teacher's Edition.

Skills Focus: Phonics

Objectives Review words with /ô/
Decode multisyllabic words with /ô/

Materials • **Student Book** "Red and Her Friends" • index cards

WORDS WITH /ô/

LA.3.1.4 Demonstrate knowledge of alphabetic principle

Model/Guided Practice

- Remind students that the letters *aw* as in *jaw*, *au* as in *launch*, and *a* as in *all* stand for the /ô/ sound.
- Write the letters *l*, *a*, *w* on the board. Say the sounds that the letters stand for: /l/ /ô/. Then blend the sounds: */lllôôô/. Say the word with me:* law.
- Repeat the routine with *au* and *fault* and *a* and *ball.*
- Ask students to provide their own examples of words with /ô/. Encourage them to include words with all three spellings of /ô/.

MULTISYLLABIC WORDS WITH /ô/

LA.3.1.4.3 Decode multi-syllabic words **LA.3.1.4.1** Use knowledge of pronunciation to decode words

- Write the word *drawing* on the board and have students identify the first syllable as containing the /ô/ sound: *draw.* Have students repeat the syllable and then blend sounds and read the whole word several times.
- Have pairs of students work together to practice decoding longer words with the /ô/ sound. Write the words below on the board and ask student pairs to copy them onto index cards or sheets of paper. *Say each word. Circle the letters that stand for the /ô/ sound. Then sort the words by spelling pattern.*

always	haunting	launches	crawling	falsify
hauling	saunter	scrawling	basketball	salted

- Check pairs for their progress and accuracy. Offer constructive feedback as necessary.

WORD HUNT: WORDS WITH /ô/ IN CONTEXT

LA.3.1.4 Apply grade level phonics to read text

- Review words with /ô/ spelled *au, aw,* and *a* with *l* in the accented first syllable.
- Have students search "Red and Her Friends" to find words with this vowel sound. Ask them to write the words and circle the syllable in each word that has /ô/.
- Check to see if students have found the following: *called, walked, paws, walk.*

Constructive Feedback

The /ô/ sound can be difficult for some students to hear and produce. Have them practice saying /ô/ in isolation and then in words, while looking at you to see how the mouth moves to produce the /ô/ sound. For example, write the word *lawn* on the board and point out the letters *aw.*

This word is lawn. *The* aw *has the sound /ô/. Say it with me: /ô/. Let's sound out, blend, and then say the word together: /lllôôônnn/,* lawn.

Repeat with /ô/ and the word *haul.*

Additional Resources

For each skill below, additional lessons are provided. You can use these lessons on consecutive days after teaching the lessons presented within the week.

- Compare Characters, Settings, Events, T1
- Idioms, T5
- Text Feature: Diagrams, T10

Decodable Text

To help students build speed and accuracy with reading multisyllabic words, use the additional decodable text on pages 87–90 of the **Teacher's Resource Book**.

Skills Focus: Fluency

Objective Read with increasing prosody and accuracy at a rate of 82–92 WCPM

Materials • index cards • **Approaching Practice Book A**, p. 115

WORD AUTOMATICITY

Have students make flashcards for the following words with /ô/: *yawn, hauls, drawing, taught, hawks, caused, salt, squawk, paused, lawn, also, crawled, false, bawls, always.*

Display the cards one at a time and have students say each word. Repeat twice more, displaying the words more quickly each time.

REPEATED READING

LA.3.1.5 Demonstrate the ability to read text orally with accuracy

Model reading the passage on **Practice Book** page 115. Have the group echo-read the passage and pay attention to punctuation. Then have partners practice reading to each other. Circulate and provide constructive feedback as needed.

TIMED READING

Tell students that they will be doing a final timed reading of the passage on Practice Book page 115. Students should

- begin reading the passage aloud when you say "Go."
- stop reading the passage after one minute when you say "Stop."

As students read, note any miscues. Help students record and graph the number of words they read correctly. Provide support and constructive feedback to students as necessary.

Constructive Feedback

If students read without sufficient expression, pauses, and attention to punctuation, reread the passage to them, one sentence at a time, exaggerating the correct expression and pauses. Have students copy your expression as they echo-read each sentence.

Skills Focus: Vocabulary

Objective Apply vocabulary word meanings

Materials • **Vocabulary Cards** • **Student Book** *Cook-A-Doodle Doo!*

VOCABULARY WORDS

LA.3.1.6.3 Use context clues to determine meanings

Use the **Vocabulary Cards** to review this week's and last week's words. Help students locate and read vocabulary words in the main selection, *Cook-A-Doodle-Doo!* Guide them to use context clues to determine or confirm meanings. For example, in the second paragraph on page 17, point out that the words "most wonderful . . . in the whole wide world" help readers figure out that *magnificent* means "grand."

recipes | magnificent | ingredient | masterpiece | tasty

Approaching Practice Book A, page 115

As I read, I will pay attention to punctuation.

There are thousands of farms across the United States.
9 But most people don't live near farms. The food has to
20 travel to reach them.
24 Food did not always travel far from farms. Travel took
34 a long time. There were no roads, only bumpy dirt trails.
45 And the only way to get around was with a wagon pulled
57 by a horse.
60 Then things began to change. New roads were built.
69 Steamboats appeared on the rivers. Railroad trains were
77 introduced. Many towns and cities were connected. Now
85 food could travel farther from the farms. 92

Comprehension Check

1. Why did it take a long time for food to travel before things began to change? **Main Idea and Details** There were no roads, and the only mode of transportation was horse and wagon.
2. What changes allowed for food to travel farther from farms? **Main Idea and Details** the building of roads and the use of steamboats and railroad trains

	Words Read	–	Number of Errors	=	Words Correct Score
First Read		–		=	
Second Read		–		=	

Approaching Level Options

Vocabulary

Review last week's vocabulary words (**instance, illustrate, style, textures, sketches, suggestions**) and this week's words (**magnificent, masterpiece, ingredient, recipes, tasty**). Have students write a sentence for each word.

Student Book, or Transparencies 16a and 16b

Skills Focus: Vocabulary

Objective Review idioms

Materials • **Student Book** *Cook-A-Doodle Doo!*

FCAT

DICTIONARY: IDIOMS

LA.3.2.1.5 Explain author's use of idiomatic language
LA.3.1.6.10 Determine meanings using a dictionary

- Write the phrase *lost your marbles* on the board. Remind students that it is an idiom, a phrase whose meaning is different from that of the words alone. Point out that dictionaries sometimes define idioms.
- Ask students to use word clues or a dictionary to figure out the meaning of *handed down* on **Student Book** page 16.

Skills Focus: Comprehension

Objective Compare and contrast story characters

Materials • **Student Book** "Red and Her Friends" • **Transparencies 16a** and **16b**

STRATEGY
MAKE INFERENCES AND ANALYZE

LA.3.1.7.3 Determine implied inference

Explain to students that to make inferences, good readers use their own experiences and clues from the story to figure out, or analyze, information that the author has left out.

FCAT

SKILL
COMPARE CHARACTERS

LA.3.2.1.2 Identify and explain character/character development

Explain/Model

Tell students that when you compare and contrast characters, you think about how they are alike and different. In this story, Ricardo and Fiona are similar in some ways but different in others.

Display **Transparencies 16a** and **16b**. Begin reading aloud "Red and Her Friends."

Think Aloud Both Fiona and Ricardo want a tasty meal and are friends with Red. That is how they are alike. Fiona is the only one willing to work in the garden with Red and to help cook the meal. That is how she is different from Ricardo.

Practice/Apply

Have students underline text that tells how the characters are alike. Have them circle text that tells how Ricardo and Fiona are different.

Leveled Reader Lesson

Objective Read to apply strategies and skills

Materials • **Leveled Reader** *Measurement* • **Student Book** *Cook-A-Doodle-Doo!*

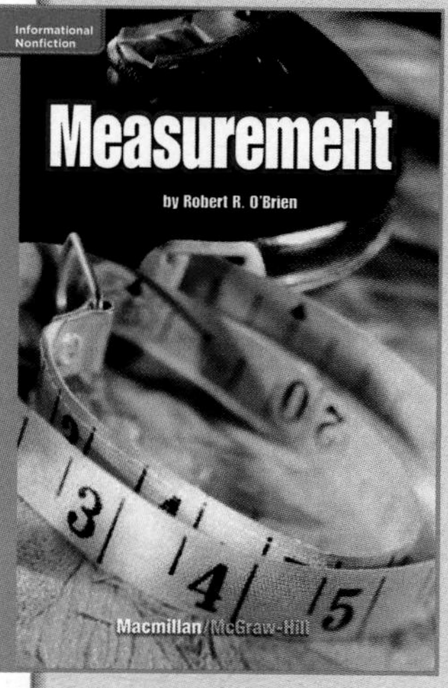

Leveled Reader

PREVIEW AND PREDICT

LA.3.1.7.1 Use text features to make predictions

Show the cover. Read the title and table of contents. Have students preview the illustrations. Discuss their predictions and questions.

VOCABULARY WORDS LA.3.1.6 Develop grade-appropriate vocabulary

As you read, help students identify, decode, and understand the vocabulary words in *Measurement*. Review meanings as necessary.

STRATEGY
MAKE INFERENCES AND ANALYZE

LA.3.1.7.3 Determine implied inference

Explain that making inferences and analyzing the text can help students understand what they read. Have students reread pages 2–3 and make inferences to answer the questions raised in the introduction. Model the strategy.

Think Aloud The introduction introduces a boy making a car that has to be a certain size. He asks how he can make sure the car he makes meets the requirements. I know from my own experience that I can use a ruler to measure length. If I look ahead to Chapter 1, I see it asks "How Long Is It?" I can infer that this section will help answer the boy's question.

FCAT

SKILL
COMPARE

LA.3.1.7 Use a variety of strategies to comprehend grade level text

As you continue reading, help students make inferences to compare and contrast different ways to measure length/distance. You may wish to have students fill in a Venn Diagram.

READ AND RESPOND

LA.3.1.6.2 Read and discuss text

Read to the end of the selection. Students can find out the measurement systems and the tools used to measure length/distance, weight, and temperature. Afterward, have them describe what they liked and disliked about this book. Was the information interesting?

MAKE CONNECTIONS ACROSS TEXTS

LA.3.1.7.7 Compare and contrast topics

Ask students to compare *Cook-A-Doodle Doo!* and *Measurement*.

- How would the characters in *Cook-A-Doodle Doo!* have used the information in *Measurement*?
- How are these books different?

ELL — **Access for All**

Chart Create a chart on the board about measuring length and measuring weight. On one side write, *How length and weight are alike*. On the other side write, *How length and weight are different*. Before beginning, discuss the concepts of alike and different to be sure students are familiar with the terms. Ask students to fill in both sides of the chart.

On Level Options

Skills Focus Phonics

Objective Decode one-syllable and multisyllabic words with /ô/

Materials • chart paper

DECODE WORDS WITH /ô/

LA.3.1.4 Demonstrate knowledge of alphabetic principle

- Remind students that the letters *aw* as in *paw*, *au* as in *fault*, and *a* as in *tall* stand for the /ô/ sound and that recognizing the letters that stand for /ô/ can help students sound out an unfamiliar word.
- Write the spelling words *caused*, *yawn*, and *salt* on chart paper. Segment and blend each word and have students echo you. Circle the letters that spell the /ô/ sound, noting the different ways the sound can be spelled.
- Have students segment, blend, and write each of these words: *falling, drawing, water.* Have them underline the letter(s) that spell the /ô/ sound.

Skills Focus Vocabulary

Objective Apply vocabulary and identify idioms

Materials **• Vocabulary Cards** **• Student Book** *Cook-A-Doodle-Doo!*

VOCABULARY WORDS

LA.3.1.6.1 Use new vocabulary

Show the **Vocabulary Cards** for *tasty*, *recipes*, *masterpiece*, *ingredient*, and *magnificent*. Ask volunteers to think of a synonym or antonym for each word, and make up a sentence that uses it.

FCAT

DICTIONARY: IDIOMS

LA.3.1.6.10 Determine meanings using a dictionary and digital tools

Read aloud the sentence with the phrase *handed down* from page 16 of *Cook-A-Doodle-Doo!* Ask students what *handed down* means. Discuss the words in the sentence that gave students a clue. (from chicken to chicken) Ask students to figure out the meanings for *lost your marbles* on page 19. They can use a print or digital dictionary to help them.

Cook-A-Doodle-Doo!
by Janet Stevens and Susan Stevens Crummel
illustrated by Janet Stevens

Student Book

Skills Focus Fluency

Objective Read fluently with good prosody at a rate of 82–102 WCPM

Materials • **On Level Practice Book O**, p. 115

REPEATED READING

LA.3.1.5 Demonstrate the ability to read text orally with expression

Model expressive reading using the fluency passage on **Practice Book** page 115. Have students echo-read each sentence after you. Have student pairs practice the passage. Remind them to show with their voices that they are interested in what they are reading.

Timed Reading Have partners time each other's reading for one minute at the end of the week and record their reading rates.

On Level Practice Book O, page 115

As I read, I will pay attention to punctuation.

Even kids can be inventors. Frank Epperson was eleven
9 years old when he proved it! One night he mixed powdered
20 fruit flavor in a cup of soda water. He stirred it with a stick.
34 That's how people made fruit drinks in 1905. But after a
44 sip or two, Frank left his drink on the back porch.
55 The night grew very cold. By morning, Frank had a
65 magnificent surprise. His fruit soda had frozen to the stick.
75 Frank showed it to his friends. At first everyone thought
85 Frank had lost his marbles. They thought he was crazy.
95 But after one lick, everyone cheered. Frank's invention was
104 a masterpiece. A work of art! Frank called it an Epsicle.
115 Frank decided to sell the icy treats. 122

Comprehension Check

1. How was a fruit drink made in 1905? **Main Idea and Details** Powdered fruit flavor was mixed with soda water.
2. How did Frank Epperson discover popsicles? **Main Idea and Details** Frank left his drink on the back porch, and it froze during the night, creating an Epsicle.

	Words Read	–	Number of Errors	=	Words Correct Score
First Read		–		=	
Second Read		–		=	

Leveled Reader Lesson

Objective Read to apply strategies and skills

Materials
- **Leveled Reader** *Measurement*
- **Student Book** *Cook-A-Doodle-Doo!*
- chart paper

Leveled Reader

PREVIEW AND PREDICT
LA.3.1.7.1 Use text features to make predictions

Show the cover of *Measurement* and read the title. Discuss students' predictions, purposes for reading, and any questions students may have.

STRATEGY
MAKE INFERENCES AND ANALYZE

LA.3.1.7.3 Determine implied inference

Explain that using text clues and knowledge from their own experiences can help students figure out information the author doesn't say directly. Read aloud pages 4–7. Model how to make inferences.

Think Aloud The text says that the first measurements came from body measurements. I know how different parts of people's bodies, such as their feet, may be different sizes. That helps me understand why people came up with standard measurements.

SKILL
COMPARE

LA.3.1.7 Use a variety of strategies to comprehend grade level text

As they read, help students find and make inferences about similarities and differences in the text. Prompt them with questions such as: *How do you measure length? How do you measure weight? In what ways are these kinds of measurements alike and different?* Students can create a Venn Diagram.

READ AND RESPOND

LA.3.1.6.3 Use context clues

Have students read to the end of Chapter 2 orally. They should look for clues that help them make inferences. Review how vocabulary words are used in context.

Then have students finish the book. Ask students how the different ways to measure amounts are alike and different.

MAKE CONNECTIONS ACROSS TEXTS

LA.3.1.7.7 Compare and contrast topics

Discuss how *Cook-A-Doodle-Doo!* and *Measurement* are alike and different. Students can think about how both selections tell about measuring amounts. Remind students that good readers compare and contrast the characters, settings, events, and information in the texts they read. Model how you make connections.

Beyond Level Options

Student Book

Skills Focus: Vocabulary

Objective Complete sentences using content vocabulary words

Materials • **Student Book** "Welcome to the Bakery!"

EXTEND VOCABULARY

LA.3.1.6.1 Use new vocabulary that is introduced and taught directly

Review the content vocabulary words listed on **Student Book** page 40: *measurements, temperature, thermometer.* Have students tell about things they may have baked with parents or other adults. As each student tells a story, he or she must use at least two of the content words. Other students should be prepared to correct the speaker if he or she uses a word incorrectly.

ELL — Access for All

Vocabulary Have students work in pairs. On the board write: *measurements, temperature, thermometer.* Ask the groups to think of working in a bakery and how each word is connected to that job. Have each pair of students co-construct one sentence for each word. Ask them to include the meaning of each vocabulary word in each sentence. Have students read their sentences aloud.

Skills Focus: Text Feature

Objective Review diagrams and create a diagram

Materials • **Student Book** "Welcome to the Bakery!"

DIAGRAMS

LA.3.2.2.3 Show understanding of main ideas through summarizing
LA.3.1.7.1 Use text features
LA.3.4.2.1 Write in expository forms

Ask students to review "Welcome to the Bakery!" on Student Book pages 40–43 and use boldfaced words and illustrations to summarize the main ideas. Review and discuss the diagram on page 41.

- What information does the diagram explain? (how to make bread)
- What do the arrows and large dots show? (the order in which to follow the steps)

Challenge individual students or pairs to invent recipes for special dishes. They should each make a diagram with step-by-step directions and explanatory drawings that show how to make the dish.

Beyond Practice Book B, page 115

As I read, I will pay attention to punctuation.

People in ancient Greece and Rome ate seasoned flat
9 bread. It looked a little like the pizza crust we know
20 today. They added herbs, spices, and oil to make the bread
31 tasty. Egyptians made flat bread like this too. They made it
42 to celebrate the Pharaoh's birthday.
47 Scientists think Roman soldiers ate something like
54 pizza. They found traces of ovens where the men once
64 lived. The ovens were over 2,000 years old. They were
73 lined with stone. They looked like early pizza ovens!
82 In the 1600s, people who lived in Italy ate
90 simple round flat bread as their main food. They had little
101 to work with besides wheat flour, olive oil, and local
111 herbs. They called the bread "focaccia" (foh•KAH•chee•uh).
117 They were the first people to put tomatoes on their
127 flat bread. The first tomatoes brought to Italy were most
137 likely yellow. Italians called them "golden apples." 144

Comprehension Check

1. Why do scientists think Roman soldiers ate something similar to pizza? **Main Idea and Details** Scientists found remains of ancient ovens where Roman soldiers once lived. These ovens looked like early pizza ovens.
2. Why were the breads used in both Greece and Italy flat? **Main Idea and Details** They were the first people to put tomatoes on their flat bread.

	Words Read	–	Number of Errors	=	Words Correct Score
First Read		–		=	
Second Read		–		=	

Skills Focus: Fluency

Objective Read fluently with good prosody at a rate of 92–102 WCPM

Materials • **Beyond Practice Book B**, p. 115

REPEATED READING

LA.3.1.5 Demonstrate the ability to read text orally with expression

Read the passage on **Practice Book** page 115 as students echo-read each sentence. Have students practice reading the passage aloud. Remind students to use their voices to show that they are interested in the text.

Timed Reading You may wish to have students do a timed reading of the passage at the end of the week and record their reading rates.

Leveled Reader Lesson

Objective Read to apply strategies and skills

Materials • **Leveled Reader** *Measurement*

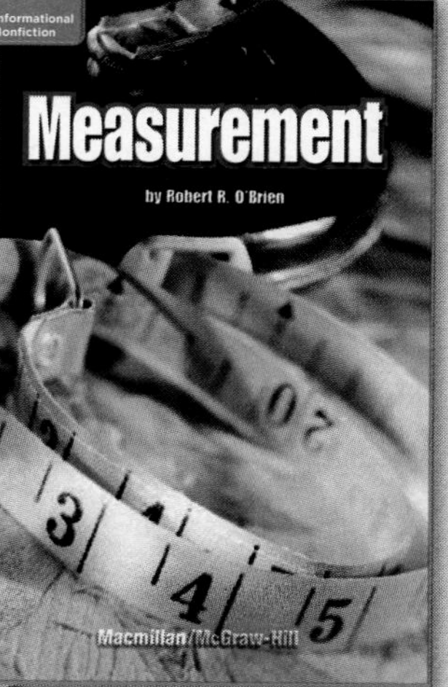

Leveled Reader

PREVIEW AND PREDICT

LA.3.1.7.1 Use text features to establish purpose for reading

Show the cover and read the title. Have students preview the table of contents. Discuss students' questions and set reading purposes.

STRATEGY
MAKE INFERENCES AND ANALYZE

LA.3.1.7.3 Determine implied inference

Remind students that using text clues and their own prior knowledge can help them figure out what the author does not state directly. Have students read pages 2–3 aloud. Discuss what clues the text gives and what questions students asked themselves as they read.

Think Aloud If I were making a Pinewood Derby car, I would use a ruler to measure its length and a scale to measure weight. But I am not sure that this is the best way. I'll read on to find out.

FCAT

SKILL
COMPARE

LA.3.2.2.3 Show understanding of main ideas through summarizing

As you read, have students summarize the text through Chapter 2. They should describe how people measure length and weight both now and in the past and how the customary system differs from the metric system.

READ AND RESPOND

LA.3.1.6.2 Read and discuss conceptually challenging text

Have students first read through Chapter 2. Tell them they will find out how the systems of measurement developed and their differences. Discuss vocabulary words as they are used in the book.

Then have students read the rest of the book. After they have finished, they can share their personal experiences about when they have had to measure to find length, weight, or temperature.

Self-Selected Reading

Objective Read independently to apply comprehension strategies and skills

Materials • Leveled Readers or trade books at students' reading levels

FCAT

READ TO COMPARE

LA.3.2.1.8 Select fiction materials to read
LA.3.2.1.6 Write a book review

Invite each student to choose a fiction title to read independently for enjoyment. For a list of theme-related titles, see pages T18–T19. As students read, they should compare elements or characters in the story.

After reading, have partners who have read the same story write a joint review in which they compare their thoughts about the story.

English Language Learners

Academic Language

Throughout the week the English language learners will need help in building their understanding of the academic language used in daily instruction and assessment instruments. The following strategies will help to increase their language proficiency and comprehension of content and instructional words.

Technology

Oral Language For additional language support and oral vocabulary development, go to www.macmillanmh.com

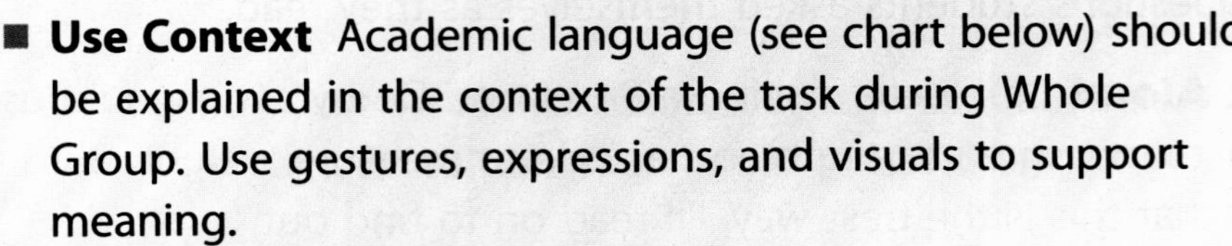

Strategies to Reinforce Academic Language

- **Use Context** Academic language (see chart below) should be explained in the context of the task during Whole Group. Use gestures, expressions, and visuals to support meaning.
- **Use Visuals** Use charts, transparencies, and graphic organizers to explain key labels to help students understand classroom language.
- **Model** Demonstrate the task using academic language in order for students to understand instruction.

Academic Language Used in Whole Group Instruction

Content/Theme Words	Skill/Strategy Words	Writing/Grammar Words
what's cooking? (p. 10)	idioms (p. 13)	narrative (p. 44)
meal (p. 11)	make inferences and analyze (p. 13A)	strong lead (p. 45B)
shortening (p. 40)	compare and contrast (p. 13A)	helping verbs (p. 45B)
yeast (p. 40)	Venn diagram (p. 13B)	present-tense forms (p. 45I)
flavor (p. 40)	diagrams (p. 40)	

ELL Leveled Reader Lesson

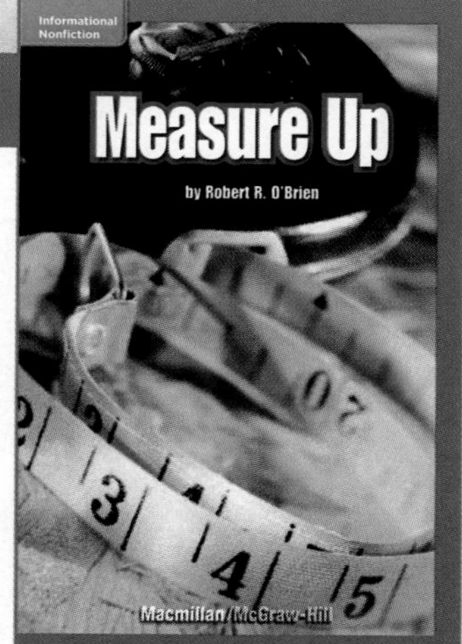

Informational Nonfiction
Measure Up
by Robert R. O'Brien
Macmillan/McGraw-Hill

Before Reading

DEVELOP ORAL LANGUAGE

Build Background Pose the questions: *How are things measured? How do we know we are using the correct amount of ingredients when we are cooking or tell how hot or cold the temperature outside is?* Divide the class into groups. Have them discuss one of the questions and share their answers.

Review Vocabulary Write the vocabulary and support words on the board and discuss their meanings. Use synonyms to help students better understand. *The cake is* tasty! *It's delicious, great, yummy!* **LA.3.1.6.8** Use knowledge of synonyms

PREVIEW AND PREDICT **LA.3.1.7.1** Use text features to make predictions; **LA.3.1.7.5** Identify text structure

Point to the cover photograph and read the title aloud. Have students make predictions. *What do you think this book is about?* Have students read the table of contents and share their predictions.

Set a Purpose for Reading Show the Venn diagram. Ask students to use similar diagrams to compare things that can be measured.

During Reading

LA.3.1.7 Use strategies to comprehend text

Choose from among the differentiated strategies below to support students' reading at all stages of language acquisition.

Beginning	Intermediate	Advanced
Shared Reading As you read, model how to infer and analyze from information that you are reading. Every few chapters, record the information in a Venn diagram.	**Read Together** Read the introduction and Chapter 1. Help students summarize. Model how to make inferences. Have students take turns reading Chapters 2 and 3. Help them record information in a Venn diagram. Repeat with Chapters 4 and 5.	**Independent Reading** Have students read the selection. Each day ask them to summarize and make inferences. At the end, ask them to choose two foods and compare them using Venn diagrams.

After Reading

LA.3.1.6.1 Use new vocabulary

Remind students to use the vocabulary and story words in their whole group activities.

Objective

- Apply vocabulary and comprehension skills

Materials

- ELL Leveled Reader

ELL 5 Day Planner

DAY 1	• Academic Language • Oral Language and Vocabulary Review
DAY 2	• Academic Language • ELL Leveled Reader
DAY 3	• Academic Language • ELL Leveled Reader
DAY 4	• Academic Language • ELL Leveled Reader
DAY 5	• Academic Language • ELL Leveled Reader Comprehension Check and Literacy Activities

ELL Teacher's Guide for students who need additional instruction

Student Book Selections

Weekly Theme: Getting Along

Week At A Glance

Whole Group

VOCABULARY
argued, beamed, fabric, possessions, purchased, quarreling

FCAT Dictionary/Multiple-Meaning Words

COMPREHENSION
Strategy: Make Inferences and Analyze
FCAT Skill: Plot Development: Draw Conclusions

WRITING
FCAT Poster

FCAT **Science**
Earth and Space

Small Group Options

Differentiated Instruction for Tested Skills

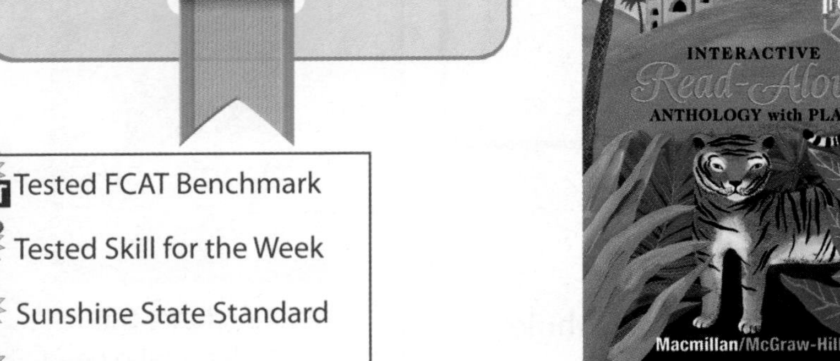

Main Selection
Genre Fable

Vocabulary/ Comprehension

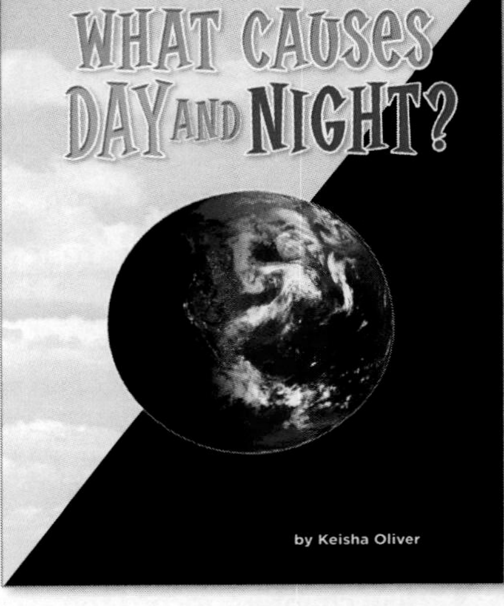

Science Link
Genre Nonfiction Article

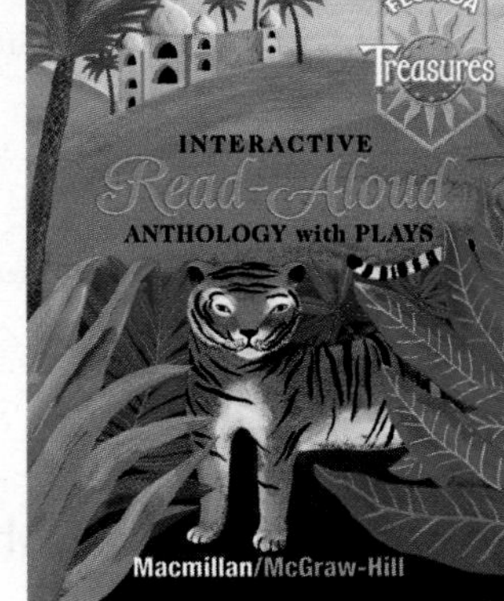

Read-Aloud Anthology
- Listening Comprehension
- Readers' Theater

Resources for Differentiated Instruction

LEVELED READERS

GR Levels M–R

Genre Folk Tale

- Same Theme
- Same Vocabulary
- Same Comprehension Skills

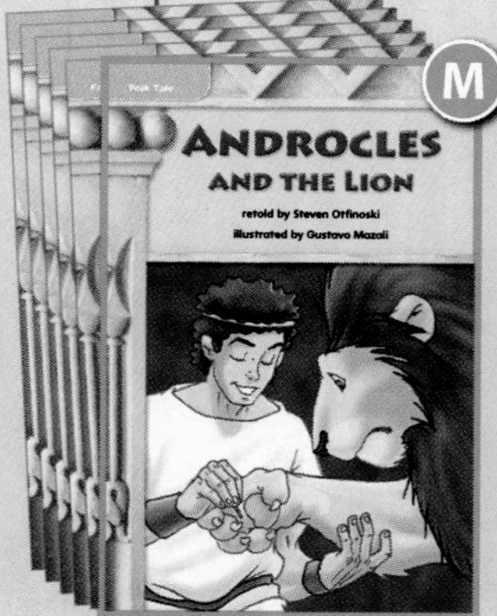

Approaching Level

On Level

Beyond Level

English Language Leveled Reader

Sheltered Readers for English Language Learners

ELL Teacher's Guide also available

LEVELED PRACTICE

Approaching

On Level

Beyond

ELL

INTERVENTION PROGRAM

- Phonics and Decoding
- Comprehension
- Vocabulary

Also available, *Reading Triumphs*, Intervention Program

CLASSROOM LIBRARY

Genre Informational Nonfiction

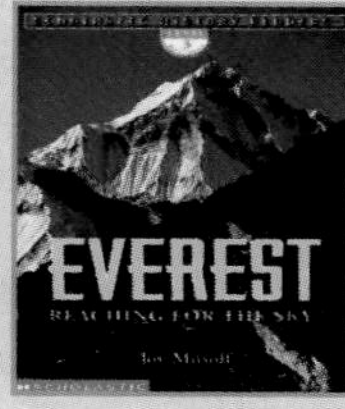

Approaching

On Level

Beyond

Trade books to apply Comprehension Skills

FCAT Success!

- **FCAT Edition**
- **Content Area Reading**

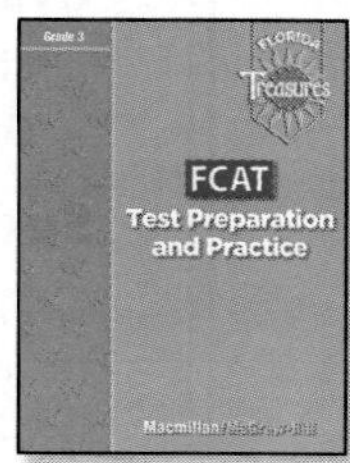

FCAT Test Preparation and Practice

FCAT Benchmark Assessments

FCAT Unit and Weekly Assessments

HOME-SCHOOL CONNECTION

- Family letters in English, Spanish, and Haitian Creole
- Take-Home Stories

FLORIDA Suggested Lesson Plan

Seven Spools of Thread, 50–71

Integrated ELL Support Every Day

Whole Group	Day 1	Day 2
ORAL LANGUAGE • Listening • Speaking • Viewing	**Listening/Speaking/Viewing** Focus Question People can have different ideas and still work together. What do you do when someone disagrees with you? LA.3.5.2 Build Background, 46 **Read Aloud:** "Arachne the Spinner," 47 LA.3.2.1	**Listening/Speaking** Focus Question How will the brothers get along at the end of the story? LA.3.5.2
WORD STUDY • Vocabulary • Phonics/Decoding	**Vocabulary** LA.3.1.6.1 *beamed, argued, possessions, fabric, purchased, quarreling,* 48 Practice Book A-O-B, 119 FCAT **Strategy:** Dictionary: Multiple-Meaning Words, 49 LA.3.1.6.9	**Vocabulary** LA.3.1.6.1 Review Vocabulary Words, 50 **Phonics** LA.3.1.4.1 Decode Words with /ou/, 77E Practice Book A-O-B, 125
READING • Develop Comprehension • Fluency	**Read** "Community Works," 48–49 LA.3.1.6.3 Student Book **Comprehension,** 49A–49B **Strategy:** Make Inferences and Analyze FCAT **Skill:** Plot Development: Draw Conclusions LA.3.1.7.3 Practice Book A-O-B, 120 **Fluency** Partner Reading, 46I Model Fluency, 47 LA.3.1.5	**Read** *Seven Spools of Thread,* 50–71 Student Book **Comprehension,** 50–71 **Strategy:** Make Inferences and Analyze FCAT **Skill:** Plot Development: Draw Conclusions LA.3.1.7.3 Practice Book A-O-B, 121 **Fluency** Partner Reading, 46I LA.3.1.5 Punctuation, 56
LANGUAGE ARTS • Writing • Grammar • Spelling	FCAT **Writing** Daily Writing: Write about someone you get along with well. Explain why you get along so well. Poster, 76–77B LA.3.4.2.1 **Grammar** Daily Language Activities, 77I Linking Verbs, 77I LA.3.3.4.5 Grammar Practice Book, 103 **Spelling** Pretest, 77G LA.3.3.4.4 Spelling Practice Book, 103–104	FCAT **Writing** Daily Writing: Write a paragraph trying to convince your readers why it is important for two people who are on the same team to get along. Poster, 76–77B LA.3.4.2.1 **Grammar** Daily Language Activities, 77I Linking Verbs, 77I LA.3.3.4.5 Grammar Practice Book, 104 **Spelling** Words with /ou/, 77G LA.3.3.4.5 Spelling Practice Book, 105
ASSESSMENT • Informal/Formal	Quick Check **Vocabulary,** 48 **Comprehension,** 49B	Quick Check **Comprehension,** 59, 71 **Phonics,** 77E
Turn the Page for **Small Group Lesson Plan**	**Differentiated Instruction 77M–77V**	**Differentiated Instruction 77M–77V**

FCAT Benchmarks

Vocabulary	Comprehension	Writing	Science
Vocabulary Words **Dictionary/Multiple-Meaning Words** **LA.3.1.6.9** Determine correct meaning of words with multiple meanings	**Strategy: Make Inferences and Analyze** **Skill: Plot Development: Draw Conclusions** **LA.3.1.7.3** Determine implied inference	**Expository/Poster** **LA.3.4.2.1** Write in informational forms	**Earth and Space** **SC.E.1.2.1.3.1** Changes in length of days

Turn the Page for **Small Group Options**

Day 3

Listening/Speaking

Focus Question How is the problem in "Community Works" similar to the problem in *Seven Spools of Thread*? How are the solutions to the problems different?

Summarize, 73 LA.3.1.7.8

Vocabulary LA.3.1.6.3

Review Vocabulary, 77C

FCAT **Strategy:** Dictionary: Multiple-Meaning Words, 77D LA.3.1.6.9

Practice Book A-O-B, 124

Phonics LA.3.1.4.3

Decode Multisyllable Words, 77E

Read *Seven Spools of Thread*, 50–71

Student Book

Comprehension

Comprehension Check, 73

FCAT **Skill:** Plot Development: Plot and Settings, 73B LA.3.1.7.3

Fluency Partner Reading, 46I LA.3.1.5

Repeated Reading, 73A

Practice Book A-O-B, 122

FCAT Writing

Daily Writing: Imagine that you were one of the seven brothers in the story. Write about what you would have suggested doing with the spools of thread.

Writer's Craft: Precise Words, 77 LA.3.3.3.1

Poster, 76–77B LA.3.4.2.1

Grammar Daily Language Activities, 77I

End Punctuation, 77J LA.3.3.4.3

Grammar Practice Book, 105

Spelling Words with /ou/, 77H LA.3.1.6.4

Spelling Practice Book, 106

Quick Check **Fluency,** 73A

Differentiated Instruction 77M–77V

Day 4

Listening/Speaking

Focus Question Why is the sun important in *Seven Spools of Thread*?

Expand Vocabulary: Getting Along, 77F LA.3.1.6.1

Vocabulary LA.3.1.6.1

Content Vocabulary: *sphere, rotates, axis,* 74

Suffix *-ly*, 77F LA.3.1.6.7

Apply Vocabulary to Writing, 77F

Phonics LA.3.1.6

Rhyming /ou/ Riddles, 77E

Read "What Causes Day and Night?" 74–75

Student Book

Comprehension

Science: Nonfiction Article

Text Feature: Rules, 74 LA.3.2.2.1

Practice Book A-O-B, 123

Fluency Partner Reading, 46I LA.3.1.5

FCAT Writing

Daily Writing: Suppose you could travel to visit the moon. Write a journal entry describing your time there.

Writing Trait: Organization, 77 LA.3.3.3.2

Poster, 76–77B LA.3.4.2.1

Grammar Daily Language Activities, 77I

Linking Verbs, 77J LA.3.3.4.4

Grammar Practice Book, 106

Spelling Words with /ou/, 77H LA.3.3.4.1

Spelling Practice Book, 107

Quick Check **Vocabulary,** 77D

Differentiated Instruction 77M–77V

Day 5 Review and Assess

Listening/Speaking

Focus Question Read the African proverb on page 71. How is this proverb similar to the sons' teamwork?

Speaking and Listening Strategies, 77A

Vocabulary LA.3.1.6

Spiral Review: Vocabulary Game Show, 77F

Read Self-Selected Reading, 46I

Student Book

Comprehension

Connect and Compare, 75

Fluency Partner Reading, 46I LA.3.1.5

FCAT Writing

Daily Writing: What rules could the seven brothers follow to prevent any more quarreling? Write a list of rules for the brothers to follow.

Poster, 76–77B LA.3.4.2.1

Grammar Daily Language Activities, 77I

Linking Verbs, 77J LA.3.3.4.4

Grammar Practice Book, 107-108

Spelling Posttest, 77H LA.3.1.6.4

Spelling Practice Book, 108

FCAT **Weekly Assessment, 201–212**

Differentiated Instruction 77M–77V

Differentiated Instruction

What do I do in small groups?

Focus on Skills

Skills Focus Use your  observations to guide additional instruction and practice.

Phonics
Decode Words with /ou/

Vocabulary
Words: beamed, argued, possessions, fabric, purchased, quarreling
FCAT **Strategy:** Dictionary/Multiple-Meaning Words

Comprehension
FCAT **Strategy:** Make Inferences and Analyze
FCAT **Skill:** Plot Development: Draw Conclusions

FCAT **Fluency**

Suggested Lesson Plan

	Day 1	Day 2
Approaching Level • **Additional Instruction/Practice** • **Tier 2 Instruction**	Fluency, 77N Vocabulary, 77N Comprehension, 77O 	Phonics, 77M Vocabulary, 77O Leveled Reader Lesson, 77P • Vocabulary • Comprehension 
On Level • **Practice**	Vocabulary, 77Q Leveled Reader Lesson, 77R • Comprehension 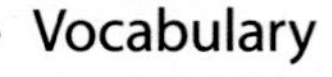 ELL Leveled Reader, 77U–77V 	Phonics, 77Q Leveled Reader Lesson, 77R • Comprehension • Vocabulary 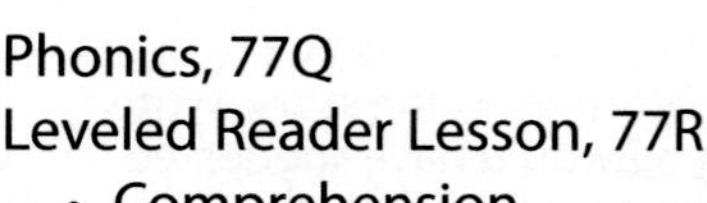
Beyond Level • **Extend**	Vocabulary, 77S Leveled Reader Lesson, 77T • Comprehension 	Leveled Reader Lesson, 77T • Comprehension • Vocabulary 

For intensive intervention see READING Triumphs

Small Group Options

Focus on Leveled Readers

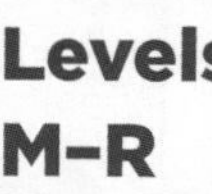

Levels M–R

Apply FCAT skills and strategies while reading appropriate leveled books.

On Level

Beyond

The Diamond

ELL

Additional Leveled Reader Resources

Leveled Reader Database
Go to www.macmillanmh.com

Search by

- Comprehension Skill
- Content Area
- Genre
- Text Feature
- Guided Reading Level
- Reading Recovery Level
- Lexile Score
- Benchmark Level

Subscription also available.

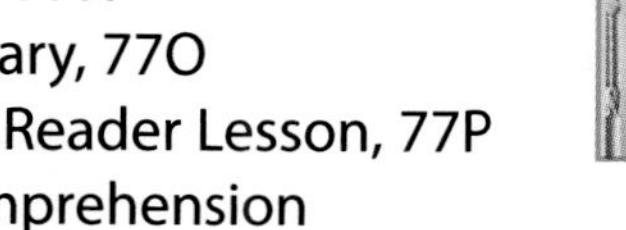

Day 3

Phonics, 77M
Fluency, 77N
Vocabulary, 77O
Leveled Reader Lesson, 77P
- Comprehension

Fluency, 77Q
Vocabulary, 77Q
Leveled Reader Lesson, 77R
- Comprehension

Fluency, 77S
Vocabulary, 77S
Leveled Reader Lesson, 77T
- Comprehension

Day 4

Phonics, 77M
Leveled Reader Lesson, 77P
- Comprehension
- ELL Skill: Plot Development: Draw Conclusions

Leveled Reader Lesson, 77R
- Comprehension

Text Feature, 77S
Leveled Reader Lesson, 77T
- Comprehension

Day 5

Fluency, 77N
Leveled Reader Lesson, 77P
- Make Connections Across Texts

Fluency, 77Q
Leveled Reader Lesson, 77R
- Make Connections Across Texts

Fluency, 77S
Self-Selected Reading, 77T

Managing the Class

What do I do with the rest of my class?

Class Management Tools

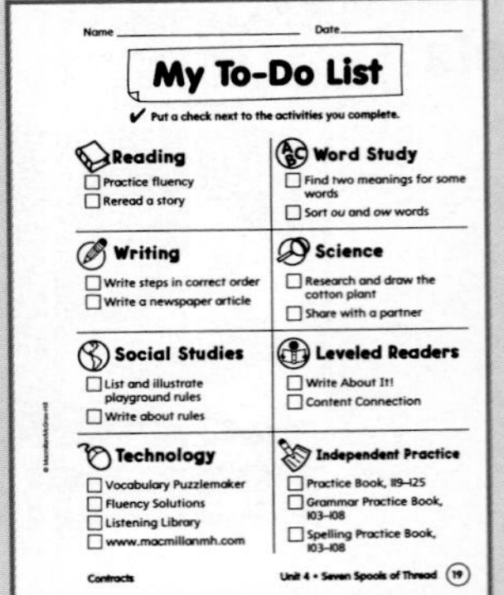

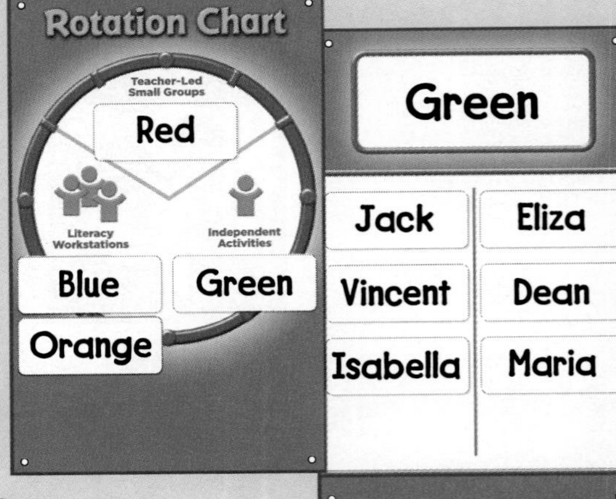

Includes:
- How-to Guide
- Rotation Chart
- Weekly Contracts

Hands-on activities for reinforcing weekly skills

Three-Pocket Foldable

Standing Cube Foldable

Independent Activities

Reinforcing Weekly Skills

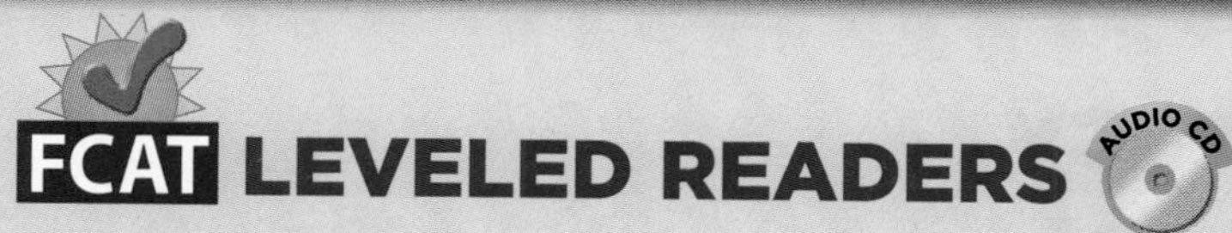

For Repeated Readings and Literacy Activities

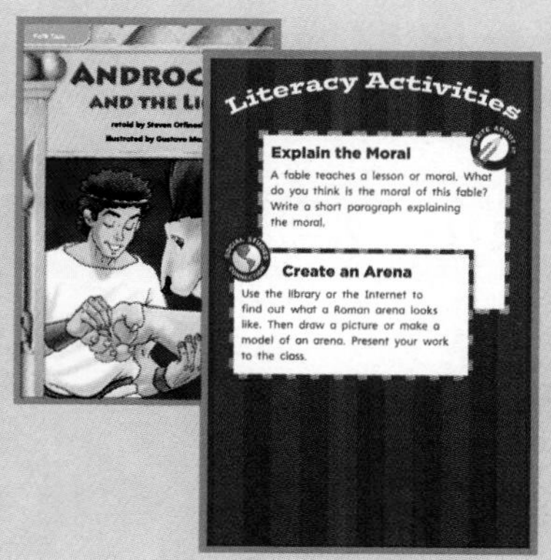

Approaching

On Level

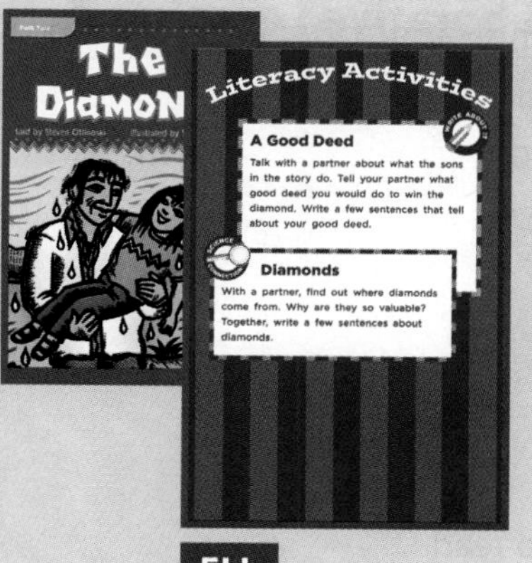

ELL

Beyond

LEVELED PRACTICE

Skills: Phonics, Vocabulary, Plot Development, Draw Conclusions, Fluency, Multiple-Meaning Words, Rules

Approaching

On Level

Beyond

ELL

Technology

ONLINE INSTRUCTION www.macmillanmh.com

- Meet the Author/Illustrator

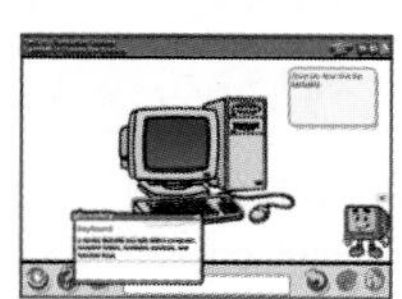

- Computer Literacy Lessons

- Research and Inquiry Activities

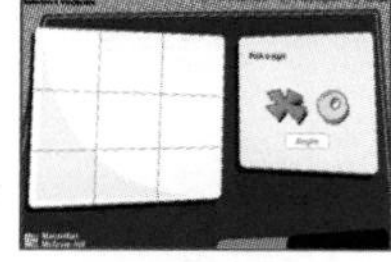

- Oral Language Activities

- Vocabulary and Spelling Activities

- Leveled Reader Database

LISTENING LIBRARY

Recordings of selections
- Main Selections
- Leveled Readers
- ELL Readers
- Intervention Anthology

FLUENCY SOLUTIONS

Recorded passages for modeling and practicing fluency

VOCABULARY PUZZLEMAKER

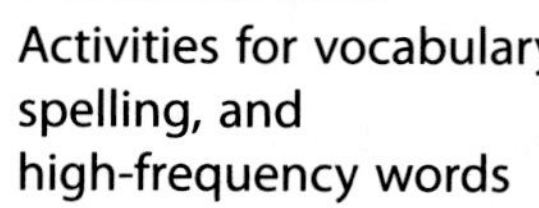

Activities for vocabulary, spelling, and high-frequency words

NEW ADVENTURES WITH BUGGLES AND BEEZY

Phonemic awareness and phonics practice

Turn the page for Literacy Workstations.

Literacy Activities

Collaborative Learning Activities

Reading

Objectives

- Time reading to practice fluency
- Draw conclusions about a character in a story
- Select fiction materials to read

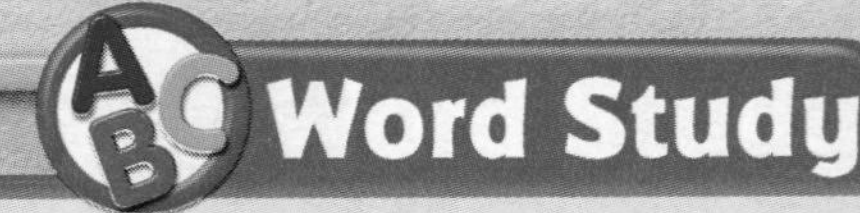

Word Study

Objectives

- Use a dictionary to find multiple meanings of given words
- Sort and match words with /ou/

LA.3.1.5 Demonstrate the ability to read grade level text

Reading **Fluency** 20 Minutes

- Choose a partner. Take turns reading aloud page 122 of your Practice Book. Notice punctuation as you read. Pause at a semicolon (;). Drop your voice at a period (.).

Extension

- Read the sentences again. This time do not pause at a semicolon. Discuss with a partner what happens to the meaning of the paragraph.
- Listen to responses to punctuation on the audio disc. Time your reading.

Things you need:
- Practice Book

Fluency Solutions
Listening Library

33

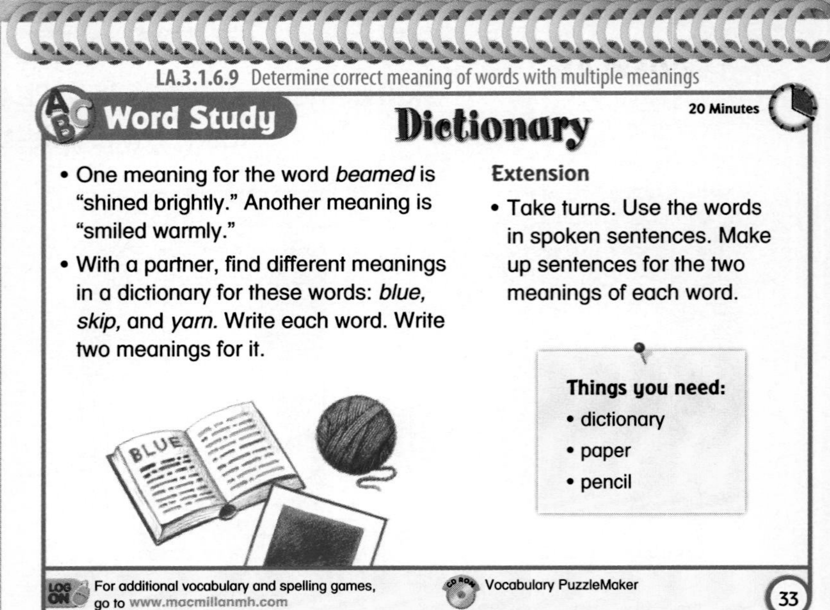

LA.3.1.6.9 Determine correct meaning of words with multiple meanings

Word Study **Dictionary** 20 Minutes

- One meaning for the word *beamed* is "shined brightly." Another meaning is "smiled warmly."
- With a partner, find different meanings in a dictionary for these words: *blue, skip,* and *yarn.* Write each word. Write two meanings for it.

Extension

- Take turns. Use the words in spoken sentences. Make up sentences for the two meanings of each word.

Things you need:
- dictionary
- paper
- pencil

For additional vocabulary and spelling games, go to www.macmillanmh.com

Vocabulary PuzzleMaker

33

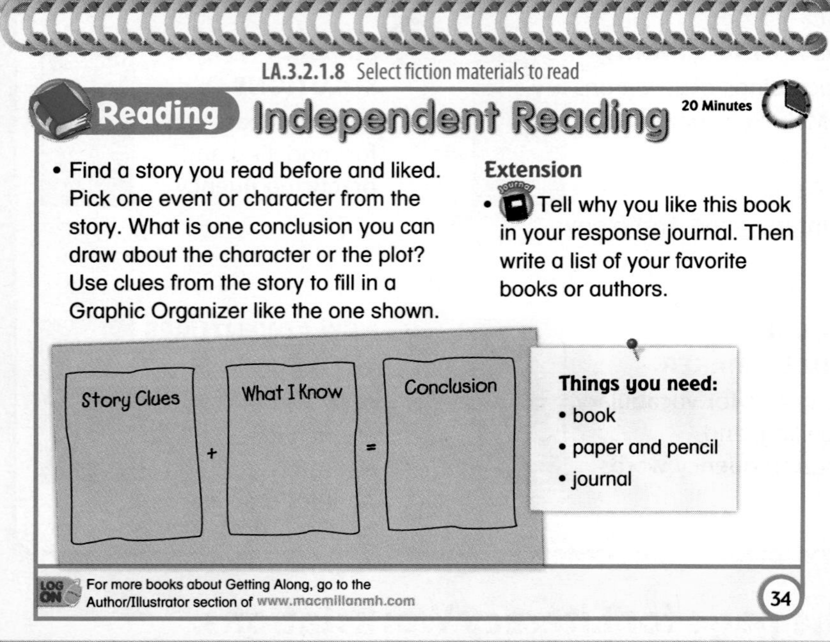

LA.3.2.1.8 Select fiction materials to read

Reading **Independent Reading** 20 Minutes

- Find a story you read before and liked. Pick one event or character from the story. What is one conclusion you can draw about the character or the plot? Use clues from the story to fill in a Graphic Organizer like the one shown.

Extension

- Tell why you like this book in your response journal. Then write a list of your favorite books or authors.

Things you need:
- book
- paper and pencil
- journal

For more books about Getting Along, go to the Author/Illustrator section of www.macmillanmh.com

34

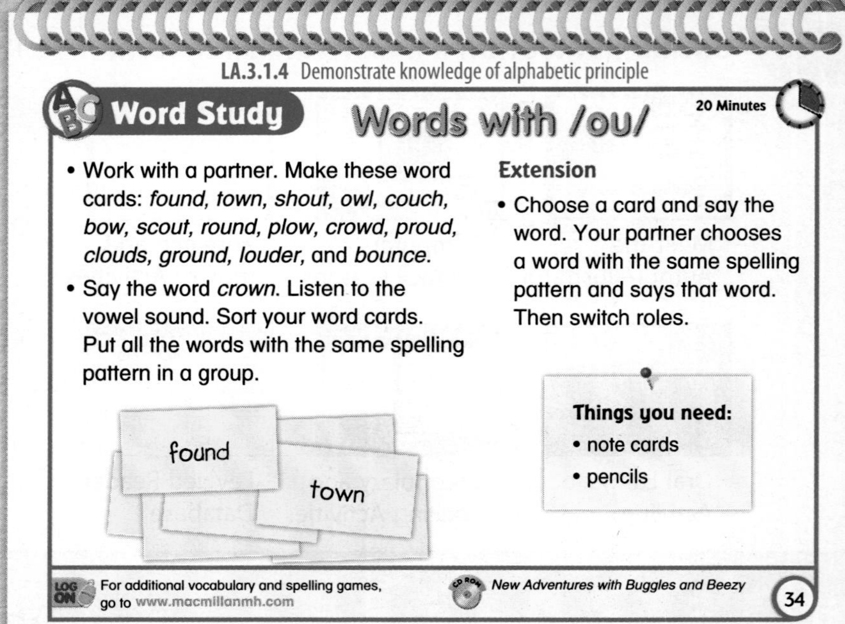

LA.3.1.4 Demonstrate knowledge of alphabetic principle

Word Study **Words with /ou/** 20 Minutes

- Work with a partner. Make these word cards: *found, town, shout, owl, couch, bow, scout, round, plow, crowd, proud, clouds, ground, louder,* and *bounce.*
- Say the word *crown.* Listen to the vowel sound. Sort your word cards. Put all the words with the same spelling pattern in a group.

Extension

- Choose a card and say the word. Your partner chooses a word with the same spelling pattern and says that word. Then switch roles.

Things you need:
- note cards
- pencils

For additional vocabulary and spelling games, go to www.macmillanmh.com

New Adventures with Buggles and Beezy

34

Literacy Workstations

Writing

Objectives

- Write a paragraph explaining how to make a class book of stories
- Write an article explaining how to keep a desk neat

Content Literacy

Objectives

- Make a list of rules for a playground
- Research to find facts about the cotton plant

LA.3.4.2.1 Write in informational /expository forms

Writing — **How to Make a Class Book** — 20 Minutes

- Write a paragraph. Explain how to make a class book of stories. Write the steps in the correct order. Use words, such as *first, next, then,* and *last,* to make the order of events clear.

Extension

- Underline the time-order words you used. Do you need to add any other time-order words? What are they?

Things you need:
- paper
- pencil

33

LA.3.6.2.3 Communicate information with visual support

Social Studies — **Playground Rules** — 20 Minutes

- A community needs to decide on rules for things. Think about playground rules for your school. Work with a partner to make a list of rules.
- Write your rules on a poster. Add drawings to make the rules clearer.

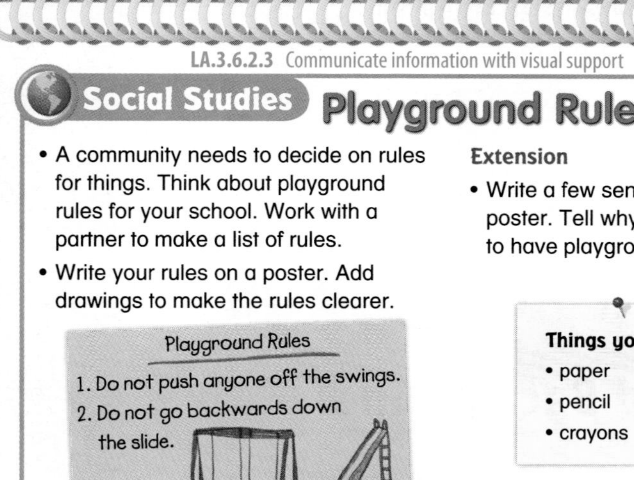
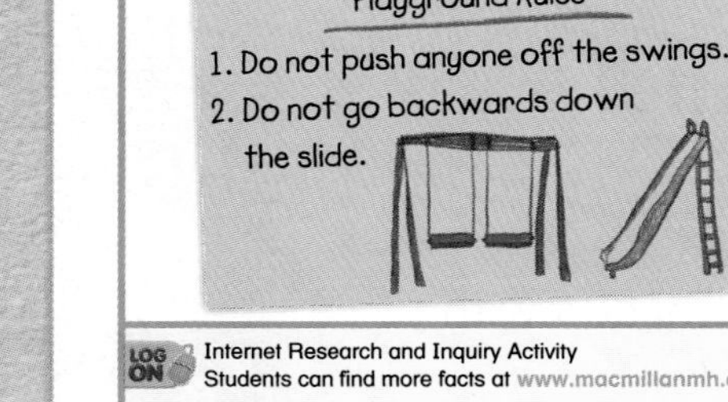

Playground Rules
1. Do not push anyone off the swings.
2. Do not go backwards down the slide.

Extension

- Write a few sentences on your poster. Tell why it is important to have playground rules.

Things you need:
- paper
- pencil
- crayons

Internet Research and Inquiry Activity
Students can find more facts at www.macmillanmh.com

33

LA.3.4.2.1 Write in informational /expository forms

Writing — **How to Keep Your Desk Neat** — 20 Minutes

- Write an article for a class newspaper. Explain how to keep a desk neat. Write the steps in a clear order.
- Before you begin to write, clean out your own desk. Note the steps.

Extension

- Ask a partner to follow your steps to clean his or her desk. If you need to, add words or sentences to make the steps clear.

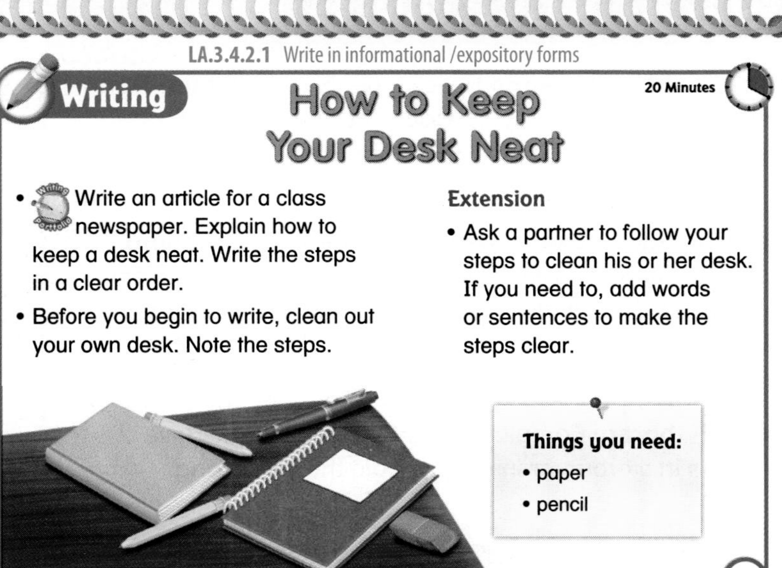

Things you need:
- paper
- pencil

34

LA.3.6.1.1 Read informational text and organize information

Science — **Cotton Thread** — 20 Minutes

- Some thread is made from cotton. Use a science book or encyclopedia to find out about the cotton plant. Write three facts you learn about this plant.
- Draw a picture to show what a cotton plant looks like.

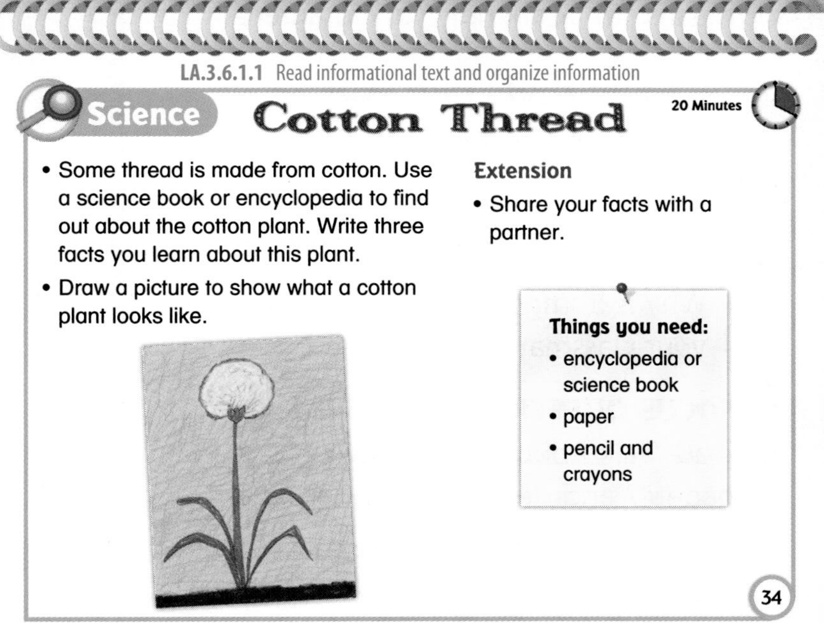

Extension

- Share your facts with a partner.

Things you need:
- encyclopedia or science book
- paper
- pencil and crayons

34

Prepare

ORAL LANGUAGE
- Build Background
- Read Aloud
- Expand Vocabulary

FCAT **VOCABULARY**
- Teach Words in Context
- Multiple-Meaning Words

COMPREHENSION
- **Strategy:** Make Inferences and Analyze
- FCAT **Skill:** Plot Development

SMALL GROUP OPTIONS
- Differentiated Instruction, pp. 77M–77V

Oral Language

Build Background

ACCESS PRIOR KNOWLEDGE

Share the following information with students:

The phrase *getting along* is an idiom. It means "to be friendly" or "to agree."

TALK ABOUT GETTING ALONG

LA.3.5.2 Apply listening and speaking strategies

Discuss the weekly theme.

- Whom do you get along with best? Why do you get along so well?
- Why is it important to get along with your classmates and teacher?

FOCUS QUESTION Have a volunteer read "Talk About It" on **Student Book** page 47 and describe the photo. Ask:

- Are the people in the photo getting along? How do you know?

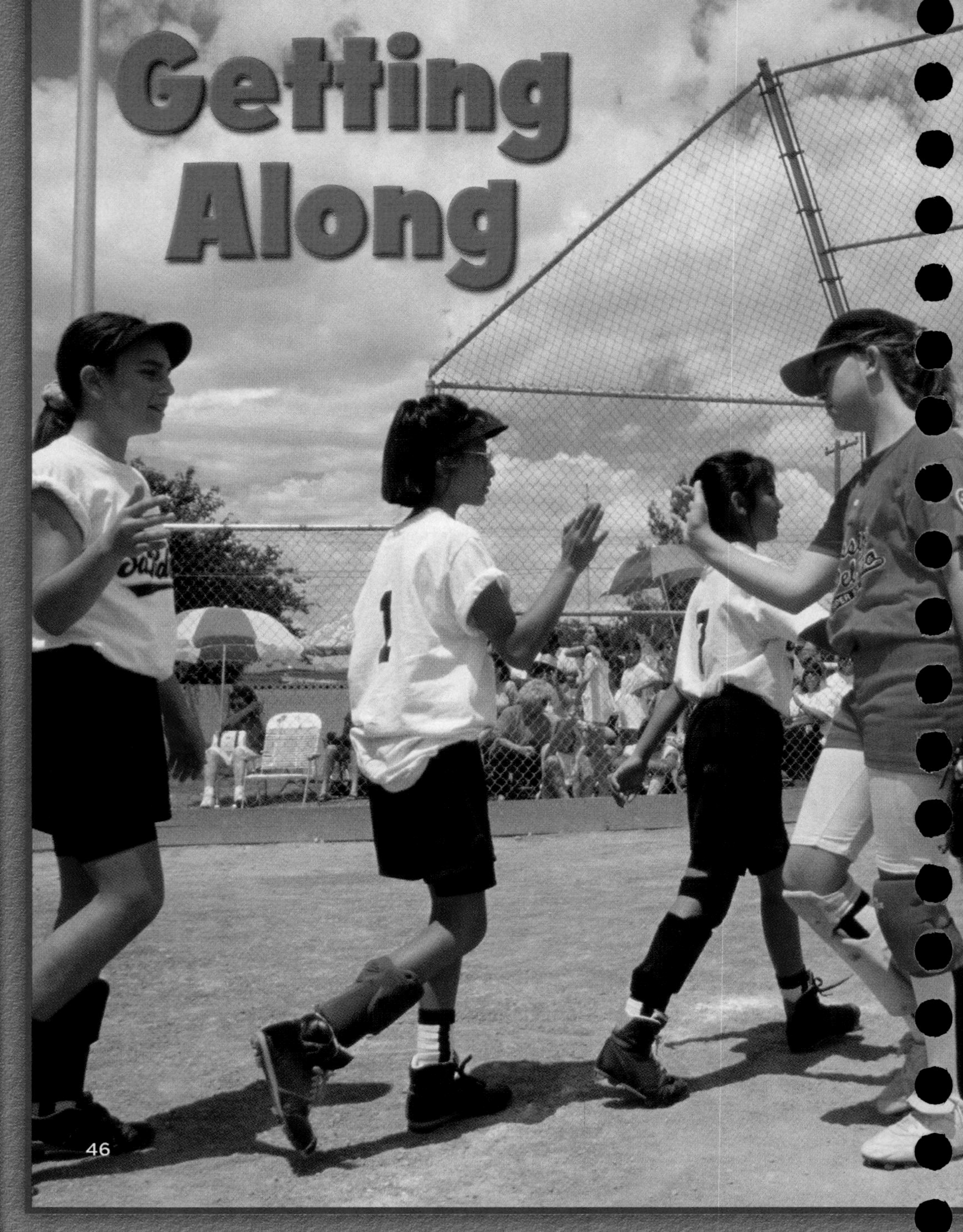

ENGLISH LANGUAGE LEARNERS

Beginning **Build Background** Have students say what they can about the photograph. Then say: *These children are on teams. Do you play on a team? Tell us about it.* Help students say what they can. Encourage the use of pantomime.

Intermediate **Share Ideas** Have students describe the photo. Say: *Teams shake hands with each other after a game. They get along.* Explain the meaning of *get along.* Say: *It's important to get along with other people. What do you do and say to get along with your classmates?* Help students express their ideas.

Advanced **Elaborate** Complete the Intermediate task. Have students discuss in a group or in class people they get along with well.

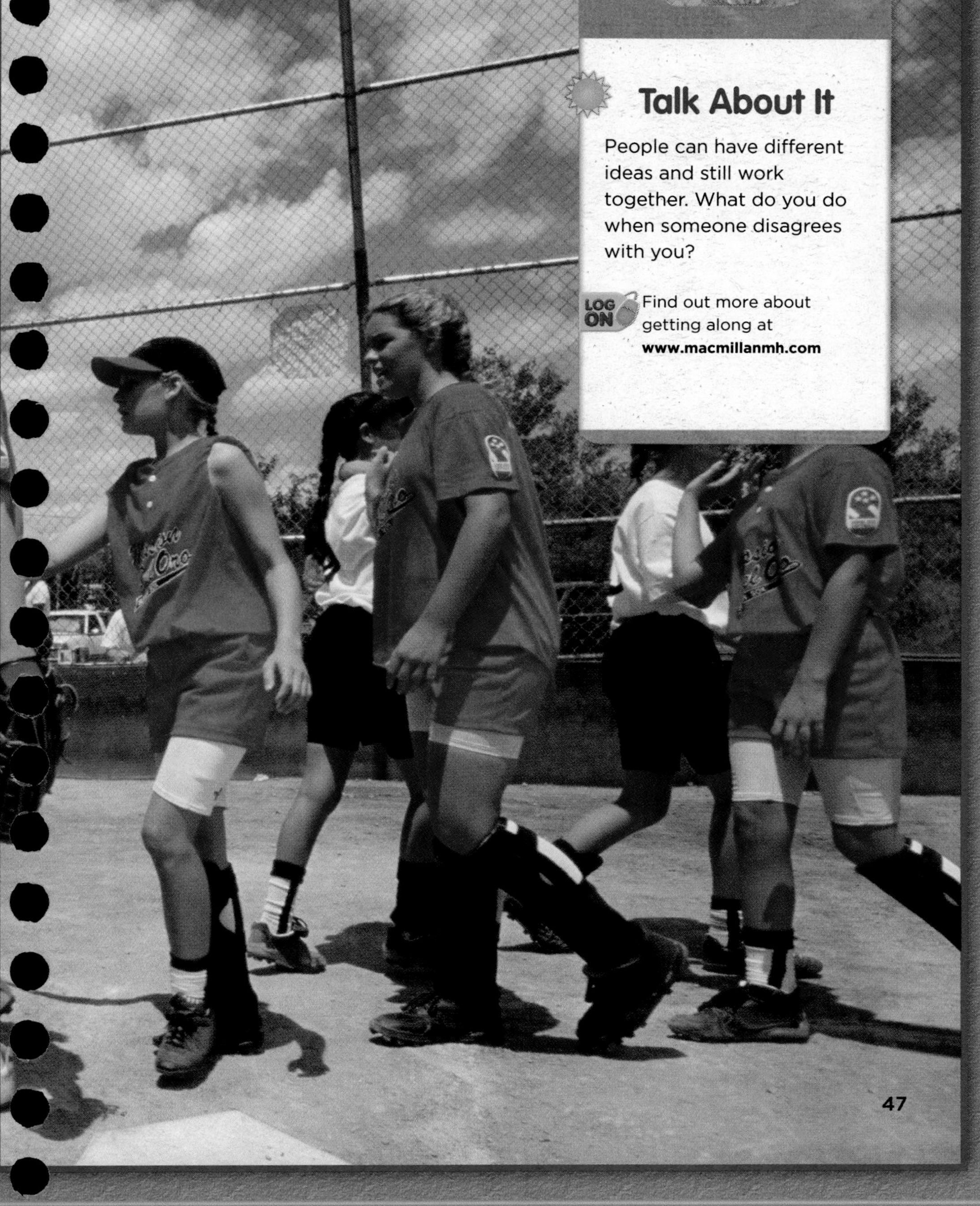

Talk About It
People can have different ideas and still work together. What do you do when someone disagrees with you?
LOG ON
Find out more about getting along at
www.macmillanmh.com
47

Read Aloud

Read "Arachne the Spinner"

LA.3.2.1 Identify elements of literary text

GENRE: Myth
Explain that myths are fiction stories that tell about Greek or Roman gods and goddesses, may have characters who do amazing things, often explain why something happens in nature

Read Aloud
pages 75–78

LISTENING FOR A PURPOSE

LA.3.1.6.2 Listen to text

Read "Arachne the Spinner" in the **Read-Aloud Anthology** and have students listen for the elements that make this story a myth. Choose from the teaching suggestions.

Fluency Ask students to listen to your phrasing, expression, and tone of voice as you read aloud.

LA.3.2.1 Develop a thoughtful response to literature

RESPOND TO THE MYTH

Ask students: What would you have done if you were Arachne? Do you think she found a good solution to her problem? Why or why not?

Expand Vocabulary

LA.3.1.7.6 Identify themes

LA.3.2.1.5 Explain author's use of descriptive language

Ask students to think about the weekly theme and the myth. Ask: What qualities does Arachne have that keep her from getting along with Athena? Discuss words from the story that describe Arachne's qualities (*bragging*, *preened*, *smug*, *pride*, *irreverence*).

Use the routine card to teach Expand Vocabulary words in the Read Aloud lesson.

Picture Prompt

Look at the photograph. Write about what the girls are doing. You can write a poem, a story, a description, or use any other type of writing you like.

LA.3.4.1 Develop and demonstrate creative writing

Technology

For an extended lesson plan, Web site activities and additional Read Alouds for **oral language** and **vocabulary development**, go to www.macmillanmh.com

Vocabulary

TEACH WORDS IN CONTEXT

LA.3.1.6.1 Use new vocabulary taught directly

Use the following routine:

LA.3.1.6.9 Determine correct meaning of words with multiple meanings

Routine

Define: If something **beamed**, it shined brightly.
Example: The sun beamed through the clouds. *Beamed* also means "smiled happily." She beamed with happiness.
Ask: What does *beamed* mean in this sentence? The child beamed when he got his new bike. MULTIPLE-MEANING WORDS

LA.3.1.6.8 Use knowledge of synonyms

- If you disagreed loudly with someone, you **argued**. They argued about what to do after school. What word has the same meaning as *argued*? *(fought)* SYNONYM
- Things that people own are called **possessions**. My books are my favorite possessions. What are your favorite possessions? EXAMPLE

- **Fabric** is cloth that is used for making clothes. My shirt is made from cotton fabric. What are some kinds of clothes that are made from fabric? EXAMPLE
- If you **purchased** something, you got it by paying money. We purchased tickets for the show. What are some things that you have purchased? EXAMPLE

LA.3.1.6.8 Use knowledge of synonyms

- If you are having an argument, you are **quarreling**. The boys were quarreling about whose turn it was to ride the bike. What word means the same thing as *quarreling*? *(arguing)* SYNONYM

Vocabulary

beamed	fabric
argued	purchased
possessions	quarreling

FCAT **Dictionary**
Multiple-Meaning Words are words that have more than one meaning.

Use a dictionary to find the meaning of *beamed* in the first sentence. Remember to look up the base word.

Community Works

by Jenna Rabin

One bright day, as the sunlight **beamed** through the windows, Mr. Turner's class started to plan the third-grade community service project.

"Okay," said Mr. Turner. "Let's share some ideas and listen to each other."

A few students raised their hands. Mr. Turner called on Mark. "We could clean up the small park—pick up trash and paint the benches," said Mark.

Rachel got annoyed. She **argued** with Mark. "You just want that park clean for yourself. Everyone else uses the big park across town. I think we should serve meals at the homeless shelter."

"Now, Rachel. Everyone should have a chance to share his or her ideas. It's okay to disagree, but we should still treat each other nicely."

48

Quick Check **Do students understand word meanings?**

During **Small Group Instruction**

If No → Approaching Level Vocabulary, p. 77N

If Yes → On Level Options, pp. 77Q–77R

Beyond Level Options, pp. 77S–77T

ELL

Reinforce Vocabulary For *fabric*, point out different kinds of fabric in clothes and other items in the room. For *possessions*, have a student name items he or she owns. Write them on the board and say: *These are [Tina's] possessions.* Ask students to discuss favorite possessions with partners.

"Sorry, Mr. Turner," Rachel said.

Jen cut in, "There are people who don't have many **possessions**, not even warm clothing. We could collect **fabric** for making nice, warm clothes for them!"

Cara added, "I read about a class that raised money and **purchased** notebooks and pencils for kids from a discount store."

"We could do crafts with people in nursing homes or hospitals," said Maria.

"Crafts?" groaned Sameer. "I'm really bad at crafts. I'm all thumbs! But how about a walkathon. I'm a fast walker, and we'd get exercise," he said. This made everyone laugh and stop their **quarreling** over who had the best idea.

Then Mr. Turner spoke. "All of your ideas are great. I'm going to write them on the board. Then we will take a class vote. This way we can choose a community service project that most people want to do."

The students agreed this was a good plan.

Reread for Comprehension

FCAT **Make Inferences and Analyze**

Plot Development Authors sometimes give readers **clues** about characters, setting, and story events. Readers should analyze these clues and **draw conclusions**. You can draw a conclusion about the characters, setting, or events by using story clues and what you already know. Reread the selection. Use your Conclusion Map to draw a conclusion about Rachel. Use Rachel's actions and reactions as your clues.

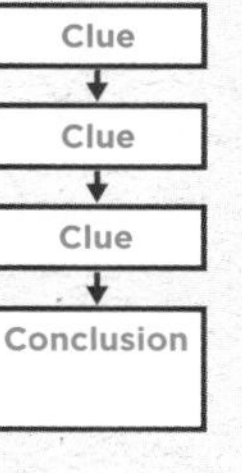

Vocabulary

FCAT **STRATEGY DICTIONARY**

LA.3.1.6.9 Determine correct meaning of words with multiple meanings in context

Multiple-Meaning Words To figure out an unfamiliar word, look for context clues in surrounding sentences or look for word parts that give clues to the word's meaning. When these strategies do not help, look up the word in a dictionary. If the unfamiliar word has prefix, a suffix, or an ending added, then figure out the base, or root, word and find that word in the dictionary.

LA.3.1.6.10 Determine meanings using a dictionary

Some words have more than one meaning. To find the meaning that fits in the sentence, first figure out what part of speech the word is. Then look at the meanings for that part of speech in a print or digital dictionary entry, and choose the meaning that best fits the sentence.

Point to the verb *beamed* on **Student Book** page 48. Help students see that this verb has the past-tense ending *-ed,* so they will have to look up the base word *beam* in a dictionary. In a dictionary, *beam* has several definitions for verbs and nouns. Look at the two verb definitions: "shine brightly" and "smile happily." Try each in the sentence. The definition that fits for *beamed* is "shined brightly."

Read "Community Works"

LA.3.1.6.3 Use context clues

As students read "Community Works," ask them to identify clues that reveal the meanings of the highlighted words. Tell students they will read these words again in *Seven Spools of Thread.*

FCAT Success!

Test Prep and Practice with vocabulary, pages 6–31

Vocabulary

Review last week's vocabulary words: **magnificent**, **masterpiece**, **ingredient**, **recipes**, and **tasty**.

On Level Practice Book O, page 119

A. Use the words below to fill in each blank in the story.

argued beamed fabric quarreling possessions purchased

One rainy day, Juan and Maria argued about what to do. "Let's look through our possessions to see what we don't need. We can give away toys we do not play with," said Juan.

Their mother beamed at his idea. "I am glad that you are not greedy children!" she said. This is a much better way to spend time than quarreling. A long time ago I purchased a lot of fabric to make a dress, and I never used it. Take it and bring it with you. Maybe some children can make costumes with it."

B. Write a definition for each vocabulary word. Possible responses provided.

1. argued disagreed loudly with someone
2. beamed shone brightly
3. fabric cloth used for making clothes
4. quarreling having an argument
5. possessions things that people own
6. purchased got something by paying for it

Approaching Practice Book A, page 119

Beyond Practice Book B, page 119

Reread for Comprehension

Objectives

- Make inferences and analyze
- Use academic language: *inference, conclusion*
- Understand plot development in a story through drawing conclusions

Materials

- Comprehension Transparencies 17a and 17b
- Graphic Organizer Transparency 17
- Leveled Practice Books, p. 120

FCAT Skills Trace

Plot Development: Draw Conclusions	
Introduce	U4: 49A–B
Practice / Apply	U4: 50–73; Leveled Practice, 120–121
Reteach / Review	U4: 77M–T; U6: 387A–B, 388–399, 403M–T; Leveled Practice, 215–216
Assess	Weekly Tests; Units 4, 5, 6 Tests; Benchmark Tests A, B
Maintain	U5: 177B; U6: 339B

ELL

Clarify To help students practice drawing conclusions, make sure they understand the text. As you read, stop to say: *Rachel is annoyed. What do you think that word means? What's another word for annoyed?* *What do you do when you serve meals? Sameer groaned. How is he feeling?*

STRATEGY
MAKE INFERENCES AND ANALYZE

LA.3.1.7.3 Determine implied inference

Authors don't always tell a reader every detail in a story. Readers have to carefully look at the information and **make inferences** about it. To make inferences, good readers use what they know and clues in the story to figure out what is missing. Making inferences helps readers understand the characters' actions and the events in a story. Readers can make inferences to help them draw conclusions.

FCAT

SKILL
PLOT DEVELOPMENT: DRAW CONCLUSIONS

LA.3.1.7.3 Determine relevant supporting details

LA.3.1.7.3 Determine implied inference

EXPLAIN

Readers often make inferences and **draw conclusions** about the characters and events in a story. To draw conclusions, readers use two or more story details and their own experiences to explain why characters act in a certain way or why something happens.

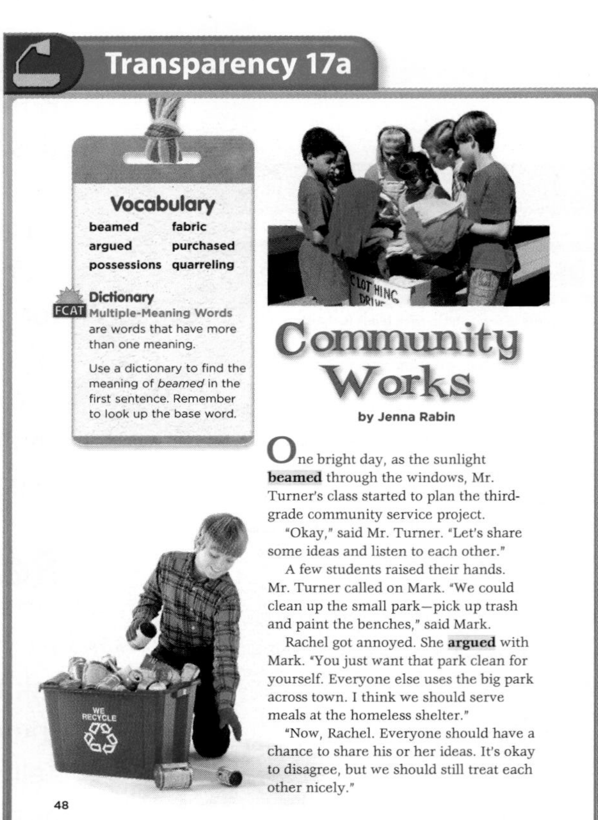

Transparency 17a

Vocabulary

beamed, fabric, argued, purchased, possessions, quarreling

FCAT **Dictionary**

Multiple-Meaning Words are words that have more than one meaning.

Use a dictionary to find the meaning of *beamed* in the first sentence. Remember to look up the base word.

Community Works

by Jenna Rabin

One bright day, as the sunlight **beamed** through the windows, Mr. Turner's class started to plan the third-grade community service project.

"Okay," said Mr. Turner. "Let's share some ideas and listen to each other."

A few students raised their hands. Mr. Turner called on Mark. "We could clean up the small park—pick up trash and paint the benches," said Mark.

Rachel got annoyed. She **argued** with Mark. "You just want that park clean for yourself. Everyone else uses the big park across town. I think we should serve meals at the homeless shelter."

"Now, Rachel. Everyone should have a chance to share his or her ideas. It's okay to disagree, but we should still treat each other nicely."

48

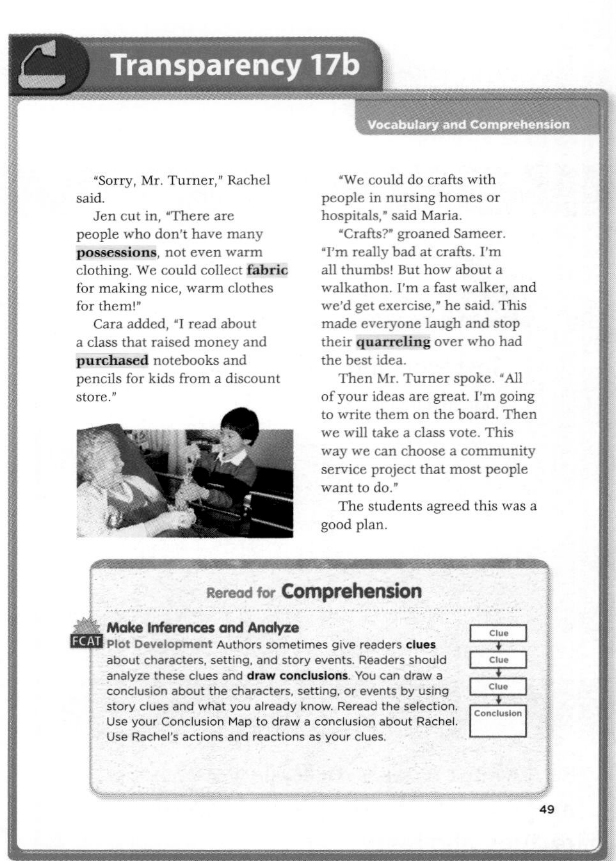

Transparency 17b

Vocabulary and Comprehension

"Sorry, Mr. Turner," Rachel said.

Jen cut in, "There are people who don't have many **possessions**, not even warm clothing. We could collect **fabric** for making nice, warm clothes for them!"

Cara added, "I read about a class that raised money and **purchased** notebooks and pencils for kids from a discount store."

"We could do crafts with people in nursing homes or hospitals," said Maria.

"Crafts?" groaned Sameer. "I'm really bad at crafts. I'm all thumbs! But how about a walkathon. I'm a fast walker, and we'd get exercise," he said. This made everyone laugh and stop their **quarreling** over who had the best idea.

Then Mr. Turner spoke. "All of your ideas are great. I'm going to write them on the board. Then we will take a class vote. This way we can choose a community service project that most people want to do."

The students agreed this was a good plan.

Reread for **Comprehension**

FCAT **Make Inferences and Analyze**

Plot Development Authors sometimes give readers **clues** about characters, setting, and story events. Readers should analyze these clues and **draw conclusions**. You can draw a conclusion about the characters, setting, or events by using story clues and what you already know. Reread the selection. Use your Conclusion Map to draw a conclusion about Rachel. Use Rachel's actions and reactions as your clues.

49

Student Book pages 48–49 available on Comprehension Transparencies 17a and 17b

MODEL

Read aloud "Community Works" on **Student Book** page 48.

Think Aloud Why does Mr. Turner tell Rachel that people should treat each other nicely? To figure out the answer, I will look at Rachel's actions. She is annoyed and tells Mark that she doesn't agree with him. I know that sometimes people sound angry when they are annoyed. I can draw the conclusion that Rachel sounded angry and maybe yelled at Mark. She was rude to him. Now I understand why Mr. Turner reminded Rachel about treating others nicely.

LA.3.2.1.2 Identify elements of story structure

GUIDED PRACTICE

Display **Transparency 17**. Remind students that a Conclusion Map can help them reach a new understanding of the events in a story or characters' actions. Also remind students that a conclusion is not directly stated in the story.

- Ask: *How does Rachel feel about Mark's idea?* Begin the Conclusion Map by writing in the first clue box: *Rachel doesn't like Mark's idea.*
- Ask: *Why doesn't Rachel like Mark's idea?* (She thinks Mark wants to clean the park just so he can use it.) Place this clue on the chart.
- Ask: *What does Rachel want the class to do?* (Rachel wants the class to serve meals at a homeless shelter.) Place this clue on the chart. Tell students to use the clues to draw a conclusion about Rachel. (Rachel wants to help people.) Add this to the Conclusion box on the chart.

LA.3.2.1.2 Identify and explain character/character development

LA.3.1.7.3 Determine implied inference

APPLY

Have students reread "Community Works" and draw a conclusion about Mr. Turner. They should conclude that Mr. Turner is very fair, using the following details: He thinks people should treat each other nicely. He listens to all the students' ideas. He has the class vote to pick the idea that they all like.

Quick Check **Can students draw conclusions about characters and events?**

During **Small Group Instruction**

If No → **Approaching Level** Comprehension, p. 77O

If Yes → **On Level** Options, pp. 77Q–77R

Beyond Level Options, pp. 77S–77T

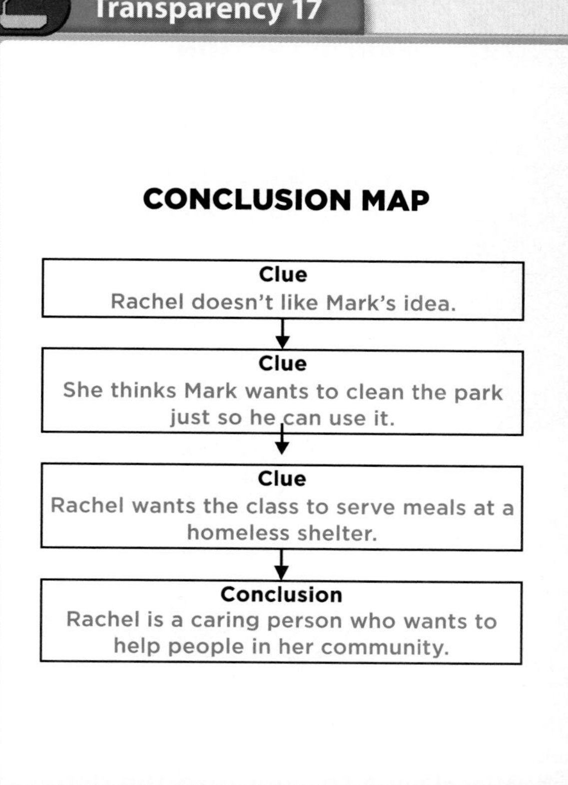

Transparency 17
CONCLUSION MAP
Clue
Rachel doesn't like Mark's idea.
Clue
She thinks Mark wants to clean the park just so he can use it.
Clue
Rachel wants the class to serve meals at a homeless shelter.
Conclusion
Rachel is a caring person who wants to help people in her community.

Graphic Organizer Transparency 17

FCAT Success!

Test Prep and Practice with plot development, pages 65–96

On Level Practice Book O, page 120

A conclusion is a decision you make after looking at all the information about a specific topic. You can **draw conclusions** by considering the information the author gives you and your own experiences. Drawing conclusions helps you understand **plot development**.

Read the information below. On the lines below each story, write a conclusion based on information given. Possible responses provided.

1. Sam walks into the classroom. There is a sign on the bulletin board that says "Welcome Sam!" The other students invite Sam to join their activity and to sit at their lunch table.
   Conclusion: Sam feels welcome in his new school.
2. Neighborhood children walk together to a park, carrying trash bags, rakes, and buckets. Three children work together picking up litter in a park. One child rakes leaves, and another shoves leaves into a trash bag. When they are finished, all the children play in the park.
   Conclusion: Children in a neighborhood cooperate to clean up a park.
3. Kayla brings her box of games over to Jen, and they open it together. They choose a game from the box and play.
   Conclusion: Kayla and Jen share well together.
4. Tyler and Grace wash the dishes, sweep the floor, rake leaves, take out the trash, take their baby brother out in his stroller.
   Conclusion: Tyler and Grace help with jobs at home.

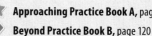

Approaching Practice Book A, page 120

Beyond Practice Book B, page 120

Read

MAIN SELECTION
- *Seven Spools of Thread*
- FCAT **Skill:** Plot Development

PAIRED SELECTION
- "What Causes Day and Night?"
- FCAT **Text Feature:** Rules

SMALL GROUP OPTIONS
- Differentiated Instruction, pp. 77M–77V

Comprehension

LA.3.2.1 Identify elements of literary text

GENRE: FABLE

Have a student read the definition of Fable on **Student Book** page 50. Students should look for a statement in the story that states the lesson, or moral, that the reader learns.

STRATEGY
MAKE INFERENCES AND ANALYZE

LA.3.1.7.3 Determine implied inference

Good readers make inferences by using clues in the story and their own experiences to figure out information the author has not told the reader.

SKILL
PLOT DEVELOPMENT

LA.3.2.1.2 Identify elements of story structure

LA.3.1.7.3 Determine implied inference

To understand how a plot develops, readers often need to **draw conclusions**. To draw conclusions, readers use two or more details from the story and what they know to come to an understanding about characters or events.

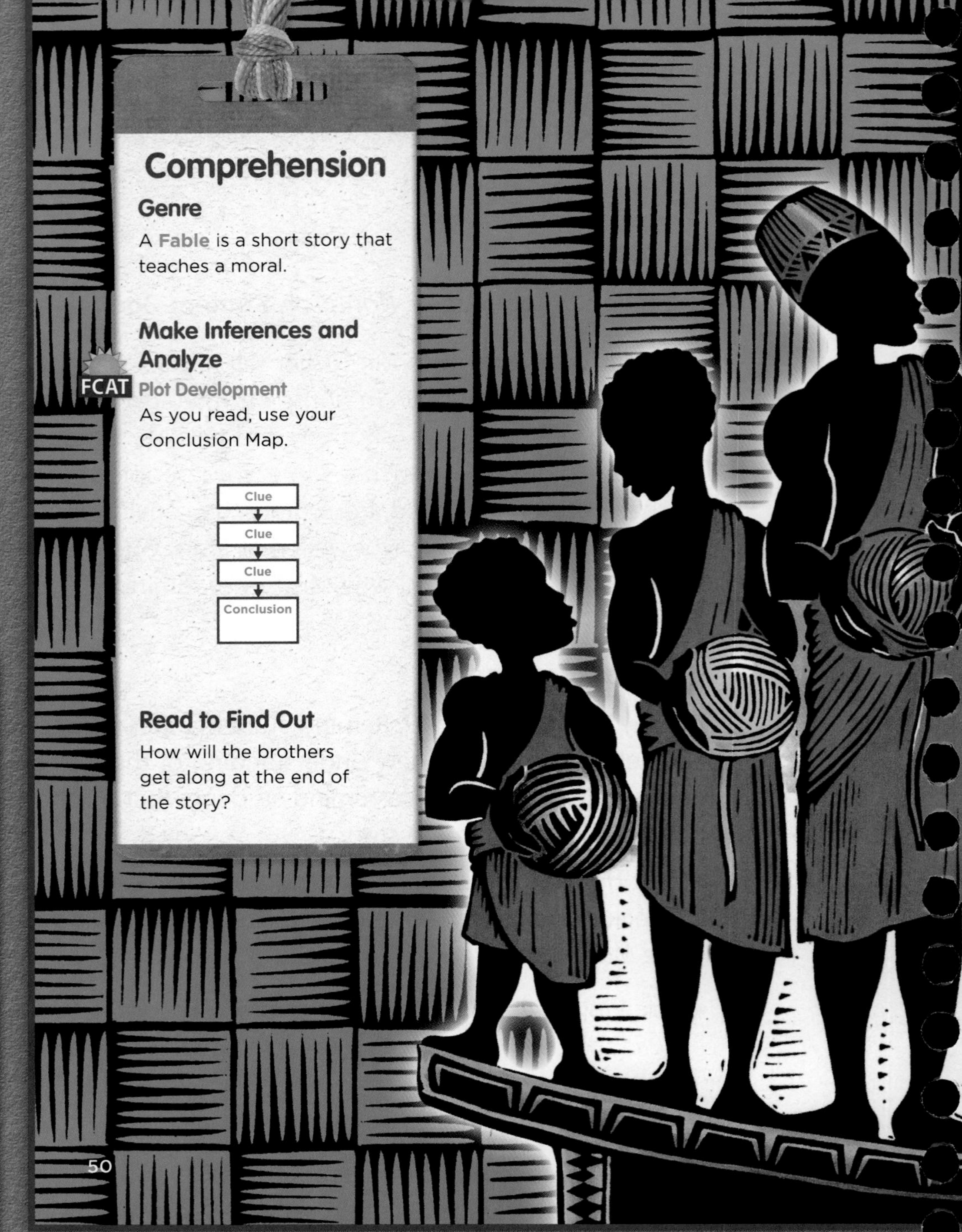

Comprehension

Genre

A **Fable** is a short story that teaches a moral.

Make Inferences and Analyze

FCAT **Plot Development**

As you read, use your Conclusion Map.

Read to Find Out

How will the brothers get along at the end of the story?

50

FCAT Vocabulary

Vocabulary Words Review the tested vocabulary words: **beamed**, **argued**, **possessions**, **fabric**, **purchased**, and **quarreling**.

Story Words Students may find these words difficult. Pronounce the words and present the meanings as necessary.

mahogany (p. 52): a certain kind of reddish-brown wood

spools (p. 56): small pieces of wood that hold thread

bolt (p. 61): a large roll of cloth

loom (p. 61): machine used to weave thread into cloth

LA.3.1.6.1 Use new vocabulary taught directly

Main Selection

Seven Spools of Thread

A Kwanzaa Story

By Angela Shelf Medearis

Illustrated by Daniel Minter

Award Winning Selection

51

LA.3.1.5.2 Adjust reading rate based on purpose; LA.3.1.7.8 Use strategies to repair comprehension

Read Together	Read Independently
If your students need support to read the Main Selection, use the prompts to guide comprehension and model how to complete the graphic organizer. Encourage students to read aloud.	If your students can read the Main Selection independently, have them read and complete the graphic organizer. Suggest that students set purposes, adjust reading rate, and choose reading strategies based on the purpose.

If your students need an alternate selection, choose the **Leveled Readers** that match their instructional levels.

Audio CD

Technology

Story available on **Listening Library Audio CD**

Preview and Predict

LA.3.1.7.1 Use text features to make predictions

Ask students to read the title, preview the illustrations, and note questions and predictions about this story. Who are the characters? What will they do? Have students write their predictions and any questions they want answered about the story.

Set Purposes

LA.3.1.7.1 Use text features to establish purpose for reading

FOCUS QUESTION Talk about the "Read to Find Out" question and discuss how to look for the answer.

Point out the Conclusion Map in the **Student Book** and on **Practice Book** page 121. Explain that students will fill it in as they read the story.

Read *Seven Spools of Thread*

LA.3.1.6.2 Read text

Use the questions and Think Alouds for additional instruction to support the comprehension strategy and skill.

On Level Practice Book O, page 121

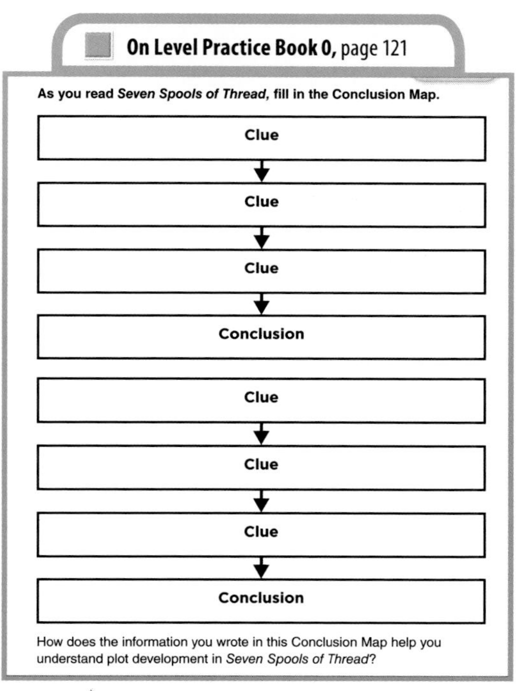
As you read *Seven Spools of Thread*, fill in the Conclusion Map.

Clue

Clue

Clue

Conclusion

Clue

Clue

Clue

Conclusion

How does the information you wrote in this Conclusion Map help you understand plot development in *Seven Spools of Thread*?

Approaching Practice Book A, page 121

Beyond Practice Book B, page 121

Develop Comprehension

1 PLOT DEVELOPMENT: SETTING

LA.3.2.1.2 Identify setting

What is the setting of this story? (The story is set in a small village in Ghana, Africa. Because it is a fable, there is no set year in which it takes place. Fables are meant to be timeless.)

2 STRATEGY DICTIONARY

LA.3.1.6.9 Determine correct meaning of words with multiple meanings

LA.3.1.6.10 Determine meanings using a dictionary

The word *limbs* has more than one meaning. How can using a **dictionary** help you figure out what it means here? (A dictionary entry gives all the meanings of a word. By trying each meaning in a sentence, I can find which one fits best. A dictionary states that limbs can be branches of a tree or a person's arms and legs. By trying each definition in the sentence, I can tell that in this case *limbs* means "a person's arms or legs.")

In a small African village in the country of Ghana there lived an old man and his seven sons. After the death of his
1 wife, the old man became both father and mother to the boys. The seven brothers were handsome young men. Their skin was as smooth and dark as the finest mahogany wood.
2 Their limbs were as straight and strong as warriors' spears.

But they were a disappointment to their father. From
3 morning until night, the family's small home was filled with the sound of the brothers' **quarreling**.

As soon as the sun brought forth a new day, the brothers began to argue. They **argued** all morning about how to tend the crops. They argued all afternoon about the weather.

"It is hot," said the middle son.

"No—a cool breeze is blowing!" said the second son.

They argued all evening about when to return home.

"It will be dark soon," the youngest said. "Let's finish this row and begin anew tomorrow."

"No, it's too early to stop," called the third son.

"Can't you see the sun is setting?" shouted the sixth son.

And so it would continue until the moon **beamed** down and the stars twinkled in the sky.

52

ELL

Explain Vocabulary Ask: *How did the father feel about his sons?* Students may not understand the word *disappointment*. Explain that the father felt sad because his sons acted badly. They fought all the time. Help students see that *disappointment* means unhappiness because something did not happen the way you wanted.

Develop Comprehension

3 STRATEGY
MAKE INFERENCES AND ANALYZE

LA.3.1.7.3 Determine implied inference

Teacher Think Aloud Sometimes an author doesn't tell readers everything that happens in a story. By using story clues and what I know, I can figure out what details were left out. By making inferences and drawing conclusions about the characters, I will better understand the story. On page 52 I read that the seven brothers "were a disappointment to their father." I'm not sure why. Then I read that the brothers fight all the time. I know that most parents do not like it when their children argue with each other. Using my own experience and a clue in the story, I can make an inference. The father in the story feels disappointed because he thinks his sons should be able to get along.

Develop Comprehension

4 PLOT DEVELOPMENT

LA.3.1.7.3 Determine implied inference

How do you think the father feels about the way his sons argue over the food? Use information from the story and your own experiences to draw a conclusion. (Earlier I learned that the father felt his sons were a disappointment. In this part of the story, he tells his arguing sons that he divided the food equally, so I know that they have nothing to argue about. I know that when people argue for no reason, it can make other people irritated or angry. So I can conclude that the father feels unhappy and maybe angry with his sons for their bad behavior.)

54

At mealtime, the young men argued until the stew was cold and the fu fu was hard.

"You gave him more than you gave me," whined the third son.

"I divided the food equally," said their father. **4**

"I will starve with only this small portion on my plate," complained the youngest.

"If you don't want it, I'll eat it!" said the oldest son. He grabbed a handful of meat from his brother's plate.

"Stop being so greedy!" said the youngest.

And so it went on every night. It was often morning before the seven brothers finished dinner.

One sad day, the old man died and was buried. At sunrise the next morning, the village Chief called the brothers before him.

"Your father has left an inheritance," said the Chief.

The brothers whispered excitedly among themselves.

"I know my father left me everything because I am the oldest son," said the oldest.

"I know my father left me everything because I am the youngest son," said the youngest.

"He left everything to me," said the middle son. "I know I was his favorite."

"Eeeh!" said the second son. "Everything is mine!"

The brothers began shouting and shoving. Soon, all seven were rolling around on the ground, hitting and kicking each other. **5**

55

Develop Comprehension

5 PLOT DEVELOPMENT

FCAT

LA.3.2.1.2 Identify character/ character development

LA.3.1.7.3 Determine implied inference

What character traits do the brothers have? What story details and personal experiences help you reach a conclusion about them? Write the clues and conclusion on your Conclusion Map. (All the brothers do is argue with each other and complain. They hit and kick one another. Each of them wants to be the only son who receives the inheritance. I know that people who act like this toward other people are mean and selfish. So I can conclude that the brothers are mean and selfish and do not seem to like each other.)

Clue
The brothers argue with one another.
Clue
The brothers kick one another.
Clue
Each brother wants to be the only one to get the inheritance.
Conclusion
The brothers are mean and selfish.

FCAT Comprehension

Plot Development: Draw Conclusions

Explain Tell students that when they draw conclusions, they use two or more details about a story and what they know to better gain understanding of characters or events. They should first gather as many clues as they can. To be sure that the conclusion they draw makes sense, they should think about how each clue fits with the other clues.

Discuss *How do the brothers act when they find out their father has left them an inheritance?* (They whisper excitedly. Each thinks that their father has left him everything.) *What do they do next?* (They roll around on the ground, fighting.) *What conclusion can you draw about the brothers?* (They are selfish and greedy.)

Apply Have students continue to draw conclusions about the brothers as they read the story.

LA.3.1.7.3 Determine implied inference

Develop Comprehension

6 PLOT DEVELOPMENT

LA.3.1.7.3 Determine implied inference

In his will, the father said that the sons had to make gold out of the thread by moonrise that night. Why did he say this? Place the clues and conclusion on a Conclusion Map. (The father did not like the way the brothers treated one another. If the brothers have to work to make gold by the time the moon rises, they will not have time to argue. From my own experiences, I know that when I am working toward a goal with someone, I don't have time to argue. I think the father said this in his will to teach the brothers to act more caringly toward one another and work together instead of fighting.)

Clue
The father was disappointed in his sons.

↓

Clue
The brothers fought all the time.

↓

Clue
The brothers will work quickly to reach their goal.

↓

Conclusion
The father wanted his sons to learn how to work together instead of fighting.

"Stop that this instant!" the Chief shouted.

The brothers stopped fighting. They shook the dust off their clothes and sat before the Chief, eyeing each other suspiciously.

"Your father has decreed that all of his property and **possessions** will be divided among you equally," said the Chief. "But first, by the time the moon rises tonight,
6 you must learn how to make gold out of these spools of silk thread. If you do not, you will be turned out of your home as beggars."

The oldest brother received blue thread. The next brother, red. The next, yellow. The middle son was given orange thread; the next, green; the next, black; and the youngest son received white thread. For once, the
7 brothers were speechless.

The Chief spoke again. "From this moment forward, you must not argue among yourselves or raise your hands in anger towards one another. If you do, your father's property and all his possessions will be divided equally among the poorest of the villagers. Go quickly; you only have a little time."

The brothers bowed to the Chief and hurried away.

FCAT **Plot Development**
Why were the brothers speechless after listening to the Chief?

56

Vocabulary

Read the sentence that contains the word **possessions**. What does the word *possessions* mean? (Possessions are things that a person owns.)

LA.3.1.6.3 Use context clues

Fluency

Punctuation

Explain When you read aloud, you pause to show punctuation. This helps others follow along as they listen. Give commas a short pause. Use a slightly longer pause for periods and semicolons.

Model Point to the second paragraph in the passage available on **Transparency 17**. Point out commas, semicolons, and the period in the fourth sentence: "The middle son was given orange thread; the next, green; the next, black; and the youngest son received white thread." Read the sentence aloud, pausing appropriately.

Practice Have students pay attention to punctuation as they read aloud with partners. One student should read a sentence. The other student echo-reads it. Then students switch roles. Remind students to tell their partners when they have done a good job.

LA.3.1.5 Demonstrate the ability to read text orally with accuracy

Develop Comprehension

7 PLOT DEVELOPMENT

LA.3.1.7.3 Determine implied message

Why were the brothers speechless after listening to the Chief? (Each brother thought that he would receive all of the inheritance without having to do anything for it. When they all found out they would have to work together, they were surprised and shocked, because all they had ever done was argue.)

ELL

Access for All

STRATEGIES FOR EXTRA SUPPORT

Question 7 PLOT DEVELOPMENT

Restate the decree in simpler terms so that students understand it: *The brothers have to make gold from thread or they will become beggars. Beggars are very poor people who have to ask people for money to live.* Explain that the brothers are speechless—they are so surprised that they can't talk. Ask: *Why are the brothers surprised? Will it be easy or hard to make gold from silk threads?*

Develop Comprehension

8 **STRATEGY**
MONITOR AND CLARIFY: SELF-CORRECT

LA.3.1.7.8 Question to repair comprehension

Do you know why the brothers are sitting down side by side? What questions can you ask yourself to make sure that you understand why this happened? (At first I thought the brothers sat down because they thought someone else would do the work. I will ask several questions to make sure I am correct. What happened earlier in the story? Why did the father give the brothers seven spools of thread? The answer is: The father died and left an inheritance, but the brothers had to turn the thread into gold to get it. They also had to stop fighting. Now the brothers are sitting side by side. They understand that they have to work together to get the money. They are trying to figure out how to do this. Thinking more closely about the story helped me correct my mistake.)

8 When the seven Ashanti brothers arrived at their farm, something unusual happened. They sat side by side, from the oldest to the youngest, without saying anything unkind to each other.

"My brothers," the oldest said after a while, "let us shake hands and make peace among ourselves."

"Let us never argue or fight again," said the youngest brother.

The brothers placed their hands together and held each other tightly.

58

FCAT Comprehension

Monitor and Clarify: *Self-Correct*

Explain/Discuss Good readers form ideas about the characters and events in a story. To make sure that their ideas are correct and to correct misunderstandings, they can ask themselves questions such as *why?* and *what if?* and *how?* Asking these questions can help explain what is happening in a story. Help students use the Self-Correct strategy. Show them how to answer question 8, using the strategy to ask *why? what if?* and *how?* Help them see how questioning can help them correct any wrong ideas about events or characters.

Apply Have students read page 59 and use the Self-Correct strategy to answer this question: *How do you think the brothers feel about not fighting with each other?* (Students should use the strategy to generate questions that help them answer this question.)

LA.3.1.7.8 Question to repair comprehension

For the first time in years, peace rested within the walls of their home.

"My brothers," said the third son quietly, "surely our father would not turn us into the world as beggars."

"I agree," said the middle son. "I do not believe our father would have given us the task of turning thread into gold if it were impossible." 9

"Could it be," said the oldest son, "that there might be small pieces of gold in this thread?"

59

Develop Comprehension

9 PLOT DEVELOPMENT

LA.3.1.7.3 Determine implied inference

LA.3.2.1.2 Identify and explain character/character development

How do the brothers feel about their father now? How do you know? (I know that the sons loved their father. The text says that they think that their father would not want them to become beggars. He would not give them an impossible task. So, I can conclude that they have kind feelings for him and are not angry.)

Have students respond to the story by confirming or revising their predictions. Encourage students to revise or write additional questions they have about the story.

Can students use clues to draw conclusions about the story? If not, see the Extra Support on this page.

Extra Support

Plot Development

FCAT

Remind students to use details from the story and their own ideas to draw conclusions about the plot. Discuss events in the story so far. Ask: *After the brothers hear that they will have to work together, what do they do?* (They begin to talk about their ideas. They listen to one another.) *Why do they do that?* (It is what their father wanted them to do.) *What does this experience teach them about their father?* (He wanted them to learn to get along because he loved them and wanted them to do better.)

If students have difficulty, review how to draw a conclusion. Remind them that they can use clues from the story and their own experiences to help them figure out how the brothers feel about their father.

LA.3.1.7.8 Use strategies to repair comprehension

Stop here if you wish to read this selection over two days.

Develop Comprehension

10 SUMMARIZE

LA.3.1.7.8 Summarize to repair comprehension

What has happened so far in this story? (The seven brothers fight all the time. Their father dies. Each brother believes that he will get all of the father's property and possessions. The Chief gives the brothers thread and tells them that they have to make gold from it or they will not get any of their inheritance. The brothers go home and act more kindly toward one another.)

11 FIGURATIVE LANGUAGE: PERSONIFICATION

LA.3.2.1.5 Explain author's use of personification

What word does the author use to make the light in the hut appear as if it is alive? (The author uses *crept* to show how the light moves. It makes the light seem alive, as if it wants to stay hidden or move quietly from place to place.)

10

The sun beamed hotly overhead. Yellow streams of light crept inside the hut. Each brother held up his spool of thread. The beautiful colors sparkled in the sunlight. But there were no nuggets of gold in these spools. 11

"I'm afraid not, my brother," said the sixth son. "But that was a good idea."

"Thank you, my brother," said the oldest.

"Could it be," said the youngest, "that by making something from this thread we could earn a fortune in gold?" 12

"Perhaps," said the oldest, "we could make cloth out of this thread and sell it. I believe we can do it."

"This is a good plan," said the middle son. "But we do not have enough of any one color to make a full bolt of cloth."

"What if," said the third son, "we weave the thread together to make a cloth of many colors?"

"But our people do not wear cloth like that," said the fifth son. "We wear only cloth of one color."

"Maybe," said the second, "we could make a cloth that is so special, everyone will want to wear it."

"My brothers," said the sixth son, "we could finish faster if we all worked together."

"I know we can succeed," said the middle son.

The seven Ashanti brothers went to work. Together they cut the wood to make a loom. The younger brothers held the pieces together while the older brothers assembled the loom.

61

Develop Comprehension

12 PLOT DEVELOPMENT

FCAT

LA.3.2.1.2 Identify and explain character/character development

How have the brothers' feelings for one another changed? Why do you think this? (Earlier in the story, the brothers didn't seem to like each other. Now they are getting along better. They even seem to like each other, and they are making plans to work together and turn the thread into gold. These are all clues that show how the brothers feel.)

Ways to Confirm Meaning

Semantic/Syntactic Cues

Explain/Model Good readers often use what they know about grammar, pronunciation of root words, and context clues to help them with a difficult word. Read the word *assembled* in context.

Think Aloud This word has an *-ed* ending. This ending added to a verb shows an action in the past. I know how to pronounce the base word, *assemble*. I know from the sentence that *assembled* is a verb—something the brothers do. I know the brothers are making a loom, so I think that *assembled* probably means "put together."

Apply Tell students to use grammatical and context clues to help them with other difficult words. Determining whether a word is a noun, adjective, or verb will help. Students may want to try to predict what the word means first and then use the clues to confirm or revise their prediction.

LA.3.1.4.3 Decode multi-syllabic words in context; **LA.3.1.4.1** Use knowledge of pronunciation of root words; **LA.3.1.6.7** Use base words and affixes; **LA.3.1.6.3** Use context clues

Develop Comprehension

13 WRITER'S CRAFT: PRECISE WORDS

LA.3.2.1.5 Examine how language describes objects

Why do you think the author chose the word *multicolored* in this sentence? Why is it a good word to describe the cloth? (*Multicolored* is a precise word that clearly describes what the cloth looks like. It has more than one color.)

They took turns weaving cloth out of their spools of thread. They made a pattern of stripes and shapes that looked like the wings of birds. They used all the colors—blue, red, yellow, orange, green, black, and white. Soon the brothers had several pieces of beautiful multicolored cloth. 13

62

When the cloth was finished, the seven brothers took turns neatly folding the brightly colored **fabric**. Then they placed it into seven baskets and put the baskets on their heads. 14

63

Develop Comprehension

14 MAKE PREDICTIONS

LA.3.1.7.8 Predict to repair comprehension

What do you think the brothers are going to do with the cloth? (The brothers put the cloth in baskets on their heads. Earlier in the story they talked about making cloth to sell. I think they will probably take it to a place where they can sell it.)

Vocabulary

Read the sentence that contains the word **fabric**. What is a synonym for *fabric*? (*cloth*)

LA.3.1.6.8 Use knowledge of synonyms

Develop Comprehension

15 CONFIRM PREDICTIONS

LA.3.1.7.8 Predict to repair comprehension

What do the brothers do with the cloth? Was your prediction correct? (The brothers take the cloth to the marketplace. They show it to the people there and offer it for sale. Students should indicate whether or not their prediction was correct.)

16 FIGURATIVE LANGUAGE: SIMILE

LA.3.2.1.5 Explain author's use of similes

To what does the author compare the multicolored cloth? What clue word tells you this figure of speech is a simile? (The cloth is compared to a rainbow. The word *like* shows that this is a simile.)

The brothers formed a line from the oldest to the youngest and began the journey to the village. The sun slowly made a golden path across the sky. The brothers hurried down the long, dusty road as quickly as they could.

15 As soon as they entered the marketplace, the seven Ashanti brothers called out, "Come and buy the most wonderful cloth in the world! Come and buy the most wonderful cloth in the world!"

They unfolded a bolt and held it up for all to see. The multicolored fabric glistened like a rainbow. A crowd
16 gathered around the seven Ashanti brothers.

"Oh," said one villager. "I have never seen cloth so beautiful! Look at the unusual pattern!"

"Ah," said another. "This is the finest fabric in all the land! Feel the texture!"

17

FCAT **Plot Development** What have the brothers learned?

64

Cross-Curricular Connection

Math

GEOMETRIC SHAPES IN KENTE CLOTH

The Ashanti people of Ghana in West Africa have been famous for their weaving for several centuries. The looms which the Ashanti use are only four inches wide, so the cloth is narrow. The narrow strips are sewn together to make fabric for clothing. The special cloth, woven for royal people, is sometimes called kente cloth.

Give students graph paper and ask them to use crayons or markers or a computer drawing program to draw some typical Ashanti patterns and then identify the geometric shapes—rectangles, squares, triangles—that make up the patterns. They can find samples of patterns on the Internet. Then challenge them to put their finished drawings together to form the largest "piece of fabric" they can on paper.

LA.3.6.4.1 Use appropriate technologies to enhance communication and achieve a purpose

Develop Comprehension

17 PLOT DEVELOPMENT

LA.3.1.7.3 Determine implied inference

What have the brothers learned? How do you know? (The brothers are working together to sell the cloth. In the illustration I see them standing together proudly as they sell the cloth. The brothers have learned that working together leads to success.)

ELL Access for All

Question 17 PLOT DEVELOPMENT

How did the brothers act toward each other at the beginning of the story? Did they get along? How are they different at the end of the story? How do they treat each other? What happened to make them act differently? What have they learned?

Develop Comprehension

18 PLOT DEVELOPMENT

LA.3.1.7.3 Determine relevant supporting details

LA.3.2.1.2 Identify plot

What does the King's treasurer do? Why is this important? (The King's treasurer decides to buy the cloth as a gift for the King. He agrees to give the sons a bag of gold as payment. This is important because it shows the sons have "made gold" out of the cloth, so they can get their inheritance.)

Cultural Perspectives

CULTURAL ELEMENTS IN FOLK LITERATURE

Reading folk literature helps students understand other country's cultures. Discuss *Seven Spools of Thread*. It takes place in Ghana, a country on the coast of western Africa, and centers around the theme that a family can solve a problem by learning to work together.

Have students listen to audio recordings or read fables and folk literature about families in many cultures from different eras including those from ancient times and identify important cultural elements and familiar themes. Then have them discuss their findings in a literature circle or class book club. They can compare and contrast families and cultural elements in the stories as well as themes and implied messages.

SS.A.2.2.3.3.1 Aspects of family life in many eras; **LA.3.1.6.2** Discuss familiar text; **LA.3.1.7.7** Compare and contrast topics, settings, characters, and problems in two texts; **LA.3.1.7.3** Determine strongly implied message; **LA.3.1.7.6** Identify themes

The brothers smiled proudly. Suddenly, a man dressed in magnificent robes pushed his way to the front of the crowd. Everyone stepped back respectfully. It was the King's treasurer. He rubbed the cloth between the palms of his hands. Then he held it up to the sunlight.

"What a thing of beauty," he said, fingering the material. "This cloth will make a wonderful gift for the King! I must have all of it."

The seven brothers whispered together.

"Cloth fit for a king," said the oldest, "should be **purchased** at a price only a king can pay. It is yours for one bag of gold." 18

"Sold," said the King's treasurer. He untied his bag of gold and spilled out many pieces for the brothers.

The seven Ashanti brothers ran out of the marketplace and back down the road to their village.

19

67

Develop Comprehension

19 STRATEGY

MAKE INFERENCES AND ANALYZE

LA.3.1.7.3 Determine implied inference

Teacher Think Aloud When an author leaves out details, I can use story clues and what I know to figure out the missing information. The author doesn't tell us how the brothers feel when the King's treasurer buys their cloth. Explain how you can figure this out.

(Encourage students to apply the strategy in a Think Aloud.)

Student Think Aloud I know the brothers really wanted to sell the cloth before the moon rose so they could get their inheritance. I know that I am very happy when I get something that I want. So I think the brothers must be very happy that they got the gold.

Develop Comprehension

20 STRATEGY
MAKE INFERENCES AND ANALYZE

LA.3.1.7.3 Determine implied inference

How can you figure out why the brothers are sweating and panting? How does this help you understand the story? Explain your thinking.

LA.3.1.7.3 Determine relevant supporting details

Student Think Aloud I know that I often hurry when I have something important to do. I also know that the brothers need to reach the Chief by first moonlight to prove they can work together. So now I know that they are panting and sweating because they ran all the way to the Chief's hut. By using clues and what I know, I understand what is happening in this part of the story.

A shining silver moon began to creep up in the sky. Panting and dripping with sweat, the brothers threw 20
themselves before the Chief's hut.

"Oh, Chief," said the oldest, "we have turned the thread into gold!"

The Chief came out of his hut and sat upon a stool.

The oldest brother poured the gold out onto the ground.

"Have you argued or fought today?" asked the Chief.

"No, my Chief," said the youngest. "We have been too busy working together to argue or fight."

"Then you have learned the lesson your father sought to teach you," said the Chief. "All that he had is now yours."

The older brothers smiled happily, but the youngest son looked sad.

"What about the poor people in the village?" he asked. "We receive an inheritance, but what will they do?"

"Perhaps," said the oldest, "we can teach them how to turn thread into gold."

The Chief smiled. "You have learned your lesson very well."

The seven Ashanti brothers taught their people carefully.
The village became famous for its beautiful, multicolored 21
cloth, and the villagers prospered.

69

Develop Comprehension

21 PLOT DEVELOPMENT

LA.3.2.1.2 Identify and explain character/character development

LA.3.1.7.3 Determine implied inference

How do you think the villagers feel about the seven brothers? Why? (The villagers are very happy. The brothers taught them how to make the fabric, and this gave the villagers a way to make money. The village prospered.)

Cross-Curricular Connection

TRADITIONAL DRESS

Seven Spools of Thread is set in Ghana, an African country famous for its kente cloth. Kente cloth is a narrow strip of colorful patterned cloth like that woven by the brothers in the story. Kente cloth strips are sewn together into traditional costumes. Have each student use several sources of informational text to research traditional dress in a country of his or her choice and write an informational essay explaining the history of the costume. Have each student include a topic sentence and supporting details in his or her essay. Then students can create paper dolls dressed in their nations' costumes. Place the dolls in the appropriate locations on a mural-sized world map.

LA.3.4.2.3 Write informational essays that include a topic sentence and supporting details; **LA.3.6.1.1** Read informational text for purpose of making a report; **LA.3.6.2.3** Communicate information in an informational report

Develop Comprehension

22 **THEME/ESSENTIAL MESSAGE**

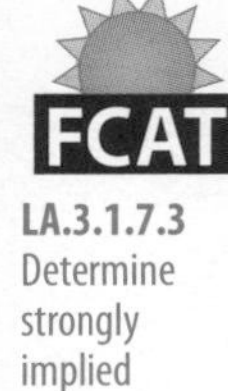

LA.3.1.7.3 Determine strongly implied message

LA.3.1.7.6 Identify themes

What does the proverb mean? How does it summarize the theme of the story? (Each stick stands for a person. When people are part of a "bundle" or group, such as a family, they have other people to support and love them. This makes all the people in the group stronger. The brothers have learned that when they work together, it is easier for them to reach their goals. They are "unbreakable" because there are many of them.)

23 **GENRE: FABLE**

LA.3.2.1 Identify and analyze elements of fiction

What lesson does this story tell? How do you know? (The story's lesson is the following: People can reach their goals when they work together instead of fighting with each other. Groups of people are stronger than individuals who try to do everything on their own or, as the proverb at the end of the story says, sticks in a bundle are unbreakable.)

From that day until this, the seven Ashanti brothers have worked together, farming the land.

And they have worked peacefully, in honor of their father.

70

FCAT Comprehension

Theme

Explain/ Discuss The author's theme is the overall message or main idea of a story. The theme can be stated or unstated. Sometimes the theme is stated as a moral or lesson at the end of the story in one sentence. Sometimes it is an implied message that the reader figures out using story clues. In *Stone Soup* (Unit 3, Week 1) one character says to the monks, "You have shown us that sharing makes us all richer." Point out that this is the stated main idea, or theme, of the story.

Apply Have students look at the last two pages of *Seven Spools of Thread*. Ask them to identify a statement that tells the story's overall idea. (Sticks in a bundle are unbreakable.) Explain that a proverb is a short saying that offers wisdom or advice. Help them understand that the proverb is the theme of the story. Then have them determine the unstated theme in another story they have read.

LA.3.1.7.3 Determine explicit ideas in grade level text; **LA.3.1.7.3** Determine implied message; **LA.3.2.1.4** Identify an author's theme

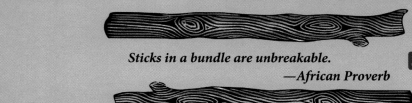

Sticks in a bundle are unbreakable.
—African Proverb

22 23

71

Develop Comprehension

LA.3.1.7.1 Use text features to confirm predictions

RETURN TO PREDICTIONS AND PURPOSES

Review students' predictions and purposes. Were they correct? Can they explain how the relationships among the brothers changed?

LA.3.1.7.3 Determine implied inference

LA.3.1.7 Use strategies to comprehend text

REVIEW READING STRATEGIES

How did making inferences and drawing conclusions about the characters and their actions help students to understand the story? Have students share any questions they have about the story. What strategies can they use to answer the questions?

LA.3.2.1.6 Write a book review that identifies the main ideas, character(s), setting, sequence of events, and problem/solution

PERSONAL RESPONSE

Have each student write a book review of *Seven Spools of Thread* that identifies the main characters, the setting, the problem, and the events that lead to the story's solution. Remind students to include a recommendation for classmates to read or not read the book and include reasons.

Quick Check **Can students draw conclusions about plot development in a story?**

During **Small Group Instruction**

If No → **Approaching Level** Leveled Reader Lesson, p. 77P

If Yes → **On Level** Options, pp. 77Q–77R

Beyond Level Options, pp. 77S–77T

Author and Illustrator

WEAVING A TALE WITH ANGELA AND DANIEL

Have students read the biographies of the author and illustrator.

DISCUSS

LA.3.1.7.2 Identify how author's perspective influences text

- Why does Angela Shelf Medearis write books about her African American heritage? How do you think Medearis's background—including her age, cultural traditions in her family, where and when she grew up, and what she learned in school—affects what she writes?

LA.3.1.7.2 Identify the author's purpose

- Why do you think Daniel Minter used woodcuts to illustrate this book?

WRITE ABOUT IT

LA.3.1.7.6 Identify themes

LA.3.4.2.4 Write a message

Discuss the main events and theme of the story. Have each student write an e-mail message to the author telling her what he or she liked about the story and how the story made him or her feel. After students have finished, invite them to share their messages with one another.

FCAT Author's Purpose

Have students use the genre (fable) and content to figure out the author's purpose. Help them to see that this is a made-up story that has a theme or message. It does not contain facts and information or try to persuade. The purpose of this story is to entertain.

LA.3.1.7.2 Identify the author's purpose

LOG ON Technology

Students can find more information about Angela Shelf Medearis at **www.macmillanmh.com**

WEAVING A TALE WITH ANGELA AND DANIEL

Author **Angela Shelf Medearis** wrote this story to celebrate the African American holiday Kwanzaa. When Angela was growing up, there were no books for her to read about her African American heritage. Today she writes books about African Americans so readers can feel proud of who they are.

Illustrator **Daniel Minter** often carves and paints on wood, just as he did for this story. Woodcarving is an important part of traditional African art. Daniel's carvings help keep these traditional arts alive.

Other books by Angela Shelf Medearis: *Too Much Talk* and *The Freedom Riddle*

LOG ON Find out more about Angela Shelf Medearis and Daniel Minter at **www.macmillanmh.com**

FCAT Author's Purpose

Did Angela Shelf Medearis write this story to explain, inform, or entertain? What clues tell you her purpose for writing?

72

Author's Craft

Figurative Language: Simile

Angela Shelf Medearis uses **figurative language**, such as similes, to help the reader picture what she is describing.

- **Similes** use the words *like* or *as* to compare two things that are not alike. For example: "Their limbs were as straight and strong as warriors' spears." (p. 52) The author wants readers to picture the brothers' arms. The arms are long and straight like spears.

Have students find and explain other similes, such as "Their skin was as smooth and dark as the finest mahogany wood." (p. 52) and "The multicolored fabric glistened like a rainbow." (p. 64) Challenge students to create similes of their own.

LA.3.2.1.5 Identify and explain author's use of similes
LA.3.2.1.5 Identify author's use of figurative language

FCAT Comprehension Check

Summarize

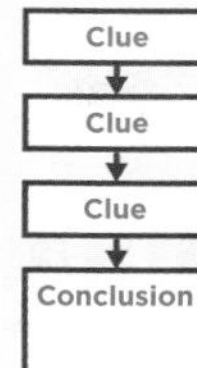

Summarize the plot of *Seven Spools of Thread*. Use your Conclusion Map to help you recall clues that tell how the brothers behave at the end.

Think and Compare

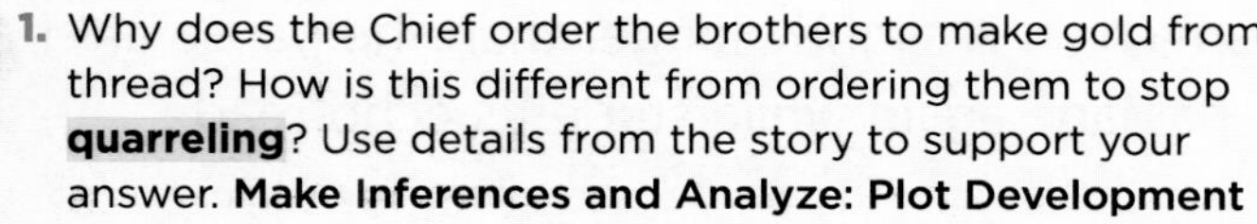

1. Why does the Chief order the brothers to make gold from thread? How is this different from ordering them to stop **quarreling**? Use details from the story to support your answer. **Make Inferences and Analyze: Plot Development**

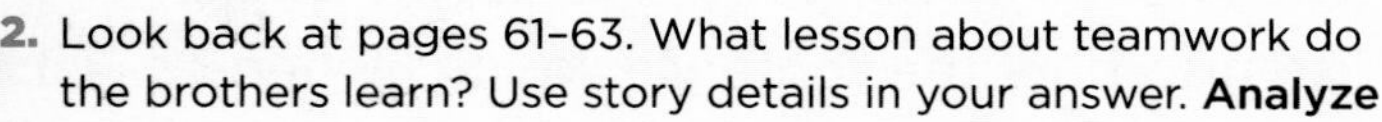

2. Look back at pages 61–63. What lesson about teamwork do the brothers learn? Use story details in your answer. **Analyze**
3. Think of a time you had to work with a friend or family member. What did you learn from your experience? **Apply**
4. The brothers teach the villagers how to weave the special cloth. Why is this better than giving the villagers money? Explain. **Evaluate**
5. Reread "Community Works" on pages 48–49. How is the problem in that story similar to the problem in *Seven Spools of Thread*? How are the solutions to the problems different? Use details from both stories in your answer. **Reading/Writing Across Texts**

73

Strategies for Answering Questions

On My Own

Model the On My Own strategy with question 3. To answer this question, students will need to think about their own experiences in relation to the story.

Question 3 Think Aloud: I worked with my family last week to clean up our basement. Not only did we get the job done fast, but we also had a great time doing it. The lesson that I learned is that working together can be enjoyable and get the job done quickly.

LA.3.1.7 Use strategies to comprehend text

Comprehension Check

SUMMARIZE

LA.3.1.7.8 Summarize to repair comprehension

Have partners identify and summarize the main events in *Seven Spools of Thread*. Remind students that their Conclusion Maps can help them organize their ideas.

THINK AND COMPARE

Sample answers are given.

LA.3.1.7.3 Determine implied inference

1. **Plot Development:** The brothers are selfish and don't get along. Making gold from thread teaches them to work together. It is better than just telling them to stop quarreling.

LA.3.1.7.3 Determine relevant supporting details

2. **Analyze:** The brothers learn that if they work together, they can find a way to make the cloth. They also learn to treat each other with respect and to share ideas.

LA.3.2.1.7 Connect text to self

3. **Text-to-Self:** Answers should explain a positive experience working with others. ON MY OWN

LA.3.2.1.7 Connect text to world

4. **Text-to-World:** After the villagers learn how to weave the special cloth, they can make it on their own and then sell it to make money. Teaching the villagers a skill is better than just giving them money.

FOCUS QUESTION

LA.3.2.1.7 Connect text to text

LA.3.1.7.7 Compare and contrast characters

5. **Text-to-Text:** The characters in both stories must stop quarreling and work together to do something. The solutions are different. In "Community Works," the students take a vote. In *Seven Spools of Thread*, the brothers learn to work together and make cloth.

Objectives

- Read accurately with appropriate pauses
- Rate: 82–102 WCPM

Materials

- Fluency Transparency 17
- Fluency Solutions Audio CD
- Leveled Practice Books, p. 122

ELL Access for All

Model Read aloud sentences that include commas or semicolons and end with a period and model pausing. Model this a few times. Then have students echo-read the sentences with you. Have students practice the sentences in pairs.

Fluency

Repeated Reading: Pauses

LA.3.1.5 Demonstrate the ability to read text orally with accuracy

EXPLAIN/MODEL Model the passage on **Transparency 17**, and point out the semicolons after *orange thread*, *green*, and *black*. Explain that the pause after a semicolon is slightly longer than the pause after a comma. Model the passage again while students echo-read.

Think Aloud I will keep my voice level and pause at each semicolon. I'll listen to how the sentence sounds when I say it out loud.

Transparency 17

"Your father has decreed that all of his property and possessions will be divided among you equally," said the Chief. "But first, by the time the moon rises tonight, you must learn how to make gold out of these spools of silk thread. If you do not, you will be turned out of your home as beggars."

The oldest brother received blue thread. The next brother, red. The next, yellow. The middle son was given orange thread; the next, green; the next, black; and the youngest son received white thread. For once, the brothers were speechless.

Fluency Transparency 17
from *Seven Spools of Thread*, page 56

PRACTICE/APPLY Divide students into two groups. One group reads each sentence. The other group echo-reads. Then they switch roles. For additional practice, have students use **Leveled Practice Book** page 122 or **Fluency Solutions Audio CD**.

Access for All

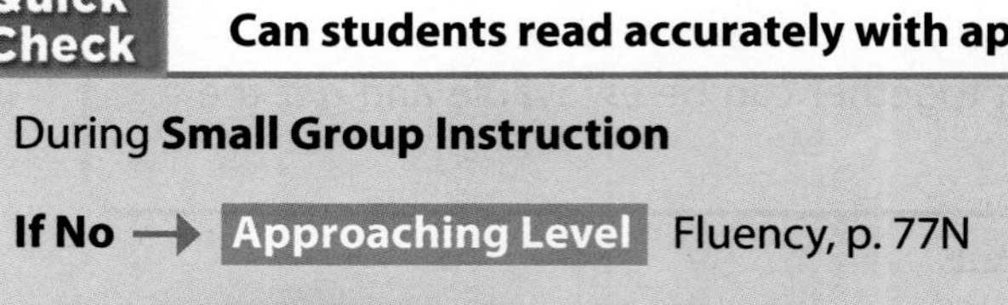

Quick Check **Can students read accurately with appropriate pauses?**

During **Small Group Instruction**

If No → Approaching Level Fluency, p. 77N

If Yes → On Level Options, pp. 77Q–77R

Beyond Level Options, pp. 77S–77T

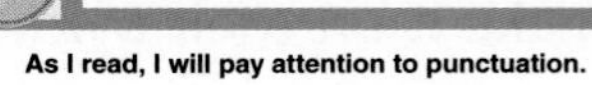

On Leveled Practice Book O, page 122

As I read, I will pay attention to punctuation.

The old man could give the diamond to only one son.
11 Which one should it be? He loved them all equally. Finally
22 he came up with a solution.
28 The next morning, the old man called his three sons
38 before him.
40 "My sons, I have a problem," he told them. "I love all
52 three of you, but I can give my most precious possession
63 to only one of you. Therefore, I will give my diamond to
75 the son that best meets my challenge."
82 "The one of you who proves to be a true hero will get
95 the diamond," said the old man.
101 "That is fair," said the three sons in unison.
110 "To decide who is the true hero, I will give you a task,"
123 said their father. 126

Comprehension Check

1. What is the old man's problem? **Problem and Solution** The old man has only one diamond and three sons. He does not know which son should get the diamond.
2. How does the old man decide which son should get the diamond? **Plot Development** The old man decides to give the diamond to the son who proves to be a hero. The sons have to complete a task that their father gives them.

	Words Read	–	Number of Errors	=	Words Correct Score
First Read		–		=	
Second Read		–		=	

Approaching Practice Book A, page 122

Beyond Practice Book B, page 122

Comprehension

REVIEW SKILL
PLOT DEVELOPMENT

LA.3.2.1.2 Identify and explain elements of story structure

EXPLAIN/MODEL

- By identifying a story's plot, characters, and setting and seeing how they fit together, a reader can understand **plot development**.

LA.3.2.1.2 Identify plot, character/ character development and setting

- A **plot** is the made-up events in a fiction story. A plot has a beginning, middle, and end.
- **Characters** are the people in a story.
- The **setting** is when and where the story takes place.

Model how to identify the characters, plot, and setting in "Community Works" on pages 48–49. Point out the characters—a teacher and his students. Help students to see that the setting is a classroom during a school day.

PRACTICE/APPLY

Ask students to discuss the questions below about *Seven Spools of Thread*. Have students use story details to support their answers. For comprehension practice, use graphic organizers on pages 99–112 in the **Teacher's Resource Book**.

LA.3.2.1.2 Identify and explain setting

- Why is the setting important to the plot? (This is a story that can only take place in a little village in Ghana. It couldn't take place in the United States.)
- What time of day is it when the Chief meets with the seven sons after their father's death? Why is this detail important? (The Chief meets with them at sunrise. The time of this meeting is important because the sons must turn the thread into gold by sunset.)

LA.3.1.7.3 Determine implied message

- Why is the marketplace important to the plot of the story? What happens here? (The marketplace is important because it is where the brothers turn the thread into gold. They sell their cloth for gold coins.)

LA.3.2.1.8 Select fiction materials to read

LA.3.1.7.3 Determine implied message

Have student pairs read another fable or folk tale aloud to each other. Ask them to discuss the plot and setting and to identify the story's theme, or implied message. Invite them to share the details of their discussions with other pairs.

Objectives

- Understand plot development in a story
- Use academic language: *plot, development, setting*

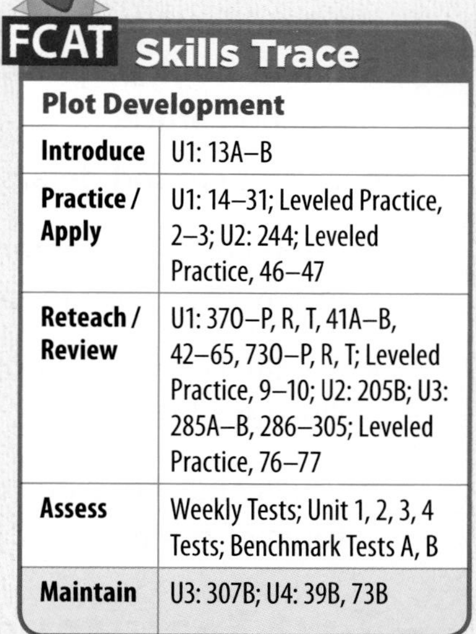

FCAT Skills Trace

Plot Development	
Introduce	U1: 13A–B
Practice / Apply	U1: 14–31; Leveled Practice, 2–3; U2: 244; Leveled Practice, 46–47
Reteach / Review	U1: 37O–P, R, T, 41A–B, 42–65, 73O–P, R, T; Leveled Practice, 9–10; U2: 205B; U3: 285A–B, 286–305; Leveled Practice, 76–77
Assess	Weekly Tests; Unit 1, 2, 3, 4 Tests; Benchmark Tests A, B
Maintain	U3: 307B; U4: 39B, 73B

RESEARCH Why It Matters

Comprehension Research shows that partner reading is a research-proven technique that provides students with the kinds of fluency practice that can improve reading achievement. Having a student read a text while a classmate listens and provides guidance and support really works.

Timothy Shanahan

Log on to **www.macmillanmh.com**

Informational Text: Science

LA.3.2.2 Identify elements of non-fiction

GENRE: NONFICTION ARTICLE

Have students read the bookmark on **Student Book** page 74. Explain that a nonfiction article

- gives facts and details about a topic;
- often contains diagrams to make information easy to understand; (LA.3.2.2.1 Explain purpose of text features)
- usually contains photographs to help illustrate the text;
- usually has headings that tell the topic of the text that follows.

Text Feature: Rules

LA.3.2.2.1 Identify and explain the purpose of text features

EXPLAIN Point out the list of rules on page 74. Explain that this set of rules is for staying safe in the sun.

- Rules tell how people should behave in certain situations and what is expected of them.
- Rules often appear in a numbered or bulleted list.
- Lists of rules usually have a title that explains what the rules will be about.

LA.3.2.2.4 Identify characteristics of texts

APPLY Have students read the list of Daytime and Nighttime Rules. Ask: How many rules are there? (three for daytime and two for nighttime) Why is each rule a short sentence? (Short rules are easy for people to remember.)

Science

Genre

Nonfiction Articles give the reader information about people, places, things, or events.

FCAT **Text Features**

Rules are a list of ways you should behave.

Content Vocabulary

sphere

rotates

axis

WHAT CAUSES DAY AND NIGHT?

by Keisha Oliver

Believe it or not, people used to think that Earth stood still while the sun traveled around it each day. It is simple to see why they thought this. The sun rises in the morning, moves across the sky, and disappears at night. Today we know much more about the movement of Sun and Earth.

1 The movement of Earth causes day and night. Earth is shaped like a ball, or **sphere**. As Earth **rotates**, or turns, there is daylight where Earth faces the sun. There is darkness where Earth is turned away from the sun.

Earth is rotating all the time, but we do not feel it. It takes 24 hours for Earth to make one full rotation. This rotation is equal to one day.

2

RULES FOR DAYTIME AND NIGHTTIME

Reading Rules

Follow these rules to help you stay safe when you are outside in the daytime or the nighttime.

Daytime Rules

1. Do not look directly at the sun.
2. Wear sunglasses when outside in daylight.
3. Wear sunscreen.

Nighttime Rules

1. Wear bright clothing so you can be seen.
2. Make sure you tell a responsible adult where you are at all times.

74

Content Vocabulary

LA.3.1.6.1 Use new vocabulary that is introduced and taught directly

Review the spelling and meaning of each content vocabulary word for "What Causes Day and Night?" on Student Book page 74: *sphere, rotates, axis.*

- A **sphere** is a body that has the shape of a ball or a globe. What objects are shaped like a sphere?
- When an object turns around and around, it **rotates**. What is one planet that rotates around the Sun?
- A real or imaginary line through the center of a spinning object is called its **axis**. Does Earth have an axis? How do you know?

EARTH MOVES!

Earth rotates around an imaginary line called an **axis**. The axis is drawn through the center of Earth. The equator is a name for the imaginary circle that goes around the middle of Earth.

Since Earth is tilted toward or away from the sun, the amount of heat and energy changes at different places. The temperature is warmer at the equator and colder at the two poles. Earth's tilt also changes the amount of light found in different places at different times of the year. This is why night can last for months in Alaska!

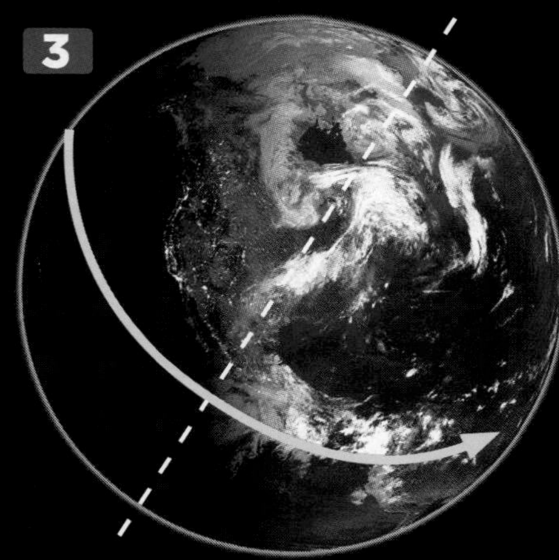

As Earth moves around the sun, it turns on its axis. Places near the equator receive nearly the same amount of sunlight all year long.

FCAT Connect and Compare

1. Look at the diagram above. Describe Earth's axis. **Reading a Diagram**
2. How long does it take Earth to make a complete rotation? Describe how this rotation affects daylight. **Recall**
3. Why is the sun important in *Seven Spools of Thread*? **Reading Across Texts**

Science Activity

Research two areas of Earth with different temperatures. Write a paragraph summarizing your research. Draw a diagram to explain how the tilt of Earth on its axis affects the temperatures in the areas you researched.

LOG ON Find out more about day and night at **www.macmillanmh.com**

75

Science Activity

Have students display their diagrams and explain how the tilt of Earth affects the temperatures. Invite them to discuss why they chose to research those areas, and how they conducted their searches for answers.

SC.E.1.2.1.3.2 Interaction and organization of Solar System affects life on Earth; **LA.3.6.2.3** Communicate information in an informational report with visual support; **LA.3.6.2.2** Select reference materials; **LA.3.5.2.2** Give an oral presentation

Technology

Internet Research and Inquiry Activity Students can find more facts at **www.macmillanmh.com**

Read "What Causes Day and Night?"

LA.3.1.6.3 Use context clues to determine meanings; **LA.3.1.6.2** Read and discuss conceptually challenging text

Remind students to apply what they have learned about rules. Have them identify clues to the meanings of the highlighted words.

1 MAIN IDEA AND DETAILS

LA.3.2.2.2 Answer questions related to main ideas

What causes day and night on planet Earth? How does this happen? (Earth's movement around the Sun causes day and night. When Earth rotates and faces the Sun it is day. When it is away from the Sun it is night.)

2 TEXT FEATURE: RULES

Why should you follow rules when you are outside during the day? (They help you keep safe from Sun's harmful rays.)

LA.3.1.7.1 Identify a text's features

3 TEXT FEATURE: READING A DIAGRAM

LA.3.2.2.1 Identify and explain the purpose of text features

Look at the diagram. What part of Earth is in daytime? How can you tell? (The east side of Earth is in daytime because it has rotated and is facing the Sun.)

Connect and Compare

LA.3.1.7.3 Determine explicit information in grade level text; **LA.3.2.2.1** Explain purpose of text features

SUGGESTED ANSWERS

1. Earth's axis is a slanted line that runs through the middle of the planet. READING A DIAGRAM
2. It takes Earth twenty-four hours to make a complete rotation around the Sun. RECALL

FOCUS QUESTION

LA.3.1.7.7 Compare and contrast texts

3. In *Seven Spools of Thread*, the brothers must turn thread into gold before the sun sets. The Sun acts as a time line. READING/WRITING ACROSS TEXTS

Connect Language Arts

WRITING
- Expository
- Writer's Craft: Precise Words

WORD STUDY
- Words in Context
- **Phonics:** Words with /ou/*ou, ow*
- Vocabulary Building

SPELLING/GRAMMAR
- Words with /ou/*ou, ow*
- Linking Verbs

SMALL GROUP OPTIONS
- Differentiated Instruction, pp. 77M–77V

Writing

Precise Words

LA.3.3.3.1 Evaluate draft for use of word choice

READ THE STUDENT MODEL

Read the bookmark about precise words. Explain that good writers choose words carefully to make their writing clear and exact. Tell students that using just the right words helps readers to understand the writer's meaning clearly.

LA.3.4.2 Develop and demonstrate technical writing

Have students turn to page 48. Discuss how precise words, such as the verb *beamed*, clearly show what happens.

Have the class read the directions and callouts. Tell students that they will write their own directions to explain how to do or make something. They will also learn to use precise words to make meaning clear.

Writer's Craft

Precise Words

A writer uses **precise words** to make the meaning clear. Precise words make writing easy to understand. This is especially important when writing instructions.

Write Directions

I choose a precise word to describe the place mat.

I use precise verbs to tell the reader what to do.

Make a Rainbow Place Mat

by Peter K.

A rainbow-colored place mat is easy to make. You will need tape, scissors, and paper in several colors.

1. Fold a piece of paper in half.
2. Starting from the fold, make five cuts that end one inch from the paper's edge. Unfold.
3. Cut one-inch-wide strips from the other pieces of paper. Then weave the strips between the cuts you made.
4. Tape the strips in place. Pound them lightly to make them stick.
5. Your place mat is ready to use!

76

Features of Directions

Directions, or instructions, explain how to do or make something step by step. Directions are often used in technical manuals or in how-to books.

- Directions a series of steps written in time-order, or sequence. The steps may be numbered, and they may contain time-order words or phrases such as *first*, *before*, *then*, *next*, *last*, and *while*. Directions begin with a topic sentence that explains what readers will learn to do and often include a list of materials needed to make or do what is being explained.

LA.3.4.2.1 Write in informational forms; **LA.3.6.1.1** Organize information for purpose of following multi-step directions; **LA.3.3.3.1** Evaluate draft for use of logical organization; **LA.3.3.2.2** Use time-order words

Writing Prompt

People write directions to tell how to do something.

Think about something you know how to do.

Now write directions to explain how to do something.

FCAT Writer's Checklist

- **Focus:** I choose a topic and identify my purpose—to explain.
- **Organization:** My directions present the steps in order. I use numbers to show the order.
- **Support:** I choose **precise words** that make the meaning clear.
- **Conventions:** I use linking verbs correctly. I use the correct punctuation at the end of complete sentences.

Transparency 65: **Sequence Chart**
Transparency 66: **Draft**
Transparency 67: **Revision**

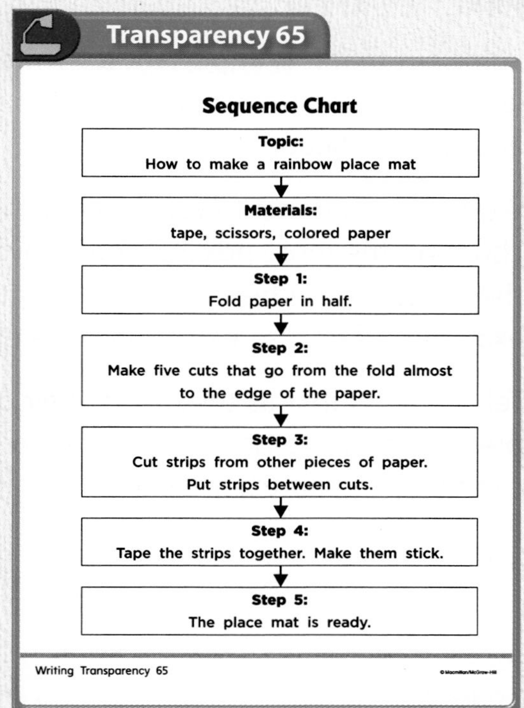

Transparency 65

Sequence Chart

Topic:
How to make a rainbow place mat

Materials:
tape, scissors, colored paper

Step 1:
Fold paper in half.

Step 2:
Make five cuts that go from the fold almost to the edge of the paper.

Step 3:
Cut strips from other pieces of paper. Put strips between cuts.

Step 4:
Tape the strips together. Make them stick.

Step 5:
The place mat is ready.

Writing Transparency 65

Writing Transparency 65

PREWRITE

LA.3.3.1 Use prewriting strategies **LA.3.3.1.2** Determine purpose and intended audience of a writing piece; **LA.3.3.1.1** Generate ideas from multiple sources **LA.3.3.1.3** Use organizational strategies to make a plan for writing

Discuss the writing prompt on page 77. Have students generate ideas using graphic organizers, reading books, or brainstorming with partners. Have them figure out the purpose (to inform) and the audience (classmates). Display **Transparency 65**. Discuss how Peter used a Sequence Chart to plan his writing. Then have students make Sequence Charts for their directions.

DRAFT

LA.3.3.2 Write a draft; **LA.3.3.2.2** Organize information into logical sequence through use of time-order words

Display **Transparency 66**. Discuss how Peter used his chart to write a draft and how he could improve the draft. Then have students use their Sequence Charts to write their directions. Have them use numbers and sequence words to make sure their steps are in order. Remind them to format their directions so they are easy to read.

REVISE

LA.3.3.3.1 Evaluate draft for use of word choice

LA.3.3.3.3 Create interest by modifying word choices

LA.3.3.3.2 Create clarity by rearranging sentences

LA.3.3.4 Edit and correct draft for standard language conventions

Present the explicit lesson on **Precise Words** on page 77A and the minilesson **Rearrange Details** on page 77B. Display **Transparency 67**. Discuss the revisions. Discuss how adding and changing words make the steps clearer. Students can revise their drafts or place them in writing portfolios to work on later. If they choose to revise, have them work in pairs to use the Writer's Checklist on page 77. Have students **proofread/edit** their writing. Before they publish, present the minilesson on **Textual Formatting** on page 77B. For **Publishing Options**, see page 77A.

For lessons on linking verbs, and spelling words with /ou/, see page 77B and **5 Day Spelling** and **Grammar** on pages 77G–77J.

Writer's Craft

LA.3.3.5.2 Add graphics where appropriate;
LA.3.5.2.2 Give an oral presentation;
LA.3.5.1.1 Demonstrate cursive writing skills

Publishing Options

Students can read aloud their directions to the class. See Speaking and Listening tips below. They can also use their best cursive to write their paragraphs. (See **Teacher's Resource Book** pages 216–221 for cursive models and practice.) Then have students make posters of their directions. Students can add drawings to illustrate the steps.

Speaking and Listening

SPEAKING STRATEGIES

- Use props and gestures to help your audience picture the steps.
- Speak slowly and clearly, pausing before you read each step.
- Emphasize sequence words such as *first*, *next*, and *then*.

LISTENING STRATEGIES

- Listen to try to understand each step.
- After the speaker is finished, summarize the steps to show your understanding. Ask the speaker any questions you have.

LA.3.5.2 Apply listening and speaking strategies;
LA.3.5.2.1 Summarize information presented orally;
LA.3.5.2.2 Use appropriate voice and body movements for presentation

6-Point Scoring Rubric

Use the rubric on page 149G to score published writing.

Writing Process

For a complete lesson, see Unit Writing on pages 149A–149F.

SUPPORT

Precise Words

EXPLAIN/MODEL

Good writers take time to choose the best words to make the meaning clear. Display **Transparency 68**.

LA.3.3.3.1 Evaluate draft for use of word choice

Think Aloud The first sentence uses the verb *put* to show what was done with the milk. It is not precise and does not clearly describe the action. The second sentence uses the verb *pour*. It is a precise verb that clearly tells the action. The precise verb *pour* helps me understand exactly what is happening.

Transparency 68

Precise Words

not precise: We put the milk into a glass.
precise: We poured the milk into a glass.

______ 1. The horse ______ across the meadow. (ran, galloped)
______ 2. The king wore a ______ robe. (magnificent, pretty)
______ 3. Tasha ate a ______ sandwich for lunch. (good, delicious)
______ 4. The table was a dark ______ color. (mahogany, brown)
______ 5. The bright stars ______ in the sky. (sat, twinkled)
______ 6. The brothers ______ loudly all afternoon. (argued, talked)

(1: galloped; 2: magnificent; 3: delicious; 4: mahogany; 5: twinkled; 6: argued)

Writing Transparency 68

PRACTICE/APPLY

LA.3.3.3.3 Create interest by modifying word choices

Point out that it is important for writers to use precise words in all kinds of writing from directions to expository articles to fairy tales and realistic fiction.

Work with students to complete each sentence in items 1–6 by choosing the most precise word. Have them explain why the word they chose is the best one in the sentence. Then have students find examples of precise words on page 69 of *Seven Spools of Thread*.

Tell students that as they write their directions, they should choose precise nouns, verbs, or adjectives to make the meaning clear. They can use a thesaurus or dictionary to help them find precise words.

Writer's Toolbox

LA.3.3.3.2 Create clarity by rearranging words, sentences LA.3.3.3.1 Evaluate draft for use of logical organization

ORGANIZATION

Writing Traits: Rearrange Details

Explain/Model In directions, details need to be in the correct order so the steps are clear. Display **Transparency 67**. Point out that the first two sentences are not in logical order, so the writer has used proofreading marks to change the order. Help students see how to use proofreading marks to mark their manuscripts when they want to rearrange the order of words, sentences, or paragraphs.

Practice/Apply As students revise their directions, have them make sure that all the steps and details are in logical order. If something is out of place, have them use proofreading to rearrange the order so it makes sense.

CONVENTIONS

Textual Formatting

Discuss the formatting of the directions on page 76. Point out that published writing is formatted so that there is proper spacing between letters in words, between words in sentences, and between sentences. When there are steps in the writing, the numbers need to line up. If there are paragraphs, they need to indent. The title goes at the top of the page and is often centered. As students revise their directions, have them pay attention to the formatting so the writing is easy to read.

LA.3.4.1.2 Employ appropriate format

Technology

Remind students that they can use the boldface feature and set tabs to help them format each step of their directions.

LA.3.3.4.3 Edit end punctuation; LA.3.3.4.5 Edit for correct use of subject/verb agreement; LA.3.3.4.4 Edit for correct use of present verb tense

CONVENTIONS

Linking Verbs

Explain/Model Explain that a linking verb connects the subject to a noun or adjective in the predicate. It does not show action. Forms of the verb *be* are often linking verbs. Read the first sentence on page 76 and identify the linking verb *is*. It joins the subject (place mat) to a description of the subject (easy to make). Point out that a linking verb must agree with the subject in the sentence.

Practice/Apply Have students look at step 5 in the directions and explain why *is* is a linking verb. For a complete lesson on linking verbs, see pages 77I–77J.

Mechanics Review how to write complete sentences with subjects and predicates and also correct end punctuation for statements, questions, commands, and exclamations.

CONVENTIONS

Spelling Words with /ou/*ou, ow*

Point out that the /ou/ sound in *pound* in step 4 on page 76 is spelled *ou*. It can also be spelled *ow*, as in *owl*. As students revise their writing, remind them to pay attention to spelling words with the /ou/ sound. Remind them that they can use a print or digital dictionary to check spelling. For a complete lesson on spelling the /ou/ sound, see pages 77G–77H.

LA.3.3.4.1 Edit for correct use of spelling; LA.3.3.4.1 Edit using a dictionary or other resources

FCAT Success!

Test Prep and Practice with Writing+, pages 180–230

Word Study

Objectives

- Apply knowledge of word meanings and context clues
- Use a dictionary to find meanings of multiple-meaning words

Materials

- Vocabulary Transparency 33
- Vocabulary Strategy Transparency 34
- Leveled Practice Books, p. 124
- dictionary

Vocabulary

beamed (p. 52) 1. shined brightly 2. smiled brightly

argued (p. 52) disagreed with someone

possessions (p. 56) things people own

fabric (p. 63) cloth

purchased (p. 67) bought

quarreling (p. 52) having an argument

ELL

Play a Game After you review the vocabulary, say: *My CD player and my watch are my ______.* Ask students to repeat the sentence with the correct vocabulary word. (*possessions*) Repeat this for the other words.

Review Vocabulary

Words in Context

LA.3.1.6.3 Use context clues to determine meaning

EXPLAIN/MODEL

Review the meanings of the vocabulary words. Display **Transparency 33**. Model how to use word meanings and context clues to fill in the first missing word.

Transparency 33

argued **fabric** **possessions**
purchased **quarreling** **beamed**

King Midas was a very rich man. He bought everything he wanted. The king (1) *purchased* things with gold coins. His (2) *possessions* filled three palaces, but he wanted more. "I want everything I touch to turn into gold," he said.

The hot sun (3) *beamed* through the palace window. The king's daughter (4) *argued* with her father. She did not agree with him. "How will you eat?" she asked. "Your food will turn to gold. When you touch your clothes, the (5) *fabric*, will turn to gold, too."

The king didn't want to fight. "Let's stop (6) *quarreling*," he said. He gave his daughter a big hug. Then she turned into a gold statue!

Vocabulary Transparency 33

Think Aloud I see that King Midas bought many things with gold coins. I know that *purchased* is another word for *bought*. The missing word is *purchased*.

PRACTICE/APPLY

Have each student use context clues to write missing words for items 2–6 on a separate piece of paper. Students can exchange papers, check answers, and explain context clues they used.

LA.3.1.6.7 Use base words and affixes
LA.3.1.6.4 Identify salient features
LA.3.1.4.2 Use knowledge of pronunciation to decode word families

Word Families The words *argued*, *purchased*, *quarreling*, *possession*, and *beamed* have base words, or root words, and suffixes. Have pairs identify and pronounce the base word, or root word, in each and use a dictionary to find other words that belong to the same word family: *purchase, purchased, purchasing, purchaser.* Remind students to use what they know about the pronunciation of the root word to pronounce other words in the family. Have pairs use the words in sentences.

STRATEGY
DICTIONARY: MULTIPLE-MEANING WORDS

LA.3.1.6.9 Determine correct meaning of words with multiple meanings

EXPLAIN/MODEL

- When students cannot figure out a word's meaning with context clues or word parts, they should look up the word in a dictionary.
- Some words are both nouns and verbs. There may be several meanings for each in a dictionary entry. Figure out what part of speech the word is. Then try the definitions listed under that part of speech in the sentence.

Read the example sentence on **Transparency 34**. Model how to figure out the meaning of the noun *thread.*

LA.3.1.6.10 Determine meanings using a dictionary

Transparency 34

Dictionary: Multiple-Meaning Words

We could make cloth out of this *thread.*

> **thread** (thred) *noun* 1. A very thin string used to sew. *He bought a spool of* ***thread.*** 2. The ridges on a screw. *The* ***thread*** *on a screw makes it hold tightly.*
> *verb* 1. To put a piece of thread through a hole. *Please* ***thread*** *the needle for me.* 2. Move through a crowd. ***Thread*** *your way through the crowd to the front.*

1. It was hard to thread the needle. (verb meaning 1)
2. The thread on the screw is worn down. (noun meaning 2)
3. He used red thread to mend the shirt. (noun meaning 1)
4. We will thread our way through the crowd. (verb meaning 2)

Vocabulary Strategy Transparency 34

PRACTICE/APPLY

Access for All

LA.3.1.6 Use multiple strategies to develop grade-appropriate vocabulary

Have students find the meaning for the underlined nouns and verbs in items 1–4. Then have each student write a sentence using one meaning of *thread*, trade sentences with a partner, and use a dictionary to figure out which meaning was used.

Quick Check **Can students use context clues to figure out word meanings and choose the correct meaning of a word in a dictionary entry?**

During **Small Group Instruction**

If No → **Approaching Level** Vocabulary, pp. 77N–77O

If Yes → **On Level** Options, pp. 77Q–77R

Beyond Level Options, pp. 77S–77T

ELL Access for All

Use Visuals Have students copy the four definitions of the word *thread*. Use gestures and draw pictures to help students understand each meaning. Use the words in other sentences. Help students distinguish the nouns and verbs.

Vocabulary

Review last week's vocabulary words. Some ingredients found in recipes are *cream, pepper,* and *nuts*. Ask students to find multiple meanings for each word and to use each meaning in a sentence.

FCAT Success!

Test Prep and Practice with vocabulary, pages 6–31

On Level Practice Book O, page 124

Some words have more than one meaning. Use a dictionary to find two meanings for each word below and write each meaning under the word. Possible responses provided.

1. **stick**
   definition 1: a long, thin piece of wood
   definition 2: to stab or poke with a pointed object
2. **corner**
   definition 1: the point or place where two lines meet
   definition 2: to force into a position where escape is impossible
3. **row**
   definition 1: a series of people or things in a straight line
   definition 2: to use oars to propel a boat
4. **raise**
   definition 1: to move something to a higher level
   definition 2: to increase in amount
5. **block**
   definition 1: a solid piece of wood or stone
   definition 2: to prevent forward movement
6. Write a sentence that uses both meanings of one of the words above. Your sentence should tell something about getting along with others.
   We had to row the boat quickly to join the long row of boats in the lake.

Approaching Practice Book A, page 124

Beyond Practice Book B, page 124

Word Study

Objectives

- Segment and blend words with /ou/
- Decode words with /ou/

Materials

- Leveled Practice Books, p. 125
- Teacher's Resource Book, pp. 91–94

ELL Access for All

Identify Sounds
Pretend to hurt your finger and say: *Ouch! Ow! That hurt!* Write *ouch* and *ow* on the board. Have students say them dramatically. Write words with the /ou/ sound on the board. Say them with students. Have volunteers underline the letters that make the sound. Co-construct sentences with students using the words, and then practice saying them.

On Level Practice Book O, page 125

When two vowel sounds are blended together in the same syllable, they are pronounced as one sound. The letters *ou* and *ow* can stand for the /ou/ sound, as in *found* or *crowd*.

Use the words in the box with the /ou/ sound to complete the sentences.

bow	shout	bounce	scout	scowl	round
doubt	towel	found	sound	proud	ground

1. The ball took a bad bounce and got past me.
2. Please do not shout in the library because many people are studying and reading.
3. The cast of the play came out and took a bow.
4. I hurt my leg when I slipped on the ice and fell on the hard ground.
5. After winning the science contest, I was very proud.
6. When Fiona got to the pool, she found the towel that she thought she had put in her bag.
7. The sound of the dog barking outside woke me up.
8. My dad had a scowl on his face when I broke the window.

★ **Approaching Practice Book A,** page 125
◆ **Beyond Practice Book B,** page 125

Phonics

Decode Words with /ou/

EXPLAIN/MODEL

LA.3.1.4.1 Use knowledge of pronunciation to decode words

- The letters *ou* and *ow* usually stand for the /ou/ sound, as in *mouse* and *town.*
- Recognizing the letters that stand for the /ou/ sound can help readers pronounce unfamiliar words.

Write the word *round.*

LA.3.1.4 Demonstrate knowledge of alphabetic principle

Think Aloud This word begins with *r,* which has the /r/ sound. The letters *o* and *u* together probably have the /ou/ sound. The next letter has the /n/ sound. The last sound is the /d/ sound. The sounds are /r/ /ou/ /n/ /d/. I'll blend these sounds together: /rrrounnnd/. The word is *round.*

PRACTICE/APPLY

LA.3.1.4.4 Use self-correction

Display *house, down, found, clown, owl,* and *blow.* Have volunteers underline the letters that stand for the /ou/ sound in each word. Have them read the words aloud. Point out that the *ow* in *down* can also have the long *o* sound, as in *blow.* Remind students to try both sounds if they have trouble sounding out a word.

LA.3.1.4.3 Decode multi-syllabic words in isolation and in context

Decode Multisyllabic Words Have students use their knowledge of phonics patterns, compound words, and word parts to decode long words. Write these words on the board: *boundary, playground, southwestern, howling, eyebrow.* Model how to decode *howling.* Then work with students to decode the other words with /ou/ and read them aloud. For more practice in decoding multisyllabic words, see decodable passages on **Teacher's Resource Book** pages 91–94.

LA.3.1.6 Use multiple strategies to develop vocabulary

Rhyming /ou/ Riddles Have students use /ou/ words and a rhyming dictionary to write hink pinks, or riddles and rhyming answers, such as: *What is a hat for a crabby person?* (a frown crown) *What does a wise bird use to dry itself after a shower?* (an owl towel)

Quick Check **Can students decode words with /ou/?**

During **Small Group Instruction**

If No → **Approaching Level** Phonics, p. 77M

If Yes → **On Level** Options, pp. 77Q–77R

Beyond Level Options, pp. 77S–77T

Vocabulary Building

LA.3.1.6 Use multiple strategies to develop vocabulary

LA.3.1.6.4 Categorize key vocabulary

Oral Language

Expand Vocabulary Have students brainstorm action words about getting along and not getting along, and write the words in a web.

ACTIONS

How to Get Along	How Not to Get Along
smile	quarreling
help	argue
share	fight
caring	frown
laugh	disagree
agree	

Vocabulary Building

Suffix *-ly* The word *proudly* in *Seven Spools of Thread* ends in the suffix *-ly*. When the suffix *-ly* is added to a describing word, or an adjective, it means "in a certain way." The word *proudly* means "in a proud way." Have students write the word parts and the meanings of *quietly*, *perfectly*, and *sadly* on a chart. Review last week's vocabulary words. Have students identify the adjectives (*magnificent, tasty*) and add *-ly* to them. Then have students use all five new words in sentences.

Word	Suffix	Meaning
quiet	-ly	in a quiet way
perfect	-ly	in a perfect way

LA.3.1.6.4 Identify salient features; LA.3.1.6.7 Use base words and affixes

LA.3.1.6.1 Use new vocabulary

Apply Vocabulary

Write a Paragraph Have each small group of students use the vocabulary words *beamed, argued, possessions, fabric, purchased*, and *quarreling* in a paragraph about getting along or a self-selected topic. Students can read their paragraphs aloud to the class.

Spiral Review

Vocabulary Game Show

Write the vocabulary words *fabric, innocent, recipes, instance, masterpiece, politely, possessions, style, tasty*, and *wearily* on the board. Choose a game host.

- The host says the definition of one of the words in the form of an answer. For example, for the word *innocent*, the host might say, "It means 'not guilty.'"
- A contestant responds in the form of a question. The contestant might say, "What does *innocent* mean?"
- A contestant who gives the correct response changes places with the host.
- The game continues until all the vocabulary words have been used.

LA.3.1.6 Develop grade-appropriate vocabulary ; LA.3.1.6.1 Use new vocabulary

Technology

Vocabulary PuzzleMaker

For additional vocabulary and spelling games, go to www.macmillanmh.com

5 Day Spelling

Spelling Words

found	bow	proud
town	scout	clouds
shout	round	ground
owl	plow	louder
couch	crowd	bounce

Review drawing, lawn, hauls

Challenge snowplow, outline

Dictation Sentences

1. Meg found shells in the sand.
2. Do you live in a small town?
3. I heard him **shout**.
4. An owl is in the tree.
5. Let's sit on the couch.
6. Actors **bow** at the end of a play.
7. We will scout for wood.
8. The moon is round.
9. Farmers plow their fields in the fall.
10. Don't get lost in the **crowd**.
11. Mom is **proud** of her work.
12. The rain clouds are dark.
13. The snow is on the **ground**.
14. Speak louder so we can hear.
15. Will the old ball bounce?

Review Words

1. I made a drawing in art class.
2. We had a picnic on the lawn.
3. The truck hauls new cars.

Challenge Words

1. Joe drives a snowplow in winter.
2. She made an outline of her hand.

Note: Words in **bold** type are from *Seven Spools of Thread*.

Display the Spelling Words throughout the week.

LA.3.3.4.1 Correctly use spelling

Words with /ou/

Day 1 Pretest

ASSESS PRIOR KNOWLEDGE

Use the Dictation Sentences. Say the underlined word, read the sentence, and repeat the word. Have students write the words on **Spelling Practice Book** page 103. For a modified list, use the first 12 Spelling Words and the 3 Review Words. For a more challenging list, use Spelling Words 3–15 and the Challenge Words. Have students correct their own tests.

Have students cut apart the Spelling Word Cards BLM on **Teacher's Resource Book** page 130 and plan a way to sort them. Have them save the cards for use during the week.

Students can use Spelling Practice Book page 104 for independent practice.

For leveled Spelling word lists, go to **www.macmillanmh.com**

Day 2 Word Sorts

TEACHER AND STUDENT SORTS

- Review the Spelling Words, point out the /ou/ spellings *ou* and *ow*, and discuss meanings.
- Use the cards on the Spelling Word Cards BLM. Attach the key words *out* and *crown* to a bulletin board.
- Model how to sort words with /ou/, and place the cards beneath the correct key words.
- Have students take turns choosing cards, sorting them, and explaining how they sorted them.
- Then have students use their own Spelling Word Cards. After placing the key words on their desks, they can sort the Spelling Words several times. Have students write their last sort on Spelling Practice Book page 105.

Spelling Practice Book, pages 103–104

Fold back the paper along the dotted line. Use the blanks to write each word as it is read aloud. When you finish the test, unfold the paper. Use the list at the right to correct any spelling mistakes.

	1. ______	1. found
	2. ______	2. town
	3. ______	3. shout
	4. ______	4. owl
	5. ______	5. couch
	6. ______	6. bow
	7. ______	7. scout
	8. ______	8. round
	9. ______	9. plow
	10. ______	10. crowd
	11. ______	11. proud
	12. ______	12. clouds
	13. ______	13. ground
	14. ______	14. louder
	15. ______	15. bounce
Review Words	16. ______	16. drawing
	17. ______	17. lawn
	18. ______	18. hauls
Challenge Words	19. ______	19. snowplow
	20. ______	20. outline

Spelling Practice Book, page 105

found	owl	scout	crowd	ground
town	couch	round	proud	louder
shout	bow	plow	clouds	bounce

Pattern Power!

This week's spelling words contain the vowel sound /ou/. Write the spelling words with the /ou/ sound spelled:

ou

1. louder
2. bounce
3. found
4. clouds
5. proud
6. couch
7. ground
8. shout
9. round
10. scout

ow

11. bow
12. crowd
13. plow
14. town
15. owl

Words Within Words

Write each spelling word in which you can find the smaller word.

16. row crowd
17. low plow
18. loud clouds
19. own town
20. round ground

LA.3.1.6.4 Categorize key vocabulary; **LA.3.3.4.1** Edit for correct use of spelling patterns

Day 3 Word Meanings

CATEGORIES

Read each group of words below. Ask students to copy the words into their word study notebooks. Have them complete each group with the correct Spelling Word.

1. eagle, hawk, owl
2. chair, sofa, couch
3. yell, cry, shout
4. dig, rake, plow
5. dirt, soil, ground

Challenge students to find rhyming words with the same or different spelling patterns.

Have partners write sentences for each Spelling Word, leaving blanks where the words should go. Then have them trade papers and write the missing words.

Day 4 Review and Proofread

SPIRAL REVIEW

Review /ô/. Display *drawing*, *lawn*, and *hauls*. Have students identify letters that spell the /ô/ sound.

PROOFREAD/EDIT

Write the sentences below. Have students proofread/edit to correct errors.

1. The farmer will plou the grownd. (plow, ground)
2. A man in the croud began to showt. (crowd, shout)

BLIND SORT

Partners use their Spelling Word Cards and each write key words *out* and *crown* on a sheet of paper. One draws cards and says the words. The other writes them under the key words. Then switch roles. After both students have finished, they can check each other's papers.

Day 5 Assess and Reteach

POSTTEST

Use the Dictation Sentences on page 77G for the Posttest.

If students have difficulty with any of the words in the lesson, have them place them on a list called "Spelling Words I Want to Remember" in their word study notebooks.

WORD STUDY NOTEBOOK

Challenge students to search for other words with the /ou/ spelling pattern in their reading for the week and write them in their word study notebooks under the heading "Other Words that Sound Like *Clown* and *Loud*."

Remind students as they proofread/edit their writing during the week to check for spelling in words with /ou/.

Spelling Practice Book, page 106

found	owl	scout	crowd	ground
town	couch	round	proud	louder
shout	bow	plow	clouds	bounce

Analogies

An analogy is a statement that compares sets of words that are alike in some way: *Night* is to *day* as *black* is to *white*. This analogy points out that *night* and *day* are opposite in the same way that *black* and *white* are opposite.

Use the spelling words to complete the analogies below.

1. *Top* is to *bottom* as *sky* is to ground.
2. *Bad* is to *good* as *lost* is to found.
3. *Quiet* is to *whisper* as *loud* is to shout.
4. *Flying disk* is to *throw* as *ball* is to bounce.
5. *Moo* is to *cow* as *hoot* is to owl.
6. *Salute* is to *general* as bow is to *audience*.

Define It!

Write the spelling word that matches each definition.

7. Large group of people crowd
8. Big soft seat to sit on couch
9. Feeling pleased about what you did proud
10. What rain falls from clouds
11. Someone who goes out to get information scout
12. Shape of a circle round
13. A place where people live town
14. Raised volume louder
15. Tool on a farm plow

Spelling Practice Book, page 107

Proofreading

There are six spelling mistakes in this paragraph. Circle the misspelled words. Write the words correctly on the lines below.

Our Class Newsletter

Our class is prowd to announce that we have come up with some new rules. The lunchroom has gotten looder over the past year. We fownd it is hard to enjoy eating our lunches. We have decided that to fix the problem we will do two things. First, everyone must sit at one of the rond tables during lunch. There must be no walking around. Second, you are not allowed to schot at each other or stomp on the growned. These new rules should make lunchtime much better. If we make the lunchroom a nicer place, everyone will want to eat there.

1. proud
2. louder
3. found
4. round
5. shout
6. ground

Writing Activity

Write an article for your class newsletter. Use at least three spelling words in your paragraph.

Spelling Practice Book, page 108

Look at the words in each set below. One word in each set is spelled correctly. Look at Sample A. The letter next to the correctly spelled word in Sample A has been shaded in. Do Sample B yourself. Shade the letter of the word that is spelled correctly. When you are sure you know what to do, go on with the rest of the page.

Sample A:
Ⓐ owt
Ⓑ ott
Ⓒ oute
● out

Sample B:
● brown
Ⓕ braun
Ⓖ bron
Ⓗ browne

1. Ⓐ fownd Ⓑ fawnd Ⓒ faund ● found
2. Ⓔ taun ● town Ⓖ tawn Ⓗ toun
3. ● shout Ⓑ showt Ⓒ shaut Ⓓ shawt
4. Ⓔ awel Ⓕ oal Ⓖ owel ● owl
5. ● couch Ⓑ cowch Ⓒ coch Ⓓ coush
6. Ⓔ bau Ⓕ bou ● bow Ⓗ baw
7. Ⓐ scowt Ⓑ scaut ● scout Ⓓ scawt
8. Ⓔ raund ● round Ⓖ rawnd Ⓗ rownd
9. ● plow Ⓕ plaugh Ⓖ plau Ⓗ plaw
10. Ⓐ craud ● crowd Ⓒ crawd Ⓓ crod
11. Ⓔ praud Ⓕ prawd ● proud Ⓗ prowd
12. Ⓐ clowds Ⓑ clawds Ⓒ clauds ● clouds
13. Ⓐ grownd ● ground Ⓒ graund Ⓓ grawnd
14. Ⓔ lowder Ⓕ lauwder Ⓖ loder ● louder
15. Ⓐ bownce Ⓑ bounse Ⓒ bownse ● bounce

5 Day Grammar

Daily Language Activities

Use these activities to introduce each day's lesson. Write the day's activities on the board or use **Transparency 17**.

DAY 1
1. ali and Sam are friends. **2.** Ali are nice to everywon. **3.** They is friendly (1: Ali; 2: is; everyone.; 3: are friendly.)

DAY 2
1. Jill am my friend. **2.** she are a scowt. **3.** She be happie! (1: is; 2: She; is; scout.; 3: is happy.)

DAY 3
1. My neighbors is my friends **2.** they am good soccer players. **3.** We was good players? 1: are; friends.; 2: They; are; 3: were; players.)

DAY 4
1. Larry were our guide in ghana. **2.** His toun were small. **3.** africa are beautiful. 1: was; Ghana.; 2: town; was; 3: Africa; is)

DAY 5
1. Dave be in texas. **2.** He are very happy? **3.** he are on a plane (1: is; Texas.; 2: is; happy.; 3: He; is; plane.)

ELL — **Access for All**

Co-construct Sentences
Write: *That girl runs. The girl is my friend.* Have students tell which sentence has an action. Explain that some verbs don't show actions but tell us something about the subject. Co-construct sentences with students using the forms of the verb *be*.

LA.3.3.4.4 Edit for correct use of present verb tense; **LA.3.3.4.5** Edit for correct use of subject/verb agreement

Linking Verbs

Day 1 Introduce the Concept

INTRODUCE LINKING VERBS

Present the following:

- An **action verb** tells what the subject does: The boy *jumps*.
- A **linking verb** does not show action. It connects the subject to a noun or an adjective in the predicate. It tells what the subject is or is like: The girl *is* my friend. The day *is* sunny.
- The verb *be* is the most common linking verb. It has special forms in the present tense: I *am*, the boy *is*, the boys *are*.

See Grammar Transparency 81 for modeling and guided practice.

Grammar Practice Book, page 103

- A **linking verb** does not show action. It connects the subject to a noun or adjective in the predicate.
- The word *be* is a common linking verb. *Be* has special forms in the present tense.
  I *am* part of a big family.
  The house *is* big and roomy.
  All my brothers *are* here.

Write *am, is,* or, *are* to finish each sentence.

1. I ___am___ on vacation with my family.
2. My brothers and I ___are___ at a park with lots of rides.
3. The rides ___are___ fast and scary.
4. But every ride ___is___ fun.
5. Sam and I ___are___ happy to stay in the water park.
6. Chris ___is___ ready to try the roller-coaster.
7. Mom and Dad ___are___ ready for lunch.
8. Fortunately, my cousins ___are___ here.
9. I ___am___ happy to see them.
10. We ___are___ eager to play together.
11. Mom and Dad ___are___ glad to be at the park.
12. Sam and Chris ___are___ at the ice cream stand.
13. I ___am___ hungry.
14. George ___is___ on the steps to the ticket booth.
15. My cousin and I ___are___ near the miniature golf course.

Day 2 Teach the Concept

REVIEW LINKING VERB *BE*

Review with students what a linking verb is. Review present-tense forms of the linking verb *be*: *am, is, are.*

INTRODUCE MORE LINKING VERBS

- The verb *be* is the most common linking verb. It has special forms in the past tense: I *was*, the boy *was*, the boys *were*.
- Use the linking verbs *is, am,* and *was* when the subject is singular: I *am* happy. The cloth *is* blue. The man *was* tall.
- Use the linking verb *am* with the subject I: I *am* a runner.
- Use the linking verbs *are* and *were* with plural subjects and *you*: The cats *are* lions. You *were* lucky.

See Grammar Transparency 82 for modeling and guided practice.

Grammar Practice Book, page 104

- The verb *be* is a common **linking verb**. *Be* has special forms in the past tense.
  Jim *was* at the door.
  My brothers and I *were* sorry.

For each sentence below, write the verb form of *be* that agrees with the subject of the sentence.

1. My brothers and I ___were___ always fighting.
2. Dad ___was___ upset about our fights.
3. The solution ___was___ to make us work together.
4. Our task ___was___ to build a tree house.
5. We all ___were___ eager to have a tree house.
6. I ___was___ in charge of measuring.
7. Dad ___was___ there to help us cut and nail.
8. We ___were___ hard at work.
9. It ___was___ all very peaceful.
10. We ___were___ glad we did something together.
11. My brothers and I ___were___ careful with the nails.
12. The wooden planks ___were___ everywhere.
13. We ___were___ out back all day.
14. Dad ___was___ happy with our progress.
15. We ___were___ thirsty in the hot sun.

LA.3.3.4.3 Edit end punctuation; LA.3.3.4.4 Edit for correct use of present and past verb tense

Day 3 Review and Practice

REVIEW LINKING VERBS

Remind students that a linking verb connects the subject to a noun or an adjective in the predicate.

MECHANICS AND USAGE: END PUNCTUATION AND COMPLETE SENTENCES

- A statement and a command, or imperative sentence, end with a period.
- A question ends with a question mark.
- An exclamation and an exclamatory sentence end with an exclamation point.
- A complete sentence has a subject and a predicate, and tells a complete thought.

See Grammar Transparency 83 for modeling and guided practice.

Grammar Practice Book, page 105

- A **sentence** is a group of words that tells a complete thought. A sentence begins with a capital letter.
- A **statement** is a sentence that tells something. It ends with a period.
- A **question** is a sentence that asks something. It ends with a question mark.
- A **command** is a sentence that tells or asks someone to do something. It ends with a period.
- An **exclamation** shows strong feeling. It ends with an exclamation point.

Rewrite the sentences with correct end punctuation and capitalization.

1. there are seven principles of Kwanzaa
   There are seven principles of Kwanzaa.
2. can you name them all
   Can you name them all?
3. work together
   Work together.
4. we will share each other's problems and responsibilities
   We will share each other's problems and responsibilities.
5. i can speak for myself
   I can speak for myself.
6. wow, that's beautiful
   Wow, that's beautiful!
7. what kind of business should we start
   What kind of business should we start?

Day 4 Review and Proofread

REVIEW LINKING VERBS

Ask students to explain what a linking verb is and give examples of sentences using past- and present-tense linking verbs. Have them explain how to punctuate statements, questions, commands or imperatives, and exclamations.

PROOFREAD/EDIT

Have students proofread/edit to correct the errors.

1. How is you feeling this morning (are; morning?)
2. What are her name. (is; name?)
3. Dena were a good artist. (was)
4. teri and Dan is fast runners. (Teri; are)
5. My vacation last year were lots of fun (was; fun.)

See Grammar Transparency 84 for modeling and guided practice.

Grammar Practice Book, page 106

- The verb *be* connects the subject to the rest of the sentence. *Be* has special forms in the present tense and the past tense.

PRESENT	PAST
I *am*	I *was*
The boy *is*	The girl *was*
The boys *are*	The girls *were*

Proofread the story. Circle any linking verbs that are not correct.

my brother and I helped Grandma decorate. She (were) having a party. I (is) the oldest, so I got the cake and presents. I arranged them in the center of the table

"That (be) my job" Carl said. "I did it last year."

Then we started yelling at each other

"Boys" said Grandma. "why don't you work together to arrange the plates and silverware"

So we did and made the table look nice. It (are) not so bad. in fact, we (be) a pretty good team

Rewrite the paragraph. Use the correct linking verbs. Make sure that all sentences begin with a capital letter and have an end mark.

My brother and I helped Grandma decorate. She was having a party. I am the oldest, so I got the cake and presents. I arranged them in the center of the table.

"That is my job," Carl said. "I did it last year."

Then we started yelling at each other.

"Boys!" said Grandma. "Why don't you work together to arrange the plates and silverware?"

So we did and made the table look nice. It was not so

Day 5 Assess and Reteach

ASSESS

Use the Daily Language Activity and page 107 of the **Grammar Practice Book** for assessment.

RETEACH

Write the linking verbs *am*, *is*, *are*, *was*, and *were* on separate index cards. Place the cards in a bag. Have each student draw a card and use the verb in a sentence, then put the card back in the bag. Encourage students to create sentences based on *Seven Spools of Thread*. Record the sentences on a chart and display them in the classroom or on a Word Wall.

Use page 108 of the Grammar Practice Book for additional reteaching.

See Grammar Transparency 85 for modeling and guided practice.

Grammar Practice Book, pages 107–108

Write the linking verb in each sentence.

1. Kwanzaa is an annual celebration. is
2. The seven principles of Kwanzaa are very important. are
3. They are part of African culture. are
4. We were part of a Kwanzaa celebration at school. were
5. I was the person in charge of decorations. was
6. The colors red, black, and green are important. are
7. What is the best way to hang these pictures? is
8. Our teacher was happy with our work. was

Choose a verb from the box to complete each sentence. Some words may be used more than once.

am   is   are   was   were

9. My brothers and I are, were always fighting.
10. I am the youngest.
11. Last night, Mom and Dad were home early.
12. We were all working on a model airplane.
13. It was surprisingly easy to work together!
14. Making things is not so hard.
15. Mom and Dad are, were proud of us.

Administer the Test

Weekly Reading Assessment, pages 201–212

ASSESSED SKILLS

- Plot Development
- Vocabulary Words
- Dictionary/Multiple-Meaning Words
- Words with /ou/
- Linking Verbs

Administer the **Weekly Assessment** from the CD-ROM or online.

Fluency

Assess fluency for one group of students per week. Use the Oral Fluency Record Sheet to track the number of words read correctly. Fluency goal for all students: **82–102 words correct per minute (WCPM)**.

Approaching Level	Weeks 1, 3, 5
On Level	Weeks 2, 4
Beyond Level	Week 6

Alternative Assessments

- **ELL Assessment**, pages 114–115

Weekly Assessment, 201–212

Fluency Assessment

ELL Assessment, 114–115

Diagnose		Prescribe
	IF . . .	**THEN . . .**
VOCABULARY WORDS **VOCABULARY STRATEGY** Dictionary/Multiple-Meaning Words Items 1, 2, 3	0–1 items correct . . .	Reteach skills using the **Additional Lessons**, page T6. LOG ON Reteach skills: Log on to **www.macmillanmh.com** CD ROM Vocabulary PuzzleMaker Evaluate for Intervention.
COMPREHENSION Skill: Plot Development Items 4, 5, 6	0–1 items correct . . .	Reteach skills using the **Additional Lessons**, page T2. Evaluate for Intervention.
GRAMMAR Linking Verbs, Items 7, 8, 9	0–1 items correct . . .	Reteach skills: **Grammar Practice Book**, page 108.
SPELLING Words with /ou/ Items 10, 11, 12	0–1 items correct . . .	LOG ON Reteach skills: Log on to **www.macmillanmh.com**
FLUENCY	73–81 WCPM 0–72 WCPM	AUDIO CD Fluency Solutions Evaluate for Intervention.

DIBELS LINK

PROGRESS MONITORING

Use your DIBELS results to inform instruction.

IF...

DIBELS Oral **R**eading **F**luency **(DORF)** 0–91

THEN...

Use the Fluency Solutions Audio CD.

TPRI LINK

PROGRESS MONITORING

Use your TPRI scores to inform instruction.

IF...

Graphophonemic Awareness	Still developing
Reading Fluency/Accuracy	Frustrational on Grade 3, Story 1
Reading Comprehension Questions	0–5 correct

THEN...

Use the Fluency Solutions Audio CD. Use the Comprehension Skills **Additional Lessons** suggestions in the above chart.

READING Triumphs Also Available

AN INTERVENTION PROGRAM

To place students in the Intervention Program, use the **Diagnostic Assessment** in the Intervention Teacher's Edition.

Skills Focus Phonics

Objectives Review words with /ou/
Decode multisyllabic words with /ou/

Materials • **Student Book** "Community Works" • index cards

WORDS WITH /ou/

LA.3.1.4 Demonstrate knowledge of alphabetic principle

Model/Guided Practice

- Remind children that the letters *ou* as in *house* and *ow* as in *cow* stand for the /ou/ sound.
- Write the letters *d*, *o*, *w*, *n* on the board. Say the sounds that the letters stand for: */d/ /ou/ /n/.* Then blend the sounds: */dounnn/. Say the word with me:* down.
- Repeat the routine with *ou* and *mouse*.
- Ask students to think of their own examples of words with the /ou/ sound spelled *ou* or *ow*.

MULTISYLLABIC WORDS WITH /ou/

LA.3.1.4.3 Decode multi-syllabic words

- Write the word *rounded* on the board and have students identify the first syllable as containing the /ou/ sound: *round*. Have students repeat the syllable and then blend and read the whole word several times.
- Have pairs of students work together to practice decoding longer words with /ou/. Write the words below on the board and ask student pairs to copy them onto index cards or sheets of paper. *Say each word. Circle the letters that stand for the /ou/ sound. Then sort the words by spelling pattern.*

louder	browner	couches	pounding
growling	crouching	plowing	underground

- Check pairs for their progress and accuracy. You may wish to invite students to extend by adding to the sort their choice of additional words with the *ou* or *ow* spellings of the /ou/ sound.

WORD HUNT: WORDS WITH /ou/ IN CONTEXT

LA.3.1.4 Apply grade level phonics to read text

- Review words with /ou/.
- Have students search "Community Works" to find words with the /ou/ sound. Ask them to write the words and circle the syllable in each word that has /ou/.
- Check to see if students have found the following: *town*, *about*.

Constructive Feedback

The /ou/ sound can be difficult for some students to hear and produce. Have them practice saying /ou/ in isolation and then in words, while looking at you to see how the mouth moves to produce the /ou/ sound. For example, write the word *down* on the board and point out the *ow*.

This word is town. *The letters* ow *together have the sound /ou/. Say it with me: /ou/. Let's sound out, blend the sounds, and say the word together: /tounnn/,* town.

Repeat with /ou/ and the word *found*.

Additional Resources

For each skill below, additional lessons are provided. You can use these lessons on consecutive days after teaching the lessons presented within the week.

- Plot Development: Conclusions, T2
- Multiple-Meaning Words, T6
- Text Feature: Diagrams, T10

Decodable Text

To help students build speed and accuracy with reading multisyllabic words, use the additional decodable text on pages 91–94 of the **Teacher's Resource Book**.

Skills Focus Fluency

Objective Read with increasing prosody and accuracy at a rate of 82–92 WCPM

Materials • index cards • **Approaching Practice Book A**, p. 122

WORD AUTOMATICITY

Have students make flashcards for the following words with /ou/: *found, bow, proud, town, scout, clouds, shout, round, ground, owl, plow, louder, couch, crowd, bounce.*

Display the cards one at a time and have students say each word. Repeat twice more, displaying the words more quickly each time.

REPEATED READING

LA.3.1.5 Demonstrate the ability to read text orally with accuracy

Model reading the passage on **Practice Book** page 122. Have the group listen for how punctuation affects your reading and echo-read. Then have partners practice reading to each other. Circulate and provide constructive feedback as needed.

TIMED READING

Tell students that they will be doing a final timed reading of the passage on Practice Book page 122. Students should

- begin reading the passage aloud when you say "Go."
- stop reading the passage after one minute when you say "Stop."

As students read, note any miscues. Help students record and graph the number of words they read correctly. Provide support and feedback.

Skills Focus Vocabulary

Objective Apply vocabulary word meanings

Materials • **Vocabulary Cards** • **Student Book** *Seven Spools of Thread*

VOCABULARY WORDS

LA.3.1.6.3 Use context clues to determine meanings

Use the **Vocabulary Cards** to review this week's and last week's words. Help students locate and read the vocabulary words in *Seven Spools of Thread*. Discuss any context clues that help them determine or confirm the meanings of the words. Share an example: *On page 52, the words* moon *and* down *helped me figure out that* beamed *means "shined" or "sent its light."*

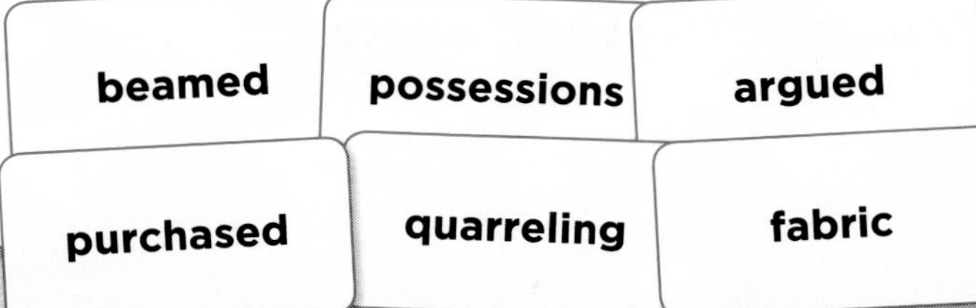

Constructive Feedback

If students read without sufficient expression, pauses, and attention to punctuation, reread the passage to them, one sentence at a time, exaggerating the correct expression and pauses. Have students copy your expression as they echo-read each sentence.

ELL Access for All

Context Clues Ask students to complete the sentence frames with these vocabulary words: *argued, beamed, purchased, quarreling, fabric*. The fabric for the skirt was blue. The light beamed down from the sun. My sister purchased some candy. The boys were quarreling about the new bike. The angry boy argued with his friend about whose turn it was. Write *possessions* on the board. Have each student write a sentence using the word.

Approaching Practice Book A, page 122

As I read, I will pay attention to punctuation.

In Rome there once lived a slave named Androcles.
9 The master who purchased him treated him poorly. One
18 day Androcles took his few possessions and ran away. In a
29 dark forest, he heard a loud roar.
36 "That sounds like a lion!" he thought.
43 He heard the roar again. Now it sounded more like a
54 moan. In a clearing, he saw the lion. Androcles was
64 frightened. But the lion didn't move.
70 The beast was in pain. Its right paw was bleeding. A
81 large thorn was stuck in it.
87 Androcles could see that the lion was hurt.
95 Androcles was scared, but he was brave. 102

Comprehension Check

1. Why did Androcles run away? **Main Idea and Details** His master treated him poorly.
2. What do you think Androcles will do next? **Plot Development** Possible response provided. Androcles will pull the thorn out of the lion's paw.

	Words Read	–	Number of Errors	=	Words Correct Score
First Read		–		=	
Second Read		–		=	

Approaching Level Options

Vocabulary

Review last week's vocabulary words (**magnificent, masterpiece, ingredient, recipes, tasty**) and this week's words (**beamed, argued, possessions, fabric, purchased, quarreling**). Have students make up silly sentences that each contain at least four of the words.

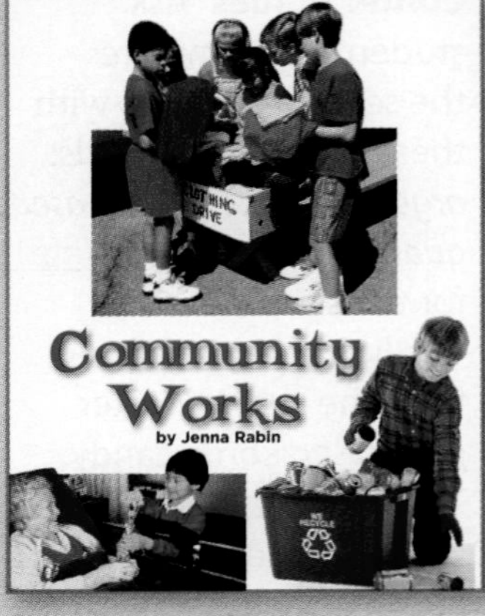

Student Book, or Transparencies 17a and 17b

Skills Focus Vocabulary

Objective Review multiple-meaning words

FCAT **DICTIONARY: MULTIPLE-MEANING WORDS**

LA.3.1.6.9 Determine correct meaning of words with multiple meanings
LA.3.1.6.10 Determine meanings using a dictionary

- Write these sentences: *Mom beamed at me and gave me a kiss when I offered to help her. The sunlight beamed through the windows.* Explain that *beamed* can mean "smiled" and "cast light."
- Ask students to say sentences for each meaning of *beamed*. Then have students use a dictionary to find two meanings for *argued* ("stated" and "fought using words") and say sentences for each meaning. Brainstorm and discuss other multiple-meaning words.

Skills Focus Comprehension

Objective Draw conclusions about a story

Materials
- **Student Book** "Community Works"
- **Transparencies 17a** and **17b**

STRATEGY
MAKE INFERENCES AND ANALYZE

LA.3.1.7.3 Determine implied inference

To make inferences, good readers use their own experiences and clues from the story to figure out information that the author has left out.

FCAT **SKILL**
PLOT DEVELOPMENT: CONCLUSIONS

LA.3.1.7 Use strategies to comprehend text

Explain/Model

Explain that when you draw conclusions, you use information from the story together with your own knowledge. Display **Transparencies 17a** and **17b**. Read the first paragraph of "Community Works" aloud again.

Think Aloud This paragraph says that Mr. Turner's class is starting to plan a community service project, but it doesn't explain further. I know that *community service* means "helping people in need." I will look for more information to help me draw a conclusion about the type of community service they choose. Is it something I am interested in, too?

Practice/Apply

Have students underline the story information that helps them draw conclusions about community service.

Leveled Reader Lesson

Objective Read to apply strategies and skills

Materials
- **Leveled Reader** *Androcles and the Lion*
- **Student Book** *Seven Spools of Thread*

Leveled Reader

PREVIEW AND PREDICT

LA.3.1.7.1 Use text features to establish purpose for reading

Show the cover. Read the title. Explain that *Androcles* (AN-druh-kleez) *and the Lion* is a fable, a story that teaches a lesson. Ask students what lesson they think they might learn. Have them set purposes for reading.

VOCABULARY WORDS

LA.3.1.6.1 Use new vocabulary

Discuss the vocabulary words and remind students to look for them as they read this story: *purchased*, *possessions*, p. 2; *fabric*, *beamed*, p. 4; *argued*, p. 7; *quarreling*, p. 8.

STRATEGY
MAKE INFERENCES AND ANALYZE

LA.3.1.7.3 Determine implied inference

Explain that authors don't always explain exactly why a story event happens or why a character does something. Suggest that as they read, students should use story clues and their own understanding of people to figure out what the character Androcles is like. Read pages 2–3 aloud and model making inferences.

Think Aloud Androcles decides to help the hurt lion even though he is scared. Story clues such as that help me make the inference that he is brave and kind. I'll look for other clues in the story that either confirm this or make me change my opinion of him.

SKILL
PLOT DEVELOPMENT: DRAW CONCLUSIONS

LA.3.1.7 Use strategies to comprehend text

Remind students that they can better understand plot development by drawing conclusions. Drawing conclusions means using details and their own experience to explain characters' actions or events in a story. During and after reading, discuss clues that help readers draw conclusions about what lesson this fable teaches. Help students create a Conclusion Map.

READ AND RESPOND

LA.3.1.6.2 Read and discuss text

Have students read to the end of the story. Review students' conclusions about the moral of the fable after reading. Ask if any students have read or seen other versions of this fable and can compare the versions.

MAKE CONNECTIONS ACROSS TEXTS

LA.3.1.7.7 Compare and contrast texts

Have students compare *Seven Spools of Thread* and *Androcles and the Lion*, including the themes and lessons the stories teach. Ask how these stories teach people to behave. (to cooperate with others; to be kind and to help those in trouble) Ask: *Would either story make a good movie?*

On Level Options

Skills Focus: Phonics

Objective Decode one-syllable and multisyllabic words with /ou/

Materials • chart paper

DECODE WORDS WITH /ou/

LA.3.1.4 Demonstrate knowledge of alphabetic principle

- Explain that knowing that the letters *ou* and *ow* stand for the /ou/ sound can help students pronounce unfamiliar words.
- Write the following: *I went downtown to hang around. The sounds were loud, and the streets were crowded.* Say the sentences and have students echo you. Underline the letters that stand for /ou/.
- Have students say, write, and sort the words *crowded, louder, shouting,* and *howling*, and then underline the letters that spell /ou/ in each word.

Skills Focus: Vocabulary

Objective Apply vocabulary and identify multiple-meaning words

Materials • **Vocabulary Cards** • **Student Book** "Community Works"

FCAT VOCABULARY WORDS

LA.3.1.6 Use multiple strategies to develop grade-appropriate vocabulary

Have students name the vocabulary word that goes with each sentence:

- The sun shone brightly down on the picnic. (*beamed*)
- They had a heated disagreement that lasted for hours. (*argued*)
- She had so many things, she didn't know where to store them. (*possessions*)
- They bought all the food they needed for the week. (*purchased*)
- Their continuous arguing upset the neighbors. (*quarreling*)

Student Book

DICTIONARY: MULTIPLE-MEANING WORDS

LA.3.1.6.9 Determine correct meaning of words with multiple meanings

Ask students what the meaning of *called* is on page 48 of "Community Works." (asked for; summoned) Ask a volunteer to confirm it using a dictionary. *Now give another meaning of* called. (made a telephone call to) Have students figure out the meanings of these words as used in the text: *raised, treat, warm, board*. They can confirm meanings using a dictionary.

Skills Focus: Fluency

Objective Read fluently with good prosody at a rate of 82–102 WCPM

Materials • **On Level Practice Book O**, p. 122

REPEATED READING

LA.3.1.5 Demonstrate the ability to read text orally with expression

Model expressive reading using the fluency passage on **Practice Book** page 122. Have students echo-read each sentence after you. Show how you pay attention to punctuation. Have students take turns reading the passage to partners and show the characters' feelings in their voices.

On Level Practice Book O, page 122

As I read, I will pay attention to punctuation.

The old man could give the diamond to only one son.
11 Which one should it be? He loved them all equally. Finally
22 he came up with a solution.
28 The next morning, the old man called his three sons
38 before him.
40 "My sons, I have a problem," he told them. "I love all
52 three of you, but I can give my most precious possession
63 to only one of you. Therefore, I will give my diamond to
75 the son that best meets my challenge."
82 "The one of you who proves to be a true hero will get
95 the diamond," said the old man.
101 "That is fair," said the three sons in unison.
110 "To decide who is the true hero, I will give you a task,"
123 said their father. 126

Comprehension Check

1. What is the old man's problem? **Problem and Solution** The old man has only one diamond and three sons. He does not know which son should get the diamond.
2. How does the old man decide which son should get the diamond? **Plot Development** The old man decides to give the diamond to the son who proves to be a hero. The sons have to complete a task that their father gives them.

	Words Read	–	Number of Errors	=	Words Correct Score
First Read		–		=	
Second Read		–		=	

Leveled Reader Lesson

Objective Read to apply strategies and skills

Materials
- **Leveled Reader** *A True Hero* • chart paper
- **Student Book** *Seven Spools of Thread*

Leveled Reader

PREVIEW AND PREDICT

LA.3.1.7.1 Use text features to make predictions

Show the cover of the book and read the title. Ask students why they think the word *true* is in the title. Discuss their predictions and set purposes for reading.

STRATEGY
MAKE INFERENCES AND ANALYZE

LA.3.1.7.3 Determine implied inference

Tell students that as they read, they should use story clues and their own experiences to figure out why the characters behave the way they do. Read aloud the table of contents and the first paragraph on page 2. Model making inferences and analyzing text.

Think Aloud In the first paragraph, I learn that the father has three sons and only one diamond to give away. Maybe the father will challenge his sons to be heroes and will give the diamond to the son who is the bravest or most generous of the three. I'll keep reading to find out.

SKILL
PLOT DEVELOPMENT: DRAW CONCLUSIONS

LA.3.1.7 Use a variety of strategies to comprehend grade level text

Help students use story clues to draw conclusions so they can understand plot development and figure out what lesson this folk tale teaches. Ask: *What is a true hero, based on this folk tale? What clues lead to that conclusion?* Students can create Conclusion Maps to help them.

ELL
Leveled Reader
Go to pages
77U–77V.

READ AND RESPOND

LA.3.2.1.7 Respond to and discuss literary selections

Have students read aloud to the end of Chapter 2. Offer fluency support and review vocabulary word meanings as needed. Ask students to find out what the father's challenge is and how it will determine a winner.

Then have students read to the end of Chapter 4. Discuss how each of the brothers' deeds were different and whether or not the father made the right decision in the end.

MAKE CONNECTIONS ACROSS TEXTS

LA.3.1.7.7 Compare and contrast texts

Have students compare *Seven Spools of Thread* and *A True Hero* and tell how they are alike and different. Encourage discussion and help students draw conclusions about how the characters' lives will continue to be different.

Beyond Level Options

Student Book

Skills Focus Vocabulary

Objective Complete sentences using content vocabulary words

Materials • **Student Book** "What Causes Day and Night?"

EXTEND VOCABULARY

LA.3.1.6.1 Use new vocabulary that is introduced and taught directly

Review content vocabulary words so students can answer questions:

- What is another name for a ball? (a sphere)
- What is another word for *spin*? (rotate)
- What is the imaginary line through the center of Earth? (axis)

Skills Focus Text Feature

Objective Review diagrams

Materials • **Student Book** "What Causes Day and Night?"

DIAGRAMS

LA.3.2.2.1 Identify purpose of text features

Ask students to review "What Causes Day and Night?" on **Student Book** pages 74–75 and use the boldfaced words and illustrations to summarize the main ideas. Review and discuss the diagram on page 75.

- What information does the diagram explain? (how Earth moves around the sun)
- What do the labels tell you? (where the axis and the equator are)

Skills Focus Fluency

Objective Read fluently with good prosody at a rate of 92–102 WCPM

Materials • **Beyond Practice Book B**, p. 122

REPEATED READING

LA.3.1.5 Demonstrate the ability to read text orally with expression

Read the passage on **Practice Book** page 122 as students echo-read each sentence. Have students imagine they are storytellers and read with expression so that the listeners stay alert and interested. Remind them to pay attention to punctuation.

Have partners take turns reading the passage and providing feedback to each other. The pairs should continue to practice reading during independent time.

Timed Reading You may wish to have students do a timed reading at the end of the week.

Beyond Practice Book B, page 122

As I read, I will pay attention to punctuation.

Once upon a time in a tiny village in southern China
11 there lived a poor woman and her son. They lived in a tiny
24 hut with few possessions. The woman made a living by
34 weaving brocade. The entire village admired her work and
43 considered her the finest weaver in the region.
51 The woman enjoyed her work and she loved her son
61 dearly. She loved him so much that she wished she could
72 do more for him. Instead of living in a poor hut, she
84 wished their home were a great house. Instead of a
94 few skinny trees, she wished their house were surrounded
103 by beautiful gardens with fine fruits and colorful flowers.
112 Instead of a few rabbits, she wished the fields were full
123 of exotic animals. Instead of a few old crows, she wished
134 that the skies above teemed with different birds with many
144 bright feathers.
146 All these things she wished for, but knew that none of
157 her wishes would come true. 162

Comprehension Check

1. What did the poor woman wish for? **Relevant Details** A great house, beautiful gardens, and exotic animals
2. Why did she wish for these things? **Main Idea and Details** She wanted to do more for her son.

	Words Read	–	Number of Errors	=	Words Correct Score
First Read		–		=	
Second Read		–		=	

Leveled Reader Lesson

Objective Read to apply strategies and skills

Materials • **Leveled Reader** *The Lost Brocade*

Leveled Reader

PREVIEW AND PREDICT

LA.3.1.7.1 Use text features to make predictions

Show the cover and read the title of the book. Ask students if they know what brocade is. Ask them what they think will happen in the story.

STRATEGY
MAKE INFERENCES AND ANALYZE

LA.3.1.7.3 Determine implied inference

Remind students to use story clues and their own prior knowledge to make inferences about things that the author did not explicitly tell. Read aloud pages 2–3. Ask students to predict what the woman will do. Model how to make inferences and analyze text.

Think Aloud The story title tells me that the poor woman's brocade is lost. Since it is the title of the story, I know that the brocade is very important. In other fairy tales, good people who are poor often become wealthy. I think the woman's brocade will somehow bring her riches.

SKILL
PLOT DEVELOPMENT: DRAW CONCLUSIONS

LA.3.1.7 Use strategies to comprehend text

Help students draw conclusions about why the woman decides to weave her special brocade. Students can create Conclusion Maps.

READ AND RESPOND

LA.3.2.1.7 Respond to and discuss literary selections

Have students read to the end of Chapter 2. Find out how the poor woman's work as she creates the brocade changes her life and her son's life at the beginning of the story. As students complete the story, ask them how the woman and her son's sacrifices have paid off. Discuss how the brocade might continue to affect their lives in the future. Discuss the vocabulary words in the story as well.

Self-Selected Reading

Objective Read independently to apply comprehension strategies and skills

Materials • Leveled Readers or trade books at students' reading levels

FCAT

READ TO UNDERSTAND PLOT DEVELOPMENT AND DRAW CONCLUSIONS

LA.3.2.1.8 Select fiction materials to read

Invite each student to choose a fiction book for independent reading. As students read, remind them to make inferences and draw conclusions. After reading, partners who have read the same book should discuss whether or not their conclusions were correct and which clues lead to their conclusions.

Academic Language

Throughout the week the English language learners will need help in building their understanding of the academic language used in daily instruction and assessment instruments. The following strategies will help to increase their language proficiency and comprehension of content and instructional words.

LOG ON Technology

Oral Language For additional language support and oral vocabulary development, go to **www.macmillanmh.com**

Strategies to Reinforce Academic Language

- **Use Context** Academic language (see chart below) should be explained in the context of the task during Whole Group. Use gestures, expressions, and visuals to support meaning.
- **Use Visuals** Use charts, transparencies, and graphic organizers to explain key labels to help students understand classroom language.
- **Model** Demonstrate the task using academic language in order for students to understand instruction.

Academic Language Used in Whole Group Instruction

Content/Theme Words	Skill/Strategy Words	Writing/Grammar Words
getting along (p. 46)	multiple-meaning words (p. 48)	directions (p. 76)
sphere (p. 74)	make inferences and analyze (p. 49A)	precise words (p. 77A)
rotates (p. 74)	plot development (p. 49A)	linking verbs (p. 77I)
axis (p. 74)	nonfiction article (p. 74)	punctuation (p. 77J)
	rules (p. 74)	

ELL Leveled Reader Lesson

Before Reading

DEVELOP ORAL LANGUAGE

Build Background Write the word *hero* on the board and have students brainstorm words they associate with it. *Who is your hero? Why?*

LA.3.1.6 Develop grade-appropriate vocabulary

Review Vocabulary Write the vocabulary and support words on the board and discuss their meanings. Use each word in a sentence. *I went shopping and* purchased *many books. Now, these books are part of my* possessions.

PREVIEW AND PREDICT

LA.3.1.7.1 Use text features to make predictions

Point to the cover illustration and read the title aloud. *What do you think this story may be about?* Read the table of contents and ask: *How many characters do you think there may be?* Have students make predictions.

Set a Purpose for Reading Show the Conclusion Map. As they read, ask students to look for and record clues that will help them reach and explain a conclusion. Drawing conclusions helps readers to understand plot development.

During Reading

LA.3.2.1.2 Identify and explain plot; **LA.3.1.7.3** Determine implied inference

Choose from among the differentiated strategies below to support students' reading at all stages of language acquisition.

Beginning

Shared Reading As you read, model how to make inferences and look for clues to draw a conclusion. At the end, review these clues and model reaching a conclusion. Have students help you fill in the Conclusion Map.

Intermediate

Read Together Read Chapter 1. Model how to look for clues that will lead you to a conclusion. Take turns reading the selection and ask students to use the strategy. At the end, have students help you fill in the map.

Advanced

Independent Reading Have students read the selection. Each day ask them to discuss it with partners and look for clues that will lead them to a conclusion. Have them use the strategy to fill in the map.

After Reading

LA.3.1.6.1 Use new vocabulary

Remind students to use the vocabulary and story words in their whole group activities.

Objective

- Apply vocabulary and comprehension skills

Materials

- ELL Leveled Reader

ELL 5 Day Planner

DAY 1	• Academic Language • Oral Language and Vocabulary Review
DAY 2	• Academic Language • ELL Leveled Reader
DAY 3	• Academic Language • ELL Leveled Reader
DAY 4	• Academic Language • ELL Leveled Reader
DAY 5	• Academic Language • ELL Leveled Reader Comprehension Check and Literacy Activities

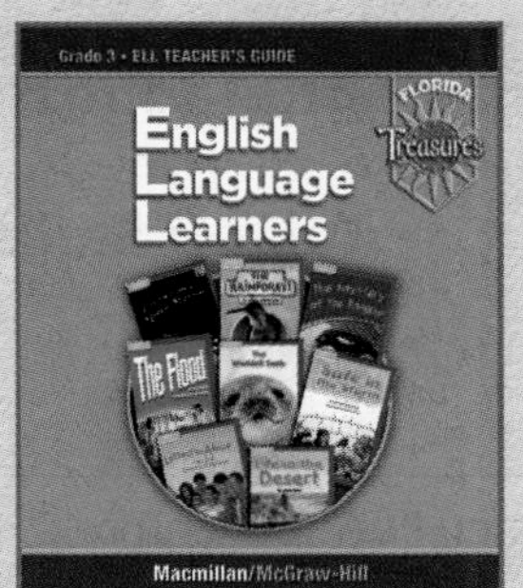

ELL Teacher's Guide for students who need additional instruction

Student Book Selections

Weekly Theme: Protecting Our Natural Resources

Week At A Glance

Whole Group

VOCABULARY
clumps, native, research, shouldn't, sprout

Word Parts/Contractions

COMPREHENSION
Strategy: Monitor Comprehension
Skill: Compare and Contrast

TEST STRATEGY
Think and Search

WRITING
Narrative/Article

Science Link
Living Things Interact with Their Environment

Small Group Options

Differentiated Instruction for Tested Skills

FCAT Tested FCAT Benchmark
Tested Skill for the Week
Sunshine State Standard
FCAT FCAT Benchmark

AUDIO CD

Comprehension

Genre
Nonfiction Articles give information about real people, places, or things.

Monitor Comprehension
FCAT Compare and Contrast
When authors compare two topics or ideas, they often use signal words, such as *alike* and *different*.

WASHINGTON WEED WHACKERS

WHAT ALIEN SPECIES IS CREEPING ALONG THE SHORES OF PUGET SOUND?

The "weed whackers" of Lincoln Elementary, in Mount Vernon, Washington

Spartina is a perfectly good plant. It creates a habitat and food for many fish and wildlife. So why do the kids at Lincoln Elementary School in Mount Vernon, Washington, want to get rid of it? It's because spartina **shouldn't** live on the West Coast. In Washington State's Puget Sound, spartina has turned into a life-choking weed.

82

Science Link
Main Selection
Genre Nonfiction Article

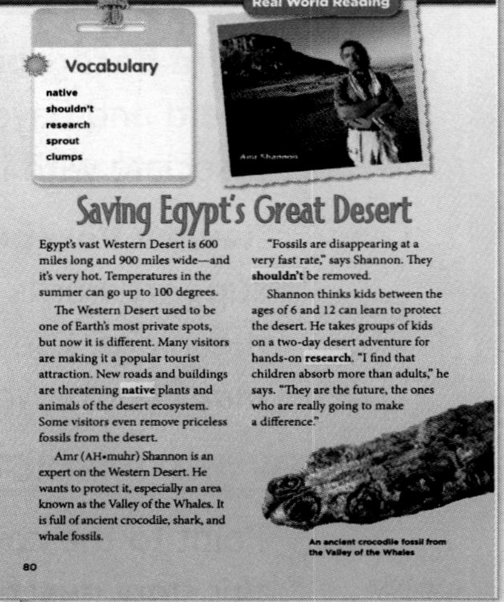
Real World Reading

Vocabulary
native
shouldn't
research
sprout
clumps

Saving Egypt's Great Desert

Egypt's vast Western Desert is 600 miles long and 900 miles wide—and it's very hot. Temperatures in the summer can go up to 100 degrees.

The Western Desert used to be one of Earth's most private spots, but now it is different. Many visitors are making it a popular tourist attraction. New roads and buildings are threatening **native** plants and animals of the desert ecosystem. Some visitors even remove priceless fossils from the desert.

Amr (AH•muhr) Shannon is an expert on the Western Desert. He wants to protect it, especially an area known as the Valley of the Whales. It is full of ancient crocodile, shark, and whale fossils.

"Fossils are disappearing at a very fast rate," says Shannon. They **shouldn't** be removed.

Shannon thinks kids between the ages of 6 and 12 can learn to protect the desert. He takes groups of kids on a two-day desert adventure for hands-on **research**. "I find that children absorb more than adults," he says. "They are the future, the ones who are really going to make a difference."

An ancient crocodile fossil from the Valley of the Whales

80

Vocabulary/ Comprehension

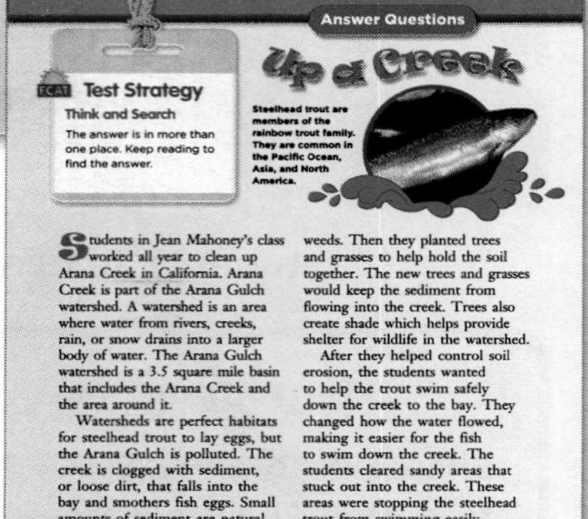
Answer Questions

FCAT **Test Strategy**
Think and Search
The answer is in more than one place. Keep reading to find the answer.

Up a Creek

Steelhead trout are members of the rainbow trout family. They are common in the Pacific Ocean, Asia, and North America.

Students in Jean Mahoney's class worked all year to clean up Arana Creek in California. Arana Creek is part of the Arana Gulch watershed. A watershed is an area where water from rivers, creeks, rain, or snow drains into a larger body of water. The Arana Gulch watershed is a 3.5 square mile basin that includes the Arana Creek and the area around it.

Watersheds are perfect habitats for steelhead trout to lay eggs, but the Arana Gulch is polluted. The creek is clogged with sediment, or loose dirt, that falls into the bay and smothers fish eggs. Small amounts of sediment are natural and do not hurt the fish eggs. But recent storms have caused too much sediment to build up.

After Ms. Mahoney's class learned about the area's plants and animals, they went to work. They picked up trash and removed weeds. Then they planted trees and grasses to help hold the soil together. The new trees and grasses would keep the sediment from flowing into the creek. Trees also create shade which helps provide shelter for wildlife in the watershed.

After they helped control soil erosion, the students wanted to help the trout swim safely down the creek to the bay. They changed how the water flowed, making it easier for the fish to swim down the creek. The students cleared sandy areas that stuck out into the creek. These areas were stopping the steelhead trout from swimming easily.

The following spring they tested the water temperature and sediment levels. Conditions were just right for the trout. Today, the watershed is tested regularly. It is once again a good place for plants and animals to call home.

86 Go on

FCAT **Test Strategy Think and Search**

Read-Aloud Anthology
- Listening Comprehension
- Readers' Theater

Resources for Differentiated Instruction

FCAT LEVELED READERS: Science

GR Levels M–R

Genre Informational Nonfiction

- Same Theme
- Same Vocabulary
- Same Comprehension Skills

Approaching Level

On Level

Beyond Level

English Language Leveled Reader

Sheltered Readers for English Language Learners

ELL Teacher's Guide also available

LEVELED PRACTICE

Approaching

On Level

Beyond

ELL

INTERVENTION PROGRAM

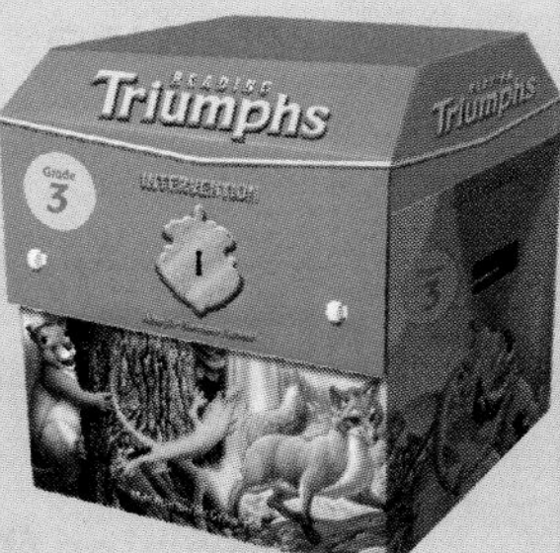

- Phonics and Decoding
- Comprehension
- Vocabulary

Also available, *Reading Triumphs*, Intervention Program

CLASSROOM LIBRARY

Genre Informational Nonfiction

Approaching

On Level

Beyond

Trade books to apply Comprehension Skills

FCAT Success!

- FCAT Edition
- Content Area Reading

FCAT Test Preparation and Practice

FCAT Benchmark Assessments

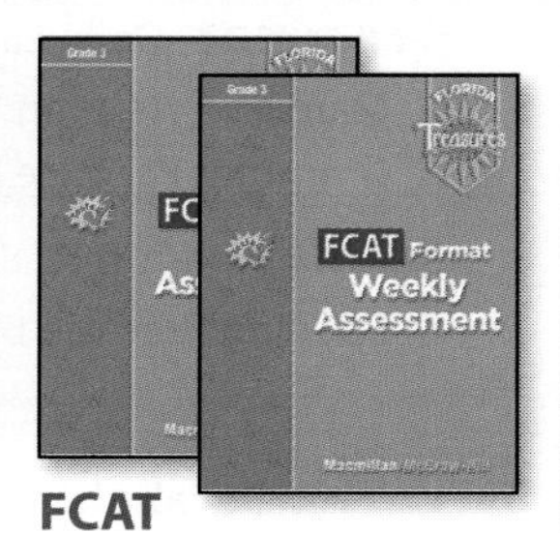

FCAT Unit and Weekly Assessments

HOME-SCHOOL CONNECTION

- Family letters in English, Spanish, and Haitian Creole
- Take-Home Stories

FLORIDA Suggested Lesson Plan

Washington Weed Whackers, 82–85

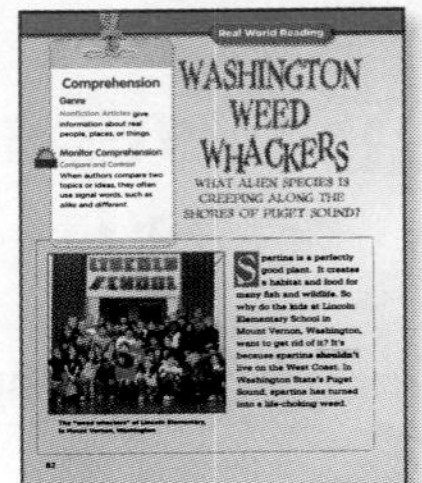

Integrated ELL Support Every Day

Whole Group	Day 1	Day 2
ORAL LANGUAGE • Listening • Speaking • Viewing	**Listening/Speaking/Viewing** Focus Question Why do people need the natural resources shown on these pages? Build Background, 78 LA.3.5.2 **Read Aloud:** "The People Who Hugged the Trees," 79 LA.3.2.1.1	**Listening/Speaking** Focus Question What alien species is creeping along the shores of Puget Sound? LA.3.5.2
WORD STUDY • Vocabulary • Phonics/Decoding	**Vocabulary** LA.3.1.6.1 *native, shouldn't, research, sprout, clumps,* 80 Practice Book A-O-B, 126 FCAT **Strategy:** Word Parts: Contractions, 81 LA.3.3.4.3	**Vocabulary** LA.3.1.6.1 Review Vocabulary, 82 **Phonics** Decode Words with Soft *c* and *g*, 89E LA.3.1.4 Practice Book A-O-B, 132
READING • Develop Comprehension • Fluency	**Read** "Saving Egypt's Great Desert," 80–81 Student Book **Comprehension,** 81A–81B **Strategy:** Monitor Comprehension FCAT **Skill:** Compare and Contrast LA.3.1.7.5 Practice Book A-O-B, 127 **Fluency** Partner Reading, 78I LA.3.1.5 Model Fluency, 79	**Read** *Washington Weed Whackers,* 82–85 Student Book **Comprehension,** 82–85 **Strategy:** Monitor Comprehension FCAT **Skill:** Compare and Contrast LA.3.1.7.5 Practice Book A-O-B, 128 **Fluency** Partner Reading, 78I LA.3.1.5
LANGUAGE ARTS • Writing • Grammar • Spelling	FCAT **Writing** LA.3.3.2.1 Daily Writing: Imagine you are an archaeologist on a dig in Egypt. What do you find? Would you bring your findings to the United States? Why? **Generate Questions:** Article, 89A **Grammar** Daily Language Activities, 89I Main and Helping Verbs, 89I LA.3.3.4.5 Grammar Practice Book, 109 **Spelling** Pretest, 89G LA.3.3.4.1 Spelling Practice Book, 109–110	FCAT **Writing** LA.3.6.2.2 Daily Writing: If all the streets were rivers, how would this change what your school looks like? How would you get to school? **Find Information:** Article, 89A **Grammar** Daily Language Activities, 89I Main and Helping Verbs, 89I LA.3.3.4.4 Grammar Practice Book, 110 **Spelling** Words with soft *c* and *g*, 89G Spelling Practice Book, 111 LA.3.1.4
ASSESSMENT • Informal/Formal	Quick Check **Vocabulary,** 80 **Comprehension,** 81B	Quick Check **Comprehension,** 85 **Phonics,** 89E
Turn the Page for **Small Group Lesson Plan**	**Differentiated Instruction 89M–89V**	**Differentiated Instruction 89M–89V**

FCAT Benchmarks

Vocabulary	Comprehension	Writing	Science
Vocabulary Words **Word Parts/ Contractions** LA.3.3.4.3 Edit for correct use of apostrophes	**Strategy: Monitor Comprehension** **Skill: Compare and Contrast** LA.3.1.7.5 Identify the text structure an author uses	**Narrative/Article** LA.3.4.2.1 Write in expository forms	**Living Things Interact with Their Environment** SC.G.1.2.1.3.1 Living things compete for resources

Turn the Page for **Small Group Options**

Day 3

Listening/Speaking

Focus Question How have people brought on the problems in "Saving Egypt's Great Desert" and *Washington Weed Whackers*?

Summarize, 85 LA.3.2.2.3

Vocabulary LA.3.1.6.3

Review Words in Context, 89C

FCAT **Strategy:** Word Parts: Contractions, 89D

Practice Book A-O-B, 131 LA.3.3.4.3

Phonics LA.3.1.4.3

Decode Multisyllable Words, 89E

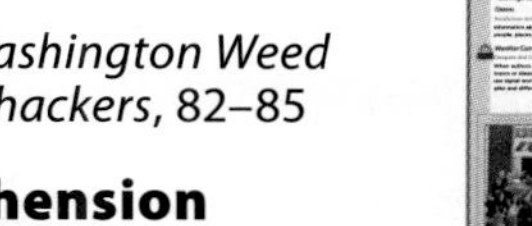

Read *Washington Weed Whackers*, 82–85

Student Book

Comprehension

Comprehension Check, 85

FCAT **Skill:** Cause and Effect, 85A LA.3.1.7.4

Fluency Partner Reading, 78I

Repeated Reading, 85A LA.3.1.5

Practice Book A-O-B, 129

FCAT Writing

Daily Writing: Your neighborhood has a bug problem. Write a journal entry describing what you would do.

Organize Information: Article, 89A LA.3.6.1.1

Grammar Daily Language Activities, 89I

Quotation Marks, 89J LA.3.3.4.3

Grammar Practice Book, 111

Spelling Words with soft *c* and *g*, 89H

Spelling Practice Book, 112 LA.3.1.6.3

Quick Check **Fluency,** 85A

Differentiated Instruction 89M–89V

Day 4

Listening/Speaking

Focus Question What are some qualities of a good volunteer? How were the students in Ms. Mahoney's class good volunteers?

Expand Vocabulary: Natural Resources, 89F LA.3.1.6.1

Vocabulary LA.3.1.6.8

Antonyms, 89F

Apply Vocabulary to Writing, 89F

Phonics

Picture Dictionary, 89E LA.3.1.6

Read "Up A Creek," 86–87

Student Book

Test Strategy: Think and Search

Research and Study Skills LA.3.6.1.1

Computer Search Engines in the Media Center, 85B

FCAT Practice Book A-O-B, 130

Fluency Partner Reading, 78I LA.3.1.5

FCAT Writing

Daily Writing: Write a short newspaper article informing people in your state about the problems spartina causes.

Synthesize and Write: Article, 89A LA.3.3.2

Grammar Daily Language Activities, 89I

Main and Helping Verbs, 89J LA.3.3.4.5

Grammar Practice Book, 112

Spelling Words with soft *c* and *g*, 89H

Spelling Practice Book, 113 LA.3.3.4.1

Quick Check **Vocabulary,** 89D

Differentiated Instruction 89M–89V

Day 5

Review and Assess

Listening/Speaking

Focus Question Both Amr Shannon in Egypt and the students in Washington want to help the environment. Compare how they are protecting these places.

Speaking and Listening Strategies, 89A LA.3.5.2

Vocabulary LA.3.1.6.1

Spiral Review: Vocabulary Concentration, 89F

Read Self-Selected Reading, 78I

Student Book

Comprehension

Strategy: Monitor Comprehension

FCAT **Skill:** Compare and Contrast LA.3.1.7.5

Fluency Partner Reading, 78I LA.3.1.5

Writing LA.3.6.1.1

Daily Writing: You are a photographer and have taken a picture of a polluted river. Write three different captions for your photo.

Share Information: Article, 89A

Grammar Daily Language Activities, 89I

Main and Helping Verbs, 89J LA.3.3.4.5

Grammar Practice Book, 113-114

Spelling Posttest, 89H

Spelling Practice Book, 114 LA.3.3.4.1

FCAT **Weekly Assessment, 213–224**

Differentiated Instruction 89M–89V

What do I do in small groups?

Focus on Skills

Skills Focus

Use your  **observations to guide additional instruction and practice.**

Phonics

Decode Words with Soft *c* and *g*

Vocabulary

Words: native, shouldn't, research, sprout, clumps

FCAT **Strategy:** Word Parts/Contractions

Comprehension

Strategy: Monitor Comprehension

FCAT **Skill:** Compare and Contrast

FCAT **Fluency**

Suggested Lesson Plan

CD ROM Instructional Navigator Interactive Lesson Planner

	Day 1	Day 2
Approaching Level • **Additional Instruction/Practice** • **Tier 2 Instruction**	Fluency, 89N Vocabulary, 89N Comprehension, 89O 	Phonics, 89M Vocabulary, 89O Leveled Reader Lesson, 89P • Vocabulary • Comprehension 
On Level • **Practice**	Vocabulary, 89Q Leveled Reader Lesson, 89R • Comprehension  ELL Leveled Reader, 89U–89V 	Phonics, 89Q Leveled Reader Lesson, 89R • Comprehension • Vocabulary  
Beyond Level • **Extend**	Vocabulary, 89S Leveled Reader Lesson, 89T • Comprehension 	Leveled Reader Lesson, 89T • Comprehension • Vocabulary 

For intensive intervention see READING Triumphs

Small Group Options

Focus on Leveled Readers

Levels M–R

Apply FCAT skills and strategies while reading appropriate leveled books.

Approaching

On Level

Beyond

N — Resources

ELL

Additional Leveled Reader Resources

Leveled Reader Database

Go to www.macmillanmh.com

Search by

- Comprehension Skill
- Content Area
- Genre
- Text Feature
- Guided Reading Level
- Reading Recovery Level
- Lexile Score
- Benchmark Level

Subscription also available.

Focus on Science

Teacher's Annotated Edition

Living Things Interact with their Environment

SC.G.1.2.1.3.1 Living things compete for resources

Additional Leveled Readers

Enjoying Our Natural Resources

Energy and Our Natural Resources

Day 3

Phonics, 89M
Fluency, 89N
Vocabulary, 89O
Leveled Reader Lesson, 89P
- Comprehension

Fluency, 89Q
Vocabulary, 89Q
Leveled Reader Lesson, 89R
- Comprehension

Fluency, 89S
Vocabulary, 89S
Leveled Reader Lesson, 89T
- Comprehension

Day 4

Phonics, 89M
Leveled Reader Lesson, 89P
- Comprehension
- ELL Skill: Compare and Contrast

Leveled Reader Lesson, 89R
- Comprehension

Study Skill, 89S
Leveled Reader Lesson, 89T
- Comprehension

Day 5

Fluency, 89N
Leveled Reader Lesson, 89P
- Make Connections Across Texts

Fluency, 89Q
Leveled Reader Lesson, 89R
- Make Connections Across Texts

Fluency, 89S
Self-Selected Reading, 89T

What do I do with the rest of my class?

Class Management Tools

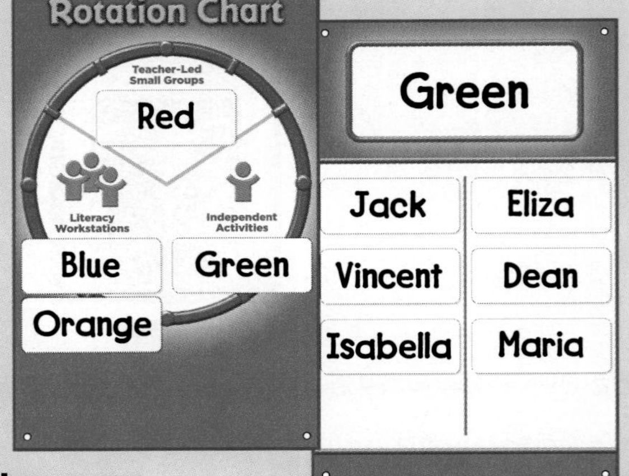

Includes:
- How-to Guide
- Rotation Chart
- Weekly Contracts

FOLDABLES™

Hands-on activities for reinforcing weekly skills

Three-Pocket Foldable

Standing Cube Foldable

Independent Activities

Reinforcing Weekly Skills

For Repeated Readings and Literacy Activities

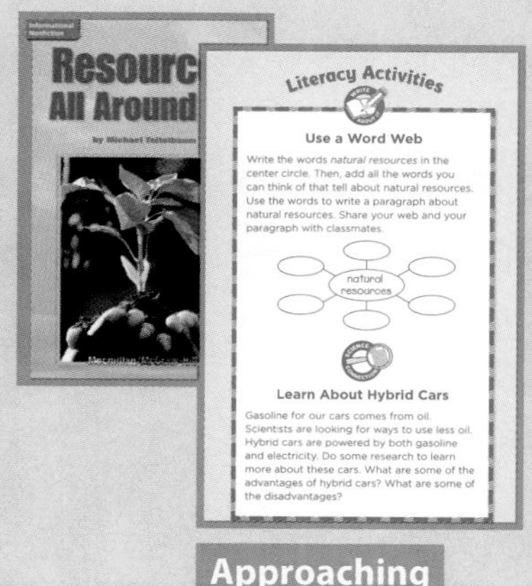

Approaching

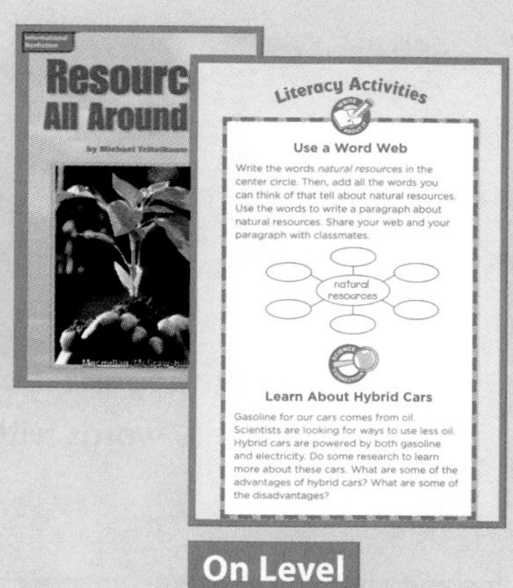

On Level

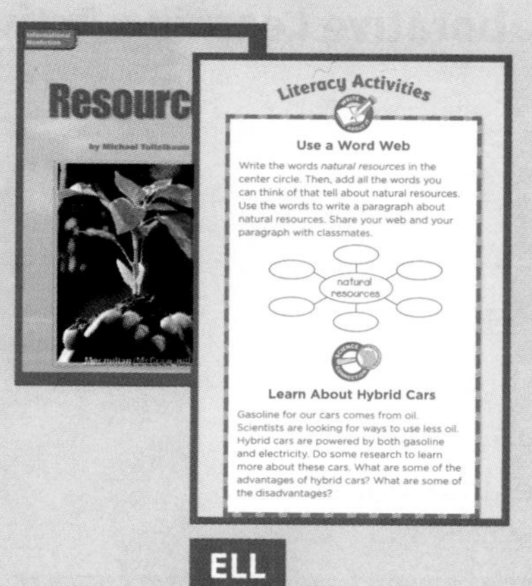

ELL

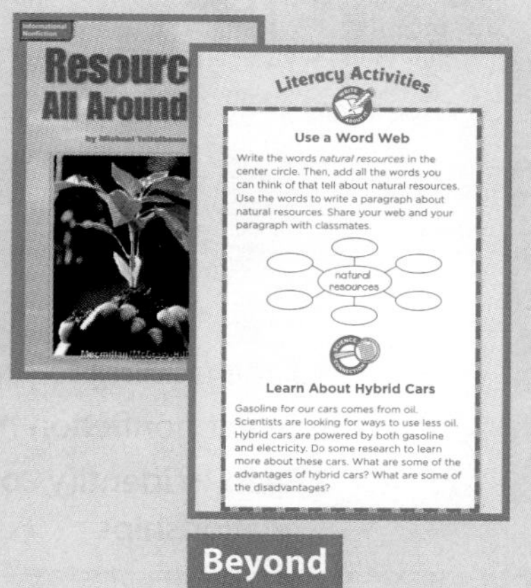

Beyond

LEVELED PRACTICE

Skills: Phonics, Vocabulary, Compare and Contrast, Fluency, Contractions, Computer Search Engines in Media Centers

Approaching

On Level

Beyond

ELL

Technology

ONLINE INSTRUCTION www.macmillanmh.com

- Meet the Author/Illustrator

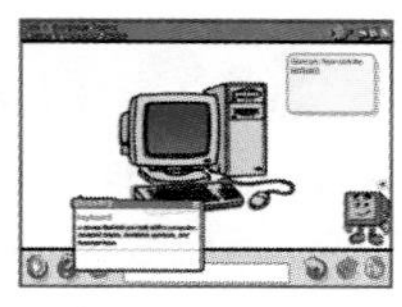

- Computer Literacy Lessons

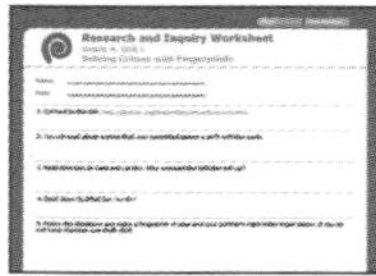

- Research and Inquiry Activities

- Oral Language Activities

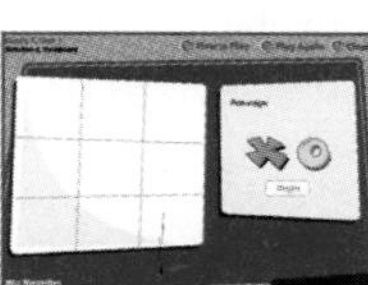

- Vocabulary and Spelling Activities

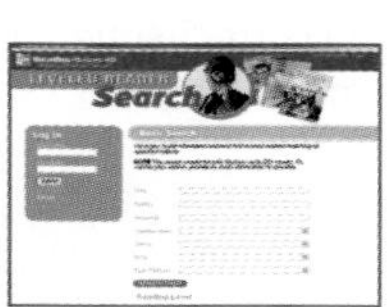

- Leveled Reader Database

LISTENING LIBRARY

Recordings of selections

- Main Selections
- Leveled Readers
- ELL Readers
- Intervention Anthology

FLUENCY SOLUTIONS

Recorded passages for modeling and practicing fluency

VOCABULARY PUZZLEMAKER

Activities for vocabulary, spelling, and high-frequency words

NEW ADVENTURES WITH BUGGLES AND BEEZY

Phonemic awareness and phonics practice

Turn the page for Literacy Workstations.

Literacy Activities

Collaborative Learning Activities

Reading

Objectives

- Time reading to practice fluency
- Select nonfiction materials to read
- Read to identify compare-and-contrast relationships

Word Study

Objectives

- Identify contractions
- Identify words with soft *c* and *g*

LA.3.1.5.1 Apply letter-sound knowledge to decode unknown words in context

Reading — **Fluency** — 20 Minutes

- Choose a reading buddy. Take turns reading aloud page 129 of your Practice Book.
- When you come to a hard word, stop. Help each other pronounce the word.

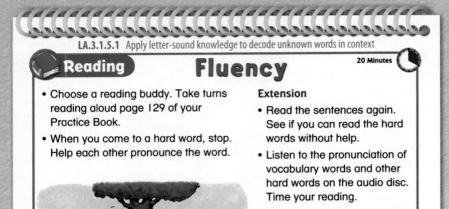

Extension

- Read the sentences again. See if you can read the hard words without help.
- Listen to the pronunciation of vocabulary words and other hard words on the audio disc. Time your reading.

Things you need:
- Practice Book

Fluency Solutions
Listening Library

35

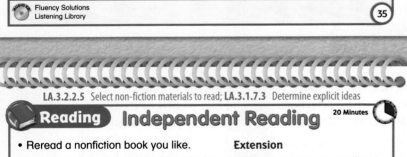

LA.3.1.4 Apply grade level phonics

Word Study — **Contractions** — 20 Minutes

- Work with a partner. Write these contractions on note cards: *shouldn't, aren't, doesn't, don't, she's,* and *it's*.
- Place the cards facedown. Take turns drawing a card.
- Read the contraction aloud. Name the missing letter.

wouldn't / would not

he's / he is

Extension

- Tell the two words each contraction stands for.
- Write the two words under the contraction.

Things you need:
- note cards
- pencil

For additional vocabulary and spelling games, go to www.macmillanmh.com

Vocabulary PuzzleMaker

35

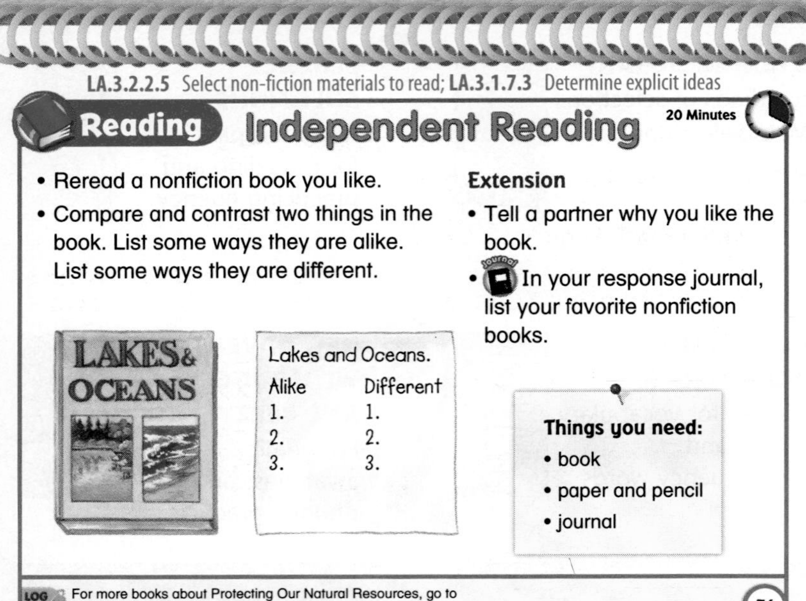

LA.3.2.2.5 Select non-fiction materials to read; LA.3.1.7.3 Determine explicit ideas

Reading — **Independent Reading** — 20 Minutes

- Reread a nonfiction book you like.
- Compare and contrast two things in the book. List some ways they are alike. List some ways they are different.

LAKES & OCEANS

Lakes and Oceans.

Alike	Different
1.	1.
2.	2.
3.	3.

Extension

- Tell a partner why you like the book.
- In your response journal, list your favorite nonfiction books.

Things you need:
- book
- paper and pencil
- journal

For more books about Protecting Our Natural Resources, go to the Author/Illustrator section at www.macmillanmh.com

36

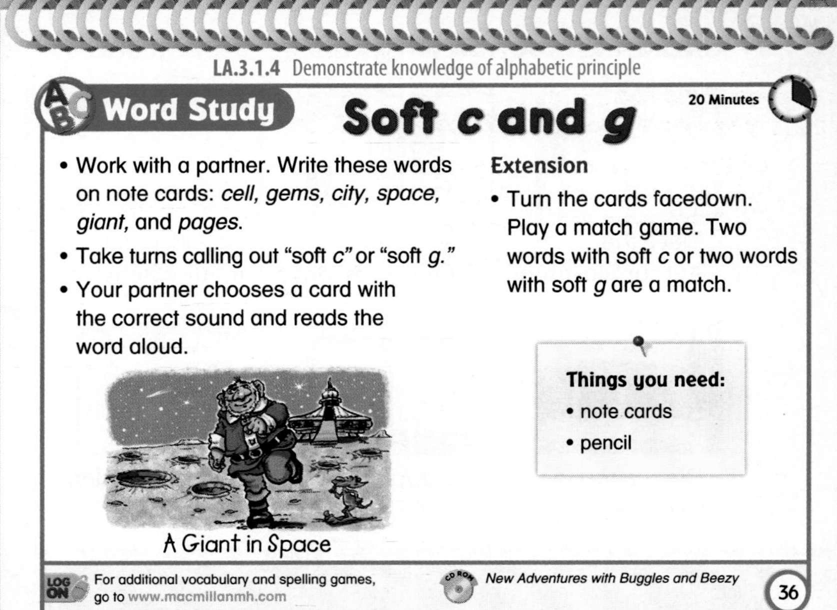

LA.3.1.4 Demonstrate knowledge of alphabetic principle

Word Study — **Soft *c* and *g*** — 20 Minutes

- Work with a partner. Write these words on note cards: *cell, gems, city, space, giant,* and *pages*.
- Take turns calling out "soft *c*" or "soft *g*."
- Your partner chooses a card with the correct sound and reads the word aloud.

A Giant in Space

Extension

- Turn the cards facedown. Play a match game. Two words with soft *c* or two words with soft *g* are a match.

Things you need:
- note cards
- pencil

For additional vocabulary and spelling games, go to www.macmillanmh.com

New Adventures with Buggles and Beezy

36

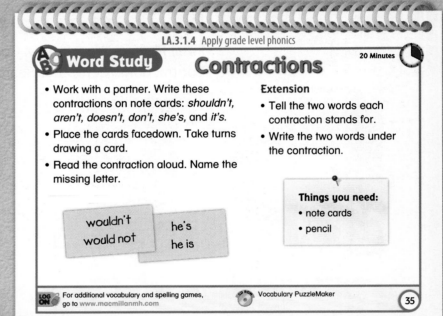

Literacy Workstations

Writing

Objectives

- Write a story and read it aloud to a partner
- Write an explanatory paragraph about natural resources

Content Literacy

Objectives

- Research information about oil spills
- Make a poster of camping rules

LA.3.4.1.1 Write narratives that include characters, setting, plot

Writing — Narrative Writing

20 Minutes

- Write a story about characters who go on a hike.
- Write a title for your story.

Extension

- Retell your story to a partner.
- List ideas for another story. It can be about any topic.

Things you need:

- paper
- pencil

35

LA.3.6.2.2 Select reference materials; LA.3.6.1.1 Read informational text for purpose of making a report

Science — Oil Spills

20 Minutes

- Use the Internet, an encyclopedia, or a science book. Learn about oil spills.
- Find answers to these questions: What is an oil spill? Why is an oil spill harmful? Take notes.

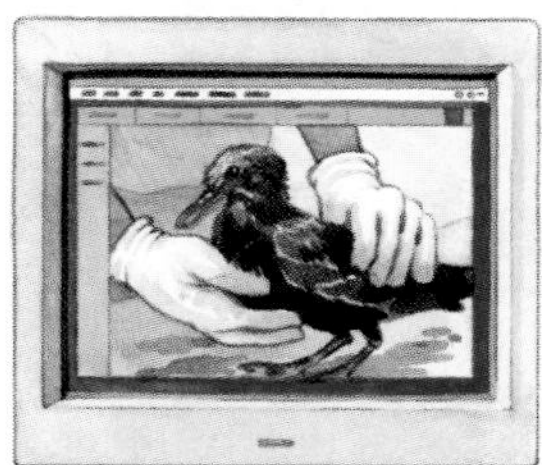

Extension

- Write a paragraph about oil spills. Use your notes.

Things you need:

- computer, encyclopedia, or science book
- paper
- pencil

LOG ON Internet Research and Inquiry Activity
Students can find more facts at www.macmillanmh.com

35

LA.3.4.2.3 Write expository essays

Writing — Our Natural Resources

20 Minutes

-  Write an explanatory paragraph. Tell why air, water, sunlight, and soil are important natural resources.
- Do research if you need information.

Extension

- Read your paragraph to a partner.
- Ask if your explanation was clear.

Things you need:

- paper
- pencil

36

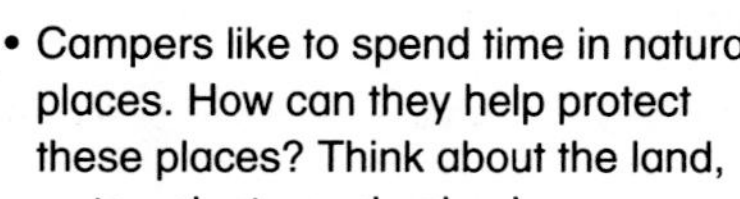

LA.3.6.2.3 Communicate information with visual support

Social Studies — Careful Campers

20 Minutes

- Campers like to spend time in natural places. How can they help protect these places? Think about the land, water, plants, and animals.
- Make a DO and DON'T poster with rules for campers.

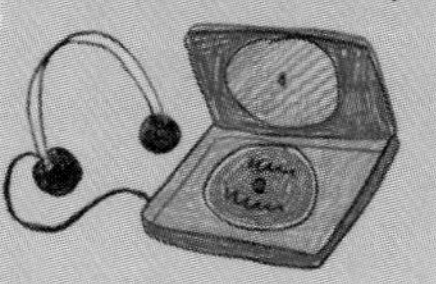

Extension

- Show your poster to classmates.
- Work with classmates. Make a classroom exhibit of posters.

Things you need:

- poster paper
- crayons or markers

36

Prepare

ORAL LANGUAGE
- Build Background
- Read Aloud
- Expand Vocabulary

FCAT **VOCABULARY**
- Teach Words in Context
- Contractions

COMPREHENSION
- **Strategy:** Monitor Comprehension
- FCAT **Skill:** Compare and Contrast

SMALL GROUP OPTIONS
- Differentiated Instruction, pp. 89M–89V

Oral Language

Build Background

ACCESS PRIOR KNOWLEDGE

Share the following information:

Natural resources are things found in nature that people use. Water is one of our most valuable natural resources. Sadly, most of the water we use goes down the drain.

LA.3.5.2 Apply listening and speaking strategies

TALK ABOUT PROTECTING OUR NATURAL RESOURCES

Discuss the weekly theme.

- What are some of Earth's natural resources? Which do you use?

FOCUS QUESTION Ask a volunteer to read "Talk About It" on **Student Book** page 78 and describe the photo.

LA.3.1.7.1 Identify a text's features

- What natural resources can you see? What are they used for?

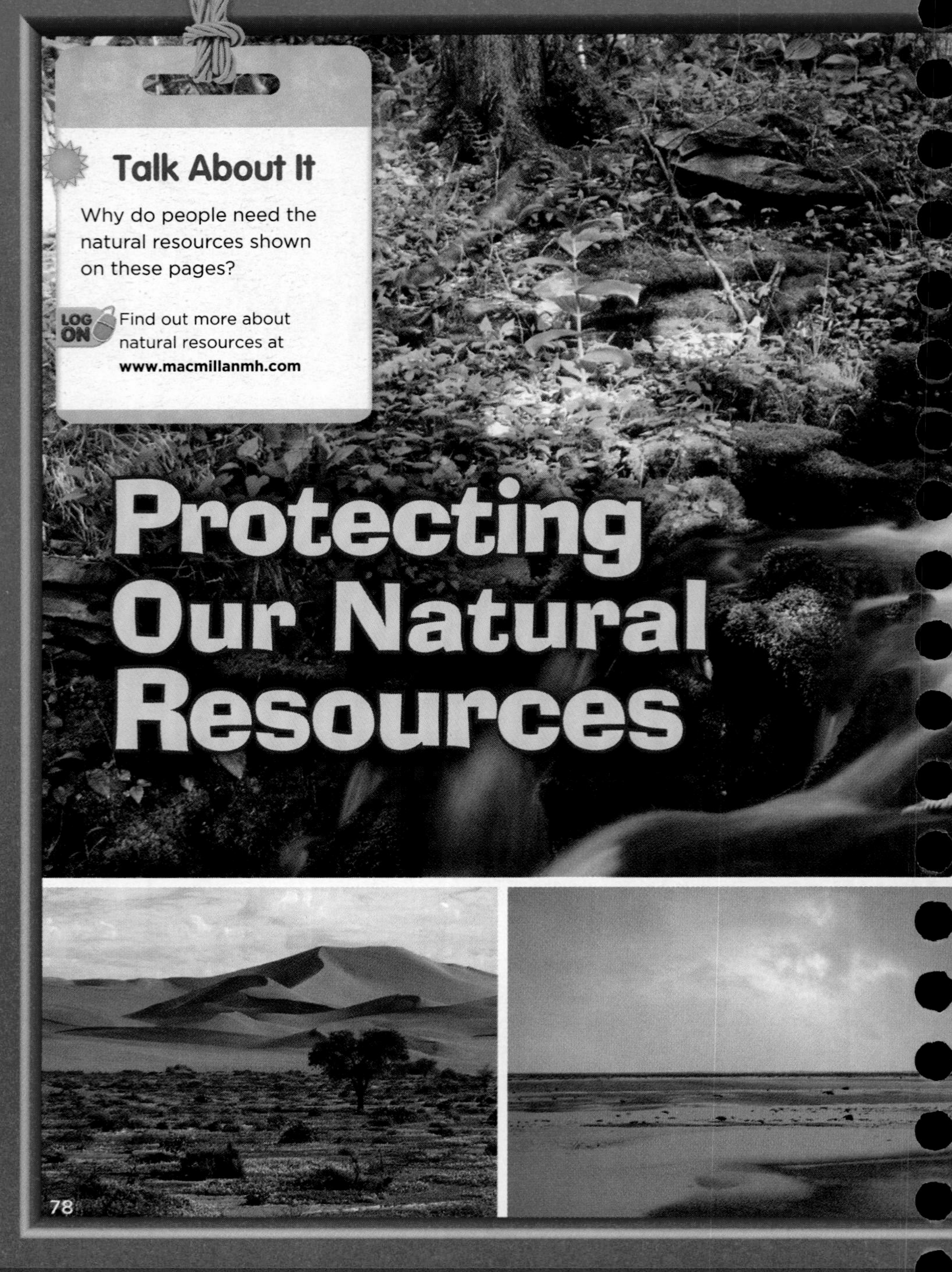

Talk About It
Why do people need the natural resources shown on these pages?
LOG ON
Find out more about natural resources at
www.macmillanmh.com
Protecting Our Natural Resources
78

ENGLISH LANGUAGE LEARNERS

Beginning **Name and Repeat** Point to the photos in the Student Book and say: *Tell me what you see in the pictures. Where is the water? Where are the mountains? These are our natural resources.* Identify unfamiliar vocabulary and have students repeat the words.

Intermediate **Preview with Pictures** Help students describe each photo. Ask: *Which places would you like to visit? Why?* Restate their responses in full sentences. Explain what natural resources are. List the natural resources students see in each photo.

Advanced **Give Opinions** Complete the Intermediate task. Then have students tell why they think we need natural resources. Model using complex language: *We need trees so that we can have oxygen to breathe.*

TIME FOR KIDS

79

Read Aloud

Read "The People Who Hugged the Trees"

LA.3.2.1.1 Understand distinguishing features of literature

GENRE: Folk Tale

Folk tales are stories that have been passed orally from generation to generation; they often teach a lesson and may be fables or legends.

Read Aloud
pages 79–83

LA.3.1.6.2 Listen to and discuss familiar text

LISTENING FOR A PURPOSE

Ask students to compare and contrast the characters, their beliefs, and their actions in "The People Who Hugged the Trees" in the **Read-Aloud Anthology**. Choose from among the teaching suggestions.

Fluency Ask students to pay attention to phrasing, expression, and tone of voice as they listen.

LA.3.2.1.7 Respond to and discuss literary selections

RESPOND TO THE FOLK TALE

Ask for students' opinions about this tale. Did they enjoy reading about the characters? Was the plot interesting? Was the story worthwhile?

Expand Vocabulary

LA.3.1.6.1 Use new vocabulary

LA.3.1.6.4 Categorize key vocabulary

Have students choose three or more words from the folk tale that relate to protecting natural resources, such as *forest, guarded, precious, build,* and *protect.* Have each student choose a natural resource and tell a partner why he or she would like to protect it, using these words.

Use routine card to teach Expand Vocabulary words in the Read Aloud lesson.

Picture Prompt

Look at the photographs. Write about the one that you like the most. You can write a poem, a story, a description, or use any other type of writing you like.

LA.3.4.1 Develop and demonstrate creative writing

Technology

For an extended lesson plan, Web site activities, and additional Read Alouds for **oral language** and **vocabulary development**, go to **www.macmillanmh.com**

Vocabulary

TEACH WORDS IN CONTEXT

Use the following routine: LA.3.1.6.1 Use new vocabulary taught directly

Routine

Define: Something that is **native** to a place grows, lives, or was born there.
Example: The elephant is native to Asia and Africa.
Ask: What is an animal that is native to the United States? EXAMPLE

- If you **shouldn't** do something, it means you should not do it. I shouldn't go to bed late, because I will be tired in the morning. What is something that you shouldn't do? EXAMPLE
- **Research** is the careful study of a particular subject. When I did research on polar bears, I learned many interesting facts about them. What is something you learned when you did library or Internet research? EXAMPLE
- LA.3.1.6.8 Use knowledge of synonyms — If a seed begins to **sprout,** it grows. Flower seeds sprout in the spring. What is a synonym for *sprout*? SYNONYM
- **Clumps** are groups or clusters of something. Clumps of weeds grew together in the empty lot. What other plants grow in clumps? EXAMPLE

Quick Check Do students understand word meanings?

During **Small Group Instruction**

If No → Approaching Level Vocabulary, p. 89N

If Yes → On Level Options, pp. 89Q–89R

Beyond Level Options, pp. 89S–89T

Real World Reading

Vocabulary
native
shouldn't
research
sprout
clumps

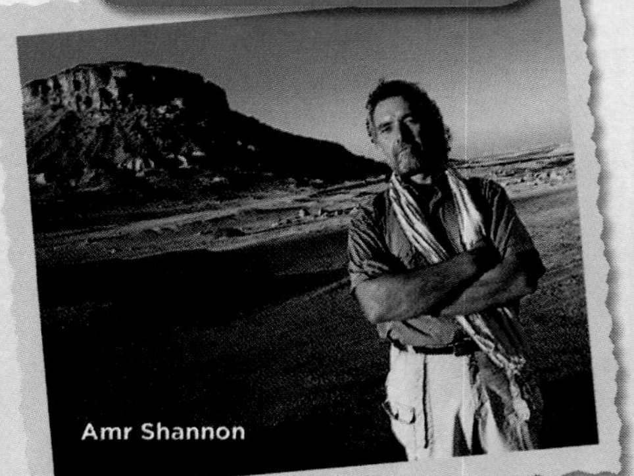
Amr Shannon

Saving Egypt's Great Desert

Egypt's vast Western Desert is 600 miles long and 900 miles wide—and it's very hot. Temperatures in the summer can go up to 100 degrees.

The Western Desert used to be one of Earth's most private spots, but now it is different. Many visitors are making it a popular tourist attraction. New roads and buildings are threatening **native** plants and animals of the desert ecosystem. Some visitors even remove priceless fossils from the desert.

Amr (AH•muhr) Shannon is an expert on the Western Desert. He wants to protect it, especially an area known as the Valley of the Whales. It is full of ancient crocodile, shark, and whale fossils.

"Fossils are disappearing at a very fast rate," says Shannon. They **shouldn't** be removed.

Shannon thinks kids between the ages of 6 and 12 can learn to protect the desert. He takes groups of kids on a two-day desert adventure for hands-on **research**. "I find that children absorb more than adults," he says. "They are the future, the ones who are really going to make a difference."

An ancient crocodile fossil from the Valley of the Whales

80

ELL Access for All

Pantomime and Gesture Pantomime going to sleep and say: *You should go to sleep early on a school night. You* (gesture "no") *shouldn't stay up late. What shouldn't you do at school?* Help students answer in full sentences.

For the word *research*, pantomime looking through a book. Say: *When you do research about a topic, you look for information in books or on the Internet.*

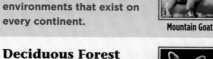

TIME FOR KIDS

Earth's Biomes

A biome is a large community of plants and animals that live in a certain type of climate. Here's a look at the seven major biomes in the world.

Polar Bear

Arctic Tundra
A cold area in the far north around the Arctic Ocean. The frozen soil makes it impossible for trees to **sprout**, or grow, from seed. It is Earth's coldest biome.

Rain Forest
A wet and humid forest that receives at least 70 inches of rain a year. **Clumps**—groups growing close together—of mosses and fungi grow on the forest floor.

Orchid

Desert
A dry area that gets very little rainfall. There are two kinds of deserts: hot and dry, or cold and dry.

Cactus

Mountains
Very cold and windy environments that exist on every continent.

Mountain Goat

Deciduous Forest
Found in mild-temperature zones. It is mostly made up of trees that lose their leaves.

Raccoon

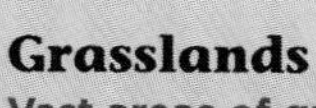

Grasslands
Vast areas of grassy fields, perfect for growing food.

Zebra

Coniferous Forest
A biome of cone-bearing trees south of the Arctic tundra.

Snowshoe Hare

Sandy Island's Best Beach

Dana Beach

Kids who live on Sandy Island in South Carolina ride to their classes on a school boat! The island has rare trees, birds, plants, and only 120 people.

When some landowners wanted to build a bridge to the mainland, the islanders feared it would ruin the natural environment. Environmentalist Dana Beach and other islanders stopped the bridge. Then he helped turn the endangered longleaf-pine forest into a nature preserve to protect it forever.

LOG ON Find out more about nature preserves at **www.macmillanmh.com**

81

FCAT Success!

Test Prep and Practice with vocabulary, pages 6–31

On Level Practice Book O, page 126

native research shouldn't sprout clumps

A. Fill in the blank in each sentence with the correct vocabulary word.

1. Students will research the climate in a desert during their trip.
2. This cactus is a native plant of the desert.
3. Visitors shouldn't harm the plant life in the desert.
4. We walked along the path among clumps of grass.
5. The weather conditions are so harsh that most plants can't sprout from seeds.

B. Write the definition next to each vocabulary word.

6. shouldn't contraction that means "should not"
7. native born in a particular place
8. clumps a group or cluster
9. sprout grow from a seed
10. research collecting information about a particular subject

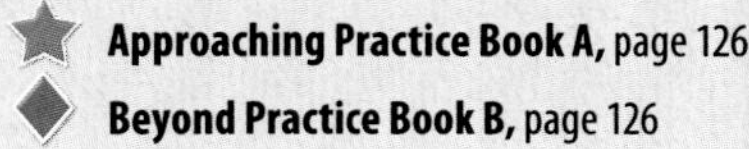
Approaching Practice Book A, page 126
Beyond Practice Book B, page 126

Vocabulary

Review last week's vocabulary words: **beamed**, **argued**, **possessions**, **fabric**, **purchased**, and **quarreling**.

LA.3.1.6 Develop grade-appropriate vocabulary

Vocabulary

LA.3.1.6 Use multiple strategies to develop grade-appropriate vocabulary

USING THE STRATEGIES

To figure out unfamiliar words, students can use phonics to decode words, look for word parts or context clues, or use a dictionary.

FCAT **STRATEGY**
WORD PARTS

LA.3.1.6.7 Use meaning of base words to determine meanings

Contractions A contraction is a word made by putting two words together and then shortening them. An apostrophe takes the place of the letters that are left out.

Point to the word *shouldn't* in "Saving Egypt's Great Desert." Explain that this is a contraction for the words *should not*. The apostrophe takes the place of the letter *o* in *not*. Write the following words and their contractions: *is not/ isn't*; *do not/don't*; *he is/he's*. Help students see that the apostrophe stands for the letter that is left out in each word.

Help students understand the difference between contractions and possessives. A contraction always contains a verb. *This isn't a book.* A possessive is always a noun that shows ownership. *This is Jan's book.*

Read "Saving Egypt's Great Desert"

LA.3.1.6 Develop grade-appropriate vocabulary

As students read "Saving Egypt's Great Desert," ask them to look for other contractions. Have them identify the words that were combined. Tell students that they will read these words again in *Washington Weed Whackers*.

Objectives

- Use the monitor comprehension strategy
- Identify the compare-and-contrast text structure
- Use academic language: *monitor comprehension, text structure, compare, contrast*

Materials

- Comprehension Transparency 18
- Leveled Practice Books, p. 127

FCAT Skills Trace

Compare and Contrast	
Introduce	U3: 347A
Practice / Apply	U3: 411B
Reteach / Review	U4: 81A–B, 82–85, 89M–T; Leveled Practice, 127–128
Assess	Weekly Tests; Unit 3, 4, 5 Tests; Benchmark Tests A, B
Maintain	U4: 281B

ELL

Use Drawings Write the word *compare* on the board. Underneath it write: *How are these things alike?* Draw a hat and a shoe on the board and have students compare them. Write the sentences on the board. Circle the signal words. Repeat the activity with the word *contrast*.

Reread for Comprehension

STRATEGY
MONITOR COMPREHENSION

LA.3.1.7.8 Use strategies to repair comprehension

Good readers **monitor comprehension** as they read. This means that they regularly stop to check that they understand what they have read. They also stop when they do not understand something. If they are confused, they can reread, read ahead, paraphrase, visualize, summarize, adjust their reading rate, or seek help to understand what they are reading. Students can use the monitor comprehension strategy to help them identify the compare-and-contrast text structure.

SKILL
COMPARE AND CONTRAST

EXPLAIN

LA.3.1.7.5 Identify how text structure impacts meaning

- Authors use the **compare-and-contrast text structure** to show how two things are alike and different.
- When authors **compare** two things, they use the signal words *like, just as, similar, both, also,* and *too.*

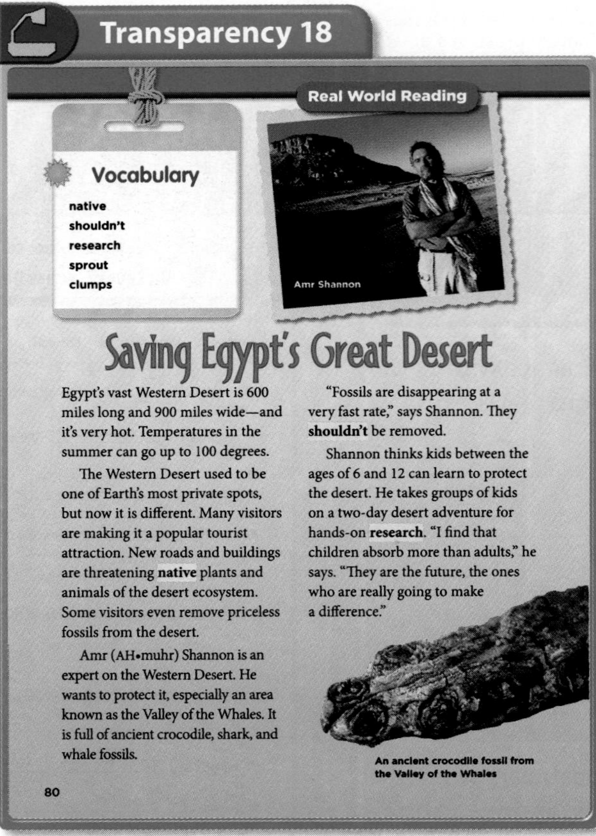

Transparency 18

Real World Reading

Vocabulary
native
shouldn't
research
sprout
clumps

Amr Shannon

Saving Egypt's Great Desert

Egypt's vast Western Desert is 600 miles long and 900 miles wide—and it's very hot. Temperatures in the summer can go up to 100 degrees.

The Western Desert used to be one of Earth's most private spots, but now it is different. Many visitors are making it a popular tourist attraction. New roads and buildings are threatening **native** plants and animals of the desert ecosystem. Some visitors even remove priceless fossils from the desert.

Amr (AH•muhr) Shannon is an expert on the Western Desert. He wants to protect it, especially an area known as the Valley of the Whales. It is full of ancient crocodile, shark, and whale fossils.

"Fossils are disappearing at a very fast rate," says Shannon. They **shouldn't** be removed.

Shannon thinks kids between the ages of 6 and 12 can learn to protect the desert. He takes groups of kids on a two-day desert adventure for hands-on **research**. "I find that children absorb more than adults," he says. "They are the future, the ones who are really going to make a difference."

An ancient crocodile fossil from the Valley of the Whales

80

Student Book page 80 available on Comprehension Transparency 18

- When authors **contrast** two things, they use the signal words *different, but,* and *on the other hand.* Identifying the compare-and-contrast text structure helps readers understand and remember nonfiction.

MODEL

Write on the board: *Today the Western Desert is very different from what it was just a few years ago. This hot, dry patch of land was once a very private place, but now it is a popular tourist attraction.*

LA.3.1.7.5 Identify the text structure an author uses

Think Aloud As I begin to read this paragraph, I notice the signal word *different.* This tells me that the author is using a compare-and-contrast text structure. Then I ask myself what is being compared and contrasted. I see that the author is contrasting how the Great Western Desert is today with how it was in the past. In the past it was very private. Today it is a popular tourist attraction. Recognizing the compare-and-contrast text structure has helped me understand this paragraph.

GUIDED PRACTICE

LA.3.1.6.2 Read and discuss conceptually challenging text

- Reread the first two paragraphs of "Saving Egypt's Great Desert" on **Student Book** page 80.
- Help students recognize other ways that the great Western Desert is different today from how it was in the past. (New roads and buildings threaten the ecosystem. Some tourists take away priceless fossils.)

APPLY

LA.3.1.7.5 Identify text structure

Have students look at the last paragraph on page 80. Ask: *How is the expert Amr Shannon like the children who visit the desert?* (Both want to protect the desert.) Then ask students: *How are the children who visit the Western Desert different from most adults who visit?* (Young people learn about the desert and find out how to protect it.)

Quick Check **Can students identify the compare-and-contrast text structure?**

During **Small Group Instruction**

If No → Approaching Level Comprehension, p. 89O

If Yes → On Level Options, pp. 89Q–89R

Beyond Level Options, pp. 89S–89T

FCAT Success!

Test Prep and Practice with compare and contrast, pages 125–152

On Level Practice Book O, page 127

When you **compare and contrast** two things, you show how they are alike and how they are different.

When comparing two things, look for signal words, such as *like, just as, similar, both, also,* and *too.*

When contrasting two things, look for signal words, such as *different, but,* and *on the other hand.*

Read this paragraph and answer the compare and contrast questions below. Possible responses provided.

My cousin lives in California, and I live in Connecticut. We enjoy visiting each other. I like the sunny, sandy beaches in California. We have sandy beaches in Connecticut, too, but they are not as big. Also it stays warm in parts of California all year long, so you can go to the beach any time you want. Back home, on the other hand, it's too cold to go to the beach in the winter.

1. What two things are compared in this selection? The beaches of California and Connecticut are compared.
2. How are the beaches alike? They are both sandy.
3. How are they different? The beaches in California are bigger. They are also sunny and warm all year long in some parts of California. People can go to beaches in Connecticut during the summer only.
4. What signal words are used to alert you that they are comparing and contrasting? too, but, on the other hand

Approaching Practice Book A, page 127

Beyond Practice Book B, page 127

Read

MAIN SELECTION
- *Washington Weed Whackers*
- FCAT **Skill:** Compare and Contrast

TEST PREP
- "Up a Creek"
- **Test Strategy:** Think and Search

SMALL GROUP OPTIONS
- Differentiated Instruction, pp. 89M–89V

Comprehension

LA.3.2.2 Identify elements of expository texts

GENRE: NONFICTION ARTICLE

Have a student read the definition of Nonfiction Article on **Student Book** page 82. Students should look for facts about the article's topic, spartina.

STRATEGY
MONITOR COMPREHENSION

LA.3.1.7.8 Use strategies to repair comprehension

To **monitor comprehension**, good readers check that they understand what they have read. If they don't understand, they can ask questions, reread, read ahead, slow down, summarize, or paraphrase.

SKILL
COMPARE AND CONTRAST

LA.3.1.7.5 Identify the text structure an author uses

Authors use the **compare-and-contrast** text structure to show how two things are alike and different. They may use signal words such as *alike*, *same*, *similar*, *both*, *different*, and *but* to show a comparison or contrast.

Real World Reading

Comprehension

Genre

Nonfiction Articles give information about real people, places, or things.

FCAT **Monitor Comprehension**

Compare and Contrast

When authors compare two topics or ideas, they often use signal words, such as *alike* and *different*.

WASHINGTON WEED WHACKERS

WHAT ALIEN SPECIES IS CREEPING ALONG THE SHORES OF PUGET SOUND?

The "weed whackers" of Lincoln Elementary, in Mount Vernon, Washington

Spartina is a perfectly good plant. It creates a habitat and food for many fish and wildlife. So why do the kids at Lincoln Elementary School in Mount Vernon, Washington, want to get rid of it? It's because spartina **shouldn't** live on the West Coast. In Washington State's Puget Sound, spartina has turned into a life-choking weed.

82

FCAT Vocabulary

Vocabulary Words Review the tested vocabulary words: **native**, **shouldn't**, **research**, **sprout**, and **clumps**.

Selection Words Students may find these words difficult. Pronounce the words and present their meanings as necessary.

alien (p. 83): something that lives in the wrong place

beds (p. 84): flat ground at the bottom of a river, lake, or sea

urging (p. 84): trying to convince or persuade someone to do something

impact (p. 85) the effect or result that one thing has on something else

LA.3.1.6.1 Use new vocabulary taught directly

TIME FOR KIDS.

Spartina is **native** to the East Coast. There, native plants and animals keep it from growing out of control. Besides providing a wetland habitat, spartina's roots stop soil from being washed away. In Washington, however, spartina is a different kind of plant. Its traits are not helpful. Spartina is an alien species since it does not grow there naturally. 2

AN ALIEN ATTACKS!

Since no animals eat spartina in Puget Sound, it grows in thick **clumps**, crowding out native plants. Its roots hurt rather than help. "It clogs up all the mud and changes the shape of the mud flats," explains student Seth Morris. In the East it creates a good habitat, but in the West, it has caused crabs, snails, salmon, and shorebirds to leave because there is less food.

This photo shows how spartina is spreading in Puget Sound and has crowded out native plants. Spartina is easy to dig up when it's young, but after a couple of years, it grows deep, thick roots and is very hard to remove.

83

Preview and Predict

LA.3.1.7.1 Use text features to make predictions

Ask students to read the title, preview text features, skim the text, ask questions before reading, and use section headers to make predictions about what weed whackers do. Have students write their predictions.

Set Purposes

LA.3.1.7.1 Use text features to establish purpose for reading

FOCUS QUESTION Discuss the question under the title of the article. Point out the Venn Diagram on **Leveled Practice Book** page 128. Students will fill it in as they read.

Read *Washington Weed Whackers*

1 **STRATEGY**
MONITOR COMPREHENSION

LA.3.1.7.8 Use strategies to repair comprehension

Teacher Think Aloud After I read the first paragraph, I'm confused. It says that spartina is a "perfectly good plant" and a "life-choking weed." Explain what you can do to better understand what you read. *(Encourage students to apply the strategy in a Think Aloud.)*

LA.3.1.7.8 Reread to repair comprehension

Student Think Aloud When I don't understand something, I stop and figure out a strategy to help me. I will reread the paragraph and look for answers. I see that spartina shouldn't live on the West Coast, but this doesn't answer my question. So I will try reading ahead. On page 83 I find the answer. Spartina is a good plant on the East Coast, but in Washington it is harmful because it is an alien species. By rereading and reading ahead, I was able to see how spartina is different in two parts of the country.

Read Together	Read Independently
If your students need support in reading the Main Selection, use the prompts to guide comprehension and model how to complete the graphic organizer. Encourage students to read aloud.	If your students can read the Main Selection independently, have them read and complete the graphic organizer. Remind students to adjust their reading rate when reading informational nonfiction.

If your students need an alternate selection, choose the **Leveled Readers** that match their instructional levels.

LA.3.1.5.2 Adjust reading rate based on purpose and text difficulty

Technology

Selection available on **Listening Library Audio CD**

Develop Comprehension

2 COMPARE AND CONTRAST

LA.3.1.7.5 Identify text structure

Look at the two paragraphs on page 83. How is spartina in the East different from spartina in Washington? How is it the same? Let's fill in a Venn Diagram. (Spartina is native to the East Coast. There it provides a wetland habitat, and its roots stop soil from being washed away. In Washington, spartina is a life-choking weed. It clogs up the mud and changes the shape of the mud flats. Spartina in Washington also causes animals to leave because there is less food. In both the East and Washington, spartina grows on the coast.)

LA.3.2.2 Analyze elements of expository texts

LA.3.6.1.1 Read informational text and organize information

LA.3.2.2.3 Organize information to show an understanding of main ideas

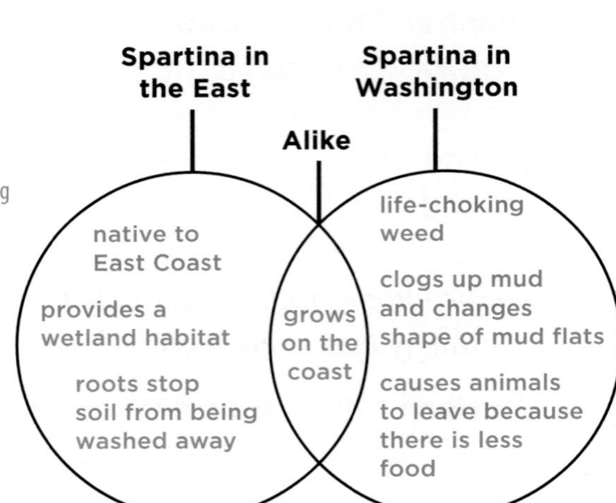

3 COMPARE AND CONTRAST

LA.3.1.7.5 Identify how text structure impacts meaning

How was the work of the student teams alike? How was it different? (All of the teams were working to help solve the problems caused by spartina. One team did research, another team made drawings, and a third team tried to get the word out. All three groups wrote letters asking for help.)

When the kids at Lincoln Elementary School took on the spartina problem, they didn't know how the plant got to the Northwest. The kids contacted local experts and hit the books to do some **research**.

WHERE DID IT COME FROM?

Students Seth Morris and Anna Hansen reported that spartina came to Puget Sound in a few ways. "Spartina goes back to the late 1800s, when it came here from the East Coast," Seth explains. Settlers wanted to raise oysters in the West. They packed them in wet spartina to keep them fresh. When the oysters were put in new beds in Puget Sound, it made spartina seeds **sprout**.

Spartina was also introduced when duck hunters planted it to attract more ducks. Engineers brought the plant in to keep soil from washing away, and farmers planted it to feed their cattle.

TAKING ACTION

3 The classes worked in teams. One team researched Padilla Bay. Another team made drawings of spartina and its effects on the shore. The third team worked to get the word out about spartina. All the kids wrote letters to state lawmakers, urging them to help.

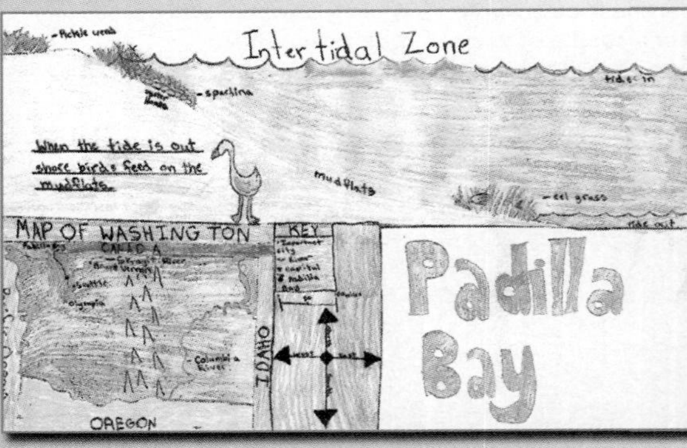

A student's drawing shows where spartina has invaded Padilla Bay.

84

FCAT Comprehension

Compare and Contrast

Explain Nonfiction authors use the compare-and-contrast text structure to show how things are alike and different. **Compare** means telling how things are alike. **Contrast** means telling how they are different. Signal words such as *alike*, *both*, and *different* tell the reader that a compare-and-contrast text structure is being used.

Discuss Write: *In the late 1800s people on the East and West Coasts had the same tastes. People on both coasts loved to eat oysters. Oysters grew on the East Coast, but they did not grow on the West Coast.* Ask: What signal words do you see? (*both*; *but*) What did people on both coasts like to eat? (oysters) What was different about the coasts? (Oysters grew in the East but not in the West.)

Apply Have students record the information in a Venn Diagram.

LA.3.1.7.5 Identify the text structure an author uses
LA.3.6.1.1 Read informational text and organize information

Getting rid of spartina takes lots of hard work and money. That's why the students wanted to teach the community about the weed. First, they held town meetings to discuss spartina's impact on the environment. They also traveled to the state capitol in Olympia to talk about the problem. The kids even headed to Padilla Bay to snip off spartina seed heads to keep the weed from spreading.

"One of the big lessons we learned from this project," says their teacher, Teresa Vaughn, "was that we can't take care of the problem by just taking care of it in our bay. This is a problem for the entire Northwest coast."

The kids know that saving Padilla Bay will be hard work. It took decades for the spartina problem to take root. It'll take many years to get rid of it.

Students from Lincoln's fifth and sixth grades became activists to fight the spartina invasion.

FCAT

Think and Compare

1. What is the difference between spartina growth in the East and in Washington?
2. Why is spartina described as an alien?
3. Why is getting rid of spartina so difficult?
4. How have people caused the problems described in "Saving Egypt's Great Desert" and "Washington Weed Whackers"?

Quick Check **Can students identify a compare-and-contrast text structure?**

During **Small Group Instruction**

If No → **Approaching Level** Leveled Reader Lesson, p. 89P

If Yes → **On Level** Options, pp. 89Q–89R

Beyond Level Options, pp. 89S–89T

PERSONAL RESPONSE

LA.3.1.7.1 Use text features to confirm predictions

Review students' predictions and purposes. Were they correct? Were they able to identify how the author compared and contrasted different elements? Have each student write a formal letter to a state senator about a natural resource he or she wants to protect.

LA.3.4.2.4 Write formal letters

Comprehension Check

SUMMARIZE

LA.3.2.2.3 Show understanding of main ideas through summarizing

Have students summarize *Washington Weed Whackers* by identifying the main ideas and relevant details. Remind students that their Venn Diagrams can help them summarize.

THINK AND COMPARE

Sample answers are given.

LA.3.1.7.5 Identify text structure

1. **Compare and Contrast:** In the East, spartina growth is kept under control by other plants and animals. In Washington, spartina grows out of control. Spartina is native to the East Coast, but is an alien species in Washington, on the West Coast.

LA.3.2.2.2 Answer questions related to relevant details

2. **Critical:** Spartina is described as an alien because it is from the East and it does not grow naturally in Washington.

LA.3.2.1.7 Connect text to self

3. **Text-to-Self:** Getting rid of spartina is difficult because it takes money, public awareness, and time. The spartina have been taking root for decades.

LA.3.2.1.7 Connect text to world

4. **Text-to-World:** Both problems have been caused by people's actions—bringing spartina to Washington, changing the Western Desert into a tourist attraction, and taking fossils from the desert.

Objectives

- Read accurately with prosody
- Rate: 82–102 WCPM
- Recognize cause-and-effect relationships

Materials

- Fluency Transparency 18
- Fluency Solutions Audio CD

Transparency 18

"Fossils are disappearing at a very fast rate," says Shannon. They shouldn't be removed.

Shannon thinks kids between the ages of 6 and 12 can learn to protect the desert. He takes groups of kids on a two-day desert adventure for hands-on research. "I find that children absorb more than adults," he says. "They are the future, the ones who are really going to make a difference."

Fluency Transparency 18

FCAT Skills Trace

Cause and Effect	
Introduce	U1: 67B
Practice / Apply	U1: 81A, 103; U3: 343A–B; Leveled Practice, 90–91
Reteach / Review	U3: 3510–P, R, T; U5: 187A–B, 188–209, 2170–P, R, T; Leveled Practice, 157–158
Assess	Weekly Tests; Unit 3 ,4, 5 Tests; Benchmark Tests A, B
Maintain	U1: 71A–B; U3: 343A–B; U4: 85A

Fluency

Repeated Reading: Pronunciation

LA.3.1.5 Demonstrate the ability to read text orally with accuracy

EXPLAIN/MODEL Model reading the passage on **Transparency 18** aloud. Point out the punctuation used in the paragraphs: periods, commas, and quotation marks. Discuss their functions: Periods indicate a full stop, commas indicate a pause, and quotation marks indicate a person speaking. Then call attention to the vocabulary word *research*, and model reading it at a slower tempo.

LA.3.1.5.2 Adjust reading rate based on text difficulty

PRACTICE/APPLY As students read aloud with you and track print, read at a moderate pace until you come to the key word *shouldn't*. Have students slowly read it aloud by themselves. Continue reading together at a moderate pace, stopping again for *research* and *absorb*. For additional practice, have students use **Leveled Practice Book** page 129 or the **Fluency Solutions Audio CD**.

Comprehension

REVIEW SKILL
CAUSE AND EFFECT

LA.3.1.7.4 Identify cause-and-effect relationships in text

EXPLAIN/MODEL

A **cause-and-effect** relationship explains how or why something happened. A **cause** is an event that makes something happen. An **effect** is something that happens because of that event or action. To identify a cause-and-effect text structure in nonfiction, look for signal words, such as *because*, *due to*, *since*, and *as a result*.

Model how to identify a cause-and-effect relationship in "Saving Egypt's Great Desert" on page 80. Point out that native plants and animals are being threatened. This is the effect. Point out how the Western Desert is now building more roads and tourist attractions. This is the cause.

PRACTICE/APPLY

LA.3.1.7.4 Identify cause-and-effect **LA.3.2.2.5** Select non-fiction materials to read **LA.3.1.7.7** Compare and contrast texts

Discuss the causes and effects in *Washington Weed Whackers*. Ask: Why do the students want to get rid of spartina? What signal word helps you figure out the cause and effect? (Spartina is a life-choking weed and should not live on the West Coast. The signal word is *because* on page 82.)

Have pairs read another short nonfiction article. Ask them to compare and contrast the two articles and the text features in the articles, and then share their findings with other pairs.

Research
Study Skills
Using Computer Search Engines in the Media Center

LA.3.6.4 Develop essential technology skills
LA.3.6.3 Develop and demonstrate an understanding of media literacy
LA.3.6.2.2 Use predetermined evaluative criteria to select reference materials
LA.3.6.1.1 Read informational text and organize information for the purpose of being informed, following multi-step directions, making a report, conducting interviews, preparing to take a test, and performing a task
LA.3.6.4.1 Use appropriate available technologies

EXPLAIN

Students can use computers in the Media Center to search the Internet for information they can read and organize.

A computer that has **Internet** access can be used as a research tool to find information about any topic. Users enter **key words** into a **search engine** and then click "Search" or type in a **URL**, or Web address, and click "Go." The search engine will show a list of Web sites that contain the key words. Users can click on a Web site's title to take them there.

Find out if the information on Web sites is trustworthy. Online encyclopedias and official sites created by universities or government agencies may be the best sources for research.

Tell students they can read and organize informational text including graphs, charts, and manuals from Web sites for the purpose of making a report, gathering information to conduct interviews, performing a task, being informed, or even taking a test.

MODEL

Display **Transparency 4**.

Think Aloud I will type in the URL for the search engine and then type in the key words *dinosaur fossils*. The search engine shows a list of sites that I can evaluate to see if I think they will be useful in my research. I think the first site looks as if it might have information I can use. The third site is just a game, so it is not useful. I will click on the boldface underlined words to go to the first site. Then I will look at the information, diagrams, charts, and illustrations, and decide if it has information about my topic.

LA.3.6.1.1 Read informational text and organize information

PRACTICE/APPLY

Ask students: Which Web site has information about dinosaur fossils in the Gobi Desert? (the second site: Dinosaur Fossils) Can you tell from the description if this site is reliable? Why or why not? (No. I don't know if an expert has helped create this site.) Which site would you go to if you wanted to learn dinosaur names? (the third site; it is a game about dinosaur names.)

Objective

- Use a computer search engine to find information

Materials

- Study Skills Transparency 4
- Leveled Practice Books, p. 130

Transparency 4

Study Skills Transparency 4

On Level Practice Book O, page 130

A **media center** in the library is a place where you can do research. One way to do research is on a computer using the Internet.
- **Search engine:** a computer program system that looks for information on the Internet using key words
- **Key words:** important words that identify a subject
- **URLs:** addresses for where you want to go on the Internet

A. Choose which URL in the box would likely have information about the topics below.

http://www.Arctictundras.com
http://www.desertplantsandanimals.com

1. How animals survive in the harsh desert climate
URL: http://www.desertplantsandanimals.com
2. Why trees cannot grow in some tundras
URL: http://www.Arctictundras.com

B. Answer the questions about key words and search engines.

3. What key words would you type in a search engine to learn about protecting oceans from pollution? pollution, water, protect
4. What key words would you type in a search engine to learn about how plants survive in a desert? desert, plants, survive

 **Approaching Practice Book A,** page 130
Beyond Practice Book B, page 130

Answer Questions

Test Strategy: Think and Search

LA.3.6.1.1 Read informational text for purpose of preparing to take a test

EXPLAIN

Good test takers know that the answer to a question is often found in more than one place.

- **Think** about what the question asks. Then, search for the answer.
- **Read** to find the information to answer the question.

Note: As students work through these test strategy pages, remind them to record their answers on separate sheets of paper.

MODEL

Question 1 Read the question and all of the answer choices.

LA.3.2.2.2 Answer questions related to relevant details

Think Aloud This question asks me to find out what pollution can do to fish in their natural habitat. I know that a fish's natural habitat is water. I need to look for information about pollution and what happens to the fish. The information may be in different places.

GUIDED PRACTICE

Have students reread parts of the selection to find words, phrases, or sentences that are helpful. Direct students' attention to the second paragraph. Make sure all students have identified and located any key phrases or sentences.

FCAT **Test Strategy**

Think and Search

The answer is in more than one place. Keep reading to find the answer.

Up a Creek

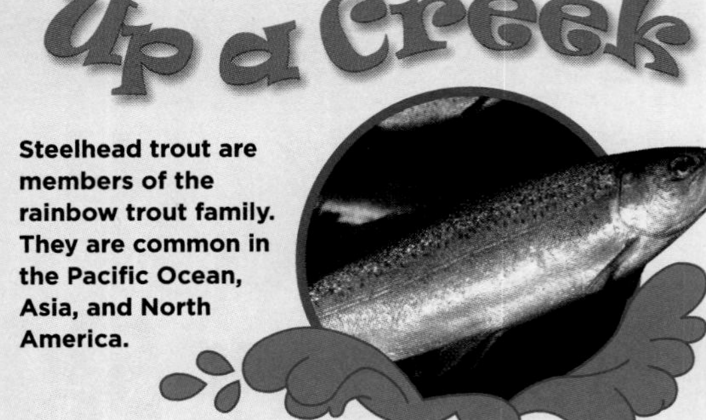

Steelhead trout are members of the rainbow trout family. They are common in the Pacific Ocean, Asia, and North America.

Students in Jean Mahoney's class worked all year to clean up Arana Creek in California. Arana Creek is part of the Arana Gulch watershed. A watershed is an area where water from rivers, creeks, rain, or snow drains into a larger body of water. The Arana Gulch watershed is a 3.5 square mile basin that includes the Arana Creek and the area around it.

Watersheds are perfect habitats for steelhead trout to lay eggs, but the Arana Gulch is polluted. The creek is clogged with sediment, or loose dirt, that falls into the bay and smothers fish eggs. Small amounts of sediment are natural and do not hurt the fish eggs. But recent storms have caused too much sediment to build up.

After Ms. Mahoney's class learned about the area's plants and animals, they went to work. They picked up trash and removed weeds. Then they planted trees and grasses to help hold the soil together. The new trees and grasses would keep the sediment from flowing into the creek. Trees also create shade which helps provide shelter for wildlife in the watershed.

After they helped control soil erosion, the students wanted to help the trout swim safely down the creek to the bay. They changed how the water flowed, making it easier for the fish to swim down the creek. The students cleared sandy areas that stuck out into the creek. These areas were stopping the steelhead trout from swimming easily.

The following spring they tested the water temperature and sediment levels. Conditions were just right for the trout. Today, the watershed is tested regularly. It is once again a good place for plants and animals to call home.

Go on

Think Aloud Paragraph 2 says the Arana Gulch area is polluted and that sediment in the creek falls into the bay, smothering fish eggs. I will keep reading. I still haven't found enough information. Paragraph 3 says students planted trees so the creek wouldn't fill up with sediment. Paragraph 4 says the water flow was changed so fish can swim easily. I know that sediment makes it hard for fish to swim. The best answer is **C**.

TIME FOR KIDS

FCAT **Now answer numbers 1 through 5. Base your answers on the article "Up a Creek."**

1. How does pollution affect fish in a natural habitat?
   - (A) It creates a watershed to protect them.
   - (B) It decreases the average water temperature.
   - (C) It makes it hard for fish to swim and for their eggs to hatch.
   - (D) It reduces the amount of sediment.

Tip
Look for key words.

2. How would you describe the students in Ms. Mahoney's class?
   - (F) excited about trout fishing
   - (G) tired of picking up trash and weeds
   - (H) interested in protecting the environment
   - (I) unhappy about working outside the classroom

3. Compare the Arana Creek before Ms. Mahoney's class cleaned it with the creek after the students helped.
   - (A) Before, the creek was part of the basin; after, it became part of a new watershed.
   - (B) Before, the creek was part of a man-made lake; after, it drained into the sea.
   - (C) Before, the creek was full of sediment; after, the water flowed easily.
   - (D) Before, the creek was 3.5 square miles; after, it was 4 miles long.

4. In what ways was Arana Creek better off after Jean Mahoney's class worked on it? Use details from the article in your answer.

5. What are some qualities of a good volunteer? How were the students in Ms. Mahoney's class good volunteers? Use information from the article in your answer.

STOP 87

FCAT Success!

Test Prep and Practice with compare and contrast, pages 125–152

LOG ON Technology

Go to **www.macmillanmh.com** for Sample Responses to questions 4 and 5.

LA.3.1.7.3 Determine explicit information

ADDITIONAL GUIDED PRACTICE

Question 2 After reading the entire question, point out that students need to reread the parts of the selection to find the answer. Tell students that this often means they need to think about what they know and search for clues. Help them see that in paragraph 1, the author mentions how hard the class worked to clean up the Arana Creek. In paragraph 3, Ms. Mahoney's class was determined to continue to protect the animals and plants by cleaning up the areas around the creek. So, the best answer is choice H.

LA.3.1.7.8 Reread to repair comprehension

Question 3 Read question 3 and all of the answer choices. Have students use the Think and Search strategy to choose an answer. After students have chosen an answer, ask: *What does the question ask you to do?* (Compare the Arana Creek before and after Ms. Mahoney's class cleaned it up.) *Where did you search for the answer?* (in paragraphs 2 and 4) *What seems to be the best answer? Why?* (C, because it describes how students helped to improve the creek.) *To choose the best answer, what did you need to do?* (keep reading) *What is the best answer?* (The best answer is C.)

LA.3.2.2.2 Answer questions related to explicitly stated relevant details

Students answer the following:

LA.3.2.2.2 Answer questions related to explicitly stated details

Question **4** and **Question 5** Read both questions aloud and point out the "Read/Think/Explain" icon in each. Note that these two questions do not include answer choices as do the first three questions. Explain that these questions require written responses.

See the Constructed Response Rubrics on page 149H.

Connect Language Arts

WRITING WORKSHOP
- Write to a Prompt
- Research and Inquiry

WORD STUDY
- Words in Context
- Contractions
- **Phonics:** Words with Soft *c* and *g*
- Vocabulary Building

SPELLING
- Words with Soft *c* and *g*

GRAMMAR
- Main and Helping Verbs

SMALL GROUP OPTIONS
- Differentiated Instruction, pp. 89M–89V

Writing Prompt

LA.3.6.1.1 Read and organize information for purpose of preparing to take a test

EXPLAIN

Tell students that often when taking a test, they will be asked to write to a prompt. Explain that a prompt introduces or gives information about a writing topic, and then provides instructions about a specific writing assignment related to the information. Explain to students that most prompts will fall under two types of writing or writing modes: expository prompts, which ask the writer to explain something, or narrative prompts, which ask the writer to tell a story.

Before students begin to write to a prompt, they need to find the following information:

- What is the mode or type of writing? Is the prompt expository or narrative?

Writing: Narrative

Write to a Prompt

FCAT Sometimes people have amazing things happen to them. Think about an amazing thing that could happen to you. Now write about this amazing thing that could happen to you.

Narrative writing tells a story about a personal or fictional experience.

To figure out if a writing prompt asks for narrative writing, look for clue words, such as write about, tell what happened, and write a story.

Below see how one student begins a response to the prompt above.

The beginning of the story explains the setting, or where the story takes place.

Today was the big day! I had volunteered to talk about our school fundraising project on TV. I entered the studio ready for my big TV break.

Soon, we went on live. First, I answered questions. Then I said, "We need to educate people about the needs of others in their communities. Local shelters should be well-stocked for emergencies. This takes time and money."

Then the host said, "We have someone here who can help you with that."

Suddenly, the President of the United States walked onto the stage. "I think I can help," he said. The President handed me a check for two million dollars!

88

- What is the **purpose** for writing? What is the actual assignment?
- Does the prompt call for a specific **form** or **format**?

LA.3.3.5.1 Prepare writing in format appropriate to audience and purpose; **LA.3.4.1.2** Employ appropriate format

Determine the Writing Mode Read the prompt above the student model aloud. Then draw students' attention to the information in the bubbles. Review the definition of narrative writing. Point out the clue words in the bubble and the specific clue words in the prompt.

Determine the Purpose Ask: *What clues tell the student what the writing should be about?* Point out the second and third sentences. Explain that the second sentence tells the student to think about the topic. (Think about an amazing thing that could happen to you.)

Writing Prompt

Respond in writing to the prompt below. Before you write, read the Writing Hints for Prompts. Remember to review the hints after you finish writing.

FCAT

People sometimes have unusual days.
Think about how a day could be unusual.
Now write a story about an unusual day.

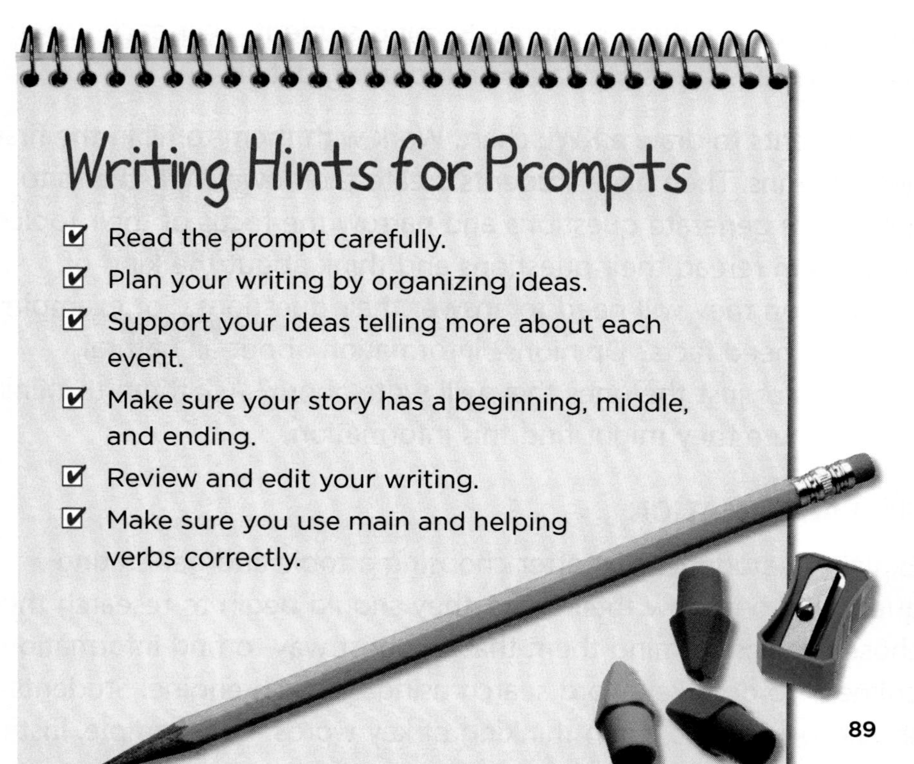

Writing Hints for Prompts

- ☑ Read the prompt carefully.
- ☑ Plan your writing by organizing ideas.
- ☑ Support your ideas telling more about each event.
- ☑ Make sure your story has a beginning, middle, and ending.
- ☑ Review and edit your writing.
- ☑ Make sure you use main and helping verbs correctly.

89

LA.3.3.1.2 Determine purpose of writing piece

PRACTICE

Work with students to read the writing prompt on **Student Book** page 89 and find the clues that determine the correct mode and purpose.

Writing Mode This is a narrative prompt. The student is being asked to tell a story.

Purpose The student is being asked to write a story about an unusual day.

LA.3.4.1.1 Write narratives based on imagined events

APPLY

Writing Prompt Students can practice writing from the prompt, simulating a test-taking situation. Distribute 3–4 sheets of paper per student for the response. After students have analyzed the prompt, tell them they will have 45 minutes to write their responses.

LA.3.3.1.3 Use organizational strategies for writing

LA.3.3.4 Edit and correct draft for standard language conventions

Tell students: You may use scrap paper to organize your thoughts before you begin to draft your essay. I will tell you when you have 15 minutes left to finish the essay. Be sure to use Writing Hints for Prompts to help you draft, revise, and edit for language conventions.

SCORING RUBRIC

6 Points	5 Points	4 Points	3 Points	2 Points	1 Point
Focus Writing is on topic and complete. **Organization** Writing is logically organized, with a variety of sentence structures used. **Support** There are ample supporting ideas and word choice is precise. **Conventions** Correct grammar and complete sentences are used.	**Focus** Writing is on topic. **Organization** Writing has a generally successful organizational pattern. **Support** Supporting details are included. Word choice is adequate but may lack precision. **Conventions** Various sentence structures have been used. Punctuation, grammar, and spelling are generally correct.	**Focus** Writing is generally on topic. Some loosely related information is included. **Organization** An organizational pattern is evident, although lapses occur. **Support** Details or ideas are not fully developed. Word choice is adequate. **Conventions** Knowledge of grammar, spelling, and punctuation is evident.	**Focus** Writing is generally on topic, although irrelevant information is included. **Organization** An organizational pattern has been attempted. **Support** Some supporting ideas are not developed. Word choice is limited. **Conventions** Knowledge of grammar, spelling, and punctuation conventions is evident. Many sentences are simple.	**Focus** Writing is somewhat related to the topic but offers few supporting details **Organization** An organizational pattern is not evident. Word choice is limited and immature. **Support** Few supporting details are offered. **Conventions** Frequent errors occur in grammar, spelling, and punctuation. Most sentences are simple constructions.	**Focus** Writing minimally address the topic. **Organization** No organizational pattern is evident. **Support** Details are irrelevant, and word choice is immature. **Conventions** Frequent errors in grammar, spelling, and punctuation impede communication. Sentence structure is simple at best.

Go to **www.macmillanmh.com** for **Anchor Papers** on the writing prompt.

Research and Inquiry

LA.3.3.5 Publish final product for intended audience

Publishing Options

To publish, students can make neat final copies using their best handwriting or use digital tools and type the articles on the computer. Students can bind their articles together to make a natural resources magazine. Students can also read aloud their articles as "authorities" on a radio or TV program, identifying their sources.

Speaking and Listening

SPEAKING STRATEGIES

- Prepare and practice your presentation.
- Use vocabulary related to the subject.
- Organize with a clear beginning, middle, and end.

LISTENING STRATEGIES

- Look at the speaker.
- Listen for the main details and essential ideas.
- Paraphrase what you hear and identify new vocabulary.

LA.3.5.2 Apply listening and speaking strategies; LA.3.5.2.2 Give an oral presentation; LA.3.5.2.1 Interpret information presented orally

6-Point Scoring Rubric

Use the rubrics on pages **149G** to score published writing.

Writing Process

For a complete lesson, see Unit Writing on pages 421A-421H. Go to **www.macmillanmh.com** for **Anchor Papers** on Narrative Writing for samples on different writing levels.

Article

LA.3.3.2.1 Use prewriting plan to develop main idea with supporting details

LA.3.6.2.1 Determine information needed by narrowing a topic

GENERATE QUESTIONS

What I Know	What I Want to Know	What I Learned
Trees help people and animals.	What would happen if there were no trees?	

Direct students to the vocabulary passage "Sandy Island's Best Beach" on **Student Book** page 81. Explain that each student will write a short magazine article about a natural resource. Remind students that each article should include a main idea and supporting details.

Ask students to draw a KWL chart. Work with them to fill in the first two columns. Then have students create their own KWL charts to help them generate questions and narrow the focus of their topics. Have them reread their questions and think about the kind of information they will need to answer their questions. For example: Will they need facts? Opinions? Information about all natural resources or just the ones they will write about? Ask them to think about where they might find this information.

LA.3.6.2.2 Select reference materials

LA.3.6.4.1 Use appropriate available technologies

LA.3.6.2.1 Identify key words

FIND INFORMATION

Explain to students that after choosing a topic and generating questions to narrow their focus, they should begin to research their chosen topics. Remind them that the best way to find information online is to do a key word search using a search engine. Students should be specific when thinking of key words. For example, instead of entering *natural resources*, enter a specific resource such as *water*.

LA.3.6.1.1 Organize information for different purposes
LA.3.6.2.4 Record basic bibliographic data and recognize intellectual property rights

ORGANIZE INFORMATION

Emphasize to students that gathering interesting and useful information about a topic is only one step in completing a research project: The information they gather must be organized. Use the **Take Notes** minilesson on the next page and **Transparency 69** to show students how to cite and organize their research to keep track of their sources. Use the **Organize Information** minilesson on the next page and **Transparency 70** to help them create flowcharts.

LA.3.3.2 Write a draft
LA.3.3.3 Revise draft
LA.3.3.2.1 Use prewriting plan to develop main idea with supporting details

SYNTHESIZE AND WRITE

Have students draft their articles, using an effective organizational pattern with main ideas and supporting details. They should give the articles interesting titles and use headings and subheadings that reflect main ideas. Show **Transparency 71** and discuss the draft. Then display **Transparency 72** and discuss changes. Have students revise their articles, exchange with partners, and review.

Writer's Toolbox

Take Notes

Explain to students that they should take notes to organize their research and keep track of sources and multiple representations of information, including encyclopedias, books, magazines, Internet, and other types of media.

- Display **Transparency 69**. Discuss how to take notes.
- For each source, students should include the author's name, the title of the book, article, or Web site, and other publishing information.
- Tell them to compare and contrast ideas they find in at least two sources.

LA.3.6.1.1 Read informational text for purpose of making a report; LA.3.4.2.2 Record information related to a topic; LA.3.6.2.2 Select multiple representations of information; LA.3.6.2.4 Record basic bibliographic data and recognize intellectual property rights

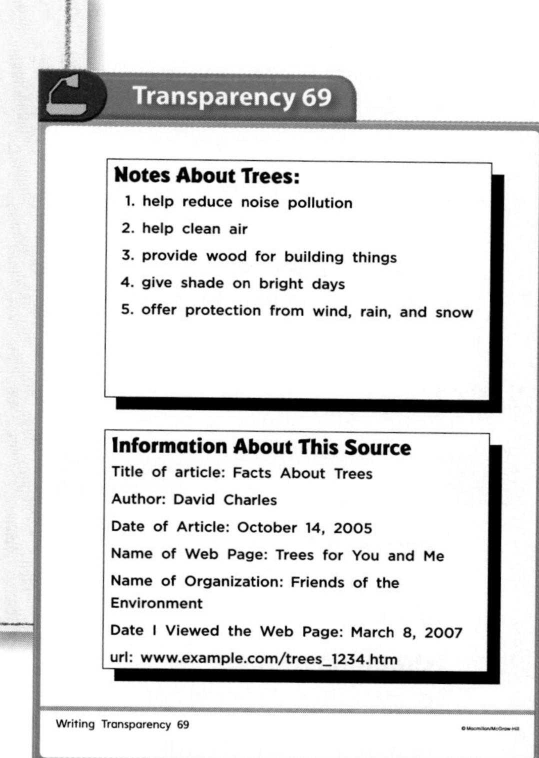
Transparency 69

Notes About Trees:
1. help reduce noise pollution
2. help clean air
3. provide wood for building things
4. give shade on bright days
5. offer protection from wind, rain, and snow

Information About This Source
Title of article: Facts About Trees
Author: David Charles
Date of Article: October 14, 2005
Name of Web Page: Trees for You and Me
Name of Organization: Friends of the Environment
Date I Viewed the Web Page: March 8, 2007
url: www.example.com/trees_1234.htm

Writing Transparency 69

Writing Transparency 69

ORGANIZATION

Flowchart

Explain to students that making a flowchart helps a writer organize information and see how it is related. Students will use their notes to make charts that will help them write their drafts.

Display **Transparency 70**. Use it to discuss with students how to create a flowchart. Point out that each section has a clear controlling main idea supported by details. The chart moves in order from beginning to middle to end.

Writing Transparency 70

LA.3.6.1.1 Organize information for purpose of making a report; LA.3.3.1.3 Use organizational strategies to make a plan for writing; LA.3.3.2.2 Organize information into logical sequence

SUPPORT

Research Tips

Remind students to evaluate the information by asking themselves these questions:

- Is the information accurate and current?
- Who is the author? Is he or she an expert source?
- Will this information help me write my report?
- Is this material too difficult to read? Do I need to find another source?

LA.3.6.2.2 Use predetermined evaluative criteria to select reference materials

Word Study

Objectives

- Apply knowledge of word meanings and context clues
- Identify and apply knowledge of contractions
- Use academic language: *contraction, apostrophe*

Materials

- Vocabulary Transparency 35
- Vocabulary Strategy Transparency 36
- Leveled Practice Books, p. 131

Vocabulary

native (p. 83) originally living or growing in a place

shouldn't (p. 82) contraction of *should not*

research (p. 84) careful study or investigation in order to learn facts

sprout (p. 84) to begin to grow

clumps (p. 83) groups or clusters, as of dirt or plants

ELL — Access for All

Word Webs Make individual word webs with *clumps, research,* and *sprout.* Prompt with: *What things can you find in clumps? What resources do you use when you do research? Name things that can sprout.*

Review

Vocabulary

Words in Context

LA.3.1.6.3 Use context clues to determine meaning

EXPLAIN/MODEL

Review the meanings of the vocabulary words. Display **Transparency 35**. Model how to use context clues and word meanings to complete the first sentence.

Transparency 35

native shouldn't research sprout clumps

1. Scientists have done much research to help them learn about plants.
2. Sometimes plants grow close together, in clumps.
3. People shouldn't let weeds take over their gardens.
4. Those plants are not native to this part of the country.
5. Give those seeds water and they will sprout into healthy plants.

Vocabulary Transparency 35

Think Aloud The first sentence tells about something scientists have done to learn about plants. I know that research has to do with learning. Would it make sense for scientists to have done research? Yes, it would. *Research* is the best word to use here.

PRACTICE/APPLY

Ask volunteers to identify clues to the missing word in item 2. Then have students complete the remaining items on their own. Partners can exchange papers, check each other's answers, and discuss what context clues they used.

Concept Definition Maps Have student groups draw concept definition maps with a vocabulary word or another word from the selection in the center and three surrounding boxes labeled *What Is It?, What Is It Like?,* and *Description.* Ask: *What is this word? What is it like? Can you describe it?* Groups can complete maps and use them to create their own definitions and sentences.

LA.3.1.6 Develop grade-appropriate vocabulary
LA.3.1.6.1 Use new vocabulary

STRATEGY
WORD PARTS: CONTRACTIONS

EXPLAIN/MODEL

LA.3.1.6 Use multiple strategies to develop grade-appropriate vocabulary

Access for All

- Explain that a **contraction** is a word made by putting two words together and then shortening them.
- Point out that an apostrophe takes the place of the letter or letters that are left out.

Point out *it's* on page 82 of *Washington Weed Whackers*. Model how the two words *it is* were combined to form this contraction. Review the contractions at the top of **Transparency 36**.

Transparency 36

WORD PARTS: CONTRACTIONS

she + is = she's	should + not = shouldn't
you + have = you've	did + not = didn't
that + is = that's	it + will = it'll

1. Mary said that she's really interested in learning about plants. (she's, she is)
2. Joe thinks that's a great thing for her to do. (that's, that is)
3. We shouldn't let weeds keep other plants from growing. (shouldn't, should not)
4. Mary says it'll take a lot of hard work to clean up the weeds. (it'll, it will)

Vocabulary Strategy Transparency 36

PRACTICE/APPLY

LA.3.1.6 Develop grade-appropriate vocabulary

Help students identify the contraction and the two words that form it in item 1. Then have students complete items 2–4 and then write their own sentences using the contractions.

Quick Check

Can students use context clues to figure out word meanings and identify and form contractions?

During **Small Group Instruction**

If No → **Approaching Level** Vocabulary, pp. 89N–89O

If Yes → **On Level** Options, pp. 89Q–89R

Beyond Level Options, pp. 89S–89T

ELL Access for All

Use Gestures To teach contractions, hold up a finger from each hand to represent each word as you say: *He is*. Repeat this with students a few times. Then put your fingers together and say the contraction. Repeat this with students a few times. Repeat for each contraction.

Vocabulary

Review last week's vocabulary words. Have students choose three words and use each in a sentence with a contraction. Have partners share their sentences.

FCAT Success!

Test Prep and Practice with vocabulary, pages 6–31

On Level Practice Book O, page 131

Contractions are made when two words are put together in a shortened form. An apostrophe is used to show that one or more letters have been left out to form the contraction.

A. Write the contraction for each pair of words.

1. I am I'm	6. that is that's
2. they are they're	7. did not didn't
3. do not don't	8. she is she's
4. we will we'll	9. have not haven't
5. we are we're	10. could not couldn't

B. Fill in the blank in each sentence with the correct contraction from the box.

they'll wouldn't it's he'll

11. When the team is ready, they'll run onto the field.
12. Everyone agrees that it's about time to go home.
13. Did Hector say when he'll be arriving?
14. It wouldn't hurt to bring an umbrella because there is a chance of rain.

Approaching Practice Book A, page 131

Beyond Practice Book B, page 131

Objectives

- Segment and blend words with soft *c* and soft *g*
- Decode words with /s/ and /j/

Materials

- Leveled Practice Books, p. 132
- Teacher's Resource Book, pp. 95–98

ELL Access for All

Mimic On the board draw pictures of a bicycle and a gem. Pronounce the words as you underline the /s/ and /j/ sounds. Write: *cell, police, ice, germ, gym, giant*. Have students repeat the words alone and in sentences.

Phonics

Decode Words with Soft *c* and *g*

EXPLAIN/MODEL

LA.3.1.4 Demonstrate knowledge of alphabetic principle

- The letter *c* can have the /k/ sound as in *cake*, or the /s/ sound as in *city*. When *c* is followed by *i*, *e*, or *y*, it usually has the /s/ sound.
- The letter *g* can have the /g/ sound as in *give*, or the /j/ sound as in *giant*, *gems*, *gyms*, and *age*. When *g* is followed by *i*, *e*, or *y*, it often has the /j/ sound.
- To pronounce a *c* or *g* in a word, try both sounds.

Write the word *gems*.

LA.3.1.4.4 Use self-correction when subsequent reading indicates an earlier misreading

Think Aloud I am not sure how to say this word. I know that *g* can have the /g/ sound in *get*, or the /j/ sound in *gyms*. I will try saying the word both ways. /g/ /e/ /m/ /z/, /gemz/. That doesn't make sense, so I'll try it with the /j/ sound. /j/ /e/ /m/ /z/, /jemz/. That's a word I know. The letter *g* has the /j/ sound in *gems*.

PRACTICE/APPLY

Write these words on the board: *cent*, *trace*, *circus*, *page*, *gym*, *giant*, *gift*. Have students underline the letters that stand for the /s/ and /j/ sounds. Segment the sounds in each word and have students repeat after you. Then have students say each word.

LA.3.1.4.3 Decode multi-syllabic words in isolation and in context

Decode Multisyllabic Words Have students use their knowledge of phonics patterns, compound words, and word parts to decode long words. Write *dangerous*, *vegetable*, *celebration*, *cyclone*, and *Pacific*. Model how to decode *dangerous*, focusing on the /j/ sound of the letter *g*. Then help students to decode the remaining words and read them aloud. For more practice in decoding multisyllabic words, see decodable passages on **Teacher's Resource Book** pages 95–98.

LA.3.1.6 Use multiple strategies to develop vocabulary

Picture Dictionary Have students make and illustrate a picture dictionary for words with soft *c* and soft *g*, such as *cent*, *circus*, *circle*, *pencil*, *giant*, and *vegetable*.

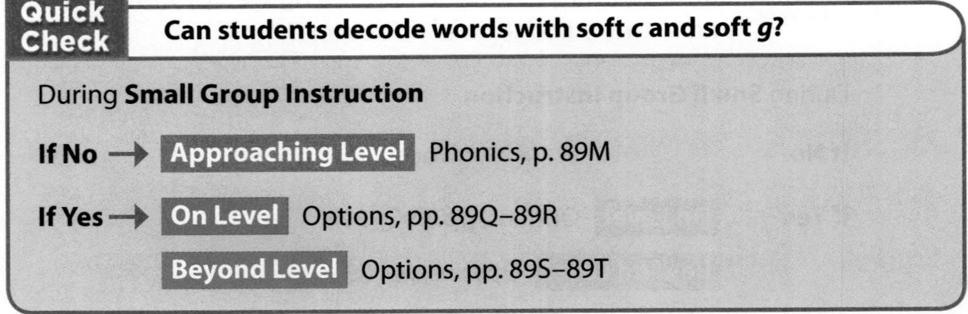

Quick Check Can students decode words with soft *c* and soft *g*?

During **Small Group Instruction**

If No → **Approaching Level** Phonics, p. 89M

If Yes → **On Level** Options, pp. 89Q–89R

Beyond Level Options, pp. 89S–89T

On Level Practice Book O, page 132

The letters *c* or *g* usually stand for a soft sound when they are followed by the vowel letters *e*, *i*, or *y*. Read the following words. Notice the **soft *c*** or **soft *g*** sound in each.

gentle engine cell city

A. Fill in the blank in each word with a *c* or a *g*.

cycle center iceberg core danger fence stage

1. The life __c__ycle of a butterfly begins with an egg.
2. It is common to see an i__c__eberg floating in the arctic waters.
3. The hot, dry climate of the desert can be a dan__g__er to a hiker who is not prepared.
4. Many rain forests are located near the __c__enter of Earth.
5. Some people build a fen__c__e to protect the flowers and trees in their yard.

B. Circle the words in each group that have a soft *c* or soft *g* sound.

6. (central) (nice) cute, cherry
7. (gem) get, (germ) garden
8. ghost, guess, (stage) (gesture)
9. (circle) can't, (celery) cactus
10. guppy, (giraffe) (gerbil) goldfish

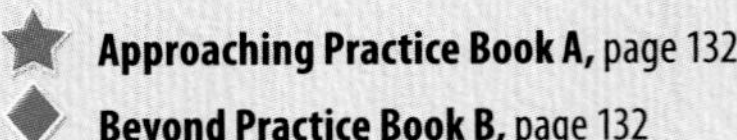

Approaching Practice Book A, page 132

Beyond Practice Book B, page 132

Vocabulary Building

LA.3.1.6 Use multiple strategies to develop vocabulary

LA.3.1.6.4 Categorize key vocabulary

Oral Language

Expand Vocabulary Work with students to brainstorm examples of natural resources and ways to protect them. Have students write the words in a chart.

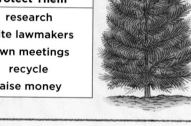

Natural Resources	
What They Are	**How to Protect Them**
air	research
water	write lawmakers
trees	town meetings
land	recycle
	raise money

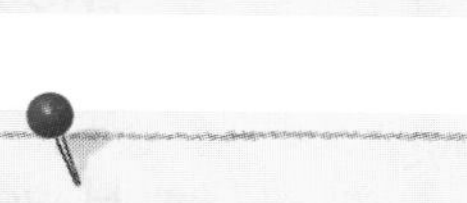

Vocabulary Building

Antonyms Antonyms are words that have opposite meanings, such as *big* and *little*. In the weekly reading, *native* and *alien* are antonyms. Have students use a thesaurus to find antonyms for *protect*, *create*, *helpful*, and *hard*. Have them record the antonyms on a chart.

Words	Antonyms
protect	harm
create	destroy; ruin
helpful	harmful
hard	easy

Create a similar chart using antonyms for last week's vocabulary words *purchased* and *argued*.

LA.3.1.6.8 Use knowledge of antonyms

LA.3.1.6.1 Use new vocabulary

Apply Vocabulary

Write a Paragraph Have each student use the words *native, shouldn't, research, sprout,* and *clumps* in a paragraph about a habitat. Students can read their paragraphs aloud to the class.

Spiral Review

Vocabulary Game Review last week's words and this week's words. Then have students play a word guessing game using the words *gnaws, package, politely, recipes, purchased, clumps, argued, possessions, purchased,* and *sprout*. Divide the class into two teams.

- Place the word cards facedown in a pile.
- A player from Team A draws a card and gives his/her teammates clues to the word's meaning.
- If the teammates guess the correct word, the team gets a point and keeps the card. If not, the card is placed at the bottom of the pile.
- Then Team B takes a turn. Play continues until the teams have defined all the words. The team with the most cards wins.

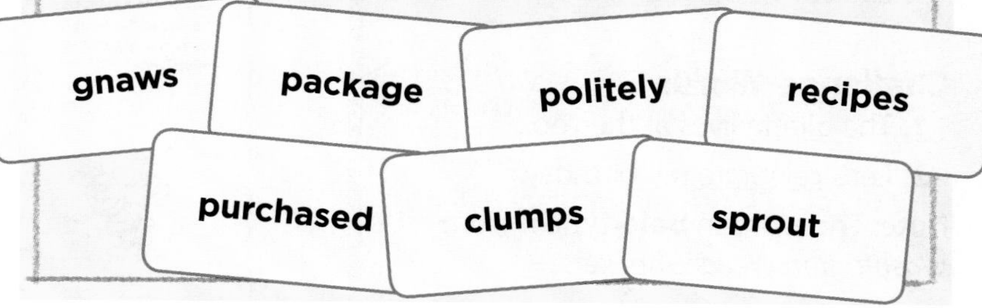

LA.3.1.6.1 Use new vocabulary

Technology

Vocabulary PuzzleMaker

For additional vocabulary and spelling games, go to www.macmillanmh.com

5 Day Spelling

Spelling Words

cell	city	giant
gems	cents	changes
age	price	pages
place	space	gentle
gyms	nice	message

Review crowd, clouds, found

Challenge giraffe, celebrate

Dictation Sentences

1 A <u>cell</u> is a small plain room.
2. Diamonds are my favorite <u>gems</u>.
3. What is your <u>age</u>?
4. Our town is a nice <u>place</u>.
5. We like going to new <u>gyms</u>.
6. We live in a large <u>city</u>.
7. Give me fifty <u>cents</u>, please.
8. What is the <u>price</u> of this book?
9. Rockets travel in <u>space</u>.
10. Those are <u>nice</u> shoes.
11. He is as tall as a <u>giant</u>.
12. Tim **<u>changes</u>** his clothes after school.
13. How many <u>pages</u> have you read?
14. Be <u>gentle</u> with the baby chick.
15. I'll give her the <u>message</u>.

Review Words

1. I saw a large <u>crowd</u> at the movies.
2. I saw rain <u>clouds</u> in the sky.
3. Look at what I <u>found</u>.

Challenge Words

1. The <u>giraffe</u> lives at the zoo.
2. Let's <u>celebrate</u> my birthday.

Note: The word in **bold** type is from *Washington Weed Whackers*.

Display the Spelling Words throughout the week.

LA.3.3.4.1 Correctly use spelling; LA.3.1.4 Demonstrate knowledge of alphabetic principle

Words with Soft *c* and *g*

Day 1 Pretest

ASSESS PRIOR KNOWLEDGE

Use the Dictation Sentences. Say the underlined word, read the sentence, and repeat the word. Have students write the words on **Spelling Practice Book** page 109. For a modified list, use the first 12 Spelling Words and the Review Words. For a more challenging list, use Spelling Words 3–15 and the Challenge Words. Have students correct their own tests.

Have students cut apart the Spelling Words Cards BLM on **Teacher's Resource Book** page 131 and find a way to sort them. Have them save the cards to use during the week.

Students can use Spelling Practice Book page 110 for independent practice.

For leveled Spelling word lists, go to **www.macmillanmh.com**

Day 2 Word Sorts

TEACHER AND STUDENT SORTS

- Review the Spelling Words, point out the soft *c* and *g* spellings, and discuss meanings. Point out the unusual spelling of *gyms*.
- Use the cards on the Spelling Word Cards BLM. Attach the key words *ice* and *germs* to a bulletin board.
- Model how to sort words with soft *c* and *g*. Place the cards beneath the correct key words.
- Have students take turns choosing cards, sorting them, and explaining how they sorted them.
- Have students use their own Spelling Word Cards. They can place the key words on their desks, sort the Spelling Words three times, and write the last sort on Spelling Practice Book page 111.

Spelling Practice Book, pages 109–110

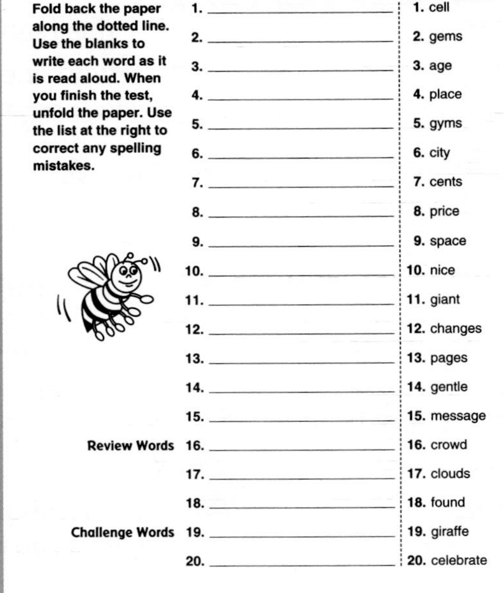

Fold back the paper along the dotted line. Use the blanks to write each word as it is read aloud. When you finish the test, unfold the paper. Use the list at the right to correct any spelling mistakes.

	1. ______	1. cell
	2. ______	2. gems
	3. ______	3. age
	4. ______	4. place
	5. ______	5. gyms
	6. ______	6. city
	7. ______	7. cents
	8. ______	8. price
	9. ______	9. space
	10. ______	10. nice
	11. ______	11. giant
	12. ______	12. changes
	13. ______	13. pages
	14. ______	14. gentle
	15. ______	15. message
Review Words	16. ______	16. crowd
	17. ______	17. clouds
	18. ______	18. found
Challenge Words	19. ______	19. giraffe
	20. ______	20. celebrate

Spelling Practice Book, page 111

cell	place	cents	nice	pages
gems	gyms	price	giant	gentle
age	city	space	changes	message

Word Sort

Write the spelling words that have soft *c* spelled:

c
1. city

ce
2. cell
3. nice
4. place
5. space
6. cents
7. price

Write the spelling words that have soft *g* spelled:

g
8. gyms
9. giant
10. gems
11. gentle

ge
12. age
13. pages
14. message

Rhyme Time

Write the spelling word that rhymes with each word below.

15. face space
16. cages pages
17. bell cell
18. pity city
19. rims gyms
20. ranges changes

LA.3.3.4.1 Edit for correct use of spelling

Day 3 Word Meanings

DEFINITIONS

Display the definitions below. Have students write the clues and the Spelling Words that go with them in their word study notebooks.

1. the opposite of mean (nice)
2. pieces of paper in a book (pages)
3. another name for pennies (cents)
4. how old a person is (age)
5. rubies are one type (gems)

Challenge students to come up with clues for other Spelling Words, including Review Words and Challenge Words.

Have partners write sentences for each Spelling Word, leaving blanks where the words should go. Then have them trade papers and write the missing words.

Day 4 Review and Proofread

SPIRAL REVIEW

Review words with /ou/. Write: *crowd, clouds, found.* Have students identify the letters that spell the /ou/ sound.

PROOFREAD/EDIT

Write the sentence below. Have students proofread/edit to correct the errors.

The prise is four dollars and fifty sents. (price, cents)

BLIND SORT

Partners use their Spelling Word Cards and each write key words *ice* and *germ* on a sheet of paper. Then students take turns. One draws cards and says the words. The other writes them under the key words. After both have finished, they can check each other's papers.

Day 5 Assess and Reteach

POSTTEST

Use the Dictation Sentences on page 89G for the Posttest.

If students have difficulty with any words in the lesson, have them place them on a list called "Spelling Words I Want to Remember" in their word study notebooks.

WORD STUDY NOTEBOOK

Challenge students to search for other words with soft *c* and *g* in their reading for the week and write them in their word study notebooks under the heading "Other Words with Soft *c* and *g*."

Students can add their words to a Word Wall.

Remind students to spell words with soft *c* and *g* correctly as they edit their weekly writing.

Spelling Practice Book, page 112

cell	place	cents	nice	pages
gems	gyms	price	giant	gentle
age	city	space	changes	message

It Takes Three

Write a spelling word that goes with the other two words.

1. cost, amount, price
2. jewelry, charms, gems
3. coins, change, cents
4. town, village, city
5. calm, tender, gentle

Words in Sentences

Write a spelling word to complete each sentence.

1. There are many pages inside a book.
2. There was a time when the Earth was a cold and frosty place.
3. Dinosaurs lived during a different age.
4. You get 5 cents for each bottle you recycle.
5. We won't cut down trees to make space for a mall.
6. You must be gentle when you pet animals.
7. There are giant trees in the redwood forest.
8. We had a "Save the Forest" meeting in each of the school gyms.
9. My sister looked at a plant cell under a microscope.
10. You cannot put a price on nature.
11. They mine for gems in those mountains.
12. I left a message on her answering machine.
13. The actor changes his costume in the play.
14. The nice woman never litters.
15. The pollution from the city is hurting the forest nearby.

Spelling Practice Book, page 113

Proofreading

There are six spelling mistakes in this paragraph. Circle the misspelled words. Write the words correctly on the lines below.

What You Can Do to Help Save the Planet

There are several ways to help take care of nature in your town. Write to your sitti mayor about a pollution problem. This will tell him or her that you are worried about the environment. You can raise money, too. Save your extra sence. Even spare change can help buy a tree. You can then plant it on your street or in a public park. Remember to always be jentl with animals. We all have to share the same natural space. You should be nys to any wildlife you find. Never litter. This only makes the roads and grassy areas dirty. Save your plastic bottles. Buy a ginte can to put them in. When you have enough, take them in for recycling. The most important thing you can do is this: Tell others about keeping our world clean. Pass on this important mesaje to everyone you know.

1. city
2. cents
3. gentle
4. nice
5. giant
6. message

Writing Activity

Write a paragraph about what you can do to help the planet. Use at least three spelling words in your paragraph.

Spelling Practice Book, page 114

Look at the words in each set below. One word in each set is spelled correctly. Look at Sample A. The letter next to the correctly spelled word in Sample A has been shaded in. Do Sample B yourself. Shade the letter of the word that is spelled correctly. When you are sure you know what to do, go on with the rest of the page.

Sample A:
Ⓐ caige
Ⓑ cage
Ⓒ caje
Ⓓ cayj

Sample B:
Ⓔ rice
Ⓕ ryse
Ⓖ ryce
Ⓗ raice

1. Ⓐ sel Ⓑ cell Ⓒ selle Ⓓ cel
2. Ⓔ jems Ⓕ jehms Ⓖ gems Ⓗ gehms
3. Ⓐ aig Ⓑ aje Ⓒ age Ⓓ adje
4. Ⓔ place Ⓕ playce Ⓖ plase Ⓗ plaise
5. Ⓐ jyms Ⓑ gyms Ⓒ jims Ⓓ gims
6. Ⓔ city Ⓕ sity Ⓖ citty Ⓗ cety
7. Ⓐ zents Ⓑ sence Ⓒ cents Ⓓ cense
8. Ⓔ pryce Ⓕ price Ⓖ prise Ⓗ pryse
9. Ⓔ spase Ⓕ spaice Ⓖ spayce Ⓗ space
10. Ⓐ nyce Ⓑ nise Ⓒ naice Ⓓ nice
11. Ⓔ jiant Ⓕ jyant Ⓖ giant Ⓗ gyant
12. Ⓐ chanjes Ⓑ chaynjes Ⓒ chainges Ⓓ changes
13. Ⓐ pages Ⓑ pajes Ⓒ payges Ⓓ paiges
14. Ⓔ jentle Ⓕ gentle Ⓖ gentel Ⓗ jentel
15. Ⓐ mecage Ⓑ mesadge Ⓒ messej Ⓓ message

Daily Language Activities

Use these activities to introduce each day's lesson. Write the day's activities on the board or use **Transparency 18.**

DAY 1
1. my uncle has open his presents.
2. our sisters had planned the party
3. We have wash the dishes. (1: My; opened; 2: Our; party.; 3: washed)

DAY 2
1. I am go to school now. **2.** we are take a test. **3.** She were helping the teacher yesterday. (1: going; 2: We; taking; 3: was)

DAY 3
1. I said, Please finish your homework. **2.** "Is Dad cleaning the garage? I asked. **3.** The message said, "She is come next Tuesday. (1: "Please; homework."; 2: garage?"; 3: coming; Tuesday.")

DAY 4
1. "Mom has return from the office? I said. **2.** She has ask my brother to clean his room **3.** He said, I is going home now. (1: returned; office,"; 2: asked; room. 3: "I am; now.")

DAY 5
1. I am invite your frend to the party.
2. The boys have make a cake for us.
3. Paul am coming later. (1: inviting; friend; 2: made; 3: is)

ELL

Practice Language
Review subject-verb agreement of *has/have.* Write the subject pronouns on the board and have students match them with the correct verb form. Students will probably have difficulty understanding when to use helping verbs, especially *has/have.*

LA.3.3.4.4 Edit for correct use of present and past verb tense; **LA.3.3.4.5** Edit for correct use of subject/verb agreement

Main and Helping Verbs

Day 1 Introduce the Concept

INTRODUCE MAIN AND HELPING VERBS

- Sometimes a verb may be more than one word: *has cleaned.*
- The **main verb** tells what the subject is or does. *Cleaned* is a main verb. The **helping verb** helps the main verb show action. *Has* is a helping verb.
- *Have, has,* and *had* can be helping verbs.
- Helping verbs must agree with the subject.

Examples:
John **has finished** his chores.
Ana and I **have washed** the car.
Matt **had played** soccer.

Day 2 Teach the Concept

REVIEW MAIN AND HELPING VERBS

Review main and helping verbs. *Have, has,* and *had* are helping verbs.

INTRODUCE MORE HELPING VERBS

- The verb forms of *be* can also act as helping verbs.
- *Is, are, am, was, were,* and *will* can be helping verbs.
- The helping verb must agree with the subject of the sentence.

Examples:
Jack **was mowing** the lawn.
Peg and Dan **are taking** a test.
The boys **were running** a race.

See Grammar Transparency 86 for modeling and guided practice.

Grammar Practice Book, page 109

- A main verb tells what the subject is or does.
  He *visited* the bay.
- A **helping verb** helps another verb show an action. *Have, has,* and *had* are helping verbs. They help to tell about things that have already happened.
  The class *has* visited the bay.
  They *had* learned about spartina.
  I *have* looked for it in the water.

Circle the correct form of the verb to complete each sentence.

1. Spartina (have, **has**) turned into a problem.
2. It (**has**, have) lived in Washington since the 1800s.
3. Now it (**has**, have) turned into a pest.
4. Our neighbor (have, **had**) found some near his house.
5. It (have, **had**) destroyed his other plants.
6. It (**has**, have) forced native plants out of the area.
7. Sea creatures (has, **have**) moved out of there.
8. The mud flats (**have**, has) disappeared.
9. People (**had**, has) traveled with spartina from the East.
10. They (has, **had**) hoped it would be useful in the West.
11. People (**have**, has) tried many ways to control spartina.
12. We (**had**, has) to watch out for any signs of this plant.
13. I (**have**, has) to do more research on it.
14. Our neighbor (have, **has**) looked into some options.
15. Now we (has, **have**) found some useful information.

See Grammar Transparency 87 for modeling and guided practice.

Grammar Practice Book, page 110

- Verb forms of *be* are *is, are, am, was, were,* and *will*. They are also **helping verbs**.
- *Is, are,* and *am* help to tell about what is happening now.
  I *am* reading about plant life.
  Jeff *is* reading about plant life.
  We *are* reading about plant life.
- *Was* and *were* help to tell about what was happening in the past.
  I *was* learning about sea creatures last week.
  We *were* learning about sea creatures last week.
- *Will* helps to tell about something that will happen.
  We *will* visit the bay tomorrow.

Write a helping verb to finish each sentence.

1. Last week we ___were___ learning about spartina.
2. I ___was___ listening to Mr. Perkins.
3. Our teacher ___was___ talking about the problems in the bay.
4. Kim and I ___were___ doing a project about native bay life.
5. I ___was___ looking for good photos to use.
6. My classmates ___were___ finding lots of interesting information.
7. Joann and Ira ___were___ trying to find a way to use it all.
8. Kim ___is___ bringing her camera to the bay tomorrow.
9. Our friend ___is___ going to take her own pictures.
10. I ___am___ looking forward to revisiting the bay.
11. Tomorrow we ___will___ look for more spartina.
12. My classmate and I ___will___ walk in muddy water again.

LA.3.3.4.3 Edit for correct use of quotation marks in dialogue; **LA.3.3.4.5** Edit for correct use of subject/verb agreement

Day 3 Review and Practice

REVIEW HELPING VERBS

Review helping verbs. Focus on helping verbs that are forms of *be*. Remind students that the main and helping verb must agree with the sentence's subject.

MECHANICS AND USAGE: QUOTATION MARKS IN DIALOGUE

- **Quotation marks** show that someone is speaking.
- They come at the beginning and end of the speaker's exact words.

Examples:

Sarah said, "Please help me clean the yard."

"I will help you," I answered.

See Grammar Transparency 88 for modeling and guided practice.

Grammar Practice Book, page 111

- Use quotation marks at the beginning and end of a person's exact words.

Write each line of dialogue correctly. Use the correct form of the irregular verb.

1. Has you heard about Washington's spartina problem? asked Kevin.
   "Have you heard about Washington's spartina problem?" asked Kevin.
2. "I has read about it, but I hadn't actually seen any," said Mom.
   "I have read about it, but I haven't actually seen any," said Mom.
3. My class have just learned about it said Kevin.
   "My class has just learned about it," said Kevin.
4. It have damaged many native plants said Mom.
   "It has damaged many native plants," said Mom.
5. We taked a trip to the bay to see the wildlife there said Kevin.
   "We took a trip to the bay to see the wildlife there," said Kevin.

Day 4 Review and Proofread

REVIEW MAIN AND HELPING VERBS AND QUOTATION MARKS

Remind students how to use correct subject-verb agreement with helping verbs and how to use quotation marks when they edit/proofread their writing.

PROOFREAD/EDIT

Have students write the sentences below and proofread/edit to correct errors.

1. She have played that game before. (has played)
2. She said, Take me home now." ("Take)
3. The girls is reading this book? (are reading; book.)
4. I asked, Can I come, too?" ("Can)

See Grammar Transparency 89 for modeling and guided practice.

Grammar Practice Book, page 112

- **Helping verbs** help other verbs show an action.
- Forms of *have—have, has,* and *had—*are used with verbs ending in *-ed*.
- Forms of *be—is, are, was,* and *were—*are used with verbs ending in *-ing*.
- *Will* helps to tell what will happen in the future.

Proofread the passage. Circle any incorrect helping verbs.

We has gotten on the buses very early at 7:00 a.m. We slept on the way to Padilla Bay. We finally arrived at 9:00 a.m.

"I has never been so tired! yawned Steph.

"Wake up! said Tory. I is planning to take a class picture."

"She have taken pictures at every class trip sighed Steph.

"Hurry up!" said Ms. Harper. We has a lot of activities planned for today.

Writing Activity

Rewrite the passage. Write the helping verbs correctly. Add commas and quotation marks where necessary.

We had gotten on the buses very early at 7:00 a.m. We slept on the way to Padilla Bay. We finally arrived at 9:00 a.m.

"I have never been so tired!" yawned Steph.

"Wake up!" said Tory. "I am planning to take a class picture."

"She has taken pictures at every class trip," sighed Steph.

"Hurry up!" said Ms. Harper. "We have a lot of activities planned for today."

Day 5 Assess and Reteach

ASSESS

Use the Daily Language Activity and page 113 of the **Grammar Practice Book** for assessment.

RETEACH

Write each helping verb for *be* and *have* on a separate index card. Place the cards in a bag. Have each student draw a card and use the helping verb and a main verb in a sentence. Record the sentences on chart paper. Cards should be put back in the bag. Display the sentences on a Word Wall.

Use page 114 of the Grammar Practice Book for additional reteaching.

See Grammar Transparency 90 for modeling and guided practice.

Grammar Practice Book, pages 113–114

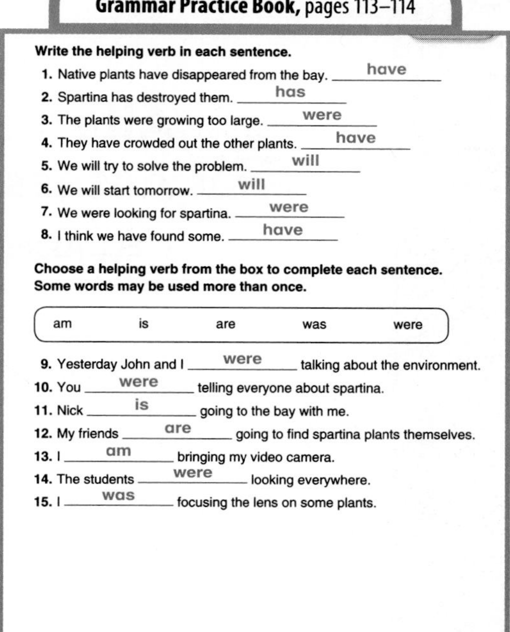

Write the helping verb in each sentence.

1. Native plants have disappeared from the bay. have
2. Spartina has destroyed them. has
3. The plants were growing too large. were
4. They have crowded out the other plants. have
5. We will try to solve the problem. will
6. We will start tomorrow. will
7. We were looking for spartina. were
8. I think we have found some. have

Choose a helping verb from the box to complete each sentence. Some words may be used more than once.

am is are was were

9. Yesterday John and I were talking about the environment.
10. You were telling everyone about spartina.
11. Nick is going to the bay with me.
12. My friends are going to find spartina plants themselves.
13. I am bringing my video camera.
14. The students were looking everywhere.
15. I was focusing the lens on some plants.

Administer the Test

Weekly Reading Assessment, pages 213–224

ASSESSED SKILLS

- Compare and Contrast
- Vocabulary Words
- Word Parts/Contractions
- Words with Soft *c* and *g*
- Main and Helping Verbs

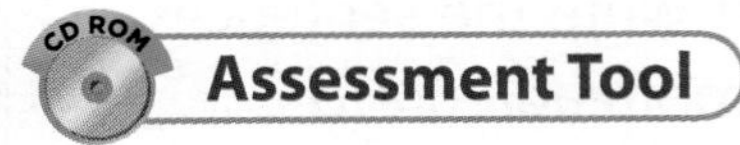

Administer the **Weekly Assessment** from the CD-ROM or online.

Weekly Assessment, 213–224

Fluency

Assess fluency for one group of students per week. Use the Oral Fluency Record Sheet to track the number of words read correctly. Fluency goal for all students: **82–102 words correct per minute (WCPM).**

Approaching Level	Weeks 1, 3, 5
On Level	Weeks 2, 4
Beyond Level	Week 6

Fluency Assessment

Alternative Assessments

- **ELL Assessment**, pages 118–119

ELL Assessment, 118–119

Diagnose		Prescribe
	IF . . .	**THEN . . .**
VOCABULARY WORDS **VOCABULARY STRATEGY** Word Parts/Contractions Items 1, 2, 3	0–1 items correct . . .	Reteach skills using the **Additional Lessons**, page T7. LOG ON Reteach skills: Log on to **www.macmillanmh.com** CD ROM Vocabulary PuzzleMaker Evaluate for Intervention.
COMPREHENSION Skill: Compare and Contrast Items 4, 5, 6	0–1 items correct . . .	Reteach skills using the **Additional Lessons**, page T1. Evaluate for Intervention.
GRAMMAR Main and Helping Verbs Items 7, 8, 9	0–1 items correct . . .	Reteach skills: **Grammar Practice Book**, page 114.
SPELLING Words with Soft *c* and *g* Items 10, 11, 12	0–1 items correct . . .	LOG ON Reteach skills: Log on to **www.macmillanmh.com**
FLUENCY	73–81 WCPM 0–72 WCPM	AUDIO CD Fluency Solutions Evaluate for Intervention.

READING Triumphs
AN INTERVENTION PROGRAM

Also Available

To place students in the Intervention Program, use the **Diagnostic Assessment** in the Intervention Teacher's Edition.

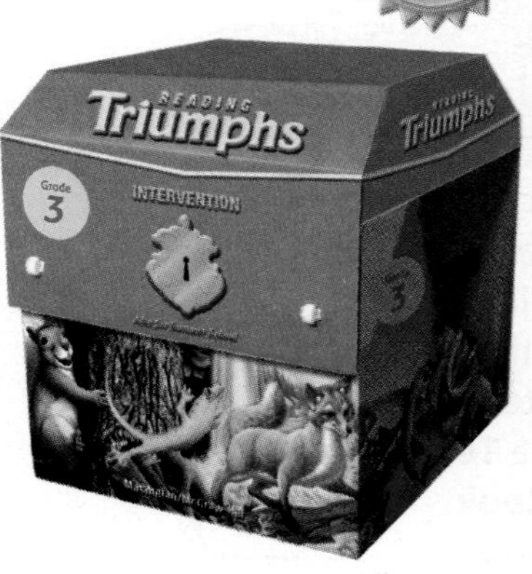

Constructive Feedback

If students have trouble deciding whether to pronounce the *c* in a word with a hard or soft sound, write *concern* on the board and say:

I notice that the first c *is followed by an* o*, so I know I must pronounce that syllable with a hard* c*, the /k/ sound. The second* c *is followed by an* e*, so I must pronounce that syllable with a soft* c*, the /s/ sound. Let's sound out and say the word together: /kooonnnsssûrrrnnn/,* concern.

Repeat as needed with other words with soft *c* and *g*.

Additional Resources

For each skill below, additional lessons are provided. You can use these lessons on consecutive days after teaching the lessons presented within the week.

- Compare, T1
- Word Parts: Contractions, T7
- Study Skills: Media Center, T11

Decodable Text

To help students build speed and accuracy with reading multisyllabic words, use the additional decodable text on pages 95–98 of the **Teacher's Resource Book.**

Skills Focus Phonics

Objectives Review words with soft *c* and *g*
Decode multisyllabic words with soft *c* and *g*

Materials • **Student Book** "Saving Egypt's Great Desert"

DECODE WORDS WITH SOFT *c* AND *g*

LA.3.1.4.1 Use knowledge of pronunciation to decode words
LA.3.1.4 Demonstrate knowledge of alphabetic principle

Model/Guided Practice

- Explain that the letter *c* can have a hard /k/ sound as in *cat* or a soft /s/ sound as in *center* when the *c* comes before the letter *e* or *i*.
- Write *city* on the board and read it aloud. Say: *The word* city *begins with a* c *followed by an* i. *I know that when* c *is followed by* i *or* e*, the* c *has a soft* c *or /s/ sound. The sounds in this word are /s/ /i/ /t/ /ē/. When I blend the sounds together, I get /sitē/. The word is* city.
- Explain that the letter *g* can have a hard /g/ sound as in *good* or a soft /j/ sound as in *germ*, usually when the *g* comes before the letter *e* or *i*.
- Write *gem* on the board and read it aloud. Say: *The word* gem *begins with a* g *followed by an* e. *I know that usually when* g *is followed by* i *or* e*, the* g *has a soft* g *or /j/ sound. The sounds in this word are /j/ /e/ /m/. When I blend the sounds together, I get /jem/. The word is* gem.

MULTISYLLABIC WORDS WITH SOFT *c* AND *g*

LA.3.1.4.3 Decode multisyllabic words

- Write the word *giant* on the board and have students identify the first syllable as containing soft *g*, or the /j/ sound: *gī*. Have students repeat the syllable and then blend and read the whole word several times.
- Have pairs of students work together to practice decoding longer words with soft *c* and *g*. Write the words below on the board and ask student pairs to copy them onto sheets of paper. Have them divide each word into syllables and then circle each silent letter. Then ask students to write sentences for each word.

circus	messages	decide	changing
concern	vegetable	fancy	ridges

- Check each pair for their progress and accuracy.

WORD HUNT: WORDS WITH SOFT *c* AND *g* IN CONTEXT

LA.3.1.4 Apply grade level phonics to read text

- Review words with soft *c* and *g*.
- Have students search "Saving Egypt's Great Desert" to find words with soft *c* and *g*. Ask them to write the words and circle the letter with the sound for soft *c* or *g*.
- Check to see if students have found the following: *Egypt*, *priceless*, *ages*, *difference.*

Skills Focus: Fluency

Objective Read with increasing prosody and accuracy at a rate of 82–92 WCPM

Materials • index cards • **Approaching Practice Book A**, p. 129

WORD AUTOMATICITY

Have students make flashcards for the following words with soft *c* and *g*: *cell, city, giant, germs, cents, changes, age, price, pages, place, space, gentle, gyms, nice, message.*

Display the cards one at a time and have students say each word. Repeat twice more, displaying the words more quickly each time.

REPEATED READING

LA.3.1.5 Demonstrate the ability to read grade level text

Model reading the passage on **Practice Book** page 129. Have the group listen for how you pronounce difficult words and then echo-read the passage. Next have partners practice reading to each other. Circulate and provide constructive feedback as needed.

TIMED READING

Tell students that they will be doing a final timed reading of the passage on Practice Book page 129. Students should

- begin reading the passage aloud when you say "Go."
- stop reading the passage after one minute when you say "Stop."

As students read, note any miscues. Help students record and graph the number of words they read correctly. Provide support and feedback.

Constructive Feedback

If students make mistakes in pronunciation while reading, pronounce each troublesome word in isolation for students and have them repeat after you. Then reread each sentence with a troublesome word and have students echo-read. Then echo-read the entire passage with students.

Skills Focus: Vocabulary

Objective Apply vocabulary word meanings

Materials • **Vocabulary Cards** • **Student Book** *Washington Weed Whackers*

VOCABULARY WORDS

LA.3.1.6.1 Use new vocabulary

Use the **Vocabulary Cards** to review this week's and last week's words. Help students locate and read vocabulary words in *Washington Weed Whackers*. Then guide them to use the words in cloze sentences. Example: *We went to the library to do some ____ on wild plants in our community.* (research) Have students exchange sentences with partners and complete the sentences with the correct words.

shouldn't | native | research | sprout | clumps

Approaching Practice Book A, page 129

As I read, I will pay attention to my pronunciation of vocabulary words and other difficult words.

Without water there can be no life. Your body needs
10 water to stay healthy. You take a bath in it to stay clean.
23 You wash your clothes in clean water.
30 Cars won't run without water. Without water, our **native**
39 plants would not grow. Animals we raise for food need
49 water too. Without water, we'd all be thirsty and hungry.
59 But where do we find water?
65 About 70 percent of Earth is covered with water. But
74 most of Earth's water is salt water. We cannot drink it
85 because it has too much salt.
91 About three percent of Earth's water is fresh. Only
100 fresh water is good for drinking. 106

Comprehension Check

1. Why is water an important natural resource? **Plot Development**
   Without water there can be no life. Every animal and plant on Earth needs water to live.
2. How much of the Earth's water is fresh? **Main Idea and Details**
   three percent

	Words Read	–	Number of Errors	=	Words Correct Score
First Read		–		=	
Second Read		–		=	

Vocabulary

Review last week's vocabulary words (**beamed**, **argued**, **possessions**, **fabric**, **purchased**, **quarreling**) and this week's words (**native**, **shouldn't**, **research**, **sprout**, **clumps**). Have students sort the words by part of speech.

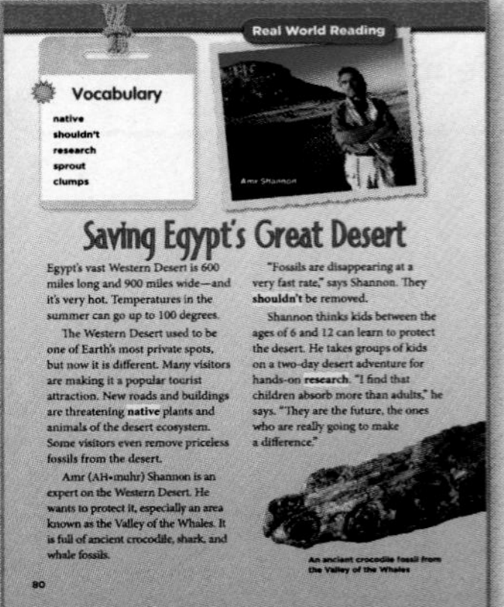

Student Book, or Transparency 18

Skills Focus: Vocabulary

Objective Review contractions

Materials • **Student Book** *Washington Weed Whackers*

FCAT **WORD PARTS: CONTRACTIONS**

LA.3.1.6 Use multiple strategies to develop grade-appropriate vocabulary

Write *shouldn't* on the board. Ask students to explain what the apostrophe stands for in this case. (the *o* in *not*) Ask students to look through *Washington Weed Whackers* and find these contractions: *it's* (p. 82); *didn't* (p. 84); *that's*, *can't*, *it'll* (p. 85). Have them explain what each contraction means. Help them identify the words combined in each contraction.

Skills Focus: Comprehension

Objective Identify comparisons and contrasts

Materials • **Student Book** "Saving Egypt's Great Desert" • **Transparency 18**

STRATEGY
MONITOR COMPREHENSION

LA.3.1.7 Use strategies to comprehend text

Remind students that to monitor comprehension, they should check to be sure they understand what they are reading.

FCAT **SKILL**
COMPARE AND CONTRAST

LA.3.1.7.5 Identify text structure

Explain/Model

Discuss comparison and contrast as a text structure.

- When an author organizes an article using a compare-and-contrast text structure, he or she shows how things are alike and different.
- To identify comparisons and contrasts, look for words such as *like*, *both*, *different*, and *but*.

Display **Transparency 18**. Read aloud "Saving Egypt's Great Desert."

Think Aloud The first sentence of the second paragraph includes *but*. That tells me the author is pointing out a contrast. Let me think about that contrast. This desert used to be private. Now it is popular.

Practice/Apply

Have students reread Amr Shannon's words in the last paragraph. Ask them to identify how Shannon thinks children visiting the desert are different from adults visiting the desert.

ELL 

Contractions Write the vocabulary word *shouldn't* on the board. Say: *This word is a contraction. It stands for the words* should not. Point to the apostrophe and say: *The apostrophe is here instead of the letter* o. Ask students to volunteer other contractions and write them on the board. Next to each contraction, write the words the contraction stands for. Have students pronounce both sets of words.

Leveled Reader Lesson

Objective Read to apply strategies and skills

Materials
- **Leveled Reader** *Resources All Around Us*
- **Student Book** *Washington Weed Whackers*

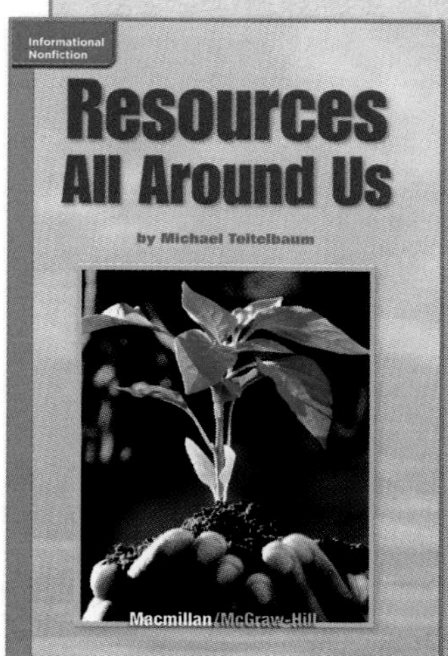

Leveled Reader

PREVIEW AND PREDICT

LA.3.1.7.1 Use text features to make predictions

Show the cover. Discuss the title and the table of contents.

- What does the author means by "resources"?
- What do you think this book is about? What questions do you have?

VOCABULARY WORDS

LA.3.1.6 Develop grade-appropriate vocabulary

Review the vocabulary words: *sprouts*, p. 2; *native*, p. 4; *clumps*, p. 11; *shouldn't*, *research*, p. 14. Discuss how each word is used in this selection and compare it to how it was used in *Washington Weed Whackers*.

STRATEGY
MONITOR COMPREHENSION

LA.3.1.7.8 Use strategies to repair comprehension

Explain that checking to make sure you understand what you are reading can help you learn more from a book. Read pages 2–3 aloud.

Think Aloud I'm having a little trouble understanding the second paragraph on page 2. It seems to be telling me to do things. Let me reread it more slowly and then read ahead to the next paragraph. Now I see. The author is listing ways that resources help us.

SKILL
COMPARE AND CONTRAST

LA.3.1.7.5 Identify text structure
LA.3.1.7 Use strategies to comprehend text

Remind students that some texts are organized with a compare-and-contrast text structure. In this book each chapter tells about a different resource. Students should look for comparisons and contrasts. Help students compare and contrast water and wood with Venn Diagrams.

Read and Respond

Read to the end of the book. Students will find out how people depend on soil and oil and how we can protect these resources. Check their understanding. Encourage them to share any questions they have as well as their opinions about using resources wisely. Discuss how they monitored their comprehension and when they might use the strategies again.

MAKE CONNECTIONS ACROSS TEXTS

LA.3.1.7.7 Compare and contrast topics

Have volunteers summarize *Washington Weed Whackers* and *Resources All Around Us*. Compare and contrast the two selections as a group.

- How are the topics the same? How are they different?
- Would you call weeds "natural resources"? Why or why not?
- What reading strategies helped you understand each selection?

On Level Options

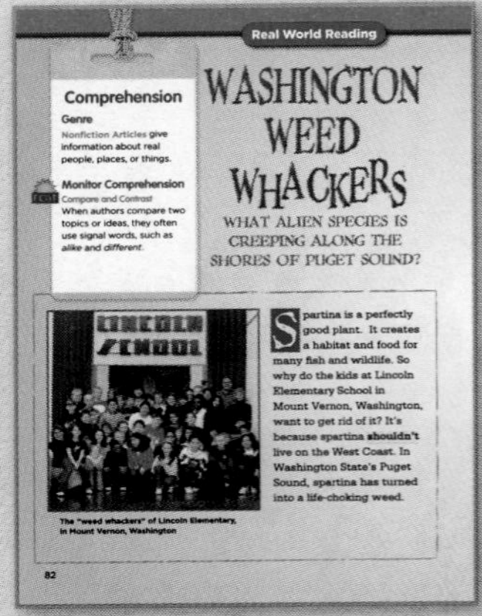

Student Book

Skills Focus: Phonics

Objective Decode one-syllable and multisyllabic words with soft *c* and *g*

Materials • chart paper

DECODE WORDS WITH SOFT *c* AND *g*

LA.3.1.4 Demonstrate knowledge of alphabetic principle

- Write, read aloud, and have students repeat this sentence: *Good, gentle cats live in this city.* Discuss how in the word *good*, the letter *g* has a hard *g* sound, but in *gentle*, it has a soft *g*, or /j/, sound. Similarly, the *c* in *cats* makes the /k/ sound (hard *c*), but the *c* in *city* has a soft *c*, or /s/, sound.
- Ask students to say aloud, write, and sort *center*, *iceberg*, *gigantic*, and *ages*, and then circle each soft *c* or *g*. Brainstorm other soft *c* or *g* words.

Skills Focus: Vocabulary

Objective Apply vocabulary and knowledge of contractions

Materials • **Vocabulary Cards** • **Student Book** *Washington Weed Whackers*

VOCABULARY WORDS

LA.3.1.6.1 Use new vocabulary

Write *native*, *shouldn't*, *research*, *sprout*, and *clumps* on the board. Give students sentences with missing words and have them fill in the blanks with the correct vocabulary words. For example:

The bengal tiger is ____ to India. It lives there naturally. (native)

Hostas are plants that grow together in big, thick bunches, or ____. (clumps)

FCAT WORD PARTS: CONTRACTIONS

LA.3.1.6 Use multiple strategies to develop grade-appropriate vocabulary

Point out these contractions in *Washington Weed Whackers*: *shouldn't* (p. 82); *didn't* (p. 84); *that's*, *can't*, *It'll* (p. 85). Have students explain the meaning of each contraction and tell how they were created.

Ask students to form contractions and write sentences for the following phrases: *they would* (they'd), *we will* (we'll), and *would not* (wouldn't).

Skills Focus: Fluency

Objective Read fluently with good prosody at a rate of 82–102 WCPM

Materials • **On Level Practice Book O**, p. 129

REPEATED READING

LA.3.1.5 Demonstrate the ability to read grade level text

Model pronouncing vocabulary and difficult words, using the fluency passage on **Practice Book** page 129. Then have partners practice reading aloud. Remind students to use their voices to show interest in the text while they read. Remind students that when they are listening, they should help partners with difficult words, let them know about mistakes, and praise what they do well.

On Level Practice Book O, page 129

As I read, I will pay attention to my pronunciation of vocabulary words and other difficult words.

Our Earth has beautiful caves that people can explore.
9 Sometimes these explorers wear harnesses and hard hats
17 and climb walls inside the caves.
23 Cave explorers may see unusual rock shapes. A stalactite
32 is a form of rock that hangs from the roof or sides of the
46 cave. A stalagmite forms on the bottom of the cave.
56 These big **clumps** of rock **sprout** and build up slowly
66 over years. They are made of limestone and water.
75 Other people like to climb rocks. Beginners use ropes
84 and put their hands and feet in holes drilled for their use.
96 Experts make their own routes up the rocks. They've
105 learned to climb without looking down. This, they say,
114 helps to keep them safe.
119 Other people enjoy nature by hiking in mountains,
127 deserts, or the deep, quiet woods. 133

Comprehension Check

1. Compare and contrast stalactites and stalagmites. **Compare and Contrast** Stalactites hang from the roof or sides. Stalagmites form on the bottom. Both are made of limestone and water.
2. What tip do expert rock climbers use? **Main Idea and Details** Expert rock climbers climb without looking down.

	Words Read	–	Number of Errors	=	Words Correct Score
First Read		–		=	
Second Read		–		=	

Leveled Reader Lesson

Objective Read to apply strategies and skills

Materials
- **Leveled Reader** *Resources All Around Us*
- **Student Book** *Washington Weed Whackers*

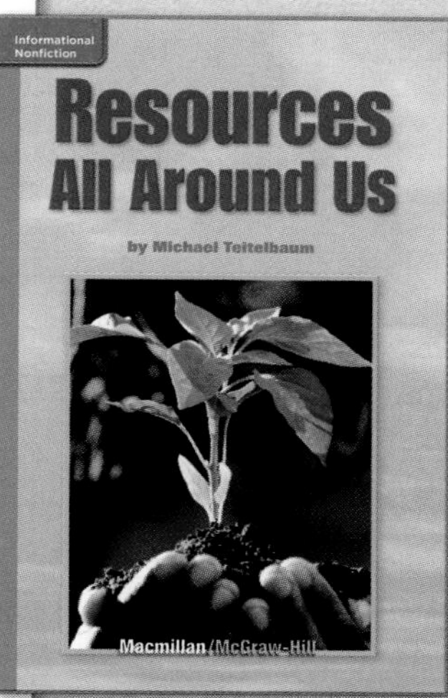

Leveled Reader

PREVIEW AND PREDICT

LA.3.1.7.1 Use text features to make predictions

Show the cover and read the title. Discuss what students already know about natural resources. Have them share predictions and questions.

STRATEGY
MONITOR COMPREHENSION

LA.3.1.7 Use strategies to comprehend text

Tell students that pausing to check their understanding of a passage can help them get more out of their reading. If they realize that they don't understand what they just read, they should reread it carefully and then read on to see if their questions are answered. Read pages 2–3 aloud. Model monitoring comprehension.

Think Aloud I'm not sure what opening the faucet and planting a flower in soil have to do with natural resources. I've already reread this passage, but that didn't really help me very much. I'll read ahead to see if I can find out the connection.

SKILL
COMPARE AND CONTRAST

LA.3.1.7.5 Identify text structure

After students have read to the end of Chapter 2, ask them to compare and contrast water and wood. Students can create Venn Diagrams to help them with their comparisons.

READ AND RESPOND

LA.3.2.1.7 Respond to and discuss literary selections

Have students finish reading the book. Discuss the vocabulary words and what students learned about using and protecting natural resources. After reading, engage students in a discussion to assess comprehension.

- What are some of the things that make up soil?
- What are some uses for oil?
- What facts did you learn about natural resources that you did not know before?
- What did you enjoy most about the book?

MAKE CONNECTIONS ACROSS TEXTS

LA.3.1.7.7 Compare and contrast texts

Have students compare how *Washington Weed Whackers* and *Resources All Around Us* are alike and different. Find out which selection students found more interesting and why. Discuss any questions that students still have and any comprehension monitoring strategies they found helpful with these selections.

Beyond Level Options

Small Group

Skills Focus: Vocabulary

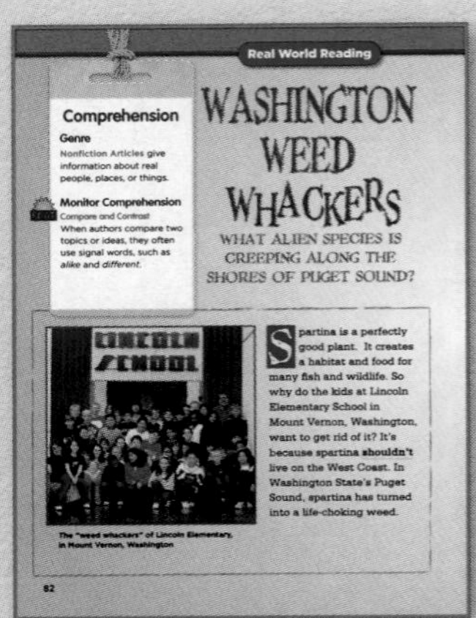

Student Book

Objective Use word associations to review and extend vocabulary

Materials • **Student Book** *Washington Weed Whackers*

EXTEND VOCABULARY

LA.3.1.6.5 Relate new vocabulary to familiar words

Review the vocabulary words as used in *Washington Weed Whackers: native, shouldn't, research, sprout, clumps.* Ask students to associate the vocabulary words with one of the following words or phrases:

- What word means "born in a certain area"? *(native)*
- What word is a synonym for *grow?* *(sprout)*
- What word might be used to describe thick masses? *(clumps)*
- What word might be done in a library? *(research)*

Skills Focus: Study Skill

Objective Use a search engine to find information

Materials • computer with Internet access • **Study Skills Transparency 4**

USING COMPUTER SEARCH ENGINES IN THE MEDIA CENTER

LA.3.6.4.1 Use appropriate technologies to achieve a purpose

Review **Transparency 4**. Have pairs of students use the media center's computer to access a search engine. Review precise key words they can use to find out information about spartina. Suggest that they use the term *spartina* first and then add the place names *Puget Sound* and *Padilla Bay* as they do their searches. Guide students to click through to reputable Web sites. They can use what they read to write reports on energy sources.

Skills Focus: Fluency

Objective Read fluently with good prosody at a rate of 92–102 WCPM

Materials • **Beyond Practice Book B**, p. 129

REPEATED READING

LA.3.1.5 Demonstrate the ability to read text orally with expression

Read the passage on **Practice Book** page 129 to model expressive reading and have students echo-read. Pay special attention to pronouncing any words that students find difficult.

Have students take turns reading the passage to partners and offering corrective feedback. Ask students to imagine that they are narrating a TV program about natural resources.

Timed Reading At the end of the week, have students read the passage and record their reading rates.

Beyond Practice Book B, page 129

As I read, I will pay attention to my pronunciation of vocabulary words and other difficult words.

Oil is found underground. A long drill digs a deep hole
11 to find the oil. The drill must pass through layers of sand
23 and rock.
25 The energy and products we get from oil make our
35 lives easier. But drilling, transporting, and using oil can
44 hurt the environment.
47 At times forests are cut down to run oil pipes under the
59 ground. Huge tankers transport oil. If the oil spills, it can
70 harm **native** fish and sea birds.
76 When oil is burned as fuel in cars or to heat our homes,
89 it gives off gases that pollute the air. **Research** on cars
100 that run on other types of fuel may change that.
110 Another source of energy, natural gas, is used to
119 cook food and to heat homes and water. Pockets of this gas
131 are trapped in the rock and soil under great pressure. By
142 getting at this trapped gas and bringing it to the surface,
153 we can use it for energy. 159

Comprehension Check

1. How can oil be harmful to the environment? **Main Idea and Details** Oil spills are harmful to wildlife, and oil used as fuel pollutes the air.
2. Compare and contrast oil and natural gas. **Compare and Contrast** both can be used to heat homes; oil is found underground; natural gas is trapped in rock and soil

	Words Read	–	Number of Errors	=	Words Correct Score
First Read		–		=	
Second Read		–		=	

Leveled Reader Lesson

Objective Read to apply strategies and skills

Materials • **Leveled Reader** *Resources All Around Us*

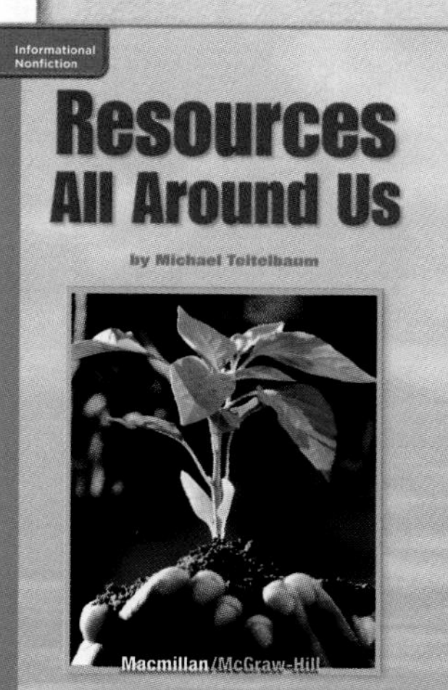

Leveled Reader

PREVIEW AND PREDICT

LA.3.1.7.1 Use text features

Show the cover of the book. Read the table of contents. Ask students what resources the book describes. Remind them to look for vocabulary words as they read. Suggest they skim the text and note questions.

STRATEGY
MONITOR COMPREHENSION

LA.3.1.7.8 Use strategies to repair comprehension

Explain that monitoring comprehension as they read can help students better understand the text. Remind them that if they don't understand a part of the text, they can reread, read ahead, or ask for help. Read pages 2–3 aloud. Model monitoring comprehension.

Think Aloud These pages talk about natural resources, but I'm still not sure what the author means by this term. I'll look at the table of contents. There I can read key words in the chapter titles: Water, Wood, Soil, and Oil. Now I understand that these things are natural resources.

SKILL
COMPARE AND CONTRAST

LA.3.1.7.5 Identify text structure

Ask students to compare and contrast different kinds of natural resources that they read about in the book, such as wood and soil. Students can create Venn Diagrams to help them with their comparisons.

READ AND RESPOND

LA.3.2.1.7 Respond to and discuss literary selections

Have students read to the end of Chapter 2. Discuss where we get water and wood, how we use these resources, and why we need to take care of them. After students finish the book, have them share personal responses.

- What do you think is the most important natural resource? Why?
- How might you try to protect natural resources in your daily life?

Self-Selected Reading

Objective Read independently to apply comprehension strategies and skills

Materials • Leveled Readers or trade books at students' reading levels

FCAT

READ TO COMPARE AND CONTRAST

LA.3.2.1.8 Select fiction materials to read

Invite each student to choose a fiction book for independent reading. As students read, remind them to stop to be sure they understand what they have read. After reading, students should discuss how the author compares and contrasts information.

Academic Language

Throughout the week the English language learners will need help in building their understanding of the academic language used in daily instruction and assessment instruments. The following strategies will help to increase their language proficiency and comprehension of content and instructional words.

LOG ON Technology

Oral Language For additional language support and oral vocabulary development, go to www.macmillanmh.com

Strategies to Reinforce Academic Language

- **Use Context** Academic language (see chart below) should be explained in the context of the task during Whole Group. Use gestures, expressions, and visuals to support meaning.
- **Use Visuals** Use charts, transparencies, and graphic organizers to explain key labels to help students understand classroom language.
- **Model** Demonstrate the task using academic language in order for students to understand instruction.

Academic Language Used in Whole Group Instruction

Content/Theme Words	Skill/Strategy Words	Writing/Grammar Words
natural resources (p. 78)	contractions (p. 81)	narrative (p. 89)
protect (p. 78)	compare (alike) (p. 81A)	article (p. 89A)
habitat (p. 82)	contrast (different) (p. 81A)	search engine (p. 89A)
impact (p. 82)	monitor comprehension (p. 81A)	flowchart (p. 89B)
		main verb (p. 89I)
		helping verb (p. 89I)
		quotation marks in dialogue (p. 89J)

ELL Leveled Reader Lesson

Before Reading

LA.3.1.7.1 Use text features

Resources
by Michael Teitelbaum
Macmillan/McGraw-Hill

DEVELOP ORAL LANGUAGE

Build Background Write the word *Resources* and brainstorm examples. Use the pictures and table of contents in the book to introduce further natural resources.

LA.3.1.6 Develop grade-appropriate vocabulary

Review Vocabulary Write the vocabulary and support words on the board and discuss their meanings. Use them in sentences that will help you write a quick definition for each. *If you want to know more about something, you can* research *it using the Internet or books. Definition: research = to look for more information.*

PREVIEW AND PREDICT

LA.3.1.7.1 Use text features to make predictions

Point to the cover photograph and read the title aloud. *In this book we are going to read about natural resources such as water, air, and rocks. Why do you think it is titled "Resources"?*

Set a Purpose for Reading Show a Venn diagram. Ask students to make similar ones and to think about how we use and enjoy natural resources as they read. Encourage them to use this information in their diagrams.

During Reading

LA.3.1.7 Use strategies to comprehend text

Choose from among the differentiated strategies below to support students' reading at all stages of language acquisition.

Beginning	Intermediate	Advanced
Shared Reading As you read, model how to identify ways in which natural resources are used. Write a list for each resource. Monitor comprehension by asking questions and referring back to the list.	**Read Together** Read Chapter 1. Model how to monitor comprehension by generating and answering questions. Use the text, pictures, and captions for reference. Take turns reading the selection. Ask students to use the strategy as they read.	**Independent Reading** Have students read the selection. Each day ask them to monitor comprehension by discussing the selection in pairs. Have them identify ways in which natural resources are used and write a list for each resource.

After Reading

LA.3.1.6.1 Use new vocabulary

Remind students to use the vocabulary and story words in their whole group activities.

Objective

- Apply vocabulary and comprehension skills

Materials

- ELL Leveled Reader

ELL 5 Day Planner

DAY 1	• Academic Language • Oral Language and Vocabulary Review
DAY 2	• Academic Language • ELL Leveled Reader
DAY 3	• Academic Language • ELL Leveled Reader
DAY 4	• Academic Language • ELL Leveled Reader
DAY 5	• Academic Language • ELL Leveled Reader Comprehension Check and Literacy Activities

ELL Teacher's Guide for students who need additional instruction

Student Book Selections

Weekly Theme: Getting Involved

Week At A Glance

Whole Group

VOCABULARY
community, deserve, grownups, interviewed, slogan, thrilled, tour, volunteers

FCAT Context Clues/Example

COMPREHENSION
Strategy: Monitor Comprehension
FCAT Skill: Author's Purpose

WRITING
FCAT Expository/Personal Essay

FCAT **Social Studies**
Government and the Citizen

Small Group Options

Differentiated Instruction for Tested Skills

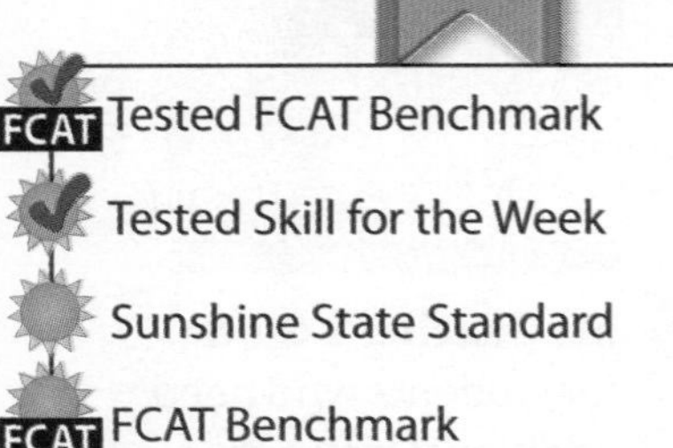

Social Studies Link
Main Selection
Genre Nonfiction Article

Vocabulary/ Comprehension

Genre Poem

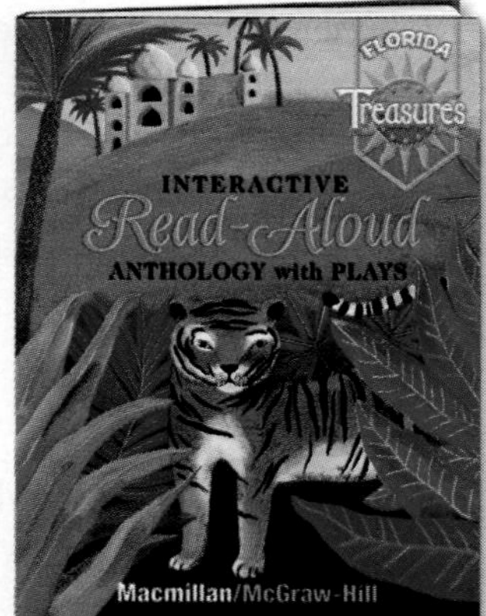

Read-Aloud Anthology
- Listening Comprehension
- Readers' Theater

Resources for Differentiated Instruction

FCAT LEVELED READERS: Social Studies

GR Levels M–R

Genre Informational Nonfiction

- **Same Theme**
- **Same Vocabulary**
- **Same Comprehension Skills**

Approaching Level

On Level

Beyond Level

English Language Leveled Reader

Sheltered Readers for English Language Learners

ELL Teacher's Guide also available

LEVELED PRACTICE

Approaching

On Level

Beyond

ELL

INTERVENTION PROGRAM

- Phonics and Decoding
- Comprehension
- Vocabulary

Also available, *Reading Triumphs*, Intervention Program

CLASSROOM LIBRARY

Genre Informational Nonfiction

Approaching

On Level

Beyond

Trade books to apply Comprehension Skills

FCAT Success!

- **FCAT Edition**
- **Content Area Reading**

FCAT Test Preparation and Practice

FCAT Benchmark Assessments

FCAT Unit and Weekly Assessments

HOME-SCHOOL CONNECTION

- Family letters in English, Spanish, and Haitian Creole
- Take-Home Stories

FLORIDA Suggested Lesson Plan

Here's My Dollar, 94–105

Integrated ELL Support Every Day

Whole Group	Day 1	Day 2
ORAL LANGUAGE • Listening • Speaking • Viewing	**Listening/Speaking/Viewing** Focus Question What are some ways that you can help your school or community? LA.3.5.2 Build Background, 90 **Read Aloud:** "The Song of the World's Last Whale," 91 LA.3.2.1.1	**Listening/Speaking** Focus Question What did the author write about Angel? LA.3.5.2 **Cross-Curricular Connection:** *Carnival of the Animals*, 100 LA.3.4.1.2
WORD STUDY • Vocabulary • Phonics/Decoding	**Vocabulary** LA.3.1.6.1 *tour, volunteers, community, thrilled, slogan, grownups, deserve, interviewed*, 92 Practice Book A-O-B, 133 FCAT **Strategy:** Context Clues: Example Clues, 93 LA.3.1.6.3	**Vocabulary** LA.3.1.6.1 Review Vocabulary Words, 94 **Phonics** Decode Homophones, 111E LA.3.1.6.8 Practice Book A-O-B, 139
READING • Develop Comprehension • Fluency	**Read** "Gorilla Garden," 92–93 LA.3.1.6.2 Student Book **Comprehension,** 93A–93B **Strategy:** Monitor Comprehension FCAT **Skill:** Author's Purpose LA.3.1.7.2 Practice Book A-O-B, 134 **Fluency** Partner Reading, 90I Model Fluency, 91 LA.3.1.5	**Read** *Here's My Dollar*, 94–105 LA.3.1.6.2 Student Book **Comprehension,** 94–105 **Strategy:** Monitor Comprehension FCAT **Skill:** Author's Purpose LA.3.1.7.2 Practice Book A-O-B, 135 **Fluency** Choral Reading, 97 LA.3.1.5 Partner Reading, 90I
LANGUAGE ARTS • Writing • Grammar • Spelling	FCAT **Writing** Daily Writing: Write about a time when you helped someone. How did you feel? How do you think the other person felt? Personal Essay, 110–111B LA.3.4.2.3 **Grammar** Daily Language Activities, 111I Irregular Verbs, 111I LA.3.3.4.4 Grammar Practice Book, 115 **Spelling** Pretest, 111G LA.3.1.6.8 Spelling Practice Book, 115–116	FCAT **Writing** Daily Writing: Imagine your class is volunteering at an animal shelter. Write a paragraph describing what your classmates can do and why. Personal Essay, 110–111B LA.3.4.2.3 **Grammar** Daily Language Activities, 111I Irregular Verbs, 111I LA.3.3.4.5 Grammar Practice Book, 116 **Spelling** Homophones, 111G LA.3.3.4.3 Spelling Practice Book, 117
ASSESSMENT • Informal/Formal	Quick Check **Vocabulary,** 92 **Comprehension,** 93B	Quick Check **Comprehension,** 101, 105 **Phonics,** 111E
Turn the Page for **Small Group Lesson Plan**	**Differentiated Instruction 111M–111V**	**Differentiated Instruction 111M–111V**

FCAT Benchmarks

Vocabulary
Vocabulary Words
Context Clues/ Examples
LA.3.1.6.3 Use context clues to determine meanings

Comprehension
Strategy: Monitor Comprehension
Skill: Author's Purpose
LA.3.1.7.2 Identify the author's purpose

Writing
Expository/ Personal Essay
LA.3.4.2.3 Write expository essays

Social Studies
Government and the Citizen
SS.C.2.2.3.1 Personal and civic responsibility

Turn the Page for **Small Group Options**

Day 3

Listening/Speaking

Focus Question How are Amelia and Angel alike? Describe the different ways they help animals. Use details from both selections in your answer. LA.3.5.2

Summarize, 107 LA.3.1.7.8

Vocabulary LA.3.1.6.3

Review Words in Context, 111C

FCAT **Strategy:** Context Clues: Example Clues, 111D

Practice Book A-O-B, 138

Phonics LA.3.1.4.3

Decode Multisyllabic Words, 111E

Read *Here's My Dollar,* 94–105 LA.3.1.6.2

Student Book

Comprehension

FCAT Comprehension Check, 107

Skill: Chronological Order, 107B LA.3.1.7.3

Fluency Partner Reading, 90I LA.3.1.5

Repeated Reading, 107A

Practice Book A-O-B, 136

FCAT Writing

Daily Writing: Write about a person who helped you in some way.

Writer's Craft: Strong Opening, 111A LA.3.3.2.1

Personal Essay, 110–111B LA.3.4.2.3

Grammar Daily Language Activities, 111I

Correct Verb Forms, 111J LA.3.3.4.4

Grammar Practice Book, 117

Spelling Homophones, 111H LA.3.1.6.8

Spelling Practice Book, 118

Quick Check **Fluency,** 107A

Differentiated Instruction 111M–111V

Day 4

Listening/Speaking/Viewing

Focus Question Compare these two poems about helping and *Here's My Dollar.* How are these selections alike? How are they different? LA.3.5.2

Media Literacy: Newspaper and Television Reporting, 102 LA.3.6.3

Expand Vocabulary: Getting Involved, 111F

Vocabulary LA.3.1.6.10

Greek and Latin Roots, 111F

Apply Vocabulary to Writing, 111F LA.3.1.6.1

Phonics LA.3.1.6

Homophone Match, 111E

Read "Neighbors" and "Recycling," 108–109

Student Book

Comprehension

Language Arts: Poetry LA.3.2.1.1

Literary Elements: Rhyme Scheme and Repetition, 108

Practice Book A-O-B, 137

Fluency Partner Reading, 90I LA.3.1.5

FCAT Writing

Daily Writing: Imagine that you are Angel and you are on a TV talk show. Write what you would tell the audience.

Writing Trait: Ideas and Content, 111B LA.3.3.3.3

Personal Essay, 110–111B LA.3.4.2.3

Grammar Daily Language Activities, 111I

Irregular Verbs, 111J LA.3.3.4.5

Grammar Practice Book, 118

Spelling Homophones, 111H LA.3.1.6.8

Spelling Practice Book, 119

Quick Check **Vocabulary,** 111D
Phonics, 111E

Differentiated Instruction 111M–111V

Day 5 Review and Assess

Listening/Speaking

Focus Question Think about the author's purpose for writing "Here's My Dollar." Do you think he believes that kids can make a difference in the world?

Speaking and Listening Strategies, 111A LA.3.5.2

Vocabulary LA.3.1.6.1

Spiral Review: Vocabulary Game, 111F

Read Self-Selected Reading, 90I LA.3.1.6.2

Student Book

Comprehension

Connect and Compare, 109 LA.3.1.7.3

Fluency Partner Reading, 90I LA.3.1.5

FCAT Writing

Daily Writing: Write about volunteer work that you would enjoy. Explain why you would enjoy it.

Personal Essay, 110–111B LA.3.4.2.3

Grammar Daily Language Activities, 111I

Irregular Verbs, 111J LA.3.3.4.4

Grammar Practice Book, 119–120

Spelling Posttest, 111H LA.3.1.6.8

Spelling Practice Book, 120

FCAT **Weekly Assessment, 225–236**

Differentiated Instruction 111M–111V

Differentiated Instruction

What do I do in small groups?

Focus on Skills

Skills Focus Use your Quick Check observations to guide additional instruction and practice.

Phonics
Decode Homophones

Vocabulary
Words: tour, volunteers, community, thrilled, slogan, grownups, deserve, interviewed
FCAT **Strategy:** Context Clues/Example

Comprehension
Strategy: Monitor Comprehension
FCAT **Skill:** Author's Purpose

FCAT **Fluency**

Suggested Lesson Plan

CD ROM Instructional Navigator Interactive Lesson Planner

	Day 1	Day 2
Approaching Level • **Additional Instruction/Practice** • **Tier 2 Instruction**	Fluency, 111N Vocabulary, 111N Comprehension, 111O 	Phonics, 111M Vocabulary, 111O Leveled Reader Lesson, 111P • Vocabulary • Comprehension 
On Level • **Practice**	Vocabulary, 111Q Leveled Reader Lesson, 111R • Comprehension ELL Leveled Reader, 111U–11V 	Phonics, 111Q Leveled Reader Lesson, 111R • Comprehension • Vocabulary 
Beyond Level • **Extend**	Vocabulary, 111S Leveled Reader Lesson, 111T • Comprehension 	Leveled Reader Lesson, 111T • Comprehension • Vocabulary 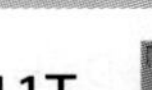 

For intensive intervention see READING Triumphs

Focus on Leveled Readers

Levels M-R

Apply FCAT skills and strategies while reading appropriate leveled books.

Approaching

On Level

Beyond

N — Kids Make a Difference

ELL

Additional Leveled Reader Resources

Leveled Reader Database
Go to **www.macmillanmh.com**

Search by

- Comprehension Skill
- Content Area
- Genre
- Text Feature
- Guided Reading Level
- Reading Recovery Level
- Lexile Score
- Benchmark Level

Subscription also available.

Focus on Social Studies

Teacher's Annotated Edition

Government and the Citizen
SS.C.2.2.2.3.1 Personal and civic responsibility

Additional Leveled Readers
Our City Gardens
Service Dogs in the Neighborhood

Day 3

Phonics, 111M
Fluency, 111N
Vocabulary, 111O
Leveled Reader Lesson, 111P
- Comprehension

Fluency, 111Q
Vocabulary, 111Q
Leveled Reader Lesson, 111R
- Comprehension

Fluency, 111S
Vocabulary, 111S
Leveled Reader Lesson, 111T
- Comprehension
- ELL Synonym Matching, 111S

Day 4

Phonics, 111M
Leveled Reader Lesson, 111P
- Comprehension
- ELL Skill: Author's Purpose

Leveled Reader Lesson, 111R
- Comprehension

Literary Elements, 111S
Leveled Reader Lesson, 111T
- Comprehension

Day 5

Fluency, 111N
Leveled Reader Lesson, 111P
- Make Connections Across Texts

Fluency, 111Q
Leveled Reader Lesson, 111R
- Make Connections Across Texts

Fluency, 111S
Self-Selected Reading, 111T

Managing the Class

What do I do with the rest of my class?

Class Management Tools

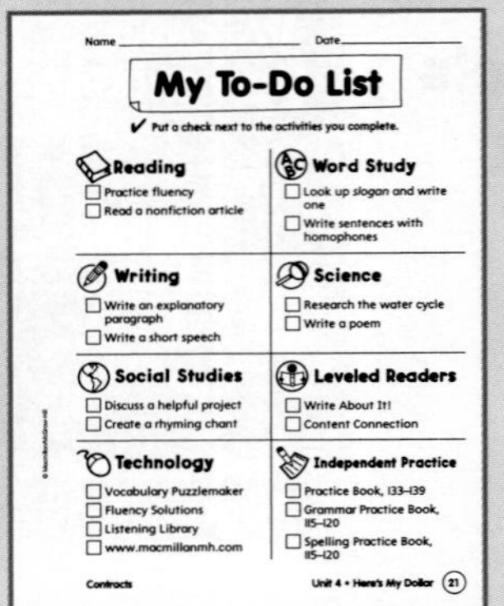

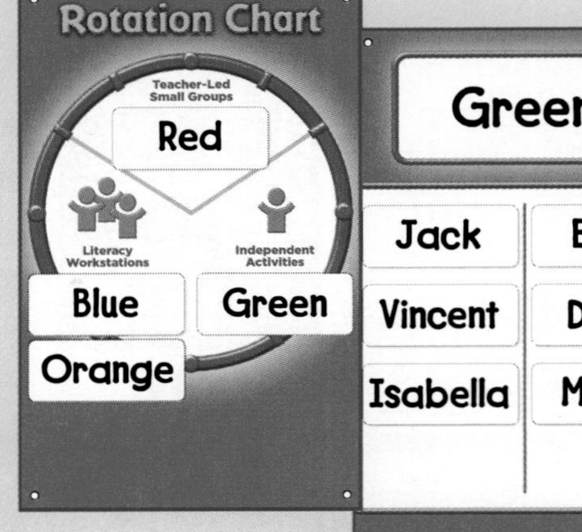

Includes:

- How-to Guide
- Rotation Chart
- Weekly Contracts

Hands-on activities for reinforcing weekly skills

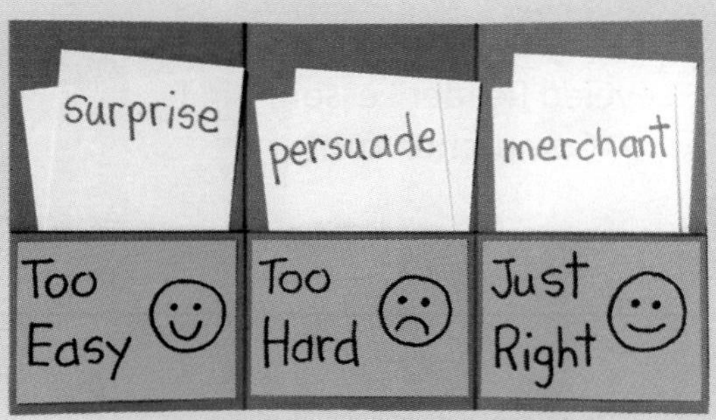

Three-Pocket Foldable

Standing Cube Foldable

Independent Activities

Reinforcing Weekly Skills

FCAT LEVELED READERS: Social Studies

For Repeated Readings and Literacy Activities

Approaching

On Level

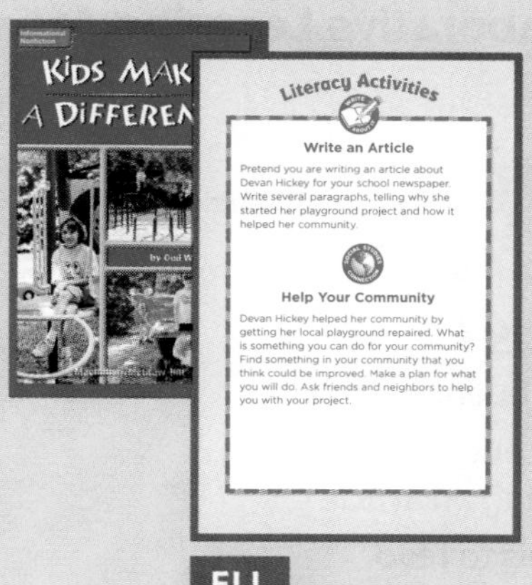

ELL

Beyond

LEVELED PRACTICE

Skills: Phonics, Vocabulary, Author's Purpose, Fluency, Example Context Clues, Rhyme Scheme and Repetition

Approaching

On Level

Beyond

ELL

Technology

ONLINE INSTRUCTION www.macmillanmh.com

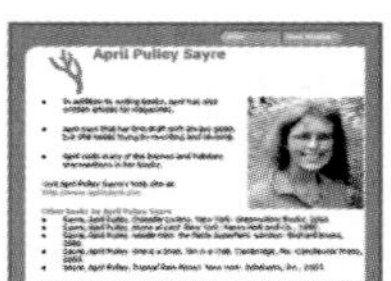

- Meet the Author/Illustrator

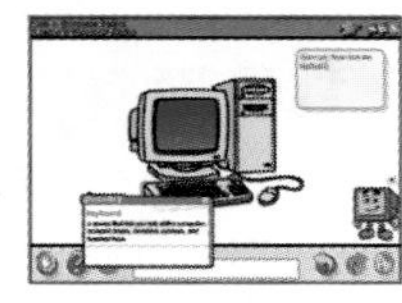

- Computer Literacy Lessons

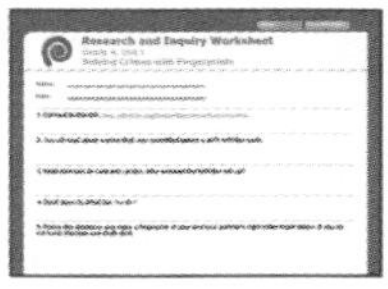

- Research and Inquiry Activities

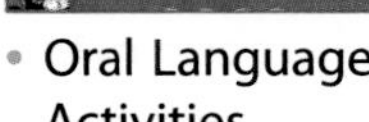

- Oral Language Activities

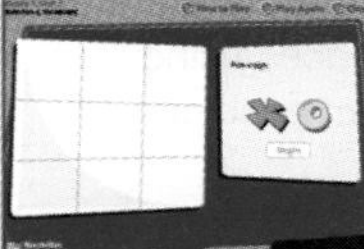

- Vocabulary and Spelling Activities

- Leveled Reader Database

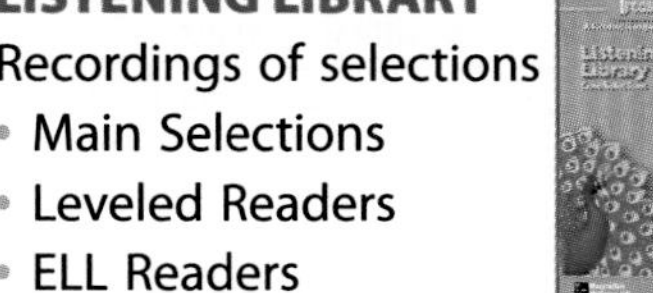

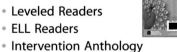

LISTENING LIBRARY

Recordings of selections

- Main Selections
- Leveled Readers
- ELL Readers
- Intervention Anthology

FLUENCY SOLUTIONS

Recorded passages for modeling and practicing fluency

VOCABULARY PUZZLEMAKER

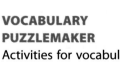

Activities for vocabulary, spelling, and high-frequency words

NEW ADVENTURES WITH BUGGLES AND BEEZY

Phonemic awareness and phonics practice

Turn the page for Literacy Workstations.

Literacy Activities

Collaborative Learning Activities

Reading

Objectives

- Time reading to practice fluency
- Read to gain information and figure out the author's purpose for writing an article
- Select nonfiction materials to read

Word Study

Objectives

- Write a sentence using the word *slogan* and include context clues
- Identify and define homophones

LA.3.1.5 Demonstrate the ability to read text orally with appropriate rate

Reading — **FLUENCY** — 20 Minutes

- Choose a reading buddy. Take turns reading aloud page 136 of your Practice Book.
- Read at a steady tempo.

Extension

- Read the passage aloud again. This time, read it aloud together at the same pace. Try not to read too quickly or too slowly.
- Listen to the pace of the reading on the audio disc. Time your reading.

Things you need:

- Practice Book

Fluency Solutions Listening Library

37

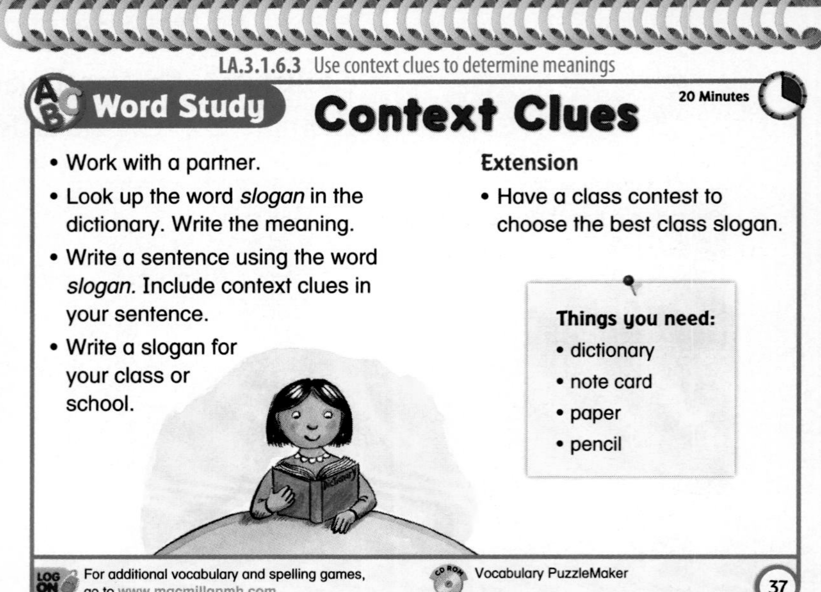

LA.3.1.6.3 Use context clues to determine meanings

Word Study — **Context Clues** — 20 Minutes

- Work with a partner.
- Look up the word *slogan* in the dictionary. Write the meaning.
- Write a sentence using the word *slogan*. Include context clues in your sentence.
- Write a slogan for your class or school.

Extension

- Have a class contest to choose the best class slogan.

Things you need:

- dictionary
- note card
- paper
- pencil

For additional vocabulary and spelling games, go to www.macmillanmh.com

Vocabulary PuzzleMaker

37

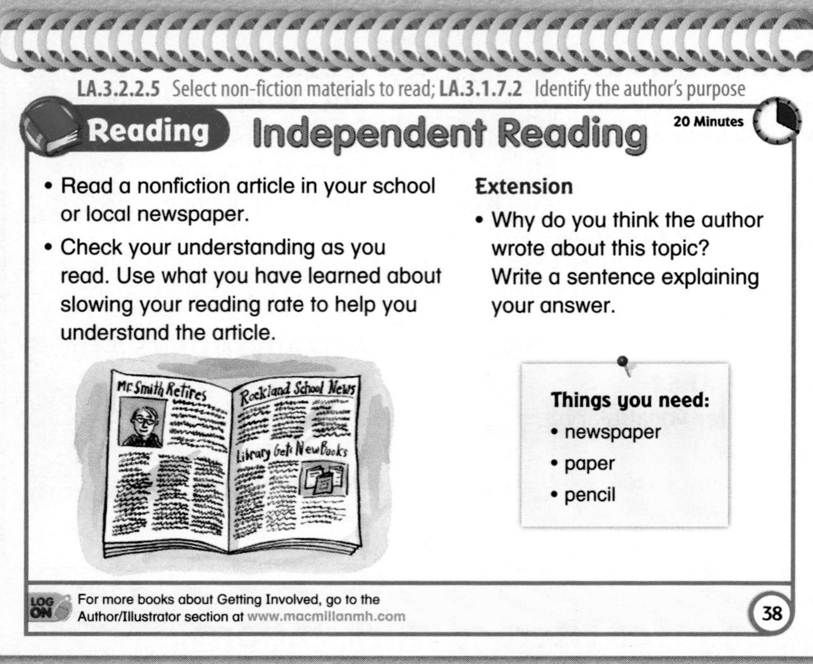

LA.3.2.2.5 Select non-fiction materials to read; LA.3.1.7.2 Identify the author's purpose

Reading — **Independent Reading** — 20 Minutes

- Read a nonfiction article in your school or local newspaper.
- Check your understanding as you read. Use what you have learned about slowing your reading rate to help you understand the article.

Extension

- Why do you think the author wrote about this topic? Write a sentence explaining your answer.

Things you need:

- newspaper
- paper
- pencil

For more books about Getting Involved, go to the Author/Illustrator section at www.macmillanmh.com

38

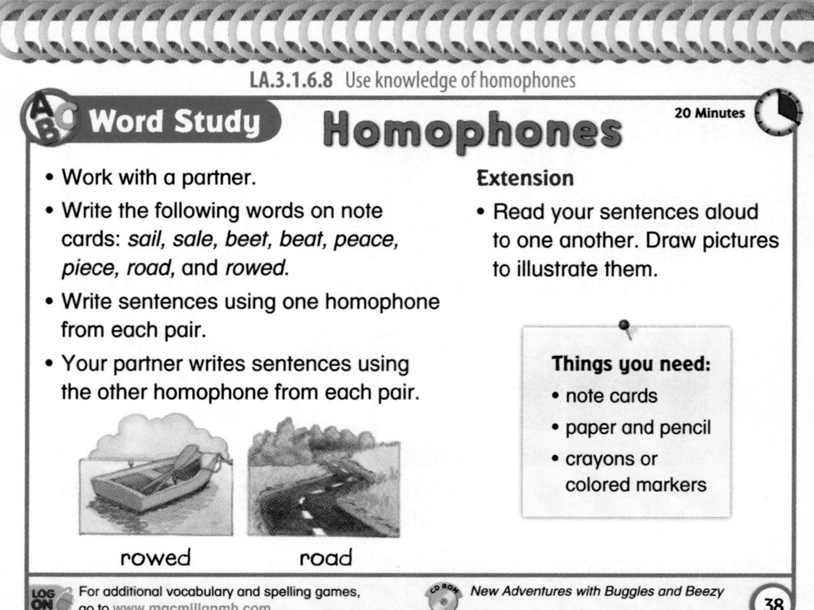

LA.3.1.6.8 Use knowledge of homophones

Word Study — **Homophones** — 20 Minutes

- Work with a partner.
- Write the following words on note cards: *sail, sale, beet, beat, peace, piece, road,* and *rowed.*
- Write sentences using one homophone from each pair.
- Your partner writes sentences using the other homophone from each pair.

Extension

- Read your sentences aloud to one another. Draw pictures to illustrate them.

Things you need:

- note cards
- paper and pencil
- crayons or colored markers

For additional vocabulary and spelling games, go to www.macmillanmh.com

New Adventures with Buggles and Beezy

38

Literacy Workstations

Writing

Objectives

- Write an explanatory paragraph about helping the community
- Write a speech about helping at school

Content Literacy

Objectives

- Research information about the water cycle
- Work with a partner to create a school or community project

---

LA.3.4.2.3 Write informational essays

Writing — **Explanatory Writing** — 20 Minutes

- Think about a time you helped a person or helped your community.
- Write a paragraph about what you did to help. Explain why you got involved.

Extension

- Draw a picture. Show what you did to help.

Things you need:
- paper
- pencil
- crayons or markers

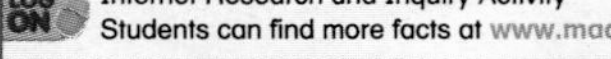
Internet Research and Inquiry Activity
Students can find more facts at www.macmillanmh.com

37

LA.3.6.1.1 Read informational text to perform a task; LA.3.4.1.2 Write expressive forms

Science — **The Water Cycle** — 20 Minutes

- Use a science book, an encyclopedia, or the Internet. Find information about how the water cycle works.
- Take notes on what happens in each step of the cycle.

Extension

- Write a poem about the water cycle. It does not need to rhyme, but you can use repetition. Repeat important words.

Things you need:
- science book, encyclopedia, or computer
- paper
- pencil

37

LA.3.4.2.3 Write informational essays; LA.3.3.5.3 Share writing with intended audience

Writing — **Speech, Speech!** — 20 Minutes

- Think of something you could do to help your school, such as cleaning up the playground or painting a classroom.
- Write a short speech. Tell what you want to do and how it will help.

Extension

- Read your speech aloud to some of your classmates.

Things you need:
- paper
- pencil

38

LA.3.2.1.5 Examine how language describes people, feelings, and objects

Social Studies — **Chant for Help** — 20 Minutes

- Work with a partner. Talk about a project you could do to help your school or community, such as starting a recycling program. Make a plan to make it happen.

Extension

- Make up a chant to get people excited about your project. Try to make your chant rhyme. Here are some words you might use: *street, neat; school, cool;* and *clean, green.*

Things you need:
- paper
- pencil

38

Prepare

ORAL LANGUAGE
- Build Background
- Read Aloud
- Expand Vocabulary

FCAT **VOCABULARY**
- Teach Words in Context
- **Context Clues:** Examples

COMPREHENSION
- **Strategy:** Monitor Comprehension
- **Skill:** Author's Purpose

FCAT

SMALL GROUP OPTIONS
- Differentiated Instruction, pp. 111M–111V

Oral Language

Build Background

ACCESS PRIOR KNOWLEDGE

Share the following information:

Volunteers are people who work for something they care about without getting paid. In 2005 more than 65 million people in the United States volunteered at least once. Volunteering is one way of "getting involved."

LA.3.5.2 Apply listening and speaking strategies

TALK ABOUT GETTING INVOLVED

Discuss the weekly theme. Ask: Have you ever helped do something for your school or your community?

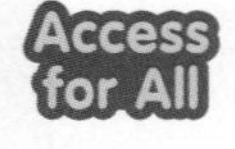

LA.3.1.7.1 Identify a text's features

FOCUS QUESTION Ask a volunteer to read "Talk About It" on **Student Book** page 91 and describe the photograph. Ask: What are these children doing to help their community?

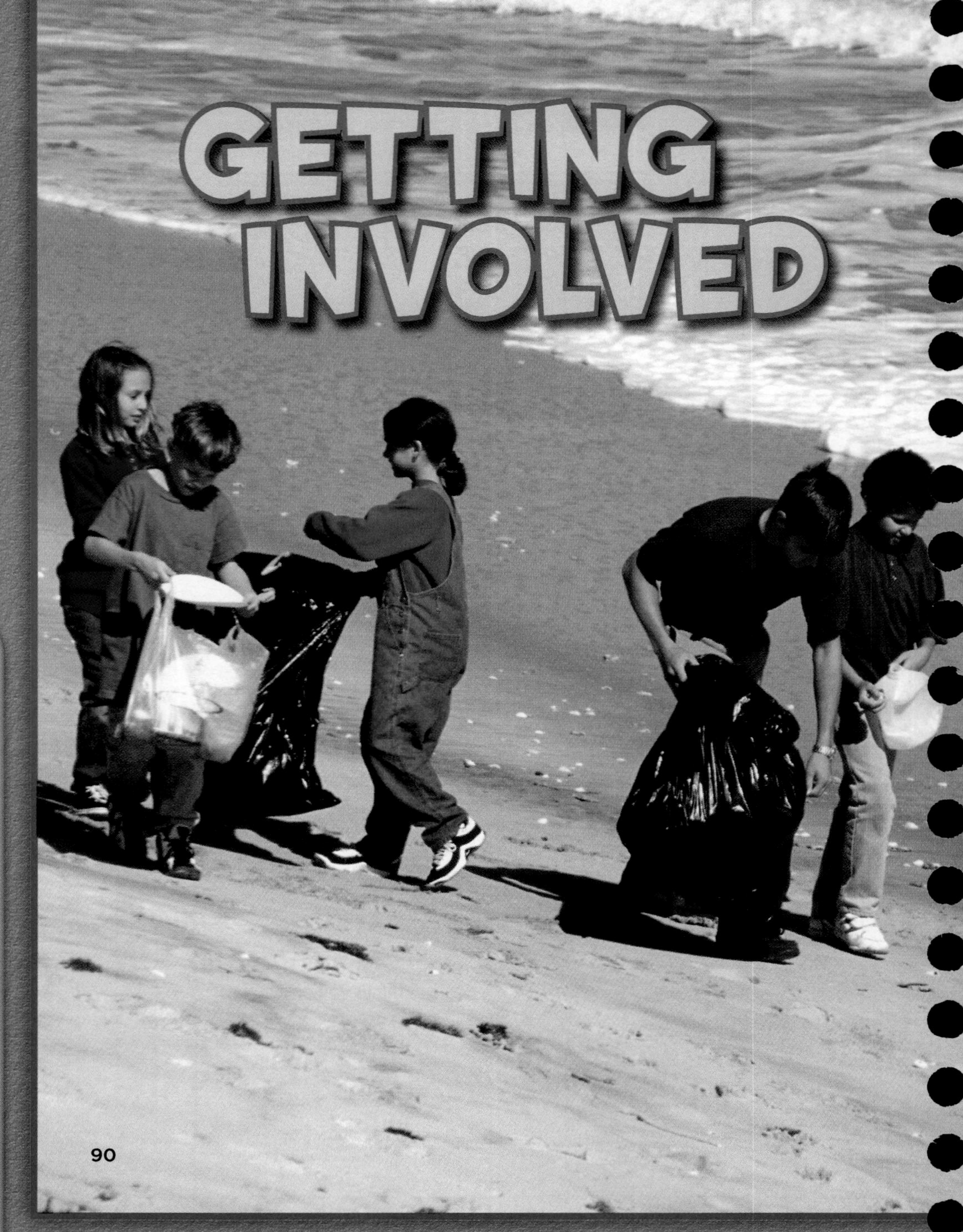

ENGLISH LANGUAGE LEARNERS

Access for All

Beginning **Ask Questions** Ask: *What do you see?* Help students answer. Say: *These people are cleaning up a beach. They are volunteers. Volunteers like to help other people. Do you like to help people? What do you do to help people?* Help students say what they can.

Intermediate **Relate to Personal Experience** Discuss the picture. Say: *These children are getting involved. They are helping their community.* Explain what a volunteer is. *What activities in your community are you involved in? How do you they help other people?*

Advanced **Share Information** Do the Intermediate task. As students talk, ask them questions to help them use more precise and descriptive language.

Talk About It

What are some ways that you can help your school or community?

LOG ON Find out more about getting involved at **www.macmillanmh.com**

91

Read Aloud

Read "The Song of the World's Last Whale"

LA.3.2.1.1 Understand distinguishing features of literature

GENRE: Folk Song Explain that folk songs may show strong feelings about a topic, usually have rhythm and rhyme, and are written in lines or stanzas.

Read Aloud pages 84–86

LA.3.1.6.2 Listen to text

LA.3.1.7.2 Identify the author's purpose

LISTENING FOR A PURPOSE

Ask students to identify the author's purpose in "The Song of the World's Last Whale" in the **Read-Aloud Anthology**. Choose from among the teaching suggestions.

Fluency Tell students to listen to your phrasing, expression, and tone of voice as you read aloud.

LA.3.2.1.7 Respond to, discuss, reflect on literary selections

RESPOND TO THE FOLK SONG

Have students retell, role-play, or reenact the song. Then ask: Why is it important to save whales? What does the poet mean when he says, "But it's upon the land/They decide my fate"? Students should support their answers with details from the folk song.

Expand Vocabulary

LA.3.1.6 Develop grade-appropriate vocabulary

Ask students to choose a few words about getting involved from the song, such as *heart*, *decide*, *feel*, and *save*.

LA.3.4.1.2 Write expressive forms

Have groups use the words to write lyrics for a song about a cause such as protecting trees or recycling.

Use the routine card to teach Expand Vocabulary words in the Read-Aloud lesson.

Picture Prompt

Look at the photograph. Write about what the children are doing. You can write a poem, a story, a description, or use any other type of writing you like.

LA.3.4.1 Develop and demonstrate creative writing

Technology

For an extended lesson plan, Web site activities, and additional Read Alouds for **oral language and vocabulary development**, go to **www.macmillanmh.com**

Vocabulary

LA.3.1.6.1 Use new vocabulary taught directly

FCAT **TEACH WORDS IN CONTEXT**

Use the following routine:

Routine

Define: A **tour** is a short trip to a place of interest with a guide.
Example: Our class took a tour of the science museum.
Ask: Have you ever been on a tour? What did you see? EXAMPLE

- **Volunteers** are people who do a job willingly without getting paid. Sometimes volunteers work in museums. Where else might volunteers work? PRIOR KNOWLEDGE
- A **community** is a group of people. The community planted trees. Why should people in a community help each other? EXPLANATION

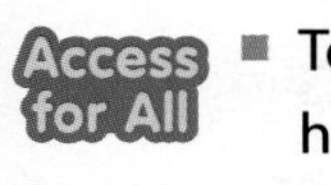

LA.3.1.6.3 Use context clues

- To be **thrilled** is to be very excited or happy. I was thrilled when everyone came to my party. When was a time that you were thrilled? EXAMPLE
- A **slogan** is an easy-to-remember phrase that is used in advertisements or by special groups or organizations. "Service with a smile" might be a good slogan for a store. Why should a slogan be easy to remember? EXPLANATION
- **Grownups** are adults. The grownups watched the children play. How are grownups different from teens? CONTRAST
- If you **deserve** something, you have a right to it. The girls deserve praise for their hard work. When do you deserve praise? EXPLANATION
- A person who is **interviewed** gives answers to questions that someone else asks. The mayor was interviewed on the radio. What would you tell about yourself if you were interviewed? DESCRIPTION

Vocabulary

tour	slogan
volunteers	grownups
community	deserve
thrilled	interviewed

FCAT **Context Clues**

Examples found in a sentence can help you figure out the meaning of some unknown words.

Use the example in the story to figure out the meaning of *slogan*.

GORILLA GARDEN

by Michael Feldman

Have you ever taken a **tour** of a zoo? If so, it's likely that the person who led you through the zoo helped you to learn a lot about the animals.

Amelia Rinas is a high school student who lives in Ohio. One day Amelia visited the Cleveland Metroparks Zoo. She worried about the gorillas she saw there. She wondered if they were getting the right foods.

Amelia read all she could about gorillas and learned what they like to eat. Then she started a "gorilla garden." She grows the fruits and vegetables that gorillas love to eat. Some of those foods are tomatoes, carrots, and strawberries. Amelia works with other **volunteers** in her **community** who use their extra time to help Amelia and the gorillas. When they take the food to the zoo, the gorillas are **thrilled**. They look so excited!

92

Quick Check **Do students understand word meanings?**

During **Small Group Instruction**

If No → **Approaching Level** Vocabulary, p. 111N

If Yes → **On Level** Options, pp. 111Q–111R

Beyond Level Options, pp. 111S–111T

ELL Access for All

Sentence Frames For the word *thrilled*, write this sentence frame to help students discuss their ideas: *I was thrilled when* ____. Give a few examples.

For *deserve*, write: *If you work hard, you deserve good grades. If you don't work hard, you don't deserve good grades.* Have students use this sentence frame to discuss their ideas: *If I* ____, *I deserve* ____.

Who is responsible for Amelia's interest in animals? Amelia is a member of Roots & Shoots. Its members are young people who care about animals and the environment. They helped Amelia understand that animals need our care, too. The **slogan** on the Roots & Shoots Web site is "Inspire, take action, make a difference." These words tell what the group is all about. The group urges kids and **grownups**, including parents and teachers, to do what they can to make a difference where they live.

Amelia believes that both people and animals **deserve** to be treated well.

When **interviewed** about her project, Amelia said, "I joined Roots & Shoots because I wanted to make a difference in the world."

There are many ways to make a difference in the world. Amelia Rinas's gorilla garden has helped make gorillas happier and healthier.

Reread for **Comprehension**

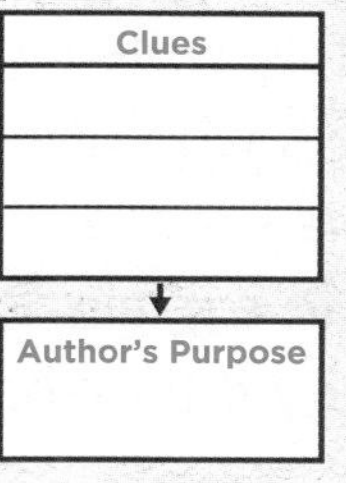

Monitor Comprehension

FCAT **Author's Purpose** An author writes to entertain, inform, or explain. Usually, an author will give readers **clues** that help readers figure out the **author's purpose**. You can help monitor your understanding of an article by thinking about the author's purpose. Reread the article. Use your Author's Purpose Chart to figure out why the author wrote this article.

Clues

↓

Author's Purpose

Prepare

Vocabulary/Comprehension Student page 93

Vocabulary

USING THE STRATEGIES

LA.3.1.4.1 Use knowledge of pronunciation to decode words

To figure out unfamiliar words, students can

LA.3.1.6.7 Use meaning of affixes to determine meanings

LA.3.1.6.10 Determine meanings using a dictionary and thesaurus

- decode words using phonics principles
- look for prefixes, suffixes, base words, and other word parts
- look for context clues
- use a dictionary or thesaurus

FCAT

STRATEGY CONTEXT CLUES

LA.3.1.6.3 Use context clues to determine meanings of unfamiliar words

Examples When students come across an unfamiliar word, they can look for clues in nearby sentences. One kind of clue is an **example**. It tells or shows exactly what the unfamiliar word is. Red and blue are examples of colors. Robins and owls are examples of birds.

Point to *slogan* on **Student Book** page 93. Read aloud the slogan for the organization Roots & Shoots, "Inspire, take action, make a difference." Help students see that this short, easy-to-remember saying is an example of a slogan. Being able to identify context clues that are examples can help students figure out unfamiliar words.

Have students find the two context clues that are examples of grownups on page 93. (parents, teachers)

Read "Gorilla Garden"

LA.3.1.6.3 Use context clues

As students read "Gorilla Garden," have them identify clues to the meanings of the highlighted words. Tell students they will read these words again in *Here's My Dollar.*

FCAT **Success!**

Test Prep and Practice with vocabulary, pages 6–31

Vocabulary

Review last week's vocabulary words: **native, shouldn't, research, sprout, clumps.** Have students name as many items as they can that *sprout.*

LA.3.1.6.1 Use new vocabulary

On Level Practice Book O, page 133

Complete each sentence with the vocabulary word that makes the most sense.

community	deserve	grownups	interviewed
slogan	thrilled	tour	volunteers

1. My friends and I are volunteers at the city food bank.
2. We were thrilled when we found out we were taking a field trip to the zoo.
3. My favorite tour at the zoo is of the reptile house.
4. To get to the zoo, ask your parents or other grownups for a ride.
5. A good motto or slogan is "Every little bit helps."
6. Everyone thinks that the zoo animals deserve a safe place to live.
7. I read in the paper that the zookeepers were interviewed by a reporter.
8. People who lived in the community helped raise money for the zoo.

 **Approaching Practice Book A,** page 133

◆ **Beyond Practice Book B,** page 133

Objectives

- Monitor comprehension
- Use academic language: *comprehension, author's purpose*
- Evaluate author's purpose

Materials

- Comprehension Transparencies 19a and 19b
- Graphic Organizer Transparency 19
- Leveled Practice Books, p. 134

FCAT Skills Trace

Author's Purpose	
Introduce	U1: 33B
Practice / Apply	U1: 11B; U2: 259A–B, 260–273
Reteach / Review	U2: 277M–T; U4: 93A–B, 94–107, 111M-T; Leveled Practice, 134–135
Assess	Weekly Tests; Unit 1, 2, 4, 6 Tests
Maintain	U3: 335B; U4: 39B; U6: 361A–B, 362–379, 383M–T; Leveled Practice, 215–216

ELL

Make Comparisons
Review the meanings of *entertain, inform*, and *explain*. Use TV examples of what entertains (comedies, cartoons), informs (news, science programs), and explains (cooking programs). Preview programs before showing to students. Draw a parallel between the purpose of different kinds of TV programs and an author's purpose.

Reread for Comprehension

STRATEGY
MONITOR COMPREHENSION

LA.3.1.7 Use strategies to comprehend text

LA.3.1.7.8 Use strategies to repair comprehension

Good readers **monitor comprehension** as they read. This means that they stop to check that they understand what they have read. They also stop when they do not understand something. If they are confused, they can reread, read ahead, paraphrase, visualize, summarize, adjust their reading rate, or seek help.

SKILL
AUTHOR'S PURPOSE

LA.3.1.7.2 Identify the author's purpose

EXPLAIN

Access for All

Author's purpose is the reason an author writes something. Authors write to entertain, to inform, or to explain. Authors who write to entertain write stories that are funny, interesting, or suspenseful. Authors who give a lot of facts write to inform. Authors who show readers how to do something or why they should do something write to explain. Readers can use the monitor comprehension strategy if they have trouble identifying the author's purpose.

Transparency 19a

Vocabulary
tour, slogan, volunteers, grownups, community, deserve, thrilled, interviewed

Context Clues
Examples found in a sentence can help you figure out the meaning of some unknown words.
Use the example in the story to figure out the meaning of *slogan*.

GORILLA GARDEN
by Michael Feldman

Have you ever taken a **tour** of a zoo? If so, it's likely that the person who led you through the zoo helped you to learn a lot about the animals.

Amelia Rinas is a high school student who lives in Ohio. One day Amelia visited the Cleveland Metroparks Zoo. She worried about the gorillas she saw there. She wondered if they were getting the right foods.

Amelia read all she could about gorillas and learned what they like to eat. Then she started a "gorilla garden." She grows the fruits and vegetables that gorillas love to eat. Some of those foods are tomatoes, carrots, and strawberries. Amelia works with other **volunteers** in her **community** who use their extra time to help Amelia and the gorillas. When they take the food to the zoo, the gorillas are **thrilled**. They look so excited!

92

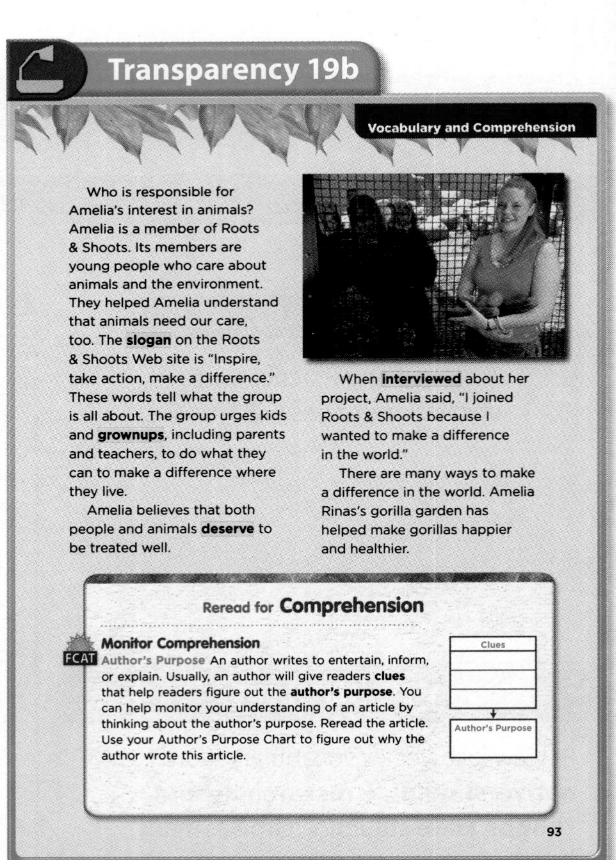

Transparency 19b

Vocabulary and Comprehension

Who is responsible for Amelia's interest in animals? Amelia is a member of Roots & Shoots. Its members are young people who care about animals and the environment. They helped Amelia understand that animals need our care, too. The **slogan** on the Roots & Shoots Web site is "Inspire, take action, make a difference." These words tell what the group is all about. The group urges kids and **grownups**, including parents and teachers, to do what they can to make a difference where they live.

Amelia believes that both people and animals **deserve** to be treated well.

When **interviewed** about her project, Amelia said, "I joined Roots & Shoots because I wanted to make a difference in the world."

There are many ways to make a difference in the world. Amelia Rinas's gorilla garden has helped make gorillas happier and healthier.

Reread for **Comprehension**

Monitor Comprehension
Author's Purpose An author writes to entertain, inform, or explain. Usually, an author will give readers **clues** that help readers figure out the **author's purpose**. You can help monitor your understanding of an article by thinking about the author's purpose. Reread the article. Use your Author's Purpose Chart to figure out why the author wrote this article.

93

Student pages 92–93 available on Comprehension Transparencies 19a and 19b

LA.3.1.7.2 Identify how author's perspective influences text

Author's perspective is how an author feels about a topic. By choosing lots of positive details, authors show that they think a topic is interesting or worthwhile.

MODEL

Read aloud the first two paragraphs of "Gorilla Garden" on page 92.

LA.3.1.7.3 Determine explicit information in grade level text

Think Aloud I see this is a nonfiction article about gorillas at a zoo. I know that authors often write nonfiction to inform or to explain, so I will look for clues to help me figure out the author's purpose. In the second paragraph on page 92, the author gives information about Amelia's trip to the zoo. I don't see any words that try to explain how to do something. So far, I think the author's purpose is to inform. I will keep reading to find out.

GUIDED PRACTICE

LA.3.1.7.2 Identify the author's purpose

- Display the Author's Purpose Chart on **Transparency 19**.
- Have students reread the second paragraph and identify its topic. On an Author's Purpose Chart, have them write this clue: *The author gives information about Amelia's trip to the zoo.* Help students identify other clues to place on the chart by asking: *Why do you think the author tells about the fruits and vegetables Amelia grows?* (The author wants readers to know what Amelia does when she is volunteering.)

APPLY

Have students reread the first paragraph on page 93. Ask: *What does the author tell about in this paragraph?* (He gives facts and details about the organization Roots & Shoots.) Add this clue to the chart. Then have students look at all the clues, figure out the author's purpose, and write it in the last box on the chart.

LA.3.1.7.2 Identify how author's perspective influences text

Ask students how the author feels about Amelia and how they can tell as they read the article. (I think the author admires Amelia because he presents a lot of interesting details about her gorilla garden.)

Quick Check **Can students identify the author's purpose in a nonfiction article?**

During **Small Group Instruction**

If No → Approaching Level Comprehension, p. 111O

If Yes → On Level Options, pp. 111Q–111R

Beyond Level Options, pp. 111S–111T

Transparency 19

AUTHOR'S PURPOSE CHART

Clues
The author gives information about Amelia's trip to the zoo.
The author tells what Amelia does while she is volunteering.
The author tells about Roots & Shoots and its members.

Author's Purpose
The author's purpose is to inform readers about a project and a group for young volunteers.

Graphic Organizer Transparency 19

FCAT Success!

Test Prep and Practice with author's purpose, pages 32–179

On Level Practice Book O, page 134

Authors write for three main reasons: to entertain, to inform, or to persuade. Identifying an **author's purpose** in writing can tell readers what to expect.

Read the following passages. Tell the author's purpose for writing each one.

1. Animals do not eat the same food as humans so some zoos sell food that you can feed to the animals. This food is part of their diet and is healthy for them. All animals need a proper diet to thrive.

   The author's purpose is ___to inform___.

2. Dad bought me a helium balloon. Suddenly, a monkey grabbed it from my hand. Off the monkey went, soaring into the air. A zookeeper sat on a giraffe to try and reach the silly monkey as it floated toward the clouds. That monkey has been grounded for a week!

   The purpose of this paragraph is ___to entertain___.

3. Keep our zoos and nature parks clean. Use the trash cans that are placed throughout the parks. Animals can cut themselves on soda cans. Their necks can get caught in plastic rings. They can swallow objects that make them choke. We need everyone's help. We all lose if we don't protect our animals.

   The purpose of this paragraph is ___to persuade___.

4. My class wanted to help out the community so we planted a vegetable garden in an empty lot near our school. We grew tomatoes, beans, and squash. We gave all the vegetables to a local food bank.

   The purpose of this paragraph is ___to inform___.

Approaching Practice Book A, page 134

Beyond Practice Book B, page 134

Read

MAIN SELECTION

- *Here's My Dollar*
- FCAT **Skill:** Author's Purpose

PAIRED SELECTION

- "Neighbors," "Recycling"
- **Literary Elements:** Rhyme Scheme and Repetition

SMALL GROUP OPTIONS

- Differentiated Instruction, pp. 111M–111V

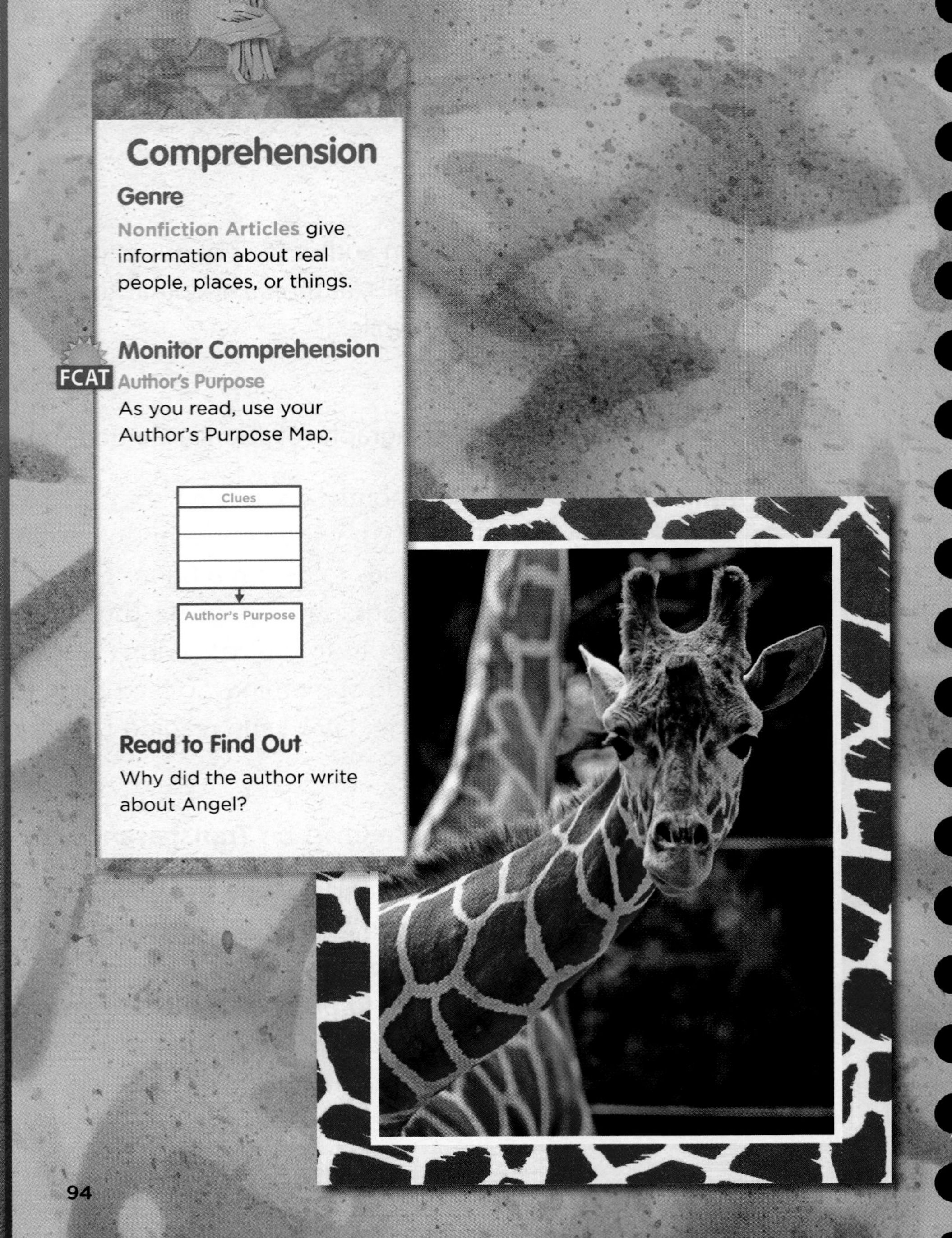

Comprehension

Genre

Nonfiction Articles give information about real people, places, or things.

Monitor Comprehension

FCAT Author's Purpose

As you read, use your Author's Purpose Map.

Read to Find Out

Why did the author write about Angel?

94

Comprehension

LA.3.2.2 Identify elements of non-fiction

LA.3.1.7.1 Identify a text's features

GENRE: NONFICTION ARTICLE

Have a student read the definition of Nonfiction Articles on **Student Book** page 94. Students should look for information about real people, places, or events in features such as photos, captions, headings, and text boxes.

LA.3.1.7 Use a variety of strategies to comprehend grade level text

LA.3.1.7.8 Use strategies to repair comprehension

STRATEGY
MONITOR COMPREHENSION

To **monitor comprehension**, good readers stop often to check that they understand what they are reading. They also learn to stop and help themselves when they don't understand what they are reading.

SKILL
AUTHOR'S PURPOSE

LA.3.1.7.2 Identify the author's purpose

Authors write to entertain, to inform, or to explain. Identifying an **author's purpose** can help readers evaluate and understand what they read.

FCAT Vocabulary

Vocabulary Words Review the tested vocabulary words: **tour, volunteers, community, thrilled, slogan, grownups, deserve, interviewed.**

Selection Words Students may find these words difficult. Pronounce the words and present their meanings as necessary.

zoologist (p. 96): someone who studies animals

plight (p. 98): a situation, especially one that is bad

LA.3.1.6.1 Use new vocabulary taught directly

Here's My Dollar

By Gary Soto

Angel poses with her cat.

How tall is a hero? If you had ever met nine-year-old Angel Arellano, you'd know a hero is four feet two inches tall. Angel's story began on Thanksgiving Day. She was in the kitchen listening to her Great-Grandmother Sandy.

Preview and Predict

LA.3.1.7.1 Use text features to make predictions

Ask students to read the title, preview the photographs and captions, note questions, and make predictions about the article. Why is a dollar important? Have students write their predictions and any questions they have about the article.

Set Purposes

LA.3.1.7.1 Use text features to establish purpose for reading

FOCUS QUESTION Talk about the "Read to Find Out" question and discuss how students can look for the answer as they read.

Point out the Author's Purpose Chart in the **Student Book** and on **Leveled Practice Book** page 135. Explain that students will fill in the chart as they read the selection.

Read *Here's My Dollar*

LA.3.1.6.2 Read text

LA.3.1.7 Use strategies to comprehend text

Use the questions and Think Alouds as additional instruction to support the comprehension strategy and skill.

On Level Practice Book O, page 135

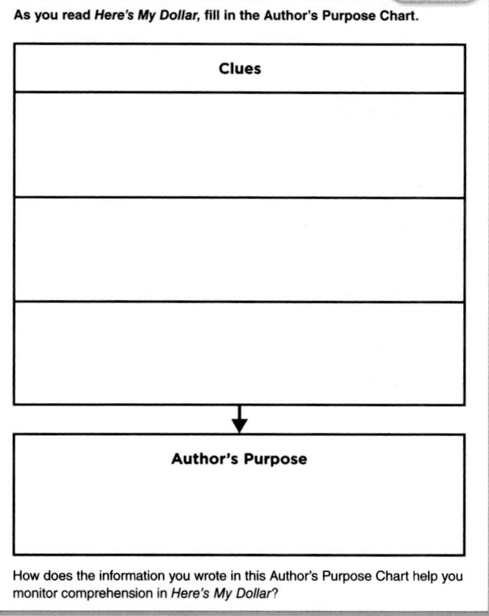
As you read *Here's My Dollar,* fill in the Author's Purpose Chart.

Clues

Author's Purpose

How does the information you wrote in this Author's Purpose Chart help you monitor comprehension in *Here's My Dollar?*

Approaching Practice Book A, page 135

Beyond Practice Book B, page 135

Read Together

If your students need support to read the Main Selection, use the prompts to guide comprehension and model how to complete the graphic organizer.

Read Independently

If your students can read the Main Selection independently, have them complete the graphic organizer. Have students set purposes and adjust their reading rate based on the purpose., text difficulty, form, and style.

If your students need an alternate selection, choose the **Leveled Readers** that match their instructional levels.

LA.3.1.5.2 Adjust reading rate based on purpose, text difficulty, form, style

Technology

Story available on **Listening Library Audio CD**

Develop Comprehension

1 STRATEGY
CONTEXT CLUES

LA.3.1.6.3 Use context clues

What other word in the sentence is an **example** of a reptile? (The word that is an example of a reptile is *boa constrictor*.)

2 AUTHOR'S PURPOSE

LA.3.1.7.2 Identify the author's purpose

Why does the author tell us about Angel's pets? Write this information in your Author's Purpose Chart. (The author shows that Angel loves animals by telling readers about her cats.)

Clues
The author shows that Angel loves animals by telling about her cats.

↓

Author's Purpose

"The zoo has money problems," Great-Grandmother Sandy remarked.

1 Angel listened. She heard that Fresno's Chaffee Zoo didn't have enough money to take care of its animals. Angel wondered what would happen to the elephants, the hippo, and her favorite reptile, the boa constrictor.

2 Angel loved animals. She planned to study them and become a zoologist when she grew up. In their own apartment in Fresno, Angel's family had four cats—Buster, Krystal, Rex, and Oreo. Angel took good care of them and made sure that they always had food and water.

FCAT Author's Purpose
Why does the author tell us about Angel's pets?

Angel holds a skink at the Chaffee Zoo.

96

ELL — Access for All

STRATEGIES FOR EXTRA SUPPORT

Question 2 AUTHOR'S PURPOSE

What pets does Angel have? How does she take care of them? Why does the author tell us this information? Why is it important to know this information about Angel?

Angel felt sorry for the zoo animals. While the **grownups** were cooking Thanksgiving dinner, Angel was cooking up a way to help the animals. She decided to write a letter to show how she felt.

When she finished writing, Angel showed the letter to her mom and her aunt. They changed some of the words and fixed the spelling. Then Angel copied her letter onto fancy stationery and added a **slogan** at the bottom: "Give a dollar, save a life." She slipped a dollar into the envelope and addressed it to *The Fresno Bee*, the local newspaper. **3**

Angel's letter to *The Fresno Bee*

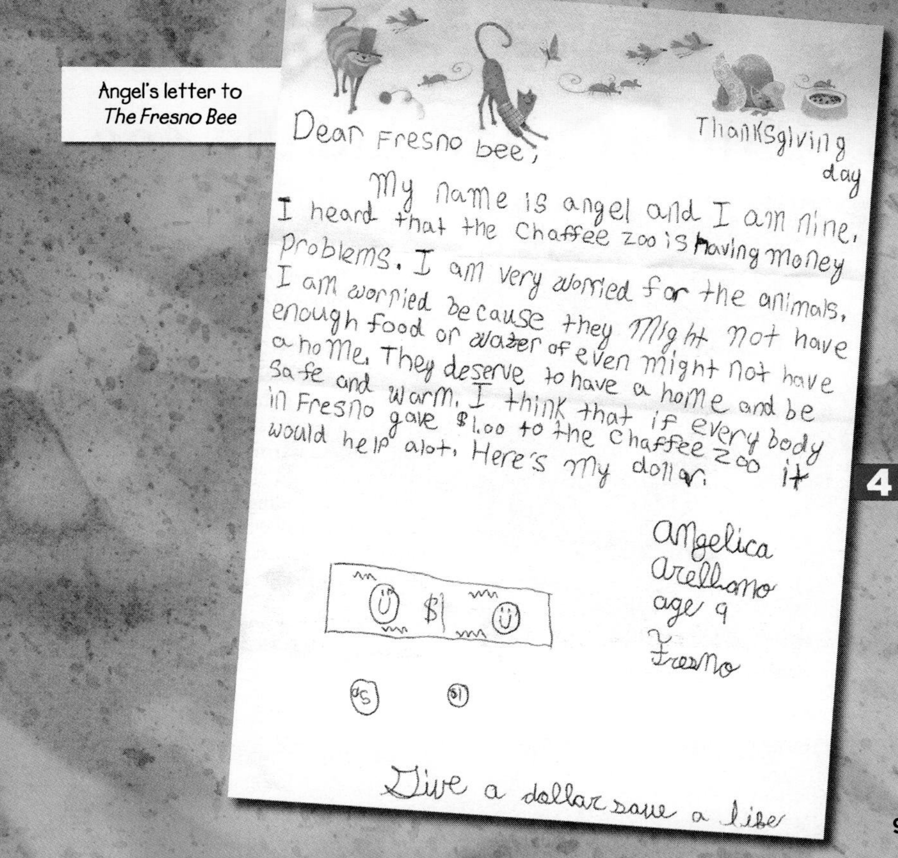

Dear Fresno bee,

Thanksgiving day

My name is angel and I am nine. I heard that the Chaffee zoo is having money problems. I am very worried for the animals. I am worried because they might not have enough food or water or even might not have a home. They deserve to have a home and be safe and warm. I think that if every body in Fresno gave $1.00 to the Chaffee zoo it would help alot. Here's my dollar.

Angelica
Arellano
age 9
Fresno

Give a dollar save a life

4

97

Develop Comprehension

3 STRATEGY
MONITOR COMPREHENSION

LA.3.1.7 Use a variety of strategies to comprehend grade level text

Teacher Think Aloud I want to make sure I understand what I am reading. On page 97 I don't understand why Angel sends her letter and a dollar to *The Fresno Bee* instead of to the zoo. I'll reread this page to look for information that can help me. I don't find the reason. Now I will read ahead and look for an answer to my question. I find an answer on the next page. I think she sent the letter to the newspaper because she hoped people would read it and help the zoo. Reading ahead helped me understand what was happening in the article.

4 AUTHOR'S PURPOSE

LA.3.1.7.2 Identify the author's purpose

What is the purpose of Angel's letter to the newspaper? What persuasive words did she use to influence readers? (Angel's purpose is to persuade people to send money to help the zoo. She used words like *worried* and *might not have a home* to influence readers.)

Fluency

Choral Reading

Explain When you read aloud, you read at a steady pace so that listeners are able to understand the information.

Model Read aloud the letter on **Student Book** page 97 available on **Transparency 19**. First, read slowly. The second time, read very fast. Finally, read at a normal tempo. Point out that this pace is just right for nonfiction because listeners can understand new information as it is read.

Apply Have students participate in a choral reading. One student should read the first sentence, then the next student joins in as the two read the second sentence together, then a third joins in, and so on. Have students continue until all students are reading together. When students reach the end of the passage, have them read again from the beginning until everyone has been included in the reading.

LA.3.1.5 Demonstrate the ability to read text orally with appropriate rate

Vocabulary

Read the sentence that contains the word **slogan**. Use *slogan* in a sentence of your own. (When the students made a poster for the talent show, they included a slogan that was easy to remember.)

LA.3.1.6.1 Use new vocabulary

Develop Comprehension

5 CHRONOLOGICAL ORDER

LA.3.1.7.3 Determine chronological order of events

What happened after Angel sent the letter to *The Fresno Bee*? How do you know? (A week after Angel sent her letter, a photographer from the paper took her picture. A few days later, her letter appeared in the paper. The signal words *a week later* and *a few days after that* show what happened after Angel sent the letter.)

6 AUTHOR'S PURPOSE

LA.3.6.3 Develop and demonstrate an understanding of media literacy

LA.3.1.7.2 Identify the author's purpose

Why does the author include the newspaper article entitled "Child's Call to Aid the Zoo" in this story? (The newspaper article shows that the events in the story really happened and that Angel is a hero. It also shows how much money Angel's letter raised for the zoo.)

Clues
The author shows that Angel loves animals by telling about her cats.
The newspaper article shows how much money Angel's letter raised for the zoo.

Author's Purpose

Angel hoped that other people might send a dollar, too, after they had read her letter. She didn't know that the zoo needed three million dollars, but that wouldn't have stopped her anyhow. Angel was a girl on a mission!

5 A week later, a man from *The Fresno Bee* came to take a picture of Angel. A few days after that, Angel's letter was published in *The Fresno Bee*. Almost immediately, people began sending in checks and dollar bills. Angel's letter was working!

6 7

Child's Call to Aid the Zoo

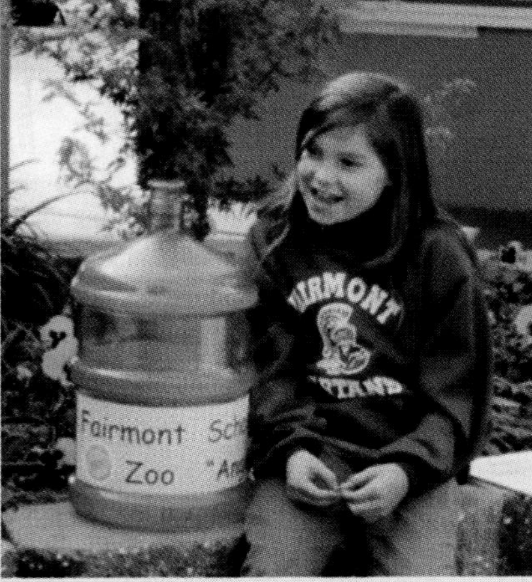

Angel Arellano collects money for the Chaffee Zoo.

By Jim Davis

Nine-year-old Angel Arellano is sparking a grass-roots effort to help the Chaffee Zoo through its financial plight. The little girl sent a letter to *The Bee* and enclosed a $1 donation for the zoo. She asked others to donate as well. "I just hope it will help," Angel said. "I want the animals to be safe and warm and let them get fed like my letter said." Dozens have followed Angel's lead, sending donations ranging from $1 to a $1,000 check that arrived Thursday. After just two days' mail, the zoo has received $5,084.

Text from an article about Angel in *The Fresno Bee*, December 6, 2003

98

FCAT Comprehension

Author's Purpose

Explain/Discuss Authors write to inform, to entertain, or to explain. When authors entertain, they tell a good story that is usually made up. When they explain, they tell how to do something. When they inform, they give facts and information about a topic.

Discuss the newspaper article on page 98. Help students see that the article gives facts about Angel's effort to help the zoo. Ask: *What is the article about?* (It is about how Angel's letter inspired other people to send money for the zoo.) What is the author's purpose for writing the article? (The author's purpose is to inform people about what Angel did.)

Apply Ask students to think about "Gorilla Garden" and explain how they would change the article to make it entertaining. (If the author use the information about helping the gorillas to make up a good fiction story, the purpose would be to entertain.)

LA.3.1.7.2 Identify the author's purpose

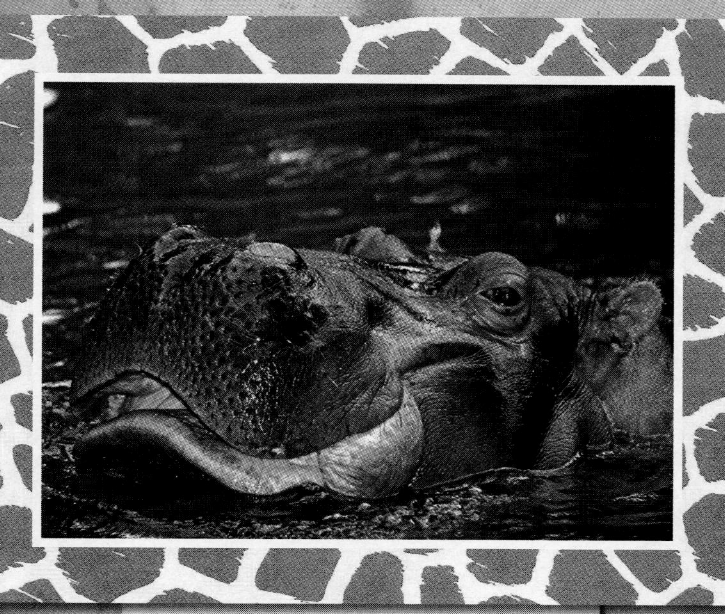

Hippos love the zoo's shallow river. 8

At school, Angel went to each classroom to read the letter that appeared in the newspaper. She asked her schoolmates to give money to the zoo. An empty water jug was placed in each classroom and in the main office. Students—and parents—began to fill the jugs with coins and dollar bills.

Angel's letter had touched the **community** of Fresno—and beyond. Donations for the Chaffee Zoo began to arrive from all over California. One donation came from as far away as England. It seemed as if the whole world wanted to help the zoo.

99

Comprehension

Make Generalizations

Explain A **generalization** is a broad conclusion that readers make from reading and from their own experiences. After reading the first paragraph on page 98, readers can make this generalization about Angel: She does not give up easily. The way she acts toward helping the zoo is probably how she acts in other situations.

Discuss What did people do when they read Angel's letter? (Many of them sent money to the zoo.) What generalization can you make about the people who sent money? (Like Angel, many people in Fresno care about animals and the Chaffee Zoo.)

Apply Help students make generalizations about the people of Fresno. Remind them to support their generalizations with specific details or examples from the text. (Many, but not all, people in Fresno gave money to help the zoo. Many people believe the zoo is important.)

LA.3.1.7 Use a variety of strategies to comprehend grade level text; **LA.3.1.7.3** Determine implied inference; **LA.3.1.7.3** Determine relevant supporting details

Develop Comprehension

7 STRATEGY
MONITOR AND CLARIFY: ADJUST READING RATE

LA.3.1.5.2 Adjust reading rate based on text difficulty

Why should you slow down to read the newspaper article on page 98? (Newspaper articles sometimes contain difficult information, so it is better to read them slowly.)

8 GENRE: NONFICTION ARTICLE

LA.3.2.2.1 Identify and explain the purpose of text features

What text features does this informational nonfiction article include? Why are they an important part of the article? (This informational nonfiction article includes photos with captions, a newspaper article about Angel, and a copy of Angel's letter. These text features give me more information and detail about the topic of the article, raising money for the zoo.)

Develop Comprehension

9 AUTHOR'S PERSPECTIVE

LA.3.1.7.2 Identify how author's perspective influences text

LA.3.1.7.3 Determine implied inference

How does the author feel about Angel? How can you tell? (The author admires Angel. I can tell because he shows that she is daring and brave. She lets a giraffe take an apple slice out of her mouth. She agrees to speak in front of large groups of people about the zoo.)

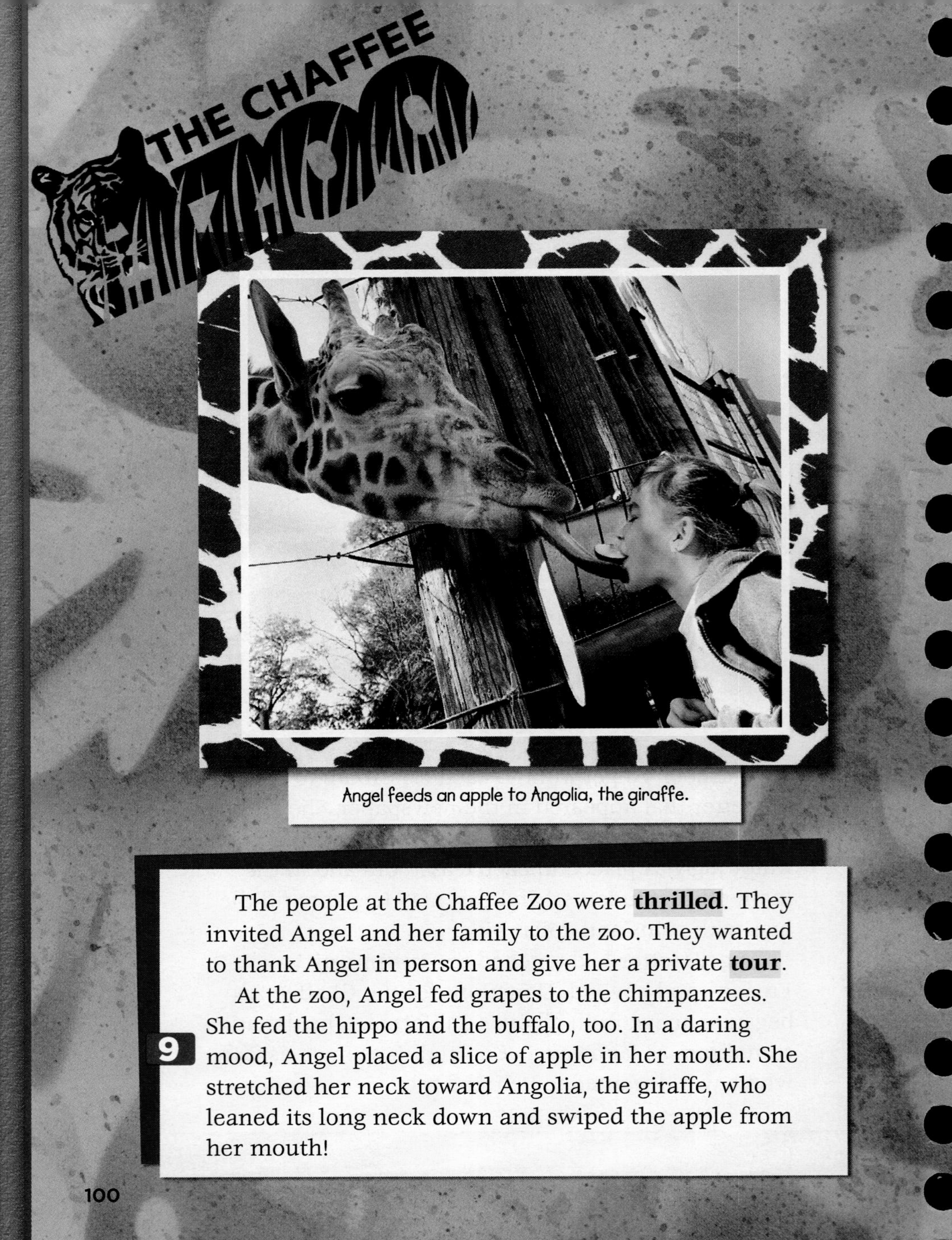

Angel feeds an apple to Angolia, the giraffe.

The people at the Chaffee Zoo were **thrilled**. They invited Angel and her family to the zoo. They wanted to thank Angel in person and give her a private **tour**.

9 At the zoo, Angel fed grapes to the chimpanzees. She fed the hippo and the buffalo, too. In a daring mood, Angel placed a slice of apple in her mouth. She stretched her neck toward Angolia, the giraffe, who leaned its long neck down and swiped the apple from her mouth!

100

Music

Cross-Curricular Connection

CARNIVAL OF THE ANIMALS

The zoo was one of French composer Camille Saint-Saëns's (1835–1921) favorite places, so he composed *Carnival of the Animals*. This amusing music includes musical portraits of a lion, elephant, fish, kangaroos, hens, and a swan.

Have students listen to a recording of *Carnival of the Animals*. Ask them each to choose an animal and explain how the sound and tempo of the music depict the animal. Then have them use the music to help them write descriptive paragraphs or poems using figurative language about their animals. Students can also put on a performance in which they take the parts of the animals as each musical "portrait" plays. Then have them take turns asking questions and analyzing the performances.

LA.3.4.1.2 Employ figurative language; LA.3.4.1.2 Write expressive forms

Angel went on being a regular kid—for a while. Before long, she was asked to make public appearances to talk about the zoo. The zoo still needed money, and Angel was happy to help. The principal of her school drove her to other schools in the area. He was just as concerned about the zoo animals as Angel.

"The zoo needs your help," Angel told the other children. "We can all make a difference."

During these appearances, Angel autographed pieces of paper, posters, and lots of shirts and caps. **10** When reporters **interviewed** her, she tried to be herself. She spoke from her heart.

Angel prepares to make a public service announcement.

101

Develop Comprehension

10 AUTHOR'S PURPOSE

FCAT

LA.3.1.7.2 Identify the author's purpose

Why does the author tell the reader about Angel's public appearances, interviews, and the items she autographed? (These details give more information about Angel. They show that she was willing to do more than just write a letter to help her local zoo.)

LA.3.1.7.1 Use text features to confirm predictions

Have students respond to the selection by confirming or revising their predictions and purposes. Encourage them to write new questions they may have about the selection.

Quick Check

Can students identify clues about the author's purpose in the article? If not, see the Extra Support on this page.

Extra Support

FCAT

Author's Purpose

Help students identify details to help them figure out the author's purpose. Ask: *Why does Angel travel to schools?* (She asks people to help.) *Do most students do things like this?* (No.) *What does this show about Angel?* (It shows she will do more than write a letter.) *Why did the author include these details?* (They give information about Angel.)

If students have difficulty identifying clues about the author's purpose, review the main reasons that authors write and ask them these questions: *When you read page 101, do you laugh?* (No.) *Is the author asking you to do something?* (No.) *Does the author give you information about Angel?* (Yes.) Ask students to identify facts about Angel's actions. Help them see that these facts give readers information.

LA.3.1.7.2 Identify the author's purpose; **LA.3.1.7.8** Question to repair comprehension

Vocabulary

Read the sentence that contains the word **interviewed**. Tell students to describe what Angel and the reporters may have talked about while Angel was being interviewed. (This can be an oral or written activity.)

LA.3.1.6.1 Use new vocabulary

Stop here if you wish to read this selection over two days.

Develop Comprehension

11 SUMMARIZE

LA.3.1.7.8 Summarize to repair comprehension

What has happened in the story so far? (Angel hears that the zoo in Fresno has money problems. She writes a letter to the newspaper and asks people in Fresno to send a dollar to the zoo. She sends the first dollar with her letter. The newspaper prints Angel's letter. Money begins to arrive. Then the zoo invites Angel and her family to visit. Soon Angel goes to other schools to talk about helping the zoo. She also gets interviewed by newspaper reporters.)

12 STRATEGY MONITOR COMPREHENSION

LA.3.1.7.8 Use strategies to repair comprehension

Teacher Think Aloud Suppose you don't understand why more donations to the zoo arrived after Angel's appearance on television. Explain what you can do to understand this part of the story.

(Encourage students to apply the strategy in a Think Aloud.)

LA.3.1.7.8 Reread to repair comprehension

Student Think Aloud First, I'll stop reading and decide what strategy to use. I'll reread this page. I find that Angel went on a popular talk show. This means that a lot of people watch the show. I think that many people saw Angel and heard about the zoo. They wanted to help, so they sent money. Now I understand why more donations came. Rereading helped me understand this part of the story.

11 Next, Angel was asked to appear on television. She was invited to be on a popular talk show. Angel flew from Fresno to Los Angeles. It was the first time she was ever on a plane!

At the television studio, Angel entered the stage to applause and her favorite rock music. She smiled and waved. The audience was rooting for her. They were rooting for the zoo animals back in Fresno, too.

More donations arrived after Angel's appearance on television. The Chaffee Zoo got larger and larger checks. One was for $10,000. Another was for $15,000. And one was for $50,000!

12 Of course, many donations were still just for one dollar. Children were sending in what they had, just as Angel had done on Thanksgiving Day.

Angel boards a plane to make a television appearance.

102

Media Literacy

Compare Media: *Newspaper and Television Reporting*

Explain/Discuss News events are reported in both newspapers and on television. The way these two medias report an event may be slightly different. Both newspaper articles and television news shows told about Angel's efforts to save the zoo. Ask students how the reports may have been different.

Apply Bring in a Grade 3-appropriate newspaper article and a video clip of a TV newscast on the same topic. Have students compare the two. Ask: *What is the main idea of each? Which details are presented in both? Which details appear in one but not the other? Which gives more information? How do these medias contribute to communication and serve an important role in people's lives?* Have each student write a short paragraph about which type of media is better and why.

LA.3.6.3 Develop and demonstrate an understanding of media literacy; **LA.3.6.3.1** Determine main content and supporting details in print media message

Zookeeper Mary helps Angel hold a boa constrictor.

Everyone was behind Angel and the zoo. High school teams held car washes to raise money. **Volunteers** showed up at the zoo to help paint and clean up. A local business made T-shirts with a picture of the zoo on the front.

The zookeepers were very happy. Ray Navarro is the person most responsible for the animals. He has hauled thousands of buckets of water for the animals. He has pushed wheelbarrows of hay for the elephants, the giraffes, and the zebras. "Angel opened the eyes of Fresno," said Ray. "She made us see that people can make a difference." **13**

FCAT **Author's Purpose**
Why did the author choose to write about Angel?

103

Develop Comprehension

13 AUTHOR'S PURPOSE

FCAT

LA.3.1.7.2 Identify the author's purpose

Why did the author choose to write about Angel? Place your ideas in the Author's Purpose box on the Author's Purpose Chart. (The author gives a lot of information about how Angel helped raise money for the zoo. I think the author admired her. The author's purpose is to inform readers about how one person like Angel can make a difference in her community.)

Clues
The author shows that Angel loves animals by telling about her cats.
The newspaper article shows how much money Angel's letter raised for the zoo.
Angel's letter and her visits to schools and television shows made other people want to help.

↓

Author's Purpose
to inform readers that one person can make a difference in her community

ELL Access for All

Understand Idioms Write on the board the first sentence on page 103: *Everyone was behind Angel and the zoo.* Point out that the sentence means that people agreed with Angel. Ask two volunteers to come to the front. Have the first student say: *We should help the zoo.* Have the second student say: *We shouldn't help the zoo.* Walk over to the first student and say: *I agree. We should help the zoo. I stand behind [say the first student's name]. I don't stand behind [say the second student's name].*

RESEARCH Why It Matters

English Language Learners Research indicates that ELLs need access to the specific types of oral and written language that are required for making academic progress, that is, academic English.

Jana Echevarria

Log on to **www.macmillanmh.com**

Develop Comprehension

14 **AUTHOR'S PURPOSE**

FCAT

LA.3.1.7.2 Identify the author's purpose

Why did the author include information about how the zoo used the donations? (The author wanted to inform readers about how the money was spent and to show how much can be done when people pitch in to help.)

15 **STRATEGY**
MONITOR COMPREHENSION

What can you do to better understand the last three sentences on page 105? Explain your thinking.

LA.3.1.7.8 Use strategies to repair comprehension

Student Think Aloud When I come to a part of the story that I don't understand, I'll stop and figure out what to do. Page 105 is the last page of the story, so I can't read ahead to find an answer. The last three sentences are short and simple, so I don't need to put them in my own words. Since this is the end, I will try summarizing. This may help me understand why the animals might thank Angel and call her a hero. When I summarize what has happened in a story, I briefly paraphrase the main events. I remember that the zoo was going to close. Angel got the community to help the zoo. They raised enough money to keep it open. This is why the zoo didn't close and the animals didn't lose their home. This is also why the animals would thank Angel and call her a hero. Summarizing and paraphrasing helped me figure out why Angel's work was so important.

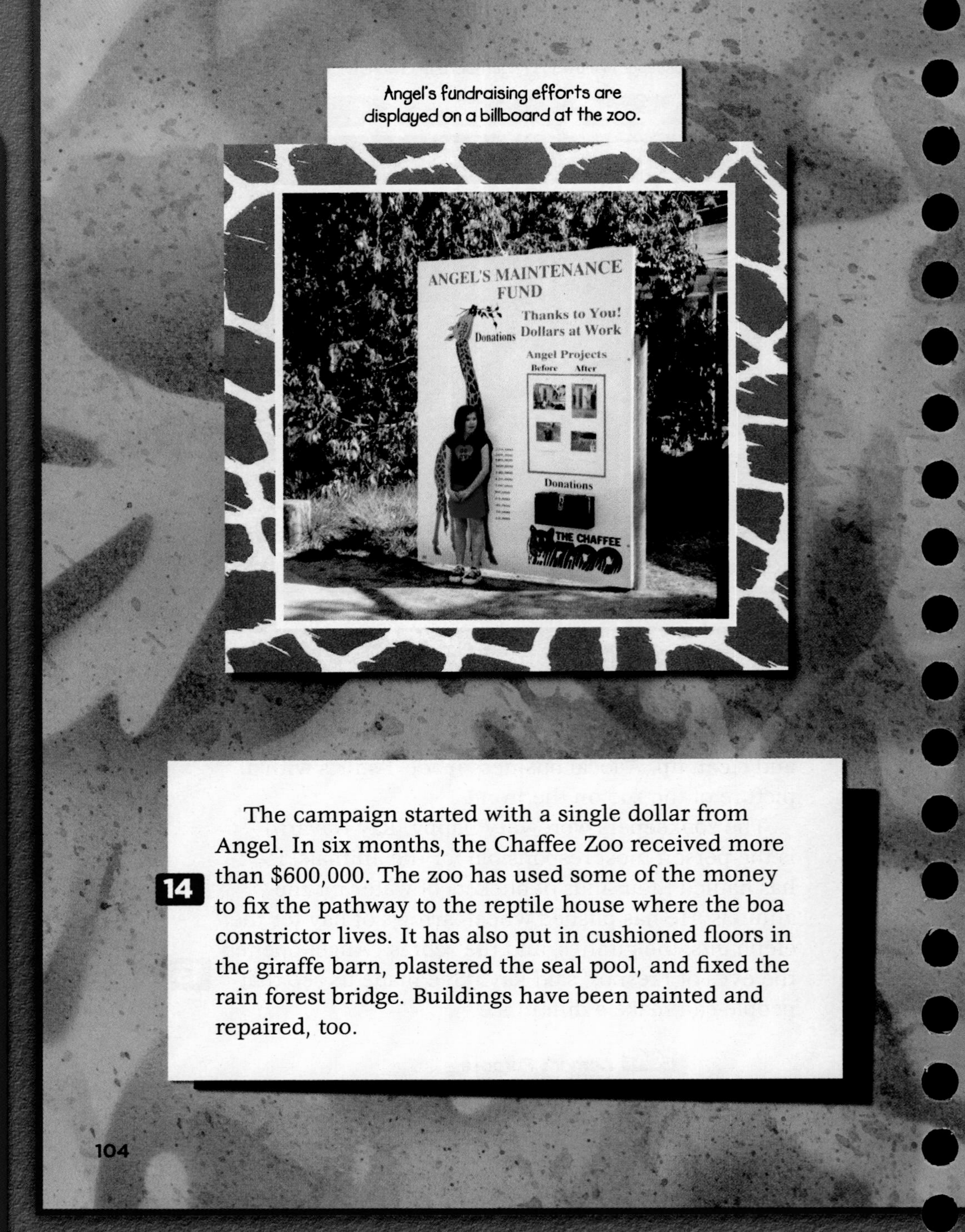

Angel's fundraising efforts are displayed on a billboard at the zoo.

14 The campaign started with a single dollar from Angel. In six months, the Chaffee Zoo received more than $600,000. The zoo has used some of the money to fix the pathway to the reptile house where the boa constrictor lives. It has also put in cushioned floors in the giraffe barn, plastered the seal pool, and fixed the rain forest bridge. Buildings have been painted and repaired, too.

104

ELL Access for All

STRATEGIES FOR EXTRA SUPPORT

Question 14 AUTHOR'S PURPOSE

How much money did the zoo collect in six months? Where did the money come from? Did many people make donations? What did the Chaffee Zoo use the money for? Why do you think the author told us how the zoo spent the money?

The campaign to save the Chaffee Zoo has been exciting. People from Fresno are proud that a young girl woke up their own community spirit. The zoo is looking better and better. And even though the zoo animals can't speak human languages, if they could, they might say, "You are a hero to us, Angel Arellano. You **deserve** our thanks for saving our zoo." 15

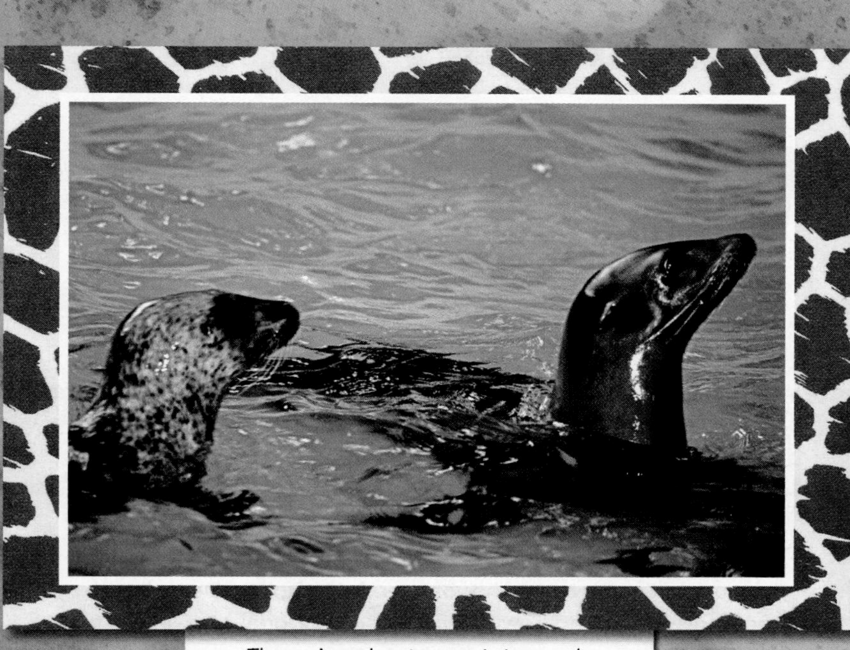

The zoo's seals enjoy a swim in a newly plastered pool, thanks to Angel.

Develop Comprehension

LA.3.1.7.1 Use text features to confirm predictions

RETURN TO PREDICTIONS AND PURPOSES

Review students' predictions and purposes. Were they correct? Did students figure out why a dollar is important in this selection?

LA.3.1.7 Use strategies to comprehend text

REVIEW READING STRATEGIES

Ask students: How did monitoring your comprehension and figuring out the author's purpose help you better understand what happened in the story?

LA.3.4.2.4 Write formal letters

LA.3.4.3.1 Write persuasive text

PERSONAL RESPONSE

Have each student write a persuasive formal letter to a local newspaper about a place in the community that needs help, such as a park, library, or zoo. Ask students to explain how people can help and to state their opinions clearly. Review the format of a formal letter. Have students mail their letters. Review how to address an envelope with the return and recipient addresses.

Quick Check **Can students identify the author's purpose for writing a selection?**

During **Small Group Instruction**

If No → Approaching Level Leveled Reader Lesson, p. 111P

If Yes → On Level Options, pp. 111Q–111R

Beyond Level Options, pp. 111S–111T

Author

HERE'S OUR AUTHOR

Have students read the author's biography.

DISCUSS

LA.3.1.7.3 Determine implied message

- In Here's My Dollar, what was Gary Soto's message to the reader? How can you tell?
- Why do you think Gary Soto visits Fresno often?

WRITE ABOUT IT

LA.3.4.2.4 Write messages

Discuss with students what they would like to do to help their community. Have each student write a message to the other students in the school asking them to join in a group project. For example, they might ask classmates to clean up a park, collect food for animal shelters, or give books to the library. Have students share their messages with partners.

FCAT Author's Purpose

Discuss with students how the author presents facts and information about a nonfiction topic. Help them to conclude that the author's purpose is to inform readers about how one girl made a huge difference in her community.

LA.3.1.7.2 Identify the author's purpose

LOG ON Technology

Students can find more information about Gary Soto at **www.macmillanmh.com**

Here's Our Author

Gary Soto was born and raised in Fresno, California, which is also the hometown of the Chaffee Zoo. He has written many poems and stories for children and adults. In his spare time, Gary loves to read, play tennis and basketball, and travel. He still visits Fresno often, and there is a library named for him at Winchell Elementary School in Fresno.

Other books by Gary Soto: *Baseball in April* and *Chato's Kitchen*

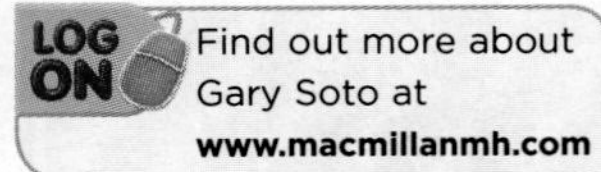

Find out more about Gary Soto at **www.macmillanmh.com**

FCAT Author's Purpose

Suppose you were the author of "Here's My Dollar." Describe why you wrote this article and how you achieved your goal. Use details from the article in your answer.

106

Author's Craft

Descriptive Details in Nonfiction

Gary Soto uses **descriptive details** to capture Angel's personality.

- Descriptive details help readers picture what Angel looks like and how she acts. For example: *How tall is a hero? If you had ever met nine-year-old Angel Arellano, you'd know a hero is four feet two inches tall.* (p. 95)
- This detail helps readers picture Angel Arellano. Ask students to find details from the selection that show how Angel acts and feels. ("But that wouldn't have stopped her. Angel was a girl on a mission"; Angel was "in a daring mood" when she fed the giraffe.)

Have students explain what these descriptive details tell about Angel. (She is "hard-working" and "brave.")

LA.3.2.1.5 Examine how language describes people; LA.3.2.1.5 Explain author's use of descriptive language

FCAT Comprehension Check

Summarize

Summarize "Here's My Dollar." Use your Author's Purpose Chart to help you.

Think and Compare

1. Why do you think Gary Soto wrote "Here's My Dollar"? Use examples and information from the article in your answer. **Monitor Comprehension: Author's Purpose**
2. Reread pages 97–99. Explain how Angel "touched the community" of Fresno and beyond. How did *The Fresno Bee* help do this? Use article details in your answer. **Analyze**
3. Think of a good cause in your own community that needs help, such as a school, library, or park. How would you encourage people to help? **Apply**
4. Why is using a **slogan** a good way to help raise money for a cause? Use information from the story to support your ideas. **Synthesize**
5. Reread "Gorilla Garden" on pages 92–93. How are Amelia and Angel alike? Describe the different ways they help animals. **Reading/ Writing Across Texts**

107

Strategies for Answering Questions

On My Own

Model the On My Own strategy with question 3. Students will not find the answers to On My Own questions in the selection. Sometimes they will be asked to form an opinion. Other times they will use information they already know.

Question 3: Think Aloud The answer to this question won't be in the story because it asks me what I would do. I'll have to think about what people did in the story and then form my opinion. I also want to think about my own community. There is a library in my town, but its books are very old. I could start a drive for books and a fundraising activity to raise money for the library to buy new books. I could also write a letter and ask our community paper to print it. That's what Angel did in *Here's My Dollar* and it worked very well. Thinking about the story and what I already know helped me to form an opinion and answer the question.

LA.3.1.7 Use strategies to comprehend text

Comprehension Check

SUMMARIZE

LA.3.1.7.8 Summarize to repair comprehension

Have students write a summary of *Here's My Dollar* by paraphrasing the main events. Remind students to use their Author's Purpose Charts.

THINK AND COMPARE

Sample answers are given.

LA.3.1.7.2 Identify the author's purpose

1. **Author's Purpose:** Gary Soto's story tells us about the things Angel did to help her community, so his purpose was to inform.

LA.3.2.2.2 Answer questions related to relevant details

2. **Analyze:** Angel touched her community by supporting something she believed in and getting others in her community to believe too. *The Fresno Bee*'s article about Angel and her cause drew a lot of attention and helped raise money for the zoo.

LA.3.2.1.7 Connect text to self

3. **Text-to-Self:** Answers will vary depending on the needs of the community. Students may choose to write letters to a local newspaper or hold a fundraiser. USE ON MY OWN

LA.3.2.1.7 Connect text to world

4. **Text-to-World:** Using a clever slogan is a successful way to get people's attention and a way to remind them to support a good cause.

FOCUS QUESTION

LA.3.2.1.7 Connect text to text

LA.3.1.7.7 Compare and contrast problems

5. **Text-to-Text:** Both Amelia and Angel worried about zoo animals and thought of ways that they could help, but they did very different things. Amelia started a garden to grow food for gorillas. She works with Roots & Shoots. Angel wrote a letter to a newspaper that asked people to give money to the zoo. She also made public appearances.

Objectives

- Read accurately with prosody
- Rate: 82–102 WCPM

Materials

- Fluency Transparency 19
- Fluency Solutions Audio CD
- Leveled Practice Books, p. 136

ELL Access for All

Read at an Appropriate Rate Ask students to explain why Angelica is worried about the zoo. Help as needed. Echo-read the passage with students at a slow but steady pace. Do this a few times, increasing the pace a bit each time.

AUDIO CD

On Level Practice Book O, page 136

As I read, I will pay attention to tempo.

All playgrounds should be safe. But some of them are
10 not. Sometimes playground equipment breaks down. And
17 a broken piece of equipment can be dangerous. Sometimes
26 there are holes in the ground where children can trip and
37 fall. Kids and even grownups don't always recognize these
46 dangers.
47 One nine-year-old girl did spot dangers on a playground,
56 and she decided to take action. She came up with a
67 wonderful plan for making the playground safe. She's
75 Devan Hickey, a fun-loving girl who lives in Bryan, Ohio.
85 First Devan got all her facts together. Then she reported
95 her plan to a group of people in her community who could
107 help her. She also asked family and friends to help out. She
119 didn't give up until the playground was safe. Read her
129 story. 130

Comprehension Check

1. How do playgrounds become unsafe? **Main Idea and Details** when equipment breaks down or when the ground has holes
2. What steps did Devan follow to make a playground safer? **Chronological Order** Devan got all her facts together, reported her plan to improve the playground, and asked for help.

	Words Read	–	Number of Errors	=	Words Correct Score
First Read		–		=	
Second Read		–		=	

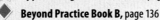

 **Approaching Practice Book A,** page 136

Beyond Practice Book B, page 136

Fluency

Repeated Reading: Tempo

LA.3.1.5 Demonstrate the ability to read text orally with appropriate rate

EXPLAIN/MODEL Model reading one or two sentences on **Fluency Transparency 19**. Pay special attention to your reading rate and prosody. First read at a faster rate, then at a slower rate, and finally at a normal tempo. Remind students that reading at a normal tempo helps increase understanding of this nonfiction material.

Transparency 19

Dear Fresno Bee,

My name is Angel and I am nine. I heard that the Chaffee Zoo is having money problems. I am very worried for the animals. I am worried because they might not have enough food or water or even might not have a home. They deserve to have a home and be safe and warm. I think that if everybody in Fresno gave $1.00 to the Chaffee Zoo it would help a lot. Here's my dollar.

Angelica Arellano
age 9
Fresno

Fluency Transparency 19 from *Here's My Dollar*, page 97

LA.3.1.5.2 Adjust reading rate

PRACTICE/APPLY Do a choral reading with students at a normal pace. Then have students do their own choral reading. First, one student reads a sentence at a slower pace. The next student joins in, then a third, and so on, until all students are reading together. When students reach the end of the passage, they should return to the beginning and continue reading until everyone has been included. Repeat this pattern at a faster, then a normal, tempo, adjusting reading rate. For additional practice, have students use **Leveled Practice Book** page 136 or the **Fluency Solutions Audio CD**.

Quick Check **Can students read accurately with prosody?**

During **Small Group Instruction**

If No → Approaching Level Fluency, p. 111N

If Yes → On Level Options, pp. 111Q–111R

Beyond Level Options, pp. 111S–111T

Comprehension

EXPLAIN/MODEL

LA.3.1.7.3 Determine chronological order of events
LA.3.1.7.5 Identify the text structure an author uses

- **Chronological order**, or **sequence**, is the order in which events happen or is a way to present information in time order. Authors use the sequence text structure when they write about events that happened in the past. They also use sequence when writing directions and steps in a process.
- Signal words such as *first*, *next*, *last*, *before*, *when*, and *after* tell readers the order in which events happen. The signal word *while* shows that two things are happening at the same time.

Model how to identify chronological order in "Gorilla Garden." Point out the chronological order in the second and third paragraphs on page 92. Help students see how the signal word *when* helps the reader understand the order of events. After learning all she could about gorillas and what they love to eat, Amelia decided to help by growing fruits and vegetables for the gorillas at a local zoo.

PRACTICE/APPLY

Work with students to identify sequence of events in *Here's My Dollar*. For comprehension practice, use graphic organizers on pages 99–112 in the **Teacher's Resource Book**.

LA.3.1.7.3 Determine chronological order of events

- What is the sequence of events on page 97? What signal words help you figure this out? (While the adults were cooking dinner, Angel wrote a letter. Then, she showed the letter to her mom and aunt. Next, they changed some of the words and fixed the spelling. Then Angel copied the letter on special paper and added a slogan. The last thing she did was put the letter in an envelope. The signal words are *while*, *when*, and *then*.)
- On page 98, what happened after Angel sent the letter? What signal words help you figure this out? (A man from a newspaper came to take a picture of Angel. Next, Angel's letter was published. Then people started sending in money. The signal words are *a week later*, *a few days after that*, and *almost immediately*.)

LA.3.3.2.2 Organize information into logical sequence
LA.3.4.2.2 Record information related to a topic

Have student pairs identify and discuss the sequence, or chronological order, of the events in this article about Angel. As a group, have them write a summary and record events in chronological order on a time line.

Objectives

- Recognize and arrange events in chronological order
- Use academic language: *chronological order, sequence, signal words*

FCAT Skills Trace

Chronological Order	
Introduce	U2: 273B
Practice / Apply	U3: 304, 335B, 387A–B; Leveled Practice, 104–105
Reteach / Review	U3: 4170–P, R, T; U5: 153A–B, 154–175, 1830–P, R, T; Leveled Practice, 150–151
Assess	Weekly Tests; Unit 2, 3, 4, 5, 6 Tests; Benchmark Tests A, B
Maintain	U4: 107B; U5: 153A–B; U6: 353A, 379B

Poetry

GENRE: POEM

LA.3.2.1.1 Understand distinguishing features of literature
LA.3.2.1.3 Identify and explain how language choice helps develop mood

Have students read the bookmark on **Student Book** page 108. Explain that a poem:

- may have repeated words, phrases, lines, or groups of lines
- often rhymes and may have figurative language or descriptive language that creates a mood

Literary Elements: Rhyme Scheme and Repetition

LA.3.2.1.5 Identify author's use of descriptive language

EXPLAIN Discuss these poetry terms:

- A rhyme is two or more words that end with the same sound, such as *ate* and *late*.
- A **rhyme scheme** is the pattern of rhymes in a poem. To find the pattern, look at the last word of each line.
- **Repetition** means that words or phrases are repeated. A repeated line in a poem is called a refrain.

LA.3.2.1.3 Identify how language choice helps develop meaning
LA.3.2.1.4 Use details to explain how author developed theme

APPLY Have students identify the repeated line in "Neighbors." ("Neighbors are friends that live just next door.") Then have students find words that rhyme. (*stew, you*; *floor, door, sore*; *down, town*) Ask students why they think the poet used repetition and rhyme. (to make the poems interesting and fun to read aloud) What is the author's theme? (being a good neighbor)

LA.3.4.1.2 Employ figurative language
LA.3.4.1.2 Employ rhythm

Have students write poems with rhyme, repetition, and figurative language and read their poems aloud, emphasizing rhythm and rhyme.

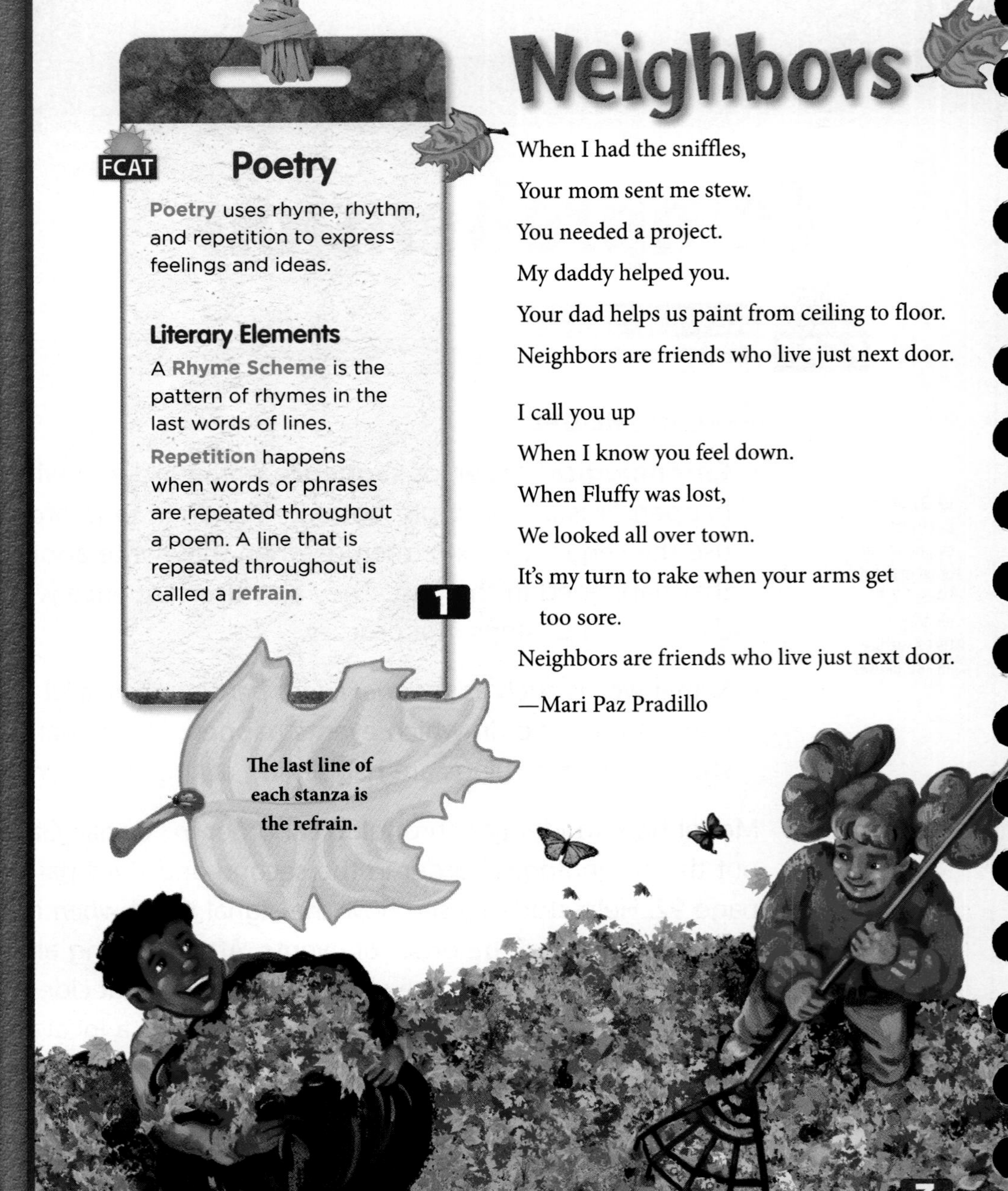

FCAT
Poetry
Poetry uses rhyme, rhythm, and repetition to express feelings and ideas.
Literary Elements
A Rhyme Scheme is the pattern of rhymes in the last words of lines.
Repetition happens when words or phrases are repeated throughout a poem. A line that is repeated throughout is called a refrain.
1
Neighbors
When I had the sniffles,
Your mom sent me stew.
You needed a project.
My daddy helped you.
Your dad helps us paint from ceiling to floor.
Neighbors are friends who live just next door.
I call you up
When I know you feel down.
When Fluffy was lost,
We looked all over town.
It's my turn to rake when your arms get too sore.
Neighbors are friends who live just next door.
—Mari Paz Pradillo
The last line of each stanza is the refrain.
3
108

ELL — Access for All

Model and Explain Read "Neighbors" aloud, emphasizing the rhythm created by rhyme and repetition as students follow along. Act out each action (paint, call, look, rake). Check students' understanding of the poem by asking questions such as, *What did one Dad do? What did the other Dad do? What things does the poet do for her friend?* Read the poem aloud a second time and encourage students to act out each action with you. Remind students of other rhymes and songs that use refrain and repetition, such as "Mary Had a Little Lamb." Discuss who is helpful in the poem. (Mom, both Dads, and the poet) Do a similar activity for "Recycling."

Recycling

Tucker Connors collected the papers
And Maya Ling tied them with string
Maya helped Tucker carry the papers
All the way to the recycling bins

Won Tan collected the cans
And Ruby Dean washed them all clean
Ruby helped Won carry the cans
All the way to the recycling bins

When we recycle, we help the plants
We help the creatures, from eagles to ants
We help make the world a healthier place
For one and for all in the human race

—J. Z. Belle

Plants and *ants* rhyme, as do *place* and *race*. The rhyme scheme for this stanza is AA BB.

2

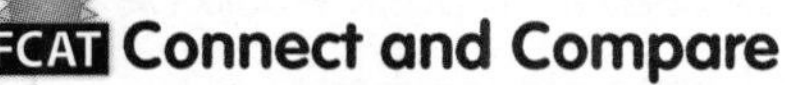

Connect and Compare

1. What are some repetitions in "Recycling"? **Repetition**
2. What does the poet want to tell you about neighbors? **Analyze**
3. Compare these two poems about helping and *Here's My Dollar*. How are these selections alike? How are they different? **Reading/Writing Across Texts**

LOG ON Find out more about poetry at **www.macmillanmh.com**

109

LOG ON Technology

Internet Research and Inquiry Activity Students can find more facts at **www.macmillanmh.com**

Read "Neighbors" and "Recycling"

LA.3.2.1.1 Understand distinguishing features of literature

As you read, remind students to apply what they have learned about refrains, rhyme scheme, and repetition to understand the poems.

1 LITERARY ELEMENT: RHYME SCHEME

What words rhyme in the second stanza of "Neighbors"? (The words *down* and *town* and *sore* and *door* in the second stanza rhyme.) LA.3.2.1.5 Identify author's use of descriptive language

2 LITERARY ELEMENT: REPETITION

What is the refrain in "Recycling"? Why is this line a refrain? ("All the way to the recycling bins" is a refrain because it repeats.)

3 MOOD

LA.3.2.1.3 Identify how language choice helps develop mood and meaning

What is the mood of "Neighbors"? What words help create the mood and meaning? (The mood is happy and positive. The poet uses words such as *helped* and *friends* to set the mood and create meaning.)

Connect and Compare

SUGGESTED ANSWERS

LA.3.1.7.3 Determine explicit information

1. The words "we help" are repeated three times in the last stanza. REPETITION
2. The poet says that neighbors should be friends who help and take care of each other. ANALYZE

FOCUS QUESTION

LA.3.1.7.7 Compare and contrast texts

LA.3.2.1.4 Identify an author's theme

3. The common theme is helping, but the kinds of help are different in each piece. In *Here's My Dollar,* Angel helps animals. In "Neighbors," there are many different types of helping. In "Recycling," people help the environment. READING/WRITING ACROSS TEXTS

Connect Language Arts

FCAT WRITING
- Expository
- Writer's Craft: Strong Opening

FCAT WORD STUDY
- Words in Context
- Context Clues: Example
- **Phonics:** Decode Homophones
- Vocabulary Building

SPELLING/GRAMMAR
- Homophones
- Irregular Verbs

SMALL GROUP OPTIONS
- Differentiated Instruction, pp. 111M–111V

Writing

FCAT A Strong Opening

LA.3.3.2.1 Use prewriting plan to develop main idea with supporting details

READ THE STUDENT MODEL

Read the bookmark about a strong opening. Explain that an opening sentence should spark readers' interest as it introduces the topic and main idea. A question, a quote, or a vivid description are all good openings.

Have students read the first sentence on page 92. Discuss how why this is a strong opening.

Have the class read the personal essay and the callouts. Tell students that they will write their own personal essays about how to improve their community. They will also learn to write a strong opening that introduces their topics and makes readers want to keep reading.

Write About Your Community

Writer's Craft

FCAT A Strong Opening
Good writers include a **strong opening** that grabs the reader's attention. A strong opening may be an interesting quote, question, or description.

I began with a question to grab my reader's attention.

I wrote directly to other kids who care about skateboarding.

No Place to Skateboard

by Carol L.

Do you dream of halfpipes and ramps? I do, but there is one problem. My town does not have a skateboard park. I think this is a big problem. Dad said I should write a letter to our mayor. I wrote and told him why I think a skateboard park would be a good and safe place where kids could have fun. Yesterday the mayor wrote back and said that he liked my idea. Now my town is going to build a special park for skateboarding. If I had not written that letter, nothing would have happened! Maybe you can write a letter and make your community better, too.

110

Features of a Personal Essay

A personal essay, or informational essay, contains facts and opinions. The writer gives her or her own point of view on a topic.

- The essay is based on the writer's own experiences, thoughts, and feelings.
- It is written in first person, using pronouns such as *I*, *me*, and *my*.
- A strong opening introduces the topic and makes readers want to keep reading.
- The essay's main idea is supported by details that are facts, opinions, reasons, and examples.

LA.3.4.2.3 Write informational essays that include a topic sentence and supporting details; **LA.3.3.3.1** Evaluate draft for use of point of view; **LA.3.3.2.1** Use supporting details that provide facts and opinions

Writing Prompt

People often make their communities better by suggesting or planning changes.

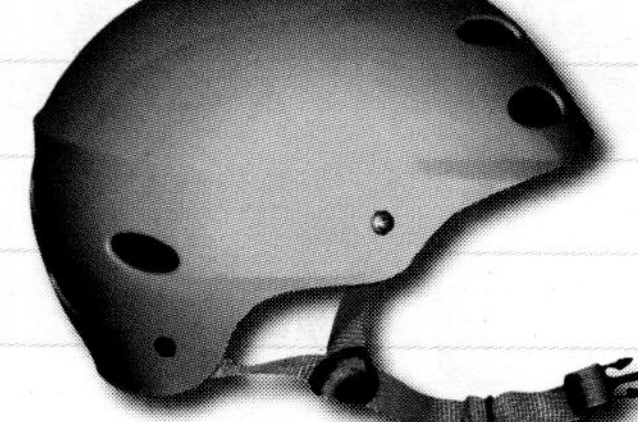

Think about a problem in your community.

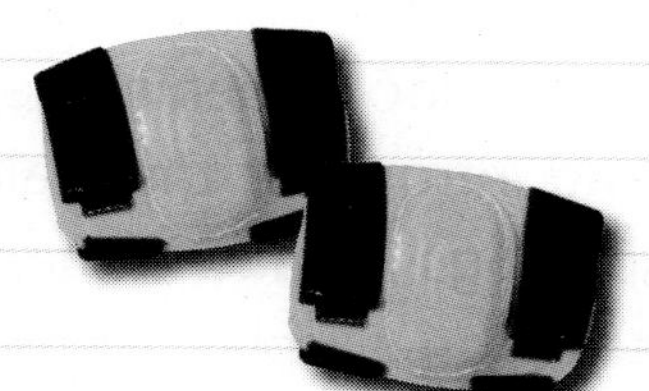

Now write about how you would solve this problem in your community.

FCAT Writer's Checklist

Focus: I write clearly about my topic.

Organization: First I tell about the problem. Then I explain how I would solve it.

Support: I include a **strong opening** to grab the reader's attention.

Conventions: I use homophones and irregular verbs correctly. All the words are spelled correctly.

111

Transparency 73: **Problem and Solution Chart**
Transparency 74: **Draft**
Transparency 75: **Revision**

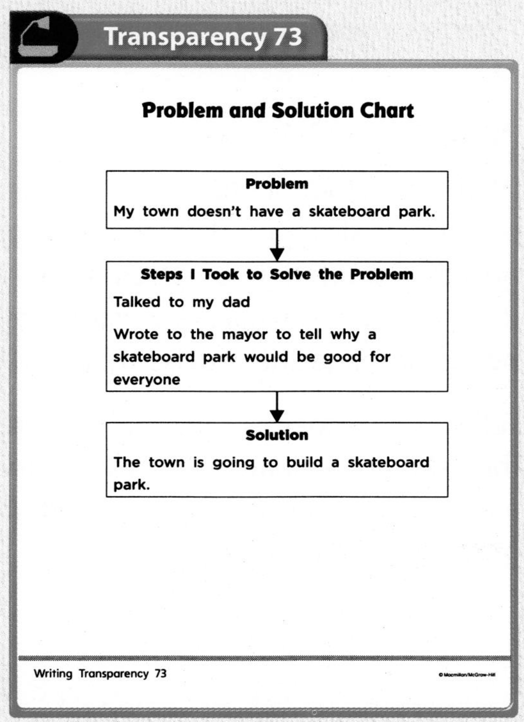

Transparency 73
Problem and Solution Chart
Problem
My town doesn't have a skateboard park.
Steps I Took to Solve the Problem
Talked to my dad
Wrote to the mayor to tell why a skateboard park would be good for everyone
Solution
The town is going to build a skateboard park.
Writing Transparency 73

Writing Transparency 73

Connect

Writing Student pages 110–111

PREWRITE

LA.3.3.1 Use prewriting strategies to formulate a plan

LA.3.3.1.2 Determine purpose and intended audience of a writing piece

LA.3.3.1.3 Use organizational strategies for writing

Discuss the writing prompt on page 111. To plan their writing, have students work independently or with partners to brainstorm topics. Have them identify their purpose and audience.

Display **Transparency 73**. Discuss how Carol used a Problem and Solution Chart to plan her essay. Have students use Problem and Solution Charts to plan their own personal essays.

DRAFT

LA.3.3.3.1 Evaluate draft for use of ideas and content
LA.3.3.2 Write a draft appropriate to topic, audience, purpose
LA.3.3.3.3 Create interest by adding supporting details

Display **Transparency 74**. Discuss how Carol used her Problem and Solution Chart. Discuss how she could improve the draft. Before students write, present the explicit lesson on **A Strong Opening** on page 111A and the minilessons on **Tone** and **Supporting Details** on page 111B. Have students use their charts to draft their essays. Ask them to start with a question, quote, or vivid detail to grab readers' attention. Remind them to keep their purpose and audience in mind.

REVISE

LA.3.3.3.1 Evaluate the draft for use of ideas and content, point of view, and word choice

LA.3.3.3.4 Apply appropriate tools or strategies to refine the draft
LA.3.3.4 Edit and correct draft for standard language conventions

Display **Transparency 75**. Discuss Carol's revisions. Students can revise their drafts or place them in writing portfolios to work on later. If they choose to revise, have them use the Writer's Checklist on page 111. They can also evaluate their essays' organization, point of view, tone, and word choice with partners. After students have completed their revisions, have them **proofread/edit** their writing. For **Publishing Options**, see page 111A.

For lessons on using irregular verbs and spelling homophones, see page 111B and **5 Day Spelling** and **Grammar** on pages 111G–111J.

Writer's Craft

SUPPORT A Strong Opening

Publishing Options

Students can present their essays to the class. See Speaking and Listening tips below. They can also use their best cursive to write their personal essays. (See **Teacher's Resource Book** pages 216–221 for cursive models and practice.) Have students work together to publish an essay collection that includes each student's essay. Students can take home the collection to share with family and friends.

LA.3.5.2.2 Give an oral presentation

Speaking and Listening

SPEAKING STRATEGIES

- Practice reading your essay in advance.
- Look at your audience as often as you can. Use your voice to emphasize the most important points.

LISTENING STRATEGIES

- Listen to try to understand the problem and suggested solution.
- Compare the speaker's views with your own views on this topic. When the speaker is done, raise your hand and asking questions.

LA.3.5.2.1 Interpret information presented orally; LA.3.5.2.2 Use appropriate voice

6-Point Scoring Rubric

Use the rubric on page 149G to score published writing.

Writing Process

For a complete lesson, see Unit Writing on pages 149A–149F.

LA.3.3.2.1 Use prewriting plan to develop main idea with supporting details

EXPLAIN/MODEL

Explain that a good opening sentence both catches the reader's interest and introduces the main idea of their writing. Three kinds of strong openings include a question, an interesting quotation, or a vivid description. Display **Transparency 76**.

Think Aloud Both of these openings are about the same topic: the importance of recycling. The first is a colorful description. It gets me interested in the topic by helping me picture a mountain of juice boxes and soup cans. The second is a simple statement. It doesn't interest me. The first opening with a description is stronger.

Transparency 76

A Strong Opening

strong: Picture a mountain of juice boxes and soup cans. If you don't recycle them, that's what you will see.

weak: Recycling juice boxes and soup cans is important.

__________ **1.** Yesterday my little sister lost her homework, her mittens, and her shoes.

__________ **2.** "I can't find my homework. Where are my mittens? Have you seen my shoes? I need help!" That's my sister!

__________ **3.** Did you ever see a sunflower that is eight feet tall? I did.

__________ **4.** I saw a sunflower that was eight feet tall in our garden.

(1: weak; 2. strong, quotation; 3. strong, question; 4. weak)

Writing Transparency 76

LA.3.3.3.1 Evaluate draft for use of ideas and content
LA.3.3.3.4 Apply appropriate strategies to refine draft

PRACTICE/APPLY

Work with students to read each pair of openings and identify the one that is stronger. Have students tell what kind of opening it is—question, quotation, or description—and discuss why it is strong and the other one is weak. Have students find more strong openings in books or magazine articles they have recently read.

Tell students that as they draft and revise their personal essays, they should evaluate their writing and make sure their opening is a description, question, or quote that tells the main idea and also grabs a readers' attention.

Writer's Toolbox

LA.3.3.3.3 Create interest by adding supporting details

ORGANIZATION

Writing Trait: Ideas and Content

Explain/Model Explain that **details** in a personal essay can give facts or opinions about the main idea. Details give important information and help readers understand the writer's point of view.

Practice/Apply Have students read the third and fourth sentences of Carol's personal essay on page 110. Explain that these sentences both give details that support Carol's main idea. The third sentence gives a fact, and the fourth sentence gives Carol's opinion. As students write their personal essays, ask them to include supporting details that give information and help readers to understand their point of view.

LA.3.3.3.1 Evaluate draft for use of voice; LA.3.3.3.3 Create interest by modifying word choices

SUPPORT

Tone

Explain/Model Tell students that tone, or voice, is the mood or personality of a piece of writing. Good writers chose words and details that create the tone they want. Most personal essays have a friendly, serious tone.

Practice/Apply Have students reread Carol's essay on page 110. Work with them to describe the essay's tone, or voice. Discuss how Carol's word choices and details work together to create and maintain this tone. As students prepare to write their essays, ask them to choose words and details that create a friendly, serious tone, and to keep the tone consistent through their entire essays.

CONVENTIONS

Irregular Verbs

Explain/Model Point out the irregular verbs *said* and *wrote* on page 110. Explain that an irregular verb has a special spelling for the past tense. Some irregular verbs have special spellings when used with helping verbs *have*, *has*, and *had*.

Practice/Apply Display: *say*, *write*, *come*, *do*. Help students write the past-tense forms and then write the forms that go with helping verbs *have*, *has*, and *had*. For a complete lesson on irregular verbs and subject-verb agreement, see pages 111I–111J.

LA.3.3.4.4 Edit for correct use of past verb tense; LA.3.3.4.5 Edit for correct use of subject/verb agreement

CONVENTIONS

Spelling Homophones

Homophones are words that sound alike but are spelled differently and have different meanings. Point out the word *write* on page 110. Display the homophones *write* and *right*. Ask volunteers to use each word in a sentence. Explain that the way a homophone is used in a sentence can help writers figure out the word's meaning, and, in turn, its spelling. Remind students that they can use a print or digital dictionary to check spelling in their drafts. For a complete lesson on spelling homophones, see pages 111G–111H.

LA.3.1.6.8 Use knowledge of homophones; LA.3.1.6.10 Determine meanings using a dictionary and digital tools

Technology

Remind students that they can use the Copy and Paste features to rearrange words, sentences, or paragraphs to create clarity instead of retyping them.

LA.3.3.3.2 Create clarity by rearranging words, sentences, paragraphs

FCAT Success!

Test Prep and Practice with Writing+, pages 180–230

Word Study

Objectives

- Apply knowledge of word meanings and context clues
- Determine word meanings using context clues including examples

Materials

- Vocabulary Transparency 37
- Vocabulary Strategy Transparency 38
- Leveled Practice Books, p. 138
- dictionary

Vocabulary

tour (p. 100) a short trip through a place to see it

volunteers (p. 103) people who offer to do jobs without pay

community (p. 99) a group of people who live in the same area

thrilled (p. 100) very excited or happy

slogan (p. 97) a phrase that is used in advertisements

grownups (p. 97) adults

deserve (p. 105) have a right to

interviewed (p. 101) met and talked with to get information

ELL

Access for All

Brainstorm Make a word web of the word *volunteers*. Have students brainstorm what volunteers are, where they can help, and what they could do.

Review Vocabulary

Words in Context

LA.3.1.6.3 Use context clues to determine meaning

EXPLAIN/MODEL

Review the meanings of the vocabulary words. Display **Transparency 37**. Model how to use word meanings and context clues to determine the missing word in item 1.

Transparency 37

tour volunteers community thrilled slogan grownups deserve interviewed

The zoo did not have much money. The zoo director put an ad in the local newspaper. The ad began with the (1) slogan "Put a Zoo in Your Life." The whole (2) community saw the ad.

Many people called. They wanted to be (3) volunteers so they could help at the zoo. The director (4) interviewed everyone who called. She explained that the zoo needed people to feed and care for the animals. "Our animals (5) deserve the best care," she said.

Some volunteers started to lead a (6) tour of the zoo. They took (7) grownups and children around to see the animals. All of the visitors were (8) thrilled to see the wonderful changes at the zoo.

Vocabulary Transparency 37

Think Aloud The first missing word comes right before a quote and describes something at the beginning of an ad. Those are good clues. I know that many ads begin with a slogan, which is a catchy phrase or quote. The missing word must be *slogan*.

PRACTICE/APPLY

Have each student write the missing words for items 2–8 on a separate piece of paper. Students can exchange papers, check answers, and explain the context clues they used.

LA.3.1.6.1 Use new vocabulary

Questions and Answers Have student pairs ask one another questions using the vocabulary words. For example: *What kind of* community *do you live in? Can you describe it?* Remind students that when answering questions, they can refer to the definition for help. Student pairs can exchange questions and answers with other pairs.

FCAT

STRATEGY
CONTEXT CLUES: EXAMPLES

LA.3.1.7
Use a variety of strategies to comprehend grade level text

LA.3.1.6.3
Use context clues

EXPLAIN/MODEL

- When students come across an unfamiliar word, they should look for context clues. One type of context clue is an **example**.
- Explain that examples can sometimes give readers a clear idea about what a word means. If an author writes that "three professions are doctor, teacher, and firefighter," readers can tell that *doctor, teacher,* and *firefighter* are examples of *professions*.

Display **Transparency 38**. Model finding examples for the word *primates*.

Transparency 38

CONTEXT CLUES: EXAMPLES

1. **Apes, monkeys, and humans are all primates.** (Primates are apes, monkeys, and humans.)
2. **You must walk around the zoo since cars, trucks, and other vehicles are not allowed.** (Cars and trucks are vehicles.)
3. **The animals come from rain forests, deserts, mountains, and many other habitats.** (Habitats are rain forests, deserts, and mountains.)
4. **Small rodents such as rats, mice, and gerbils are in a special room.** (Rodents are animals like rats, mice, and gerbils.)
5. **In the wild, wolves, lions, and hawks are all predators.** (Wolves, lions, and hawks are kinds of predators.)

Vocabulary Strategy Transparency 38

LA.3.1.6.3
Use context clues to determine meanings of unfamiliar words

PRACTICE/APPLY

Access for All

Have students identify context clues for the underlined words in sentences 2–5 and check meanings in a dictionary.

Quick Check **Can students use context clues to determine word meanings?**

During **Small Group Instruction**

If No → Approaching Level Vocabulary, pp. 111N–111O

If Yes → On Level Options, pp. 111Q–111R

Beyond Level Options, pp. 111S–111T

ELL Access for All

Context Clues Have students work in small groups to complete the Practice activity so that they can share their thinking and help each other look up the words. Challenge students to think of another example for each category word (*primates, vehicles,* etc.).

Vocabulary

Review last week's vocabulary words. Have students do a Think, Pair, Share on examples of people who are *native* to their community, state, or country. Help students form sentences for *native* using these example clues.

FCAT Success!

Test Prep and Practice with vocabulary, pages 6–31

On Level Practice Book O, page 138

When you are reading, you sometimes come across an unknown word. You can often figure out its meaning by looking at context clues, the words and phrases around it. Some context clues will contain **examples** of the unfamiliar word. Example clues help readers better understand unfamiliar words by providing related information about the unfamiliar words.

Circle the example clues that help you understand each underlined word. Then write a possible definition for the underlined word. Check your work using a dictionary.

1. The panel was made up of people of all occupations, including lawyers, physical therapists, and hairdressers.
   Meaning: areas of work
2. My best friend has two siblings, but I have four: two brothers and two sisters.
   Meaning: brothers and sisters
3. From our window we could see many structures such as bridges, skyscrapers, and docks.
   Meaning: something that is built
4. Every cello, clarinet, trombone, and violin in the orchestra sounded beautiful during the grand finale.
   Meaning: a group of musicians playing different instruments

Approaching Practice Book A, page 138

Beyond Practice Book B, page 138

Phonics

Decode Homophones

Objective

- Recognize and decode homophones

Materials

- Leveled Practice Books, p. 139

ELL Access for All

Draw/Write Sentences Have students volunteer pairs of homophones. Write the pairs of words on the board. Group students in pairs. Each student writes one sentence for one of the homophone pairs. Pairs can read their sentences aloud.

LA.3.1.6.8 Use knowledge of homophones

EXPLAIN/MODEL

- **Homophones** (also known as homonyms) are words that sound alike but are spelled differently and have different meanings, as in *their* and *there.*
- The way a homophone is used in a sentence can help readers figure out its meaning.

Write these sentences and read them aloud, emphasizing *sale* and *sail*: *The store is having a* sale. *We will* sail *our boat on the lake.*

LA.3.1.6.3 Use context clues

Think Aloud The words *sale* and *sail* are pronounced the same way, /sāl/, but they have different spellings. I can look at the words around them to figure out what they mean. I see the word *store* in the first sentence. So *sale* spelled *s-a-l-e* has to do with selling things. I see the word *boat* in the second sentence, so *sail* spelled *s-a-i-l* means "to move through or travel over the water."

LA.3.1.6.1 Use new vocabulary

PRACTICE/APPLY

Display the following homophones and their definitions: *right*—to be correct; *write*—to send a letter; *rode*—traveled in a car; and *road*—a strip of ground that cars drive on. Have students say each homophone and use it in a sentence.

LA.3.1.4.3 Decode multisyllabic words

Decode Multisyllabic Words Have students use their knowledge of phonics patterns, compound words, and word parts to decode multisyllabic words. Display homophones: *ceiling/sealing*; *patients/patience*. Model how to determine the meaning of each word by pointing to each word and using it in a clear context sentence. Then have students say the words and use them in their own sentences.

LA.3.1.6 Use multiple strategies to develop vocabulary

Homophone Match Write six pairs of homophones on index cards. Place the cards in a 3 × 4 array facedown. Students then take turns trying to match two cards that are homophones. If a student fails, he or she turns cards face down and another student takes a turn.

Quick Check **Can students decode homophones?**

During **Small Group Instruction**

If No → **Approaching Level** Phonics, p. 111M

If Yes → **On Level** Options, pp. 111Q–111R

Beyond Level Options, pp. 111S–111T

On Level Practice Book O, page 139

A **homophone** is a word that has the same sound of another word, but the words are spelled differently and have different meanings.

Underline the two homophones in each of these sentences. Then write the definition of each homophone. Accept reasonable definitions.

1. Your donations to our zoo helped so much that you're invited to visit the zoo whenever you wish.
2. I need to know where we are going so I can decide what to wear.
3. I pretended that I was on the high sea and could see other parts of the world.
4. Have you seen the scene in the movie where the kids win the soccer game?

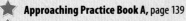

Approaching Practice Book A, page 139

Beyond Practice Book B, page 139

Vocabulary Building

LA.3.1.6 Use multiple strategies to develop vocabulary; LA.3.1.6.4 Categorize key vocabulary; LA.3.1.6.1 Use new vocabulary; LA.3.1.6 Develop grade-appropriate vocabulary; LA.3.1.6.10 Determine meanings using a dictionary; LA.3.1.6.4 Categorize key vocabulary and identify salient features

Oral Language

Expand Vocabulary Work with students to brainstorm words about getting involved. Write the words in a chart like the one below.

Getting Involved	
Who	**Where**
volunteers	community
grownups	environment
students	school

Save our Park!

Apply Vocabulary

Write a Paragraph Have each student use the vocabulary words *tour, volunteers, community, thrilled, slogan, grownups, deserve,* and *interviewed* in a paragraph about volunteering. Students can read their paragraphs aloud.

Vocabulary Building

Greek and Latin Roots The word *autographed* is made up of the Greek roots, or word parts, *auto* and *graph*. *Auto* = "self" and *graph* = "write." An autograph is a person's signature. Display the Greek roots on the chart. Have students use them to predict the meanings of *photograph, biography, autobiography,* and *photocopy*. They can use a dictionary to check their predictions. Then have them categorize the words according to the roots.

Greek Roots	
auto = self	*phot* = light
graph = write	*bio* = life

Write the Latin root *natus* on the board. Have students find which of last week's vocabulary words is made from this root.

Spiral Review

Vocabulary Game

Have students play a word game of "Fill in the Blank" using the **Vocabulary Cards** for *argued, interviewed, magnificent, native, purchased, research, tasty, volunteers,* and *thrilled.*

- Divide the class into three teams. Give each team three cards. Have the teams write context sentences using each word.
- Teams take turns copying their sentences onto the board, leaving blanks for the vocabulary words. The other teams try to guess the missing words. Teams can give clues.
- The team that guesses each missing word earns a point. Continue until all words have been used. The team with the most points wins.

Technology

Vocabulary PuzzleMaker

For additional vocabulary and spelling games, go to www.macmillanmh.com

5 Day Spelling

LA.3.1.6.8 Use knowledge of homophones; LA.3.3.4.3 Edit for correct use of apostrophes

Homophones

Spelling Words

sale	road	you're
sail	rowed	there
beet	its	they're
beat	it's	peace
rode	your	piece

Review city, gems, space

Challenge seen, scene

Dictation Sentences

1. We had a bake sale in school.
2. The boat has a sail.
3. Beet soup is red.
4. Nora beat Kate in the race.
5. Sue rode on a donkey.
6. We drove on the dirt road.
7. Have you ever rowed a boat?
8. The dog wagged **its** tail.
9. It's time to go home.
10. The zoo needs **your** dollar.
11. You're on time for the show.
12. The bears are over there.
13. They're helping the animals.
14. The baby needs peace and quiet.
15. I ate a piece of an apple.

Review Words

1. She lives in the city.
2. We looked at gems and rocks.
3. Tigers need space to run.

Challenge Words

1. Have you seen Tom?
2. I liked the first scene of the play.

Note: The words in **bold** type are from *Here's My Dollar.*

Display the Spelling Words throughout the week.

Day 1 Pretest

ASSESS PRIOR KNOWLEDGE

Use the Dictation Sentences. Say the underlined word, read the sentence, and repeat the word. Have students write the words on **Spelling Practice Book** page 115. For a modified list, use the first 12 Spelling Words and the 3 Review Words. For a more challenging list, use Spelling Words 3–15 and the Challenge Words. Have students correct their own tests.

Have students cut apart the Spelling Word Cards BLM on **Teacher's Resource Book** page 132 and figure out a way to sort them. Have them save the cards for use throughout the week.

Students can use Spelling Practice Book page 116 for independent practice.

For leveled Spelling word lists, go to **www.macmillanmh.com**

Spelling Practice Book, pages 115–116

Fold back the paper along the dotted line. Use the blanks to write each word as it is read aloud. When you finish the test, unfold the paper. Use the list at the right to correct any spelling mistakes.

	1. ______	1. sale
	2. ______	2. sail
	3. ______	3. beet
	4. ______	4. beat
	5. ______	5. rode
	6. ______	6. road
	7. ______	7. rowed
	8. ______	8. its
	9. ______	9. it's
	10. ______	10. your
	11. ______	11. you're
	12. ______	12. there
	13. ______	13. they're
	14. ______	14. peace
	15. ______	15. piece
Review Words	16. ______	16. city
	17. ______	17. gems
	18. ______	18. space
Challenge Words	19. ______	19. seen
	20. ______	20. scene

Day 2 Word Sorts

TEACHER AND STUDENT SORTS

- Review the Spelling Words, explain that they are homophones (sometimes called homonyms), and discuss meanings. Point out that the contractions *it's*, *you're*, and *they're* are homophones. Point out the apostrophes.
- Use the cards on the Spelling Word Cards BLM. Attach the headings long *a*, long *e*, long *o*, and *other homophones* to a bulletin board.
- Model how to sort the homophones by vowel sound.
- Have students take turns choosing cards, sorting them, and explaining how they sorted them.
- Have students sort their Spelling Word Cards under the headings three times and write their last sort on Spelling Practice Book page 117.

Spelling Practice Book, page 117

sale	beat	rowed	your	they're
sail	rode	its	you're	peace
beet	road	it's	there	piece

Homophones are words that sound alike but have different spellings and different meanings. Write the spelling words that are homophones of the words below.

1. there they're
2. peace piece
3. sale sail
4. beet beat
5. rowed road rode
6. it's its
7. your you're

Which spelling words are contractions?

8. you're 9. it's 10. they're

Write the spelling words that have the sounds below.

long *e*

11. beat 12. peace
13. beet 14. piece

long *a*

15. sail 16. sale

long *o*

17. rode 18. road 19. rowed

LA.3.1.6.8 Use knowledge of homophones

Day 3 Word Meanings

DEFINITIONS

Display the definitions below. Have students write in their word study notebooks the clues and the Spelling Words that go with them.

1. a large piece of cloth on a boat (sail)
2. a type of vegetable (beet)
3. a path that cars travel on (road)
4. the contraction for the words *it is* (it's)
5. one part of a whole thing (piece)

Challenge students to come up with clues for other Spelling Words, including Review Words and Challenge Words.

Have partners write sentences for each homophone pair, leaving a blank where each word should go. Then have them trade papers and fill in the correct words.

Day 4 Review and Proofread

SPIRAL REVIEW

Review the soft *c* and soft *g* patterns. Write *city*, *gems*, and *space*. Have students identify the letters that spell soft *c* and soft *g*.

PROOFREAD/EDIT

Write the sentences below. Have students correct the errors.

1. The rode was bumpy. (road)
2. Hand me you're coat. (your)

BLIND SORT

Partners use their Spelling Word Cards. They each write the headings long *a*, long *e*, long *o*, and *other homophones* on a sheet of paper. Then students take turns. One draws cards and says the words. The other writes them under the headings. After both have finished, they can check each other's papers.

Day 5 Assess and Reteach

POSTTEST

Use the Dictation Sentences on page 111G for the Posttest.

If students have difficulty with any of the words in the lesson, have them place them on a list called "Spelling Words I Want to Remember" in their word study notebooks.

WORD STUDY NOTEBOOK

Challenge students to search for other homophones, such as *to*, *two*, and *too*, in their reading for the week and write them in their word study notebooks under the heading "Other Homophones."

Homophone examples from *Here's My Dollar* include *write*, *stationery*, *read*, *for*, *one*, *whole*, *principal*, *plane*, and *hay*.

Spelling Practice Book, page 118

sale	beat	rowed	your	they're
sail	rode	its	you're	peace
beet	road	it's	there	piece

Homophones are words that sound alike but have different spellings and different meanings. In each sentence below, a homophone is used incorrectly. Circle the incorrect homophone and write the correct homophone on the line following the sentence.

1. Its important to help people that need you. It's
2. All of the cakes and pies were on sail for a good cause. sale
3. Is that you're mother on TV? your
4. The rowed was long and dark. road
5. Someday there will be piece on earth. peace
6. My family used a beat and a carrot from our garden to make soup. beet
7. At camp we learned how to sale a boat. sail
8. We were allowed to feed the chimp a peace of banana. piece
9. The gorilla scratched it's head. its
10. There going to open a new community center in our town. They're
11. The group road through the jungle in a truck. rode
12. We beet last year's record by raising even more money for the zoo. beat
13. They're are many volunteers who help at the soup kitchen. There
14. Your so good at listening to others. You're
15. We all road the boat to shore. rowed

Spelling Practice Book, page 119

Proofreading

There are seven spelling mistakes in this paragraph. Circle the misspelled words. Write the words correctly on the lines below.

Volunteer Fair

Yo're invited to our annual volunteer fair. We will have lots of ideas about how to help your community. You could adopt a raod. You could raise money for an animal shelter by holding a bake sael. You could even help build a pease of the new community center. Thire are so many ideas, you won't know where to start. Its going to be quite a fair. So please join us this Friday. Yore community needs you.

1. You're
2. road
3. sale
4. piece
5. There
6. It's
7. Your

Writing Activity

Write ideas you have for helping your community. Use at least three spelling words in your paragraph.

Spelling Practice Book, page 120

Look at the words in each set below. One word in each set is spelled correctly. Look at Sample A. The letter next to the correctly spelled word in Sample A has been shaded in. Do Sample B yourself. Shade the letter of the word that is spelled correctly. When you are sure you know what to do, go on with the rest of the page.

Sample A:	Sample B:
Ⓐ soe	Ⓔ soe
Ⓑ sowe	Ⓕ sew
Ⓒ soh	Ⓖ sowe
Ⓓ so	Ⓗ soh

1. Ⓐ sale	6. Ⓔ rowd	11. Ⓔ yure
Ⓑ sayle	Ⓕ roud	Ⓕ you're
Ⓒ saile	Ⓖ road	Ⓖ your'e
Ⓓ sayel	Ⓗ raud	Ⓗ yowr
2. Ⓔ sayle	7. Ⓐ roed	12. Ⓐ thier
Ⓕ sail	Ⓑ wrowd	Ⓑ thare
Ⓖ cayle	Ⓒ rowed	Ⓒ there
Ⓗ sayel	Ⓓ roud	Ⓓ theyr'e
3. Ⓐ beet	8. Ⓔ ets	13. Ⓐ thier
Ⓑ beete	Ⓕ i'ts	Ⓑ theyr'e
Ⓒ biet	Ⓖ its	Ⓒ thare
Ⓓ beit	Ⓗ itz	Ⓓ they're
4. Ⓔ beete	9. Ⓔ itz	14. Ⓔ peace
Ⓕ beat	Ⓕ i'ts	Ⓕ peise
Ⓖ beit	Ⓖ ets	Ⓖ peice
Ⓗ biet	Ⓗ it's	Ⓗ pease
5. Ⓐ wroad	10. Ⓐ your	15. Ⓐ peice
Ⓑ raud	Ⓑ yure	Ⓑ peise
Ⓒ rowd	Ⓒ your'e	Ⓒ piece
Ⓓ rode	Ⓓ yowr	Ⓓ pease

5 Day Grammar

Daily Language Activities

Use these activities to introduce each day's lesson. Write the day's activities on the board or use **Transparency 19.**

DAY 1
1. The children comed to our concert last night. **2.** Sam sanged in the band. **3.** The band leader sayd the music was wonderful. (1: came; 2: sang; 3: said)

DAY 2
1. jenny has came to the zoo. **2.** She has went to the zoo before. **3.** She has see the lions and tigers. (1: Jenny; come; 2: gone; 3: seen)

DAY 3
1. We comed to see the new lion cubs? **2.** I seed the new cubs last week. **3.** They have began to play with the others lions. (1: came; cubs.; 2: saw; 3: begun; other)

DAY 4
1. Cam builded a clubhouse. **2.** Cam has did a good job. **3.** I have ate lunch in his clubhouse. (1: built; 2: done; 3: eaten)

DAY 5
1. On friday I road my bike to the zoo. **2.** I had ran to the zoo the last time I goed. **3.** The lion cubs have growed. (1: Friday; rode; 2: run; went; 3: grown)

ELL **Access for All**

Tell Stories Ask a student to tell about a recent past event. Write the verbs on the board as the student says them. Have students notice the two kinds of verbs (regular and irregular). Then have students tell their own stories in pairs.

LA.3.3.4.4 Edit for correct use of past verb tense; **LA.3.3.4.5** Edit for correct use of subject/verb agreement

Irregular Verbs

Day 1 Introduce the Concept

INTRODUCE IRREGULAR VERBS

- Not all verbs add *-ed* to form the past tense.
- An **irregular verb** has a special spelling for the past tense.

Present	Past
come	came
do	did
say	said
go	went
run	ran
see	saw
give	gave
eat	ate
sing	sang

Examples:
Present tense: We **go** to the zoo.
Past tense: We **went** to the zoo.

See Grammar Transparency 91 for modeling and guided practice.

Grammar Practice Book, page 115

- Remember that an **irregular verb** has a special meaning to show the past tense.

Rewrite these sentences in the past tense.

1. We go to the zoo often during the summer.
We went to the zoo often during the summer.
2. We see a special bird exhibit.
We saw a special bird exhibit.
3. The colorful birds sing loudly.
The colorful birds sang loudly.
4. They eat worms and seeds.
They ate worms and seeds.
5. I do visit the zoo often.
I did visit the zoo often.

Finish each sentence with the correct past-tense form of the verb.

6. We ___came___ to the zoo one morning. come came
7. We ___saw___ the polar bears being fed. see saw
8. The zoo attendants ___said___ many animals live there. say said
9. She carefully ___gave___ the food to the bears. give gave
10. The bears ___ate___ with their big paws. eat ate

Day 2 Teach the Concept

REVIEW IRREGULAR VERBS

Remind students that all verbs do not end in *-ed* to show past tense. Review some irregular verbs with students.

INTRODUCE FORMS WITH *HAVE*

Some irregular verbs have a special spelling when used with the helping verbs *have*, *has*, or *had*.

Past tense with *have, has,* or *had*

has **come**	have **given**	has **run**
had **done**	has **gone**	has **sung**
has **said**	have **seen**	have **begun**

Examples:
Tina **has gone** to the zoo.
The students **have seen** the tiger.

Remind students to check subjects and helping verbs *has* and *have* for agreement: *Jim has come. I have come. They have come.*

See Grammar Transparency 92 for modeling and guided practice.

Grammar Practice Book, page 116

- An **irregular verb** has a special spelling to show the past tense.
- Some **irregular verbs** have a special spelling when used with the helping verb *have*.

PRESENT	PAST	PAST
I do	I did	I have done
you see	you saw	you have seen
she comes	she came	she has come
we go	we went	we have gone
they bring	they brought	they have brought
I run	I ran	I have run
he gives	he gave	he has given
we sing	we sang	we have sung
they begin	they began	they have begun
I eat	I ate	I have eaten
it grows	it grew	it has grown

Write the correct past-tense form of the verb to finish the sentence.

1. come People ___came___ to the zoo.
2. see They ___saw___ all the different animals.
3. sing The birds had ___sung___ for them a thousand times.
4. go They ___went___ without thinking about the zoo's problems.
5. grow They ___grew___ bigger and bigger each year.
6. bring She has ___brought___ the zoo's problems to people's attention.
7. run The newspaper ___ran___ her letter.
8. give Angel ___gave___ a dollar to help the zoo.
9. do Other people have ___done___ the same thing.
10. begin Now the zoo has ___begun___ to fix its problems.

LA.3.3.4.5 Edit for correct use of subject/verb agreement in simple and compound sentences;
LA.3.3.4.4 Edit for correct use of past verb tense

Day 3 Review and Practice

REVIEW FORMS WITH *HAVE*

Review irregular past-tense verb forms with helping verbs *have*, *has*, or *had* and subject-verb agreement in simple and compound sentences.

MECHANICS AND USAGE: CORRECT VERB FORMS

- Irregular verbs have a special spelling to show that an action happened in the past.
- Some verbs have a special spelling when used with *have*, *has*, or *had*. Irregular past-tense verbs must agree with their subjects.

Examples:

Ray **gave** money to the zoo.

The class **had given** money to help the zoo.

See Grammar Transparency 93 for modeling and guided practice.

Grammar Practice Book, page 117

- A present-tense verb tells what happens now.
- A past-tense verb tells about an action that already happened.
- A verb in the future tense tells about an action that is going to happen. To write about the future, use the special verb *will*.
- An irregular verb has a special spelling to show the past tense.
- Some irregular verbs have a special spelling when used with the helping verb *have*.

Rewrite the sentences using the correct form of the verb in parentheses.

1. I have (go) to the zoo twice before.
   I have gone to the zoo twice before.
2. My little brother Jeff (come) to the zoo with us.
   My little brother Jeff came to the zoo with us.
3. He (run) as fast as he could to see the chimpanzees.
   He ran as fast as he could to see the chimpanzees.
4. I have never (see) him look so surprised.
   I have never seen him look so surprised.
5. Jeff (sing) a song back to the chimps.
   Jeff sang a song back to the chimps.
6. The zoo workers had (give) the chimps bananas.
   The zoo workers had given the chimps bananas.
7. The chimps have (eat) bananas before.
   The chimps have eaten bananas before.
8. I have never (see) Jeff laugh so hard!
   I have never seen Jeff laugh so hard!

Day 4 Review and Proofread

REVIEW IRREGULAR VERBS

Review irregular past-tense verbs. Ask students to name the irregular past-tense forms of *go* and *say* and use them in sentences.

PROOFREAD/EDIT

Have students correct errors in the sentences below.

1. Our class goed to the zoo last friday. (went; Friday.)
2. Jenny comed after we left. (came)
3. Grandma runned in the park (ran; park.)
4. Don had seed the lion cubs playing. (seen)

Remind students to proofread/edit for correct forms of irregular past-tense verbs and subject-verb agreement

See Grammar Transparency 94 for modeling and guided practice.

Grammar Practice Book, page 118

- An irregular verb has a special spelling to show the past tense.
- Some irregular verbs have a special spelling when used with the helping verb *have*.

Proofread the paragraphs. Circle any incorrect irregular verbs.

In class, we read about Angel Arellano. She (seen) that the Chaffee Zoo was having money problems. She worried about the animals at the zoo. She wrote a letter to her local newspaper. It (bringed) attention to the zoo. Angel (have) a suggestion. She (has gave) a dollar to the zoo. She hoped everyone else would give a dollar, too. People (begun) to donate money. It helped the zoo survive.

We wondered what we could change. If we all (given) a dollar, who could we help?

Writing Activity

Rewrite the paragraphs. Write the irregular verbs correctly. Make sure other verbs are also written in the correct tense.

In class, we read about Angel Arellano. She saw that the Chaffee Zoo was having money problems. She worried about the animals at the zoo. She wrote a letter to her local newspaper. It brought attention to the zoo. Angel had a suggestion. She gave a dollar to the zoo. She hoped everyone else would give a dollar, too. People began to donate money. It helped the zoo survive.

We wondered what we could change. If we all gave a dollar, who could we help?

Day 5 Assess and Reteach

ASSESS

Use the Daily Language Activity and page 119 of the **Grammar Practice Book** for assessment.

RETEACH

Have partners play an irregular verb game. On the board, list *go*, *say*, *come*, *run*, *eat*, and *sing*. Player A says one of the verbs such as *go*. Player B says the past-tense form and uses it in a sentence. Right answers get one point. Then Player B takes a turn.

Use page 120 of the Grammar Practice Book for additional reteaching.

See Grammar Transparency 95 for modeling and guided practice.

Grammar Practice Book, pages 119–120

Choose the verb form that goes with *have* or *had*. Mark your answer.

1. We have __A__ on trips to the zoo.
   a. gone b. go c. went
2. I had __A__ something special there this time.
   a. done b. do c. did
3. The zoo keepers had __B__ us a tour of the zoo.
   a. give b. given c. gave
4. My friends and I have __B__ how the zoo workers keep the zoo running.
   a. see b. seen c. saw
5. They had __C__ to the end of the tour and thanked the zoo keepers.
   a. comes b. came c. come

Choose the correct past-tense form.

6. Yesterday we __C__ to the zoo to see the new panda bears.
   a. go b. gone c. went
7. The bears __B__ to the zoo from China.
   a. come b. came c. comes
8. The people there __C__ the bears as a gift to our zoo.
   a. give b. given c. gave
9. I __C__ the bears in their new zoo habitat.
   a. see b. seen c. saw
10. They __A__ bamboo shoots and stared at us.
    a. ate b. eat c. eaten
11. We were pleased that we __B__ to the zoo.
    a. come b. came c. comes
12. Other plants and trees __B__ in the habitat.
    a. grows b. grew c. grown

Administer the Test

Weekly Reading Assessment, pages 225–236

ASSESSED SKILLS

- Author's Purpose
- Vocabulary Words
- Context Clues/Example
- Homophones
- Irregular Verbs

Administer the **Weekly Assessment** from the CD-ROM or online.

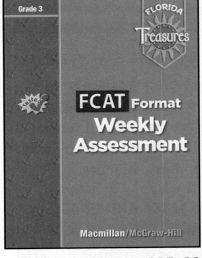

Weekly Assessment, 225–236

Fluency

Assess fluency for one group of students per week. Use the Oral Fluency Record Sheet to track the number of words read correctly. Fluency goal for all students:
82–102 words correct per minute (WCPM).

Approaching Level	Weeks 1, 3, 5
On Level	Weeks 2, 4
Beyond Level	Week 6

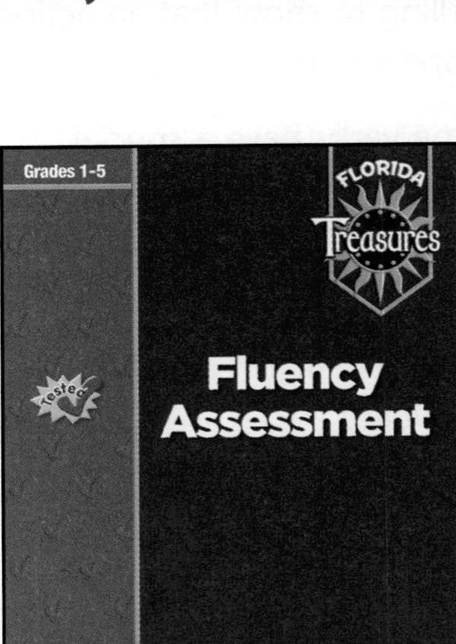

Fluency Assessment

Alternative Assessments

- **ELL Assessment**, pages 122–123

ELL Assessment, 122–123

Diagnose	IF . . .	Prescribe THEN . . .
VOCABULARY WORDS **VOCABULARY STRATEGY** Context Clues/Example Items 1, 2, 3	0–1 items correct . . .	Reteach skills using the **Additional Lessons**, page T8. LOG ON Reteach skills: Log on to **www.macmillanmh.com** CD ROM Vocabulary PuzzleMaker Evaluate for Intervention.
COMPREHENSION Skill: Author's Purpose, Items 4, 5, 6	0–1 items correct . . .	Reteach skills using the **Additional Lessons**, page T3. Evaluate for Intervention.
GRAMMAR Irregular Verbs, Items 7, 8, 9	0–1 items correct . . .	Reteach skills: **Grammar Practice Book**, page 120.
SPELLING Homophones, Items 10, 11, 12	0–1 items correct . . .	LOG ON Reteach skills: Log on to **www.macmillanmh.com**
FLUENCY	73–81 WCPM 0–72 WCPM	AUDIO CD Fluency Solutions Evaluate for Intervention.

DIBELS LINK

PROGRESS MONITORING

Use your DIBELS results to inform instruction.

IF . . .

DIBELS Oral **R**eading **F**luency (**DORF**) 0–91

THEN . . .

Use the Fluency Solutions Audio CD.

TPRI LINK

PROGRESS MONITORING

Use your TPRI scores to inform instruction.

IF . . .

Graphophonemic Awareness	Still developing
Reading Fluency/Accuracy	Frustrational on Grade 3, Story 1
Reading Comprehension Questions	0–5 correct

THEN . . .

Use the Fluency Solutions Audio CD. Use the Comprehension Skills **Additional Lessons** suggestions in the above chart.

READING **Triumphs** Also Available

AN INTERVENTION PROGRAM

To place students in the Intervention Program, use the **Diagnostic Assessment** in the Intervention Teacher's Edition.

Skills Focus: Phonics

Objectives Review homophones
Decode multisyllabic homophones

Materials • **Student Book** "Gorilla Garden"

DECODE HOMOPHONES

LA.3.1.6.8 Use knowledge of homophones to determine meaning
LA.3.1.6.1 Use new vocabulary

Model/Guided Practice

- Explain that homophones are words that sound alike but are spelled differently and have different meanings, such as *sail* and *sale*. Tell students that they can figure out the meaning of a homophone by looking at how it is used in a sentence.
- Write these sentences on the board and read them aloud, emphasizing *right* and *write*: *The opposite of* left *is* right. *I* write *my name with a* pen.
- Say: *The words* right *and* write *are pronounced the same /rīt/, but have different spellings. I can look at the sentences to figure out what they mean. I see the word* left *in the first sentence, so I know that* right, *spelled* r-i-g-h-t, *is a direction word like* left. *I see the word* pen *in the second sentence, so I know that* write, *spelled* w-r-i-t-e, *means "to form letters or words."*
- Ask students to provide their own examples of homophones and sample sentences that give clues to the meanings of the words.

MULTISYLLABIC HOMOPHONES

LA.3.1.4.3 Decode multisyllabic words

- Write the words *aloud* and *allowed* on the board and model how to determine the meaning of each word by using it in a clear context sentence.
- Have pairs of students work together to decode and determine the meanings of the pairs of homophones below. Tell them to use a dictionary as necessary. Then ask each student pair to select a homophone pair and write a sentence for each homophone.

assistance/assistants	braking/breaking	cellar/seller
presence/presents	weather/whether	basis/bases

- Check pairs for their progress and accuracy. Provide constructive feedback as necessary

WORD HUNT: HOMOPHONES IN CONTEXT

LA.3.1.6.8 Use knowledge of homophones

- Review homophones.
- Have students search "Gorilla Garden" to find homophones. Ask them to write each word and its homophone.
- Check to see if students have found the following homophones: *you (ewe), it's (its), led (lead), through (threw), to (two, too), right* (*write*), *read* (*red*), *some* (*sum*), *their* (*there, they're*), *so* (*sew*), *for* (*four*), *our* (*hour*), *where* (*wear*).

Constructive Feedback

If students have trouble figuring out the meaning of a homophone from the context of a sentence, have them try out the different meanings to see which makes sense. Write this sentence on the board: *She will meet me here.* Say:

I can replace meet *with "something to eat" and see that this meaning does not make sense. I can replace it with "get together with" and see that this meaning makes sense. So the word is* meet, m-e-e-t.

Repeat as needed with other homophones.

Additional Resources

For each skill below, additional lessons are provided. You can use these lessons on consecutive days after teaching the lessons presented within the week.

- Author's Purpose, T3
- Context Clues, T8

Skills Focus Fluency

Objective Read with increasing prosody and accuracy at a rate of 82–92 WCPM

Materials • index cards • **Approaching Practice Book A**, p. 136

WORD AUTOMATICITY

Have students make flashcards for the following homophones: *sale, road, you're, sail, rowed, there, beet, its, they're, beat, it's, peace, rode, your, piece.*

Display the cards one at a time and have students say each word. Repeat twice more, displaying the words more quickly each time. Ask volunteers to match the pairs of homophones.

REPEATED READING

LA.3.1.5 Demonstrate the ability to read grade level text

Model reading aloud the fluency passage reproduced on **Practice Book** page 136. Have the group echo-read the passage and then have partners practice reading it to each other. Circulate and listen for their tempo. Provide any constructive feedback necessary.

TIMED READING

Tell students that they will be doing a final timed reading of the passage on Practice Book page 136. Students should

- begin reading the passage aloud when you say "Go."
- stop reading the passage after one minute when you say "Stop."

As students read, note any miscues. Help students record and graph the number of words they read correctly. Provide feedback as needed.

Skills Focus Vocabulary

Objective Apply vocabulary word meanings

Materials • **Vocabulary Cards**

VOCABULARY WORDS

LA.3.1.6 Use multiple strategies to develop grade-appropriate vocabulary

Read aloud each vocabulary word from this week and last and review its definition. Then play a guessing game. Provide clues like the ones below for at least two of the words and have volunteers provide clues for the rest.

- I am thinking of a two-syllable word that begins like *dessert* and ends like *nerve*. It has to do with earning privileges or treats. (*deserve*)
- I am thinking of a three-syllable word that begins like *Internet* and ends like *chewed*. It has to do with asking questions. (*interviewed*)

tour | volunteers | community | thrilled | slogan | grownups | deserve | interviewed

Constructive Feedback

If students read too quickly or too slowly, reread the passage aloud at the correct tempo. Then lead the class in a choral reading so they can follow your model in reading at an appropriate rate. Repeat choral reading as necessary.

ELL Access for All

Cloze Completion Write the following vocabulary words on the board: *volunteers, interviewed, deserve, community.* Ask students to use the vocabulary words to complete the story: When the people in our community were interviewed by reporters about their needs, the people said, "We deserve a new town park! We will all work as volunteers to get the park finished."

Approaching Practice Book A, page 136

As I read, I will pay attention to tempo.

What do green guerillas do? Green Guerillas work to
9 change things. They change New York City lots into
18 community gardens.
20 They help in three ways. First they help the "garden
30 dreamers" form their own group. They look at the space
40 and help plan a garden.
45 Second, the Green Guerillas help get supplies. Soil,
53 plants, and tools cost money. They share ideas for raising
63 money.
64 The third job is to help each group get volunteers. At
75 first most of the **volunteers** were **grownups**. But Green
84 Guerillas wanted to get everyone involved. They wanted to
93 see young people in the gardens. 99

Comprehension Check

1. Who are the Green Guerillas? **Main Idea and Details** a group of people who change New York City lots into community gardens
2. What are the steps the Green Guerillas take to help create a garden? **Chronological Order** First they form a group. Next, they help the group get supplies. Then they help the group get volunteers.

	Words Read	–	Number of Errors	=	Words Correct Score
First Read		–		=	
Second Read		–		=	

Vocabulary

Review last week's vocabulary words (**native, shouldn't, research, sprout, clumps**) and this week's words (**tour, volunteers, community, thrilled, slogan, grownups, deserve, interviewed**). Brainstorm memory aids for any words students find difficult.

Student Book, or Transparencies 19a and 19b

Skills Focus Vocabulary

Objective Review context clues

Materials • **Student Book** *Here's My Dollar*

FCAT CONTEXT CLUES: EXAMPLES

LA.3.1.6.3 Use context clues

Read aloud the letter on page 97 of *Here's My Dollar* as students follow along. Explain that "Give a dollar, save a life" is a slogan that Angel invented. Based on this example, students should understand that a slogan is an attention-getting phrase that tries to persuade, or convince, people to do or buy something.

Help students think of sentences including example clues that help define *tour*, *community*, *grownups*, and *volunteers*.

Skills Focus Comprehension

Objective Identify author's purpose

Materials • **Student Book** "Gorilla Garden" • **Transparencies 19a** and **19b**

STRATEGY MONITOR COMPREHENSION

LA.3.1.7 Use strategies to comprehend text

Remind students that to monitor your own comprehension, you should check to be sure you understand what you are reading.

FCAT SKILL AUTHOR'S PURPOSE

LA.3.1.7.2 Identify the author's purpose

Explain/Model

Remind students that authors write to entertain, inform, or explain something to readers. The author of "Gorilla Garden" tells how Amelia Rinas makes a difference in the world.

Display **Transparencies 19a** and **19b**. Read aloud the last two paragraphs.

Think Aloud The author quotes Amelia explaining why she joined Roots & Shoots. Then he says there are many ways to make a difference in the world. I think here he is trying to inform readers of the many ways people can get involved in their communities.

Practice/Apply

Have students underline clues to the author's purpose in the article. Encourage students to compare their findings and discuss any differences of opinion.

Leveled Reader Lesson

Objective Read to apply strategies and skills

Materials
- **Leveled Reader** *Patching a Playground*
- **Student Book** *Here's My Dollar*
- **Vocabulary Cards**

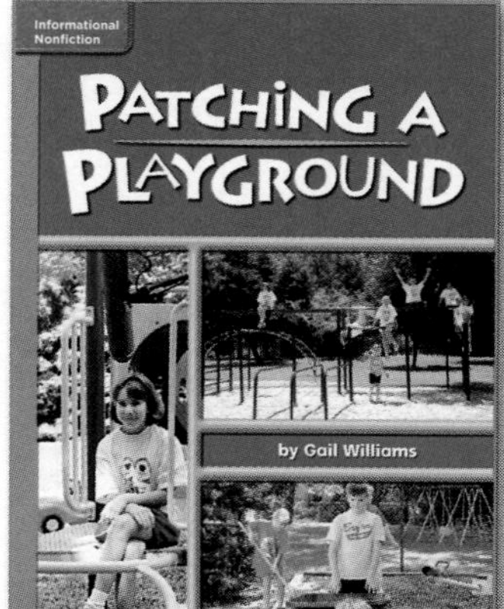

Leveled Reader

PREVIEW AND PREDICT

LA.3.1.7.1 Use text features

Show the cover. Discuss the title and table of contents with students.

- What does the author mean by "patching a playground"?
- What do you think this book is about? What questions do you have?

VOCABULARY WORDS

LA.3.1.6 Use multiple strategies to develop grade-appropriate vocabulary

Display the **Vocabulary Cards** and review the words. Have each student locate one of the words in *Patching a Playground*. Each student should read the sentence aloud, explain what the word means, and name another word or phrase that could be used instead without changing the meaning of the sentence.

STRATEGY
MONITOR COMPREHENSION

LA.3.1.7.8 Use strategies to repair comprehension

Explain why checking for understanding can help readers get more out of a selection. Suggest that as students read, they ask themselves questions, visualize, and reread any part that's not clear. Read pages 2–3 aloud.

Think Aloud I don't understand what the author means by "got her facts together" on page 3. I'll go back and reread the previous paragraph. I'll picture in my mind what happened. Maybe Devan wrote down facts about all the dangerous conditions she saw on the playground.

FCAT

SKILL
AUTHOR'S PURPOSE

LA.3.1.7.2 Identify the author's purpose

Remind students that an author's purpose is his or her reason for writing. Guide students to think about whether the author wrote this book to entertain readers, to inform them, or to explain something to them. Help students create an Author's Purpose Chart.

READ AND RESPOND

LA.3.2.1.7 Connect text to self
LA.3.2.1.7 Reflect on literary selections

Have the group finish the book to find out what Devan did to make her local playground safe. Remind students to reread or ask for help if they do not understand any part of the text. Ask students to describe problems they see in their community. What could they do to help solve them?

MAKE CONNECTIONS ACROSS TEXTS

LA.3.1.7.7 Compare and contrast texts

Have the group summarize and discuss *Here's My Dollar* and *Patching a Playground*. Ask students to compare and contrast the topics and authors' purposes.

- Are the authors' reasons for writing the same or different?
- What do Devan Hickey and Angel Arellano have in common?

On Level Options

Skills Focus: Phonics

Objective Review homophones

Materials • chart paper

DECODE HOMOPHONES

LA.3.1.6.8 Use knowledge of homophones

- Write on the board and read aloud *Please take your sweater if you're going outside.* Explain that *your* and *you're* are homophones, or words that sound the same but have different spellings and meanings. Point out that *you're* is a contraction that means "you are"; *your* shows ownership.
- Write *they're, there, it's,* and *its* on chart paper. Help students write a sentence that contains both words in each homophone pair. Examples:

They're right over there by the car. *It's fun to watch a cat wash its face.*

Skills Focus: Vocabulary

Objective Apply vocabulary and knowledge of contractions

Materials • **Vocabulary Cards** • **Student Book** *Here's My Dollar*

VOCABULARY WORDS

LA.3.1.6.1 Use new vocabulary

Use the **Vocabulary Cards** to review the words. Show the cards for *grownups, community, deserve, interviewed, volunteers, thrilled,* and *tour* one by one. Have students use an example in a sentence to define each. For instance: *Our* community, *or neighborhood, is called Potrero Hill.*

Student Book

FCAT CONTEXT CLUES: EXAMPLES

LA.3.1.6.3 Use context clues

Ask students to locate each of these in *Here's My Dollar* and to make a chart that includes the word or phrase and the example from the text: *slogan* (p. 97); *public appearances, interviewed* (p. 101); *donations* (p. 102).

Challenge students to write a definition of each term based on the example. They can work independently or in pairs.

Skills Focus: Fluency

Objective Read fluently with good prosody at a rate of 82–102 WCPM

Materials • **On Level Practice Book O**, p. 136

REPEATED READING

LA.3.1.5 Demonstrate the ability to read text orally with appropriate rate

Model reading the fluency passage on **Practice Book** page 136 with an even rhythm and meaningful breaks. Have students follow along and then echo-read each sentence. Then have students practice reading the passage in groups of three. One student can read each paragraph.

Timed Reading At the end of the week, have each student do a final timed reading. Track how many words each reads correctly in one minute.

On Level Practice Book O, page 136

As I read, I will pay attention to tempo.

All playgrounds should be safe. But some of them are
10 not. Sometimes playground equipment breaks down. And
17 a broken piece of equipment can be dangerous. Sometimes
26 there are holes in the ground where children can trip and
37 fall. Kids and even grownups don't always recognize these
46 dangers.
47 One nine-year-old girl did spot dangers on a playground,
56 and she decided to take action. She came up with a
67 wonderful plan for making the playground safe. She's
75 Devan Hickey, a fun-loving girl who lives in Bryan, Ohio.
85 First Devan got all her facts together. Then she reported
95 her plan to a group of people in her community who could
107 help her. She also asked family and friends to help out. She
119 didn't give up until the playground was safe. Read her
129 story. 130

Comprehension Check

1. How do playgrounds become unsafe? **Main Idea and Details** when equipment breaks down or when the ground has holes
2. What steps did Devan follow to make a playground safer? **Chronological Order** Devan got all her facts together, reported her plan to improve the playground, and asked for help.

	Words Read	–	Number of Errors	=	Words Correct Score
First Read		–		=	
Second Read		–		=	

Leveled Reader Lesson

Objective Read to apply strategies and skills

Materials • **Leveled Reader** *Patching a Playground* • **Student Book** *Here's My Dollar*

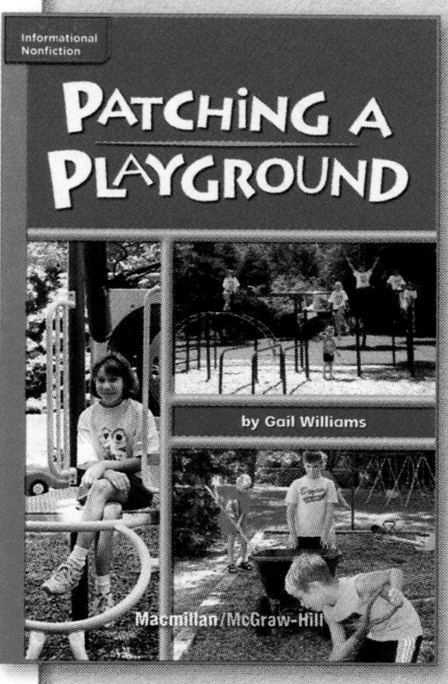

Leveled Reader

PREVIEW AND PREDICT

LA.3.1.7.1 Use text features to establish purpose for reading

Discuss the cover and the title of the book. Ask students if they know what *patching* means. Ask why they think a playground might need patching. Have students generate questions before reading and use them to set purposes for reading.

STRATEGY
MONITOR COMPREHENSION

LA.3.1.7 Use strategies to comprehend text

Tell students that while reading, they should pause regularly to check their understanding. Explain that as they read, they will check that they understand why Devan is concerned about playground safety. Read pages 2–3 aloud. Model how to monitor comprehension.

Think Aloud I don't understand why Devan, who was only nine, had to take charge of fixing up the playground. Why didn't the grownups in charge of parks fix it? I'll read ahead to see if I can find out.

SKILL
AUTHOR'S PURPOSE

LA.3.1.7.2 Identify the author's purpose

Ask a volunteer to explain what an author's purpose might be. Discuss the author's purpose for this selection. Ask students if the author has written to entertain, to inform, or to explain. Students can create Author's Purpose Charts to assist them and fill them in as they read.

READ AND RESPOND

LA.3.1.6.2 Read and discuss text

Have students read to the end of Chapter 2. Discuss why Devan thought the playground was unsafe and what she planned to do about the problem. Discuss how vocabulary words are used.

After students have read the book, discuss the steps Devan took to get the playground fixed. Ask students if they have ever done a community service project or if there is one they would like to start.

MAKE CONNECTIONS ACROSS TEXTS

LA.3.1.7.7 Compare and contrast characters

Have students compare the two girls featured in *Here's My Dollar* and *Patching a Playground*. Ask students how the girls work to make a difference. Discuss whether the purpose of the authors who wrote about Angel and Devan was the same or different.

Beyond Level Options

Student Book

Skills Focus: Vocabulary

Objective Use word associations to review and extend vocabulary

Materials • **Vocabulary Cards**

EXTEND VOCABULARY

LA.3.1.6 Use multiple strategies to develop grade-appropriate vocabulary

Review the vocabulary words using the **Vocabulary Cards**: *tour, volunteers, community, thrilled, slogan, grownups, deserve, interviewed.* Have students create cloze sentences with vocabulary words. For example:

- The guide led an exciting ____ of the museum's exhibits that left both kids and ____ breathless. (tour, grownups)
- I was so ____ when I won first prize that I couldn't stop smiling when they ____ me for the school paper. (thrilled, interviewed)

ELL Access for All

Synonym Matching
Display the following words: *tour, volunteers, deserve, community, thrilled, slogan, excited, saying, earn, visit, helpers, neighborhood.* Tell students that each of the vocabulary words has a synonym in this list of words. Pronounce the vocabulary words one at a time. Then ask: *What is the synonym of this word?* Continue with all words on the list.

Skills Focus: Literary Elements

Objectives Identify rhyme scheme, repetition, and refrain
Write poems with refrains

Materials • **Student Book** "Neighbors" and "Recycling"

RHYME SCHEME AND REPETITION

LA.3.2.1.1 Understand distinguishing features of literature

Have students reread the poems "Neighbors" and "Recycling" on **Student Book** pages 108–109 and review their rhyme scheme and repetition.

- If I told you that the rhyme scheme of "Neighbors" is *abcbdd*, can you explain it?
- How does the refrain help the poem linger in the mind of the reader?

Have students write poems with refrains on the topic of helping out around the house. The poems should have a rhyme scheme and repetition.

Skills Focus: Fluency

Objective Read fluently with good prosody at a rate of 92–102 WCPM

Materials • **Beyond Practice Book B**, p. 136

REPEATED READING

LA.3.1.5 Demonstrate the ability to read text orally with appropriate rate

Read aloud the fluency passage aloud on **Practice Book** page 136 with appropriate expression and tempo, as students echo-read.

Have students take turns reading the passage aloud. Tell them to allow their feelings about what they are reading to show in their voices as they read. Remind them to read at a comfortable tempo. Students should continue to practice reading during independent time.

Timed Reading You may wish to have students do a timed reading at the end of the week and record their reading rates.

 **Beyond Practice Book B,** page 136

As I read, I will pay attention to tempo.

The history of service dogs began near the end of
10 World War I. Dogs were trained to guide soldiers who had
20 lost their eyesight. These animals were called guide dogs.
29 During World War II many Americans gave up their
37 dogs so the dogs could defend their country. These former
47 pet dogs kept watch around the beaches and airfields
56 looking for spies. Some went with the troops overseas.
65 They carried notes and guarded army camps at night.
74 Trainers were surprised by the many things dogs could
83 learn to do. Guide dogs can guide their owners away
93 from construction sites or other dangers. The dogs know
102 when it is safe to cross the street.
110 Soon, people learned that dogs could help people in
119 many ways. Today, service dogs are being trained by
128 **volunteers** to do even more to help people. 136

Comprehension Check

1. How did dogs help during World War II? **Summarize** Dogs kept watch looking for spies, carried notes, and guarded army camps at night.
2. How do guide dogs help blind people? **Main Idea and Details** by guiding their owners away from dangers and helping them cross the street

	Words Read	–	Number of Errors	=	Words Correct Score
First Read		–		=	
Second Read		–		=	

Leveled Reader Lesson

Objective Read to apply strategies and skills

Materials • **Leveled Reader** *Patching a Playground*

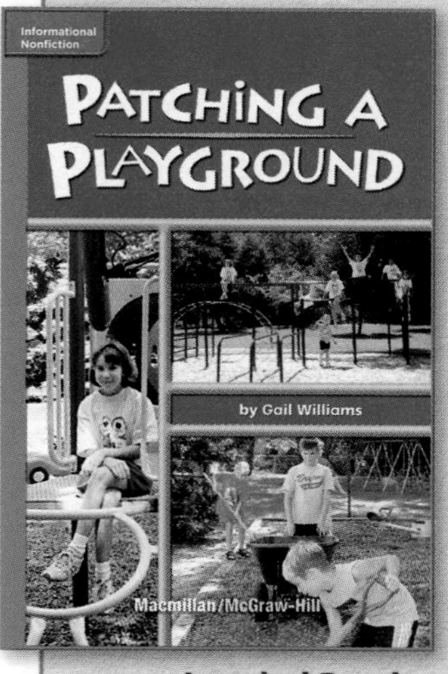

Leveled Reader

PREVIEW AND PREDICT

LA.3.1.7.1 Use text features to establish purpose for reading

Show the cover and read the title. Remind students to watch for vocabulary words and to set and adjust purposes for reading. Note students' questions.

STRATEGY
MONITOR COMPREHENSION

LA.3.1.7.8 Use strategies to repair comprehension

Remind students to stop reading occasionally to make sure they understand the text. If they don't understand, they should reread the section, read more slowly, read ahead to find more information, or ask questions. Read page 3 aloud. Model how to monitor comprehension.

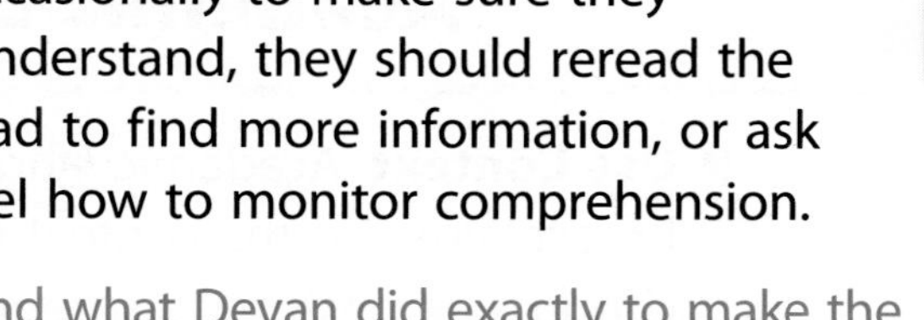

Think Aloud I still don't understand what Devan did exactly to make the playground safe. Maybe if I keep reading the next chapter, I'll find out.

SKILL
AUTHOR'S PURPOSE

LA.3.1.7.2 Identify the author's purpose

Discuss Chapter 1 including what Devan saw at her playground that was unsafe and the playground safety tips in the sidebar. Ask why the author might have written that information. Help students find other clues that tell what the author's purpose might be. Students can complete an Author's Purpose Chart to assist them.

READ AND RESPOND

LA.3.2.1.7 Respond to and discuss literary selections

Have students read the rest of the book. After students finish the selection, have them share their thoughts about what Devan did to help her community. Ask why communities need people like Devan. Have students think about what they might do to help their community.

Self-Selected Reading

Objective Read independently to apply comprehension strategies and skills

Materials • Leveled Readers or trade books at students' reading levels

FCAT READ TO UNDERSTAND AUTHOR'S PURPOSE

LA.3.2.2.5 Select non-fiction materials to read

LA.3.1.7.2 Identify the author's purpose

Invite each student to choose a nonfiction book for independent reading. For a list of theme-related titles, see pages T18–T19. Students can fill in Author's Purpose Charts to help them take note of the clues.

After reading, if students have read the same book they can discuss what they think the author's purpose was. Have students describe how they could rewrite the piece with a different purpose. Afterward, discuss students' reading preferences and any universal themes in the books.

Academic Language

Throughout the week the English language learners will need help in building their understanding of the academic language used in daily instruction and assessment instruments. The following strategies will help to increase their language proficiency and comprehension of content and instructional words.

Technology

Oral Language For additional language support and oral vocabulary development, go to **www.macmillanmh.com**

Strategies to Reinforce Academic Language

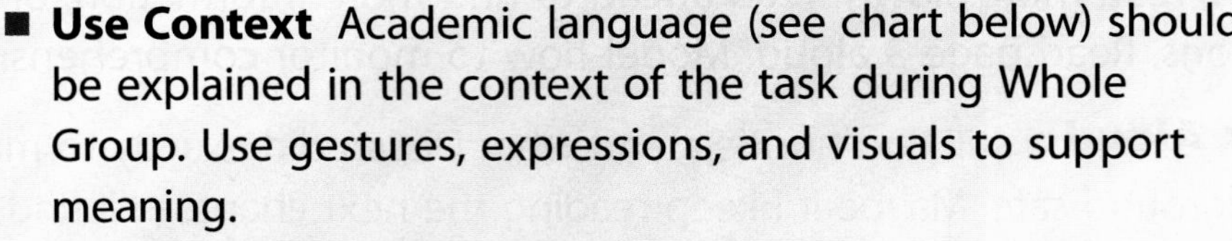

- **Use Context** Academic language (see chart below) should be explained in the context of the task during Whole Group. Use gestures, expressions, and visuals to support meaning.
- **Use Visuals** Use charts, transparencies, and graphic organizers to explain key labels to help students understand classroom language.
- **Model** Demonstrate the task using academic language in order for students to understand instruction.

Academic Language Used in Whole Group Instruction

Content/Theme Words	Skill/Strategy Words	Writing/Grammar Words
getting involved (p. 90)	monitor comprehension (p. 93A)	personal essay (p. 110)
community (p. 91)	author's purpose (p. 93A)	tone (p. 111B)
refrain (p. 108)	explain, entertain, or inform (p. 93A)	irregular verbs (p. 111I)
rhyme scheme (p. 108)	chronological order (p. 107B)	
repetition (p. 108)	rhyme (p. 108)	
recycling (p. 109)		

ELL Leveled Reader Lesson

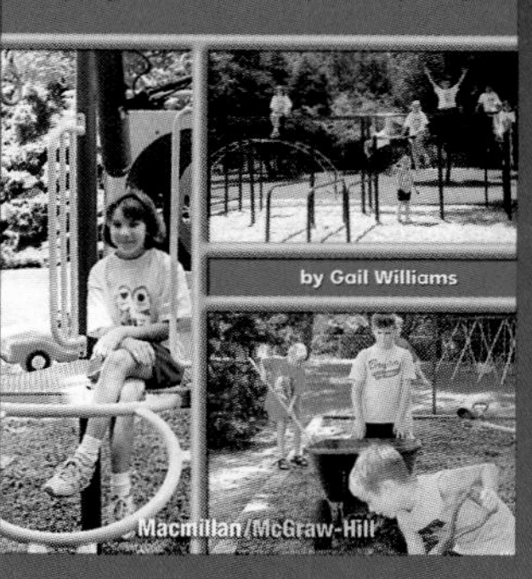

Informational Nonfiction
KIDS MAKE A DIFFERENCE
by Gail Williams
Macmillan/McGraw-Hill

Before Reading

DEVELOP ORAL LANGUAGE

Build Background Ask students to think of a time when they fixed something. *How did you "make it better"? Did you work alone, or as part of a team?* Discuss.

Review Vocabulary Write the vocabulary and support words on the board and discuss their meanings. Use each word in a sentence. *How many* grownups, *or adults, are in this room? I was so* thrilled *to see my friend. I was so happy!* LA.3.1.6 Develop grade-appropriate vocabulary

PREVIEW AND PREDICT

LA.3.1.7.1 Use text features to make predictions
LA.3.1.7.2 Identify the author's purpose

Point to the cover photographs and read the title aloud. *What is special about the photograph on the cover?* (Kids are working together.) *What do you think this book may be about?*

Set a Purpose for Reading Show the Author's Purpose Chart. Ask students to complete similar ones. Have them ask themselves: *What can I learn from this book?* Remind them to look for clues that will help them identify the author's purpose.

During Reading

LA.3.1.7 Use strategies to comprehend text; LA.3.1.7.2 Identify the author's purpose

Choose from among the differentiated strategies below to support students' reading at all stages of language acquisition.

Beginning	Intermediate	Advanced
Shared Reading Do a shared reading of the selection. After each chapter, read it aloud and model how to monitor reading. Think aloud as you look for clues that help you identify the author's purpose. Model filling in the chart as you read.	**Read Together** Read Chapter 1. Help students look for clues that help identify the author's purpose. Model how to monitor your reading and fill in the chart. Take turns reading the selection. Ask students to use the strategy.	**Independent Reading** Have students read the selection. Each day ask them to discuss: *Why did the author write this? What can we learn from it?* Have them look for clues and fill in the Author's Purpose Chart.

After Reading

LA.3.1.6.1 Use new vocabulary

Remind students to use the vocabulary and story words in their whole group activities.

Objective

- Apply vocabulary and comprehension skills

Materials

- ELL Leveled Reader

ELL 5 Day Planner

DAY 1	• Academic Language • Oral Language and Vocabulary Review
DAY 2	• Academic Language • ELL Leveled Reader
DAY 3	• Academic Language • ELL Leveled Reader
DAY 4	• Academic Language • ELL Leveled Reader
DAY 5	• Academic Language • ELL Leveled Reader Comprehension Check and Literacy Activities

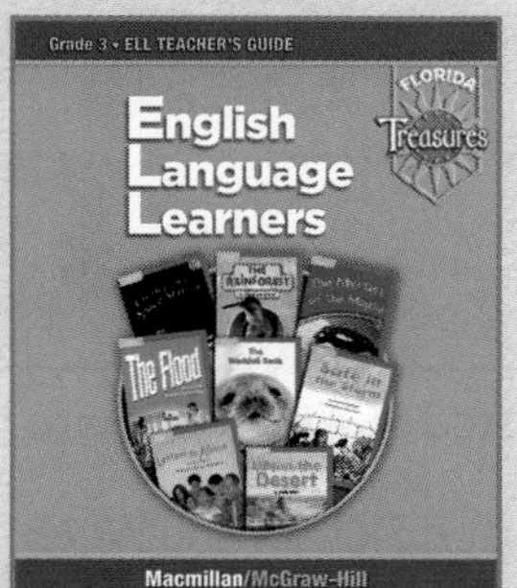

ELL Teacher's Guide for students who need additional instruction

Student Book Selections

Weekly Theme: A Place of My Own

Week At A Glance

Whole Group

VOCABULARY
crate, determination, exact, luckiest, ruined, separate, storage

FCAT Word Parts: Endings *-er, -est*

COMPREHENSION
Strategy: Monitor Comprehension
FCAT Skill: Plot Development: Make Predictions

WRITING

FCAT Expository/Directions

FCAT **Science**
The Nature of Matter

Small Group Options

Differentiated Instruction for Tested Skills

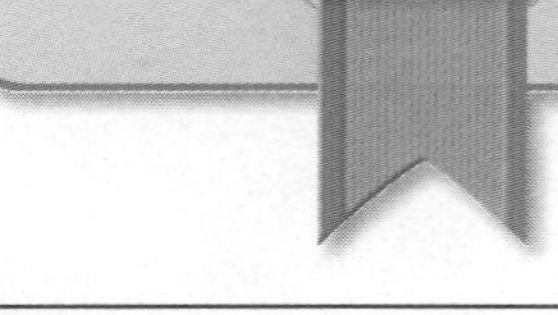

Main Selection
Genre Realistic Fiction

Vocabulary/ Comprehension

Science Link
Genre Encyclopedia Article

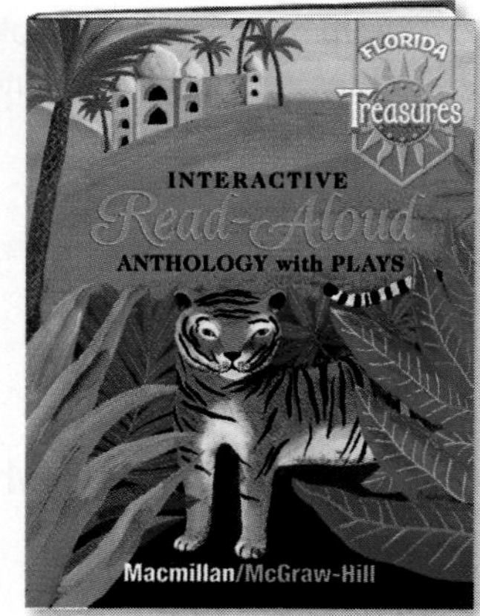

Read-Aloud Anthology
- Listening Comprehension
- Readers' Theater

FCAT Tested FCAT Benchmark
Tested Skill for the Week
Sunshine State Standard
FCAT FCAT Benchmark

Resources for Differentiated Instruction

FCAT LEVELED READERS

GR Levels M–R

Genre Realistic Fiction

- **Same Theme**
- **Same Vocabulary**
- **Same Comprehension Skills**

Approaching Level

On Level

Beyond Level

English Language Leveled Reader

Sheltered Readers for English Language Learners

ELL Teacher's Guide also available

LEVELED PRACTICE

Approaching

On Level

Beyond

ELL

INTERVENTION PROGRAM

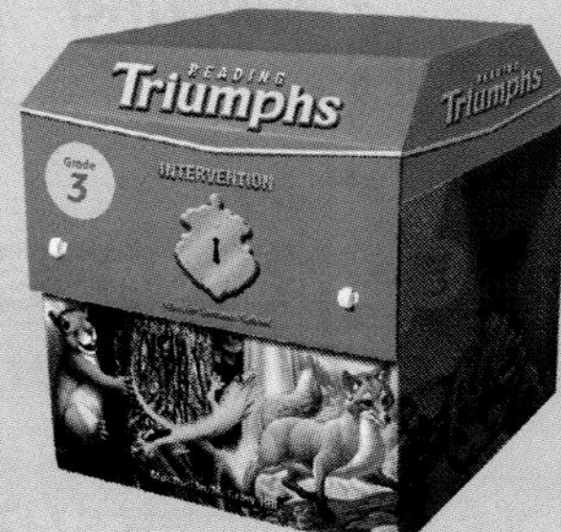

- Phonics and Decoding
- Comprehension
- Vocabulary

Also available, *Reading Triumphs*, Intervention Program

CLASSROOM LIBRARY

Genre Informational Nonfiction

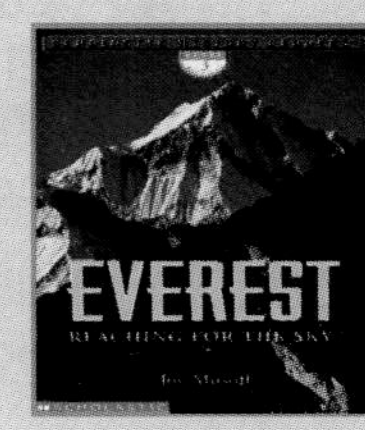

Approaching

On Level

Beyond

Trade books to apply Comprehension Skills

FCAT Success!

- **FCAT Edition**
- **Content Area Reading**

FCAT Test Preparation and Practice

FCAT Benchmark Assessments

FCAT Unit and Weekly Assessments

HOME-SCHOOL CONNECTION

- Family letters in English, Spanish, and Haitian Creole
- Take-Home Stories

FLORIDA Suggested Lesson Plan

My Very Own Room, 116–137

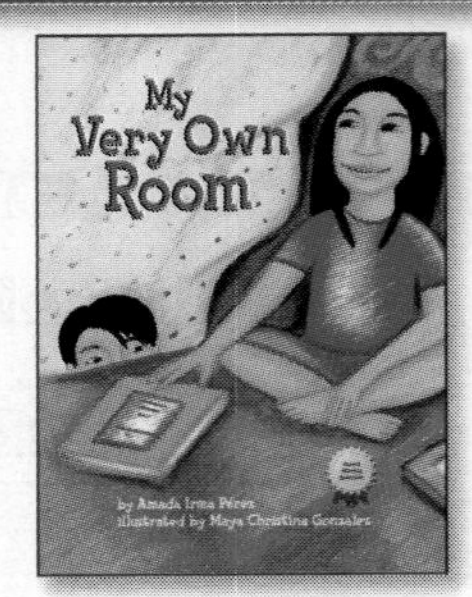

Integrated ELL Support Every Day

Whole Group	Day 1	Day 2
ORAL LANGUAGE • Listening • Speaking • Viewing	**Listening/Speaking/Viewing** Focus Question If you could have a place of your own, where would it be and what would it look like? LA.3.5.2 Build Background, 112 **Read Aloud:** "Under the Back Porch," 113 LA.3.2.1.1	**Listening/Speaking** Focus Question How does the girl get her own room? LA.3.5.2
WORD STUDY • Vocabulary • Phonics/Decoding	**Vocabulary** LA.3.1.6.1 *separate, determination, storage, crate, exact, ruined, luckiest,* 114 Practice Book A-O-B, 140 FCAT **Strategy:** Word Parts: Endings *-er, -est,* 115 LA.3.1.6	**Vocabulary** LA.3.1.6.1 Review Vocabulary Words, 116 **Phonics** Decode Plurals, 145E LA.3.1.4 Practice Book A-O-B, 146
READING • Develop Comprehension • Fluency	**Read** "Pond Street Clubhouse," 114–115 Student Book **Comprehension,** 115A–115B **Strategy:** Monitor Comprehension FCAT **Skill:** Plot Development: Make Predictions LA.3.1.7.3 Practice Book A-O-B, 141 **Fluency** Partner Reading, 112I Model Fluency, 113 LA.3.1.5	**Read** *My Very Own Room,* 116–137 LA.3.1.6.2 Student Book **Comprehension,** 116–137 **Strategy:** Monitor Comprehension FCAT **Skill:** Plot Development: Make Predictions LA.3.2.1.2 Practice Book A-O-B, 142 **Fluency** Partner Reading, 112I LA.3.1.5 Attention to Punctuation, 126
LANGUAGE ARTS • Writing • Grammar • Spelling	FCAT **Writing** Daily Writing: Write a description of an ideal place of your own. Directions, 144–145B LA.3.4.2.1 **Grammar** Daily Language Activities, 145I Contractions with *Not,* 145I LA.3.3.4.3 Grammar Practice Book, 121 **Spelling** Pretest, 145G LA.3.3.4.1 Spelling Practice Book, 121–122	FCAT **Writing** Daily Writing: Think of a place where you spend a lot of time. Write a paragraph about it and what you do there. Directions, 144–145B LA.3.4.2.1 **Grammar** Daily Language Activities, 145I Contractions with *Not,* 145I LA.3.3.4.3 Grammar Practice Book, 122 **Spelling** Plurals, 145G LA.3.3.4.1 Spelling Practice Book, 123
ASSESSMENT • Informal/Formal	Quick Check **Vocabulary,** 114 **Comprehension,** 115B	Quick Check **Comprehension,** 127, 137 **Phonics,** 145E
Turn the Page for **Small Group Lesson Plan**	**Differentiated Instruction 145M–145V**	**Differentiated Instruction 145M–145V**

FCAT Benchmarks

Vocabulary
Vocabulary Words
Word Parts/Endings *-er* and *-est*
LA.3.1.6.7 Use base words and affixes

Comprehension
Strategy: Monitor Comprehension
Skill: Plot Development: Make Predictions
LA.3.2.1.2 Identify plot

Writing
Expository/Directions
LA.3.4.2.1 Write in expository forms

Science
The Nature of Matter
SC.A.1.2.1.3.1 Measurement

Turn the Page for **Small Group Options**

Day 3

Listening/Speaking

Focus Question Explain how the characters of "Pond Street Clubhouse" and *My Very Own Room* both wanted a place of their own. LA.3.5.2

Summarize, 139 LA.3.1.7.8

Vocabulary LA.3.1.6.3

Review Words in Context, 145C

FCAT **Strategy:** Word Parts: Endings *-er, -est,* 145D

Practice Book A-O-B, 145 LA.3.1.6.7

Phonics

Decode Multisyllable Words, 145E LA.3.1.4.3

Read *My Very Own Room,* 116–137 LA.3.1.7

Student Book

Comprehension

FCAT Comprehension Check, 139

Skill: Compare Characters, Settings, and Events, 139B LA.3.2.1.2

Fluency Partner Reading, 121I

Repeated Reading, 139A LA.3.1.5

Practice Book A-O-B, 143

FCAT Writing

Daily Writing: Write a paragraph about how you would build a place of your own. What materials would you use? Who would help you?

Writer's Craft: Time-Order Words, 145 LA.3.3.2.2

Directions, 144–145B LA.3.4.2.1

Grammar Daily Language Activities, 145I

Spelling Contractions, 145J LA.3.3.4.3

Grammar Practice Book, 123

Spelling Plurals, 145H LA.3.1.6.3

Spelling Practice Book, 124

Quick Check **Fluency,** 139A

Differentiated Instruction 145M–145V

Day 4

Listening/Speaking

Focus Question Think about this article and *My Very Own Room.* How did the family know that the bed would fit in the storage space? LA.3.5.2

Expand Vocabulary: A Place of My Own, 145F LA.3.1.6.1

Vocabulary LA.3.1.6.1

Content Vocabulary: *matter, property, mass, volume,* 140

Synonyms, 145F LA.3.1.6.8

Apply Vocabulary to Writing, 145F

Phonics

Plural Match, 145E LA.3.1.6

Read "Matter Matters!" 140–143 LA.3.6.1.1

Student Book

Comprehension LA.3.2.2

Science: Encyclopedia Article

FCAT **Text Features:** Features of an Encyclopedia, 142

Practice Book A-O-B, 144

Fluency Partner Reading, 121I LA.3.1.5

FCAT Writing

Daily Writing: Describe the matter you can see in the room around you. Tell how the different items feel, weigh, and look.

Writing Trait: Topic Sentence, 145 LA.3.3.2.1

Directions, 144–145B LA.3.4.2.1

Grammar Daily Language Activities, 145I

Contractions with *Not,* 145J LA.3.3.4.3

Grammar Practice Book, 124

Spelling Plurals, 145H LA.3.1.6.8

Spelling Practice Book, 125

Quick Check **Vocabulary,** 145D

Differentiated Instruction 145M–145V

Day 5 Review and Assess

Listening/Speaking

Focus Question Describe the different types of matter found in "Pond Street Clubhouse" and *My Very Own Room.*

Speaking and Listening Strategies, 145A

Vocabulary LA.3.1.6.1

Spiral Review: Vocabulary Game, 145F

Read Self-Selected Reading, 112I

Student Book

Comprehension

Connect and Compare, 143 LA.3.1.7.3

Fluency Partner Reading, 112I LA.3.1.5

FCAT Writing

Daily Writing: Pretend you are one of the brothers in the story *My Very Own Room.* Write how you feel about your sister getting a room of her own.

Directions, 144–145B LA.3.4.2.1

Grammar Daily Language Activities, 145I

Contractions with *Not,* 145J LA.3.3.4

Grammar Practice Book, 125–126

Spelling Posttest, 145H LA.3.1.6.3

Spelling Practice Book, 126

FCAT **Weekly Assessment, 237–248**

Differentiated Instruction 145M–145V

Differentiated Instruction

What do I do in small groups?

Focus on Skills

Skills Focus **Use your  observations to guide additional instruction and practice.**

Phonics
Decode Plurals

Vocabulary
Words: separate, determination, storage, crate, exact, ruined, luckiest
FCAT **Strategy:** Word Parts/Inflectional Endings

Comprehension
FCAT **Strategy:** Monitor Comprehension
FCAT **Skill:** Plot Development: Make Predictions

 FCAT **Fluency**

Suggested Lesson Plan

CD ROM Instructional Navigator Interactive Lesson Planner

	Day 1	Day 2
Approaching Level • **Additional Instruction/Practice** • **Tier 2 Instruction**	Fluency, 145N Vocabulary, 145N Comprehension, 145O 	Phonics, 145M Vocabulary, 145O Leveled Reader Lesson, 145P • Vocabulary • Comprehension 
On Level • **Practice**	Vocabulary, 145Q Leveled Reader Lesson, 145R • Comprehension 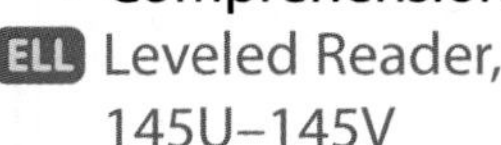 ELL Leveled Reader, 145U–145V 	Phonics, 145Q Leveled Reader Lesson, 145R • Comprehension • Vocabulary 
Beyond Level • **Extend**	Vocabulary, 145S Leveled Reader Lesson, 145T • Comprehension 	 Leveled Reader Lesson, 145T • Comprehension • Vocabulary 

For intensive intervention see READING Triumphs

Focus on Leveled Readers

Levels M–R

Apply FCAT skills and strategies while reading appropriate leveled books.

Approaching

On Level

Beyond

Safe in the Storm

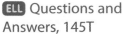

ELL

Additional Leveled Reader Resources

Leveled Reader Database

Go to www.macmillanmh.com

Search by

- Comprehension Skill
- Content Area
- Genre
- Text Feature
- Guided Reading Level
- Reading Recovery Level
- Lexile Score
- Benchmark Level

Subscription also available.

Day 3	Day 4	Day 5
Phonics, 145M Fluency, 145N Vocabulary, 145O Leveled Reader Lesson, 145P • Comprehension 	Phonics, 145M Leveled Reader Lesson, 145P • Comprehension • ELL Skill: Plot Development: Make Predictions	Fluency, 145N Leveled Reader Lesson, 145P • Make Connections Across Texts 
Fluency, 145Q Vocabulary, 145Q Leveled Reader Lesson, 145R • Comprehension   	Leveled Reader Lesson, 145R • Comprehension	Fluency, 145Q Leveled Reader Lesson, 145R • Make Connections Across Texts 
Fluency, 145S Vocabulary, 145S Leveled Reader Lesson, 145T • Comprehension	Text Feature, 145S Leveled Reader Lesson, 145T • Comprehension ELL Questions and Answers, 145T 	Fluency, 145S Self-Selected Reading, 145T 

What do I do with the rest of my class?

Class Management Tools

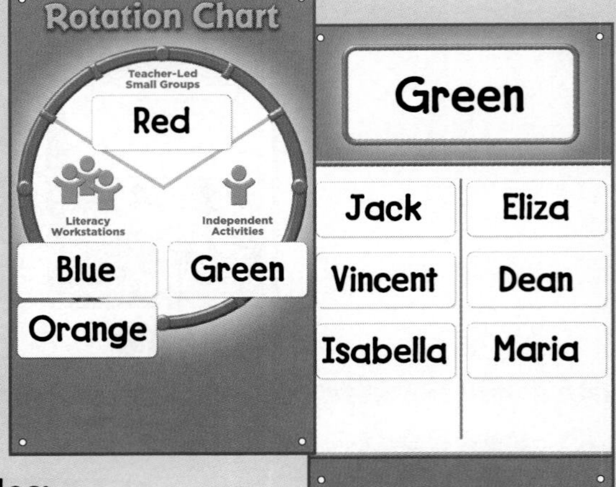

Includes:

- How-to Guide
- Rotation Chart
- Weekly Contracts

Hands-on activities for reinforcing weekly skills

Three-Pocket Foldable

Standing Cube Foldable

Independent Activities

Reinforcing Weekly Skills

FCAT LEVELED READERS

For Repeated Readings and Literacy Activities

Approaching

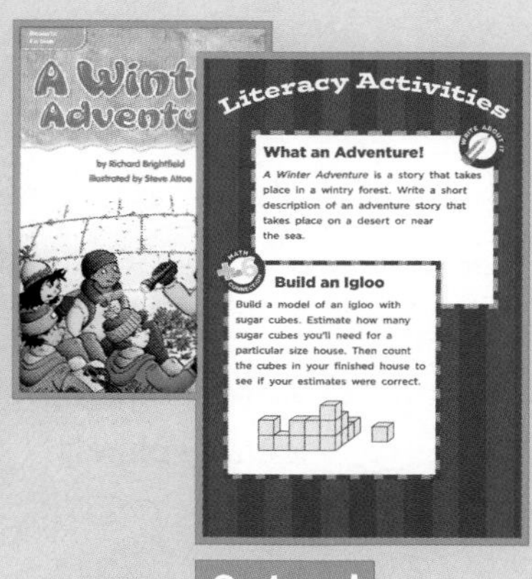

On Level

ELL

Beyond

LEVELED PRACTICE

Skills: Phonics, Vocabulary, Plot Development, Fluency, Endings *-er* and *-est*, Features of an Encyclopedia

Approaching

On Level

Beyond

ELL

Technology

ONLINE INSTRUCTION www.macmillanmh.com

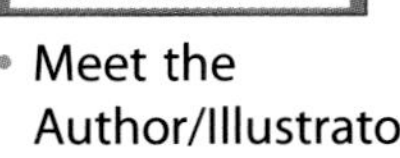

- Meet the Author/Illustrator

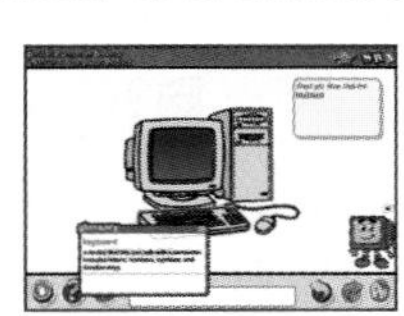

- Computer Literacy Lessons

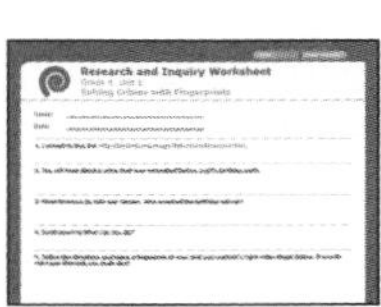

- Research and Inquiry Activities

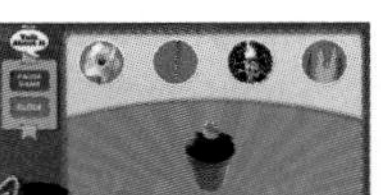

- Oral Language Activities

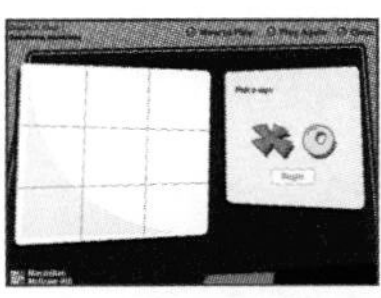

- Vocabulary and Spelling Activities

- Leveled Reader Database

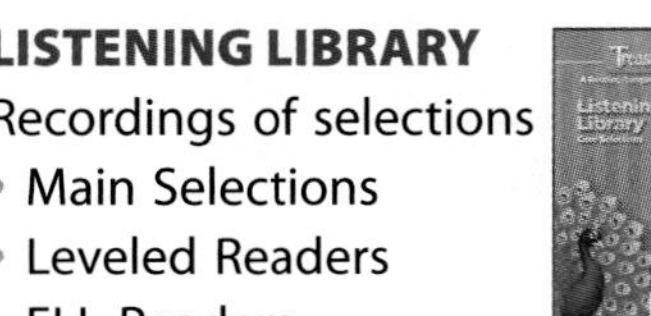

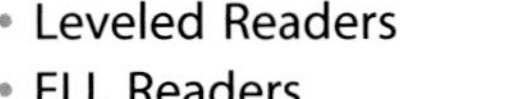

LISTENING LIBRARY

Recordings of selections

- Main Selections
- Leveled Readers
- ELL Readers
- Intervention Anthology

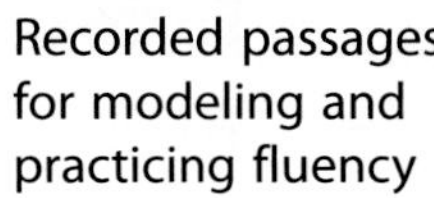

FLUENCY SOLUTIONS

Recorded passages for modeling and practicing fluency

VOCABULARY PUZZLEMAKER

Activities for vocabulary, spelling, and high-frequency words

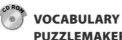

NEW ADVENTURES WITH BUGGLES AND BEEZY

Phonemic awareness and phonics practice

Turn the page for Literacy Workstations.

Literacy Activities

Collaborative Learning Activities

Reading

Objectives

- Practice fluency with Readers Theatre
- Predict what will happen next in a story
- Select fiction materials to read

Word Study

Objectives

- Write comparatives and superlatives
- Identify plurals

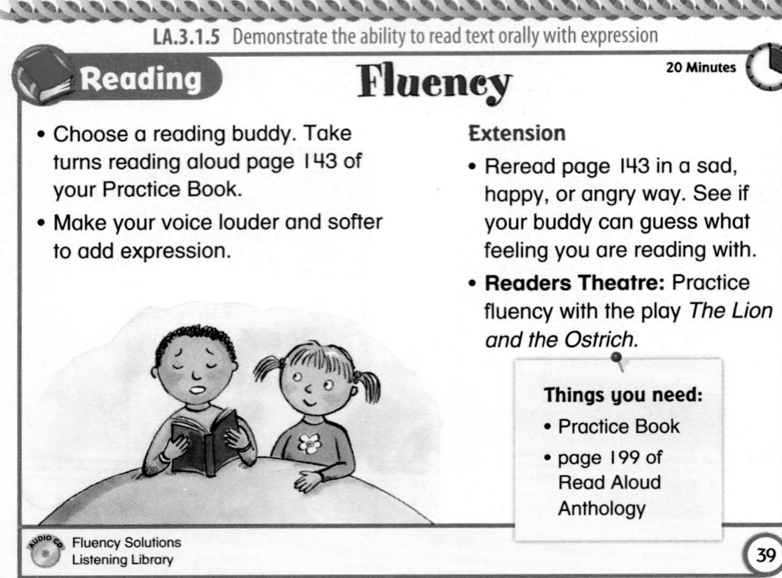

LA.3.1.5 Demonstrate the ability to read text orally with expression

Reading — **Fluency** — 20 Minutes

- Choose a reading buddy. Take turns reading aloud page 143 of your Practice Book.
- Make your voice louder and softer to add expression.

Extension

- Reread page 143 in a sad, happy, or angry way. See if your buddy can guess what feeling you are reading with.
- **Readers Theatre:** Practice fluency with the play *The Lion and the Ostrich*.

Things you need:

- Practice Book
- page 199 of Read Aloud Anthology

Fluency Solutions Listening Library

39

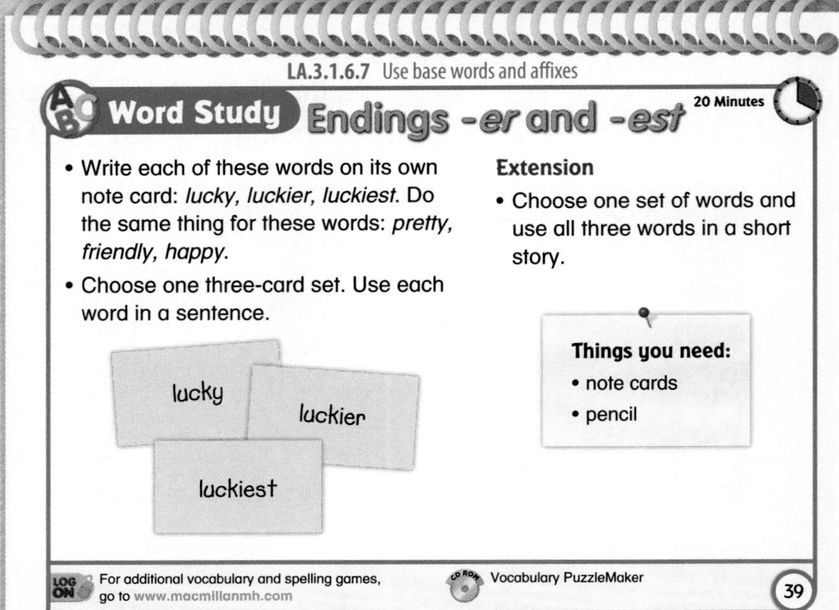

LA.3.1.6.7 Use base words and affixes

Word Study — **Endings -er and -est** — 20 Minutes

- Write each of these words on its own note card: *lucky, luckier, luckiest.* Do the same thing for these words: *pretty, friendly, happy.*
- Choose one three-card set. Use each word in a sentence.

Extension

- Choose one set of words and use all three words in a short story.

Things you need:

- note cards
- pencil

LOG ON For additional vocabulary and spelling games, go to www.macmillanmh.com

Vocabulary PuzzleMaker

39

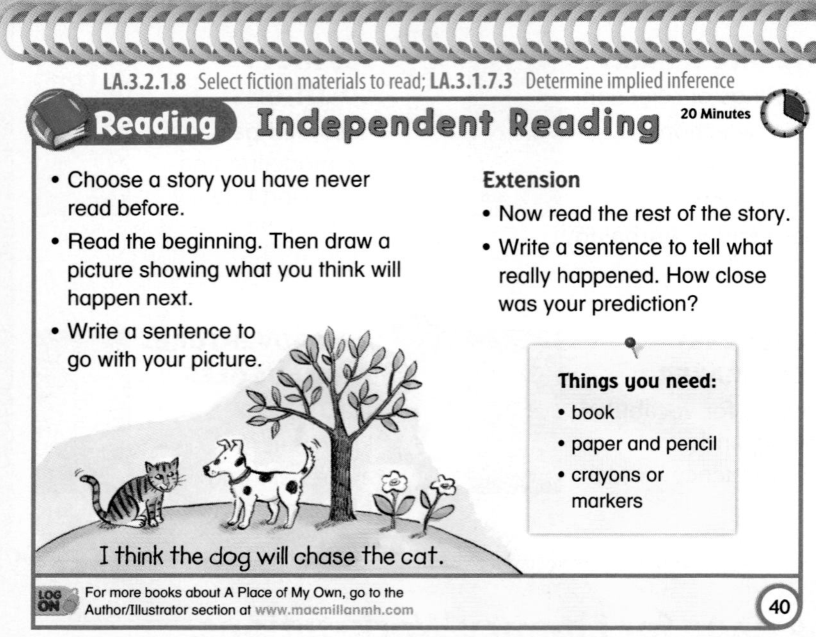

LA.3.2.1.8 Select fiction materials to read; LA.3.1.7.3 Determine implied inference

Reading — **Independent Reading** — 20 Minutes

- Choose a story you have never read before.
- Read the beginning. Then draw a picture showing what you think will happen next.
- Write a sentence to go with your picture.

Extension

- Now read the rest of the story.
- Write a sentence to tell what really happened. How close was your prediction?

Things you need:

- book
- paper and pencil
- crayons or markers

LOG ON For more books about A Place of My Own, go to the Author/Illustrator section at www.macmillanmh.com

40

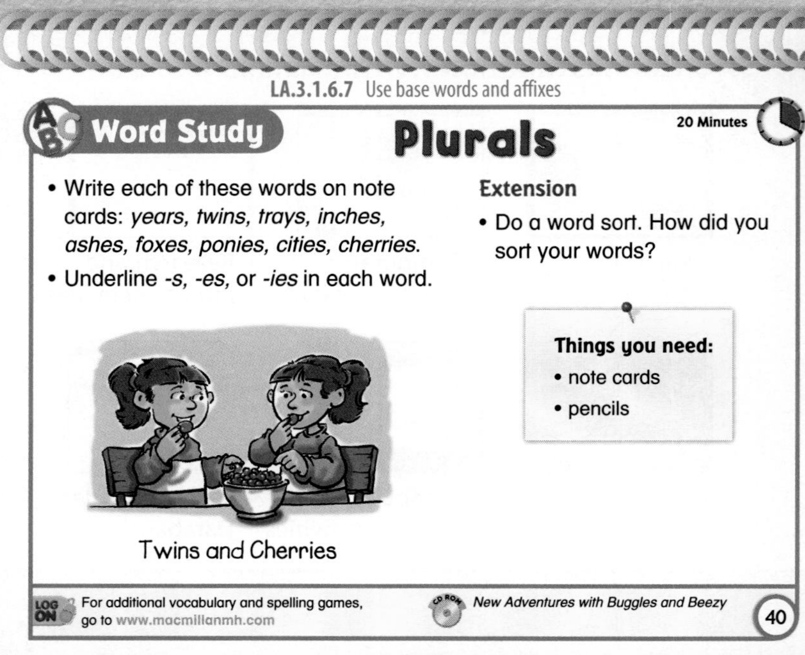

LA.3.1.6.7 Use base words and affixes

Word Study — **Plurals** — 20 Minutes

- Write each of these words on note cards: *years, twins, trays, inches, ashes, foxes, ponies, cities, cherries.*
- Underline *-s, -es,* or *-ies* in each word.

Twins and Cherries

Extension

- Do a word sort. How did you sort your words?

Things you need:

- note cards
- pencils

LOG ON For additional vocabulary and spelling games, go to www.macmillanmh.com

New Adventures with Buggles and Beezy

40

Literacy Workstations

Writing

Objectives

- Write about an after-school activity
- Write step-by-step instructions about making a snack

Content Literacy

Objectives

- Research information about beavers
- Research information about architects

LA.3.4.2.1 Write in informational /expository forms

Writing — **Explanatory Writing** — 20 Minutes

- Think about an after-school activity you enjoy doing, such as playing on a sports team or playing a musical instrument.
- Write a paragraph. Tell how you do the activity, from the first step to the last.

Extension

- Read your paragraph to a partner.
- Ask your partner how you did. Was your explanation clear?

Things you need:
- paper
- pencil

39

LA.3.4.2.2 Record information related to a topic; LA.3.4.2.2 Include visual aids as appropriate

Science — **A Special Home** — 20 Minutes

- Beavers work hard to make their own homes.
- Use an encyclopedia or the Internet to find out how beavers make dams and lodges.
- Take notes on what you find.

Extension

- Draw a picture of a beaver's dam and lodge, label its parts, and write an interesting caption.

Things you need:
- encyclopedia or computer
- paper and pencil
- crayons or markers

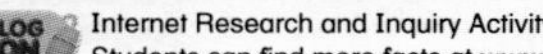

LOG ON Internet Research and Inquiry Activity
Students can find more facts at www.macmillanmh.com

39

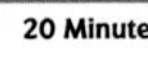

LA.3.4.2.1 Write expository forms; LA.3.4.2.2 Include visual aids as appropriate

Writing — **My Favorite Snack** — 20 Minutes

- Think of a favorite snack you know how to make, such as a tuna fish sandwich.
- Design a cookbook page. Tell others how to make the snack. List the ingredients and number the steps in order. Add a picture.

Extension

- Gather other cookbook pages from your classmates. Make a cover and make a class cookbook.

Things you need:
- paper
- pencil
- crayons or markers

40

LA.3.4.2.2 Record information related to a topic; LA.3.6.1.1 Read informational text to perform a task

Social Studies — **ARCHITECTS AT WORK** — 20 Minutes

- What do architects do at their jobs? Use an encyclopedia or the Internet to find out.
- Take notes on what you find.

New House

Extension

- Now suppose that you are an architect! Design a new house. Draw a picture of it. Where would you put a bedroom, kitchen, living room, and bathroom?

Things you need:
- encyclopedia or computer
- paper and crayons

40

Prepare

ORAL LANGUAGE
- Build Background
- Read Aloud
- Expand Vocabulary

FCAT **VOCABULARY**
- Teach Words in Context
- **Word Parts:** Endings *-er* and *-est*

COMPREHENSION
- **Strategy:** Monitor Comprehension
- FCAT **Skill:** Plot Development

SMALL GROUP OPTIONS
- Differentiated Instruction, pp. 145M–145V

Oral Language

Build Background

ACCESS PRIOR KNOWLEDGE

Share the following information:

Children like to build hideaways, such as tree houses, forts, huts, or tents, using wood, cardboard boxes, or even old bed sheets.

LA.3.5.2 Apply listening and speaking strategies

TALK ABOUT A PLACE OF MY OWN

Discuss the weekly theme.

- What does "a place of my own" mean?
- Do you have a special place of your own? Where is it? What is it like?

FOCUS QUESTION Ask a volunteer to read "Talk About It" on **Student Book** page 113 and describe the photograph. Ask: What do you think the boy in the tree house is saying?

ENGLISH LANGUAGE LEARNERS

Beginning **Build Language** Point to and name items in the photo and have students repeat. Then help students say what they can about it. Guide students to elaborate: *I see a boy* → *I see a boy in a tree house.*

Intermediate **Ask Questions** Ask: *Where is the boy? How do you think he feels? Have you ever been in a tree house? Would you like to go in a tree house? Do you have a special place of your own?* As students talk, restate what they say to model correct usage.

Advanced **Share Experiences** Complete the Intermediate task. Have students brainstorm items that their perfect places would have. Then have students choose their top three items and explain why.

A PLACE OF MY OWN

Talk About It

If you could have a place of your own, where would it be and what would it look like?

LOG ON Find out more about creating special places at **www.macmillanmh.com**

113

Picture Prompt

Look at the photograph. Write about the tree house. You can write a poem, story, description, or use any other type of writing you like.

LA.3.4.1 Develop and demonstrate creative writing

Technology

For an extended lesson plan, Web site activities, and additional Read Alouds for **oral language** and **vocabulary development**, go to www.macmillanmh.com

Read Aloud

Read "Under the Back Porch"

LA.3.2.1.1 Understand distinguishing features of literature
LA.3.2.1.5 Examine how language describes people, feelings, and objects
LA.3.2.1.5 Identify author's use of figurative language

GENRE: Poetry

Poetry can describe feelings, objects, animals, people, or events. A poem is written in lines. Sometimes poetry has rhyme and/or rhythm and may include imagery and figurative language.

Read Aloud
pages 87–89

LA.3.2.1.5 Identify author's use of descriptive language
LA.3.2.1.3 Identify how language choice helps develop mood

LISTENING FOR A PURPOSE

Ask students to listen for words that help develop a mood in "Under the Back Porch" in the **Read-Aloud Anthology**. Choose from among the teaching suggestions.

Fluency Ask students to listen carefully to your phrasing, expression, and tone of voice as you read aloud.

LA.3.2.1.5 Examine how language describes objects

RESPOND TO THE POEM

Ask: How does the poet describe sunlight? (slants through the slats in long strips of light) What does it smell like under the porch? (moist green)

Expand Vocabulary

LA.3.4.1.2 Write a variety of expressive forms

Ask students to choose three or more words or phrases from the poem that tell about the weekly theme, such as, *my*, *place*, *back porch*, *alone*, *shaded*, *underneath*, and *all mine*. Have students use some of these words or phrases to write short poems about a secret place. Ask them to memorize and recite their poems for the class.

Use the routine card to teach Expand Vocabulary words in the Read-Aloud lesson.

Vocabulary

LA.3.1.6.1 Use new vocabulary taught directly

TEACH WORDS IN CONTEXT

Use the following routine:

Routine

Define: If you **separate** things, you keep them apart.
Example: Fences separate the soccer field from the playground.
Ask: How do people usually separate the rooms of a house? EXPLANATION

- Someone who has **determination** has a firm purpose. He ran the race with determination. What have you done with determination? EXAMPLE
- Access for All: Things that people don't need every day are put in **storage** areas. Basements are often used for storage. What other spaces are used for storage? EXAMPLE
- A **crate** is a box made of wood. I packed my books in a crate. How is a crate similar to a box, and how is it different? COMPARE AND CONTRAST
- If something is **exact**, it is correct or precise. To get the exact measurement of a room, you can use a tape measure. How can you find the exact weight of something? PRIOR KNOWLEDGE
- If something is **ruined**, you can no longer use it. The homes were ruined by a hurricane. What is a synonym for *ruined*? (*destroyed*) SYNONYM
- The **luckiest** person has more luck than anyone else. Ted thought he was the luckiest boy alive when his parents gave him a puppy. What would make you feel like the luckiest person? DESCRIPTION

LA.3.1.6 Use multiple strategies to develop grade-appropriate vocabulary

Vocabulary

separate **exact**
determination **ruined**
storage **luckiest**
crate

FCAT **Word Parts**

Inflectional Endings

-er and *-est* show comparison. The ending *-er* means "more." The ending *-est* means "most."

luckiest = most lucky

Pond Street Clubhouse

by Sylvia Medrano

On Saturday I went to the lumberyard with Dad to order lumber for the new garage. I saw the wood and got an idea.

"Hey, Dad," I said. "Could we build a clubhouse?"

"Probably not," said Dad. "I'll be too busy with the garage."

"But, Dad," I said, "you had a clubhouse when you were young."

Dad said, "I know, but first we have to build the garage."

I had to think of a way to get Dad to agree. "We can **separate** the clubhouse into two rooms," I said with **determination**. "One can be used as a **storage** room."

114

Quick Check **Do students understand word meanings?**

During **Small Group Instruction**

If No → Approaching Level Vocabulary, p. 145N

If Yes → On Level Options, pp. 145Q–145R

Beyond Level Options, pp. 145S–145T

ELL Access for All

Demonstrate For the word *separate*, demonstrate things you might separate: broken crayons and new crayons, boys and girls, a binder into separate subjects. Ask: *What's in your desk that you can separate?*

For *storage*, say: *I use the classroom closet for storage. I put paper and supplies in there to use later.* Ask: *What do you keep in storage at home?*

Dad thought about it for a moment. Then he said, "Let's wait to see if there is enough extra wood."

The garage supplies came the following weekend. There were huge piles of wood and a big box. It was a **crate** of nails and shingles for the roof. It looked like more than enough. When the truck left, Dad said, "Good news! We'll be able to build your clubhouse with the leftover wood when the garage is finished."

After a few weeks, it was time to start. A bunch of neighborhood kids came to help.

Dad let us measure the wood. Measuring has to be **exact** or else the pieces won't fit together. If Dad cut the wood too long or too short, our plans could be **ruined**. I knew we couldn't buy any extra wood.

When the clubhouse was finally finished, I was so thrilled. I made a sign and nailed it on the door. It said, "Pond Street Clubhouse—Welcome!" Now I have a great place to play. Am I the **luckiest** kid in town, or what?

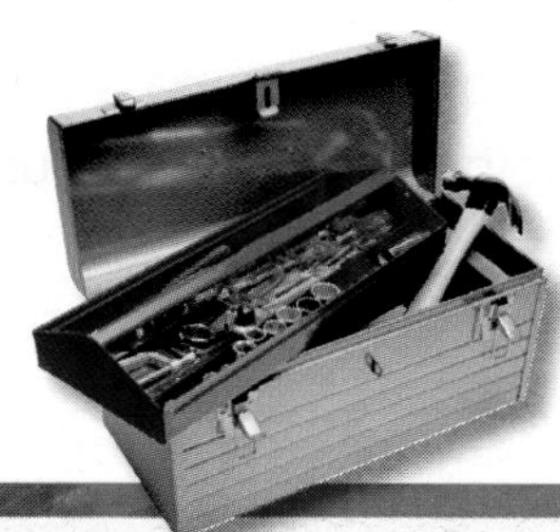

Reread for **Comprehension**

Monitor Comprehension

FCAT **Plot Development** One way to monitor, or check, your understanding of plot in a story is to **make predictions**. You can make predictions about what characters might do or what events might happen. Reread the selection. Use your Predictions Chart to keep track of your predictions about characters and events. Then check to see if your predictions were correct by writing **what happens**.

What I Predict	What Happens

115

Vocabulary

LA.3.1.4.1 Use knowledge of pronunciation to decode words

USING THE STRATEGIES

Students can figure out unfamiliar words, by using their knowledge of phonics, by looking for affixes and base words, or context clues. If these strategies don't work, students can use a dictionary to look up the word.

FCAT **STRATEGY**
WORD PARTS

LA.3.1.6.7 Use base words and affixes

Endings *-er* and *-est* An adjective is a word that describes a noun. Explain that when the ending *-er* is added to a base word that is an adjective, it means "more." When the ending *-est* is added to a base word that is an adjective, it means "most." For example, the base word *small* + *-er* (*smaller*) means "more small" and *small* + *-est* (*smallest*) means "most small." When the endings *-er* and *-est* are added to a base word that ends in consonant *y*, the *y* changes to *i*, as in *happiest*. When the endings *-er* and *-est* are added to a word that ends in a vowel and a consonant, the consonant doubles, as in *biggest*.

An adjective with an *-er* ending compares two things. An adjective with an *-est* ending compares three or more things. Point to *luckiest* on page 115. Have students identify the base word and the ending, and tell what the word means. (*lucky* + *-est*; most lucky)

Read "Pond Street Clubhouse"

LA.3.1.6.3 Use context clues to determine meanings

As students read "Pond Street Clubhouse," have them identify clues to the meanings of the highlighted words. Tell students they will read these words again in *My Very Own Room*.

FCAT **Success!**

Test Prep and Practice with vocabulary, pages 6–31

On Level Practice Book O, page 140

determination	ruined	storage	crate
exact	separate	luckiest	

A. Fill in the blank with the word from the box that best completes each sentence.

1. Rose's family had planned their trip with great determination.
2. Rose wrapped a few boxes and packed them in a wooden crate.
3. The family's furniture was put into a room for storage on the ship.
4. The ship sailed at the exact time it was supposed to leave.
5. Rose used a sheet to separate her space from the rest of her family.
6. She thought she was the luckiest person on the ship. She had her own quiet space to write in her journal.
7. Rose unpacked at her new home. Some boxes had been squashed. Nothing had been broken or ruined during the move.

B. Write a sentence using one of the vocabulary words. Possible response provided.

8. I was so happy to have my own room because I could put my stuff in the exact spot I wanted it.

Approaching Practice Book A, page 140

Beyond Practice Book B, page 140

Vocabulary

Review last week's vocabulary words: **tour, volunteers, community, thrilled, slogan, grownups, deserve, interviewed.**

LA.3.1.6.1 Use new vocabulary

Objectives

- Monitor comprehension
- Make and confirm predictions to understand plot development
- Use academic language: *predictions*

Materials

- Comprehension Transparencies 20a and 20b
- Graphic Organizer Transparency 20
- Leveled Practice Books, p. 141

FCAT Skills Trace

Plot Development: Make Predictions	
Introduce	U4: 115A–B
Practice / Apply	U4: 116–139; Practice Book, 141–142
Reteach / Review	U4: 145M–T; U5: 233A–B, 234–253, 259M–T; Leveled Practice, 171–172
Assess	Weekly Tests; Unit 4, 5 Tests; Benchmark Tests A, B
Maintain	U5: 233A–B

ELL — Access for All

Academic Vocabulary
Place a pen on the edge of a table. Tell students you will blow on the pen. Ask what will happen. (It will roll off.) Help students see that they are using their experience and what they see to make a prediction. Introduce words to make predictions: *will, won't, might, probably, could*. Help students use the words to talk about predictions.

Reread for Comprehension

STRATEGY
MONITOR COMPREHENSION

LA.3.1.7 Use strategies to comprehend text

LA.3.1.7.8 Use strategies to repair comprehension

Good readers **monitor comprehension** as they read. They stop to check that they understand what they have read. They also figure out what to do when the text is confusing. They can reread, read ahead, ask questions, paraphrase, visualize, adjust their reading rate, or seek help. Students may use the monitor comprehension strategy as they make predictions.

FCAT SKILL
PLOT DEVELOPMENT: MAKE PREDICTIONS

LA.3.1.7.1 Use text features to make predictions

EXPLAIN

Tell students:

- To better understand how a plot develops, you can **make predictions** about what will happen in a story. To make predictions, you can make inferences using story clues, including the title and illustrations, and your own knowledge.

Transparency 20a

Vocabulary
separate, determination, storage, crate, exact, ruined, luckiest

FCAT Word Parts
Inflectional Endings
-er and *-est* show comparison. The ending *-er* means "more." The ending *-est* means "most."
luckiest = most lucky

Pond Street Clubhouse

by Sylvia Medrano

On Saturday I went to the lumberyard with Dad to order lumber for the new garage. I saw the wood and got an idea.

"Hey, Dad," I said. "Could we build a clubhouse?"

"Probably not," said Dad. "I'll be too busy with the garage."

"But, Dad," I said, "you had a clubhouse when you were young."

Dad said, "I know, but first we have to build the garage."

I had to think of a way to get Dad to agree. "We can **separate** the clubhouse into two rooms," I said with **determination**. "One can be used as a **storage** room."

114

Transparency 20b

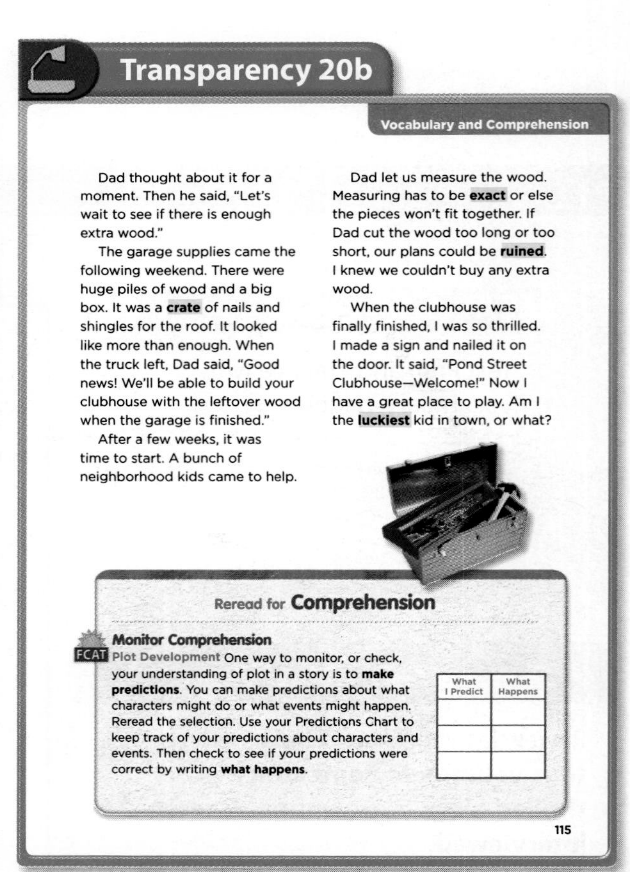

Vocabulary and Comprehension

Dad thought about it for a moment. Then he said, "Let's wait to see if there is enough extra wood."

The garage supplies came the following weekend. There were huge piles of wood and a big box. It was a **crate** of nails and shingles for the roof. It looked like more than enough. When the truck left, Dad said, "Good news! We'll be able to build your clubhouse with the leftover wood when the garage is finished."

After a few weeks, it was time to start. A bunch of neighborhood kids came to help.

Dad let us measure the wood. Measuring has to be **exact** or else the pieces won't fit together. If Dad cut the wood too long or too short, our plans could be **ruined**. I knew we couldn't buy any extra wood.

When the clubhouse was finally finished, I was so thrilled. I made a sign and nailed it on the door. It said, "Pond Street Clubhouse—Welcome!" Now I have a great place to play. Am I the **luckiest** kid in town, or what?

Reread for Comprehension

Monitor Comprehension
FCAT Plot Development One way to monitor, or check, your understanding of plot in a story is to **make predictions**. You can make predictions about what characters might do or what events might happen. Reread the selection. Use your Predictions Chart to keep track of your predictions about characters and events. Then check to see if your predictions were correct by writing **what happens**.

What I Predict	What Happens

115

Student Book pages 114–115 available on Comprehension Transparencies 20a and 20b

LA.3.1.7.3 Determine relevant supporting details

- Read on to **confirm** the prediction, or see if it is correct. If you are wrong, **revise**, or correct, your prediction—or make a new prediction.

LA.3.1.6.2 Read familiar text

MODEL

Read aloud the first page of "Pond Street Clubhouse" on **Student Book** page 114.

LA.3.2.1.2 Identify plot

Think Aloud After reading the first page, I predict that the boy will be able to build the clubhouse. To make this prediction, I can use the story title, what happened so far, and my own experience. The title is "Pond Street Clubhouse." This tells me that there might be a clubhouse in the story. The boy gives his father several reasons to build the clubhouse. I know that good reasons can help persuade someone to do something. From my own experience, I also think that the father will want to make his son happy. I will read on to see if my prediction is correct.

GUIDED PRACTICE

- Display the Predictions Chart on **Transparency 20**. Remind students that they can use a Predictions Chart to keep track of and to confirm predictions.
- After reading page 114, write the first prediction on the Predictions Chart: *The narrator's father will agree to build a clubhouse.* Remind students to look for information that confirms their prediction or, if the prediction was wrong, revise it. Then complete the What Happens box on the right. (The narrator's father agrees to build a clubhouse.)

LA.3.1.7.3 Determine implied inference

APPLY

Have students make another prediction about whether or not there will be enough lumber to build the clubhouse. Ask them to make inferences about what will happen using clues from the story and their own experience. Then have them add this second prediction, and, its confirmation or revision, to the Predictions Chart.

Quick Check **Can students understand plot development by making predictions?**

During **Small Group Instruction**

If No → Approaching Level Comprehension, p. 145O

If Yes → On Level Options, pp. 145Q–145R

Beyond Level Options, pp. 145S–145T

Transparency 20

PREDICTIONS CHART

What I Predict	What Happens
The narrator's father will agree to build a clubhouse.	The narrator's father agrees to build a clubhouse.
There will not be enough extra wood.	There was enough extra wood.

Graphic Organizer Transparency 20

FCAT Success!

Test Prep and Practice with plot development, pages 65–96

On Level Practice Book O, page 141

When you make a **prediction,** you tell what will probably happen next. As you continue reading, you can **confirm** your prediction, or find out if you were right.

Each poem tells about characters who spend time in a place of their own. Read the poem. Read the title of the poem to help you predict what will happen. Choose the words that tell what will probably happen next and write the words on the line.

1. **Finally We Can Play**

Rain has fallen for days and days.
We've been bored in many ways.
The sun is finally out today.
We can't wait to run out and play.

a. for the sky to turn gray.
(b.) to run out and play.

2. **The Tired Queen**

The queen went to sleep late last night.
She stayed up almost 'til dawn.
When she wakes up late this morning,
You'll probably see her yawn.

a. find her mowing her lawn.
(b.) probably see her yawn.

Approaching Practice Book A, page 141

Beyond Practice Book B, page 141

Read

MAIN SELECTION
- *My Very Own Room*
- FCAT **Skill:** Plot Development

PAIRED SELECTION
- "Matter Matters!"
- FCAT **Text Feature:** Encyclopedia Article

SMALL GROUP OPTIONS
- Differentiated Instruction, pp. 145M–145V

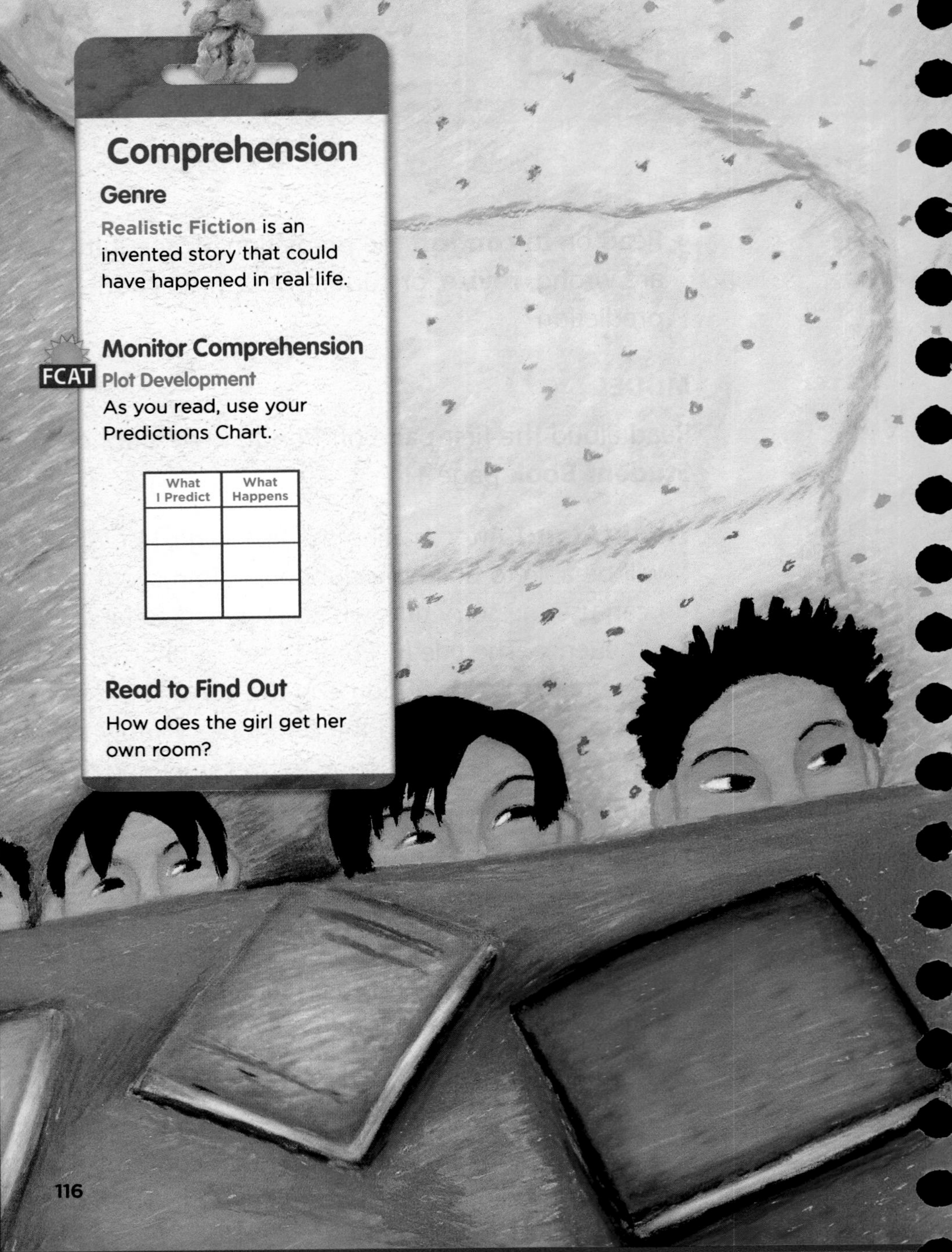

Comprehension
Genre
Realistic Fiction is an invented story that could have happened in real life.
Monitor Comprehension
FCAT
Plot Development
As you read, use your Predictions Chart.
What I Predict
What Happens
Read to Find Out
How does the girl get her own room?
116

Comprehension

LA.3.2.1 Identify and analyze elements of fiction

GENRE: REALISTIC FICTION

Have a student read the definition of Realistic Fiction on **Student Book** page 116. Students should look for characters that are like real people and events that could happen in real life.

STRATEGY
MONITOR COMPREHENSION

LA.3.1.7.8 Use strategies to repair comprehension

Good readers **monitor their comprehension**. They stop often to make sure they understand what they are reading. When something is unclear, they may reread or read ahead to find an answer to their questions.

SKILL
PLOT DEVELOPMENT: PREDICTIONS

LA.3.2.1.2 Explain plot

To understand how a plot develops, readers **make predictions**. To make a prediction, readers use text features, story clues and their own experiences to make inferences about what will happen in a story.

FCAT Vocabulary

Vocabulary Words Review the tested vocabulary words: **separate**, **determination**, **storage**, **crate**, **exact**, **ruined**, **luckiest**.

Story Words Students may find these words difficult. Pronounce the words and present the meanings as necessary.

curtain (p. 122) a hanging cloth panel sometimes used to divide a room

dainty (p. 133) small and beautiful

LA.3.1.6.1 Use new vocabulary taught directly

My Very Own Room

Award Winning Selection

by Amada Irma Pérez
illustrated by Maya Christina Gonzalez

117

Read Together	Read Independently
If your students need support to read the Main Selection, use the prompts to guide comprehension and model how to complete the graphic organizer.	If your students can read the Main Selection independently, have them read and complete the graphic organizer. Suggest that students set purposes and adjust their reading rate based on their purposes for reading.

If your students need an alternate selection, choose the **Leveled Readers** that match their instructional levels.

LA.3.1.5.2 Adjust reading rate based on purpose

Technology

Story available on **Listening Library Audio CD**

Preview and Predict

LA.3.1.7.1 Use text features to make predictions

Ask students to read the title, preview the illustrations, and note questions and predictions about what this story will be about. Who is the main character? What will she do? Have students record their predictions and any questions they have about the story.

Set Purposes

LA.3.1.7.1 Use text features to establish purpose for reading

FOCUS QUESTION Discuss the "Read to Find Out" question and talk about how to look for the answer while reading. Point out the Predictions Chart in the **Student Book** and on **Leveled Practice Book** page 142. Explain that students will fill it in as they read.

Read *My Very Own Room*

LA.3.1.7 Use strategies to comprehend text

Use the questions and Think Alouds for additional instruction to support the comprehension strategy and skill.

On Level Practice Book O, page 142

As you read *My Very Own Room*, fill in the Predictions Chart.

What I Predict	What Happens

How does the information you wrote in this Predictions Chart help you understand plot development in *My Very Own Room*?

Approaching Practice Book A, page 142

Beyond Practice Book B, page 142

Develop Comprehension

1 GENRE: REALISTIC FICTION

LA.3.2.1 Identify and analyze elements of fiction

How can you tell that this story is realistic fiction? (This is a made-up story that is being told by a nine-year-old girl. It seems to be set in the present in a house. So far, I know that the girl wants a room of her own. I can tell the story is realistic fiction because it is about characters who are like real people, and events that could really happen.)

2 STRATEGY
MONITOR AND CLARIFY: SELF-CORRECT

LA.3.1.7.8 Use strategies to repair comprehension

What can you do to make sure you understand why the girl wants a room of her own? What strategy can you use if you still don't understand what is happening? (After reading the first time, I think that the girl might not like to share, but that doesn't make sense. So I will ask myself questions about the text and then reread and try to answer them. I ask: What happens in this room? I find that the girl wakes up in a crowded room. How does the main character feel? She feels tired of sharing her room. Why does she feel this way? She thinks she is too old to share a room. Now I have more information. My first idea was wrong, so I will correct it. The girl wants a room because she is too old to share.)

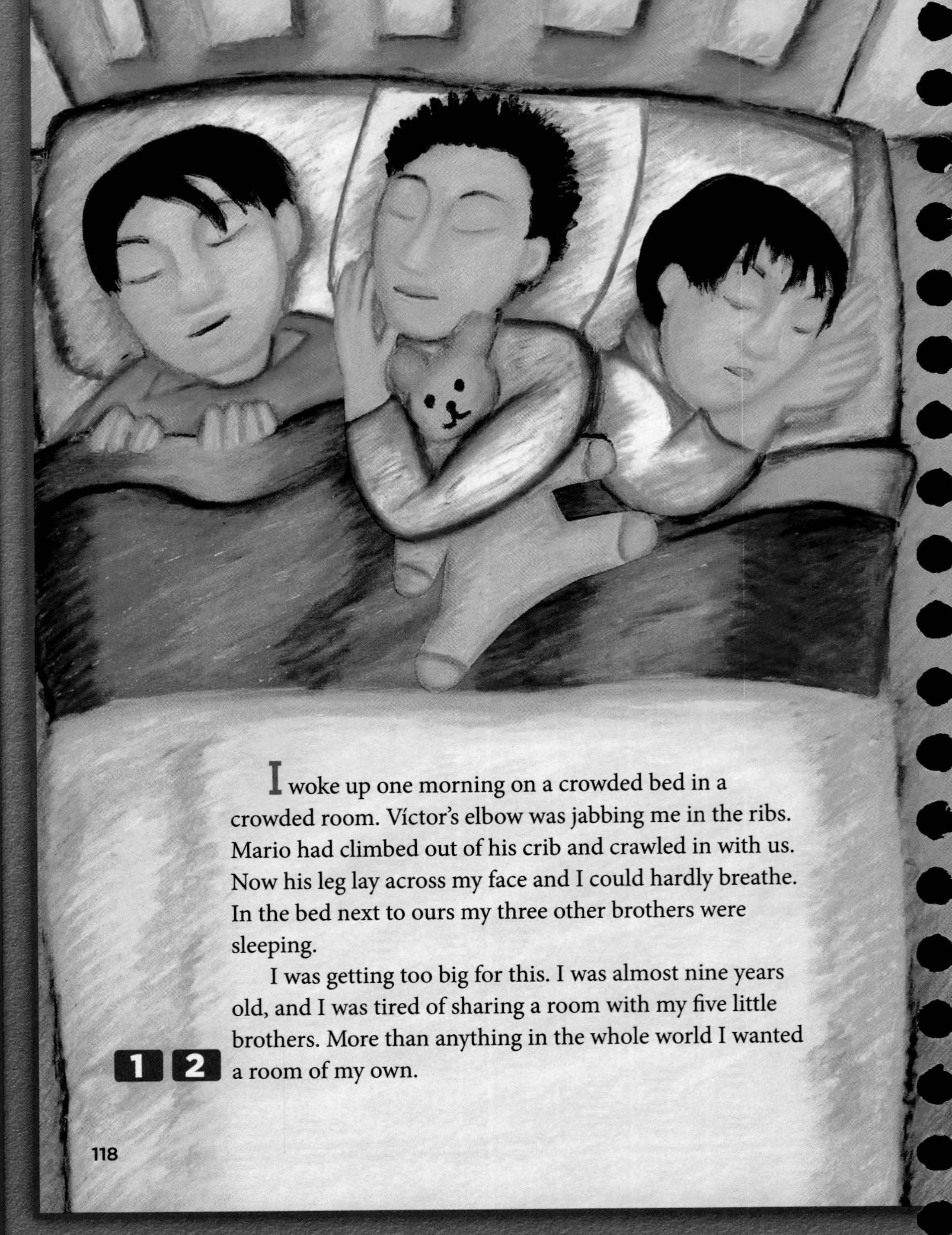

I woke up one morning on a crowded bed in a crowded room. Víctor's elbow was jabbing me in the ribs. Mario had climbed out of his crib and crawled in with us. Now his leg lay across my face and I could hardly breathe. In the bed next to ours my three other brothers were sleeping.
I was getting too big for this. I was almost nine years old, and I was tired of sharing a room with my five little brothers. More than anything in the whole world I wanted a room of my own.
1 2
118

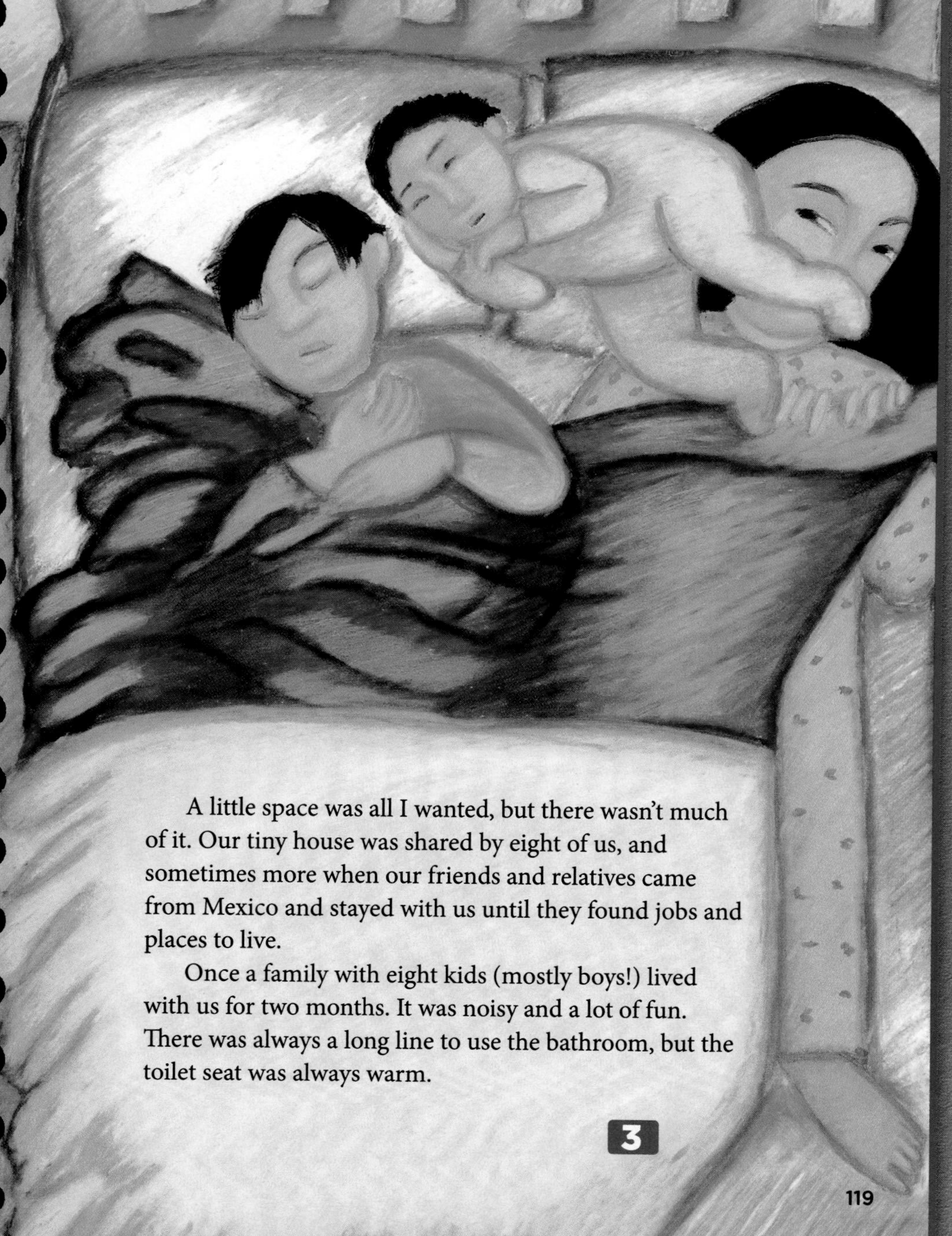

A little space was all I wanted, but there wasn't much of it. Our tiny house was shared by eight of us, and sometimes more when our friends and relatives came from Mexico and stayed with us until they found jobs and places to live.

Once a family with eight kids (mostly boys!) lived with us for two months. It was noisy and a lot of fun. There was always a long line to use the bathroom, but the toilet seat was always warm.

3

119

ENGLISH LANGUAGE LEARNERS

Access for All

STRATEGIES FOR EXTRA SUPPORT

Question 3 PLOT DEVELOPMENT

Write: *She'll probably get her own room because _____. She may get her own room because _____.* Point out the differences in certainty between the words *probably* and *may*. Have students use the sentences to explain their answers. Ask students whether or not the title of the story helps them make their predictions. Ask: *Do you agree with the author that having your own room when you get older is important? Why or why not? Do you think her parents will agree that it is important too?* Restate students' ideas in full sentences.

Develop Comprehension

3 PLOT DEVELOPMENT

FCAT

LA.3.2.1.2 Identify and explain plot

Do you think the girl will get her own room? Why or why not? (The girl will probably get her own room because she says that is what she wants more than anything in the whole world. I know that when I want something, I usually work very hard to get it, and I am usually successful. Also, the title of the story, *My Very Own Room*, gives a clue that she will get her own room.) Put your prediction under What I Predict on your Predictions Chart.

What I Predict	What Happens
The girl will get her own room.	

Develop Comprehension

4 STRATEGY MONITOR COMPREHENSION

LA.3.1.7.8 Reread to repair comprehension

Teacher Think Aloud I don't understand why the girl is sitting in the tree, so I'll stop to try to figure out why she's there. First, I'll reread page 119. The very first sentence begins with, "A little space was all I wanted." This page also tells me that her house is very crowded. I can picture the crowded house and I know how I would feel. I would want to get away and sit in a tree, too. Now I understand why she is in the tree. She just wants some time to be by herself. Rereading and visualizing helped me understand this part of the story.

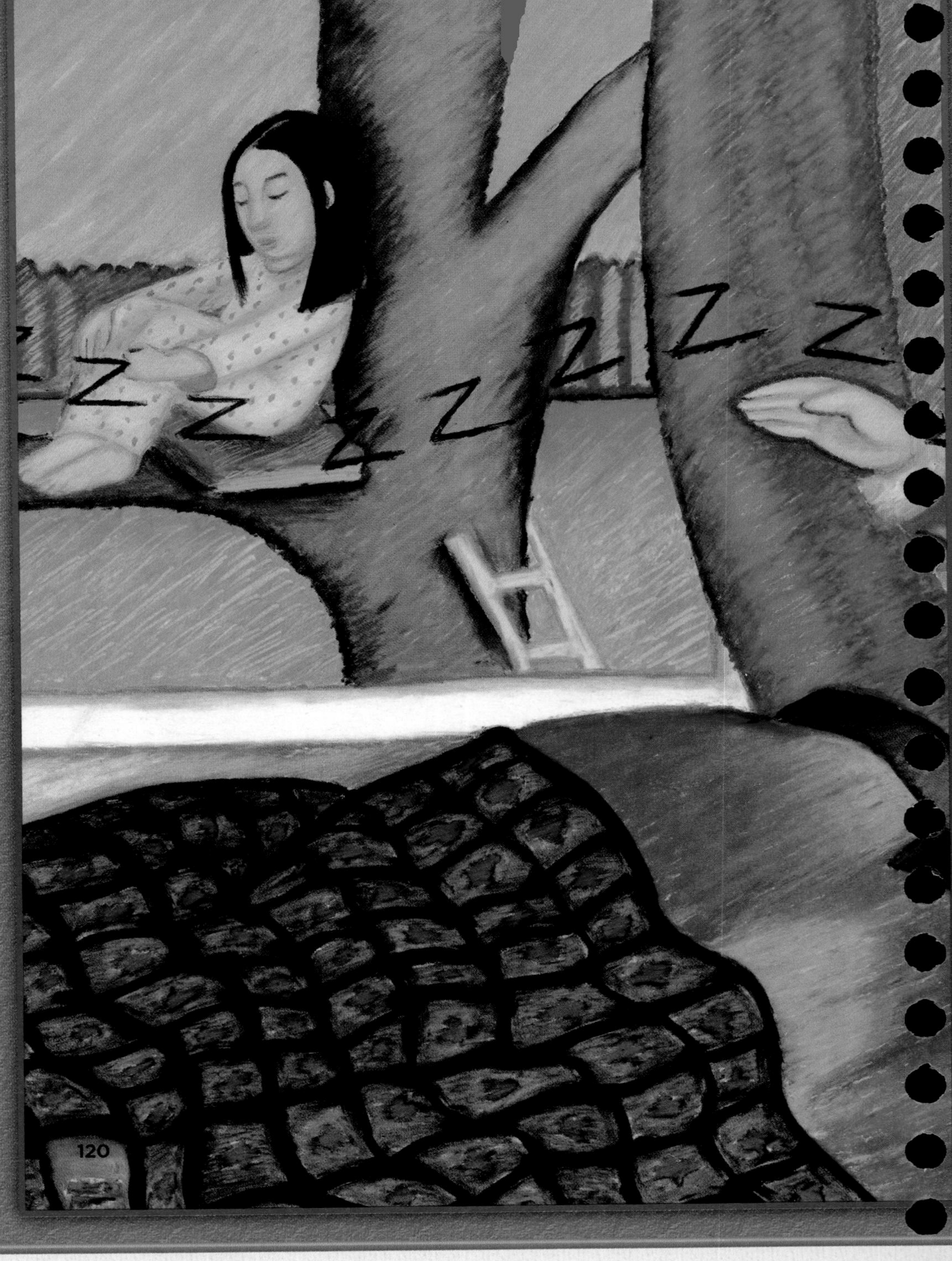

Sometimes very early in the morning while everyone was still sleeping, I would climb up the crooked ladder that leaned against the elm tree in our backyard. I would sit on a little board, pretending it was a bench, and just think. I could hear my father snoring. He worked all night at the factory and went to bed just before dawn. **4**

I loved my brothers. It wasn't that I didn't want to be near them. I just needed a place of my own. **5**

121

Develop Comprehension

5 AUTHOR'S PURPOSE

FCAT

LA.3.1.7.2 Identify the author's purpose

Think about what you have read so far. What do you think the author's purpose was for writing this story? Why do you think this? (I think the author's purpose is to entertain. I think this because *My Very Own Room* is an interesting story about made-up characters.)

Develop Comprehension

6 MONITOR AND CLARIFY: SELF CORRECT

LA.3.1.4.1 Use knowledge of pronunciation to decode words

LA.3.1.4.4 Use self-correction

Look at the last word in the first paragraph. Use what you know about letters and the sounds they stand for. How do you think this word is pronounced? If the word doesn't sound right or make sense in the sentence, what can you do to figure out how to say it? (I see the letters *close* in the word. I think they are pronounced /klōz/. But this word ends in a *t*, and /klōzt/ doesn't make sense. I will try to say the word again. This time I will divide it into two syllables. In the first syllable, I'll use the short vowel sound /o/ in *hot* for the *o*, and I'll pronounce *et* together in a second syllable: /kloz/ /it/. That makes sense, and it is a word I know.)

Vocabulary

Read the sentence that contains the word **separate**. How is it pronounced? What is another way to pronounce it? Think of a sentence for each pronunciation. (We put up doors to separate the kitchen from the living room. Then we had two separate rooms.)

LA.3.1.6.8 Use knowledge of homographs to determine meaning

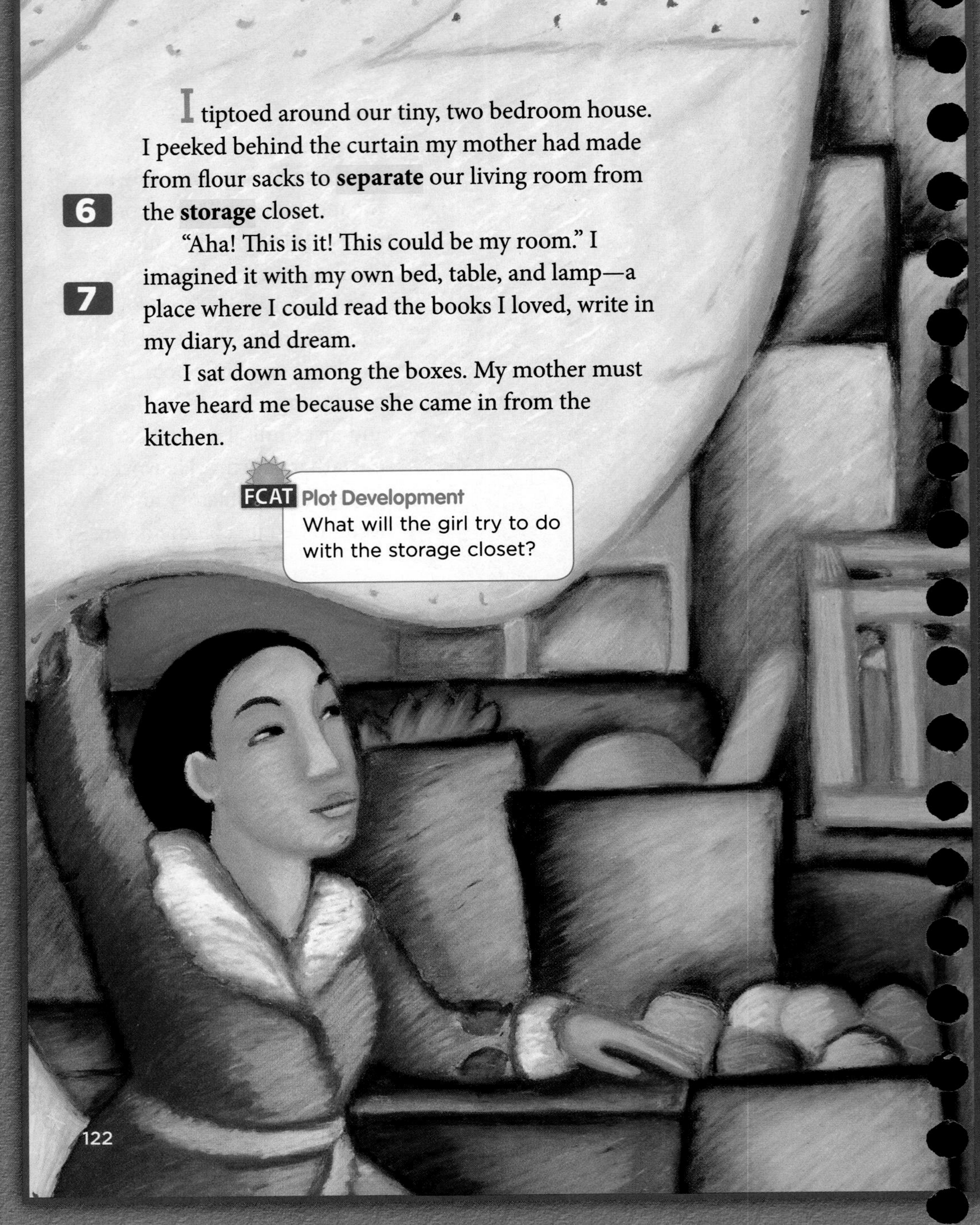

6 I tiptoed around our tiny, two bedroom house. I peeked behind the curtain my mother had made from flour sacks to **separate** our living room from the **storage** closet.
7 "Aha! This is it! This could be my room." I imagined it with my own bed, table, and lamp—a place where I could read the books I loved, write in my diary, and dream.
I sat down among the boxes. My mother must have heard me because she came in from the kitchen.
FCAT Plot Development
What will the girl try to do with the storage closet?
122

"Mamá, it's perfect," I said, and I told her my idea.

"Ay, *mijita*, you do not understand. We are storing my sister's sewing machine and your uncle's garden tools. Someday they will need their things to make a better living in this new country. And there's the furniture and old clothes," she said. Slowly she shook her head.

123

Develop Comprehension

7 PLOT DEVELOPMENT

FCAT LA.3.2.1.2 Identify and explain plot

What will the girl try to do with the storage closet? Why do you think this? (She will ask to make the storage closet into a bedroom. She thinks the storage closet would make a good room. It is also the only place in the house where she could make a room. From my own experience, I know that I would ask to use the closet as a room, too.) Let's add another prediction to our Predictions Chart.

What I Predict	What Happens
The girl will get her own room.	
The girl will try to make the storage closet into a bedroom.	

FCAT Comprehension

Plot Development

Explain/ Discuss Tell students that to better understand a story, they can make predictions. To do this, readers use story clues and what they know to figure out what will happen in a story. If they find the prediction is not correct, they can revise it. Ask students: *Do you think the girl will get a room? Why?* (Yes, because she really wants one and because the story is called *My Very Own Room*.) Ask students to read page 123. Ask: *Does it look like your prediction is correct? Why?* (No. The mother is explaining why the items in the storage room need to stay there.)

Apply Have students read on to find out what the mother will do. Then have students tell if their original predictions were correct. If not, have them revise them.

LA.3.1.7.1 Use text features to make and confirm predictions

Develop Comprehension

8 STRATEGY
MONITOR COMPREHENSION

Teacher Think Aloud When I don't understand something in a story, I stop reading and try to figure out what is happening. In this part of the story, it isn't clear why Mamá has changed her mind about letting the girl have her own room. How can you find out why the mother does this?

(Encourage students to apply the strategy in a Think Aloud.)

LA.3.1.7.8 Reread to repair comprehension

Student Think Aloud I need to reread this part of the story to find out why Mamá changed her mind. Mamá sees the determination on her daughter's face and the tears in her eyes. The daughter's face shows how important having her own room is to her. The look on her daughter's face makes Mamá change her mind and decide to move the things out of the storage closet so that it can be a bedroom.

Vocabulary

Read the sentence that contains the word **determination**. Describe how people with *determination* act. (People who have determination try very hard to reach their goals.)

LA.3.1.6.3 Use context clues

Then she saw the **determination** on my face and the tears forming in my eyes. "Wait," she said,
8 seriously thinking. "Maybe we could put these things on the back porch and cover them with old blankets."

"And we could put a tarp on top so nothing would get **ruined**," I added.

"Yes, I think we can do it. Let's take everything
9 out and see how much space there is."

I gave her a great big hug and she kissed me.

124

Develop Comprehension

9 WRITER'S CRAFT: DIALOGUE

LA.3.2.1.2 Identify character/character development

LA.3.2.1.5 Examine how language describes feelings

How does dialogue on pages 122–124 help you figure out what kind of person the girl's mother is? What does it show about the mother's feelings for her daughter? (The dialogue shows how thoughtful and caring the mother is. It shows how she begins to change her mind as she talks about changing the closet into a bedroom. It shows how much she loves her daughter.)

Develop Comprehension

10 CHRONOLOGICAL ORDER

LA.3.1.7.3 Determine chronological order of events

When did the family start moving the furniture to the back porch? How can you tell? (The signal word *after* shows that the family gets to work after they have finished breakfast.)

11 FIGURATIVE LANGUAGE: ALLITERATION

LA.3.2.1.5 Identify author's use of figurative language

Which two words in the second sentence of the second paragraph begin with the same sounds? How does this special sound language help you understand what is happening in this part of the story? (The two words are *bulging* and *bags*. These words help me picture how much stuff the family has to move to clean out the room.)

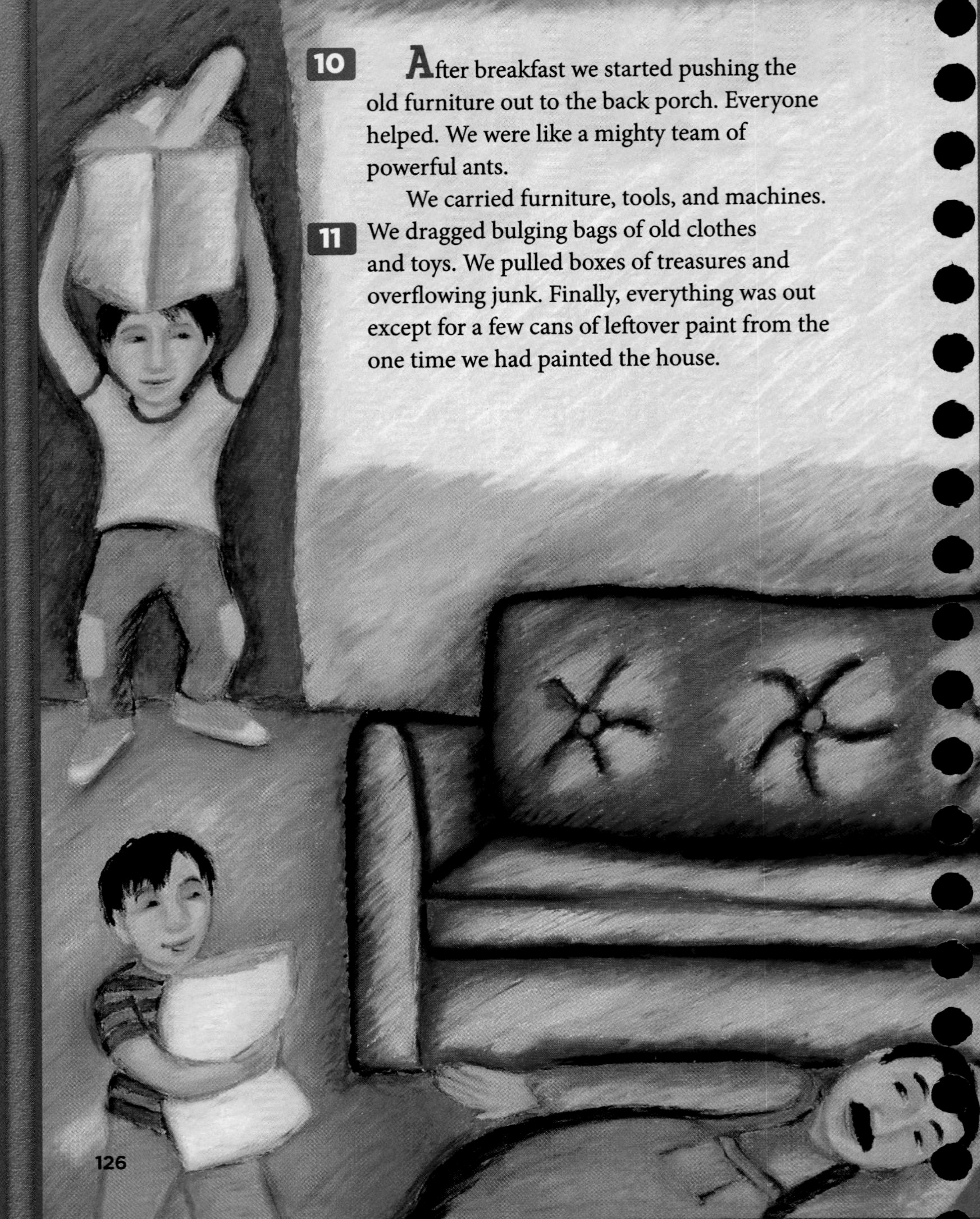

10 After breakfast we started pushing the old furniture out to the back porch. Everyone helped. We were like a mighty team of powerful ants.

We carried furniture, tools, and machines.
11 We dragged bulging bags of old clothes and toys. We pulled boxes of treasures and overflowing junk. Finally, everything was out except for a few cans of leftover paint from the one time we had painted the house.

126

Fluency

Attention to Punctuation

Explain Punctuation in a text helps you know when to pause. You should pause for a short time after a comma and a slightly longer time after a period.

Model Point out that in this passage, available on **Transparency 20**, the pause after a comma is marked with one slash. The pause after a period is marked with two slashes. Read the passage, pausing appropriately to show punctuation.

Apply Have students raise their hands when they hear you pause, and lower them when you continue reading. Ask students to identify the punctuation marks after you finish reading a sentence.

LA.3.1.5 Demonstrate the ability to read text orally with accuracy

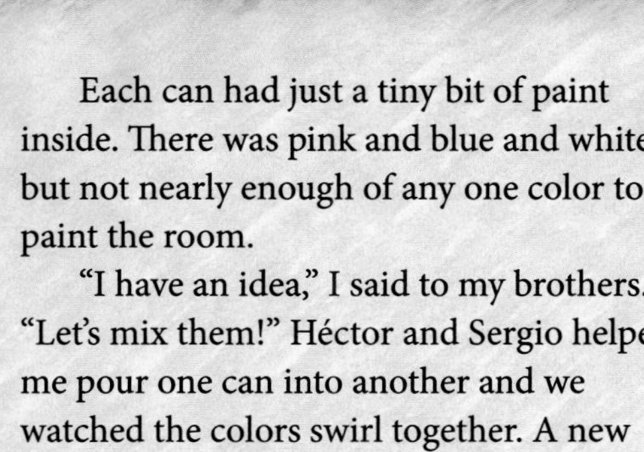

Each can had just a tiny bit of paint inside. There was pink and blue and white, but not nearly enough of any one color to paint the room.

"I have an idea," I said to my brothers. "Let's mix them!" Héctor and Sergio helped me pour one can into another and we watched the colors swirl together. A new color began to appear, a little like purple and much stronger than pink. Magenta!

We painted and painted until we ran out of paint. 12

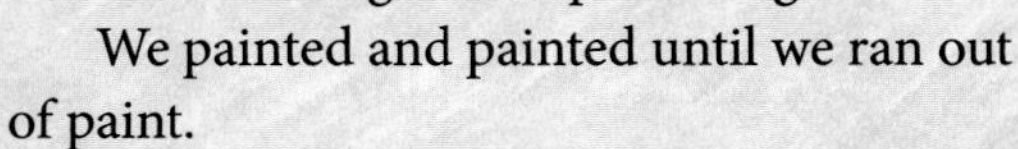

127

Develop Comprehension

12 PLOT DEVELOPMENT

FCAT
LA.3.2.1.2 Explain plot

So far, which of your predictions were correct? Fill in the right column of the Predictions Chart for each of them. (I correctly predicted that the girl would get her own room, but I did not think she would be able to use the storage room.)

What I Predict	What Happens
The girl will get her own room.	The girl does get her own room.
The girl will try to make the storage closet into a bedroom.	Mamá agrees to let her daughter use the storage closet for a bedroom. The family cleans out the room and paints it.

Journal

Have students respond to the story by confirming or revising their predictions. Encourage them to write any new questions they may have about the story.

Quick Check

Can students understand plot development by making predictions about events in the story? If not, see the Extra Support on this page.

Extra Support

FCAT

Plot Development Review how to make predictions. Remind students that if their predictions are not correct, they can revise them. If students have difficulty making and confirming predictions, have them reread pages 124–127. Tell students: *A prediction is what you think will happen next. What did you think would happen after the mother decides the girl can use the storage room?* (I thought the girl would clean up the room and move into it.) *What clue appears on page 124?* (The girl's mother talks about moving things from the storage room to the back porch.) *From your own experience, what might this clue mean?* (I know that sometimes adults need to take time to think things over. I think the girl will get the room but not right away.) *If this is what you expected to happen, your prediction was correct. If you predicted that something else would happen, think about why you made that prediction.* Point out that students need to revise their original predictions if they were wrong.

LA.3.2.1.2 Identify and explain plot

Stop here if you wish to read this selection over two days.

Develop Comprehension

13 SUMMARIZE

LA.3.1.7.8 Summarize to repair comprehension

What has happened in the story so far? (A nine-year-old girl wants a room of her own. She looks around the house for a space that can become her room. She asks her mother if she can move into a storage closet. At first her mother does not like the idea, but then she changes her mind. The family moves the old furniture out of the storage closet. Then they use leftover paint to paint the girl's new room.)

14 STRATEGY MONITOR AND CLARIFY: SEEK HELP

LA.3.1.7.8 Clarify by checking other resources

How can you figure out the meaning of the Spanish word *Tío* on page 128? (I can ask someone, like my teacher or a librarian, if they know what this word means, or I can ask someone who speaks Spanish. I can also try to find it in a Spanish and English dictionary.)

13

Mamá showed me how to measure my new magenta wall with a piece of bright yellow yarn left over from the last baby blanket she had crocheted. Tío Pancho was going back to Mexico and said I could have his bed, but we had to let him know if it would fit.

14 We cut off the piece of yarn that showed us just how big the bed could be. We all ran to Tío Pancho's waving the piece of yarn. We measured his bed. Perfect! That yellow piece of yarn was magical.

128

Cultural Perspectives

EXPRESSING IDEAS ABOUT DIFFERENT CULTURES

When authors and illustrators create books about other cultures, they use their own experiences and ideas to create details that help the reader experience those cultures. Authors may include words from a culture's language or describe dress or customs. Illustrators may choose an artistic style that mirrors art in that culture.

Have students find examples of ways authors and illustrators express ideas about culture and cultural traditions in *My Very Own Room* or other stories they have read about other groups or cultures. Have students choose one author or illustrator and write persuasive paragraphs about why the cultural depictions by that author or illustrator are successful or not successful. Then have students form a literature circle and discuss their findings.

LA.3.1.7.3 Determine explicit ideas and information in grade level text; **LA.3.4.3.1** Write persuasive text; **LA.3.5.2** Apply listening and speaking strategies

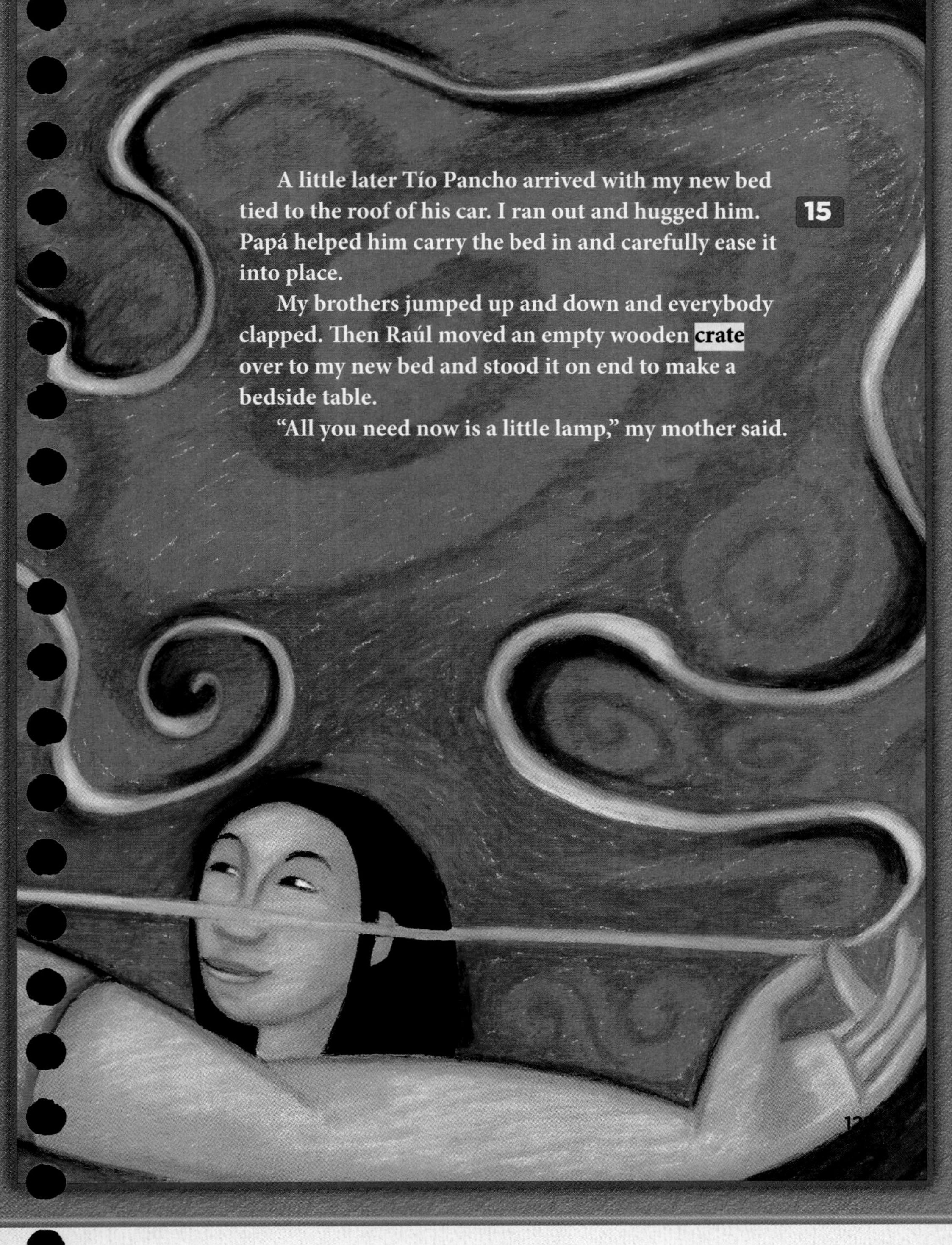

A little later Tío Pancho arrived with my new bed tied to the roof of his car. I ran out and hugged him. 15
Papá helped him carry the bed in and carefully ease it into place.
My brothers jumped up and down and everybody clapped. Then Raúl moved an empty wooden crate over to my new bed and stood it on end to make a bedside table.
"All you need now is a little lamp," my mother said.

Develop Comprehension

15 MAKE INFERENCES

LA.3.1.7.3 Determine implied inference

How does Tío Pancho feel about the narrator? How can you tell? (I think that he really cares for the girl. He agrees to give her his bed to use, if it fits in the space, and then he delivers the bed to her house. I know that when someone puts a lot of effort into helping me with something I need or want, that person really likes me.)

Develop Comprehension

16 COMPARE EVENTS

FCAT
LA.3.1.7.3 Determine implied inference

How is using Blue Chip stamps like spending money? How is using them different? (Using stamps is like spending money because people can use them to get things. They are different because the stamps can only be used in special stores and money can be spent anywhere.)

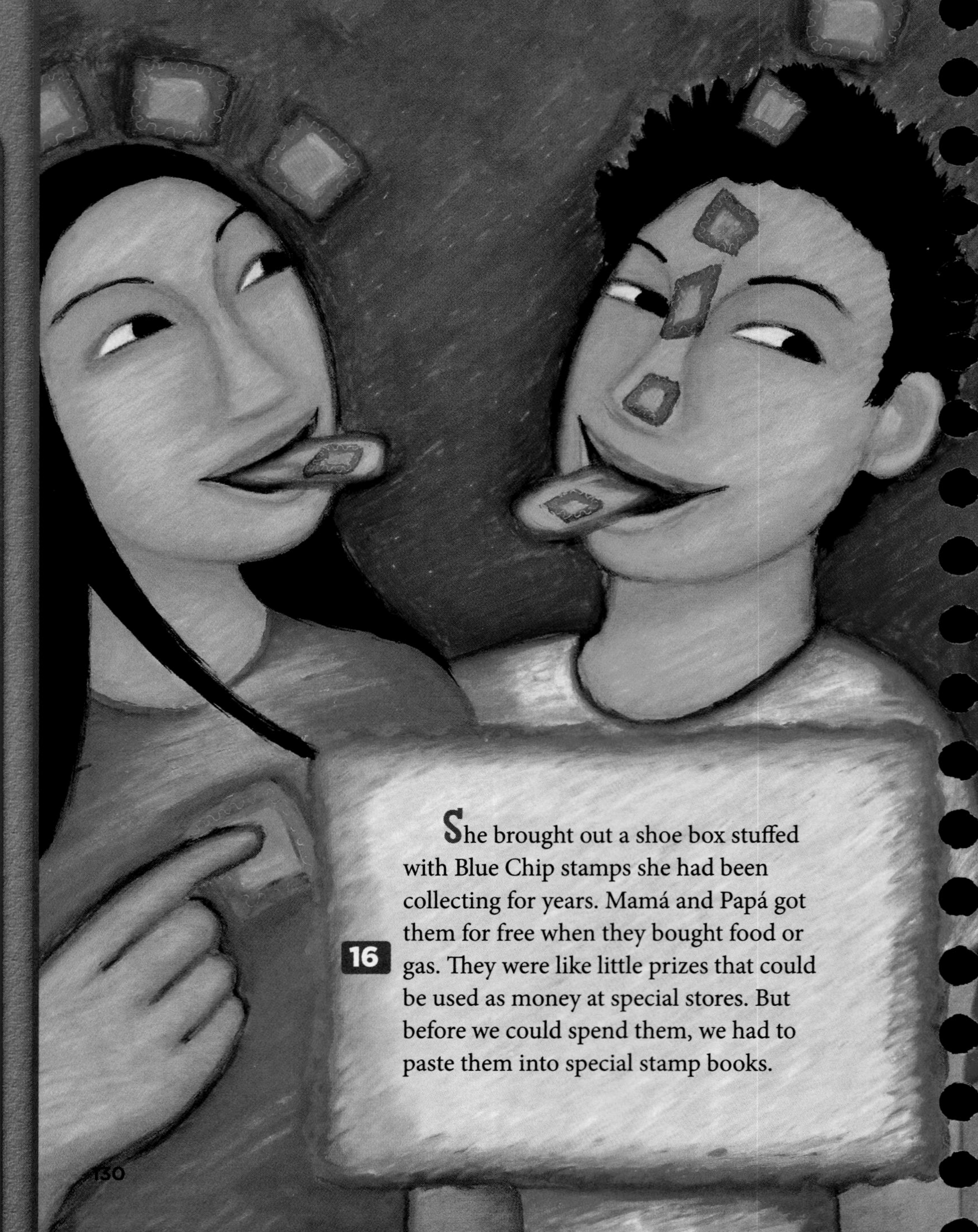

She brought out a shoe box stuffed with Blue Chip stamps she had been collecting for years. Mamá and Papá got them for free when they bought food or
16 gas. They were like little prizes that could be used as money at special stores. But before we could spend them, we had to paste them into special stamp books.

130

Art

Cross-Curricular Connection

ART APPRECIATION

Tell students that the illustrations, or artwork, in *My Very Own Room* picture a Mexican-American family. Then show students pictures of famous works of art from different cultures and times that show families or children. Compare the families or children pictured in the art and discuss how they appear to be different but still share common experiences and attitudes. Ask students what they like about the art and how it helps them understand the cultures and times that are pictured.

Have students create works of art from their own points of view that show families celebrating or working together. Then have them create a class art gallery in which they display their drawings and paintings. Have students analyze their own work as well as their classmates' work, describe what they see, how the art makes them feel, and what they like about it.

SS.A.2.2.3.3.1 Aspects of family life in many eras; **LA.3.5.2** Apply listening and speaking strategies; **LA.3.1.7.1** Identify a text's features

We licked and licked and pasted and pasted. When we were done, Papá drove us to the stamp store.

FCAT **Plot Development** What will the girl do with the Blue Chip stamps? 17

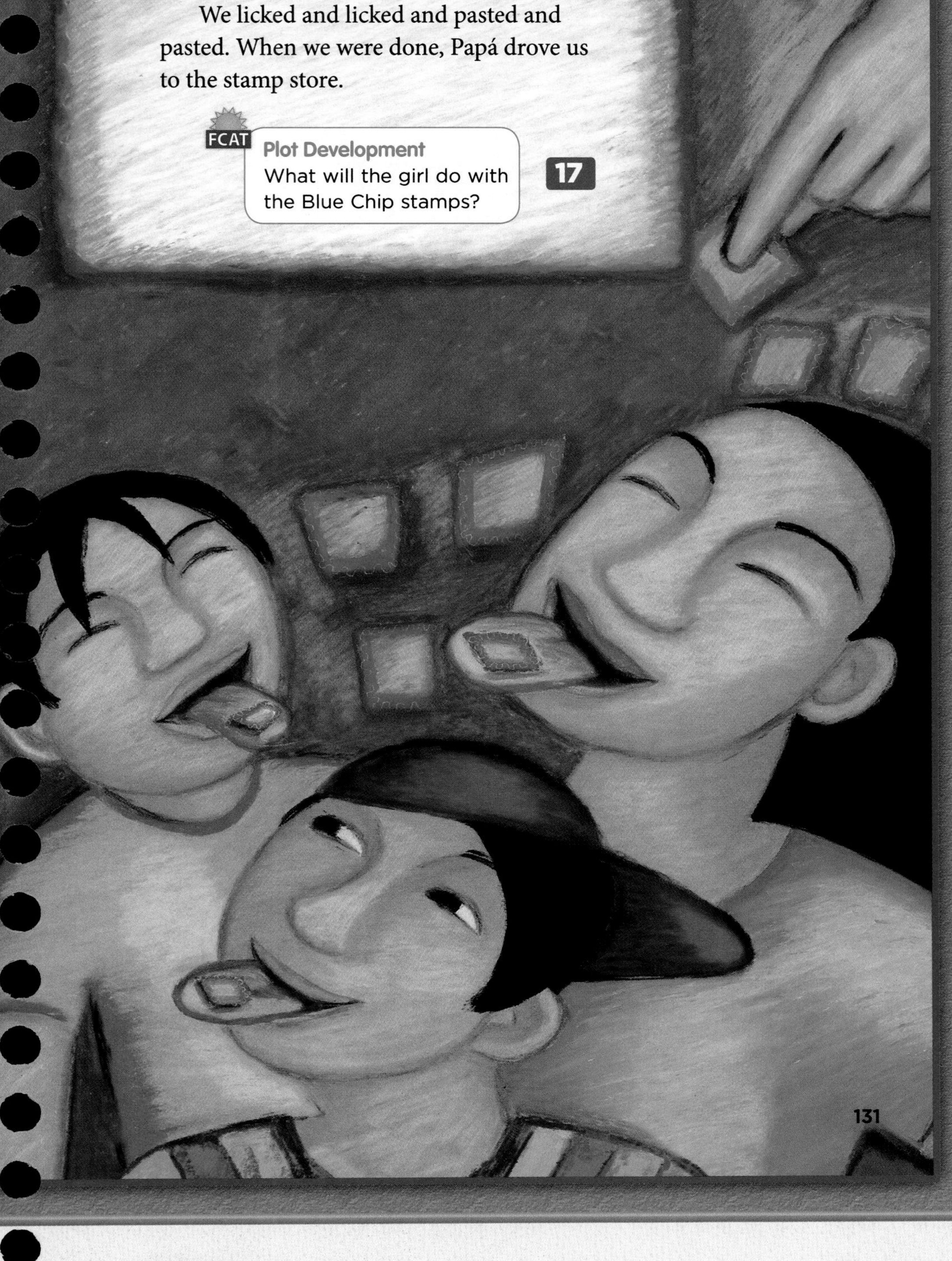

131

Develop Comprehension

17 PLOT DEVELOPMENT

FCAT LA.3.2.1.2 Identify plot

What will the girl do with the Blue Chip stamps? Add this prediction to your Predictions Chart. (The girl's room is very important to her. It makes sense that she would use the stamps to buy something for the room. She knows that the room needs a lamp, so she will probably use the Blue Chip stamps to buy one.)

What I Predict	What Happens
The girl will get her own room.	The girl does get her own room.
The girl will try to make the storage closet into a bedroom.	Mamá lets her daughter use the storage closet for a bedroom. The family cleans out the room and paints it.
The girl will buy a lamp with the stamps.	

ELL Access for All

STRATEGIES FOR EXTRA SUPPORT

Question 17 PLOT DEVELOPMENT
Have students reread page 129. Ask: *What is the girl missing in her room? What does her mother say she needs?* Have students read page 130. Ask: *What are the stamps for?*

Develop Comprehension

18 PLOT DEVELOPMENT

LA.3.1.7.1 Use text features to confirm predictions

Look at the illustration. Read page 133. Was your prediction about the lamp correct? Add this information to the What Happens column of your Predictions Chart. (Yes. The girl used the stamps to purchase a lamp for her new room.)

What I Predict	What Happens
The girl will get her own room.	The girl does get her own room.
The girl will try to make the storage closet into a bedroom.	Mamá lets her daughter use the storage closet for a bedroom. The family cleans out the room and paints it.
The girl will buy a lamp with the stamps.	The girl buys a pretty lamp for her room.

Art

Cross-Curricular Connection

ROOM DESIGN

Have students think about how they would decorate an empty room. Ask: *How would you decorate the room? What color would you paint the walls? What would you hang on them? What kind of furniture would go in it?*

Give students empty shoe boxes, paper, crayons, colored pencils, old magazines, scissors, and glue. Have them decorate, using the four sides and the bottom of the shoe box as the walls and floor of the room. Have them create furniture too.

When the rooms are complete, have students present them to the class, explain what they did, and tell why.

LA.3.5.2 Apply listening and speaking strategies; **LA.3.5.2.2** Give an oral presentation

I saw the lamp I wanted right away. It was as dainty as a beautiful ballerina, made of white ceramic glass with a shade that had ruffles around the top and bottom. 18

I shut my eyes. I was so excited yet so afraid we wouldn't have enough stamps to get it. Then I heard my mother's voice. "Yes, *mijita*. We have enough."

When we got home, I carefully set the new lamp on my bedside table. Then I lay on my new bed and stared at the ceiling, thinking. Something was still missing, the most important thing …

19

133

Develop Comprehension

19 PLOT DEVELOPMENT

FCAT

LA.3.1.7.3 Determine implied inference

LA.3.2.1.2 Explain plot

Something is still missing from the girl's room. What do you think it is? What do you think she will do? Why do you think this? (I think that the girl is missing a desk for writing, because at the beginning of the story she said she liked to write in her diary. I think she will find a way to get the thing that is missing. So far, she has found everything else that she needs for the room. I know that when I want something, I usually figure out a way to get it.)

ELL Access for All

Plot Development Have students make predictions about what will happen in the story using these sentence frames: ____ *will happen because* ____ *I think she will* ____ *because* ____. Help students use complete sentences in their predictions.

Develop Comprehension

20 PLOT DEVELOPMENT

LA.3.2.1.2 Identify and explain plot

What did the girl do about the one thing that was missing? Was your prediction correct? (Books were missing, so the girl went to the library and checked out six of them. My prediction about what the girl would do was correct because I knew that the girl would find a way to get what was missing, but I was wrong about what she would get. My prediction about the desk was wrong. She was missing books, not a desk. So now I know what is important to her.)

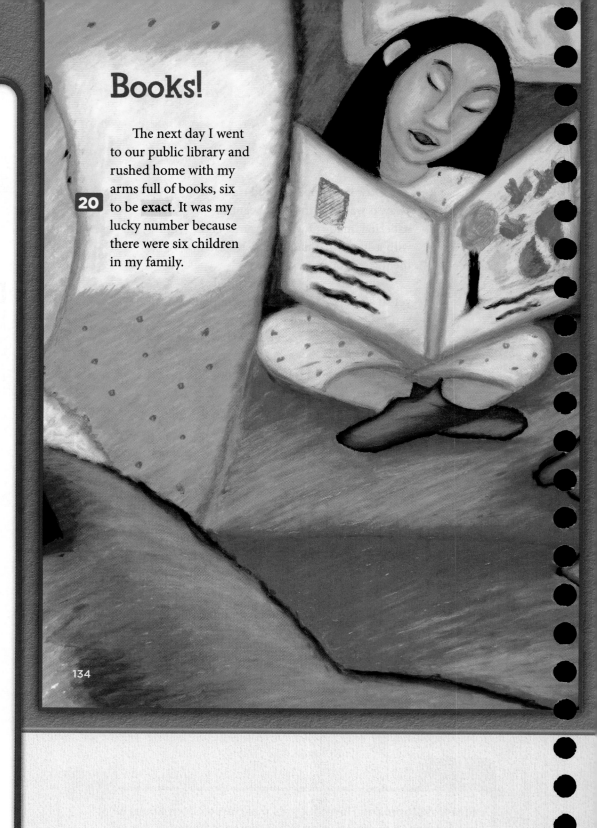

Books!

20 The next day I went to our public library and rushed home with my arms full of books, six to be **exact**. It was my lucky number because there were six children in my family.

134

That evening, I turned on my new lamp and read and read. My two littlest brothers, Mario and Víctor, stood in the doorway holding back the flour-sack curtain. I invited them in. They cuddled up on my new bed and I read them a story. Then we said goodnight and they went back to their room. **21**

Develop Comprehension

21 STRATEGY
MONITOR COMPREHENSION

LA.3.1.7 Use strategies to comprehend text

At the beginning of the story, the girl doesn't want to be around her brothers. How does she feel about them now? Explain what strategy you can use to figure out the way she feels.

LA.3.1.7.8 Reread to repair comprehension

Student Think Aloud I will reread pages 134 and 135 to see what I can learn. I see that her little brothers wait at the doorway until they are invited in. They stay to listen to the girl read them a story. Then they say good-bye and leave. The girl seems to enjoy being with them more now that she has her own room. Her feelings toward her brothers are getting better. This makes sense, because I like my family more when I don't see them all the time. I think the girl really loves her brothers. Rereading these pages helped me figure out how she feels.

Develop Comprehension

22 TEXT FEATURES: ILLUSTRATIONS

LA.3.1.7.1 Identify a text's features

How does the illustration on pages 136 and 137 help you better understand the story? (The girl looks happy, like she did when her mother agreed to let her make a bedroom out of the storage room. She is in her bed, which she does not have to share with anyone. She has books around her. The newly painted walls, the wooden crate, and the new lamp are all in the illustration. The story tells how she got each of these things. The illustration helps me understand how happy the girl is to be alone in her very own room.)

23 STRATEGY
WORD PARTS

LA.3.1.6.7 Use meaning of base words, affixes to determine meanings

What does the word *luckiest* mean? Use what you know about base words and the meaning of the suffix *-est* to help you figure it out. (The word *luckiest* means "most lucky." It has the base word *lucky* and the suffix *-est*.)

22

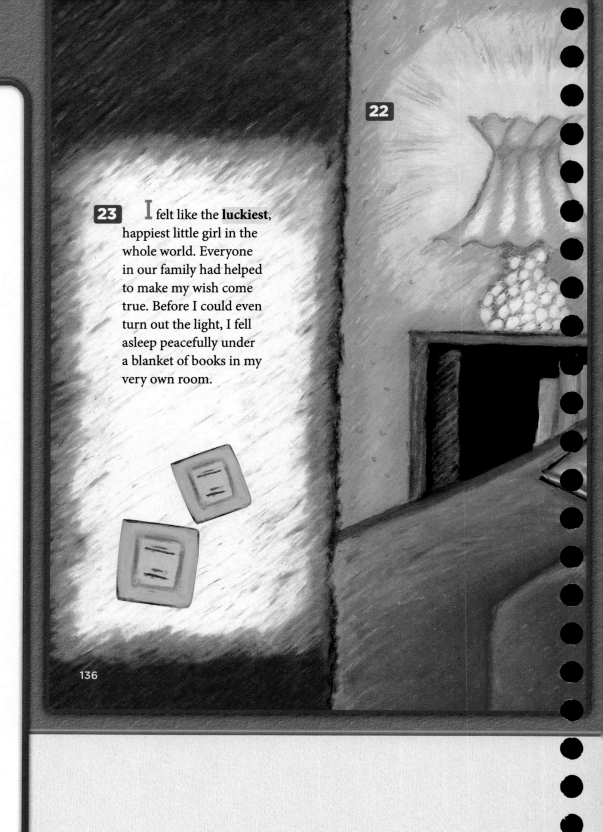

23 I felt like the **luckiest**, happiest little girl in the whole world. Everyone in our family had helped to make my wish come true. Before I could even turn out the light, I fell asleep peacefully under a blanket of books in my very own room.

136

Develop Comprehension

LA.3.1.7.1
Use text features to confirm predictions

RETURN TO PREDICTIONS AND PURPOSES

Review students' predictions and purposes. Were they correct? Did students find clues that helped them predict whether or not the main character would get a room of her own?

LA.3.1.7
Use strategies to comprehend text

REVIEW READING STRATEGIES

Ask students: How did making predictions about whether or not the girl would get her own room help you keep track of events in the story? What strategies did you use when you came to difficult words?

PERSONAL RESPONSE

LA.3.4.2.3
Write informational essays that include a topic sentence and supporting details

Ask each student to write a short informational essay about why it is important to have "a room of your own." Remind students to begin with a topic sentence and to add supporting details. After students have finished writing, have them read their essays to partners, or to the class.

Quick Check **Can students understand plot development by making predictions?**

During **Small Group Instruction**

If No → **Approaching Level** Leveled Reader Lesson, p. 145P

If Yes → **On Level** Options, pp. 145Q–145R

Beyond Level Options, pp. 145S–145T

Author and Illustrator

AMADA AND MAYA'S ROOM

Have students read the biographies of the author and illustrator.

DISCUSS

LA.3.1.7.2 Identify how author's perspective influences text

- How was Amada Irma Pérez's childhood like that of the girl in the story?
- Why do you think Maya Christina Gonzalez became an illustrator?

WRITE ABOUT IT

LA.3.5.1 Write to communicate ideas and experiences

Discuss the main character's favorite new place. Have each student write about his or her favorite place and tell why it is special. Remind students to make good word choices and use vivid language.

FCAT Author's Purpose

Discuss how the author does not give facts and details about a nonfiction topic and does not explain how to do something. Help students conclude that the author's purpose was to write an entertaining story about a girl who wanted a special place of her own.

LA.3.1.7.2 Identify the author's purpose

LOG ON Technology

Tell students they can find more information about Amada Irma Pérez and Maya Christina Gonzalez at **www.macmillanmh.com**

LA.3.6.4 Develop essential technology skills

Amada and Maya's Room

Author Amada Irma Pérez grew up in a family just like the one in this story. Because her parents were unable to get the family a bigger house, there was not much room for Amada and her five brothers. But they did give Amada and her brothers lots of love and encouraged them to study and work hard.

Another book **by Amada Irma Pérez:** ***My Diary from Here to There/Mi diario de aquí hasta allá***

Illustrator Maya Christina Gonzalez has always loved to draw and paint. She has also always been very proud of being Mexican. In fact, as a child, Maya would draw her face on the blank page in the back of books because she wanted someone in the books to look like her.

LOG ON Find out more about Amada Irma Pérez and Maya Christina Gonzalez at **www.macmillanmh.com**

FCAT Author's Purpose

What was the author's purpose for writing *My Very Own Room*? Did Amada Irma Pérez want to entertain or inform? Use details from the story in your answer.

138

Author's Craft

Figurative Language: Simile

Amada Irma Pérez uses similes to make her writing more interesting.

- Similes use *like* or *as* to compare two things. For example: *We were like a mighty team of powerful ants.* (p. 126) The family is like a team of ants because they work together. This simile helps readers understand that the family is large and hardworking, like the ants in an ant colony.

Have students find another simile on page 133. (The new lamp is "as dainty as a beautiful ballerina.") Then have students write similes of their own.

LA.3.2.1.5 Identify author's use of similes

FCAT Comprehension Check

Summarize

Summarize *My Very Own Room*. Use your Predictions Chart to help you tell about events in the story that you predicted and what actually happens.

What I Predict	What Happens

Think and Compare

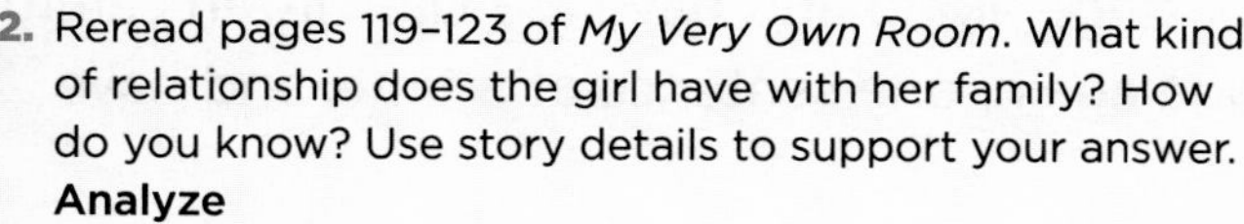

1. What story details help you predict whether the girl will get a room of her own? Use your Predictions Chart to help you answer. **Monitor Comprehension: Plot Development**
2. Reread pages 119–123 of *My Very Own Room*. What kind of relationship does the girl have with her family? How do you know? Use story details to support your answer. **Analyze**
3. What are some reasons why you might want a quiet space of your own? **Evaluate**
4. Why is it good for a whole family to help one family member with a problem? **Apply**
5. Reread "Pond Street Clubhouse" on pages 114–115. Think about how the main character is like the girl in *My Very Own Room*. Why is **determination** an important character trait in both characters? **Reading/Writing Across Texts**

139

Strategies for Answering Questions

Think and Search

Model the Think and Search strategy with question 5. The answer can be found in the story but will require students to look in more than one place.

Question 5 Think Aloud I need to look in both stories to find the answer. I know that both of the main characters are determined to make their own special place, but each wants the special place for different reasons. On page 118, I see that the main character of *My Very Own Room* wants more space because she is tired of sharing a room with her brothers. In the last paragraph of page 115, I see that the boy in "Pond Street Clubhouse" wants a place where he can play. I had to look in several places to find this information, but it was there in the stories.

LA.3.1.7 Use strategies to comprehend text

Comprehension Check

SUMMARIZE

FCAT **LA.3.1.7.8** Summarize to repair comprehension

Have partners summarize *My Very Own Room* by paraphrasing the main events. Remind students that their Predictions Charts can help them organize their summaries.

THINK AND COMPARE

Sample answers are given.

FCAT **LA.3.2.1.2** Identify and explain plot

1. **Plot Development:** First, she finds the closet that she can turn into a room. She shows her mother how much she wants a room of her own. She works hard to move the furniture, paint the walls, and measure the space for the bed.

LA.3.1.7.3 Determine implied inference

2. **Analyze:** The girl has a very close relationship with her family. They are all willing to pitch in and help turn the closet into a room that is just for her.

LA.3.2.1.7 Connect text to self

3. **Text-to-Self:** Students may say they might like a quiet space to read, draw, or study.

LA.3.2.1.7 Connect text to world

4. **Text-to-World:** Sometimes it is easier to solve a problem when several people help out. It is also important for people to help, because when a problem is solved, everyone in the family feels good about it.

FOCUS QUESTION

LA.3.2.1.7 Connect text to text

LA.3.1.7.7 Compare and contrast characters

5. **Text-to-Text:** The boy in "Pond Street Clubhouse" wanted a place of his own to play and be with friends. The girl in *My Very Own Room* wanted a quiet place to read, think, and sleep without the noise of her brothers. Both characters' determination helped them get what they wanted. USE THINK AND SEARCH

Objectives

- Read accurately with good prosody
- Rate: 82–102 WCPM

Materials

- Fluency Transparency 20
- Fluency Solutions Audio CD
- Leveled Practice Books, p. 143

RESEARCH
Why It Matters

Fluency
Oral reading practice appears to be superior to silent reading practice in stimulating improvement in learning to read.

Timothy Shanahan

Log on to
www.macmillanmh.com

On Level Practice Book O, page 143

As I read, I will pay attention to dialogue.

"What are your plans for today?" Mr. Sanchez asked his
10 son Carlo.
12 "I'm hiking with my nature club," Carlo said, "from
21 the state park entrance to Turtle Lake. Jimmy's father,
30 Mr. Gordon, is going with us."
36 "It's colder than yesterday," his mother said. "Please
44 take your warmest jacket and your gloves."
51 "Hold on," Carlo's father said. "I need to get your warm
62 blue jacket from the storage crate in the attic. Then I'll
73 drop you off."
76 A short time later, Carlo met up with Mr. Gordon and
87 the other members of the club, Jimmy, Julie, and Tyrone.
97 Mr. Gordon packed them in his van and drove them to
108 the state park.
111 When they arrived he checked his compass. "The
119 old logging trail is somewhere directly west of here,"
128 he said. 130

Comprehension Check

1. What are Carlo's plans? **Main Idea and Details** Carlo is going hiking in the state park with his nature club.
2. What is the weather like? **Plot Development** The weather is very cold.

	Words Read	–	Number of Errors	=	Words Correct Score
First Read		–		=	
Second Read		–		=	

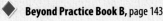

Approaching Practice Book A, page 143

Beyond Practice Book B, page 143

LA.3.1.5 Demonstrate the ability to read text orally with accuracy

Fluency

Repeated Reading: Pauses and Stops

EXPLAIN/MODEL Tell students that good readers learn to read groups of words together in phrases. Explain that the text on **Transparency 20** has been marked with slashes that indicate pauses and stops. A single slash indicates a pause, usually between phrases. A double slash indicates a full stop, usually between sentences. Model reading the passage aloud and have the class listen carefully. Then read the passage again, one sentence at a time, and have students echo-read.

Transparency 20

After breakfast we started pushing the old furniture out to the back porch.// Everyone helped.// We were like a mighty team of powerful ants.//

We carried furniture,/ tools,/ and machines.// We dragged bulging bags of old clothes and toys.// We pulled boxes of treasures and overflowing junk.// Finally, / everything was out except for a few cans of leftover paint from the one time we had painted the house.//

Fluency Transparency 20
from *My Very Own Room*, page 126

PRACTICE/APPLY Divide students into two groups. Have groups alternate echo-reading sentences. Remind students to pay attention to the pauses and stops, as indicated by the slash marks.

Cooperative Learning

For additional practice, have students use **Leveled Practice Book** page 143 or the **Fluency Solutions Audio CD**.

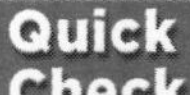

Quick Check **Can students read accurately with good prosody?**

During **Small Group Instruction**

If No → **Approaching Level** Fluency, p. 145N

If Yes → **On Level** Options, pp. 145Q–145R

Beyond Level Options, pp. 145S–145T

Comprehension

FCAT **REVIEW SKILL**
COMPARE CHARACTERS, SETTINGS, EVENTS

EXPLAIN/MODEL

LA.3.2.1.2 Identify and explain elements of story structure

- To **compare** characters, settings, or events, tell how they are alike.
- To **contrast** characters, settings, or events, tell how they are different.

Model how to compare and contrast characters in "Pond Street Playhouse" on pages 114–115. Point out how the narrator and his father are different: The father wants to build a garage. The narrator wants to build a clubhouse. Then discuss how the two are alike: At the end of the story, the narrator has a clubhouse, just like the father did when he was a boy.

PRACTICE/APPLY

Help students compare and contrast characters, settings, and events in *My Very Own Room*. For comprehension practice, use graphic organizers on pages 99–112 in the **Teacher's Resource Book**.

LA.3.1.7.3 Determine explicit ideas and information in grade level text

- What did the storage closet look like before the family worked on it? How did it look when the girl moved in? (At first, the storage closet was filled with tools, furniture, and old clothes. After the family worked on it, it was a small bedroom for a young girl, with newly painted walls, a bed, a bedside table, and a reading lamp.)
- How is the girl different at the end of the story? (At the beginning of the story, the girl is unhappy because she is sharing a room. At the end of the story, she is happy because she has her own room.)

LA.3.2.1.2 Explain character/character development

LA.3.2.1.7 Respond to, discuss, reflect on literary selections

Have students form a literature circle and discuss the story events in *My Very Own Room*. Then ask students to work in pairs to identify the similarities and differences between the girl's family and the boy's father in "Pond Street Clubhouse." Students may wish to use a Venn diagram to make the comparisons. Then have them compare their findings with other pairs.

Objectives

- Identifies similarities and differences among characters, settings, and events
- Use academic language: *compare, contrast*

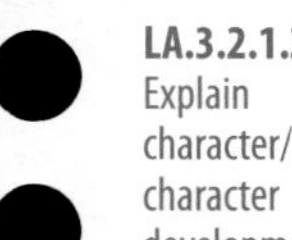

FCAT Skills Trace

Compare Characters, Settings, Events	
Introduce	U2: 181A–B
Practice / Apply	U2: 244; Leveled Practice, 46–47
Reteach / Review	U2: 2110–P, R, T; U4: 450–P, R, T; Leveled Practice, 113–114
Assess	Weekly Tests; Unit 2, 3, 4 Tests; Benchmark Tests A, B
Maintain	U3: 307B; U4: 139B

Informational Text: Science

LA.3.6.1.1 Read informational text to be informed

LA.3.1.6.2 Read conceptually challenging text

GENRE: NONFICTION ARTICLE

Have students read the bookmark on page 140. Explain that a nonfiction article gives facts and information about a topic. Nonfiction articles often have text features, such as headings, photographs, illustrations and captions.

Text Feature: Encyclopedia Article

LA.3.2.2 Identify elements of informational texts

EXPLAIN Point out the encyclopedia article on page 142.

- A print **encyclopedia** is a set of books that contains information on many subjects. Each book in a set is called a **volume**. Volumes are arranged in alphabetical order. Most encyclopedias have a volume for the index that tells which volumes contain information about a topic. Encyclopedia volumes contain **guide words** at the top of each page to help readers locate information. Digital encyclopedias can be found on CD-ROMs or online.

LA.3.6.4.1 Use appropriate available technologies

- **Encyclopedia articles** appear in alphabetical order in each volume. The articles' text features that make them easy to read include **headings**, subheadings, and illustrations with **captions**.

LA.3.2.2.2 Answer questions related to main ideas and relevant details

APPLY Have students identify the topic of the encyclopedia article on page 142 and the volume in which it is found. (The article is in volume C and gives information about a caliper.)

Science

Genre

Encyclopedia Articles provide detailed information about a specific topic.

FCAT **Text Feature**

Guide Words, **Headings**, and **Captions** are features of an encyclopedia. Topics in an encyclopedia are listed in alphabetical order.

Content Vocabulary

matter
property
mass
volume

Matter Matters!

by Karen O'Malley

Everything you see in your classroom is made of **matter**. Books, desks, pencils, and even you and the other students all take up space. Every object you see is an example of matter.

1 **Properties of Matter**

Not all matter is the same. You can describe matter and compare it with other types of matter by looking at its properties. A **property** is a characteristic that you can see or measure. Color and shape are properties. Look around your classroom at all the colors and shapes of the matter you see.

140

Content Vocabulary

LA.3.1.6.1 Use new vocabulary that is introduced and taught directly

Review the spelling and meaning of each content vocabulary word for "Matter Matters!"

- **Mass** is the amount of matter in an object. What object has greater mass—a paper clip or a basketball?
- Any characteristic of matter that you can observe is called its **property**. Can you identify a property of a crayon?
- Anything that takes up space and has mass is called **matter**. Is the pencil on your desk matter?
- The measure of how much space matter takes up is called **volume**.

Measuring Matter

You can compare matter by measuring it. Look at your desk. Use a ruler to measure the sides. This will tell you the length and width. **2**

You can also describe an object by looking at its **mass**. Mass tells how much matter is in an object. A heavy object has more mass than a light object. You can measure mass with a balance or scale.

Comparing Mass

A larger item does not always have more mass than a smaller one. Think about a beach ball and a bowling ball. Both objects take up about the same amount of space. However, the bowling ball has a much greater mass.

In the bowling ball, the tiny pieces of matter are packed more tightly than the matter in the beach ball. This is why the bowling ball is heavier. Now you know why a bowling ball is heavy enough to knock down the bowling pins. A beach ball could never do that!

These objects are about the same size. Which has the greater mass? 3

ENGLISH LANGUAGE LEARNERS

Access for All

Beginning Use Visuals Help students describe the photos. Use the photos to explain the difference between objects and how they are measured.

Intermediate Build Background/Compare Complete the Beginning task. Write the words *volume* and *mass* on the board. Discuss and compare. Then point to each feature of the encyclopedia article and discuss its importance. Model using the headings to predict the content of the article.

Advanced Context Clues Complete the Intermediate task. As you read, ask students to tell you the word clues that help identify the meaning of each word in bold type.

Informational Text

Read "Matter Matters!"

Access for All

LA.3.1.6.3 Use context clues to determine meanings; LA.3.1.7.1 Identify a text's features

As they read, remind students to apply what they have learned about text features of nonfiction articles and encyclopedia articles. Also have them identify clues to the meanings of the highlighted words.

1 TEXT FEATURES: HEADINGS

What heading do you see on page 140? What does it tell you? (The heading is "Properties of Matter." It tells me that the topic and main idea of this section is the properties of matter.)

2 MAIN IDEA AND DETAILS

LA.3.1.7.3 Determine explicit information in grade level text

What are some ways you can measure matter? What tools can you use to measure it? (I can measure the length and width of matter with a ruler. I can also measure its mass, or how heavy it is, with a balance or scale.)

3 TEXT FEATURES: PHOTOS WITH CAPTIONS

How does the photo and caption at the bottom of page 141 help you understand what mass is? (This photo and caption shows a bowling ball and a beach ball, which are both about the same size. Using the text above and the photo and caption, I can see that two objects that are about the same size do not have the same mass. The bowling ball is heavier because it has more mass.)

Informational Text

4 TEXT FEATURE: ENCYCLOPEDIA ARTICLE

FCAT LA.3.2.2.1 Identify and explain the purpose of text features

What is the guide word for this encyclopedia article? What is the purpose of guide words? (The guide word is Caliper. Guide words are arranged alphabetically and tell the first subject on that page.)

5 TEXT FEATURE: ENCYCLOPEDIA ARTICLE

FCAT LA.3.2.2.1 Identify and explain the purpose of text features

What is the subheading of the article? What does it tell you? Why do you think it is important? (The sub-head is "Uses of Calipers." It tells about who uses calipers and their importance to growing fruit crops.)

6 RELEVANT DETAILS

FCAT LA.3.1.7.3 Determine relevant supporting details LA.3.2.2.2 Answer questions related to relevant details

What units of measure are used to measure mass? What units of measure are used to measure volume? (To measure the mass of small, light objects, use grams. To measure the mass of heavier objects, use kilograms. To measure volume, use mililiters and liters.)

LA.3.6.4.2 Use digital tools LA.3.6.4.1 Use appropriate available technologies

Encourage students to use digital tools such as the Internet to practice viewing encyclopedia articles online.

An Encyclopedia Article

Reading an Encyclopedia Article

Encyclopedia articles are arranged alphabetically in each volume, or book.

page number guide word heading caption

103 **Caliper** 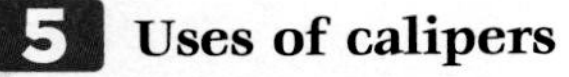

Caliper

This caliper measures the diameter of the orange with a precise number. Farmers read the measurement on a digital display.

A caliper is an instrument that measures the thickness or diameter of an object. It has a fixed arm and a second arm that moves along a graduated scale.

5 Uses of calipers

Calipers are used by orange growers in Florida. Growers need to know whether the size of the fruit in of their crops stays the same, increases, or decreases. Calipers are useful because they can measure very small changes in the size of the oranges.

This article is from Volume C of an encyclopedia.

142

On Level Practice Book O, page 144

An encyclopedia is a set of books filled with articles. The articles are in alphabetical order and give information about many subjects. On the top of each page is a **guide word** that tells the reader what will be on that page. Some articles have **headings** and subheadings in boldface type to summarize information and make it easy to find. Sometimes there are pictures with **captions** which explain the pictures.

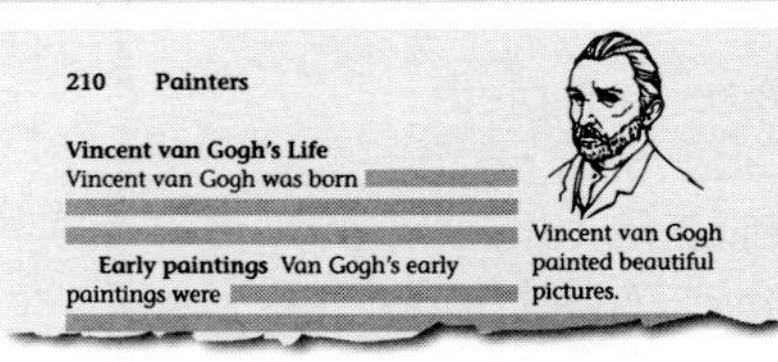

210 Painters
Vincent van Gogh's Life
Vincent van Gogh was born
Early paintings Van Gogh's early paintings were
Vincent van Gogh painted beautiful pictures.

Answer the following questions about this encyclopedia article below.

1. What is the page number 210
2. What is the guide word? Painters
3. What is the heading? Vincent van Gogh's Life
4. What is the subheading? Early paintings.
5. What is the caption? Vincent van Gogh painted beautiful pictures.

 **Approaching Practice Book A,** page 144

Beyond Practice Book B, page 144

Measuring Mass and Volume 6

You can measure mass in different ways. For small, light objects, the unit of measurement is a gram (g). For larger, heavier objects, you use a kilogram (kg).

You measure liquids by volume. **Volume** is how much space the liquid takes up. Liquids are measured in measuring cups called beakers. The units of measure are milliliter (ml) and liter (L).

Measuring matter is an important part of the job for scientists, cooks, electricians, and many workers. For people who use measurement every day, the mass and volume of matter really matter!

Each of these paper clips has a mass of about 1 gram.

FCAT Connect and Compare

1. Why are calipers a useful measurement tool for Florida orange growers? **Reading an Encyclopedia Article**
2. According to the article, what unit of measurement could you use to describe the weight of an elephant? A handful of sand? A jug of water? **Analyze**
3. In *My Very Own Room*, how did the family know the bed would fit in the storage space? **Reading Across Texts**

Science Activity

List different ways you can measure the length of an object if you do not have a ruler. Hint: Think about how the main character and her mother measure the bed in *My Very Own Room*.

LOG ON Find out more about measurement at **www.macmillanmh.com**

143

Research and Inquiry

PROPERTIES OF MATTER

Tell students that properties of matter can be observed as shape, color, length, mass, and even temperature.

Divide students into groups. Ask groups to choose three objects with different properties of matter to observe. Have them record each object and its properties in a chart. Remind them to use different tools for measurement, such as a ruler, a thermometer, or other objects if these items are not available.

Ask each group to give an oral presentation about their observations. Each group should explain their choice for the three objects, what they used as forms of measurement, and use the chart to show the similarities and differences among properties.

Encourage the audience to take notes and ask a member of the student group questions at the end.

SC.A.1.2.1.3.1 Physical properties of matter; **LA.3.5.2.2** Give an oral presentation; **LA.3.6.1.1** Organize information for different purposes; **LA.3.4.2.2** Record information related to a topic

Informational Text

Connect and Compare

SUGGESTED ANSWERS

FCAT

LA.3.1.7.3 Determine explicit information in grade level text

1. Calipers are useful for orange growers because they measure the thickness, or diameter of oranges. READING AN ENCYCLOPEDIA ARTICLE

LA.3.2.2.2 Answer questions related to relevant details

2. The weight of an elephant would be measured in kilograms and a handful of sand would be measured in grams. A mililiter or liter could be used to measure a jug of water. APPLY

FOCUS QUESTION

LA.3.2.1.7 Connect text to text

3. The family knew the bed would fit because the girl measured the length and width of the walls in her room and then measured the length and width of the bed to make sure it would fit. READING/WRITING ACROSS TEXTS

LA.3.5.2 Apply listening and speaking strategies

Science Activity

Have students share their ideas with the class. Then invite them to discuss what can be measured in the classroom and how they would measure the objects using their previous suggestions. Remind the student audience to ask questions.

SC.A.1.2.1.3.1 Physical properties of matter

LOG ON Technology

Internet Research and Inquiry Activity
Students can find more facts at **www.macmillanmh.com**

Connect Language Arts

FCAT WRITING
- Expository
- Writer's Craft: Time-Order Words

FCAT WORD STUDY
- Words in Context
- Word Parts: Endings *-er, -est*
- **Phonics:** Plural Nouns
- Vocabulary Building

SPELLING/GRAMMAR
- Plural Nouns
- Contractions with *Not*

SMALL GROUP OPTIONS
- Differentiated Instruction, pp. 145M–145V

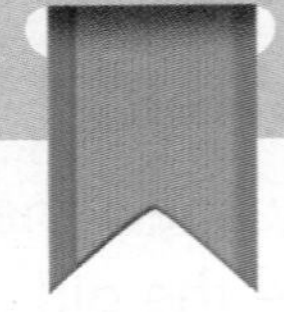

Writing

FCAT Time-Order Words

LA.3.3.2.2 Organize information through use of time-order words

READ THE STUDENT MODEL

Read the bookmark about time-order words. Good writers make directions easy to follow by including sequence words such as *first, next, after, then,* and *last.*

Have students turn to page 115. Discuss how the use of time-order words makes sequence clear.

LA.3.4.2 Develop and demonstrate technical writing
LA.3.3.2.2 Organize information into logical sequence

Then have the class read Robert H.'s directions and the callouts. Tell students that they will write their own directions to explain how to do or make something. They will also learn to use time-order words to tell about sequence and make their directions easy to follow.

Write Directions

Writer's Craft

FCAT Time-Order Words

Words such as *first, next, then,* and *last* tell the order in which things happen. Writers use these **time-order words** to show the sequence in which things should be done.

I used time-order words to show the sequence in which things should be done.

I completed my directions with the time-order word "last."

How to Make a Study Place

by Robert H.

Studying for a test is easier when you have a quiet place of your own. Here's how to make one. First, find a chair that's comfortable and put it in a quiet corner that isn't too close to the TV, radio, or phone. Next, get a healthful snack so you'll think about studying, not sandwiches. Then, gather the materials you'll need. The last thing to do is to tell everyone in the house that you need peace and quiet.

144

Features of Directions

A set of directions, or instructions, tells how to make or do something.

- A topic sentence explains what the directions will teach readers to make or do.
- Details describe clearly what to do in each step.
- Directions are written in steps that are presented in time order.
- The writer uses sequence words such as *first, before, then, next, last,* and *while* to explain in what order things should happen.

LA.3.4.2.1 Write in informational /expository forms; **LA.3.6.1.1** Organize information for purpose of following multi-step directions; **LA.3.3.3.3** Create interest by adding supporting details

Writing Prompt

People often write directions in order to explain how to do or make something.

Think about something you know how to do or make.

Now write directions explaining how to do or make something.

FCAT Writer's Checklist

- **Focus:** I write clearly about one topic.
- **Organization:** I include **time-order words**, such as *first* and *last*, that show the sequence of the steps in my directions.
- **Support:** I use specific words and details in my steps.
- **Conventions:** I use contractions correctly. All my words are spelled correctly.

PREWRITE

LA.3.3.1.1 Generate ideas from multiple sources

LA.3.3.1.2 Determine purpose and intended audience of a writing piece

LA.3.3.1.3 Use organizational strategies to make a plan for writing

Read and discuss the writing prompt on page 145. Explain that directions are written to explain how to do or make something. Students can work independently or in small groups to brainstorm writing topics. Have them identify the purpose (inform) and audience (classmates and teacher). Display **Transparency 77**. Discuss how Robert created a Sequence Chart to plan his writing. Have students use Sequence Charts to plan theirs.

DRAFT

LA.3.4.2.1 Write in informational /expository forms

LA.3.3.2.2 Organize information through use of time-order words

LA.3.3.2.1 Use prewriting plan to develop main idea with supporting details

Display **Transparency 78**. Discuss how Robert used his chart to write a draft and how he could improve it. Before students draft their directions, present the explicit lesson on **Time-Order Words** on page 145A and the **Topic Sentence** minilesson on 145B. Then have students use their charts to write their directions with main ideas and supporting details.

REVISE

LA.3.3.3 Revise draft

LA.3.3.3.2 Create clarity by rearranging words and sentences

LA.3.3.3.4 Apply appropriate tools or strategies to refine draft

LA.3.3.4 Edit and correct draft for standard language conventions

Present the **Rearrange Information** minilesson on page 145B. Then display **Transparency 79**. Discuss Robert's revisions and how these changes make the directions easier to follow. Students can revise their drafts or place them in writing portfolios to work on later. If they choose to revise, have them work with partners to use the Writer's Checklist on page 145 and to evaluate each other's work. Then have students **proofread/edit** their writing. For **Publishing Options**, see page 145A.

For lessons on contractions with *not* and spelling plurals, see page 145B and **5 Day Spelling** and **Grammar** on pages 145G–145J.

Transparency 77: **Sequence Chart**
Transparency 78: **Draft**
Transparency 79: **Revision**

Transparency 77

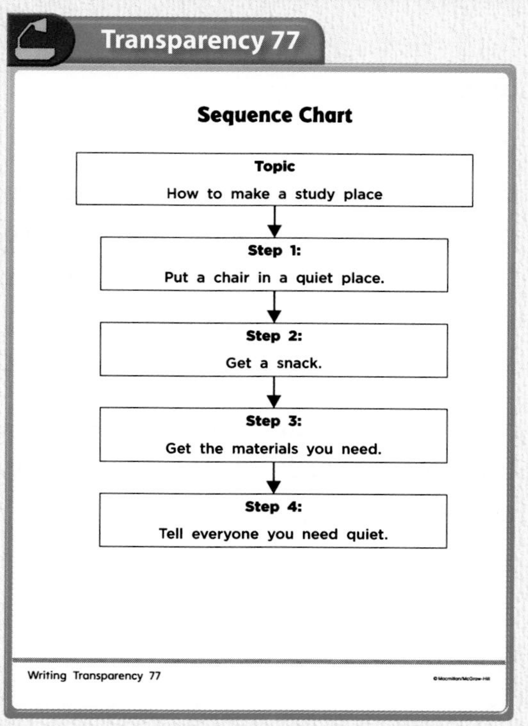

Sequence Chart
Topic
How to make a study place
Step 1:
Put a chair in a quiet place.
Step 2:
Get a snack.
Step 3:
Get the materials you need.
Step 4:
Tell everyone you need quiet.
Writing Transparency 77

Writing Transparency 77

Writer's Craft

SUPPORT Time-Order Words

Publishing Options

Students can read aloud their directions to the class. See Speaking and Listening tips below. They can also use their best cursive to write their paragraphs. (See **Teacher's Resource Book** pages 216–221 for cursive models and practice.) Then invite students to make illustrated brochures for their directions. Students should add drawings or other images that show each step.

LA.3.3.5.3 Share writing with intended audience; **LA.3.3.5.2** Add graphics where appropriate

Speaking and Listening

SPEAKING STRATEGIES

- Speak slowly and clearly, pausing before you read each step.
- Emphasize sequence words such as *first*, *next*, and *then*.
- Look up at your audience often.

LISTENING STRATEGIES

- Listen to hear what should happen in each step.
- Try to picture the steps happening in time order.
- If you have a question, wait until the speaker is done, then raise your hand and ask.

LA.3.5.2 Apply listening and speaking strategies; **LA.3.5.2.2** Use appropriate voice

6-Point Scoring Rubric

Use the rubric on page 145G to score published writing.

Writing Process

For a complete lesson, see Unit Writing on pages 145A–145F.

LA.3.3.2.2 Organize information into logical sequence through use of time-order words

EXPLAIN/MODEL

Good writers use sequence words and phrases, such as *first*, *next*, *then*, *in a while*, and *after that* to help readers understand what should happen step by step. Display **Transparency 80**.

Think Aloud These directions are easy to follow because they tell me clearly what to do in what order. The first sentence starts with the word *first*. The next sentence starts with *next*. Each step is described clearly, and each has a time-order word that helps me understand when to do each step.

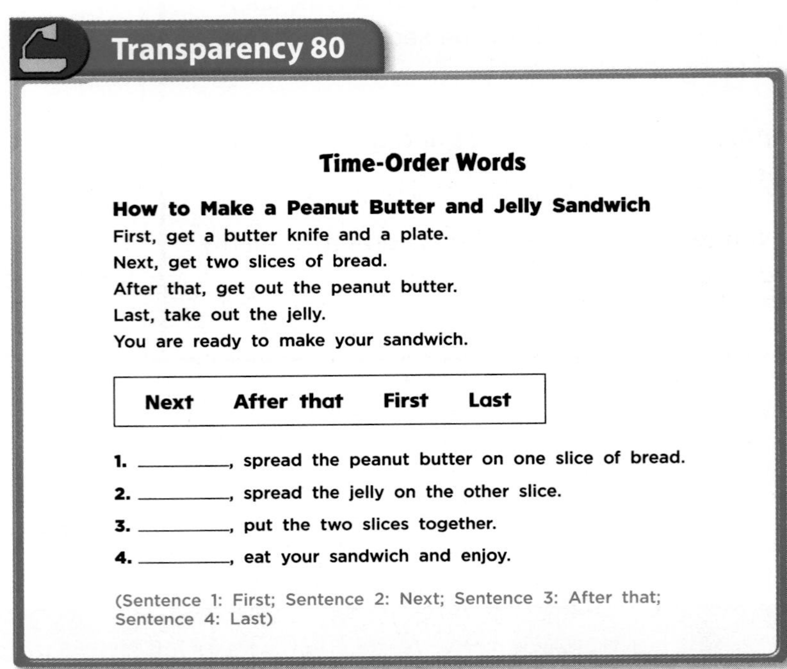

Transparency 80

Time-Order Words

How to Make a Peanut Butter and Jelly Sandwich

First, get a butter knife and a plate.
Next, get two slices of bread.
After that, get out the peanut butter.
Last, take out the jelly.
You are ready to make your sandwich.

Next	After that	First	Last

1. ________, spread the peanut butter on one slice of bread.
2. ________, spread the jelly on the other slice.
3. ________, put the two slices together.
4. ________, eat your sandwich and enjoy.

(Sentence 1: First; Sentence 2: Next; Sentence 3: After that; Sentence 4: Last)

Writing Transparency 80

LA.3.3.2.2 Use time-order words

LA.3.3.3.1 Evaluate draft for use of logical organization

PRACTICE/APPLY

Work with students to read the next four sentences of the directions. Have students suggest the best time-order word or phrase from the box to fill in each blank. When they are finished, have them read the completed sentences to make sure the sequence is as clear as possible. Then have students identify time-order words in another set of directions they have read recently.

Tell students that as they draft their directions, they should include time-order words and phrases that will help readers to follow their directions easily.

Writer's Toolbox

LA.3.3.2.1 Use supporting details that describe

ORGANIZATION

Writing Trait: Organization

Explain/Model Remind students that good writers begin informational or expository writing with a topic sentence. A topic sentence tells the main idea of the writing.

Practice/Apply Point out the topic sentence at the beginning of the directions on page 144. It tells the reader that studying for a test is easier in a quiet place. Point out that all the details in the paragraph tell how to create a quiet study place. As students draft and revise, have them check to make sure that they have good topic sentences with supporting details that tell about them.

FOCUS

Rearrange Information

Explain/Model Directions are easy to follow if all the information is in the right order. Display two sentences that are not in order. Show students how to use proofreading marks to show how to rearrange text that is out of order.

Practice/Apply As students revise, remind them to check that words, sentences, and paragraphs make sense in the order they appear. If they need to move information, they can use proofreading marks to rearrange words, sentences, and paragraphs so their writing makes sense.

LA.3.3.2.2 Organize information into logical sequence; LA.3.3.3.2 Create clarity by rearranging words, sentences, paragraphs

Technology

Remind students that as they draft, revise, and proofread, they can use the Spelling and Grammar features to check their work.

LA.3.6.4.2 Use digital tools

LA.3.3.4.3 Edit for correct use of apostrophes

CONVENTIONS

Contractions with *Not*

Explain/Model A contraction is a word that is made from two words put together with one or more letters left out; an apostrophe takes the place of left-out letters. Many contractions are formed from a verb and the word *not*.

Practice/Apply Have students read the third sentence on page 144. Help them identify a contraction made with the word *not—isn't*. Point out that an apostrophe replaces the missing letter *o* in *not*. As students proofread/edit, have them check that the apostrophe is in the correct place in each contraction they use. For a complete lesson on contractions with *not*, see pages 145I–145J.

CONVENTIONS

Spelling Plural Nouns

Point out plural nouns *materials* and *sandwiches* on page 144. Review the rules for forming plurals: In most words add *-s*; add *-es* to words ending in *x*, *sh*, *ch*; and in words ending in *y*, change *y* to *i* and add *-es*. Have students pay attention when spelling plural nouns. Remind them that they can use a print or online dictionary to check spelling in their drafts. For a complete lesson on spelling plural nouns, see pages 145G–145H.

LA.3.3.4.1 Correctly use spelling; LA.3.3.4.1 Edit using a dictionary or other resources

FCAT Success!

Test Prep and Practice with Writing+, pages 180–230

Word Study

Review Vocabulary

Words in Context

Objectives

- Apply knowledge of word meanings and context clues
- Apply knowledge of comparative and superlative endings *-er* and *-est*

Materials

- Vocabulary Transparency 39
- Vocabulary Strategy Transparency 40
- Leveled Practice Books, p. 145

Vocabulary

separate (p. 122) to set apart or keep apart

determination (p. 124) a firm purpose

storage (p. 122) a place for keeping things for future use

crate (p. 129) a box made of pieces of wood

exact (p. 134) very accurate

ruined (p. 124) damaged greatly or destroyed

luckiest (p. 136) having the most good luck

ELL

Personalize the Vocabulary Write: *I would be the luckiest person if _____.* Write a few examples and ask students for others. Then have students discuss their ideas in pairs.

LA.3.1.6.3 Use context clues to determine meaning

EXPLAIN/MODEL

Review the meanings of the vocabulary words. Display **Transparency 39**. Model how to use word meanings and context clues to fill in the first missing word.

Transparency 39

separate determination storage crate exact ruined luckiest

"Come help me clean out the (1) *storage* shed," Dad said to Lou. "Some of the things stored there are (2) *ruined*. Now they are good for nothing."

Lou and Dad took boxes out of the shed. One big (3) *crate* was filled with old record albums. Lou started to (4) *separate* the broken records from the ones in good shape.

"Let's sell the good ones!" Lou said. "They could be worth something." He spoke with (5) *determination*. "The music store buys old records. These may be the (6) *exact* kind they want."

Dad drove Lou to the store. The owner bought the records. Lou thought he was the (7) *luckiest* boy in town.

Vocabulary Transparency 39

Think Aloud In the first paragraph, I see the word *stored.* I also see the word *shed.* I know that people often store things in sheds. I can tell the missing word is *storage.*

PRACTICE/APPLY

LA.3.1.6.1 Use new vocabulary

Access for All Have each student use context clues to write missing words for items 2–7 on a separate piece of paper. Students can exchange papers, check answers, and explain context clues they used.

LA.3.1.6 Use multiple strategies to develop grade-appropriate vocabulary

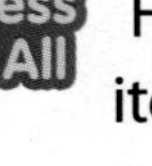

Word Maps Have student pairs create word maps with a vocabulary word or another story word in the center and four surrounding boxes labeled *synonym*, *antonym*, *example*, and *nonexample*. For example, *ruined*: *destroyed/fixed/a burnt meal, a good meal*. They may use a dictionary/thesaurus for help. When pairs have finished, they can share their word maps with classmates.

STRATEGY
WORD PARTS: ENDINGS *-ER, -EST*

EXPLAIN/MODEL

LA.3.1.6.7 Use meaning of base words, affixes to determine meanings

An adjective is a word that describes a noun. The ending, or morpheme, *-er* at the end of an adjective means "more." The ending *-est* at the end of an adjective means "most." Adjectives that end in *-er* compare two things. Adjectives that end in *-est* compare more than two things. Remind students that some base words have spelling changes when the affixes *-er* and *-est* are added.

Display **Transparency 40**. Review the examples at the top. Then help students identify the words with *-er* or *-est* endings in item 1 stating the base word, the endings, and the words' meanings.

Transparency 40

Endings *-er, -est*

young = young + er = younger (more young)
young + est = youngest (most young)

happy = happi + er = happier (more happy)
happi + est = happiest (most happy)

1. Her room was smaller than the kitchen. (small + er, more small)
   Her room was the smallest room in the house. (small + est, most small)
2. The bed was softer than her old bed. (soft + er, more soft)
   The bed was the softest bed in the world! (soft + est, most soft)
3. The bedside lamp was prettier than the living room lamp. (pretti + er, more pretty). It was the prettiest lamp in the home. (pretti + est, most pretty)

Vocabulary Strategy Transparency 40

PRACTICE/APPLY

LA.3.1.6.7 Use meaning of base words to determine meanings

Ask students to complete items 2 and 3 by identifying the base word, the endings, and the meanings.

Quick Check Can students apply knowledge of word meanings, context clues, and endings *-er* and *-est*?

During **Small Group Instruction**

If No → **Approaching Level** Vocabulary, pp. 145N–145O

If Yes → **On Level** Options, pp. 145Q–145R

Beyond Level Options, pp. 145S–145T

ELL Access for All

Make Comparisons
Ask three students to stand in a row. Compare the students: *Maria is tall. Paulo is taller. Jessica is the tallest.* Write the sentences. Compare classroom objects, animals, or other familiar items.

Vocabulary

Review last week's vocabulary words. Have students identify the plurals. (*volunteers, grownups*) Then have them pluralize *tour, community,* and *slogan.*

FCAT Success!

Test Prep and Practice with vocabulary, pages 6–31

On Level Practice Book O, page 145

The **inflectional endings** *-er* and *-est* show comparison. The ending *-er* means "more." The ending *-est* means "most."

A. Fill in the blank with the correct form of the adjective that follows each sentence. Use *-er* or *-est* to compare the items.

1. The giraffe was the tallest (tall) of all the giraffes in the zoo.
2. She had the longest (long) neck of all of the animals in the zoo.
3. She was even bigger (big) than her brother.
4. She thought that the leaves at the very tops of the trees were the sweetest (sweet).
5. She shared the largest (large) of the three spaces in their home with two other giraffes.
6. The breezes were cooler (cool) at night than in the day.
7. When the giraffe grew a little older (old), she got a big surprise. She got her own space!

Possible response provided.

B. Add *-er* or *-est* to the word *great* and use it in a sentence.

8. This is the greatest apple pie I have ever eaten.

Approaching Practice Book A, page 145

Beyond Practice Book B, page 145

Word Study

Objective

- Decode plurals

Materials

- Leveled Practice Books, p. 146

ELL **Access for All**

Game Write on the board the singular and plural forms of words: *lunch/lunches*, *puppy/puppies*, and so on. Assign each student a plural form to write on an index card. Say a singular form of a word. The student(s) with the plural form stands and says the word.

On Level Practice Book O, page 146

The **plural** of many nouns is formed by adding *-s* to the base word, as in *pears*. Nouns ending in *x*, *ch*, and *sh* form the plural by adding *-es*, as in *wishes*.

To form the plural of most nouns that end in a consonant plus *y*, change the *y* to *i* and add *-es*.

Write the plural form of each word. Then use each plural form in a sentence. Accept reasonable sentences.

rock
1. Plural form rocks

branch
2. Plural form branches

bush
3. Plural form bushes

country
4. Plural form countries

library
5. Plural form libraries

Approaching Practice Book A, page 146
Beyond Practice Book B, page 146

Phonics

Decode Plurals

LA.3.1.4.1 Use knowledge of pronunciation of root words to decode

EXPLAIN/MODEL

- A root, or base, word is a word that has no word parts added, such as *pear*. Knowing how to pronounce a root word can help students pronounce those root words with affixes added.
- Add *-s* or *-es* to a noun that is a root, or base, word to make it plural. These endings mean "more than one." The plural of many nouns is formed by adding *-s* to the base word, as in *pears*. Nouns ending in *x*, *ch*, or *sh* form the plural by adding *-es*, as in *wishes*. Nouns ending with a consonant and *y* form the plural by changing the *y* to *i* and adding *-es*, as in *puppies*.

Write: *We ate the berries for breakfast.*

Think Aloud I see that the noun *berries* ends in *-ies*. I think that the base word is *berry* because *y* changes to *i* when the plural ending *-es* is added. *Berries* fits that pattern, so I know that this word is the plural form of the word *berry*.

PRACTICE/APPLY

Write: *lunches*, *ponies*, *years*, *alleys*, *cities*. Have students circle the plural endings. Have them say the base word and tell its meaning.

LA.3.1.4.3 Decode multisyllabic words

Decode Multisyllabic Words Have students use their knowledge of phonics patterns, compound words, and word parts to decode long words. Display: *monkeys*, *melodies*, *dictionaries*, *toothbrushes*, *wristwatches*. Model how to decode *monkeys*, focusing on the base word and the plural ending. Have students decode the other nouns.

LA.3.1.6 Use multiple strategies to develop vocabulary

Plural Match Write base words and plurals on index cards: *city*, *cities*, *play*, *plays*, *lunch*, *lunches*, *daisy*, *daisies*, *fox*, *foxes*, *alley*, *alleys*. Place the cards in a 3 x 4 array. A student turns over two cards at a time to match the plural and base word. If it is not a match, the student turns the cards over, and another student takes a turn.

Quick Check **Can students decode plurals?**

During **Small Group Instruction**

If No → **Approaching Level** Phonics, p. 145M

If Yes → **On Level** Options, pp. 145Q–145R

Beyond Level Options, pp. 145S–145T

Vocabulary Building

LA.3.1.6 Use multiple strategies to develop vocabulary; LA.3.1.6 Develop grade-appropriate vocabulary; LA.3.1.6.1 Use new vocabulary; LA.3.1.6.4 Categorize key vocabulary; LA.3.1.6.8 Use knowledge of synonyms; LA.3.1.6.6 Identify "shades of meaning" in related words

Oral Language

Expand Vocabulary Work with students to brainstorm words about a place of their own. Have them suggest words about where it might be located and what the place might be like. Then ask them to write the words on an idea web.

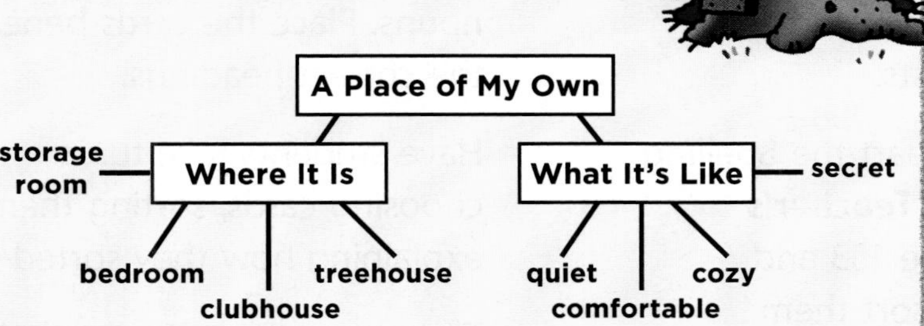

Vocabulary Building

Synonyms The word *warm* in *My Very Own Room.* is similar in meaning to the word *hot*. Help students brainstorm synonyms for *warm*, write them on a web, and discuss shades of meanings.

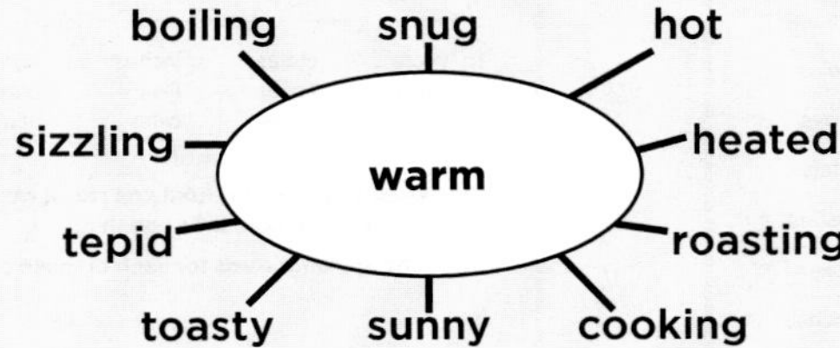

Have students do a synonym web for *thrilled* or *tour* from last week's vocabulary words.

Apply Vocabulary

Write a Paragraph Have each student use the vocabulary words *separate, determination, storage, crate, exact, ruined,* and *luckiest* in a paragraph about a special place of their own or have them self-select a topic.

Spiral Review

Vocabulary Game

Use **Vocabulary Cards** for the words *luckiest, clumps, deserve, quarreling, research, separate, sprout, thrilled,* and *volunteers.*

- Have students stand in a circle for this version of the game Hot Potato.
- Hand a word card, facedown, to one player.
- Players pass the card until you say "Stop!"
- The player holding the card turns it over, reads the word aloud, and uses it in a meaningful sentence. Continue until all words have been used.

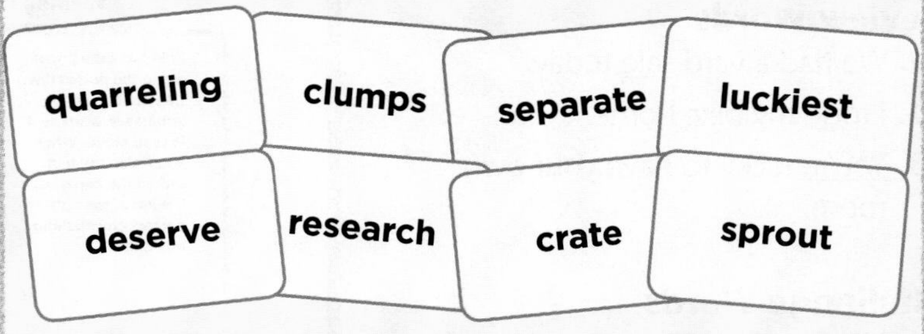

Technology

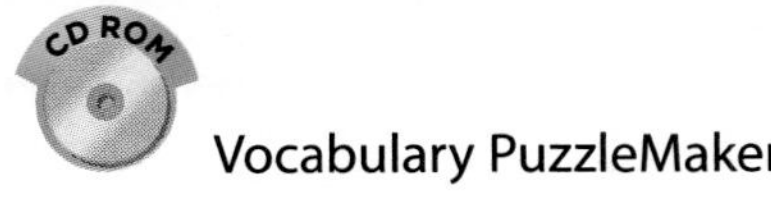

Vocabulary PuzzleMaker

For additional vocabulary and spelling games, go to www.macmillanmh.com

5 Day Spelling

Spelling Words

years	foxes	bunches
twins	inches	alleys
trays	flies	lunches
states	cities	cherries
ashes	ponies	daisies

Review sale, rode, you're

Challenge heroes, libraries

Dictation Sentences

1. They are five **years** old.
2. My brothers are twins.
3. I put fruit on the trays.
4. We have lived in two states.
5. The fire burned to ashes.
6. Baby foxes live in a den.
7. My sister grew two inches.
8. Flies are insects.
9. Do you like big cities?
10. There are ponies at the farm.
11. I picked three bunches of flowers.
12. Alleys are small streets.
13. Jim and I brought our lunches to school.
14. We had cherries for a snack.
15. Daisies grow in the garden.

Review Words

1. We had a yard sale today.
2. I rode my bike home.
3. You're lucky to have your own room.

Challenge Words

1. My parents are my heroes.
2. I like reading books in libraries.

Note: The word in **bold** type is from *My Very Own Room*.

Display the Spelling Words throughout the week.

LA.3.3.4.1 Correctly use spelling

Plurals

Day 1 Pretest

ASSESS PRIOR KNOWLEDGE

Use the Dictation Sentences. Say the underlined word, read the sentence, and repeat the word. Have students write the words on **Spelling Practice Book** page 121. For a modified list, use the first 12 Spelling Words and the 3 Review Words. For a more challenging list, use Spelling Words 3–15 and the Challenge Words. Have students correct their own tests.

Have students cut apart the Spelling Word Cards BLM on **Teacher's Resource Book** page 133 and figure out a way to sort them. Have them save the cards for use throughout the week.

Students can use Spelling Practice Book page 122 for independent practice.

For leveled Spelling word lists, go to **www.macmillanmh.com**

Spelling Practice Book, pages 121–122

Fold back the paper along the dotted line. Use the blanks to write each word as it is read aloud. When you finish the test, unfold the paper. Use the list at the right to correct any spelling mistakes.

1. ________ 1. years
2. ________ 2. twins
3. ________ 3. trays
4. ________ 4. states
5. ________ 5. ashes
6. ________ 6. foxes
7. ________ 7. inches
8. ________ 8. flies
9. ________ 9. cities
10. ________ 10. ponies
11. ________ 11. bunches
12. ________ 12. alleys
13. ________ 13. lunches
14. ________ 14. cherries
15. ________ 15. daisies

Review Words
16. ________ 16. sale
17. ________ 17. rode
18. ________ 18. you're

Challenge Words
19. ________ 19. heroes
20. ________ 20. libraries

Day 2 Word Sorts

TEACHER AND STUDENT SORTS

- Review the Spelling Words, point out the plural endings, and discuss meanings.
- Use the cards on the Spelling Word Cards BLM. Attach the headings *add -s*, *add -es*, and *y to i + -es* to a bulletin board.
- Model how to sort the plural nouns. Place the cards beneath the correct headings.
- Have students take turns choosing cards, sorting them, and explaining how they sorted them.
- Then have students use their own Spelling Word Cards. After placing the headings on their desks, they can sort the Spelling Words three times. Have students write their last sort on Spelling Practice Book page 123.

Spelling Practice Book, page 123

years	states	inches	ponies	lunches
twins	ashes	flies	bunches	cherries
trays	foxes	cities	alleys	daisies

This week's spelling list contains plural words. Plurals are words that name more than one thing.

Write the spelling words for each of these plural endings.

s
1. alleys
2. trays
3. years
4. twins

y to i + -es
5. cherries
6. daisies
7. ponies
8. cities
9. flies

es
10. ashes
11. inches
12. lunches
13. bunches
14. states
15. foxes

Find the Base Word

Write the base word of each plural noun.

16. flies fly
17. ponies pony
18. bunches bunch

LA.3.1.6.8 Use knowledge of homophones

Day 3 Word Meanings

DEFINITIONS

Display the definitions below. Have students write the clues and the Spelling Words that go with them in their word study notebooks.

1. wild animals that look like small dogs (foxes)
2. insects with thin wings (flies)
3. places where people live (cities)
4. small horses (ponies)
5. flowers with round yellow centers (daisies)

Challenge students to come up with clues for other Spelling Words, including Review Words and Challenge Words.

Have partners write sentences for each Spelling Word, leaving blanks where the words should go. Then have them trade papers and write the missing words.

Day 4 Review and Proofread

SPIRAL REVIEW

Review homophones. Display *sale*, *rode*, and *you're*. Have students state each word's homophone and use each word in a sentence.

PROOFREAD/EDIT

Write the sentences below. Have students proofread/edit to correct the errors.

1. Flys annoy ponys. (Flies, ponies)
2. Foxs don't like citys. (Foxes, cities)

BLIND SORT

Partners use their Spelling Word Cards and each write the headings *add -s*, *add -es*, and *y to i + -es* on a sheet of paper. Then students take turns. One draws cards and says the words. The other writes them under the headings. After both have finished, they can check each other's papers.

Day 5 Assess and Reteach

POSTTEST

Use the Dictation Sentences on page 145G for the Posttest.

If students have difficulty with any of the words in the lesson, have them place them on a list called "Spelling Words I Want to Remember" in their word study notebooks.

WORD STUDY NOTEBOOK

Challenge students to search for other plural nouns in their reading for the week and write them in their word study notebooks under the heading "Other Plural Nouns."

Spelling Practice Book, page 124

years	states	inches	ponies	lunches
twins	ashes	flies	bunches	cherries
trays	foxes	cities	alleys	daisies

Part of the Group

Add the spelling word that belongs in each group below.

Fruits
1. apples, grapes, cherries

Baby animals
2. calves, kittens, ponies

Places to live
3. towns, villages, cities

Units of time
4. days, months, years

Animals
5. sheep, bears, foxes

Flowers
6. roses, lilies, daisies

A Clue for You

7. They are small streets behind buildings. alleys
8. You carry food on them. trays
9. There are 50 of these in the United States. states
10. They buzz through the air. flies
11. What is left after something burns. ashes
12. What students bring to school to eat. lunches
13. Groups of something. bunches
14. There are 12 of these in 1 foot. inches
15. Two people who look exactly alike. twins

Spelling Practice Book, page 125

Proofreading

There are six spelling mistakes in this paragraph. Circle the misspelled words. Write the words correctly on the lines below.

Melody and Melissa were tooins, but they couldn't have been more different. Melody loved picking daisys, arranging flowers, and playing with her stuffed poonys. Melissa loved flis and insects and crawling around in the dirt. The problem was that they shared a room. Melody liked the room to be neat with boonchs of flowers in all the windows. Melissa was far from neat. She tracked in mud and brought bugs into the room. It had been a problem for many years. One day Melody decided that maybe she and Melissa should divide the room in two. That way they could both get what they wanted. Melissa thought it was a great idea. They hung a white sheet a few inshs from the ceiling. Now Melody's room is always beautiful, and Melissa's room is always messy. They are the happiest sisters around.

1. twins
2. daisies
3. ponies
4. flies
5. bunches
6. inches

Writing Activity

If you could have your dream room, what would it be like? Use at least three spelling words in your paragraph.

Spelling Practice Book, page 126

Look at the words in each set below. One word in each set is spelled correctly. Look at Sample A. The letter next to the correctly spelled word in Sample A has been shaded in. Do Sample B yourself. Shade the letter of the word that is spelled correctly. When you are sure you know what to do, go on with the rest of the page.

Sample A:
Ⓐ keys
Ⓑ keeze
Ⓒ keyes
Ⓓ keies

Sample B:
Ⓔ ladys
Ⓕ ladees
Ⓖ laides
Ⓗ ladies

1. Ⓐ yeares Ⓑ yiers Ⓒ years Ⓓ yeirs
2. Ⓔ twins Ⓕ twinz Ⓖ twiness Ⓗ twyns
3. Ⓐ traies Ⓑ trays Ⓒ trayies Ⓓ traes
4. Ⓔ staties Ⓕ statez Ⓖ states Ⓗ statses
5. Ⓐ ashs Ⓑ ashies Ⓒ ashez Ⓓ ashes
6. Ⓔ foxes Ⓕ foxies Ⓖ foxs Ⓗ foxses
7. Ⓐ inchs Ⓑ inchies Ⓒ inchez Ⓓ inches
8. Ⓔ flys Ⓕ flyes Ⓖ flies Ⓗ fliez
9. Ⓔ cityies Ⓕ cities Ⓖ citys Ⓗ citees
10. Ⓐ poneis Ⓑ poneese Ⓒ poneez Ⓓ ponies
11. Ⓔ bunches Ⓕ bunchs Ⓖ bunschs Ⓗ bunchez
12. Ⓐ alleyies Ⓑ alleyes Ⓒ alleys Ⓓ alleies
13. Ⓐ lunchs Ⓑ lunches Ⓒ lunschs Ⓓ lunchez
14. Ⓔ cherrys Ⓕ cherryis Ⓖ cherryies Ⓗ cherries
15. Ⓐ daisys Ⓑ daisees Ⓒ daisies Ⓓ daysies

5 Day Grammar

Daily Language Activities

Use these activities to introduce each day's lesson. Write the day's activities on the board or use **Transparency 20**.

DAY 1

1. Flo isnt' at the store. **2.** The girl could'nt find the address. **3.** Jenna did n't buy the vegetables. (1: isn't; 2: couldn't; 3: didn't)

DAY 2

1. Why is'nt Sue happy? **2.** She does'nt have her own room. **3.** She ca'nt find a quite place to study. (1: isn't; 2: doesn't; 3: can't; quiet)

DAY 3

1. Sara and laura dont look alike. **2.** You would'nt know there twins. **3.** Most people arenn't able to tell them apart. (1: Laura; don't; 2: wouldn't; they're; 3: aren't)

DAY 4

1. Those cherrys willn't last long. **2.** My little brother haven't stopped eating them. **3.** We shoul'dnt let him eat all of them. (1: cherries; won't; 2: hasn't; 3: shouldn't)

DAY 5

1. Paul and Toby havnt' helped me pick daisys yet. **2.** Wont you help me. **3.** I cann't do it alone. (1: haven't; daisies; 2: Won't; me?; 3: can't)

ELL — **Access for All**

Compare/Contrast Write the words *is not* and *isn't* on the board. Say the words with students. Have students tell you how they are the same and different. Co-construct sentences for both words. Repeat this activity with other contractions.

LA.3.3.4 Edit and correct draft for standard language conventions; **LA.3.3.4.3** Edit for correct use of apostrophes

Contractions with *Not*

Day 1 Introduce the Concept

INTRODUCE CONTRACTIONS WITH *NOT*

Present the following:

- A **contraction** is a shortened form of two words.
- An **apostrophe** takes the place of one or more letters.
- Some contractions are formed with forms of the verbs *be*, *do*, *have*, and *not*. These verbs do not usually change their spellings in a contraction with *not*.
- *Won't* is a special contraction for *will not*. The spelling of the verb *will* changes.

Examples:

is not → isn't
has not → hasn't
will not → won't

See Grammar Transparency 96 for modeling and guided practice.

Grammar Practice Book, page 121

- A **contraction** is a shortened form of two words.
- An **apostrophe** (') shows where one or more letters have been left out. In most contractions with *not*, the apostrophe takes the place of *o*.

is not	isn't	have not	haven't
are not	aren't	had not	hadn't
was not	wasn't	do not	don't
were not	weren't	does not	doesn't
has not	hasn't	did not	didn't

- *Can't* and *won't* are different. The apostrophe in *can't* takes the place of two letters: *n* and *o*. In *won't*, three letters disappear and the *o* changes position

cannot can't
will not won't

Circle the contraction in each sentence. Write the words that form the contraction.

1. I don't have my own room yet. do not
2. We didn't have time to finish it. did not
3. I can't get any peace and quiet! cannot
4. I won't complain. will not
5. We haven't much left to do. have not
6. Dad just hasn't had time to finish my room. has not
7. We weren't expecting a difficult task! were not
8. I hadn't known much about a building before now. had not
9. We aren't going to quit. are not
10. It doesn't take long if we work together. does not

Day 2 Teach the Concept

REVIEW CONTRACTIONS WITH *NOT*

Review with students what a contraction is and how to place an apostrophe.

INTRODUCE MORE CONTRACTIONS WITH *NOT*

- A **contraction** is a shortened form of two words.
- An **apostrophe** takes the place of one or more letters.

Examples:

cannot/can't	is not/isn't
are not/aren't	was not/wasn't
have not/haven't	has not/hasn't
does not/doesn't	do not/don't
did not/didn't	will not/won't

See Grammar Transparency 97 for modeling and guided practice.

Grammar Practice Book, page 122

- A **contraction** is a shortened form of two words
- An **apostrophe** (') shows where one or more letters have been left out. In most contractions with *not*, the apostrophe takes the place of *o*.

Rewrite each sentence using a contraction in place of the underlined verb and *not*.

1. I did not want to share a room with my brothers.
   I didn't want to share a room with my brothers.
2. There was not enough space for all of us.
   There wasn't enough space for all of us.
3. There is not a place in the house for me to call my own.
   There isn't a place in the house for me to call my own.
4. At first, we were not sure what to do.
   At first, we weren't sure what to do.
5. "I do not mind using the storage room," I told Mom.
   "I don't mind using the storage room," I told Mom.
6. "I will not mind," said Mom.
   "I won't mind," said Mom.
7. I have not had a room of my own yet.
   I haven't had a room of my own yet.
8. I was not sure how to fix it up.
   I wasn't sure how to fix it up.
9. I will not have a bed until tomorrow.
   I won't have a bed until tomorrow.

LA.3.3.4 Edit and correct draft for standard language conventions; **LA.3.3.4.3** Edit for correct use of apostrophes

Day 3 Review and Practice

REVIEW MORE CONTRACTIONS WITH *NOT*

Review how to form contractions with *not*.

MECHANICS AND USAGE: SPELLING CONTRACTIONS

- An **apostrophe** shows where letters are left out.
- Sometimes an apostrophe takes the place of one letter.
- Sometimes an apostrophe takes the place of more than one letter.
- When spelling contractions, make sure the apostrophe is in the correct place.

Examples:
cannot → **can't**
has not → **hasn't**

See Grammar Transparency 98 for modeling and guided practice.

Grammar Practice Book, page 123

- An **apostrophe** takes the place of letters left out of a contraction.

Rewrite these sentences. Add apostrophes to the contractions.

1. My part of the room isnt like my sisters' part.
   My part of the room isn't like my sisters' part.
2. You cant find any empty space on her walls.
   You can't find any empty space on her walls.
3. There isnt room for another poster or photograph.
   There isn't room for another poster or photograph.
4. There arent any posters or pictures on my wall.
   There aren't any posters or pictures on my wall.
5. I dont need anything but paint and a brush.
   I don't need anything but paint and a brush.
6. I didnt paint pictures.
   I didn't paint pictures.
7. I havent painted anything but colorful shapes.
   I haven't painted anything but colorful shapes.
8. Eileen and Leah say it doesnt make sense.
   Eileen and Leah say it doesn't make sense.
9. I hadnt meant for my wall to look perfect.
   I hadn't meant for my wall to look perfect.
10. I wont mind as long as its my very own space.
    I won't mind as long as it's my very own space.

Day 4 Review and Proofread

REVIEW CONTRACTIONS WITH *NOT*

Ask students to form contractions for *is not*, *do not*, and *will not*. Have them identify which letter the apostrophe stands for in each.

PROOFREAD/EDIT

Have students proofread/edit the sentences to correct the errors.

1. Zane can'not come over tomorrow. (can't)
2. dont leave your toys on the floor. (Don't)
3. Richard does'nt have his own room. (doesn't)
4. Sally hasnot' been to the library yet. (hasn't)
5. I woont be able to play today. (won't)

See Grammar Transparency 99 for modeling and guided practice.

Grammar Practice Book, page 124

- A **contraction** is a shortened form of two words.
- An **apostrophe** (') shows where one or more letters have been left out.

Proofread these paragraphs. Circle any contractions that are not correctly written. Add the apostrophes where they belong.

Its very difficult to share a room. You dont have any space of your own. You cant ever have the whole place to yourself. I had this problem. I shared my room with my brothers. They came in and played when I tried to do homework. We fought all the time. I didnt have a way to get away from everyone!

Then I had an idea. Our attic hadnt been used much. Mom and Dad said that they werent planning to use all the space. I cleared out an area in the attic. I put up curtains to make it private. I found old furniture that wasnt being used. Suddenly I had an office. Its my own special place. Best of all, my brothers and I arent fighting anymore! So if you havent got a place of your own, look around. There might be a special place just waiting for you to find it!

Writing Activity

Write a short poem that describes a space of your own. Use at least two contractions.

Poems will vary. Be sure that the contractions are used correctly.

Day 5 Assess and Reteach

ASSESS

Use the Daily Language Activity and page 125 of the **Grammar Practice Book** for assessment.

RETEACH

Write the following on index cards: *is*, *are*, *was*, *were*, *have*, *has*, *will*, and a few with *not*. Then write apostrophes on sticky notes. Students should take turns choosing a card and a *not* and creating contractions by placing the sticky notes over letters replaced by an apostrophe. Have them record their contractions, use them in sentences, and explain the oddball *will* + *not*.

Use page 126 of the Grammar Practice Book for additional reteaching.

See Grammar Transparency 100 for modeling and guided practice.

Grammar Practice Book, pages 125–126

Write the contraction for each pair of words.

1. does not doesn't
2. will not won't
3. cannot can't
4. have not haven't
5. are not aren't
6. did not didn't
7. is not isn't
8. do not don't
9. were not weren't
10. has not hasn't
11. had not hadn't
12. was not wasn't

Write the words that form the contraction in each sentence.

13. I hadn't ever lived alone. had not
14. I don't remember ever being alone. do not
15. I wasn't sure what a room of my own would be like. was not
16. Now I can't imagine going back to sharing! cannot
17. How come you haven't had that problem? have not
18. I didn't get much furniture. did not
19. My room doesn't have any pictures on the walls. does not
20. My sisters aren't allowed to barge into my room are not

Administer the Test

Weekly Reading Assessment, pages 237–248

Weekly Assessment, 237–248

ASSESSED SKILLS

- Plot Development
- Vocabulary Words
- Word Parts/Endings *-er, -est*
- Plurals
- Contractions with *Not*

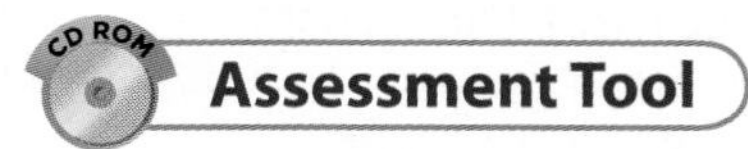

Administer the **Weekly Assessment** from the CD-ROM or online.

Fluency

Fluency Assessment

Assess fluency for one group of students per week. Use the Oral Fluency Record Sheet to track the number of words read correctly. Fluency goal for all students: **82–102 words correct per minute (WCPM)**.

Approaching Level	Weeks 1, 3, 5
On Level	Weeks 2, 4
Beyond Level	Week 6

Alternative Assessments

- **ELL Assessment**, pages 126–127

ELL Assessment, 126–127

Diagnose		Prescribe
	IF . . .	**THEN . . .**
VOCABULARY WORDS **VOCABULARY STRATEGY** Word Parts/Endings *-er, -est* Items 1, 2, 3	0–1 items correct . . .	Reteach skills using the **Additional Lessons**, page T9. LOG ON Reteach skills: Log on to **www.macmillanmh.com** CD ROM Vocabulary PuzzleMaker Evaluate for Intervention.
COMPREHENSION Skill: Plot Development Items 4, 5, 6	0–1 items correct . . .	Reteach skills using the **Additional Lessons**, page T4. Evaluate for Intervention.
GRAMMAR Contractions with *Not* Items 7, 8, 9	0–1 items correct . . .	Reteach skills: **Grammar Practice Book**, page 126.
SPELLING Plurals Items 10, 11, 12	0–1 items correct . . .	LOG ON Reteach skills: Log on to **www.macmillanmh.com**
FLUENCY	73–81 WCPM 0–72 WCPM	AUDIO CD Fluency Solutions Evaluate for Intervention.

Also Available

To place students in the Intervention Program, use the **Diagnostic Assessment** in the Intervention Teacher's Edition.

Skills Focus Phonics

Objectives Review plurals
Decode multisyllabic plurals

Materials • **Student Book** "Pond Street Clubhouse"

DECODE PLURALS

LA.3.1.4 Demonstrate knowledge of alphabetic principle

Model/Guided Practice

Explain the rules for forming most plural words:

- Make most words plural by adding *-s*.
- Words that end in *sh*, *ch*, *s*, *ss*, or *x* are made plural by adding *-es*.
- Words that end with a consonant and *y* are usually made plural by changing the *y* to *i* and adding *-es*.
- Words that end with a vowel and *y* are made plural by adding *-s*.

Write *ponies* on the board and read it aloud. Say: *I can figure out that this word is plural because it ends in* -s. *I see that the letters just before that are* i-e, *so the singular form must have ended in* y. *I know that the singular is* pony.

Repeat the procedure with the word *bunches*.

MULTISYLLABIC PLURAL WORDS

LA.3.1.4.3 Decode multi-syllabic words

- Write the word *countries* on the board, read it aloud, and have students explain how this plural was formed. Then ask them to say the singular: *country*.
- Have pairs of students work together to practice decoding longer plural words. Write the words below on the board and ask student pairs to copy them onto sheets of paper. Have them underline the plural ending of each word and then write the singular form of the word.

lunches	wristwatches	dictionaries	toothbrushes
bushes	boxes	cherries	wishes

- Check pairs for their progress and accuracy.
- Extend by providing a variety of singular forms and having students practice forming the plural forms correctly.

WORD HUNT: PLURALS IN CONTEXT

LA.3.1.4 Apply grade level phonics to read text

- Review plurals and how they are formed.
- Have students search "Pond Street Clubhouse" to find plural words.
- Check to see if students have found the following: *rooms*, *supplies*, *piles*, *nails*, *shingles*, *news*, *weeks*, *kids*, *pieces*, *plans*.

Constructive Feedback

If students have trouble remembering the rules for forming plurals, provide additional practice. Write the following words on the board: *bush*, *crutch*, *bus*, *kiss*, *box*, *cry*, *day*. Read the words aloud. Circle the last letter or letters in each word and help students use the circled letter or letters to help them decide how to form the plural. Then write the plural forms of the above words (*bushes*, *crutches*, *buses*, *kisses*, *boxes*, *cries*, *days*) and ask students to say and write the singular form of each.

Additional Resources

For each skill below, additional lessons are provided. You can use these lessons on consecutive days after teaching the lessons presented within the week.

- Plot Development: Predictions, T4
- Word Parts: Endings *-er* and *-est*, T9
- Text Feature: Encyclopedia, T11

Skills Focus Fluency

Objective Read with increasing prosody and accuracy at a rate of 82–92 WCPM

Materials • index cards • **Approaching Practice Book A**, p. 143

WORD AUTOMATICITY

Have students make flashcards for the following plurals: *years, foxes, bunches, twins, inches, alleys, trays, flies, lunches, states, cities, cherries, ashes, ponies, daisies.*

Display the cards one at a time and have students say each word. Repeat twice more, displaying the words more quickly each time.

REPEATED READING

LA.3.1.5 Demonstrate the ability to read grade level text

Model reading the passage on **Practice Book** page 143. Have the group echo-read it and then have partners practice reading to each other. Circulate and provide constructive feedback as necessary. Focus on dialogue.

TIMED READING

Tell students that they will be doing a final timed reading of the passage on Practice Book page 143. Students should

- begin reading the passage aloud when you say "Go."
- stop reading the passage after one minute when you say "Stop."

As students read, note any miscues. Help students record and graph the number of words they read correctly. Provide support and constructive feedback.

Constructive Feedback

If students read dialogue without sufficient expression, pauses, and attention to punctuation, reread the passage to them, one sentence at a time, exaggerating the correct expression and pauses. Have students copy your expression as they echo-read each sentence.

Approaching Practice Book A, page 143

As I read, I will pay attention to dialogue.

Shatima and Jamal were on their back porch looking at
10 magazines.
11 "I really like these pictures of tree houses," Shatima
20 said. "I wish we had one."
26 "We have a tree," Jamal said. "I'll bet we could build a
38 tree house."
40 "Mom and Dad won't let us," Shatima said.
48 "You are probably right," said Jamal. "They'll come up
57 with some reason we can't do it."
64 Katrina, their friend who lived next door, came over.
73 "What are you reading about?" she asked.
80 "Tree houses," Shatima said.
84 "We want to build one, but Mom and Dad won't go for
96 it," Jamal said.
99 "Try them," Katrina said. "You'll never know unless
107 you ask." 109

Comprehension Check

1. What do Shatima and Jamal want to build? **Main Idea and Details** Shatima and Jamal want to build a tree house.
2. What advice does Katrina give Shatima and Jamal? **Main Idea and Details** to ask their parents about building a tree house and not assume they will say no

	Words Read	–	Number of Errors	=	Words Correct Score
First Read		–		=	
Second Read		–		=	

Skills Focus Vocabulary

Objective Apply vocabulary word meanings

Materials • **Vocabulary Cards** • **Student Book** *My Very Own Room*

VOCABULARY WORDS

LA.3.1.6.3 Use context clues to determine meanings

Read aloud each vocabulary word from this week and last week and review all definitions. Then have students locate the vocabulary words in *My Very Own Room*. Help them use context to figure out the meanings of unfamiliar words. Have students find a synonym or antonym for each word, using a thesaurus as appropriate. Examples: *determination/certainty, ruined/repaired, storage/closet space, exact/sloppy, luckiest/unluckiest, crate/box, separate/divide.*

Approaching Level Options

Vocabulary

Review last week's vocabulary words **(tour, volunteers, community, thrilled, slogan, grownups, deserve, interviewed)** and this week's words **(separate, determination, storage, crate, exact, ruined, luckiest).** Have students write clues for each word.

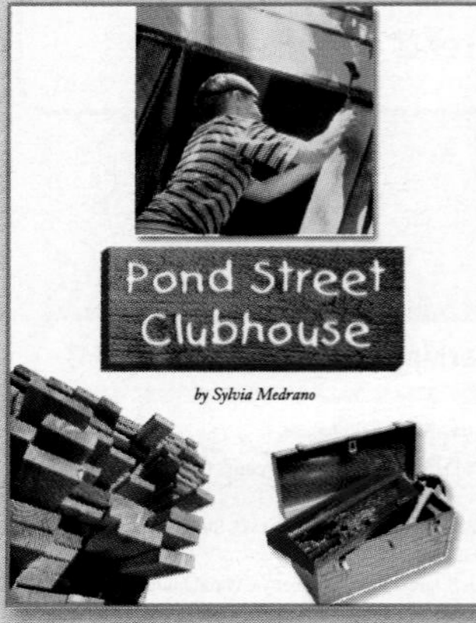

Student Book, or Transparencies 20a and 20b

ELL — Access for All

Practice Using Language Write the words *lucky*, *luckier*, and *luckiest* on the board. Use each word in a sentence to show its meaning. Explain that adjectives, or describing words, often end in *-er* and *-est*. Give examples of other adjectives, such as *small*, *dark*, and *nice*. Then have students volunteer their own examples as they pronounce the adjectives with each ending.

Skills Focus — Vocabulary

Objective Review word endings *-er* and *-est*

FCAT **WORD PARTS: ENDINGS *-ER* AND *-EST***

LA.3.1.6 Develop grade-appropriate vocabulary

Write, read aloud, and have students repeat:

Pablo was <u>lucky</u> when he found a dime. Anna was <u>luckier</u> when she found a quarter. I was the <u>luckiest</u> when my aunt gave me a dollar.

Ask students what each underlined word means. Explain that an adjective ending with *-er* usually compares two things; one ending with *-est* usually compares three or more. Brainstorm other adjectives with these endings.

Skills Focus — Comprehension

Objective Make predictions

Materials
- **Student Book** "Pond Street Clubhouse"
- **Transparencies 20a** and **20b**

STRATEGY
MONITOR COMPREHENSION

LA.3.1.7 Use strategies to comprehend text

Review the following with students:

- To monitor comprehension, you check to be sure you understand what you are reading.

FCAT **SKILL**
PLOT DEVELOPMENT: MAKE PREDICTIONS

LA.3.2.1.2 Identify elements of story structure

Explain/Model

Discuss how the characters and other story details provide clues to help readers make predictions about the events that happen in a story.

Display **Transparencies 20a** and **20b**. Read aloud the first six paragraphs of "Pond Street Clubhouse."

Think Aloud When the narrator says, "I had to think of a way to get Dad to agree," it sounds like that boy is experienced at talking the father into things. I would predict that the father helps build the clubhouse.

Practice/Apply

Guide students to make other predictions based on what they can tell about the characters. Have them confirm their predictions as they read.

Leveled Reader Lesson

Objective Read to apply strategies and skills

Materials
- **Leveled Reader** *The Slightly Tipping Tree House*
- **Vocabulary Cards**
- **Student Book** *My Very Own Room*

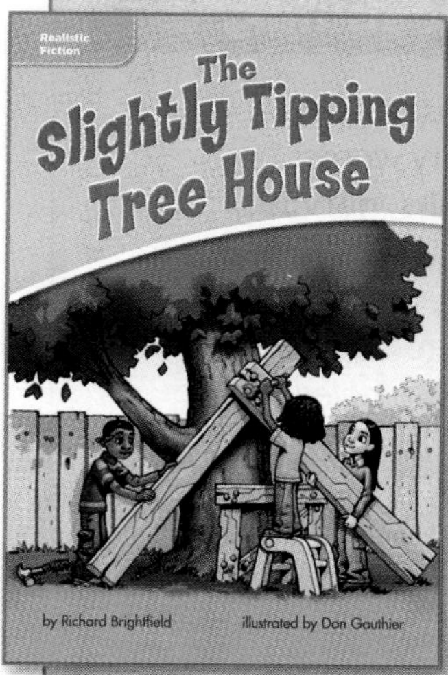

Leveled Reader

PREVIEW AND PREDICT

LA.3.1.7.1 Use text features

Show the cover and illustrations. Read the title and table of contents. Discuss why a tree house might be described as "slightly tipping."

VOCABULARY WORDS

LA.3.1.6 Develop grade-appropriate vocabulary

Display **Vocabulary Cards**. As you read, have volunteers locate the words: *storage*, p. 4; *exact*, p. 7; *ruined*, *separate*, p. 8; *crate*, p. 13; *determination*, p. 14; *luckiest*, p. 15. Students should read the sentence aloud, explain what the word means, and name another word or phrase that could be used in the sentence without changing the meaning.

STRATEGY
MONITOR COMPREHENSION

LA.3.1.7.8 Use strategies to repair comprehension

Reiterate that monitoring their comprehension can help students get more out of reading. As students read, they should pause periodically to ask themselves questions. If they don't understand something, they should reread that part and continue reading more slowly. Read page 2 aloud.

Think Aloud I don't understand how the kids are related. I'll go back and reread some parts. I see now that Shatima and Jamal are brother and sister. I can tell because, when speaking to Jamal, Shatima calls her parents "Mom and Dad." Katrina is their friend from next door.

SKILL
PLOT DEVELOPMENT: MAKE PREDICTIONS

LA.3.2.1.2 Identify elements of story structure

Help students to make, confirm, and revise predictions as they read and to create Predictions Charts. Discuss what might happen when the children ask their parents about a tree house. Later review what really happens.

READ AND RESPOND

LA.3.2.1.7 Respond to and discuss literary selections
LA.3.2.1.7 Connect text to self

Guide students' reading through the end of the book. Remind them that if they do not understand a part, they can reread it, read more slowly, read ahead, or ask for help. Have students share personal responses.

- How do you feel when you accomplish what you really wanted to do?
- Would you like to build a tree house? Why or why not?

MAKE CONNECTIONS ACROSS TEXTS

LA.3.1.7.7 Compare and contrast texts

Help the group compare *My Very Own Room* and *The Slightly Tipping Tree House*. Review students' predictions for each story.

On Level Options

Small Group

Vocabulary

Review last week's vocabulary words: **downstairs, nervous, chuckled, nonsense, fumbled,** and **trudged**. Ask students to discuss the last time they *fumbled*.

Skills Focus Phonics

Objective Review plurals

DECODE PLURALS

LA.3.1.4 Apply grade level phonics to read text

- Write and read aloud: *one city, two cities*. Underline the *-y* and *-ies* endings. Point out that the singular noun *city* ends with a consonant + *y*. Circle the *y* in *city*. Explain that to make *city* plural, you change the *y* to an *i* and add *-es*.
- Write *fly, pony, daisy,* and *cherry*. Ask students to change each singular noun into a plural noun following the model. Have them say each word.

fly	pony	daisy	cherry
flies	ponies	daisies	cherries

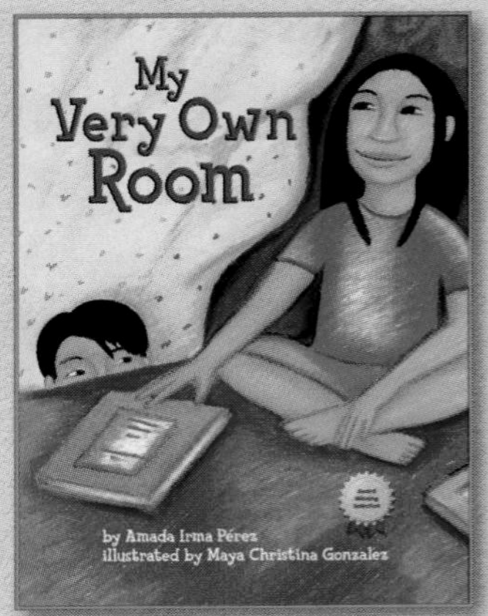

Student Book

Skills Focus Vocabulary

Objective Apply vocabulary and knowledge of word parts

Materials • **Vocabulary Cards** • **Student Book** *My Very Own Room*

VOCABULARY WORDS

LA.3.1.6.1 Use new vocabulary

Show each **Vocabulary Card** and have a volunteer create a sentence that uses that word. Other students can try to think of a sentence that better defines the word in context. For example, the first student may say, "My sister and I have to separate our laundry." Then the second may say, "We had to separate our laundry into two piles: light clothes and darks clothes."

FCAT

WORD PARTS: ENDINGS *-ER* AND *-EST*

LA.3.1.6 Develop grade-appropriate vocabulary

Remind students that the endings *-er* and *-est* can be added to an adjective or adverb. Ask them to find these words in *My Very Own Room* and tell what each means: *stronger* (p. 127); *luckiest, happiest* (p. 136).

On Level Practice Book O, page 143

As I read, I will pay attention to dialogue.

"What are your plans for today?" Mr. Sanchez asked his
10 son Carlo.
12 "I'm hiking with my nature club," Carlo said, "from
21 the state park entrance to Turtle Lake. Jimmy's father,
30 Mr. Gordon, is going with us."
36 "It's colder than yesterday," his mother said. "Please
44 take your warmest jacket and your gloves."
51 "Hold on," Carlo's father said. "I need to get your warm
62 blue jacket from the storage crate in the attic. Then I'll
73 drop you off."
76 A short time later, Carlo met up with Mr. Gordon and
87 the other members of the club, Jimmy, Julie, and Tyrone.
97 Mr. Gordon packed them in his van and drove them to
108 the state park.
111 When they arrived he checked his compass. "The
119 old logging trail is somewhere directly west of here,"
128 he said. 130

Comprehension Check

1. What are Carlo's plans? **Main Idea and Details** Carlo is going hiking in the state park with his nature club.
2. What is the weather like? **Plot Development** The weather is very cold.

	Words Read	–	Number of Errors	=	Words Correct Score
First Read		–		=	
Second Read		–		=	

Skills Focus Fluency

Objective Read fluently with good prosody at a rate of 82–102 WCPM

Materials • **On Level Practice Book O**, p. 143

REPEATED READING

LA.3.1.5 Demonstrate the ability to read text orally with expression

Model reading the fluency passage expressively, using different voices for different characters. Tell students they are to read the passage from the **Practice Book**. As they read the passage, they should change their voices to show when a different character is speaking.

Timed Reading At the end of the week, have partners time each other and note how many words they read correctly in one minute.

Leveled Reader Lesson

Objective Read to apply strategies and skills

Materials
- **Leveled Reader** *A Winter Adventure*
- **Student Book** *My Very Own Room*
- chart paper

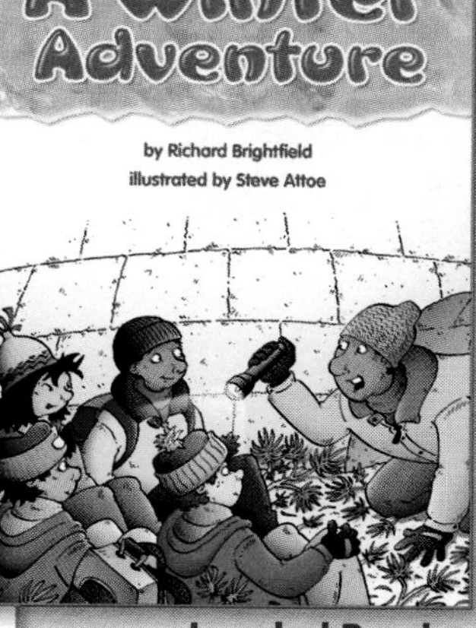

Leveled Reader

PREVIEW AND PREDICT
LA.3.1.7.1 Use text features to establish purpose for reading and make predictions

Show the cover and read the title. Ask what kind of winter adventure students think the characters will have. Have students set purposes.

STRATEGY
MONITOR COMPREHENSION

LA.3.1.7.8 Use strategies to repair comprehension

Explain that checking for understanding can help students get more out of reading. Tell students to make sure they understood what they read. They can then reread a passage, slow down, read ahead, or seek help if necessary. Read pages 2–3 aloud. Model the strategy.

Think Aloud These pages introduce a lot of characters and details about their plans. I'm going to reread these pages to get straight in my mind which characters are going where, and why.

SKILL
PLOT DEVELOPMENT: MAKE PREDICTIONS

LA.3.2.1.2 Identify elements of story structure
LA.3.1.7.8 Predict to repair comprehension

After students read Chapter 1, discuss how the story begins. Have students predict how the hiking trip will be affected by the sudden snowfall. Students can create a Predictions Chart to help them. After reading the entire story, they can confirm or revise their predictions. Remind them to use comprehension monitoring strategies to help them check and revise their predictions.

READ AND RESPOND

LA.3.2.1.7 Respond to, discuss, reflect on literary selections

Read to the end of Chapter 2. Discuss what actions the characters take after the big blizzard begins. Ask students to make more predictions about what the outcome of the hike will be. Review this week's vocabulary words as they come up.

After students read the end, have them paraphrase the main events and discuss whether or not the solutions the campers thought of were ones they had envisioned, and what other things the hikers could have done to prepare for an unexpected situation.

MAKE CONNECTIONS ACROSS TEXTS

LA.3.1.7.7 Compare and contrast texts

Have students compare and contrast the plots of *My Very Own Room* and *A Winter Adventure*. Ask if students were able to predict the resolutions and have them explain how. Find out if they enjoy reading stories with surprising plots. What would they ask or tell each author?

Beyond Level Options

Small Group

Student Book

Skills Focus: Vocabulary

Objective Use word associations to review and extend content vocabulary words

Materials • **Student Book** "Matter Matters!"

EXTEND VOCABULARY

LA.3.1.6 Use multiple strategies to develop grade-appropriate vocabulary

Review the content vocabulary words *matter*, *property*, and *mass* from "Matter Matters!" Have students create word association sentences for others to guess.

- Which word goes with "takes up space"? (*matter*)
- Which word goes with "characteristic"? (*property*)
- Which word goes with "how much matter an object has"? (*mass*)

ELL — Access for All

Questions and Answers Review as a class what students have learned about matter. Then have each child write three questions about matter or about measuring matter. When students are finished writing their questions, place them in groups of three. Have them take turns reading their questions and having other students in the group answer the questions orally.

Skills Focus: Text Feature

Objective Review encyclopedia articles and write an encyclopedia article

Materials • **Student Book** "Matter Matters!" • reference materials

ENCYCLOPEDIA ARTICLE

LA.3.6.1 Comprehend informational text
LA.3.4.2.1 Write in informational/expository forms

Ask students to review "Matter Matters!" and summarize the main ideas. Review and discuss the encyclopedia article on page 142.

- How are articles arranged in an encyclopedia? (alphabetically)
- Why does the encyclopedia page have guide words? (so readers can find articles more easily)
- What is a volume? (a single book in the encyclopedia)

Ask each student to choose a topic of interest. Students may work in pairs or independently. Provide books and magazines for reference. Students will write short articles that could be included in an encyclopedia. The articles should have titles and drawings with captions and should include facts, not opinions. Have students collate their articles, alphabetize them, and number the pages. Students may read the articles during free time.

Beyond Practice Book B, page 143

As I read, I will pay attention to dialogue.

"It's time to get ready for the science fair," Ms. Thomas, the
12 science teacher, announced to the science club. "But this year, we'll
23 work in teams, rather than each on your own."
32 "How many teams?" Erin asked.
37 "Let's see," Ms. Thomas said. "There will be five teams, each with
49 three members."
51 "That's only five exhibits," said Ari.
57 "How are we going to pick the teams?" Tanya asked.
67 "We'll pick names out of a hat," Ms. Thomas said.
77 Soon everyone was part of a team.
84 "The fair is in two weeks," Ms. Thomas said. "With hard work and
97 determination, you'll all be done in time. There will be a prize for the
111 best exhibit."
113 "What's the prize?" Ari asked.
118 "I'll keep that as a surprise," Ms. Thomas said. "I predict that this
131 year's fair will be our best yet."
138 Tanya, Erin, and Ari, who were on the same team, met in
150 the school cafeteria.
153 "Who has an idea for the exhibit?" Tanya asked. 162

Comprehension Check

1. What is the science club preparing for? **Main Idea and Details** the science fair
2. How many students will participate in the science fair? **Plot Development** 15 students

	Words Read	–	Number of Errors	=	Words Correct Score
First Read		–		=	
Second Read		–		=	

Skills Focus: Fluency

Objective Read fluently with good prosody at a rate of 92–102 WCPM

Materials • **Beyond Practice Book B**, p. 143

REPEATED READING

LA.3.1.5 Demonstrate the ability to read text orally with expression

Read aloud the fluency passage on **Practice Book** page 143 to model expressive reading. Have students take turns practicing the passage, and encourage them to continue practicing it throughout the week. As students read, tell them that they should imagine that they are storytellers or actors. They should read each character's dialogue in a different voice. Circulate and provide constructive feedback as needed.

Leveled Reader Lesson

Objective Read to apply strategies and skills

Materials • **Leveled Reader** *The Science Fair*

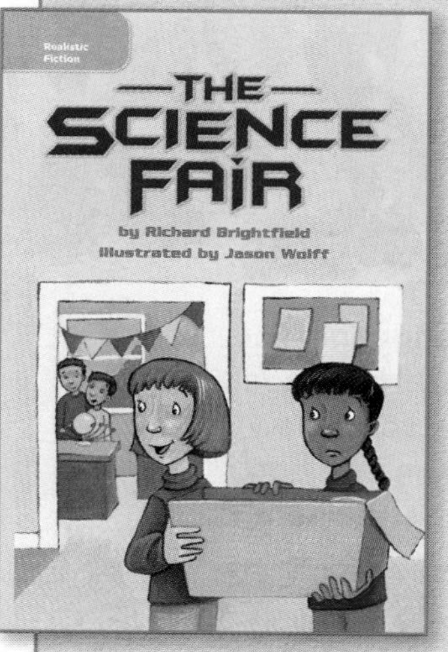

Leveled Reader

PREVIEW AND PREDICT

LA.3.1.7.1 Use text features

Show the cover and read the title of the book. Ask students to tell what they know about science fairs. Review vocabulary words as needed. Suggest that students skim the text and note questions.

STRATEGY
MONITOR COMPREHENSION

LA.3.1.7.8 Use strategies to repair comprehension

Remind students if they do not understand a section, they should reread the last part, read more slowly, read ahead to see if there is more information that can help them, or seek help. Read pages 2–4 aloud. Model how to monitor comprehension.

Think Aloud I don't understand how Erin, Tanya, and Ari ended up on the same team. I'll go back and reread page 3 to figure out what I missed. Oh, I see. The teacher must have picked their names out of a hat.

FCAT

SKILL
PLOT DEVELOPMENT: MAKE PREDICTIONS

LA.3.1.7 Use strategies to comprehend text

Discuss how the team finds a project idea that is worth pursuing. As students read, have them predict whether their project will turn out well or not. Have them explain the clues they use to make their predictions.

READ AND RESPOND

LA.3.2.1.7 Respond to, discuss, reflect on literary selections

Have students read to the end of Chapter 2. Find out what kind of project the team members decide to work on, and whether or not they work well together. Then have students finish reading, paraphrase the main events of the story, and share personal responses.

- What would you do for a science fair project?
- How could the team members have avoided the problems that they faced?

Self-Selected Reading

Objective Read independently to apply comprehension strategies and skills

Materials • Leveled Readers or trade books at students' reading levels

FCAT

READ TO UNDERSTAND PLOT DEVELOPMENT

LA.3.2.1.8 Select fiction materials to read

Invite each student to choose a fiction book for independent reading. For a list of theme-related titles, see pages T18–T19. Have students get together to discuss the books, the predictions they made, how they made them, and if they were correct. Have them discuss their interpretations of the stories.

English Language Learners

Academic Language

Throughout the week the English language learners will need help in building their understanding of the academic language used in daily instruction and assessment instruments. The following strategies will help to increase their language proficiency and comprehension of content and instructional words.

Technology

Oral Language For additional language support and oral vocabulary development, go to **www.macmillanmh.com**

Strategies to Reinforce Academic Language

- **Use Context** Academic language (see chart below) should be explained in the context of the task during Whole Group. Use gestures, expressions, and visuals to support meaning.
- **Use Visuals** Use charts, transparencies, and graphic organizers to explain key labels to help students understand classroom language.
- **Model** Demonstrate the task using academic language in order for students to understand instruction.

Academic Language Used in Whole Group Instruction

Content/Theme Words	Skill/Strategy Words	Writing/Grammar Words
a place of my own (p. 113)	monitor comprehension (p. 115A)	directions (p. 144)
matter (p. 140)	make predictions (p. 115A)	time-order words (p. 145A)
property (p. 140)	encyclopedia article (p. 140)	plural nouns (p. 145G)
mass (p. 140)	guide words (p. 140)	contraction (p. 145I)
volume (p.140)	captions (p. 140)	apostrophe (p. 145J)

ELL Leveled Reader Lesson

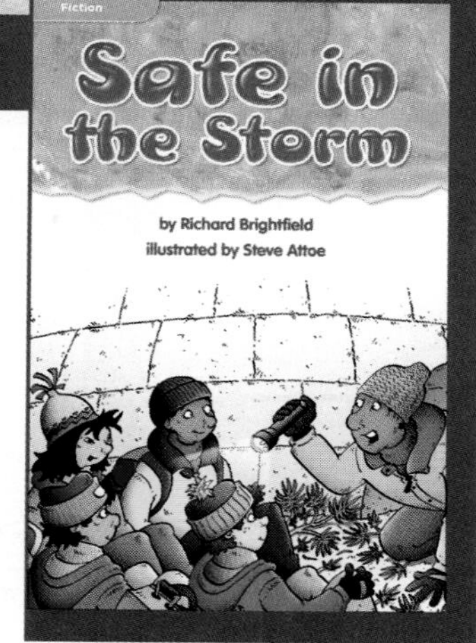

Realistic Fiction
Safe in the Storm
by Richard Brightfield
illustrated by Steve Attoe

Before Reading

DEVELOP ORAL LANGUAGE

Build Background Ask students about hiking trips. *Have you ever been hiking—or walking—in the mountains? What was the weather like? How far did you go?*

Review Vocabulary Before class, write a definition for each word on a sentence strip. Write the vocabulary and support words on the board. Read each definition and have students help you pair them to the words. Model each in a sentence. *I am the* luckiest *person in the world because I have a nice teacher.*

LA.3.1.6 Use multiple strategies to develop grade-appropriate vocabulary

PREVIEW AND PREDICT

LA.3.1.7.1 Use text features to make predictions

Point to the cover illustration and read the title aloud. Ask: *What are they wearing? What do you think the weather is like? Look at the background: Where are they?* Based on this information, have students make predictions about what the selection may be about.

Set a Purpose for Reading Show the Predictions Chart. Ask students to complete similar charts to make and confirm their predictions. Remind them to stop at different times and make predictions about what may happen. Making predictions helps readers understand plot development.

During Reading

LA.3.1.7 Use strategies to comprehend text; **LA.3.1.7.1** Use text features to make predictions

Choose from among the differentiated strategies below to support students' reading at all stages of language acquisition.

Beginning	Intermediate	Advanced
Shared Reading As you read, model how to make a prediction about what may happen next. Refer to text and pictures. Model how to confirm or revise your prediction and fill in the chart.	**Read Together** Read Chapter 1. Help students retell it. Model how to make a prediction, using text and pictures as reference. Fill in the chart. Take turns reading the selection with students and ask them to use the strategy.	**Independent Reading** Have students read the selection and stop at different times to make and check predictions. *How does Tyrone know it is getting colder?* Ask them to fill in the chart as they read.

After Reading

LA.3.1.6.1 Use new vocabulary

Remind students to use the vocabulary and story words in their whole group activities.

Objective

- Apply vocabulary and comprehension skills

Materials

- ELL Leveled Reader

ELL 5 Day Planner

DAY 1	• Academic Language • Oral Language and Vocabulary Review
DAY 2	• Academic Language • ELL Leveled Reader
DAY 3	• Academic Language • ELL Leveled Reader
DAY 4	• Academic Language • ELL Leveled Reader
DAY 5	• Academic Language • ELL Leveled Reader Comprehension Check and Literacy Activities

Grade 3 • ELL TEACHER'S GUIDE
English Language Learners
Florida Treasures
Macmillan/McGraw-Hill

ELL Teacher's Guide for students who need additional instruction

Show What You Know

FCAT Spiral Review

Show What You Know provides a spiral review of selected skills and strategies through Unit 4. After reading short fiction and nonfiction selections, students take short tests—in FCAT format—that assess reading comprehension in the context of unit skills and strategies.

Have students turn to page 146 in the **Student Book** and read "World Cup Worries" independently. Distribute **Show What You Know** pages 17–18. Have students complete the assessment. See pages 86–87 if students need a review of the test format.

Share Your Thinking

LA.3.1.7 Use a variety of strategies to comprehend grade level text

After students have completed the assessment, model your own thinking to show students how they can use test-taking, comprehension, vocabulary, and study skills and strategies to arrive at correct answers.

LA.3.1.7.3 Determine explicit ideas and information in grade level text

Question 1 Compare and Contrast *How are Fabio and his father ALIKE?*

Point out the last two paragraphs, which show that both Fabio and his dad love soccer. The correct answer is A. (A, think and search)

Show What You Know

FCAT **Review**

Draw Conclusions
Compare and Contrast
Author's Purpose
Context Clues
Multiple-Meaning Words
Time Line

World Cup Worries

Fabio was all set to watch the World Cup match. His favorite team was playing—Brazil. Just as he sat down, Fabio's father called, "Fabio, come here, please."

"But Dad, the World Cup is starting!" cried Fabio.

"That may be," said Mr. Silva. "But that doesn't change the fact that you have chores to do."

Work during the big match? Fabio really wanted to ignore his father and watch the game. He decided that if he did his chores really fast, he could still catch most of the match.

"What do you need me to do, Dad?" asked Fabio.

"You can start by cleaning your room," Mr. Silva said.

"Okay," said Fabio. He was relieved because he knew he could get that job done fast. He threw clothes in the hamper, put

146

Review

Apply Test Strategies

Right There You can find the answer right on the page. Words in the question and answer are usually the same.

Think and Search The answer is in more than one place. You need to put all the information together to answer the question.

Author and Me The answer is not stated. You have to use what you know and what you read to answer the question.

Apply Comprehension Strategies Review these comprehension strategies that students learned in this and previous units: Make Inferences and Analyze and Monitor Comprehension. Before they read, remind them to choose from the reading strategies they know to help them better understand the passage.

LA.3.1.7 Use a variety of strategies to comprehend grade level text books on the bookshelf, and straightened up his shoes. In 20 minutes, his room looked tidy—sort of.

"I'm done, Dad!" yelled Fabio. He hurried into the other room to turn on the television.

"Great," said Mr. Silva. "Now you can help me with the yard work."

Fabio sighed. He knew that yard work could take the rest of the day. "Dad, that means we'll miss the whole match!"

"This is more important," said Mr. Silva. He gave Fabio some gardening gloves and some trash bags, and put him to work cleaning up.

"Dad, I thought you loved watching the World Cup," said Fabio.

"I do," said Mr. Silva, "but work should be done while the sun shines."

After a few hours of hard work, Mr. Silva said that it was time for a break. Fabio was gloomy since he'd missed the whole match. He barely said a word as his father fixed him a snack.

"Fabio, I know you wanted to watch the match," said Mr. Silva. "I appreciate that you made the choice to help me, instead."

"I'm not sure I had a choice, Dad," replied Fabio.

"You can always choose to do the wrong thing," explained his father, "but you didn't. Now, here's the good news. I taped the game while we worked. Let's watch it while we eat!"

"All right! That sounds like a great choice, Dad," laughed Fabio.

147

Show What You Know, pages 17–18

Student Name ____________

Now answer Numbers 1 through 5. Base your answers on the story "World Cup Worries."

1. How are Fabio and his father ALIKE?
   - Ⓐ They both love soccer.
   - Ⓑ They both love cleaning.
   - Ⓒ They both love yard work.
   - Ⓓ They both love doing chores while the sun shines.

2. Read this sentence from the story.

   He was *relieved* because he could get that job done fast.

   This sentence means that Fabio felt
   - Ⓕ worried and anxious.
   - Ⓖ angry and annoyed.
   - Ⓗ jealous and spiteful.
   - Ⓘ pleased and calmed.

3. Why did the author write "World Cup Worries"?
   - Ⓐ to persuade readers to clean their rooms
   - Ⓑ to teach readers about the game of soccer
   - Ⓒ to teach readers about how to do yard work
   - Ⓓ to entertain readers with a good story that has a lesson

Go On ▶

LOG ON Technology

Go to **www.macmillanmh.com** for Sample Responses to question 5.

Spiral Review FCAT

Student page 147

LA.3.1.6.3 Use context clues to determine meanings

Question 2 Context Clues

Read this sentence from the story: "He was relieved *because he could get the job done fast." This sentence means that Fabio felt ________.*

Tell students that being relieved is a good feeling. Also if they were Fabio, they would feel pleased to get the job done and watch the soccer game. The correct answer is I. (I, author and me)

LA.3.1.7.2 Identify the author's purpose

Question 3 Author's Purpose

Why did the author write "World Cup Worries"?

Point out that fiction is usually written to entertain. The correct answer is A. (A, author and me)

LA.3.1.6.9 Determine correct meaning of words with multiple meanings

Question 4 Multiple-Meaning Words

Which word from the story can mean both "to take a rest from work" AND "to damage"?

Tell students to look for a word with two meanings and think about the meanings each answer choice can have. The answer is H. (H, think and search)

LA.3.1.7 Use strategies to comprehend text

Question 5 Draw Conclusions

What conclusions about Fabio's father can you draw from the fact that he made Fabio work during the match AND from the fact that he taped the soccer match?

Help students recognize that Mr. Silva believes in hard work. He also believes in making good choices. The fact that Fabio's father taped the soccer match shows how much he loved soccer too. Fabio's father may have used the soccer game tape as a reward for his son choosing to do the right thing.

See the Extended Response Rubric on page 149H.

FCAT **Spiral Review**

Student page 148

Share Your Thinking

LA.3.6.1.1 Read informational text for purpose of preparing to take a test

Have students turn to page 148 in the **Student Book** and read "Susan B. Anthony: A Pioneer for Women's Rights" independently. Distribute **Show What You Know** pages 19–20. Have students complete the assessment.

LA.3.1.6.2 Discuss text

After students have completed the assessment, model your own thinking to show students how they can use test-taking, comprehension, vocabulary, and study skills and strategies to arrive at correct answers.

Question 1 Compare and Contrast
According to the article, Susan B. Anthony and Elizabeth Cady Stanton were ALIKE in that they both ________.

LA.3.1.7.3 Determine relevant supporting details

Students must look for information that is true about both women. The answer is right there in the second paragraph where it says that Anthony and Stanton were leaders in the women's suffrage movement. The correct answer is B. (B, right there)

LA.3.1.7.2 Identify the author's purpose

Question 2 Author's Purpose
Why do you think Maja James wrote this article?

Help students think and search to understand that most of the information in the article is about Susan B. Anthony. The correct answer is G. (G, think and search)

Show What You Know

Susan B. Anthony

A Pioneer for Women's Rights

SUSAN B. ANTHONY was born to a Quaker family. Quakers believe in justice and fair treatment for everyone. In the early 1800s, most girls were not given an education equal to that of boys, but the Quakers allowed both boys and girls to have equal educations. In religious meetings both Quaker girls and boys could speak out. And women could vote on church matters.

After Susan B. Anthony met Elizabeth Cady Stanton, they became close friends and leaders in the women's suffrage movement. The suffrage movement worked to get women the right to vote. Anthony and Stanton were a great team. Their goal was to change the United States Constitution and give women the right to vote.

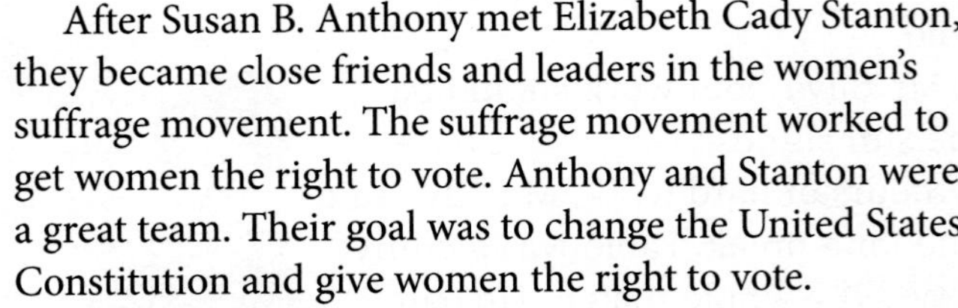

In 1872, Anthony brought 15 women to vote in a

Women Can Vote!

This time line shows important dates in Susan B. Anthony's life and in the women's suffrage movement.

Susan B. Anthony born February 15		Arrested for voting		Meets President Theodore Roosevelt
1820	1851	1872	1881	1905
	Meets Elizabeth Cady Stanton		Writes book about women's rights	

148

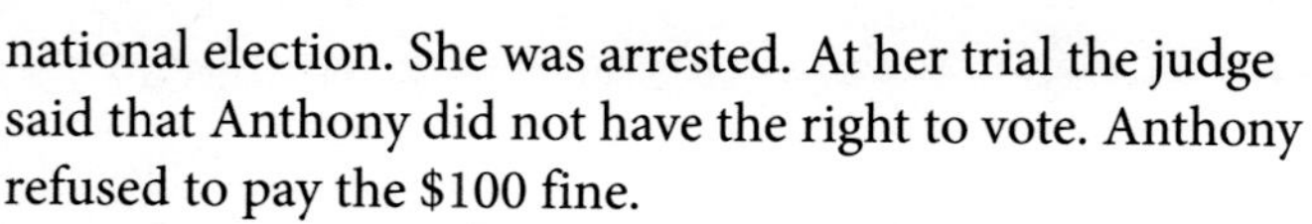

national election. She was arrested. At her trial the judge said that Anthony did not have the right to vote. Anthony refused to pay the $100 fine.

Anthony continued to work for women's suffrage throughout her life. She made many trips across the country and gave lectures about why women's rights were important. During her life Anthony published several newspapers. With Elizabeth Stanton and Matilda Gage, she wrote a book about the suffrage movement.

Susan B. Anthony died in 1906. In 1920 the Nineteenth Amendment was finally passed. This amendment gave women the right to vote. Because of all of Anthony's hard work, this law is sometimes called the Susan B. Anthony Amendment.

	19th Amendment passes		Susan B. Anthony dollar coin created
1906	1920	1920	1978
Dies March 13		Over eight million women vote	

149

Spiral Review FCAT

Student page 149

LA.3.1.7.3 Determine chronological order of events

Question 3 Time Line

According to the time line, which of the following events happened FIRST?

Tell students that the question asks them to look at the time line for the answer. The word FIRST tells students to find the date of each event and choose the event with the earliest date on the time line. The correct answer is C. (C, right there)

LA.3.1.7.3 Determine explicit ideas and information in grade level text

Question 4 Draw Conclusions

Why is the Nineteenth Amendment sometimes called the Susan B. Anthony Amendment? Use facts and information from the article to support your answer.

Help students find the last paragraph, which tells about the Nineteenth Amendment. Then point out parts of the article that tell about the work that Susan B. Anthony did for the suffrage movement. Together, this information supports a conclusion that the Nineteenth Amendment is sometimes called the Susan B. Anthony Amendment to honor a woman that helped get the law passed.

See the Short Response Rubric on page 149H.

Show What You Know, pages 19–20

Student Name ____________________

Now answer Numbers 1 through 4. Base your answers on the article "Susan B. Anthony."

1. Susan B. Anthony and Elizabeth Cady Stanton were ALIKE in that they both
   - Ⓐ were lawyers.
   - Ⓑ were Quakers.
   - Ⓒ believed in women's suffrage.
   - Ⓓ lived to see the 19th Amendment pass.

2. Why do you think Maja James wrote this article?
   - Ⓕ to persuade readers to vote
   - Ⓖ to inform readers of an important historical figure
   - Ⓗ to persuade readers to work for equal rights for women
   - Ⓘ to entertain readers with an amusing story about a woman

3. Which of the following events happened FIRST?
   - Ⓐ Susan B. Anthony is arrested.
   - Ⓑ A Susan B. Anthony dollar coin is created.
   - Ⓒ Susan B. Anthony meets Elizabeth Cady Stanton.
   - Ⓓ Susan B. Anthony meets President Theodore Roosevelt.

Go On

Florida Show What You Know • Grade 3 • Unit 4 19

LOG ON Technology

Go to www.macmillanmh.com for Sample Responses to question 4.

Unit 4 Writing Workshop

Objectives

- Identify features of a how-to article
- Plan and organize ideas for a how-to article
- Draft and revise expository writing that tells how to do something
- Proofread, publish, and present a how-to article

Materials

- Unit Writing Transparencies 19–24

Features of a How-to Article

- It explains **how to do a certain task** or **activity.**
- It presents **step-by-step directions** in a logical order.
- It gives **clear details.**
- It uses **time-order** or **space-order words.**
- It may use a variety of **transitional signals,** such as bullets, graphics, and headings.

LA.3.2.2 Identify elements of expository texts

ELL Access for All

Use a Chart Ask students to fold a paper lengthwise in half twice and unfold it to make a chart with four boxes (eight boxes if they use the other side of the page). Ask them to visualize the activity and write and/or draw the steps. Then have them discuss the steps in their chart with a partner. Encourage partners to ask each other questions to help clarify the task.

Expository: How-to Article

Read Like a Writer

LA.3.2.2 Analyze elements of expository texts

Read aloud the excerpt from **Student Book** page 31 from *Cook-A-Doodle-Doo!* by Janet Stevens and Susan Stevens Crummel. Explain to students that this excerpt is an example of expository writing. It gives information about preparing the strawberries for use in baking a strawberry shortcake. Ask students to listen for

LA.3.3.2.2 Use time-order words

LA.3.3.3.3 Create interest by adding supporting details

- **the task or activity**
- **step-by-step directions** for doing the activity
- **clear details** to clarify when and how to do each step
- **time-order** and **space-order words**

Cook-A-Doodle-Doo!

Wash the strawberries first and cut off their tops. Use a cutting board and cut each strawberry in half, then cut each half in half. (How many pieces do you have now?) Watch out for your fingers!

Discuss the Features

LA.3.1.6.2 Discuss text; LA.3.1.7.3 Determine explicit ideas and information in grade level text

After reading, discuss the following questions with students:

- **What is the topic of this paragraph?** (cutting strawberries)
- **What is the first step of the activity?** (washing the strawberries)
- **What details does the writer include?** (how to cut them in half, then in half again, and to be careful)
- **What time-order words has the writer used?** (*first* and *then*)

Prewrite LA.3.3.1 Use prewriting strategies

Access for All

LA.3.3.1.2 Determine purpose and intended audience of writing piece

Set a Purpose Remind students that the purpose for writing a how-to article is to explain how to do something.

Know the Audience Have students think about who will read their articles, such as classmates and family members. Ask: *Why do you want to help others learn to do this activity?*

LA.3.6.2.1 Narrow a topic

Choose a Topic Have students brainstorm tasks or activities they like to do or have done well in the past. Ask the following questions to help students narrow their focus on a topic:

- What do you like to do or make? Think about games you play or things you can make. Would others want to learn how to do this activity?
- Can you explain the activity in a few simple steps?

Remind students to **focus** and **plan** their how-to article about an activity they know how to explain easily.

Minilesson Organization

LA.3.3.1.3 Use organizational strategies to make a plan for writing that includes a main idea

Display **Transparency 19**. Explain that together you will follow Alex N.'s progress as he develops a how-to article. Point out the main idea and details in Alex's Main Idea and Details Chart:

- The main idea is to explain **how to** decorate a bedroom.
- He gives step-by-step directions in a logical order.
- He supports his main idea with clear details, using examples from his own experience.
- He uses time-order words, such as *first*, *next*, and *finally*.

Organize Ideas Ask students to create a Main Idea and Details Chart to plan their own how-to articles. Use Transparency 19 to demonstrate how to organize ideas.

Peer Review

LA.3.3.1 Use prewriting strategies to generate ideas and formulate a plan

Think, Pair, Share Ask students to discuss their Main Idea and Details Charts with partners. Have students identify details on a partner's chart that need to be explained more clearly. Ask volunteers to share how a partner's suggestions helped them.

Flexible Pairing Option Consider encouraging students to partner with someone who has different interests from their own.

Writing Topic

Write a how-to article that explains how to do a certain task or activity. You might write about an activity you did once, such as decorating your room. You might write about an activity you do often, such as making a favorite snack. Be sure to include step-by-step directions and clear details to help your readers understand how to do the activity.

LA.3.4.2.1 Write in informational/expository forms

Transparency 19

Main Idea and Details Chart

Main Idea	Details
How to Decorate Your Bedroom	First, pick a theme for your room. My brother and I picked basketball.
	Look for anything you own that fits the theme. We used an old basketball hoop.
	Next, hang your favorite posters or draw pictures to put up.
	Finally, enjoy your special room!

Unit Writing Transparency 19

Unit Writing Transparency 19

Draft LA.3.3.2 Write a draft

ELL Access for All

Think, Pair, Share Point out on the transparency the ways the author includes his experiences and expresses his enthusiasm. You may want students to briefly think about and then discuss their experiences doing the activity they have chosen. Encourage them to help each other come up with a few examples of their experiences for their stories.

Access for All

Minilesson Main Idea

Display **Transparency 20** and point out the following details in Alex N.'s first draft:

LA.3.3.2.1 Use prewriting plan to develop main idea with supporting details

- When I read this draft, I notice that Alex N. tells his main idea—the **activity** he is going to explain—in the topic sentence of his first paragraph.

LA.3.3.2.2 Organize information through use of time-order words

- He gives **step-by-step directions** for doing the activity.
- He uses **time-order words**, such as *first* and *next*, and the **space-order words** *on top of* to clarify the steps.

LA.3.3.2.1 Use supporting details that describe

- He includes **clear details** from his own experience that describe what to do in each step of the process.

Tell students that Alex will have the chance to revise and proofread his draft in later stages.

LA.3.3.2.1 Use prewriting plan to develop main idea with supporting details

Review Your Main Idea and Details Chart Have students review their Main Idea and Details Charts. Tell them to refer to their charts often as they write to keep their main idea and supporting details in mind.

LA.3.3.2 Write a draft appropriate to topic, audience, purpose

Write the Draft Remind students that their goal in writing a first draft is to get their thoughts on paper. They will have time to revise and proofread their work later. Share the following tips as students begin to write:

LA.3.6.1.1 Organize information for purpose of following multi-step directions

- Write about an activity you like to do. Keep in mind the purpose—to inform—and the audience—classmates.
- Include step-by-step directions for completing the activity.
- Provide clear details as well as time-order and space-order words to guide readers.

Transparency 20

How to Decorate Your Bedroom

By Alex N.

You can have a great time decorating your bedroom. My brother and I doed it. You can do the same thing.

First, choose a theme for your room. Is there anything you love. We both love basketball. Picked basketball as our theme. Look around for anything you own that fits your theme. We found an old basketball hoop and put it on our waste basket. We can take a shot every time we throw something out! We lined up our collection of basketball trading cards on top of our desks.

Next, hang posters on the walls. My posters show basketball stars. You can also make your own pictures. For example, if you like music, you can draw pictures of your favorite musicians.

Unit Writing Transparency 20

Unit Writing Transparency 20

Writer's Resources

Use a Thesaurus

Tell students that one way to vary word choice is to use a thesaurus. Explain that a thesaurus lists words in alphabetical order and offers synonyms and antonyms for each entry. Ask students to think of synonyms for the word *decorate* and list their suggestions on the board.

As students write a draft, they may wish to circle words they would like to replace. During revision, they can consult the thesaurus and find appropriate substitutes.

LA.3.1.6.8 Use knowledge of antonyms and synonyms

Revise LA.3.3.3 Revise draft

Mini Lesson Support

Display **Transparency 21** and discuss how Alex N. revises a good how-to article to make it excellent.

LA.3.3.3.1 Evaluate draft for use of voice

- He adds an exclamation and informal language in the first paragraph to show his enthusiasm. (Voice)

LA.3.3.3.1 Evaluate draft for use of ideas and content

- He uses a friendly tone by addressing readers directly in his first and last paragraphs. (Voice)
- He adds details about hanging pictures, and inserts a missing step about consulting his parents. (Ideas and Content)

LA.3.3.3.1 Evaluate draft for use of word choice

- He adds the time order word *then* and the space-order words *over, top,* and *underneath.* (Word Choice/Organization)

Note that Alex will need to proofread his how-to article to make final corrections.

Guide students to think about the following writing elements as they evaluate and revise their how-to articles.

LA.3.3.3.1 Evaluate draft for use of logical organization

Focus Do you explain all the **steps and details**? Do the details show the sequence of each step?

LA.3.3.3.2 Create clarity by rearranging sentences

Organization Did you tell your main idea in the topic sentence of your first paragraph? Did you present the **step-by-step directions** in a **logical order**? Does each sentence fit into the **flow** of ideas? Do you need to rearrange the order of any sentences so your instructions are easier to follow?

LA.3.3.3 Revise and refine draft for clarity and effectiveness

Support Do the details create interest? Do you address your audience directly with **precise words**? Have you included **time-order** and **space-order words** to help explain the process?

Conventions Do your sentences flow smoothly when you read them aloud? Can you use conjunctions to combine sentences? Did you use linking verbs properly?

Peer Review

LA.3.3.3.4 Apply appropriate tools or strategies to refine the draft

Think, Pair, Share Suggest that students read their revised drafts aloud to partners. Partners can point out which steps were easy to follow and which were more difficult. Have partners discuss revisions to clarify the steps and improve organization.

Flexible Pairing Option Try pairing students who have different learning strategies. For example, pair a visual learner with a kinesthetic learner.

ELL — Access for All

Discuss Sequence Words and Sentence Structures Ask students to identify the sequence words on the transparency. Underline the sentences in which they appear and lead students into realizing that the sentences are commands, or imperative sentences, since they start with a verb instead of a noun. Encourage students to use the sequence words and sentence structure where appropriate in their essays. Provide help as needed.

Transparency 21

How to Decorate Your Bedroom

By Alex N.

You can have a great time decorating your bedroom. My brother and I doed it. [We had fun! You can do the same thing.]

First, choose a theme for your room. Is there anything you love. We both love basketball. Picked basketball as our theme. [Then,] Look around for anything you own that fits your theme. [We went through our closet and desks.] We found an old basketball hoop and put it ~~on~~ [over the top of] our waste basket. We can take a shot every time we throw something out! We lined up our collection of basketball trading cards [underneath the glass] on top of our desks.

Next, [ask your parents if you can] hang posters on the walls. [If they say yes, ask them to help you hang them.] My posters show basketball stars. You can also make your own pictures~~.~~[, using paper, crayons, or markers.] For example, if you like music, you can draw pictures of your favorite musicians. [Finally, enjoy your special room!]

Unit Writing Transparency 21

Unit Writing Transparency 21

Unit 4 Writing Workshop

Speaking and Listening

Have students read their how-to articles aloud. Share these strategies.

SPEAKING STRATEGIES

- Look at your audience directly and use gestures.
- Emphasize time-order and space-order words. If you are using props or illustrations, organize them ahead of time.

LISTENING STRATEGIES

- Listen for directions.
- Ask questions about the directions after the speaker has finished. be ready to summarize.the steps in the process.

LA.3.5.2 Apply listening and speaking strategies

Transparency 22

How to Decorate Your Bedroom

By Alex N.

You can have a great time decorating your bedroom. My brother and I ~~doed~~ [did] it. [We had fun! You can do the same thing.]

First, choose a theme for your room. Is there anything you love~~.~~[?] We both love basketball~~.~~[, so we] ~~P~~picked basketball as our theme. [Then,] ~~L~~look around for anything you own that fits your theme. [We went through our closet and desks.] We found an old basketball hoop and put it ~~on~~ [over the top of] our waste basket. We can take a shot every time we throw something out! We lined up our collection of basketball trading cards [underneath the glass] on top of our desks.

Next, [ask your parents if you can] hang posters on the walls. [If they say yes, ask them to help you hang them.] My posters show basketball stars. You can also make your own pictures~~.~~[, using paper, crayons, or markers.] For example, if you like music, you can draw pictures of your favorite musicians. [Finally, enjoy your special room!]

Unit Writing Transparency 22 ©Macmillan/McGraw-Hill

Unit Writing Transparency 22

Proofread/Edit

LA.3.3.4 Edit and correct draft for standard language conventions

Minilesson Conventions

LA.3.3.4 Edit and correct draft for standard language conventions

LA.3.3.4.3 Edit end punctuation

LA.3.3.4.5 Edit for correct use of subject/verb agreement

Display **Transparency 22** to point out examples of Alex N.'s proofreading corrections.

- He corrects his use of a verb form by changing *doed* to *did*.
- He changes a period to a question mark.
- He corrects a verb so that the subject and verb agree.

Have students read and reread their how-to articles to find and correct usage errors. Review the use of proofreading marks on **Teacher's Resources Book** page 200. Have students apply them as they proofread. Remind students to use correct verb forms and to check for apostrophes in contractions.

LA.3.3.4.6 Edit for correct use of end punctuation for declarative, interrogative, and exclamatory sentences

Peer Review

Think, Pair, Share Have students read a partner's revised article and make any necessary proofreading corrections. Encourage students to check especially for correct punctuation of declarative, exclamatory, interrogatory, and imperative sentences.

TEACHER CONFERENCE

Use the rubric on page 149G to evaluate student writing and help you formulate questions to foster self-assessment. Ask:

- Do you include a main idea and supporting details, time-order words, explanations, and examples?
- Are your steps clearly written and easy to follow?

Publish

LA.3.3.5 Publish final product for intended audience; **LA.3.4.1.2** Employ appropriate format; **LA.3.3.5.3** Share writing with intended audience

Ask students to write their how-to articles in an appropriate format. If they write in cursive, remind them to form letters correctly, to include appropriate spacing between words and sentences, and to indent paragraphs. They can also type a final copy on the computer. Encourage students to publish one of their other weekly writing assignments.

PRESENTATION Invite students to do a demonstration of their how-to activity, using illustrations they create or props they bring to class.

Author's Chair Invite students who have written how-to articles that might be of particular interest to the class to share their articles from the Author's Chair.

Raising Scores

LA.3.3.3.4 Apply appropriate tools or strategies to refine draft

READ AND SCORE

Display **Transparency 23** and tell students to follow along as your or a volunteer read the how-to article aloud. Then have students use their student rubric for Expository: How-to Article on **Teacher's Resource Book** page 204 to assess the writing sample. Guide students to understand that this how-to article is a fair writing sample, which would score only a 3, and that they will work together in groups to improve it.

LA.3.3.3.1 Evaluate draft for use of ideas and content and use of word choice

RAISE THE SCORE

Point out the following shortfalls in the writing sample.

Focus Kelsey's main idea is clear, but she needs to add more details to make the activity easy for readers to follow. (Ideas and Content)

Organization After she explains the first step, there is no clear sequence of steps to follow. Kelsey needs to find a way to make the sequence more clear to her readers. (Organization)

Support The article lacks space-order words to show how to do the task. Inserting space-order words would make the directions more specific. (Support)

LA.3.3.4 Edit and correct draft

Ask students to work in small groups and revise the article to raise the score. Remind them to refer to the student rubric.

SHARE AND COMPARE

Ask groups to share their revised versions with the class, explaining how they improved the writing. Then display **Transparency 24** to show the same how-to article written at an excellent level. Have each group compare its revised version with the transparency. Remind students that although two versions vary, they may both be considered excellent papers. Then have students review their own how-to articles to raise their scores.

Objective

- Revise a how-to article to raise the writing score from a 3 to a 6

CREATE A RUBRIC

Distribute copies of the blank rubric on Teacher's Resource Book page 208. Remind students that the rubric should assess whether the how-to article tells how to do an activity; includes step-by-step directions and clear details; has time-order and space-order words; is logically organized, includes ample development of supporting ideas; and demonstrates a strong command of language and conventions.

Transparency 24

A Place for Treasures

By Kelsey C.

A treasures box is a fun and easy gift to make. I made one for my mom's birthday. She loved it! First, look around the house for a cardboard box. Lots of things come in cardboard boxes. Before you take one, check with your parents to be sure you can have it. They will probably say yes.

After you have your box, find a great picture. It might be a family photograph. It might be a picture you draw or cut out of a magazine. Then, collect things that will make nice decorations. Decorations can include stickers, buttons, beads, shells or even bottle caps.

Next, paste your picture on the lid of the box. Use crayons or markers to write TREASURES BOX underneath the picture. Paste the other decorations around the sides of the box. Finally, give the box to the person you made it for. That person will love it!

Unit Writing Transparency 24

Unit Writing Transparency 24

6-Point Writing Rubric

LA.3.3.3.4 Apply appropriate tools or strategies to refine draft

Use this six-point rubric to assess student writing.

SCORING RUBRIC					
6 Points	5 Points	4 Points	3 Points	2 Points	1 Point
Focus Writing is well focused on the topic and demonstrates a strong sense of command and completeness or wholeness.	**Focus** Writing is focused on the topic and demonstrates a sense of completeness or wholeness.	**Focus** Writing is generally focused on the topic, although some loosely related information may be included.	**Focus** Writing is generally focused on the topic, although irrelevant and extraneous information is included.	**Focus** Writing is somewhat related to the topic, but offers little relevant information.	**Focus** Writing minimally addresses the topic, with little or no relevant information offered.
Organization Writing is logically organized, and includes transitional devices. An interesting variety of sentence structures has been used.	**Organization** Writing has a generally successful organizational pattern. Various sentence structures have been used.	**Organization** An organizational pattern is evident. Lapses in the pattern may occur, however. An effort to vary sentences is evident, but several sentences are of simple construction.	**Organization** An organizational pattern has been attempted, but lapses occur. Some sentence variety appears, but many sentences are of simple construction.	**Organization** An organizational pattern is hardly evident. Most sentences are of simple construction.	**Organization** No organizational pattern is evident. Sentence structure is simple at best.
Support The topic is supported by ample details and ideas. Word choice is intelligent and precise.	**Support** Adequate supporting ideas and details are included. Word choice is adequate but may not be precise.	**Support** Some supporting details and ideas are not fully developed or are not specific. Word choice is generally adequate.	**Support** Some supporting ideas are included, but ideas are not developed. Word choice is limited, predictable, and often vague.	**Support** For the writing related to the topic, few supporting details or examples are offered. Word choice is limited and immature.	**Support** Few if any supporting details appear or are developed; ideas and examples that do appear are irrelevant. Word choice is immature.
Conventions Grammar is correct, as is punctuation and spelling. All sentences are complete, except when fragments are used purposefully.	**Conventions** Punctuation, grammar, and spelling are generally correct. Most sentences are complete, although some fragments appear.	**Conventions** Knowledge of grammar, spelling, and punctuation conventions is evident. Sentence fragments appear.	**Conventions** Although knowledge of grammar, spelling, and punctuation conventions is evident, errors occur. Several sentence fragments appear.	**Conventions** Frequent errors occur in basic grammar, spelling, and punctuation. A number of sentence fragments impede communication.	**Conventions** Frequent errors in grammar, spelling, and punctuation impede communication, as do numerous sentence fragments.

U Writing that is unscorable or unrelated to the topic or is illegible.

Go to **www.macmillanmh.com** for Anchor Papers on Expository Writing: How-to for samples on different writing levels.

Portfolio

Invite students to place their finished how-to articles in their portfolios. Remind students that portfolios should include more than just finished work. Encourage students to review and evaluate their personal collection of work to determine progress and set goals for improvement. They can also discuss their work with teachers and parents/caregivers. Have them jot down ideas for future writing assignments or tell what they learned about explanatory writing to include in their portfolios.

Constructed Response Rubrics

Use these rubrics to assess short and extended responses.

FCAT Reading Short-Response Rubric	
Score	**Description**
2	The student's response demonstrates a thorough understanding of the comprehension skills needed to answer the question. Details and examples are used to support the answer and clearly come from the text.
1	The student's response demonstrates a partial understanding of the comprehension skills needed to answer the question. Some of the support and important details and/or examples are too general or are left out.
0	The student's response demonstrates a complete lack of understanding of the question or the student has left the answer blank.

See Anchor Papers for short responses on the **FCAT Anchor Papers** CD-ROM.

FCAT Reading Extended-Response Rubric	
Score	**Description**
4	The student's response demonstrates a thorough understanding of the comprehension skills needed to answer the question. Details and examples are used to support the answer and clearly come from the text.
3	The student's response demonstrates an understanding of the comprehension skills needed to answer the question. Details and examples used as support are not complete or are not text-based.
2	The student's response demonstrates a partial understanding of the comprehension skills needed to answer the question. Some of the support and important details and/or examples are too general or are left out.
1	The student's response is incomplete and does not demonstrate an understanding of the question.
0	The student's response demonstrates a complete lack of understanding of the question or the student has left the answer blank.

See Anchor Papers for extended responses on the **FCAT Anchor Papers** CD-ROM.

Using a Spreadsheet

Objectives

- Learn about spreadsheet features
- Create a spreadsheet and enter data into it
- Graph the data in a spreadsheet

Materials

- www.macmillanmh.com
- spreadsheet application such as Microsoft Excel®

Vocabulary

spreadsheet a computer program that organizes information in columns and rows

cell a box that contains information and data; the box formed where a column and row meet

row an arrangement of data across a page; identified by numbers

column an arrangement of data down a page; identified by letters

graph an illustration that shows the relationship between different categories of information

ACCESS PRIOR KNOWLEDGE

Discuss with students:

LA.3.6.1.1 Organize information for different purposes
LA.3.4.2.2 Record information related to a topic

- After you gather information or data about something, how can you organize it?
- Does it help to be able to show information on a chart or spreadsheet? What can you do to make your data more interesting?

EXPLAIN

Introduce the lesson vocabulary by writing each word on the board and asking for its definition.

LA.3.1.6 Develop grade-appropriate vocabulary

- Tell students that a **spreadsheet** is a computer program that organizes information, such as numbers.
- A spreadsheet is organized into **cells**, which are boxes that contain information; **rows**, which are groups of cells that run across a page; and **columns**, which are groups of cells that run down a page.
- You can turn the information or data in a spreadsheet into a **graph**. Graphs are illustrations that condense and display information, making it easier to understand.

MODEL LA.3.6.4.2 Use digital tools; LA.3.6.4.1 Use appropriate technologies to achieve a purpose

- Show students how to open a **spreadsheet** program.
- Then show how to create a new spreadsheet by inputting numerical data into the **cells**.
- Show students how to use the **graph** function to create a graph displaying the numerical data.

Technology Has Changed Lives

- Technology has made an impact on everyday life, often making our lives easier and saving us time.
- Computers are convenient for everything from writing documents and graphing information to storing multimedia. Brainstorm with students and make a list of technology they use every day.

LA.3.6.4.1 Use appropriate technologies to achieve a purpose

GUIDED PRACTICE

Have students connect to **www.macmillanmh.com** and go to the Computer Literacy Lesson for Grade 3 Unit 4.

The online practice lesson is an excerpt from SRA TechKnowledge. For information about the full SRA TechKnowledge program, go to **www.sratechknowledge.com**

Remind students always to check with an adult if they're not sure how to use a piece of technology they encounter. If they ignore this, they could break something or injure themselves or others.

Leveled Practice

Approaching Level

Give students a topic and related data. Have students open a spreadsheet application and create a spreadsheet file. Have them practice entering data into the spreadsheet cells.

On Level

Have students think about different types of technology they use. Have them create a spreadsheet to track what the piece of technology is, and how often they use it.

Beyond Level

Have students perform a Web search to find out how much different pieces of technology cost, such as clocks, computers, and robots. Have them enter the average price into a spreadsheet and create a graph.

LA.3.6.4.2 Use digital tools; **LA.3.6.4** Develop essential technology skills

Theme Project Wrap-Up

Research and Inquiry

LA.3.6.2 Use a systematic research process; LA.3.6.2.3 Communicate information in an informational report with visual support

After students complete step 1, step 2, step 3, and step 4 of their project, have them work on the following.

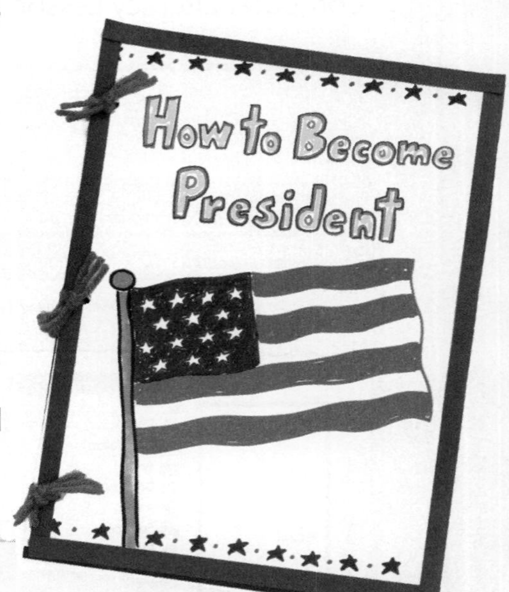

LA.3.6.4.2 Use digital tools to present and publish in a variety of media formats

Step 5 **Create the Presentation** Have students share what they have learned by creating a booklet that shows and tells about reaching their goal. Students should use digital tools, such as multimedia authoring, web tools, photos, illustrations and charts.

Step 6 **Review and Evaluate** Use these questions to help you and students evaluate their research and presentation. Students may revise future presentations based on feedback from you and their peers.

Teacher Checklist

Assess the Research Process

Planning the Project

- ✔ Participated in discussion of key words.
- ✔ Narrowed or broadened research focus.
- ✔ Identified several sources

Doing the Project

- ✔ Used text features and aids to find information within books.
- ✔ Used multiple sources.
- ✔ Took good notes.

Assess the Presentation

Speaking

- ✔ Presented project clearly.
- ✔ Expressed a clear viewpoint.
- ✔ Responded to questions with appropriate information.

Representing

- ✔ Visuals helped illustrate important information.
- ✔ Visuals and text matched.
- ✔ Visuals added interest.

Assess the Listener

Listening

- ✔ Focused on the speaker.
- ✔ Made constructive comments.
- ✔ Clarified the speaker's information or point of view by asking follow-up questions.
- ✔ Connected and related prior experiences and ideas to those of the speaker.

Student Checklist

Research Process

- ✔ Did you examine at least three sources?
- ✔ Did you take good notes?

Presenting

Speaking

- ✔ Did you speak slowly and clearly?
- ✔ Did you list questions to help you focus your research?

Representing

- ✔ Did your words and pictures work together?
- ✔ Did you include labels, captions, or other helpful information?

LA.3.4.2.2 Record information related to a topic; LA.3.4.2.2 Include visual aids as appropriate; LA.3.5.2.2 Use appropriate voice for presentation

LA.3.5.2 Apply listening and speaking strategies; LA.3.3.3.3 Create interest by using resources and reference materials; LA.3.6.2.3 Communicate information in an informational report with visual support; LA.3.1.7.1 Use text features; LA.3.6.2.1 Determine information needed for a search by narrowing or broadening a topic, identify key words

SCORING RUBRIC			
4 Excellent	3 Good	2 Fair	1 Unsatisfactory
The student: • presents the information in a clear and interesting way. • uses visuals that effectively present important information. • may offer sophisticated reflections.	The student: • presents the information in a fairly clear way. • uses visuals that present relevant information. • may offer thoughtful reflections.	The student: • struggles to present the information clearly. • may use few, adequate visuals. • may offer irrelevant reflections.	The student: • may not grasp the task. • may present sketchy information in a disorganized way. • may have extreme difficulty with research.

LA.3.5.2.2 Give an oral presentation

LA.3.6.4.1 Use appropriate available technologies to enhance communication and achieve a purpose

Home-School Connection

Invite family members, other students, and members of the community to the presentation of the projects.

- Introduce each guest by name and describe his or her relationship to the school community. Remind students to respect the age, gender, social position, and cultural traditions of those viewing their presentations.
- Videotape the presentations for family members to borrow or to show at the parent/teacher conferences.
- As part of your character-building feature, remind students to be responsible by doing their best.

Monitoring Progress

Administer the Test

Unit 4 Reading Assessment, pp. 111-144

TESTED SKILLS AND STRATEGIES

COMPREHENSION STRATEGIES AND SKILLS

- Strategies: Make Inferences and Analyze, Monitor Comprehension
- Skills: Compare Characters, Settings, Events; Plot Development; Author's Purpose; Compare and Contrast

VOCABULARY STRATEGIES

- Dictionary
- Word parts
- Context clues

TEXT FEATURES AND STUDY SKILLS

- Diagrams
- Using computer search engines in the media center
- Guide words, headings, and captions (encyclopedia articles)

GRAMMAR, MECHANICS, USAGE

- Linking, helping, and irregular verbs
- Contractions with *not*
- Subject-verb agreement
- End punctuation and complete sentences
- Quotation marks in dialogue
- Correct verb forms

WRITING

- Expository

Use Multiple Assessments for Instructional Planning

To create instructional profiles for your students, look for patterns in the results from any of the following assessments.

Fluency Assessment

Plan appropriate fluency-building activities and practice to help all students achieve the following goal: **82–102 WCPM**.

Running Records

Running Records
LEVELS: REBUS–80
Macmillan/McGraw-Hill

Use the instructional reading level determined by the Running Record calculations for regrouping decisions.

Benchmark Assessment

Administer tests four times a year as an additional measure of both student progress and the effectiveness of the instructional program.

Technology

Assessment Tool

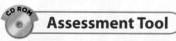

- Administer the **Unit Assessment** electronically.
- Score all tests electronically.
- Available on CD-ROM or online.

Analyze the Data

Use information from a variety of informal and formal assessments, as well as your own judgment, to assist in your instructional planning. Students who consistently score at the lowest end of each range should be evaluated for Intervention. Use the **Diagnostic Assessment** in the Intervention Teacher's Edition.

Diagnose		Prescribe
ASSESSMENTS	**IF...**	**THEN...**
UNIT TEST	0–23 questions correct	Reteach tested skills using the **Additional Lessons** (pp. T1–T11).
FLUENCY ASSESSMENT		
Oral Reading Fluency	73–81 WCPM 0–72 WCPM	Fluency Solutions Evaluate for Intervention.
RUNNING RECORDS	Level 30 or below	Reteach comprehension skills using the **Additional Lessons** (pp. T1–T4). Provide additional Fluency activities.

DIBELS LINK

PROGRESS MONITORING

Use your DIBELS results to inform instruction.

IF...

DIBELS **O**ral **R**eading **F**luency (**DORF**) 0–91

THEN...

Use the Fluency Solutions Audio CD.

TPRI LINK

PROGRESS MONITORING

Use your TPRI scores to inform instruction.

IF...

Graphophonemic Awareness — Still developing

Reading Fluency/Accuracy — Frustrational on Grade 3, Story 1

Reading Comprehension Questions — 0–5 correct

THEN...

Use the Fluency Solutions Audio CD. Use the Comprehension Skills **Additional Lessons** suggestions in the above chart.

READING **Triumphs**

AN INTERVENTION PROGRAM

To place students in the Intervention Program, use the **Diagnostic Assessment** in the Intervention Teacher's Edition.

Glossary

Glossary

INTRODUCTION

Introduce students to the Glossary by reading through the introduction and looking over the pages with them. Encourage the class to talk about what they see.

Words in a glossary, like words in a dictionary, are listed in **alphabetical order.** Point out the **guide words** at the top of each page that tell the first and last words appearing on that page.

ENTRIES

Point out examples of **main entries,** or entry words and entries. Read through a sample entry with the class, identifying each part. Have students note the order in which information is given: entry word(s) with syllable division, pronunciation respelling, part of speech, definition(s), example sentence(s).

Note that if more than one definition is given for a word, the definitions are numbered. Note also the format used for a word that is more than one part of speech.

Review the **parts of speech** by identifying each in a sentence:

Interjection	***article***	***noun***	***conjunction***	***adjective***	***noun***
Wow!	A	dictionary	and	handy	glossary

verb	***adverb***	***pronoun***	***preposition***	***noun***
tell	almost	everything	about	words!

HOMOGRAPHS/HOMOPHONES/HOMONYMS

Point out that some entries are for multiple-meaning words called **homographs.** Homographs have the same spellings but have different origins and meanings, and, in some cases, different pronunciations.

Explain that students should not confuse homographs with **homophones** or **homonyms.** Homophones are words that have the same pronunciation but have different spellings and meanings. Homonyms are words that have the same pronunciation and spelling but have different meanings. Provide students with examples.

PRONUNCIATION KEY

Explain the use of the pronunciation key (either the short key, at the bottom of every other page, or the long key, at the beginning of the Glossary). Demonstrate the difference between primary stress and secondary stress by pronouncing a word with both. Pronounce the words both correctly and incorrectly to give students a clearer understanding of the proper pronunciations.

WORD HISTORY

The Word History feature explains the **etymology** of select words. Explain to students that etymology is the history of a word from its origin to its present form. A word's etymology explains which language it comes from and what changes have occurred in its spelling and/or meaning. Many English words are derivatives of words from other languages, such as Latin or Greek. Derivatives are formed from base or root words. Many everyday words have interesting and surprising stories behind them. Note that word histories can help us remember the meanings of difficult words.

Allow time for students to further explore the Glossary and make their own discoveries.

Glossary

What Is a Glossary?

A Glossary can help you find the **meanings** of words in this book that you may not know. The words in the Glossary are listed in **alphabetical order**. **Guide words** at the top of each page tell you the first and last words on the page.

Each word is divided into syllables. The way to pronounce the word is given next. You can understand the pronunciation respelling by using the **pronunciation key** on page 409. A shorter key appears at the bottom of every other page. When a word has more than one syllable, a dark accent mark (´) shows which syllable is stressed. In some words, a light accent mark (´) shows which syllable has a less heavy stress. Sometimes an entry includes a second meaning for the word.

Guide Words

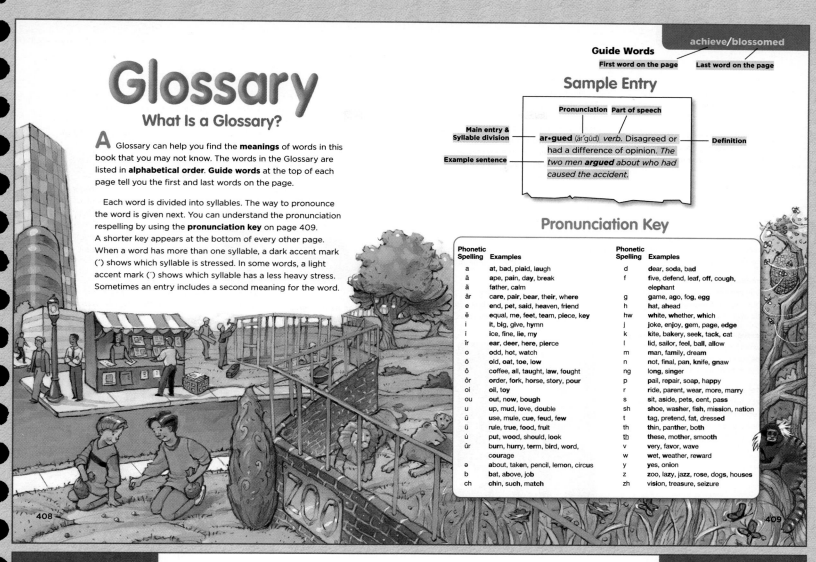

First word on the page — Last word on the page

Sample Entry

Main entry & Syllable division — Pronunciation — Part of speech — Definition — Example sentence

ar•gued (är´gūd) *verb.* Disagreed or had a difference of opinion. *The two men **argued** about who had caused the accident.*

Pronunciation Key

Phonetic Spelling	Examples	Phonetic Spelling	Examples
a	at, bad, plaid, laugh	d	dear, soda, bad
ā	ape, pain, day, break	f	five, defend, leaf, off, cough, elephant
ä	father, calm	g	game, ago, fog, egg
âr	care, pair, bear, their, where	h	hat, ahead
e	end, pet, said, heaven, friend	hw	white, whether, which
ē	equal, me, feet, team, piece, key	j	joke, enjoy, gem, page, edge
i	it, big, give, hymn	k	kite, bakery, seek, tack, cat
ī	ice, fine, lie, my	l	lid, sailor, feel, ball, allow
îr	ear, deer, here, pierce	m	man, family, dream
o	odd, hot, watch	n	not, final, pan, knife, gnaw
ō	old, oat, toe, low	ng	long, singer
ô	coffee, all, taught, law, fought	p	pail, repair, soap, happy
ôr	order, fork, horse, story, pour	r	ride, parent, wear, more, marry
oi	oil, toy	s	sit, aside, pets, cent, pass
ou	out, now, bough	sh	shoe, washer, fish, mission, nation
u	up, mud, love, double	t	tag, pretend, fat, dressed
ū	use, mule, cue, feud, few	th	thin, panther, both
ü	rule, true, food, fruit	t͟h	these, mother, smooth
ù	put, wood, should, look	v	very, favor, wave
ûr	burn, hurry, term, bird, word, courage	w	wet, weather, reward
ə	about, taken, pencil, lemon, circus	y	yes, onion
b	bat, above, job	z	zoo, lazy, jazz, rose, dogs, houses
ch	chin, such, match	zh	vision, treasure, seizure

Aa

a·chieve (ə chēv´) *verb.* To do or carry out successfully. *Did Thomas **achieve** his goal of cleaning his desk before the bell rang?*

ap·pli·an·ces (ə plī´əns əz) *plural noun.* Small machines or devices that have particular uses, such as toasters, refrigerators, and washing machines. *The store was crowded because of the sale on kitchen **appliances**.*

ar·chi·tects (är´ki tekts´) *plural noun.* People who design buildings and supervise their construction. *A group of **architects** showed up at the empty lot and began planning the building they wanted to make there.*

ar·gued (är´gūd) *verb.* Disagreed or had a difference of opinion. *The two men **argued** about who had caused the accident.*

art·ist's (är´tists) *possessive noun.* Belonging to a person who is skilled in painting, music, literature, or any other form of art. *The chef uses an **artist's** touch when he puts the toppings on his famous desserts.*

au·to·mat·i·cal·ly (ô´tə ma´ti klē) *adverb.* Gets done without a person's control. *Digestion takes place in the body **automatically**.*

ax·is (ak´sis) *noun.* A real or imaginary straight line through the center of a spinning object. *Earth spins on its imaginary **axis**.*

Bb

batch·es (bach´əz) *plural noun.* Groups of things prepared or gathered together. *Tracey and Darryl made several **batches** of cookies for the bake sale at the library.*

beamed (bēmd) *verb.* **1.** Shined brightly. *The sun **beamed** down on the field.* **2.** Smiled brightly. *Marleigh **beamed** when she thought about the joke Raffi told yesterday.*

blos·somed (blos´əmd) *verb.* Grew or developed. *The student kept practicing until she **blossomed** into a wonderful violinist.*

boast·ing (bōs´ting) *verb.* Talking with too much pride. *Everyone got annoyed when Lisa started **boasting** about her new bicycle.*

busi·ness (biz´nis) *noun.* **1.** The work a person does to earn a living. *Kenneth worked in the fashion **business** for eight years.* **2.** The buying and selling of things; trade. *The kite shop does good **business** in the summer.*

Cc

cap·ture (kap´chər) *verb.* To catch and hold a person, animal, or thing. *The park rangers were trying to **capture** the bear that was roaming the picnic area.*

clumps (klumps) *plural noun.* Groups or clusters. *After Jennifer went swimming, she had **clumps** of knots in her long hair.*

com·bine (kəm bīn´) *verb.* To join together; unite. We will ***combine** eggs, flour, and milk to make batter for pancakes.*

com·mu·ni·ty (kə mū´ni tē) *noun.* **1.** A group of people who live together in the same place. *Our **community** voted to build a new library.* **2.** A group of people who share a common interest. *The scientific **community** is involved in important research projects.*

con·struc·tion (kən struk´shən) *noun.* The act or process of building something. *It was interesting to watch the **construction** of our town's new grocery store.*

con·tain (kən tān´) *verb.* To hold inside. *The storage boxes **contain** clothes.*

con·ver·sa·tion (kon´vər sā´shən) *noun.* Talk between two or more people. *It was difficult to have a **conversation** with Jerry because of all the loud construction noises.*

at; āpe; fär; câre; end; mē; it; īce; pîerce; hot; ōld; sông; fôrk; oil; out; up; ūse; rüle; pùll; tûrn; chin; sing; shop; thin; t͟his; hw in white; zh in treasure.

The symbol ə stands for the unstressed vowel sound in about, taken, pencil, lemon, and circus.

crate (krāt) *noun.* A box made of pieces of wood. *The grocery store worker emptied the **crate** filled with grapes onto the fruit stand.*

crouch (krouch) *verb.* To stoop or bend low with the knees bent. *The firefighters had to **crouch** to pick up the hose.*

Dd

de·clared (di klârd´) *verb.* Stated strongly and firmly. *They **declared** that they were right and nothing would change their minds.*

de·mand (di mand´) *noun.* An urgent requirement or need. *Katie knew there was a **demand** for blankets at the dog shelter.*

de·serve (di zûrv´) *verb.* To have a right to something. *I believe I **deserve** to be on the soccer team because I practiced after school and on weekends.*

de·ter·mi·na·tion (di tûr´mə nā´shən) *noun.* A firm purpose. *Miguel's **determination** made him study very hard to get the best test score in the class.*

di·rec·tions (di rek´shənz) *plural noun.* **1.** Lines leading to a place or point. *The class decided to walk in two different **directions**: the boys headed for the lake, and the girls went toward the woods.* **2.** Orders or instructions on how to do something or how to act. *Follow the **directions** on the package to cook the soup.*

dis·ap·pear (dis´ə pîr´) *verb.* To stop existing or become extinct. *Elephants began to **disappear** because so many people hunted them for their tusks.*

dis·pute (di spūt´) *noun.* A disagreement. *I had a **dispute** with my sister about her messiness.*

down·town (doun´toun´) *adjective.* Located in the main part or business district of a town. *My mother works in the **downtown** office.*

Ee

en·clo·sure (en klō´zhər) *noun.* A place that is surrounded by a fence or wall on all sides. *The animals were kept in an **enclosure** until their owners came to pick them up.*

e·quip·ment (i kwip´mənt) *noun.* Anything that is provided for a special purpose or use. *The firefighters showed the class all the different **equipment** they have and how it is used.*

es·cape (e skāp´) *verb.* To become free. *The students wanted the bell to ring so they could **escape** the heat of the classroom.*

ex·act (eg zakt´) *adjective.* Very accurate. *I need to know the **exact** time because I can't be one minute late.*

ex·isted (eg zis´təd) *verb.* Was real. *Tyler couldn't believe that a movie theater once **existed** where his house now stood.*

Ff

fab·ric (fab´rik) *noun.* A material made from fibers, such as cotton, silk, or nylon. *My mother bought the **fabric** to make our costumes.*

Word History

Fabric has a complicated history, from the Latin *faber*, meaning "workman," and *fabrica*, "craft" or "workshop," to the Old French *fabrique*, and finally the Middle English *fabryke*, which meant "something constructed."

fled (fled) *verb.* Ran away from something. *Many families **fled** the hurricane coming toward them.*

Gg

gift (gift) *noun.* Something given to someone, such as a present. *Nigel received a special **gift** on his birthday.*

grace (grās) *noun.* Beautiful movement, or style. *The dancer moved with **grace** on the stage.*

at; āpe; fär; câre; end; mē; it; īce; pîerce; hot; ōld; sông; fôrk; oil; out; up; ūse; rüle; pu̇ll; tûrn; chin; sing; shop; thin; <u>th</u>is; hw in white; zh in treasure.

The symbol ə stands for the unstressed vowel sound in about, taken, pencil, lemon, and circus.

grown·ups (grōn´ups) *plural noun.* Adults. *The children were playing games while the **grownups** prepared the dessert.*

grum·bled (grum´bəld) *verb.* Complained in a low voice. *The class **grumbled** when the teacher gave them a lot of homework to do over the holiday.*

Hh

harm·ing (härm´ing) *verb.* Doing damage to or hurting. *The construction company was told that it was **harming** the environment because it cut down so many trees.*

har·vest·ing (här´vis ting) *verb.* Gathering a crop when it is ripe. *Our town farmers begin **harvesting** pumpkins in August.*

his·tor·i·cal (hi stôr´i kəl) *adjective.* Having to do with history. *This book contains **historical** information, such as how our town began and a list of its leaders.*

hives (hīvz) *plural noun.* Boxes or houses for bees to live in. *We were warned about the bees and to stay away from the **hives** in the park.*

Ii

im·age (im´ij) *noun.* A picture of a person or thing. *I still have an **image** in my head of the beautiful sunset at the beach.*

Word History

Image comes from the Latin *imago*, or *imitari*, "to imitate."

in·di·vid·u·al (in´də vij´ü əl) *adjective.* Single; separate. *The coffee was served with **individual** packets of sugar.*

in·gre·di·ent (in grē´dē ənt) *noun.* Any one of the parts used in a recipe or mixture. *The baker was missing one **ingredient** for making a cake.*

in·ter·rupt·ed (in´tə rup´təd) *verb.* Broke in upon or stopped something or someone. *A loud car alarm **interrupted** our teacher from speaking.*

in·ter·viewed (in´tər vūd´) *verb.* Obtained information from someone by asking questions. *Last night my favorite actress was **interviewed** on television.*

in·volved (in volvd´) *verb.* Taken up with. *Many students said that they wanted to become **involved** in raising money for the park.*

Kk

kind·heart·ed (kīnd´här´tid) *adjective.* Having or showing a friendly or gentle nature. *The **kindhearted** woman put food outside her house for birds to eat during the winter.*

Ll

leak·y (lē´kē) *adjective.* Having a hole or small opening that water, light, or air can pass through. *The **leaky** hose caused a big puddle whenever I tried to water the plants.*

lone·some (lōn´səm) *adjective.* Not often visited by people; deserted. *The **lonesome** house in the swamp was a sad sight.*

luck·i·est (luk´ē est) *adjective.* Having or bringing the most good luck. *Of all the contest winners, James was the **luckiest**; he won the grand prize.*

Mm

mag·nif·i·cent (mag nif´ə sənt) *adjective.* Very beautiful and grand. *We walked through the **magnificent** garden and admired all the beautiful flowers.*

mar·mo·sets (mär´mə zets´) *plural noun.* Small tropical monkeys with claws, soft thick fur, tufted ears, and long tails. *Michael enjoyed watching the **marmosets** at play.*

mass (mas) *noun.* The amount of matter in an object. *The bowling ball's **mass** was greater than the marble's.*

mas·ter·piece (mas´tər pēs´) *noun.* **1.** A great work of art. *The painting* Mona Lisa *by Da Vinci is thought to be a **masterpiece**.* **2.** Something done with great skill. *Her plan to surprise her brother on his birthday was a **masterpiece**.*

mat·ter (mat´ər) *noun.* Anything that takes up space and has weight. *Water, clay, rocks, and trees are all examples of **matter**.*

at; āpe; fär; câre; end; mē; it; īce; pîerce; hot; ōld; sông; fôrk; oil; out; up; ūse; rüle; pu̇ll; tûrn; chin; sing; shop; thin; <u>th</u>is; hw in white; zh in treasure.

The symbol ə stands for the unstressed vowel sound in about, taken, pencil, lemon, and circus.

meas·ure·ments (mezh′ər mənts) *plural noun.* The sizes, weights, or temperatures of things. *Callie used a ruler to find the* ***measurements*** *of her bookshelf.*

me·chan·i·cal (mə kan′i kəl) *adjective.* Relating to machinery or tools. *Duane bought a* ***mechanical*** *piggy bank that sorts his change for him.*

Nn

na·tive (nā′tiv) *adjective.* Originally living or growing in a region or country. *The cheetah is* ***native*** *to sub-Saharan Africa.*

news·pa·per (nüz′pā′pər) *noun.* A publication printed on sheets of paper that contains news and is published every day or every week. *Many people read the* ***newspaper*** *every morning on the way to work.*

numb (num) *adjective.* Lacking feelings. *The members of the basketball team were* ***numb*** *after they lost the championship game.*

Oo

of·fi·cial (ə fish′əl) *adjective.* Coming from or approved by authority. *The referee announced the* ***official*** *score of the basketball game.*

o·rig·i·nal (ə rij′ə nəl) *adjective.* **1.** Made, done, thought of, or used for the first time; new. *There are not many* ***original*** *ideas coming out of Hollywood anymore.* **2.** Able to do, make, or think of something new or different. *One doesn't need to be an* ***original*** *thinker to watch television.* **3.** Relating to or belonging to the origin or beginning of something; first. *The* ***original*** *owners moved out of the house years ago.*

own·ers (ō′nərz) *plural noun.* People who possess something. *Sarah was very proud that the knitting shop was doing well because she was one of the* ***owners***.

Pp

per·son·al·i·ty (pûr′sə nal′i tē) *noun.* All the qualities, traits, habits, and behavior of a person. *It was in her* ***personality*** *to always be cheerful.*

pitch (pich) *noun.* How high or low a sound is. *Melanie sang the parts of the song that were in a high* ***pitch***.

pit·i·ful (pit′i fəl) *adjective.* Making people feel sorrow for. *The boy standing outside in the cold without his coat looked* ***pitiful***.

pos·ses·sions (pə zesh′ənz) *plural noun.* Things that are owned by someone. *Many of his* ***possessions*** *were stolen by thieves who broke into his house.*

pow·ered (pou′ərd) *verb.* Filled with the energy to function or operate. *The toy truck was* ***powered*** *by batteries.*

pride (prīd) *noun.* **1.** A person's feeling of self-respect, dignity, and self-worth. *Although Rhonda did not score an A in science class, she never lost her sense of* ***pride***. **2.** A company of lions. *The antelope were startled by a small* ***pride*** *moving in their direction.*

pro·duce (prə düs′ *for verb;* prod′üs *for noun*) **1.** *verb. To make or create something. The class was asked to* ***produce*** *a play about the signing of the Declaration of Independence.* **2.** *noun.* Farm products, such as fruits and vegetables. *Mom likes to buy fresh* ***produce*** *from the farmers' market.*

prop·er·ties (prop′ər tēz) *plural noun.* Qualities or characteristics that can be seen or measured. *Mass and temperature are* ***properties*** *of matter.*

pro·tect (prə tekt′) *verb.* To defend from harm. *Mr. Trang put on a heavy overcoat to* ***protect*** *himself from the cold.*

pur·chased (pûr′chəst) *verb.* Got something by paying money for it. *Lester's mother* ***purchased*** *a bicycle to give to him for his birthday.*

at; āpe; fär; câre; end; mē; it; īce; pîerce; hot; ōld; sông; fôrk; oil; out; up; ūse; rüle; pu̇ll; tûrn; chin; sing; shop; thin; <u>th</u>is; hw in white; zh in treasure. The symbol ə stands for the unstressed vowel sound in about, taken, pencil, lemon, and circus.

Qq

quar·rel·ing (kwôr′əl ing) *verb.* Having a heated argument. *My uncles were always* ***quarreling*** *about which baseball team was better.*

Rr

re·build (rē bild′) *verb.* To build again or repair. *The farmer wanted to* ***rebuild*** *his shed after the storm blew it down.*

rec·i·pes (res′ə pēz′) *plural noun.* Lists of ingredients and instructions for making something to eat or drink. *My mother has many cookie* ***recipes***.

re·quire·ments (ri kwīr′mənts) *plural noun.* Things that are necessary; demands or needs. *There were certain* ***requirements*** *the students had to meet before they could move on to the next grade.*

re·search (ri sûrch′ *or* rē′sûrch′) *noun.* A careful study or investigation in order to learn facts. *A lot of* ***research*** *had to be done before the paper could be written.*

Word History

The Old French *recercher*, which means "to search closely," is where the word **research** comes from.

re·treats (ri trēts′) **1.** *verb. Goes back or withdraws, as from danger. A tigress* ***retreats*** *when it realizes it is outnumbered.* **2.** *plural noun.* Places to go to for safety, peace, and comfort. *Staying in* ***retreats*** *was a helpful way for Bob to leave his problems behind him.*

ro·tates (rō′tāts) *verb.* Turns around. *Marissa's ballet teacher* ***rotates*** *perfectly on her toes.*

ru·ined (rü′ind) *verb.* Damaged greatly or harmed. *The flood* ***ruined*** *all our carpets in the basement.*

Ss

school·house (skül′hous′) *noun.* A building used as a school. *On Friday night, a dance was held at the* ***schoolhouse***.

scram·bled (skram′bəld) *verb.* Moved or climbed quickly. *We all* ***scrambled*** *to the finish line in the three-legged race.*

screamed (skrēmd) *verb.* Made a loud cry or sound. *The woman* ***screamed*** *when she saw her baby crawling close to the pool.*

seized (sēzd) *verb.* Took hold of or grabbed. *The guard* ***seized*** *the money out of the thief's hand.*

sep·a·rate (sep′ə rāt′) *verb.* To set apart or place apart. *After the big fight, we had to* ***separate*** *the cat and the dog and put them in different rooms.*

ser·vi·ces (sûr′vis əz) *plural noun.* A variety of tasks or acts done for others, usually for pay. *The car wash provided other* ***services***, *such as dusting and vacuuming inside the car.*

shal·low (shal′ō) *adjective.* Not deep. *All the young children were playing in the* ***shallow*** *part of the pool.*

shel·ter (shel′tər) *noun.* Something that covers or protects. *Once it began to rain, the group immediately looked for* ***shelter***.

should·n't (shu̇d′ənt) *verb.* Contraction of *should not. You* ***shouldn't*** *run with scissors in your hands.*

shud·dered (shud′ərd) *verb.* Trembled suddenly. *The house* ***shuddered*** *during the earthquake.*

side·walks (sīd′wôks) *plural noun.* Paths by the side of the street or road, usually made of cement. *Vladimir and Bill were paid to shovel snow off the* ***sidewalks*** *around their apartment building.*

at; āpe; fär; câre; end; mē; it; īce; pîerce; hot; ōld; sông; fôrk; oil; out; up; ūse; rüle; pu̇ll; tûrn; chin; sing; shop; thin; <u>th</u>is; hw in white; zh in treasure. The symbol ə stands for the unstressed vowel sound in about, taken, pencil, lemon, and circus.

Glossary

sleek (slēk) *adjective.* Looking healthy and well cared for. *Everyone admired the **sleek** poodle at the dog show.*

sleep·y (slē'pē) *adjective.* Ready for or needing sleep. *After a big dinner, Raymond felt very **sleepy** and sat down on the couch.*

slo·gan (slō'gən) *noun.* A phrase, statement, or motto. *Today our teacher asked us to think up a **slogan** for our science club.*

sphere (sfîr) *noun.* A round, 3-dimensional shape; a globe. *Each planet is a **sphere** that revolves around the sun.*

sprout (sprout) **1.** *verb.* To begin to grow. *Maria was pleased to see that the sunflower seeds she planted were finally beginning to **sprout**.* **2.** *noun.* A new growth on a plant; a bud or shoot. *There was a **sprout** on the plant that would soon become a leaf.*

stor·age (stôr'ij) *noun.* A place for keeping things for future use. *Mr. Chen used his garage mainly for **storage**.*

strolled (strōld) *verb.* Walked in a slow, relaxed manner. *The tourists **strolled** through the streets looking at all the big buildings and store windows.*

struc·tures (struk'chərz) *plural noun.* Things that are built, such as buildings. *From so far away, the **structures** on the horizon were hard to make out.*

Word History

Structure comes from the Latin word *struere*, which means "to construct."

stur·dy (stûr'dē) *adjective.* Strong or solid. *The new table is very **sturdy**, and we are able to put many heavy boxes on it.*

sup·ply (sə plī') *noun.* An amount of something needed or available for use. *We had a **supply** of candles and batteries in the closet in case of an emergency.*

sway (swā) *verb.* To move or swing back and forth or side to side. *The trees began to gently **sway** in the tropical wind.*

Tt

tast·y (tās'tē) *adjective.* Having a pleasant flavor. *The freshly baked brownies were very **tasty**.*

tem·per·a·ture (tem'pər ə chər *or* tem'prə chər) *noun.* How hot or cold something is. *Jen ate the soup once the **temperature** was just right.*

tend (tend) *verb.* To look after or take care of something. *It was the farmer's job to **tend** to the cows and chickens and make sure they had enough food.*

ther·mom·e·ter (thər mom'i tər) *noun.* A device for measuring temperature. *The doctor used a thermometer to measure my body temperature.*

thrilled (thrild) *verb.* Filled with pleasure or excitement. *The team members were **thrilled** when they heard their best player was not badly injured.*

tools (tülz) *plural noun.* Things that help you do work. *Dad's **tools** were stored in a big box in the garage.*

tour (tůr) *noun.* A trip or journey in which many places are visited or many things are seen. *The guide led a **tour** through the museum and explained all the famous artwork.*

trad·ers (trā'dərz) *plural noun.* People who buy and sell things as a business. *The **traders** went to the settlers to sell them blankets and clothes.*

at; āpe; fär; câre; end; mē; it; īce; pîerce; hot; ōld; sông; fôrk; oil; out; up; ūse; rüle; půll; tûrn; chin; sing; shop; thin; this; hw in white; zh in treasure.

The symbol ə stands for the unstressed vowel sound in about, taken, pencil, lemon, and circus.

Vv

vi·bra·tions (vī brā'shənz) *plural noun.* Quick movements back and forth. *Jordan plucked the guitar string and watched the **vibrations**.*

vol·un·teers (vol'ən tîrz') *plural noun.* People who offer to do things by choice and often without pay. *Several **volunteers** showed up to help clean up the park and paint the fence.*

Ww

wailed (wāld) *verb.* Made a long and sad cry, especially to show grief or pain. *The baby **wailed** when she dropped her toy.*

waves (wāvz) *plural noun.* Curves or ripples. *Our ears pick up sound **waves** and turn them into sounds in our brain.*

Yy

ya·poks (yə poks') *plural noun.* Tropical aquatic opossums with dense fur, webbed feet, and long tails. *The young **yapoks** huddled together beneath the shade of the palm tree.*

yearned (yûrnd) *verb.* Felt a strong and deep desire. *The school team **yearned** for the chance to play.*

Additional Lessons and Resources

CONTENTS

Objective: Demonstrate understanding of compare and contrast
LA.3.2.1.2 Identify plot, character/character development and setting; LA.3.1.7.5 Identify the text structure an author uses

Compare Characters/Compare and Contrast

Intervention/Remediation Compare Characters, Settings, Events

Materials **Student Book:** *Cook-A-Doodle-Doo!* pp. 14–37

Review Ask: *How is a window like a door? How is a window different from a door?*

Explain Say: *When we compare things, we tell how they are alike. When we contrast things, we tell how they are different.* Read page 21 aloud. Ask students to compare and contrast a cookbook and *Cook-A-Doodle-Doo!*

Model Say: *A cookbook and* Cook-A-Doodle-Doo! *are both books. A cookbook is nonfiction.* Cook-A-Doodle-Doo! *is fiction.*

Guided Practice Read aloud page 24. Ask: *How is the way that Iguana measures flour different from the way that Rooster measures flour?* Fill in a Venn diagram to show the differences.

Constructive Feedback

If students are unable to understand the concept of compare and contrast, ask: *What tool does Iguana use to measure the flour? What tool does Rooster use?*

Practice Have students reread pages 19–20 to compare and contrast Cat and Pig.

Constructive Feedback

If students have trouble comparing and contrasting, review the definitions and have students restate them in their own words. Then have students complete cloze sentences such as: *Both Cat and Pig are ______. Cat says _____, but Pig says ______.*

Intervention/Remediation Compare and Contrast

Explain Display this paragraph: *Ted and Joe are similar in many ways. They both like baseball and both play on a team. Ted likes to read books on baseball. Joe collects baseball cards.* Read the paragraph aloud with students. Tell them that they will compare and contrast the two boys and look for signal words: *similar, alike, different.*

Guided Practice Draw a Venn diagram with labels *Ted* and *Joe*. Fill in the diagram as you ask: *What are the signal words?* (similar, like, different) *How are the two boys alike?* (They like baseball. They play on a team.) Ask: *How are they different?* (Ted reads baseball books; Joe collects cards.)

Practice Have students draw Venn diagrams. Have them label one oval *Jenn* and the other *Tina*. Show them photographs of two girls of different ages, one labeled *Jenn* and one *Tina*, each doing a different activity. Have students compare the two girls using Venn diagrams. Visual

Act It Out

Materials baseball hats and paper party hats

Explain Students will show how the two hats are alike and different by using pantomime/acting.

Guided Practice Have students work in pairs to decide how the ways the two hats are used are similar and different. Have them share their ideas in Venn diagrams. Then have each pair pantomime or show one way these hats' uses are similar and one way their uses are different. Kinesthetic/Visual

For five additional consecutive lessons on this skill, use the three lessons above. Go to **www.macmillanmh.com** for two additional lessons.

Comprehension

Objective: Understand plot development by drawing conclusions
LA.3.1.7.3 Determine implied inference

Plot Development: Draw Conclusions

Intervention/Remediation

Materials **Student Book:** *Seven Spools of Thread*, pp. 50–71

Review Ask: *If I come inside wearing a dripping wet raincoat, what would you think the weather is?*

Explain Say: *When you put two story facts together with experience, you are drawing a conclusion. Drawing conclusions can help you understand the development of the plot.* Read aloud page 64 and have students draw a conclusion about why the villagers are excited about the cloth.

Model Say: *When the brothers spread out their cloth, the text says that it was like a rainbow and had unusual patterns. I think the villagers are excited because the cloth was beautiful and unusual.*

Guided Practice Read page 67 aloud. Ask: *Why do the brothers ask for a bag of gold? What task were the brothers given at the beginning?*

Constructive Feedback

If students have difficulty drawing conclusions, ask: *What would the brothers need gold for? Why might you need money?*

Practice Read aloud the text on page 69. Have students draw a conclusion about why the oldest brother suggested that the brothers teach the poorest villagers to make cloth like theirs.

Constructive Feedback

If students have trouble drawing conclusions, review the definition. Ask: *How did the brothers earn money? How will poor villagers benefit from making cloth?*

Plot Development

Explain Write this paragraph on the board: *It was Angie's first day at her new school. As she sat down, her pencils rolled off the desk and clattered all over the floor. Angie turned bright red. She looked down as she picked up the pencils.* Tell students they will draw conclusions to understand the development of the plot.

Guided Practice Read the paragraph aloud then ask: *Why did Angie turn bright red?* (She was embarrassed.) *Why did she looked down?* (She didn't want to look at people.) *Why is Angie so embarrassed?* (It's her first day. She may not know anyone.) Auditory

Practice Write this paragraph on the board: *Rob threw his test paper on the kitchen counter and flung open the refrigerator. He dug around and then slammed it shut. "Why isn't there ever anything I like! This just hasn't been my day!"* Read the paragraph aloud. Then ask: *How well do you think Rob did on his test? How did you decide?* (He probably did poorly; he seems upset.)

What's My Job? Riddles

Materials pencils, paper

Explain Tell students they will create riddles about people who have different jobs so their classmates can draw conclusions.

Guided Practice Share the following riddle: *I take people where they want to go. I drive a vehicle, which stops and starts all day. People wait for me outside. What am I?* (a bus driver) Have partners write job description riddles. Auditory

For five additional consecutive lessons on this skill, use the three lessons above. Go to **www.macmillanmh.com** for two additional lessons.

Comprehension

Objective: Understand author's purpose

LA.3.1.7.2 Identify author's purpose

Author's Purpose

Intervention/Remediation

Materials **Student Book:** *Here's My Dollar,* pp. 94–105; ads or editorials from a magazine or newspaper

Review Remind students authors write to entertain, inform, or explain.

Explain Say: *As I read, I try to identify the author's purpose to evaluate what the author wrote.* Read aloud the letter on page 97. Ask why Angel wrote it.

Model Say: *I think that Angel is trying to explain why people should contribute to the Chaffee Zoo. Angel gave reasons why she was giving money. She even came up with a slogan.*

Guided Practice Have students look at the picture on page 104. Read the caption aloud. Ask: *Why did the author include this picture?*

Constructive Feedback

If students have trouble identifying the author's purpose, ask: *Does this selection teach something? Does this try to get you to do or think something? Is this an entertaining story?*

Practice Choose a newspaper or magazine ad or previously read nonfiction and fiction selections. Have students summarize each selection and identify the author's purpose.

Constructive Feedback

If students are unable to identify purpose, have them look for facts or entertaining parts or opinions.

Author's Purpose

Explain Write the following on the board: *Many people wear helmets when they ride bikes. Falling from a bike can be dangerous. A helmet can protect a rider's head.* Read the text with students. Tell students they will determine the author's purpose.

Guided Practice Read the paragraph and ask the following: *Does the author give facts and information?* (Yes.) *Why does the author present this information?* (to give the reader information) *What is the author's purpose?* (to inform) Auditory

Practice Read the following paragraph aloud and have students listen for the author's purpose: *Harborplace is a wonderful place to vacation. There are over 100 shops and many seafood restaurants. During the day, you don't have to go to the beach. You can enjoy a water slide or miniature golf. Every Friday night, there are fireworks.* Ask: *What is the author's purpose?* (to inform)

Slogans for a Cause

Materials drawing paper, markers

Explain Remind students that Gary Soto wrote about Angel to inform readers about the important thing that she did.

Guided Practice Have students think of people who have done important things. Have them each draw a picture of a person doing that important thing and then write sentences below the illustration giving facts and details that show the viewer/reader why that person is important. Visual

For five additional consecutive lessons on this skill, use the three lessons above. Go to **www.macmillanmh.com** for two additional lessons.

Comprehension

Objective: Make and confirm predictions to understand plot development
LA.3.1.7.1 Use text features to make predictions; **LA.3.1.7.8** Predict to repair comprehension

Plot Development: Make Predictions

Intervention/Remediation

Materials **Student Book:** *My Very Own Room*, pp. 116–137

Review Aim a piece of paper toward the garbage. Ask students to predict what you might do.

Explain Say: *Good readers make predictions or guesses about what might happen later in a story. They use clues in the text and illustrations and their own experiences. Making predictions can help readers understand the development of the plot.* Display pages 116–117 and talk about clues that could help make predictions.

Model Say: *I see a girl with five boys peeking at her. The title is* My Very Own Room. *I predict it will be about the girl getting her own room.*

Guided Practice Read aloud the first paragraph on page 130. Ask students to predict what the girl will do with the Blue Chip stamps.

Constructive Feedback

If students have trouble making predictions, ask: *What do you do with something that is like money?*

Practice Have students read page 133, and use a Prediction Chart to predict what thing the girl's room is missing.

Constructive Feedback

If students still have trouble, remind them to look for clues that tell what someone might do, or how something might happen.

Plot Development

Explain Write the following on the board: *Bob and Fred went hiking. Near the top of the hill, they found a cave. It looked very dark and damp inside. The two boys stood outside the cave. "Go on in," Fred said. Bob hesitated.* Tell students they will read the text and make a prediction to help them understand the development of the plot.

Guided Practice Read the text aloud and have students predict what will happen next and tell what clues they used. Then write this and read it aloud: *Bob said, "I don't think it's safe. I don't think it's a good idea to go inside. Fred said, "I agree. Let's hike a bit farther up the trail."* Auditory

Practice Have students compare their predictions with what happened in the story. Then have them revise their predictions.

Story Board

Materials paper, crayons or colored pencils

Explain Tell students they will practice predicting story events and outcomes with partners. They will draw pictures to show what happens next in a story.

Guided Practice Write story starters on strips for pairs of students. Have each pair create a storyboard, or a series of pictures, that continues the story and tells how the story ends. As students present their storyboards to the class, have them show only one frame at a time to give classmates time to make predictions.
Visual

For five additional consecutive lessons on this skill, use the three lessons above. Go to **www.macmillanmh.com** for two additional lessons.

Objective: Understand and use idioms
LA.3.1.6.10 Determine meanings using a dicitonary and digital tools

Idioms

Intervention/Remediation

Materials **Student Book:** *Cook-A-Doodle-Doo!* pp. 14–37

Review Tell students that the phrase *a piece of cake* means "a task is simple."

Explain Say: *An idiom is a phrase that has a meaning apart from the meaning of each word in it.* Read aloud the first two paragraphs on page 16 and have students identify the meaning of *sick of.*

Model Say: *Rooster eats the same thing every day and says he's sick of chicken feed. I think* sick of *means "bored with."*

Guided Practice Read aloud the last paragraph on page 16. Ask what *look high and low* means. Ask students to think about where Rooster was searching. Explain that students can use context clues and a dictionary to figure out idioms.

Constructive Feedback

Ask: *Did Rooster only look in high places and low places? When you search for something where or how do you look?*

Practice Have students tell the meanings of the following idioms using context and a dictionary: *Rooster was ready to take the plunge and bake something new. He whipped up a strawberry shortcake in no time at all. The delicious cake really hit the spot!*

Constructive Feedback

Review the meaning of idioms. Ask students to look for sentence clues that tell them what the idioms mean. They can also look up the key word in the dictionary, such as *plunge, whip,* and *spot.*

Idioms

Explain Write the following on the board: *If my brother finds out that we borrowed his camera without permission, and we broke it too, we're out of the frying pan and into the fire!* Read the sentence aloud and then have a volunteer read aloud the underlined idiom.

Guided Practice Have students predict what they think *out of the frying pan and into the fire* means based on the sentence clues. Say: *They have borrowed a camera without permission. That's bad. They have also broken it. That's worse.* Then explain that the idiom means "going from a bad situation to a worse one." Visual/Auditory

Practice Write the following sentence on the board and have students identify the idiom and tell what it means using context and a dictionary. *We didn't clean our rooms, so we're in the doghouse.* (in trouble)

Act It Out

Materials paper, pencils

Explain Tell students they will act out the meaning of idioms.

Guided Practice Write on strips of paper sentences that contain idioms such as these: *We're leaving for the soccer game now, so you'd better shake a leg! This painting you made is going to knock their socks off. When your brother tells you that he just won a contest, you think he is pulling your leg.* Have partners work together and act out the meaning of the sentences. Visual

For five additional consecutive lessons on this skill, use the three lessons above. Go to **www.macmillanmh.com** for two additional lessons.

Objective: Identify multiple-meaning words

LA.3.1.6.9 Determine correct meaning of words with multiple meanings in context

Multiple-Meaning Words

Intervention/Remediation

Materials **Student Book:** "Community Works," pp. 48–49; dictionaries

Review Say: *Some words have more than one meaning. These are multiple-meaning words.*

Explain Say: *Knowing if a word is used as a noun, verb, adjective, or adverb can help you use a dictionary to find the right meaning.* Read aloud the first sentence in the third paragraph on page 48. Ask students what *hands* means.

Mode Say: *In this sentence,* hands *is a noun that means "the end part of your arm."*

Guided Practice Write the word *raised*. Ask volunteers to read the meanings and parts of speech of *raised* from the dictionary. Then read the first sentence in the third paragraph on page 48 aloud again and have students decide on its meaning.

Constructive Feedback

In this sentence does raised *mean "lifted up" or "increased in amount, pay, or price"?*

Practice Have students find the words *paint*, *park*, *warm*, *laugh*, and *vote* on pages 48–49. Tell them to use a dictionary to find definitions for the correct parts of speech that make sense in the sentences.

Constructive Feedback

Review that a word might be used as a noun, verb, adjective, or adverb and that students need to check in the dictionary for the correct definition.

Multiple-Meaning Words

Materials dictionaries

Explain Write the following on the board: *The* finish *on the old table was scratched and worn. Will you* finish *your work on time?* Read the sentences aloud. Tell students they will use clues in the sentences to determine each meaning of *finish*.

Guided Practice Ask students which part of speech *finish* is in the first sentence. Based on the context, ask them what they think the meaning in this sentence is. Have them check their guesses in a dictionary. (noun; the surface) Then have them repeat the process to find the part of speech and meaning of *finish* in the second sentence. (verb; to bring to an end) Kinesthetic/Visual

Practice Write the following sentences on the board and have students use context clues or the dictionary to figure out the meaning for *steer: Dad will* steer *the car to the right side of the road. The* steer *chomped grass in the field.*

Draw a Dictionary

Materials paper, pencils, crayons or markers

Explain Tell students that they will make a picture dictionary for multiple-meaning words.

Guided Practice List multiple-meaning words such as *setting*, *stew*, *thread*, *shake*, *turn*, *light*, and *pay*. Have partners work together to draw pictures that illustrate two different parts of speech and meanings for each word. For example, for *setting* they might show the stage setting for a play and someone setting a table. After drawing the illustrations, have them write captions that use the words to show the meanings of their illustrations. Visual

Objective: Identify and use contractions
LA.3.1.6.7 Use meanings of base words to determine meanings

Contractions

Intervention/Remediation

Materials **Student Book:** Washington Weed Whackers, pp. 82–85; **Letter Cards**

Review Say: *Contractions are words like* can't, don't, doesn't, haven't, *or* I'll.

Explain Write *can not* on the board. Say: *A contraction puts a verb and another small word together. The words* can *and* not *form the contraction* can't. *The apostrophe takes the place of missing letters.* Read aloud the text on page 82. Have students decide whether *shouldn't* or *State's* is a contraction.

Model Say: Shouldn't *is a contraction for* should not *because it contains a verb.* State's *is a possessive.*

Guided Practice Read aloud the second sentence on page 85 and have students identify the contraction (that's) and break it into two words (that is). Have students break apart two more contractions on page 85.

Constructive Feedback

If students have trouble making contractions, use **Letter Cards** to show them how to use an apostrophe in place of letters in contractions.

Practice Have students scan familiar books to find contractions. Have them write the two small words that formed each contraction and underline the verb in each.

Constructive Feedback

Review the definition of contractions and have students restate it in their own words. Then have students match contractions and the words that formed them.

Contractions

Explain Write the following on the board: *I would go there, but I can not find the place on the map.* Tell students that they will replace words in the sentence with contractions.

Guided Practice Read the sentence aloud. Then underscore *I would* and show students how you can erase the *woul* and replace it with an apostrophe. Now read the sentence aloud with *I'd*. Have a volunteer repeat the process for *can not*. Auditory/Visual

Practice Write these sentences on the board and have students replace appropriate words with a contraction: *We are going soon. They have got to go with us! She will bring the sandwiches. He had better come now!* (We're, They've, She'll, He'd)

Contraction Steps

Explain Tell students they will play a game. You will say a sentence. If the sentence contains a contraction, they will take a step forward. If it does not, they will take a step backward.

Guided Practice Have students stand in a straight line in a large open area. Say sentences like the ones below and have students take a step forward if you say a sentence with a contraction and a step backward when you do not. Students can take a bonus step if they name the two words that formed the contraction. Play the game until students come to a predetermined spot. Use sentences such as the following: *She's going to be a star. It's the best sandwich. You've got to go see the movie. Dan's mother is a teacher. They're not here yet.*
Auditory

FCAT Vocabulary

Objective: Identify and use example context clues
LA.3.1.6.3 Use context clues to determine meanings of unfamiliar words

Context Clues: Examples

Intervention/Remediation

Materials **Student Book:** *Here's My Dollar*, pp. 94–105

Review Say: *Sometimes we come across an unfamiliar word. We can use nearby clues to figure it out.*

Explain Say: *One kind of context clue is an example. The example shows the word's meaning.* On page 97, read aloud the last two sentences and have students find an example for *slogan*.

Model Say: *Angel's slogan is "Give a dollar, save a life." This example shows that a slogan is a short saying with a message.*

Guided Practice Read aloud the last two sentences on page 98 and tell students to listen for examples of *donations*. ($1, $1,000, $5,084) Then use the example to find the meaning. (money given for a cause)

Constructive Feedback

If students can't identify examples, ask: *Which of these is a slogan:* "Give a dollar, save a life" *or* The Fresno Bee*?*

Practice Have students identify examples of *daring* and *public appearances* on page 100–101, and write each word's meaning.

Constructive Feedback

Review that examples show a word's exact meaning in the text. Help students find examples and use them to understand meaning.

Context Clues

Explain Write the following on the board: *The farmers grew citrus fruit. Oranges, lemons, and grapefruit grew on the hundreds of trees on the farm.* Tell students they will use context clue examples to figure out the meanings of *citrus*.

Guided Practice Read the sentences aloud. Ask students what they think *citrus* means. Then have them circle the examples that give a clue to the word's meaning. (oranges, lemons, grapefruit) Visual/Kinesthetic

Practice Write these sentences on the board: *Look in the gazette to see who is running for mayor.* The Main Street Rag *is sure to have that news on the front page.*

Mom asked us to put our overshoes away. She didn't like all those boots cluttering up the hall.

Have partners use context clues to figure out the meaning of the underlined words.

A Picture's Worth

Materials old magazines, scissors, glue or tape, drawing paper, pencils

Explain Tell students that they will create picture clues to show a word's meaning.

Guided Practice Write the following words on the board: *transportation, fabric, clumps, exercise.* Have each student choose one word and create a collage of pictures that shows examples of the word. Then have each student write a sentence or two that uses the word. Visual

Objective: Identify comparatives and superlatives with *-er, -est*
LA.3.1.6.7 Use meanings of base words, affixes to determine meanings

Endings *-er, -est*

Intervention/Remediation

Materials **Student Book:** *My Very Own Room*, pp. 116–137

Review Say: *When we want to compare two or more things, we add* -er *or* -est.

Explain Write: *Max is a small dog. Taffy is smaller than Max, but Rose is the smallest of the three dogs.* Say: -er *compares two things.* -est *compares three or more. For words ending in* y, *change the* y *to an* i *before the ending:* silly, sillier, silliest. *For words ending in a single vowel and consonant, double the final consonant:* slim, slimmer, slimmest. Read aloud the first sentence on page 136. Ask what *happiest* and *luckiest* compare.

Model Say: *Because* happiest *and* luckiest *end in* -est, *they are comparing more than two things.*

Guided Practice Write on the board: *Ray's T-shirt is big.* Read the words and sentence aloud. Ask volunteers to share sentences that compare using *-er* and *-est*.

Constructive Feedback

If students have trouble figuring out whether to add *-er* or *-est*, ask: *Are you comparing two or more things?*

Practice Have students write sentences for *tiny* and *wet* comparing two or more things.

Constructive Feedback

Remind them of the rules for comparing and have them restate each. Have students take turns comparing with *-er* and *-est*, noting any necessary spelling changes.

Endings *-er, -est*

Explain Write the following on the board: *My brother is short. I am shorter than my brother. I am the shortest person in my family.*

Guided Practice Read the sentences aloud. Have students tell how many people are being compared in each sentence and why each ending is used. Have students describe any spelling changes. Auditory

Practice Write the following sentences on the board and have students complete them with *small, smaller,* or *largest*: *Eric's pet is a _____ cat. Jenny has a _______ pet. She has a gerbil. Hal has the ______ pet of all. It is a pony.*

Triples

Materials drawing paper, markers or crayons

Explain Tell students that they will draw pictures that illustrate adjectives.

Guided Practice Write these words in a three-column chart: Column 1: *bright, fast, high*; Column 2: *early, funny, sunny*; Column 3: *red, fat, wet*. Tell students to add *-er* and *-est* to each word. Remind them they will need to change *y* to *i* before endings *-er* and *-est*, and with words that end in a vowel and consonant, they will need to double the consonant. Then have students draw pictures to illustrate each adjective. Visual

Study Skill

Objective: Understand and use diagrams and rules

LA.3.1.7.1 Identify a text's features

Diagrams and Rules

Intervention/Remediation: Diagrams

Materials **Student Book:** "Welcome to the Bakery!" pp. 40–43

Review Say: *Diagrams are pictures or illustrations that help you understand what you read.*

Explain Display the diagram on page 41. Say: *When you look at a diagram, first read the title so you'll know what the diagram is all about. Look for arrows or numbers to show you the order in which you should read. Then look at labels and captions that help you understand the pictures.* Read aloud the captions on page 41. Ask: *What is this diagram all about? How can you tell where to start reading this diagram? How many steps are there in all?*

Constructive Feedback

If students have trouble locating information in the diagram, isolate one caption for students to explain.

Practice Read aloud the text on page 43 and have students brainstorm five steps a baker might follow to run a bakery. Have each students use the steps to draw a diagram with captions and/or labels.

Constructive Feedback

If students have trouble creating diagrams of how to run a bakery, have them use the steps they brainstormed and act out being the baker. As they do each step, have them sketch it and write a label or caption for it.

Intervention/Remediation: Rules

Materials **Student Book:** "What Causes Day and Night," pp. 74–75

Review Say: *Rules help us do things in an orderly way. Different places and activities have different kinds of rules.* Ask students to tell some of the rules they use in the classroom or at home.

Explain Read aloud the Rules for Daytime and Nighttime on page 74. Say: *Rules often use numbers or bullets to make the rules easy to read. Notice how few rules there are. Fewer rules are easier to remember than a great many rules. It's also easier to remember short rules than long rules.* Have a volunteer read aloud Daytime Rules. Discuss why these rules are a good idea and why it is important that students read rules like these carefully. (to prevent harm or to keep safe) Then discuss the Nighttime Rules.

Guided Practice Have students tell the rules for eating in the school lunchroom or rules for crossing a street with a street light. Record their rules on the board. Then have students discuss other places where they have seen rules posted.

Constructive Feedback

If students have difficulty identifying classroom or school rules, have them act out following one of the rules. Then have them discuss the importance of reading rules and following them.

FCAT **Study Skill**

Objective: Learn to use a media center and encyclopedia

LA.3.6.4.1 Use appropriate technologies to achieve a purpose; **LA.3.2.2** Identify elements of informational texts

Media Center and Encyclopedia

Intervention/Remediation: Media Center

Materials media center, computer with Internet access

Review Say: *When you go to the media center, a computer with Internet access is a good tool to use to find out information you wish to know.* Have students share what they know about finding information on the Internet.

Explain Using a computer, open the browser to locate a search engine. Demonstrate the steps as you talk about them. Say: *Sometimes when you want to find information on the Internet, you know the URL or web address of the site you want, so you type it in the address bar and click Go. Sometimes you need to use a search engine. Suppose I want to know about the geography of Egypt. In the search box, I'll type the key words* Egypt *and* geography. *The search engine lists all the Web sites it finds that tell about that topic. Clicking on a title in the list opens that Web site. To make sure the information in a Web site can be trusted, check that it was published by experts such as universities or a government.*

Guided Practice Have students work in groups of three. Have them use the search engine to find information on the people, wildlife, or deserts of Egypt. Have them visit two Web sites and write a fact from each one.

Constructive Feedback

If students have difficulty finding information on the Internet, have them check the key words they used. They should confirm the spelling of the key words and check that they are clicking on the title of the site they want to view.

Intervention/Remediation: Encyclopedia

Materials print encyclopedias

Review Say: *An encyclopedia gives a lot of information about a subject or topic. I can look up the names of famous people or places and things that interest me.*

Explain Say: *An encyclopedia is a set of books. Each book is called a volume, and is organized in alphabetical order. To do research or obtain information, find the volume that starts with the letter of the topic or subject. For a person's name, such as Frank Lloyd Wright, use the initial of their last name:* W. *To find out about pyramids, choose the* P *volume. Inside each volume, articles are arranged in alphabetical order, with guide words like those found in a dictionary. Articles often include headings, pictures, diagrams, and captions. Some encyclopedias are on CD-ROM and on the Internet.*

Guided Practice Have students work in pairs and choose three topics to research. One topic should be a person, another should be a famous place or city, and the other should be a subject they find interesting. Have them use encyclopedias to find and write two facts about each topic.

Constructive Feedback

If students have difficulty locating the subject in the encyclopedia, have them broaden the search or use another search name. For example, if they are looking up *bugs*, they might want to use the word *insects*.

Objectives

- Monitor comprehension
- Recognize the use of comparison and contrast
- Identify author's purpose

Genre Informational Nonfiction

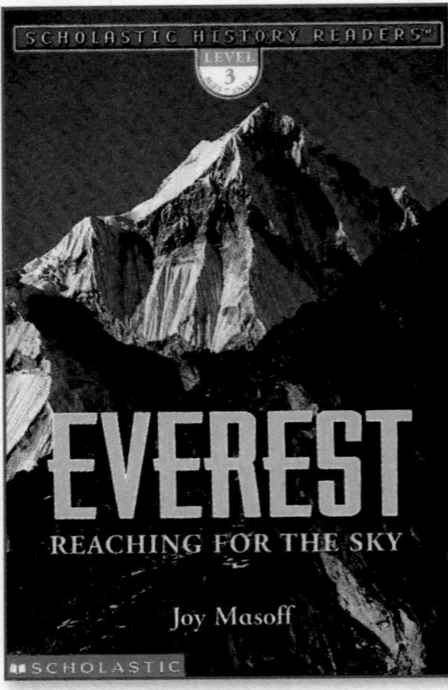

Approaching Level

Summary

This nonfiction book details Edmund Hillary and Tenzing Norgay's successful attempt to become the first people to reach the summit of Mount Everest, the tallest mountain on Earth. It also provides information about Mount Everest, the Himalayas, and later expeditions to the summit. Text features include a chronology, glossary, and index.

FYI for your information

Tenzing Norgay and Edmund Hillary were the first people to reach the summit of Everest. Norgay was a Sherpa—a native of Nepal, a small country next to China and India, and the home of Mount Everest. Sherpas have lived in the shadow of Everest for about five hundred years. They have become used to the altitude, so it does not affect them as much as it does others.

Everest: Reaching for the Sky

by Joy Masoff

Before Reading

BUILD BACKGROUND

Tell students they will be reading about the first successful attempt to climb Mount Everest, the tallest mountain in the world. Explain that Everest is 29,035 feet high, almost five vertical miles. Brainstorm a concept web with students about what the difficulties of climbing a mountain might be. Ask:

- Why do you think it might be dangerous to climb a very high mountain? (Students may note the danger of being up so high and possibly falling.)
- What do you think it takes to climb the highest mountain on Earth? (Students might mention a knowledge of the mountain, special gear, guides, and being physically fit.)

PREVIEW AND SET PURPOSES

Ask students to look at the cover of the book and read the title. Preview the book with students, pointing out pictures and reading captions. Then have students set a purpose for reading, such as to find out who made the first trip up Everest.

During Reading

APPLY COMPREHENSION SKILLS AND STRATEGIES

Students can read this book in smaller, more manageable sections as suggested below. For each section, Think Alouds and discussion questions are provided. Use these to review comprehension strategies and skills taught in this unit.

Chapters 1–2

STRATEGY
MONITOR COMPREHENSION

LA.3.1.7.8 Use strategies to repair comprehension

Think Aloud I know it is good to pause every now and again to make sure I understand what I have read. If I have trouble, I can reread or try to summarize what I have read. When I reread the first two chapters, I see the author describes how hard it is to climb Everest. She also introduces the two men who are trying to climb it, Edmund Hillary and Tenzing Norgay, and tells why they want to climb Mount Everest. Rereading helped me check my understanding. Next time I might try summarizing.

FCAT

LA.3.1.7.3 Determine explicit ideas

Compare and Contrast How are Edmund Hillary and Tenzing Norgay alike? How are they different? (They are both very good climbers, and both have a dream to climb Mount Everest. They are different because Hillary is from New Zealand and Norgay is from Nepal.)

Chapters 3–4

STRATEGY

MONITOR COMPREHENSION

LA.3.1.7.8 Use strategies to repair comprehension

Think Aloud I like to stop and think about what I have read to be sure I understand. As I read these two chapters, I learn that just to get to Everest from Kathmandu took months. Hillary and Norgay had to go through jungles and cross narrow rope bridges. Stopping as I read helps me to remember the most important information.

FCAT

LA.3.1.7.3 Determine explicit ideas

Compare and Contrast Compare what it's like at the lower altitudes with what it's like at the higher altitudes. What do the climbers do to adjust? (Down below there are "steamy jungles" full of animals. At higher altitudes, it's colder and the air is thinner. The climbers set up camps and move up the mountain bit by bit so their bodies can adjust to the thinner air.)

Chapter 5

STRATEGY

MONITOR COMPREHENSION

LA.3.1.7.8 Use strategies to repair comprehension

Think Aloud I want to make sure that I understand the main ideas in the last chapter. I can summarize to see if I remember the main ideas. Hillary and Norgay both became famous after they climbed Everest. Then they helped build schools and hospitals in Nepal. Summarizing helped me to check my comprehension.

FCAT

LA.3.1.7.2 Identify the author's purpose

Author's Purpose Is this book fiction or nonfiction? Was the author's purpose to entertain, to inform, or to explain? (It is nonfiction. The book includes facts about real people, places, and events: Edmund Hillary and Tenzing Norgay's attempt to climb Mount Everest. The author's purpose was to inform.)

LA.3.2.1.7 Respond to and discuss literary selections

After Reading

LITERATURE CIRCLES

Use page 222 in the **Teacher's Resource Book** to review Speaking and Listening guidelines for a discussion. Have students discuss the book in small groups.

- How do Hillary and Norgay help the people of Nepal after they climb Mount Everest?
- Why is it so hard to climb Mount Everest?

Write About It

Point out that Edmund Hillary and Tenzing Norgay did something that had never been done before. Have students think of a time they tried something new. They might write about how they learned to play an instrument or a new sport. Have students reread their writing to see that they have used correct verb forms.

Cross-Curricular Connection

Mountain Graph

What are the world's other tallest mountains? How tall is each one? Have students find the peak altitudes of the ten tallest mountains in an almanac or on the Internet. Invite them to use the information to draw and label a graph that shows the different heights. Have students create math questions based on their graphs.

Cross-Curricular Connection

Map It

Mount Everest is in Nepal, but where is Nepal? Have students find Nepal and the surrounding countries on a map. Ask them to locate the Himalayas and Mount Everest.

Classroom Library

Objectives

- Monitor comprehension
- Recognize the use of comparison and contrast
- Identify author's purpose

Genre Informational Nonfiction

On Level

Summary

This biography tells the story of the life of Bessie Coleman, the first African American to earn a pilot's license.

FYI for your information

Bessie Coleman was born in 1892, the tenth of thirteen children. She became the first person in her family to learn to read. At the age of twenty-eight, Bessie set off for France, intent on learning how to fly at a French flying school. Less than a year later, she earned her pilot's license, becoming the first African American to do so. She began performing at air shows and was an inspiration to young people wherever she went.

Fly High! The Story of Bessie Coleman

by Louise Borden and Mary Kay Kroeger

Before Reading

BUILD BACKGROUND

Explain that for many years after the Civil War ended in 1865, opportunities for African Americans were limited. In 1921, when Bessie Coleman got her pilot's license, she became the first African American to do so. She even had to go to France to take her lessons. Brainstorm a list of reasons that Bessie found it difficult to pursue her dream in the United States and discuss if those reasons still exist. Ask students:

- Why did Bessie go to France to earn her pilot's license?
- Would this be necessary today? Why or why not?

PREVIEW AND SET PURPOSES

Ask students to look at the cover and read the title. Remind students that the book is a biography, a type of nonfiction that tells the true story of someone's life. Then have students set a purpose for reading, such as to find out why Bessie wanted to learn how to fly.

During Reading

APPLY COMPREHENSION SKILLS AND STRATEGIES

Students can read this book in smaller, more manageable sections as suggested below. For each section, Think Alouds and discussion questions are provided. Use these to review comprehension strategies and skills taught in this unit.

Pages 1–10

STRATEGY
MONITOR COMPREHENSION

LA.3.1.7.8 Use strategies to repair comprehension

Think Aloud As I read, I like to stop and visualize what is happening. Bessie was the only person in her family who learned to read and she earned money so she could continue attending school. When I picture this, it seems to me that Bessie really wanted to do something with her life other than work on a farm. I will look for more information that helps me visualize and understand what she was like.

FCAT

LA.3.1.7.3 Determine explicit ideas

Compare and Contrast How was Bessie Coleman like her mother? How was she different? (Like her mother, Bessie was a hard worker and loved her family. Bessie was different from her mother because she learned to read and she went to school.)

Pages 11–24

STRATEGY
MONITOR COMPREHENSION

LA.3.1.7.8 Use strategies to repair comprehension

Think Aloud This story includes a lot of facts. To make sure I understand the story, I can slow down as I read and gather all of the facts. I read, first, Bessie went to Chicago where she heard stories about French women who flew airplanes. She decided she wanted to fly herself, so she learned French and set off for France. There, she earned her pilot's license. Slowing down as I read helps me to understand information in the book.

LA.3.1.7.2 Identify the author's purpose

Author's Purpose Why do you think the author includes details about Robert Abbott? (Robert Abbott was Bessie's friend. He helped her get into flight school in France, so he was a very important person in Bessie Coleman's life.)

Pages 25–end

STRATEGY
MONITOR COMPREHENSION

LA.3.1.7.8 Use strategies to repair comprehension

Think Aloud I want to remember what I read. When I reread the last section, I see that Bessie was the first African American to earn a pilot's license. She performed air shows all over the country. She died at the age of 34. Rereading helped me remember these facts.

Author's Purpose What kind of book is this? What do you think the authors' purpose was? (It is a biography. The authors' purpose was to inform readers about Bessie Coleman's life.)

LA.3.1.7.2 Identify the author's purpose
LA.3.2.1.7 Respond to and discuss literary selections

After Reading

LITERATURE CIRCLES

Use page 222 in the **Teacher's Resource Book** to review Speaking and Listening guidelines for a discussion. Discuss the book in small groups, using questions such as these:

- Who was Bessie Coleman? Why did she become famous?
- What was it like for her growing up? What did she have to do to get an education?
- Do you think Bessie Coleman accomplished her goal of becoming somebody? Explain why or why not.

Write About It

Bessie Coleman decides that she really wants to fly airplanes. Ask students to write about something they really want to do and explain why. Students might write about playing an instrument or participating in a sport. Remind students to check their use of irregular verbs when they are finished.

Cross-Curricular Connection

Math Then and Now

Point out that Bessie's interest in numbers and math probably helped her become a good pilot. Tell students that early pilots like Bessie had to calculate wind speed, gas mileage, and distances to help them fly safely. They also had to read maps to get from one place to another. Now, computers and radar do much of this work for pilots. Talk about other kinds of hobbies or jobs that would require math skills (architect, engineer, truck driver, sales clerk) How are computers or other forms of technology changing those jobs?

Cross-Curricular Connection

Time Line

Have students create time lines that show events in the life of Bessie Coleman. The book includes many dates that students can plot on their time lines. (Refer to the Author's Note for Bessie Coleman's birth date.) Challenge students to locate dates about related events that are mentioned in the book, such as the end of the Civil War and when World War I occurred. They can add these dates to their time lines.

Classroom Library

Objectives

- Monitor comprehension
- Recognize the use of comparison and contrast
- Identify author's purpose

Genre Informational Nonfiction

Beyond Level

Summary

Recycle! explains the process of recycling from start to finish and discusses what happens to paper, glass, aluminum, and plastic when they are recycled into new products. The book includes facts and statistics about recycling. It also contains a section entitled "What You Can Do," offering tips and suggestions to help students reduce the amount of resources they use and recycle the ones they do.

Solid waste includes household items, containers and packaging, food wastes, and yard wastes. As of 2005, 32% of waste was being recycled or composted, 15.9% was being incinerated, and 52.1% was being put into landfills. Each person in the United States generates an average of 4.5 pounds of waste each day.

Recycle! A Handbook for Kids

by Gail Gibbons

Before Reading

BUILD BACKGROUND

Explain that *recycling* means reusing materials instead of throwing them away. One way we recycle is to put some types of trash aside so they can be remade into new products. Paper and cardboard, aluminum, some plastics, and glass can be recycled. Point out that this book was made from recycled paper. Brainstorm a list of recycled materials. Ask:

- What do you recycle?
- What items do you buy that have been recycled or are made out of recycled materials?

PREVIEW AND SET PURPOSES

Ask students to look at the cover and read the title and the name of the author. Read a page or two aloud to give students a sense of what the book might be about. Point out pictures and diagrams. Ask students to think about the topic of the book. Then have them set a purpose for reading, such as to find out how they can recycle.

During Reading

APPLY COMPREHENSION SKILLS AND STRATEGIES

Students may want to read this book in smaller, more manageable sections as suggested below. For each section, use the Think Alouds and discussion questions provided to review comprehension strategies and skills taught in this unit.

Pages 1–9

STRATEGY
MONITOR COMPREHENSION

LA.3.1.7.8 Use strategies to repair comprehension

Think Aloud I want to be sure I understand what I am reading, so I will ask myself questions to check what I learned. Some questions I can ask are: Where does all the trash go? What is a landfill? What can people do so there is less trash? Asking and answering these questions can help me understand what I am reading.

LA.3.1.7.2 Identify the author's purpose

Author's Purpose Why do you think the author wrote this book? Was her purpose to entertain, to inform, or to explain? How do you know? (The author includes a lot of facts and information about recycling. She doesn't try to tell a funny story or explain how to do something, so her purpose is to inform.)

Pages 10–17

STRATEGY

MONITOR COMPREHENSION

LA.3.1.7.8 Use strategies to repair comprehension

Think Aloud I want to stop and make sure I understand what I have read. I can do this by looking back. When I reread I see that glass and aluminum cans are both recyclable. Making new aluminum cans and glass bottles out of old ones creates less pollution and uses less energy. I can recycle by saving used bottles and cans and taking them to a recycling center. Rereading helped me to understand these facts.

FCAT

LA.3.1.7.3 Determine explicit ideas

Compare and Contrast Why is it better to make glass bottles out of recycled glass than to use new glass? (It takes less energy and creates less pollution. Forests and fields don't have to be destroyed to dig up new sand, lime, and ash.)

Pages 18–28

STRATEGY

MONITOR COMPREHENSION

Think Aloud Looking in other places can help me to understand the information in a book. In the last section, I came across the word *polystyrene*. By reading carefully I think it is a type of packing material that is harmful to the environment and is very hard to recycle. I can check in another source such as a dictionary or encyclopedia.

FCAT

Compare and Contrast How is polystyrene like paper or glass? How is it different? (Like paper, polystyrene is used for packaging and packing materials. Unlike paper and glass, polystyrene does not biodegrade, is not recyclable, and creates poisonous gases if burned.)

LA.3.1.7.3 Determine explicit ideas; LA.3.2.1.7 Respond to and discuss literary selections

After Reading

LITERATURE CIRCLES

Use page 222 in the **Teacher's Resource Book** to review Speaking and Listening guidelines for a discussion. Have students discuss the book in small groups. Ask:

- What happens when you recycle paper, glass, aluminum, or plastic? What happens to trash that doesn't get recycled?
- What are some ways we can help reduce the amount of trash that goes to landfills?

Write About It

Recycle! includes tips that help make recycling easier. Have students make a poster that teaches people how to recycle. Have students use pictures and words to present their ideas on posters. Point out the "What You Can Do" section to help generate ideas. Remind students to check their writing to make sure they use linking verbs correctly.

Cross-Curricular Connection

Call on the Community

Tell students that they can help their friends, family, and neighbors learn about recycling. Have students use simple props and put on skits in which they pretend to stop someone who is about to throw away a recyclable item and explain to the person why it should be recycled instead. Videotape the skits and present them to community audiences as public service announcements.

Cross-Curricular Connection

Trash Graph

Have students work together to collect data on the classroom trash for a week or a month. At the end of each day, have a student weigh the trash can. Subtract the weight of the empty trash can and record the weight of the trash. Let students decide the type of graph (bar, line, or pictograph) they want to use to record and display their data. Challenge students to calculate how much trash the entire school generates, based on your classroom's data.

Additional Readings

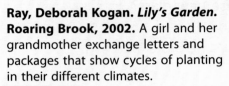

	WEEK 1	WEEK 2
By the Authors and Illustrators	**Stevens, Janet, and Stevens Crummel, Susan. *Jackalope.* Harcourt, 2003.** Jackrabbit asks his fairy godrabbit for horns and becomes the first jackalope. ON LEVEL	**Medearis, Angela Shelf. *The Freedom Riddle.* School Specialty Children's Publishing, 2003.** Based on a true story, Jim, an enslaved person, uses cleverness and ingenuity to obtain his freedom. BEYOND
Related to the Theme	**Ray, Deborah Kogan. *Lily's Garden.* Roaring Brook, 2002.** A girl and her grandmother exchange letters and packages that show cycles of planting in their different climates. APPROACHING	**Slawson, Michele. *Apple Picking Time.* Dragonfly Books, 1998.** Anna joins her friends and family in the orchard to pick apples before they spoil. APPROACHING
	Speed, Toby. *Brave Potatoes.* Putnam's, 2000. The potatoes sneak out to enjoy a carnival ride but are spotted by a chef who needs potatoes for his soup. APPROACHING	**Wheeler, Lisa. *Old Cricket.* Atheneum, 2003.** Old Cricket doesn't feel like helping his wife and neighbors prepare for the winter, so he pretends he is not well. APPROACHING
	Partridge, Elizabeth. *Annie and Bo and the Big Surprise.* Dutton, 2001. Bo bakes a full moon cake as a surprise for his friend Annie, but the outcome is unexpected. ON LEVEL	**Paul, Ann Whitford. *Mañana Iguana.* Holiday House, 2004.** This book tells the Mexican version of "The Little Red Hen." Iguana needs help preparing for a party. ON LEVEL
	Tate, Lindsey. *Teatime with Emma Buttersnap.* Henry Holt, 1998. The history of tea and tea parties is presented along with recipes for accompanying treats. ON LEVEL	**Segal, Lore Groszmann. *Why Mole Shouted and Other Stories.* Farrar, Straus and Giroux, 2004.** Stories tell about a mole and his grandmother living together and getting along. ON LEVEL
	Arnold, Ann. *The Adventurous Chef: Alexis Soyer.* Frances Foster Books, 2002. A remarkable Frenchman establishes a soup kitchen in Ireland and works with Florence Nightingale. BEYOND	**Chan, Harvey. *Three Monks, No Water.* Annick Press, 1997.** One monk is good at getting his own water, but when two more monks join him it becomes difficult to complete the task. BEYOND
	Williamson, Sarah. *Bake the Best-Ever Cookies.* Williamson Publishing, 2001. Baking procedures, ingredients, and kitchen supplies are described and followed in 26 recipes. BEYOND	**Haddix, Margaret Peterson. *Say What?* Simon & Schuster, 2004.** Three siblings get mad when they think their parents say the wrong things in response to their bad behavior. BEYOND

WEEK 3	WEEK 4	WEEK 5
Editors of TIME for Kids. *TIME for Kids: Thomas Edison.* HarperTrophy, 2005. This biography tells about an inventor who patented over 1,000 inventions. BEYOND	**Soto, Gary. *Baseball in April and Other Stories.* Harcourt, 2000.** This book presents 11 short stories about the problems of growing up in the United States. BEYOND	**Pérez, Amada Irma. *My Diary from Here to There.* Children's Press, 2002.** A girl discovers her strengths and weaknesses as she is about to move from Mexico to Los Angeles. ON LEVEL
Cosgrove, Stephen. *The Puddle Pine.* Price Stern Sloan, 2005. Three beavers discuss whether or not to chop down a pine tree from a forest that has seen much destruction. APPROACHING	**Cazet, Denys. *Minnie & Moo and the Seven Wonders of the World.* Atheneum, 2003.** Two misguided cows decide to help save their farm by creating spectacular environments. APPROACHING	**MacLachlan, Patricia. *What You Know First.* HarperCollins, 1995.** A girl's family must move away from their farm, but first she gathers mementos. APPROACHING
Nelson, Robin. *We Use Water.* Lerner, 2003. This simple text shows how we use water for fighting fires, washing hands, and making ice cubes, and stresses the importance of conserving it. APPROACHING	**Curtis, Gavin. *The Bat Boy & His Violin.* Simon & Schuster, 2001.** Reginald finds an unusual way to help his father's baseball team in the Negro League games of 1948. APPROACHING	**Ziefert, Harriet. *One Smart Skunk.* Blue Apple Books, 2004.** Rebecca the skunk is the unwelcome visitor who lives under a suburban family's deck. APPROACHING
Atkins, Jeannine. *Aani and the Tree Huggers.* Lee & Low Books, 2000. Aani and other residents of her village try to stop loggers from cutting down the trees near their homes. ON LEVEL	**Brenner, Barbara. *The Boy Who Loved to Draw: Benjamin West.* Houghton, 1999.** The childhood of the great American painter, and how he first became an artist is described. ON LEVEL	**Harrington, Janice N. *Going North.* Farrar, Straus and Giroux, 2004.** A young African American girl and her family leave their home in Alabama and move to Lincoln, Nebraska. ON LEVEL
Ray, Mary Lyn. *Pumpkins: A Story for a Field.* Voyager, 1996. This story tells of a man and his personal efforts to save a piece of land that he loves from development. ON LEVEL	**Fleming, Candace. *Boxes for Katje.* Farrar, Straus and Giroux, 2003.** Two people, one in the United States and one in the Netherlands, decide to share letters, thoughts, food, and warm clothes. ON LEVEL	**Grindley, Sally. *A New Room for William.* Candlewick Press, 2000.** When William and his mother move, he is unhappy about having a new room, but soon he changes his mind. ON LEVEL
George, Jean Craighead. *The Case of the Missing Cutthroats.* HarperCollins, 1996. Spinner and her cousin search for information about an endangered fish. BEYOND	**Banks, Jacqueline. *A Day for Vincent Chin.* Houghton, 2001.** Although Tommy has doubts about his mother's social activism, he finds a cause of his own one day. BEYOND	**Gantos, Jack. *Jack Adrift: Fourth Grade Without a Clue.* Farrar, Straus and Giroux, 2003.** Nine-year-old Jack moves with his family to Cape Hatteras when his father rejoins the Navy. BEYOND
Grupper, Jonathan. *Destination: Rain Forest.* National Geographic Society, 1997. This book explores the environment of the world's tropical rain forests and how to preserve them. BEYOND	**Mitchell, Elizabeth. *Journey to the Bottomless Pit: The Story of Stephen Bishop & the Mammoth Cave.* Viking, 2004.** An African American slave guides tours of the famous attraction. BEYOND	**Kelly, Katy. *Lucy Rose: Here's the Thing About Me.* Delacorte Press, 2004.** Eight-year-old Lucy Rose has just moved to Washington, D.C., and is struggling to fit in at her new school. BEYOND

Selection Honors, Prizes, and Awards

Cook-A-Doodle Doo!

Unit 4, p. 14
by ***Janet Stevens and Susan Stevens Crummel***

Texas Bluebonnet Award (2001)

Author/Illustrator: *Janet Stevens*, Caldecott Honor (1995) for *Tops and Bottoms*, American Booksellers Book of the Year (ABBY) Honor (1997) for *To Market, To Market*
Author: *Susan Stevens Crummel*, ALA Notable Children's Book (2002), California Young Reader Medal (2004) for *And the Dish Ran Away with the Spoon*; Storytelling World Award (2004) for *Jackalope*

Seven Spools of Thread

Unit 4, p. 50
by ***Angela Shelf Medearis***

ALA Notable Children's Book (2001), Notable Children's Trade Book in Social Studies (2001)

Author: *Angela Shelf Medearis*, winner of the Carter G. Woodson Book Award (1998) from the National Council for the Social Studies for *Princess of the Press: The Story of Ida B. Wells-Barnett*; North Carolina Children's Book Award (2000) for *The Ghost of Sifty Sifty Sam*

Here's My Dollar

Unit 4, p. 94
by ***Gary Soto***

Author: *Gary Soto*, winner of George G. Stone Center for Children's Books Recognition of Merit Award (1993) and Pura Belpré Honor Award (1996) for *Baseball in April and Other Stories*; Society of School Librarians International (SSLI) Book Award (1995) for *Jesse*; Parents' Choice Silver Award (1995) for *Chato's Kitchen*

My Very Own Room

Unit 4, p. 116
by ***Amada Irma Pérez***

Tomás Rivera Award (2000), Americas Award for Children's and Young Adult Literature Honorable Mention (2000)

Unit 1

Week		Vocabulary	Spelling			
1	**First Day Jitters** *The New House* *The New Kid* *The New Hometown* *The First Day*	downstairs nervous fumbled chuckled nonsense trudged	clap step **sick** rock	luck crop snack **mess**	**head** shut miss stamp	jump click pond
			Review Words:	cat	man	can
			Challenge Words:	bathtub	anthill	
2	**Dear Juno** *The E-Mail Pals* *Dear Ghana* *Faraway Home* *Letters to Africa*	crackle announced soared starry envelope photograph	date **fine** rose lake	life home safe rice	globe **plane** wise smoke	grade **smile** **come**
			Review Words:	clap	sick	crop
			Challenge Words:	sneeze	escape	
3	**Whose Habitat Is It?** **Approaching, On Level, Beyond:** *Saving the Rainforest* **English Language Learners:** *The Rainforest*	neighborhood content addressing resort	fail bay pail ray	plain tray trail May	braid sway gray plays	**paint** snail great
			Review Words:	safe	rice	globe
			Challenge Words:	lady	afraid	
4	**Penguin Chick** **Approaching, On Level, Beyond:** *The Weddell Seals of Antarctica* **English Language Learners:** *The Weddell Seals*	fierce whips echoes shuffles huddle junior down	gold bowl soak sold	**snow** loaf roast coast	scold coal slow **grows**	show float blow
			Review Words:	snail	plain	gray
			Challenge Words:	window	program	
5	**The Perfect Pet** *The Rescue* *Charlie's Pet Problem* *Dan's Idea* *Charlie Has a Problem*	perfect challenge healthy satisfy manage scratch appetite	mild sky pie might	**find** fight ties **right**	fry tight child flight	bright buy dye
			Review Words:	soak	bowl	gold
			Challenge Words:	wind	children	

LOG ON Go to www.macmillanmh.com for **Leveled Spelling Lists.**

Unit 2

Week	Vocabulary	Spelling			
1 **The Strongest One** *How Fly Saved the River* *Clever John* *Dorje and the Lost Treasure* *John's Plan*	decorated symbol darkened gnaws securing weakest	heel seal **weak** week	bean creek speaks team	free green clean cream	street **freeze** field
		Review Words:	right	pie	child
		Challenge Words:	sixteen	peanut	
2 **Wolf!** *Running with Wolves* *Katie and the Wolf* *A Dog's Life* *The Wolf*	passion admire concentrate splendid bothering dangerous ached	**chick** **much** pitch teacher	chum lunch ditch cheek	hatch cheese bench chunk	stretch watching crunching
		Review Words:	weak	green	seal
		Challenge Words:	catcher	sandwich	
3 **What's in Store for the Future?** **Approaching, On Level, Beyond:** *Incredible Inventions: Everyday Wonders* **English Language Learners:** *Inventions*	objects entertainment predictions computers	thick **this** truth whales	shock **fish** **what** sixth	**them** washing wheel pathway	month dishpan weather
		Review Words:	lunch	chick	pitch
		Challenge Words:	shadow	thicken	
4 **The Planets in Our Solar System** **Approaching, On Level, Beyond:** *What's in the Sky?* **English Language Learners:** *In the Sky*	solar system easily farther main dim temperatures telescope probably	thread scrubs spree screams	stream scratch spread throne	three screens spray throw	strong scraped strength
		Review Words:	thick	washing	whales
		Challenge Words:	streamer	scribble	
5 **Author: A True Story** **Approaching, On Level, Beyond:** *Storytellers of the World* **English Language Learners:** *Storytellers*	talented single proper excitement acceptance useful	wrap knit gnat wrists	knots **wrote** knight sign	knock wreck know wring	gnaws **write** **wrong**
		Review Words:	throw	spray	scratch
		Challenge Words:	wristwatch	knapsack	

Key Spelling words in bold appear in the selection.

LOG ON Go to **www.macmillanmh.com** for **Leveled Spelling Lists**.

Unit 3

Week	Vocabulary	Spelling			
1 Stone Soup *The Popcorn Dancers* *The Fox's Banquet* *The Duke's Banquet* *The Fox's Dinner*	guests banquet agreeable curiosity gaze untrusting	bark shorts sharp sore	**hard** storms **yard** sport	sharks porch pour **story**	chore wore carve
		Review Words:	knots	sign	wrong
		Challenge Words:	orchard	artist	
2 One Riddle, One Answer *The Monster's Riddle* *Magpie's Mystery* *Adding with Kevin* *The Mystery of the Magpie*	wearily depart suitable increase observed advised discouraged	stairs mare bear bare	share wear dares chairs	glare pairs hare **their**	pears square haircut
		Review Words:	sport	sore	hard
		Challenge Words:	airport	beware	
3 Saving the Sand Dunes **Approaching, On Level, Beyond:** *Water in the Desert* **English Language Learners:** *Life in the Desert*	preserve restore suffered rainfall	turns first herds learn	purr third earn nurse	perch girls firm word	**world** serve worth
		Review Words:	bare	bear	stairs
		Challenge Words:	perfect	Thursday	
4 The Jones Family Express *A Different World* *Storm Surprise* *A Long Way to Go* *The Hurricane*	annual potential expensive politely package wrapping innocent aisles	loop rude **look** clue	spoon tube **shook** blue	cubes goose mules gloom	true shoe stew
		Review Words:	firm	turns	learn
		Challenge Words:	classroom	childhood	
5 What Do Illustrators Do? **Approaching, On Level, Beyond:** *Old and New: Painting Through Time* **English Language Learners:** *Painting Through Time*	instance illustrate style textures sketches suggestions	coy soil foil toil	coins **point** noise loyal	boiled spoiled enjoys voice	choice soybean joyful
		Review Words:	spoon	rude	shook
		Challenge Words:	noisy	checkpoint	

LOG ON Go to www.macmillanmh.com for **Leveled Spelling Lists.**

Unit 4

Week		Vocabulary	Spelling			
1	**Cook-A-Doodle-Doo!** **Approaching, On Level, Beyond:** *Measurement* **English Language Learners:** *Measure Up*	magnificent masterpiece ingredient recipes tasty	yawn taught **salt** lawn	halls hauls hawks **squawk**	bought bawls drawing caused	paused crawled coughing
			Review Words:	joyful	coins	spoiled
			Challenge Words:	walrus	autumn	
2	**Seven Spools of Thread** *Androcles and the Lion* *A True Hero* *The Lost Brocade* *The Diamond*	beamed argued possessions fabric purchased quarreling	found town **shout** owl	couch **bow** scout round	plow **crowd** **proud** clouds	**ground** louder bounce
			Review Words:	drawing	lawn	hauls
			Challenge Words:	snowplow	outline	
3	**Washington Weed Whackers** **Approaching, On Level, Beyond:** *Resources All Around Us* **English Language Learners:** *Resources*	native shouldn't research sprout clumps	cell gems age place	gyms city cents price	space nice giant **changes**	pages gentle message
			Review Words:	crowd	clouds	found
			Challenge Words:	giraffe	celebrate	
4	**Here's My Dollar** **Approaching, On Level, Beyond:** *Patching a Playground* **English Language Learners:** *Kids Make a Difference*	tour volunteers community thrilled slogan grownups deserve interviewed	sale sail beet beat	rode road rowed **its**	it's **your** you're there	they're peace piece
			Review Words:	city	gems	space
			Challenge Words:	seen	scene	
5	**My Very Own Room** *The Slightly Tipping Tree House* *A Winter Adventure* *The Science Fair* *Safe in the Storm*	separate determination storage crate exact ruined luckiest	**years** twins trays states	ashes foxes inches flies	cities ponies bunches alleys	lunches cherries daisies
			Review Words:	sale	rode	you're
			Challenge Words:	heroes	libraries	

Key Spelling words in bold appear in the selection.

LOG ON Go to www.macmillanmh.com for **Leveled Spelling Lists**.

Unit 5

Word List

Week	Vocabulary	Spelling
1 Boom Town **Approaching, On Level, Beyond:** *Start Your Own Business!* **English Language Learners:** *Dog Wash*	sidewalks grumbled traders blossomed wailed lonesome	airplane, daytime, birthday, daylight, hairdo, notebook, birdhouse, barefoot, headlight, sometime, **someone**, newspaper, **sidewalks**, basketball, **stagecoach** **Review Words:** states, inches, cities **Challenge Words:** somebody, handwriting
2 Beatrice's Goat **Approaching, On Level, Beyond:** *Bright Ideas: Inventions That Changed History* **English Language Learners:** *Bright Ideas*	gift yearned tend produce sturdy schoolhouse kindhearted	names, **named**, naming, hopes, hoped, hoping, dances, danced, **dancing**, drops, dropped, dropping, wraps, wrapped, wrapping **Review Words:** airplane, birthday, newspaper **Challenge Words:** driving, traded
3 A Carousel of Dreams **Approaching, On Level, Beyond:** *Thrills and Chills* **English Language Learners:** *What a Ride!*	powered declared existed artist's pride	tries, tried, trying, dries, dried, drying, hurries, hurried, hurrying, studies, studied, studying, plays, played, playing **Review Words:** dances, hoping, wrapping **Challenge Words:** obeyed, worrying
4 The Printer **Approaching, On Level, Beyond:** *Energy!* **English Language Learners:** *See It, Feel It, Hear It*	screamed numb escape fled shuddered image newspaper	basket, rabbit, napkin, **letter**, invite, **bedtime**, mammal, number, **fellow**, chapter, follow, problem, chicken, butter, Sunday **Review Words:** tried, studies, drying **Challenge Words:** splendid, complete
5 Animal Homes **Approaching, On Level, Beyond:** *Amazing Bird Builders* **English Language Learners:** *Bird Builders*	hives architects structures contain retreats shallow shelter	pilot, diner, tiger, favor, lemon, planet, model, shady, robot, **tiny**, label, cozy, silent, **spider**, frozen **Review Words:** follow, basket, Sunday **Challenge Words:** melon, stomach

LOG ON Go to www.macmillanmh.com for **Leveled Spelling Lists**.

Unit 6

Week	Vocabulary	Spelling			
1 A Castle on Viola Street *Heat Wave* *Emergency!* *New Neighbors* *The Flood*	downtown appliances owners construction equipment leaky	able purple riddle handle	towel eagle puzzle **castle**	**little** nickel camel pickle	travel tunnel squirrel
		Review Words:	spider	tiny	planet
		Challenge Words:	motel	couple	
2 Wilbur's Boast *The Elephant's Boast* *Mike's Surprise* *The Grizzly and the Frigate Bird* *Animal Friends*	conversation interrupted boasting sway scrambled seized rebuild	**untied** repay disagree preheat	unafraid **return** preschool dislike	disappear resell precook prepay	unbeaten reprint unwrap
		Review Words:	nickel	handle	pickle
		Challenge Words:	unlucky	recover	
3 An American Hero Flies Again **Approaching, On Level, Beyond:** *Getting Out the Vote* **English Language Learners:** *Vote!*	historical dispute automatically requirements	sister sailor dollar toaster	winter doctor **later** dancer	mayor writer silver cellar	trailer December author
		Review Words:	resell	prepay	unwrap
		Challenge Words:	circular	editor	
4 Mother to Tigers *Painting Birds: The Life of John James Audubon* *Jane Goodall* *Gerald Durrell* *Jane Goodall and the Chimpanzees*	strolled pitiful sleepy crouch official sleek grace	careful cheerful helpful colorful	harmful peaceful **pitiful** painless	priceless helpless sleepless rainless	helplessly carefully peacefully
		Review Words:	doctor	dollar	December
		Challenge Words:	wonderful	cloudless	
5 Home-Grown Butterflies **Approaching, On Level, Beyond:** *Purple Loosestrife: The Beautiful Invader* **English Language Learners:** *The Marsh Monster*	disappear protect harming involved supply capture enclosure	**because** rubber **about** puddle	**alive** behind before **around**	better **attract** kettle hammer	attend tickle **people**
		Review Words:	peaceful	helpless	carefully
		Challenge Words:	believe	beaver	

Key Spelling words in bold appear in the selection.

LOG ON Go to **www.macmillanmh.com** for **Leveled Spelling Lists**.

Index

Aa

Index

Bb

Key 3.1 = Grade 3, Book 1

Cc

Key 3.1 = Grade 3, Book 1

Dd

Ee

Key 3.1 = Grade 3, Book 1

Ff

Gg

Key 3.1 = Grade 3, Book 1

Jj

Index

Key 3.1 = Grade 3, Book 1

Mm

Index

Nn

Oo

Pp

Key 3.1 = Grade 3, Book 1

Index

Qq

Rr

Key 3.1 = Grade 3, Book 1

Ss

Index

Key 3.1 = Grade 3, Book 1

Tt

Index

Key 3.1 = Grade 3, Book 1

Uu

Vv

Index

Key 3.1 = Grade 3, Book 1

Ww

Index

Key 3.1 = Grade 3, Book 1

Acknowledgments

The publisher gratefully acknowledges permission to reprint the following copyrighted material:

"A Bear in the Family" by Ben Mikaelsen from *Boys' Life*, February 1997, Vol. 87 Issue 2. Copyright © 1997 by Boy Scouts of America. Used by permission of Boy Scouts of America.

Illustration Credits

10B: Renato Alarcao. 45F: (l) Deborah Melmon; (r) Erika LeBarre. 45U: Gideon Kendall. 73B: Lin Wang. 77F: (l) Bob Dorsey; (r) Erika LeBarre. 77U: Gideon Kendall. 89F: Mark Stephens. 89U: Gideon Kendall. 107B: Greg Harris. 111F: Ken Bowser. 111U: Gideon Kendall. 145F: Ken Bowser. 145U: Gideon Kendall. 149K: Jenny Vainisi. T18: Renato Alarcao.

Acknowledgments

The publisher gratefully acknowledges permission to reprint the following copyrighted material:

"Animal Homes" by Ann O. Squire. Copyright © 2001 by Children's Press®, a Division of Scholastic Inc. All rights reserved. Reprinted by permission.

"Beatrice's Goat" by Page McBrier, illustrations by Lori Lohstoeter. Text copyright © 2001 by Page McBrier. Illustrations copyright © 2001 by Lori Lohstoeter. Reprinted by permission of Atheneum Books for Young Readers, an imprint of Simon & Schuster Children's Publishing Division.

"Boom Town" by Sonia Levitin, illustrations by Cat Bowman Smith. Text copyright © 1998 by Sonia Levitin. Illustrations copyright © 1998 by Cat Bowman Smith. Reprinted with permission by Orchard Books a Grolier Company.

"A Castle on Viola Street" by DyAnne DiSalvo. Copyright © 2001 by DyAnne DiSalvo. Reprinted with permission of HarperCollins Children's Books, a division of HarperCollins Publishers.

"The Caterpillar" by Christina Rossetti from BOOK OF POEMS by Tomie dePaola. Text copyright © 1988 by Tomie dePaola. Reprinted with permission.

"A Child's Call to Aid the Zoo" by Jim Davis. Copyright © 2003 by Jim Davis. Reprinted with permission by The Fresno Bee, a division of the The McClatchy Company.

"Cook-a-Doodle Doo!" by Janet Stevens and Susan Stevens Crummel, illustrations by Janet Stevens. Text copyright © 1999 by Janet Stevens and Susan Stevens Crummel. Illustrations copyright © 1999 by Janet Stevens. Reprinted with permission of Harcourt Brace & Company.

"Home Sweet Home" by John Ciardi from THE HOPEFUL TROUT AND OTHER LIMERICKS by John Ciardi. Text copyright © 1989 by Myra J. Ciardi. Reprinted with permission by Houghton Mifflin Company.

"Home-Grown Butterflies" by Deborah Churchman from RANGER RICK®. Copyright © 1998 by National Wildlife Federation. Reprinted with permission of the National Wildlife Federation, May 1998.

"Monarch Butterfly" by Marilyn Singer from FIREFLIES AT MIDNIGHT by Marilyn Singer. Text copyright © 2003 by Marilyn Singer. Reprinted with permission by Atheneum Books for Young Readers, an imprint of Simon & Schuster Children's Publishing Division.

"Mother to Tigers" by George Ella Lyon, illustrations by Peter Catalanotto. Text copyright © 2003 by George Ella Lyon. Illustrations copyright © 2003 by Peter Catalanotto. Reprinted by permission of Atheneum Books for Young Readers, an imprint of Simon & Schuster Children's Publishing Division.

"My Very Own Room" by Amada Irma Pérez, illustrations by Maya Christina Gonzalez. Text copyright © 2000 by Amada Irma Pérez. Illustrations copyright © 2000 by Maya Christina Gonzalez. Reprinted with permission by Children's Book Press.

"The Printer" by Myron Uhlberg, illustrations by Henri Sørensen. Text copyright © 2003 Myron Uhlberg. Illustrations copyright © 2003 by Henri Sørensen. Reprinted with permission of Peachtree Publishers.

"Seven Spools of Thread: A Kwanzaa Story" by Angela Shelf Medearis, illustrations by Daniel Minter. Text copyright © 2000 by Angela Shelf Medearis. Illustrations copyright © 2000 by Daniel Minter. Reprinted with permission by Albert Whitman & Company.

"Think of darkness" by David McCord from MORE RHYMES OF THE NEVER WAS AND ALWAYS IS by David McCord. Copyright © 1979, 1980 by David McCord. Reprinted with permission of Little, Brown and Company (Canada) Limited.

"Wilbur's Boast" (from "CHARLOTTE'S WEB") by E. B. White, illustrations by Garth Williams. Text copyright © 1952 by E. B. White. Text copyright © renewed 1980 by E. B. White. Illustrations copyright © renewed 1980 by Estate of Garth Williams. Reprinted with permission by HarperCollins Publishers, a division of HarperCollins Publishers.

ILLUSTRATIONS

Cover Illustration: Scott Gustafson

12-13: Shane McGowan. 14-39: Janet Stevens. 44: Tim Johnson. 50-73: Daniel Minter. 76: Tim Johnson. 83: Rick Nease for TFK. 84: Jack Thomas. 108-109: Traci Van Wagoner. 110: Tim Johnson. 116-139: Maya Christina Gonzalez. 142: Wetzel & Company. 144: Tim Johnson. 146-147: Sally Springer. 148-149: Wetzel & Company. 154-177: Cat Bowman Smith. 180: Wetzel & Company. 182: Tim Johnson. 188-211: Lori Lohstoeter. 216: Tim Johnson. 221: (tl) Topham/The Image Works. 222: (cr) Mario Ruiz/Time Life Pictures/Getty Images. 234-253: Henri Sørensen. 257: Barb Cousins. 258: Tim Johnson. 282-283: Amy Ning. 284: Tim Johnson. 286: Kathleen Kemly. 294-315: DyAnne DiSalvo. 320: Tim Johnson. 326-338: Garth Williams. 344: Tim Johnson. 354: Library of Congress, Prints & Photographs Division. 362-379: Peter Catalanotto. 380-381: Nicole Rutten. 382: (bc) Tim Johnson. 402: Tim Johnson. 404: Philomena O'Neill. 407: Joe Taylor. 408-409: Lindy Burnett.

PHOTOGRAPHY

All Photographs are by Macmillan/McGraw Hill (MMH) except as noted below:

10-11: Blend/PunchStock. 11: (inset) C Squared Studios/Getty Images. 38: Courtesy Susan Stevens Crummel. 40: (bkgd) Photodisc/PunchStock; (bl) Comstock Images/Alamy. 41: (b) Premium Stock/CORBIS; (bkgd) Photodisc/PunchStock. 42: (tl) Foodpix. 43: (bkgd) Photodisc/PunchStock. 44: (bkgd) Wetzel&Company; (b) Michael Newman/Photo Edit Inc. 45: Judd Pilossof/FoodPix/Getty Images. 46-47: (bkgd) James Marshall/CORBIS. 47: (inset) Royalty-Free/CORBIS. 48: (t) Myrleen Ferguson Cate/Photo Edit Inc; (bl) Richard Hutchings/Photo Edit Inc. 49: Myrleen Ferguson Cate/Photo Edit Inc. 72: (tcl) Courtesy Angela Meaderis; (cr) Courtesy Daniel Minter. 74: (bkgd) Don Farrall/Getty Images. 75: (tr) Douglas Pulsipher/Alamy. 76: Royalty-Free/CORBIS. 77: (tl) Tom McCarthy/ Photo Edit Inc; (tc) Emma Lee/LifeFile Photos Ltd./Alamy; (tr) Photodisc/Getty Images. 78: (bl) Peter Lillie/OSF/Animals Animals; (br) Wolfgang Kaehler/CORBIS. 78-79: (t) Michael Gadomski/Animals Animals. 79: (bl) David Hall/Photo Researchers; (br) Doug Wechsler/Animals Animals. 80: Barry Iverson for TFK. 81: (tl) Don Enger/Animals Animals; (tr) W. Perry Conway/CORBIS; (tcl) Nature's Images/Photo Researchers; (tcr) S. Michael Bisceglie/Animals Animals; (cl) Gregory Ochocki/Photo Researchers; (cr) Nigel Dennis/APBL/Animals Animals; (bcr) Photolink/Photodisc/Getty Images; (bl) Stephanie Harvin. 82: Jack Thomas. 83: Joel W. Rogers/CORBIS. 85: Jack Thomas. 86: (cl) Tom Myers/Photo Researchers; (bl) Courtesy Jean Mahoney. 88: SuperStock/AGE Fotostock. 89: (bkgd) Dian Lofton for TFK. 89: (c) Burke/Triolo Productions/Brand X/Alamy. (cr) Tracy Montana/PhotoLink/Getty Images; 90-91: Creatas/PunchStock. 91: (inset) Photodisc/Getty Images. 92: (bl) Peter Kaplan/Photo Researchers. 92-93: (t) Nancy Rotenberg/Animals Animals/Earth Scenes. 93: Heifer International. 94: (bc) Robert Cranston/RJ's Images of Nature. 94-95: (bkgd) Wetzel & Company. 95: (c) Darrell Wong/The Fresno Bee. 96: (bc) Courtesy Stacey L. Caha. 96-97: (bkgd) Wetzel & Company. 97: (bc) Courtesy of The Fresno Bee. 98: (bl) Courtesy Stacey L. Caha. 98-99: (bkgd) Wetzel & Company. 99: (tc) Robert Cranston/RJ's Images of Nature. 100: (tc) David Hunter/The Fresno Bee. 100-101: (bkgd) Wetzel & Company. 101: (bc) Courtesy Stacey L. Caha. 102: (bc) Courtesy Stacey L. Caha. 102-103: (bkgd) Wetzel & Company. 103: (tc) Courtesy Stacey L. Caha. 104: (tc) Courtesy Stacey L. Caha. 104-105: (bkgd) Wetzel & Company. 105: (bc) Robert Cranston/RJ's Images of Nature. 106: (tcl) Courtesy Gary Soto. 106-107: (bkgd) Wetzel & Company. 107: (br) Robert Cranston/RJ's Images of Nature. 110: Superstock/Alamy. 111: (tcl)

Steve Gorton/DK Images; (2) Thinkstock/Alamy. 112-113: (bkgd) Michael Mancuso/Omni-Photo Communications Inc. 113: (inset) Comstock. 114: (t) Tom Stewart/CORBIS; (b) Michael Pole/CORBIS. 115: C Squared Studios/Getty Images. 138: Courtesy Children's Book Press. 140: (b) Myrleen Ferguson Cate/PhotoEdit. 141: (bl) Stockdisc/PunchStock; (br) Brand X Pictures/PunchStock. 142: (cr) Chris Gibson/Alamy. 143: (tr) NiKreationS/Alamy. 144: Scholastic Studio 10/Index Stock Imagery. 145: Royalty-Free/CORBIS. 149: (bl) Library of Congress; (br) Bettmann/CORBIS. 150-151: Daniel Bosler/Getty Images. 151: (inset) Photodisc/Getty Images. 152: (t) Charles O'Rear/CORBIS; (cl) Michael Newman/Photo Edit Inc; (bl) David Young-Wolff/ Photo Edit Inc. 153: Michael Newman/ Photo Edit Inc. 176: (tcl) Courtesy Scholastic; (cl) Courtesy Cat Bowman Smith. 178: Bronwyn Kidd/Getty Images. 179: Lynda Richardson/CORBIS. 181: Ariel Skelley/CORBIS. 182: Amy Etra/Photo Edit Inc. 183: PhotoLink/Getty Images. 184-185: Jeff Greenberg/PhotoEdit. 185: (inset) David Buffington/Getty Images. 186: (t) Courtesy of the Heifer Organization; (bl) Gunter Marx Photography/CORBIS. 187: Tom Stewart/CORBIS. 210: (tr) Courtesy Simon & Schuster; (cl) Image Farm; (inset) Courtesy Simon & Schuster. 212: (tc) Courtesy of Heifer International; (tr) Freeman Patterson/Masterfile. 212-213: (bl) Freeman Patterson/Masterfile. 213: (br) Courtesy of Heifer International. 214: (cr) Courtesy of Heifer International. 214-215: (t) Freeman Patterson/Masterfile. 215: (c) Courtesy of Heifer International. 216: (cl) David Young-Wolff/Photo Edit. 217: (tr) Andy Crawford/Getty Images. 218-219: (bkgd) Orion Press/Stone/Getty Images. 220: (tl) Library of Congress, Prints and Photographs Division; (tr) NASA; (bl) Bettmann/CORBIS; (br) Gianni Dagli Orti/CORBIS. 221: (tr) AP-Wide World Photos; (c) C Squared Studios/Photodisc/Punchstock; (bcl) SSPL/The Image Works; (bl) James Keyser/Time Life Pictures/Getty Images. 222: Christopher Hornsby. 223: Mario Ruiz/Time Life Pictures/Getty Images. 224: Courtesy of Libertyland Amusement Park, TN. 226: (tcl) Ross W. Hamilton/The Oregonian; (bcl) AP-Wide World Photos. 228: Ryan McVay/Photodisc/Punchstock. 229: (c) Photodisc/Getty Images; (cr) C Squared Studios/Getty Images; (br) Ryan McVay/Photodisc/Getty Images; (b) Dian Lofton for TFK. 230-231: (bkgd) © Philip Rostron/Masterfile. 231: (inset) Siede Preis/Getty Images. 232: Jim Vecchi/CORBIS. 233: L. Rue III/Bruce Coleman. 252: (tcl) Courtesy Peachtree Publishers, Ltd; (cl) Courtesy Peachtree Publishers, Ltd. 254: (b) Phil Degginger/Alamy. 255: (r) Jamie D. Travis/Getty Images; (tl) Stocksearch/Alamy. 256: (bl) Michael Newman/PhotoEdit; (tl) Ladi Kirn/Alamy. 258: Bob Daemmrich/The Image Works. 259: Steve Cole/Getty Images. 260-261: (bkgd) MITSUHIKO IMAMORI /MINDEN PICTURES. 261: (inset) C Squared Studios/Getty Images. 262: (t) Gerry Ellis/Minden Pictures; (bl) Adam Wolfitt/CORBIS. 263: (tl) Pat O'Hara/CORBIS; (cr) Joe McDonald/CORBIS. 264-265: (bkgd) Diana L. Stratton/Tom Stack and Associates. 265: (l) Esselte/Phototone/Earthlink Textures. 266: Fritz Polking/Peter Arnold. 267: (bc) Ken Kavenaugh/Photo Researchers; (inset) Scott Camazine/Photo Researchers. 268: Jerry L. Ferrara/Photo Researchers. 269: (cl) John D. Cunningham/Visuals Unlimited; (b) Leonard Lee Roe III/Photo Researchers. 270: © SuperStock / SuperStock. 271: David Hosking/Stone/Getty Images. 272: (tl) Mark Boulton/Photo Researchers; (br) Kjell B. Sandved/Visuals Unlimited. 273: (tcl) © SuperStock / SuperStock; (tr) Bruce M. Herman/Photo Researchers; (bcr) Michael Giannechini/Photo Researchers. 274: Glen Oliver/Visuals Unlimited. 275: E. R. Degginger. 276: (tl) Jeff Lepone/Photo Researchers; (tcr) E. R. Degginger/Photo Researchers. 277: Craig K. Lorenz/Photo Researchers. 278: (tl) Randy Wells/CORBIS; (tc) David M. Schleser/Natures Images Inc/Photo Researchers; (b) Kim Heacox/Stone/Getty Images. 279: (tc) M. H. Sharp/Photo Researchers; (cl) M. H. Sharp/Photo Researchers; (br) Joe McDonald/Visuals Unlimited. 280: (l) SuperStock; (tl) Courtesy Scholastic; (bc) Gary Meszaros/Dembinsky Photo Associates; (bcr) SuperStock. 280-281: (bkgd) Raymond Gehman/CORBIS. 281: (tc) M. H. Sharp/Photo Researchers; (b) Kim Heacox/Stone/Getty Images. 284: Photodisc Blue/Getty Images. 285: (bkgd) Wetzel and company; (tr) Anup Shah/The Image Bank/Getty Images. 288: (br) Jim Reed photography; (tr) Gene Rhoden/Alamy. 289: (tr) Gene Rhoden/Alamy. 290-291: David Young-Wolff/PhotoEdit. 291: (inset) C. Borland/PhotoLink/Getty Images. 292: (t) Siede Preis/Getty Images; (b) Henry Diltz/CORBIS. 293: (cl) Dennis MacDonald/Photo Edit Inc; (cr) David Hiller/Photodisc blue/Getty Images. 314: Courtesy DyAnne Disalvo-Ryan. 316: (bc) Image Source/PunchStock; (bl) Darren Matthews/Alamy. 316-317: (bkgd) Craig D. Wood/Panoramic Images. 317: (c) Darrell Sparks. 318: (br) Beth Haller; (cl) Brad Haire, University of Georgia/Forestryimages.org. 318-319: (bkgd) Craig D. Wood/Panoramic Images. 320: Michael Newman/Photo Edit Inc. 321: CheapShots/Alamy Images. 322-323: (bkgd) Chuck Place/Place Stock. 323: (inset) Photodisc/Getty Images. 324: (t) G.K. & Vikki Hart/Getty Images; (bl) Premium Stock/CORBIS. 325: Juniors Bildarchiv/Alamy. 338: (l) Photo by Donald E. Johnson; (2) Courtesy Estate of Garth Williams c/o Frost National Bank. 340: Lawrence Manning/CORBIS. 341: Philippe McClelland/Stone/Getty Images. 342: (t) Agnes Overbaugh; (b) Siede Preis/Getty Images. 343: Rick Friedman/CORBIS. 344: Ryam McVay/Getty Images. 346-347: Photodisc/Getty Images. 348: Stephen Jaffe/AFP Photo/NewsCom. 349: (tr) Kim Kulish/CORBIS. 350: (bkgd) AP-Wide World Photos; (bl) Courtesy NASA. 351: (bc) NASA; (br) Time Life Pictures/Getty Images. 352: (b) NASA/Getty Images/NewsCom. 353: (tc) Courtesy NASA; (tr) NASA/Reuters/NewsCom. 354: Library of Congress, Prints & Photographs Division. 356: Digital Vision/Punchstock. 357: (tc) Burke/Triolo Productions/Brand X/Alamy; (cr) Nancy R. Cohen/Getty Images; (b) C Squared Studios/Getty Images; (bkgd) Dian Lofton for TFK. 358-359: Per Eriksson/Getty Images. 359: (inset) G.K. & Vikki Hart/Getty Images. 360: Frank Siteman/Photo Edit Inc. 361: (tcr) Courtesy of Texas Hearing and Service Dogs; (cr) Lawrence Migdale/Photo Researchers. 378: Courtesy Simon & Schuster. 382: Frank Siteman/Photo Edit Inc. 384-385: (bkgd) Adam Jones/Visuals Unlimited. 385: (inset) Pat Powers and Cherryl Schafer/Getty Images. 386: Millard H. Sharp/Photo Researchers. 387: (tr) Ken Thomas/Photo Researchers; (c) Valerie Giles/Photo Researchers. 388-389: William Dow/CORBIS. 390: (c) Ralph A. Clever/CORBIS; (bl) J.H. Pete Carmichael; (br) J.H. Pete Carmichael. 391: J.H. Pete Carmichael. 392-393: (t) J.H. Pete Carmichael. 393: (bl) Whit Bronaugh. 394-395: Whit Bronaugh. 395: (tl) J.H. Pete Carmichael. 396-397: Craig W. Racicot/Game Day Pictures. 398: (l) J.H. Pete Carmichael; (2) Ralph A. Clever/CORBIS; (3) J.H. Pete Carmichael. 398-399: (bkgd) Getty Images. 399: (l) Craig W. Racicot/Game Day Pictures; (2) Whit Bronaugh. 400: (b) Bill Beatty/Animals Animals/Earth Scenes. 400-401: (bkgd) Craig Tuttle/CORBIS. 401: (t) Sharon Cummings/Dembinsky Photo Associates; (c) MENDEZ, RAYMOND/Animals Animals/Earth Scenes. 402: Barry Willis/Getty Images. 403: Gay Bumgarner/Jupiter Images. 406-407: (all) Steve Ruark/Syracuse Newspapers/The Image Works. 410: Robert Glusic/Getty Images. 411: Skip Nall/Getty Images. 412: Steve Mason/Getty Images. 413: (l) Siede Preis/Getty Images. 413: (2) Siede Preis/Getty Images. 414: (l) Steve Cole/Getty Images; (r) David Seed Photography/Taxi/Getty Images. 416: Tom J. Ulrich/Visuals Unlimited. 417: Doug Cheeseman/Peter Arnold. 418: Photolink/Getty Images. 420: Michael T. Sedam/CORBIS. 421: Siede Preis/Getty Images. 422: (t) MedioImages/Picture Quest; (b) Margot Granitsas/The Image Works.

Teacher's Notes

Correlations to the Sunshine State Standards

- FCAT Reading Assessed Benchmarks
- FCAT Writing + Assessed Benchmarks
- Reading and Language Arts
- Science
- Social Studies
- Mathematics

FCAT Reading Assessed Benchmarks

The chart below correlates the FCAT Reading Assessed Benchmarks with the new Grade 3 Sunshine State Standards.

FCAT READING ASSESSED BENCHMARKS GRADES 3–5	GRADE 3 SUNSHINE STATE STANDARDS
LA.A.1.2.3 Uses simple strategies to determine meaning and increase vocabulary for reading, including the use of prefixes, suffixes, root words, multiple meanings, antonyms, synonyms, and word relationships.	**LA.3.1.6.3** - use context clues to determine meanings of unfamiliar words **LA.3.1.6.7** - use meaning of familiar base words and affixes (prefixes and suffixes) to determine meanings of unfamiliar complex words **LA.3.1.6.8** - use knowledge of antonyms, synonyms, homophones, and homographs to determine meanings of words
LA.A.2.2.1 Reads text and determines the main idea or essential message, identifies relevant supporting details and facts, and arranges events in chronological order.	**LA.3.1.7.3** - determine explicit ideas and information in grade-level text, including but not limited to main idea, relevant supporting details, strongly implied message and inference, and chronological order of events **LA.3.2.2.2** - use information form the text to answer questions related to explicitly stated main ideas or relevant details
LA.A.2.2.2 Identifies the author's purpose in a simple text. (Includes **LA.A.2.2.3** Recognizes when a text is primarily intended to persuade.)	**LA.3.1.7.2** - identify the author's purpose (e.g., to inform, entertain, or explain) in text and how an author's perspective influences text
LA.A.2.2.7 Recognizes the use of comparison and contrast in a text.	**L.A.3.1.7.5** - identify the text structure an author uses (e.g., comparison/contrast, cause/effect, and sequence of events) and explain how it impacts meaning in text
LA.A.2.2.8 Selects and uses a variety of appropriate reference materials, including multiple representations of information such as maps, charts, and photos, to gather information for research projects. (Includes LA.A.2.2.5 Reads and organizes information for a variety of purposes, including making a report, conducting interviews, taking a test, and performing an authentic task.)	**LA.3.1.7.1** - identify a text's features (e.g., title, subheadings, captions, illustrations), use them to make and confirm predictions, and establish a purpose for reading **LA.3.2.2.1** - identify and explain the purpose of text features (e.g., table of contents, glossary, headings, charts, graphs, diagrams, illustrations) **LA.3.6.1.1** - The student will read informational text (e.g., graphs, charts, manuals) and organize information for different purposes, including but not limited to being informed, following multi-step directions, making a report, conducting interviews, preparing to take a test, and performing a task.
LA.E.1.2.2 Understands the development of plot and how conflicts are resolved in a story.	**LA.3.2.1.2.** - identify and explain the elements of story structure, including character/character development, setting, plot, and problem/resolution in a variety of fiction
LA.E.1.2.3 Knows the similarities and differences among the characters, settings, and events presented in various texts.	**LA.3.1.7.7** - compare and contrast topics, settings, characters, and problems in two texts
LA.E.2.2.1 Recognizes cause-and-effect relationships in literary texts. (Applies to fiction, nonfiction, poetry, and drama.)	**LA.3.1.7.4** - identify cause-and-effect relationships in text

FCAT Writing + Assessed Benchmarks

The chart below correlates the FCAT Writing + Assessed Benchmarks with the new Grade 3 Sunshine State Standards.

FCAT ASSESSED WRITING BENCHMARKS GRADES 3 – 5	GRADE 3 SUNSHINE STATE STANDARDS FOR WRITING
LA.B.1.2.1 The student prepares for writing by recording thoughts, focusing on central idea, grouping related ideas, and identifying the purpose for writing.	**LA.3.3.2.1** using a pre-writing plan to develop the main idea with supporting details that describe or provide facts and/or opinions; and **Alt:** LA.3.3.1 Student will use prewriting strategies to generate ideas and formulate a plan. **Alt:** LA.3.3.1.1 generating ideas from multiple sources (e.g., text, brainstorming, graphic organizer, drawing, writer's notebook, group discussion, printed material);
LA.B.1.2.2 The student drafts and revises writing in cursive that focuses on the topic; has a logical organization pattern, including a beginning, middle, conclusion, and transitional devices; has ample development of supporting ideas; demonstrates a completeness of wholeness; demonstrates a command of language, including precision in word choice; generally has correct verb and noun forms; with few exceptions, has sentences that are complete, except when fragments are used purposefully; uses a variety of sentence structures; and generally follows the conventions of punctuation, capitalization, and spelling.	**L.A.3.3.2** The student will write a draft appropriate to the topic, audience, purpose. **L.A.3.3.3** The student will revise and refine the draft for clarity and effectiveness **Alt:** LA.3.3.3.1 evaluating the draft for use of ideas and content, logical organization, voice (e.g., formal or informal), point of view, and word choice;
LA.B.1.2.3 Student produces final documents that have been edited for correct spelling; correct use of punctuation, including commas in a series, dates, and addresses, and beginning and ending quotation marks; correct capitalization of proper nouns, correct usage of subject/verb agreement, verb and noun forms, and sentence structure.	**LA.3.3.5** The student will write a final product for the intended audience. **Alt:** LA.3.3.4.1 spelling, using spelling patterns and generalizations (e.g., word families, diphthong, consonant digraphs, CVC words, CCVC words, CVCC words, affixes) and using a dictionary or other resources as necessary **Alt:** LA.3.3.4.2 capitalization for proper nouns, including holidays, product names, titles used with someone's name, initials, and geographic locations; **Alt:** LA.3.3.4.3 punctuation, including end punctuation, apostrophes, commas, colons, quotation marks in dialogue, and apostrophes in singular possessives **Alt:** LA.3.3.5.1 prepare writing in a format appropriate to audience and purpose (e.g., manuscript, multimedia); **Alt.** LA.3.3.4 The student will edit and correct the draft for standard language conventions.

Reading & Language Arts Sunshine State Standards Grade 3

Each standard is coded in the following manner

LA.	3.	1.	1.	1.
Subject	Grade	Strand	Standard	Benchmark

KEY	TE = Teacher's Edition	LR = Leveled Readers	TFK FCAT = Time for Kids FCAT Edition	FCAT Test Prep = FCAT Test Prep and Practice

READING PROCESS		Macmillan/McGraw-Hill FLORIDA TREASURES
Phonics/Word Analysis: LA.3.1.4	**The student demonstrates knowledge of the alphabetic principle and applies grade level phonics skills to read text.**	
LA.3.1.4.1	use knowledge of the pronunciation of root words and other morphemes (e.g., prefixes, suffixes, derivational endings) to decode words;	**TE:** 3.1–3.3: 22, 26, 37M, 37Q, 61, 73E, 73F, 74I, 85E, 115E, 115F, 147E, 177E, 211E, 212I, 223E, 223M, 223Q, 234, 236, 255E, 268, 277E, 277M, 277Q, 282I, 313E, 313M, 313Q, 339E, 351E, 351Q, 355, 387, 417E, 417M, 417Q; 3.4–3.6: 45E, 45M, 61, 77E, 77G, 89E, 89M, 93, 115, 122, 145E, 153, 187, 217E, 229E, 229M, 229P, 285M, 345E, 357M, 383E, 403E, 403M
LA.3.1.4.2	use knowledge of the pronunciation of complex word families (e.g., -ieve, -ield) to decode words in these families;	**TE:** 3.1–3.3: 85E, 115E, 115M, 115Q, 147E, 147G-147H, 147M, 147Q, 177E, 177G-177H, 211E, 255E, 339E, 351E, 351M, 417E, 3.4–3.6: 45E, 77C,77E, 192, 229E
LA.3.1.4.3	decode multi-syllabic words in isolation and in context; and	**TE:** 3.1–3.3: 37E, 37M, 37Q, 73E, 73M, 85E, 85M, 115E, 115M, 147E, 147M, 177E, 177M, 177Q, 211E, 211M, 211Q, 223E, 223M, 255E, 255M, 277E, 277M, 313E, 313M, 313Q, 339E, 339M, 339Q, 351E, 351M, 383E, 383M, 383Q, 417E, 417M, 417Q; 3.4–3.6: 45E, 45M, 61, 77E, 77M, 89E, 89M, 111E, 111M, 145E, 145M, 183E, 183M, 1830, 183Q, 217E, 217M, 229E, 229F, 229M, 230I, 259E, 259M, 259Q, 285E, 285M, 285Q, 290R, 307, 321E, 321M, 321Q, 331, 334, 345E, 345M, 346I, 357E, 357M, 357Q, 358I, 383E, 383M, 383Q, 384I, 403E, 403M, 403Q
LA.3.1.4.4	use self-correction when subsequent reading indicates an earlier misreading.	**TE:** 3.1–3.3: 147E, 287, 319, 383E; 3.4–3.6: 89E, 122, 183E, 245, 285E, 285M, 307, 345E, 403E
Fluency: LA.3.1.5	**The student demonstrates the ability to read grade level text orally with accuracy, appropriate rate, and expression.**	
LA.3.1.5.1	apply letter-sound knowledge to decode unknown words quickly and accurately in context; and	**TE:** 3.1–3.3: 10R, 16, 37E, 37M, 37Q, 38I, 73E, 73M, 73Q, 74I, 85E, 85M, 85Q, 86I, 99, 115E, 115M, 115Q, 116I, 147E, 147M, 147Q, 152R, 177E, 177M, 197, 211E, 211M, 223E, 223M, 255E, 255M, 277E, 277M, 313E, 313M, 339E, 339M, 340I, 351E, 351M, 383E, 383M, 384I, 417E, 417M, 3.4–3.6: 45E, 45M, 77E, 77M, 78I, 89E, 89M, 111E, 111M, 145E, 145M, 183E, 183M, 217E, 217M, 229E, 229M, 259E, 259M, 263, 285E, 285M, 312, 321E, 321M, 345E, 345M, 357E, 357M, 368, 383E, 383M, 399A, 403E, 403M

Key 3.1 = Grade 3, Unit 1

LA.3.1.5.2	adjust reading rate based on purpose, text difficulty, form, and style.	**TE:** 3.1–3.3: 10R, 30, 33A, 37L, 37N, 37Q, 37S, 38I, 43, 51, 67A, 73L, 73N, 73Q, 73S, 74I, 79, 81A, 85L, 85N, 85Q, 85S, 86I, 91, 99, 111A, 115L, 115N, 115Q, 115S, 116I, 132, 141A, 147L, 147N, 147Q, 147S, 152R, 157, 171A, 177L, 177N, 177Q, 177S, 178I, 183, 205A, 211L, 211N, 211Q, 211S, 212I, 217, 219A, 223L, 223N, 223Q, 223S, 224I, 229, 249A, 255L, 255N, 255Q, 255S, 256I, 261, 273A, 277L, 277N, 277Q, 277S, 282R, 287, 307A, 313L, 313N, 313Q, 313S, 314I, 319, 324, 329, 335A, 339L, 339N, 339Q, 339S, 340I, 345, 347A, 351L, 351N, 351Q, 351S, 352I, 379A, 383L, 383N, 383Q, 383S, 384I, 389, 411A, 417L, 417N, 417Q, 417S, 3.4–3.6: 10R, 31, 39A, 45L, 45N, 45Q, 45S, 46I, 51, 73A, 77L, 77N, 77Q, 77S, 78I, 83, 85A, 89L, 89N, 89Q, 89S, 90I, 95, 99, 107A, 112I, 111L, 111N, 111Q, 111S, 117, 139A, 145L, 145N, 145Q, 145S, 150R, 177A, 183L, 183N. 183O, 183S, 184I, 189, 211A, 217L, 217N, 217Q, 217S, 218I, 223, 225A, 229L, 229N, 229Q, 229S, 230I, 253A, 259L, 259N, 259Q, 259S, 260I, 265, 268, 271, 281A, 285L, 285N, 285Q, 285S, 290R, 295, 315A, 321L, 321N, 321Q, 321S, 322I, 327, 339A, 345L, 345N, 345Q, 345S, 346I, 351, 353A, 357L, 357N. 357Q, 357S, 358I, 363, 379A, 383L, 383N, 383Q, 383S, 384I, 389, 399A, 403L, 403N, 403Q, 403S
Vocabulary Development: LA.3.1.6	**The student uses multiple strategies to develop grade appropriate vocabulary.**	
LA.3.1.6.1	use new vocabulary that is introduced and taught directly;	**TE:** 3.1–3.3: 11, 12, 13, 34, 37C, 37D, 37F, 37N, 37O, 37P, 37Q, 37R, 37S, 37V, 40, 41, 68, 69, 73C, 73D, 73F, 73N, 73O. 73P, 73Q, 73R, 73S, 73V, 76, 77, 85C, 85D, 85F, 85N, 85O, 85P, 85Q, 85R, 85S, 85V, 88, 89, 115C, 115D, 115F, 115N, 115O, 115P, 115Q, 115R, 115S, 115V, 118, 119, 142, 147C, 147D, 147F, 147N, 147O, 147P, 147Q, 147R, 147S, 147V, 153, 154, 155, 156, 158, 159, 172, 177C, 177D, 177F, 177N, 177O, 177P, 177Q, 177R, 177S, 177V, 180, 181, 182, 206, 211C, 211D, 211F, 211N, 211O, 211P, 211Q, 211R, 211S, 211V, 214, 215, 216, 223C, 223D, 223F, 223N, 223O, 223P, 223Q, 223R, 223S, 223V, 226, 227, 228, 250, 255C, 255D, 255F, 255N, 255O, 255P, 255Q, 255R, 255S, 255V, 258, 259, 260, 268, 277C, 277D, 277F, 277N, 277O, 277P, 277Q, 277R, 277S, 277V, 284, 285, 286, 290, 297, 313C, 313D, 313F, 313N, 313O, 313P, 313Q, 313R, 313S, 313V, 316, 317, 318, 339C, 339D, 339F, 339N, 339O, 339P, 339Q, 339R, 339S, 339V, 342, 343, 344, 351C, 351D, 351F, 351N, 351O, 351P, 351Q, 351R, 351S, 351V, 354, 355, 356, 360, 368, 383C, 383D, 383F, 383N, 383O, 383P, 383Q, 383R, 383S, 383V, 384I, 385, 386, 387, 388, 390, 404, 412, 417C, 417D, 417F, 417N, 417O, 417P, 417Q, 417R, 417S, 417V; 3.4–3.6: 12, 13, 14, 40, 45D, 45D, 45F, 45N, 45O, 45P, 45Q, 45R, 45S, 45V, 48, 49, 50, 77F, 77P, 77S, 77V, 79, 80, 81, 82, 89C, 89D, 89F, 89N, 89O, 89P, 89Q, 89R, 89S, 89V, 92, 93, 94, 97, 101, 111C, 111D, 111E, 111F, 111M, 111N, 111O, 111P, 111Q, 111R, 111S, 111V, 112, 113, 114, 115, 115B, 116, 140, 145C, 145D, 145F, 145N, 145O, 145P, 145Q, 145R, 145S, 145V, 152, 153, 154, 157, 178, 183, 183C, 183D, 183F, 183N, 183O, 183P, 183Q, 183R, 183S, 183V, 185, 186, 187, 187C, 212, 217C, 217D, 217F, 217N, 217O, 217P, 217Q, 217R, 217S, 217V, 220, 221, 222, 229C, 229D, 229F, 229N, 229O, 229P, 229Q, 229R, 229S, 229V, 232, 233, 234, 244, 246, 254, 259C, 259D, 259F, 259N, 259O, 259P,

		259Q, 259R, 259S, 259V, 262, 263, 264, 271, 285C, 285D, 285F, 285N, 285O, 285P, 285Q, 285R, 285S, 285V, 292, 293, 294, 299, 308, 316, 321B, 321C, 321D, 321F, 321N, 321O, 321P, 321Q, 321R, 321S, 321V, 324, 325, 326, 328, 330, 340, 345C, 345D, 345F, 345N, 345O, 345P, 345Q, 345R, 345S, 345V, 348, 349, 350, 357C, 357D, 357F, 357N, 357O, 357P, 357Q, 357R, 357S, 357V, 360, 361, 362, 367, 368, 383C, 383D, 383F, 383N, 383O, 383P, 383Q, 383R, 383S, 383V, 386, 387, 388, 395, 396, 403C, 403D, 403F, 403N, 403O, 403P, 403Q, 403R, 403S, 403V, 407I
LA.3.1.6.2	listen to, read, and discuss familiar and conceptually challenging text;	**TE:** 3.1–3.3: 10R, 11, 12-13, 13A, 14-31, 33, 34-35, 37P, 37R, 37T, 37V, 38I, 39, 40-41, 41A, 42-65, 67, 68-71, 73P, 73R, 73T, 73V, 74I, 75, 76, 77A, 78-81, 85P, 85R, 85T, 85V, 86I, 87, 88, 89, 89A, 90-109, 111, 115P, 115R, 115T, 115V, 116I, 117, 118, 119, 119A, 120-139, 141, 142-145, 147P, 147R, 147T, 147V, 3.1: T11-T16, 152R, 153, 154, 155, 155A, 156-169, 171, 172-175, 177P, 177R, 177T, 177V, 178I, 179, 180, 181, 181A, 182-203, 205, 206-209, 211P, 211R, 211T, 211V, 212I, 213, 214, 215, 215A, 216-219, 223P, 223R, 223T, 223V, 224I, 225, 226, 227, 227A, 228-247, 249, 250-253, 255P, 255R, 255T, 255V, 256I, 257, 258, 259, 259A, 260-271, 273, 274-275, 277P, 277R, 277T, 277V, 3.2: T12-T17, 282R, 283, 284, 285, 285A, 286-305, 307, 308-311, 313P, 313R, 313T, 313V, 314I, 315, 316, 317, 317A, 318-333, 335, 336-337, 339P, 339R, 339T, 339V, 340I, 341, 342, 343, 343A, 344-347, 351P, 351R, 351T, 351V, 352I, 353, 354, 355, 355A, 356-377, 373, 383P, 383R, 383T, 383V, 384I, 385, 386, 387, 387A, 388-409, 411, 412-415, 417P, 417R, 417T, 417V, T12-T17; 3.4–3.6: 10R, 11, 12, 13, 13A, 14-37, 39, 40-43, 45P, 45R, 45T, 45V, 46I, 47, 48, 49, 49A, 50-71, 73, 74-75, 77P, 77R, 77T, 77V, 78I, 79, 80, 81, 81A, 82-85, 89P, 89R, 89T, 89V, 90I, 91, 92, 93, 93A, 94-105, 107, 108-109, 111P, 111R, 111T, 111V, 112I, 113, 114, 115, 115A, 116-137, 139, 140-143, 145P, 145R, 145T, 145V, 3.4: T12-T17, 150R, 151, 152, 153, 153A, 154-175, 177, 178-181, 183P, 183R, 183T, 183V, 184I, 185, 186, 187, 187A, 188-209, 211, 212-215, 217P, 217R, 217T, 217V, 218I, 219, 220, 221, 221A, 222-225, 229P, 229R, 229T, 229V, 230I, 231, 232, 233, 233A, 234-251, 253, 254-257, 259P, 259R, 259T, 259V, 260I, 261, 262, 263, 263A, 264-279, 281, 282-283, 285P, 285R, 285T, 285V, 3.5: T13-T18, 290R, 291, 292, 293, 293A, 294-313, 315, 316-319, 321P, 321R, 321T, 321V, 322I, 323, 324, 325, 325A, 326-337, 339, 340-343, 345P, 345R, 345T, 345V, 346I, 347, 348, 349, 349A, 350-353, 357P, 357R, 357T, 357V, 358I, 359, 360, 361, 361A, 362-377, 379, 380-381, 383P, 383R, 383T, 383V, 384I, 385, 386, 387, 387A, 388-397, 399, 400-401, 403P, 403R, 403T, 403V, T13-T18
LA.3.1.6.3	use context clues to determine meanings of unfamiliar words;	**TE:** 3.1–3.3: 12, 13, 22, 37C, 40, 41,44, 48, 73C, 73D, 73O, 73Q, 73N, 76, 77, 85C, 85O, 88, 89, 107, 115C, 118, 119, 147C, 154, 155, 160, 173, 177C, 177F, 177M, 177N, 177P, 180, 181, 197, 211C, 211P, 211R, 214, 215, 223C, 223P, 223Q, 226, 227, 232, 234, 238, 255C, 255D, 255N, 255O, 255Q, 256I, 258, 259, 266, 277C, 277D, 277E, 277N, 277O, 277P, 277Q, 277R, 277S, 284, 285, 290, 313C, 313N, 313O, 316, 317, 333, 339C, 339P, 339R, 339V, 342, 343, 351C, 351N, 351P, 354, 355, 355A, 355B, 368, 383C, 383P, 383R, 386, 387, 391, 413, 417C. 417D, 417O, 417Q;

Key 3.1 = Grade 3, Unit 1

		3.4–3.6: 13, 29, 41, 45C, 45D, 45N, 45R, 48, 49, 56, 61, 77C, 77N, 80, 81, 89C, 90I, 92, 93, 96, 111C, 111D, 111E, 111O, 111Q, 114, 115, 124, 141, 145C, 145N, 147, 152, 153, 159, 179, 183C, 183P, 186, 187, 213, 217C, 217N, 220, 221, 229C, 230I, 232, 233, 237, 242, 245, 255, 259C, 259D, 259N, 259O, 259P, 259Q, 262, 263, 278, 285C, 285N, 285P, 287, 288, 290R, 292, 293, 299, 306, 317, 321C, 321D, 321O, 321P, 321Q, 321R, 324, 325, 345C, 345R, 348, 349, 357C, 357N, 360, 361, 383C, 383N, 383R, 386, 387, 403C, 403R, 405 **TFK FCAT:** Issue 3, 5, 9, 10, 15 **FCAT Test Prep**: 6-31
LA.3.1.6.4	categorize key vocabulary and identify salient features;	**TE:** 3.1–3.3: 11, 13, 24, 26, 37D, 37F, 37O, 37Q, 39, 41, 73D, 73F, 75, 77, 85D, 85F, 87, 89, 115D, 115F, 117, 119, 147D, 147F, 153, 155, 177D, 177F, 179, 181, 211D, 211F, 213, 215, 223D, 223F, 224I, 225, 227, 255D, 255F, 257, 259, 277D, 277F, 277Q, 283, 285, 313D, 313F, 315, 317, 339D, 339F, 341, 343, 351D, 351F, 353, 355, 383C, 383D, 383F, 383H, 385, 387, 417D, 417F, 3.3: T5–T9, 3.4–3.6: 11, 13, 45D, 45F, 47, 49, 77C, 77F, 77H, 79, 81, 89D, 89F, 91, 93, 111D, 111F, 113, 145D, 145F, 151, 153, 183D, 183F, 185, 187, 217D, 217F, 217O, 219, 221, 229D, 229F, 231, 233, 259D, 259F, 261, 263, 285D, 285F, 291, 293, 321D, 321F, 322I, 323, 325, 345D, 345F, 347, 349, 357D, 357F, 359, 361, 383D, 383F, 384I, 385, 387, 403D, 403F
LA.3.1.6.5	relate new vocabulary to familiar words;	**TE:** 3.1–3.3: 11, 37F, 39, 60, 73F, 75, 85F, 85N, 85O, 85P, 87, 104, 115F, 117, 147F, 153, 177C, 177F, 179, 211F, 213, 223F, 225, 255F, 257, 277F, 282R, 283, 285, 294, 313D, 313F, 313O, 313Q, 315, 322, 339F, 341, 351F, 353, 383F, 385, 396, 417F, 3.4–3.6: 11, 45F, 47, 63, 77F, 79, 89F, 89S, 91, 111F, 113, 145F, 151, 183F, 185, 217F, 217N, 219, 229F, 231, 259F, 261, 285F, 291, 321F, 323, 345F, 347, 357F, 357Q, 359, 383F, 385, 403F
LA.3.1.6.6	identify "shades of meaning" in related words (e.g., blaring, loud);	**TE:** 3.1–3.3: 20, 37F, 60, 151D, 223F, 313A, 313D, 3.4–3.6: 45C, 145F, 152, 230I, 259C, 321F, 383F
LA.3.1.6.7	use meaning of familiar base words and affixes (prefixes and suffixes) to determine meanings of unfamiliar complex words;	**TE:** 3.1–3.3: 24, 26, 37D, 37F, 58, 60, 61, 73F, 85F, 104, 105, 115F, 147F, 159, 160, 177F, 211F, 212I, 215, 223D, 223F, 262, 268, 277F, 291, 293, 313F, 313N, 328, 329, 333, 339F, 351F, 351S, 383F; 3.1: T4; 3.2: T7; 3.4–3.6: 13, 61, 77C, 77F, 81, 93, 112I, 115, 136, 145D, 183D, 183E, 184I, 187, 217D, 217M, 217Q, 218I, 221, 229D, 229E, 229F, 245, 322I, 325, 328, 334, 335, 345D, 345E, 345M, 345O, 345Q, 357Q, 358I, 361, 373, 383D, 383M, 383O, 383Q, 395, 403F, 405; 3.4: T7, T9; 3.5 T6, T7, T9; 3.6: T7, T9 **TFK FCAT:** Issue 1, 2, 4, 7, 8, 12
LA.3.1.6.8	use knowledge of antonyms, synonyms, homophones, and homographs to determine meanings of words;	**TE:** 3.1–3.3: 20, 37N, 37O, 52R, 85N, 85O, 85P, 86I, 88, 89, 97, 115D, 115H, 115N, 115O, 115Q, 125, 152R, 154, 155, 162, 177C, 177D, 177O, 177Q, 185, 211F, 234, 255P, 262, 277F, 284, 285, 290, 313A, 313D, 313Q, 316, 329, 339C, 339H, 351F, 352I, 354, 355, 383D, 383O, 383Q, 387, 394, 396; 3.1: T7; 3.2: T5; 3.3: T8, 3.4–3.6: 12, 17, 34, 38, 45C, 45F, 45V, 48, 63, 80, 89F, 90I, 111B, 111E, 111G, 111H, 111M, 111Q, 122, 145F, 145H, 149C, 165, 186, 193, 206, 217C, 220, 232, 262, 263, 268, 285D, 321F, 324, 345F, 348, 357C, 357F, 360, 386; 3.5: T10 **TFK FCAT:** Issue 6, 11, 14

LA.3.1.6.9	determine the correct meaning of words with multiple meanings in context; and	**TE:** 3.1–3.3: 81B, 85S, 89, 97, 104, 115D, 115O, 116I, 119, 128, 147D, 147O, 147Q, 178I, 180, 181, 194, 200, 211D, 211N, 327, 339D, 340I, 343, 346, 351D, 351O, 351Q, 368, 3.2: T6; 3.3: T7; 3.4–3.6: 27, 38, 46I, 48, 49, 52, 77D, 77O, 77Q, 147, 152, 387, 392, 403D, 403O, 403Q, 3.4: T6; 3.6: T10
LA.3.1.6.10	determine meanings of unfamiliar words by using a dictionary, thesaurus, and digital tools.	**TE:** 3.1–3.3: 37F, 48, 73D, 74I, 77, 81B, 85D, 85O, 85Q, 85S, 97, 115D, 115Q, 119, 128, 140, 147D, 147F, 151C, 155, 177D, 181, 200, 211D, 211O, 211Q, 224I, 256I, 285, 313A, 313D, 314I, 317, 327, 339D, 339O, 339Q, 339S, 343, 346, 351D, 351Q, 355, 368, 383B, 383D, 383F, 387, 417D, 417F, 3.1: T6, T8, T10; 3.3: T5, T6; 3.4–3.6: 10R, 13, 18, 45D, 45O, 45Q, 49, 52, 77D, 77O, 93, 111B, 111F, 150R, 153, 170, 183D, 187, 217F, 217N, 259C, 325, 357O, 384I, 403B, 403D, 403O, 403Q, 403S; 3.4: T5
Reading Comprehension: **LA.3.1.7**	**The student uses a variety of strategies to comprehend grade level text.**	**TE:** 3.1–3.3: 49A–49B, 50–71, 73, 73B, 77A–77B, 77O, 77P, 77R, 77T, 78–81, 85O, 85P, 85R, 85T, 89A–89B, 90–109, 115O, 115P, 115R, 115T, 130, 171, 194, 197, 198, 199, 201, 205, 211O, 215A–215B, 216–219, 223O, 223P, 223R, 234, 246, 259A–259B, 260–271, 273, 277O, 277P, 277R, 277T, 285A–285B, 286–305, 307, 313O, 313P, 313R, 313T, 317, 328, 331, 333, 335, 347, 355A–355B, 356–377, 379, 383O, 383P, 383R, 383T, 387, 399, 401, 402, 404, 406, 411, 3.4–3.6: 13A–13B, 14–37, 39, 45O, 45P, 45R, 49A–49B, 50–71, 73, 77O, 77P, 77R, 77T, 85, 93A, 102, 107, 111D, 111O, 115A–115B, 116–137, 145O, 145P, 145R, 145T, 147, 149, 153A–153B, 154–175, 177, 177B, 183O, 183P, 183R, 183T, 187A–187B, 188–209, 211, 213, 217O, 217P, 217R, 217T, 221A–221B, 222–225, 225A, 229O, 229P, 229R, 229T, 229V, 230I, 233A–233B, 234–251, 253, 259O, 259P, 259R, 259T, 263A–263B, 264–279, 285O, 285P, 285R, 285T, 301, 302, 303, 306, 313, 315, 325A–325B, 326–337, 339, 339B, 342, 345O, 345P, 345R, 345T, 353, 353A, 371, 372, 376, 379, 394, 399, 404
LA.3.1.7.1	identify a text's features (e.g., title, subheadings, captions, illustrations), use them to make and confirm predictions, and establish a purpose for reading;	**TE:** 3.1–3.3: 15, 37P, 37R, 37T, 37V, 43, 49, 73P, 73R, 73T, 73V, 74, 79, 80, 81, 85P, 85R, 85T, 85V, 91, 101, 109, 115P, 115R, 115T, 115V, 121, 124, 131, 133, 136, 139, 143, 147P, 147R, 147T, 147V, 152, 157, 169, 170, 174, 177P, 177R, 177S, 177T, 177V, 183, 203, 211P, 211R, 211S, 211T, 211V, 212, 217, 218, 219, 223P, 223R, 223S, 223T, 223V, 224, 229, 239, 247, 255P, 255Q, 255R, 255T, 255V, 256, 261, 271, 277P, 277R, 277T, 277V, 281K, 287, 305, 313P, 313R, 313T, 313V, 314, 319, 326, 333, 339P, 339R, 339T, 339V, 340, 345, 347, 351P, 351R, 351T, 351V, 352, 357, 367, 377, 383P, 383R, 383T, 383V, 384, 389, 393, 394, 401, 409, 417P, 417R, 417T, 417V, 3.4–3.6: 15, 25, 34, 37, 45P, 45R, 45S, 45T, 45V, 51, 53, 71, 77P, 77R, 77T, 77V, 78, 83, 85, 89P, 89R, 89T, 89V, 90, 94, 95, 101, 105, 111P, 111R, 111T, 111V, 112, 115A, 117, 123, 130, 132, 136, 137, 141, 145P, 145R, 145T, 145V, 149K, 150, 155, 156, 175, 178, 179, 183P, 183R, 183S, 183T, 183V, 189, 196, 209, 217O, 217P, 217R, 217T, 217V, 218, 223, 229P, 229R, 229T, 229V, 235, 251, 259P, 259R, 259T, 259V, 265, 279, 285P, 285R, 285T, 285V, 289, 295, 313, 321P, 321R, 321S, 321T, 321V, 327, 337, 345P, 345R, 345T, 345V, 351, 357P, 357R, 357T, 357V, 363, 370, 377, 383P, 383R, 383T, 383V, 389, 395, 397, 403P, 403R, 403T, 403V, 406

Key 3.1 = Grade 3, Unit 1

LA.3.1.7.2	identify the author's purpose (e.g., to inform, entertain, or explain) in text and how an author's perspective influences text;	**TE:** 3.1–3.3: 32, 66, 81, 110, 111B, 140, 144, 151C, 158, 170, 204, 221, 240, 248, 259A–259B, 260–271, 272, 273, 277O, 277P, 277R, 277T, 281C, 306, 334, 378, 395, 410; 3.2: T4; 3.3: T2; 3.4–3.6: 23, 26, 34, 38, 39B, 72, 90I, 91, 93A, 93B, 94–105, 106, 107, 111O, 111P, 111R, 111T, 121, 138, 147, 148, 176, 208, 210, 227, 252, 280, 314, 338, 358I, 361A, 361B, 362–377, 378, 379, 383O, 383P, 383R, 383T, 383V, 398; 3.4: T3; 3.6: T4 **TFK FCAT:** Issue 1, 4 **FCAT Test Prep**: 32-179
LA.3.1.7.3	determine explicit ideas and information in grade-level text, including but not limited to: main idea, relevant supporting details, strongly implied message and inference, and chronological order of events;	**TE:** 3.1–3.3: 21, 23, 24, 26, 33, 49, 52, 54, 58, 60, 62, 67, 71, 77A, 77B, 78, 79, 80, 81, 82, 83, 85O, 85R, 85T, 85V, 89A, 89B, 90, 93, 94, 96, 97, 101, 106, 108, 111, 115O, 125, 140, 141, 146, 155A, 155B, 156, 159, 164, 167, 168, 171, 171B, 173, 177O, 177P, 177R, 177T, 194, 198, 201, 204, 205, 209, 215A, 215B, 216, 219, 219A, 220, 221, 223O, 227A, 227B, 228, 232, 233, 234, 235, 237, 238, 243, 244, 245, 249, 251, 255O, 255P, 255Q, 255T, 264, 269, 273, 273B, 277P, 281A, 282I, 285A, 285B, 286, 288, 292, 293, 295, 296, 297, 299, 301, 302, 304, 307, 309, 313O, 313P, 313R, 313T, 313V, 317B, 322, 327, 330, 331, 332, 334, 335B, 346, 347A, 348, 349, 352I, 355A, 355B, 356, 357, 359, 362, 364, 366, 367, 368, 370, 373, 375, 376, 379, 379B, 313O, 383P, 383R, 383T, 383V, 384I, 387A, 387B, 388, 391, 397, 399, 401, 403, 404, 405, 406, 407, 411, 412, 415, 417O, 417P, 417R, 417T, 417V; 3.1: T2; 3.2: T1, T3; 3.3: T1, T4; 3.4–3.6: 13A, 14, 17, 19, 20, 25, 28, 29, 32, 35, 36, 39, 41, 42, 43, 45O, 45P, 45R, 45T, 45V, 49A, 49B, 50, 54, 55, 56, 57, 59, 65, 66, 67, 68, 69, 70, 71, 73, 73B, 77O, 77P, 77R, 77T, 77V, 78I, 87, 93B, 98, 99, 100, 106, 107B, 109, 112I, 115B, 126, 128, 129, 130, 133, 139, 139B, 141, 142, 143, 146, 148, 149, 149A, 150R, 153A, 153B, 154, 157, 158, 159, 160, 161, 162, 163, 164, 166, 167, 168, 170, 171, 173, 174, 176, 177, 177B, 180, 182, 183O, 183P, 183R, 183T, 183V, 187A, 187B, 187C, 191, 194, 195, 198, 199, 200, 202, 204, 206, 208, 210, 211, 211B, 213, 215, 217O, 217N, 217R, 217T, 221A, 221B, 222, 223, 224, 225, 225A, 225B, 226, 227, 229O, 229P, 229R, 229S, 229T, 230J, 236, 239, 242, 248, 253, 253B, 254, 257, 259O, 259P, 259R, 259T, 261, 263A, 263B, 264, 267, 268, 269, 271, 273, 275, 276, 277, 278, 280, 281, 281B, 285O, 285P, 285R, 285T, 285V, 287, 288, 289, 293A, 293B, 294, 297, 298, 305, 308, 311, 312, 315, 321O, 321P, 321R, 321V, 323, 335, 336, 338, 339, 339B, 342, 343, 346I, 349A, 349B, 350, 351, 352, 353, 353A, 354, 355, 357O, 357P, 357R, 357S, 357T, 357V, 367, 378, 379, 379B, 381, 384I, 387A, 387B, 391, 393, 394, 396, 398, 399, 399B, 403O, 403P, 403R, 403T, 403V, 405, 407; 3.4: T2; 3.5: T1, T5; 3.6: T3, T5 **TFK FCAT:** Issue 3, 5, 6, 8, 9, 10, 12, 14 **FCAT**: 32-64
LA.3.1.7.4	identify cause-and-effect relationships in text;	**TE:** 3.1–3.3: 63, 81A, 103, 191, 340I, 343A, 343B, 344, 345, 346, 347, 351O, 351P, 351R, 351T, 351V, 369, 383B; 3.3: T3; 3.4–3.6: 85A, 187A, 187B, 188, 189, 190, 193, 197, 201, 204, 207, 209, 211, 217O, 217N, 217O, 217R, 217T, 217V, 256, 286, 288, 299, 318, 395; 3.5 T2 **TFK FCAT:** 97-124 **FCAT Test Prep**: Issue 2, 13

FLORIDA Correlations

LA.3.1.7.5	identify the text structure an author uses (e.g., comparison/contrast, cause/effect, and sequence of events) and explain how it impacts meaning in text;	**TE:** 3.1–3.3: 343A, 343B, 344, 345, 347A, 351O, 351P, 351R, 351T, 351V, 387A, 387B, 388, 390, 391, 397, 402, 408, 417O, 417P, 417R, 417T, 3.4–3.6: 19, 45V, 81A, 81B, 82, 84, 89O, 89P, 89R, 89T, 107B, 263A, 263B, 268, 281B, 285R, 321V, 349A, 349B, 350, 351, 352, 357O, 357P, 357R, 357T, 357V, 379B, 406 **TFK FCAT:** Issue 7, 11, 15 **FCAT Test Prep**: 125-152
LA.3.1.7.6	identify themes or topics across a variety of fiction and non-fiction selections;	**TE:** 3.1–3.3: 10H, 11, 33, 85T, 92, 116, 147P, 201, 299, 304, 413; 3.4–3.6: 66, 70, 72, 198, 225A, 263B, 290R, 305, 311, 315, 321O, 321P, 321R, 321T, 321V, 330, 390, 396, 399B, 405, 406
LA.3.1.7.7	compare and contrast topics, settings, characters, and problems in two texts; and	**TE:** 3.1–3.3: 10H, 33, 37P, 37R, 67, 71, 73P, 73R, 81, 85P, 85R, 111, 115P, 115R, 119B, 141, 147P, 147R, 166, 169, 171, 177P, 177R, 178I, 205, 209, 211P, 211R, 211T, 219, 223P, 223R, 249, 255P, 255Q, 255R, 273, 277P, 277R, 307, 313P, 313R, 331, 335, 339P, 339R, 347, 351P, 351R, 379, 383P, 383R, 411, 415, 417P, 417R, 3.4–3.6: 10R, 16, 39, 45P, 45R, 66, 73, 77P, 77R, 78I, 85, 85A, 87, 89P, 89R, 107, 109, 111P, 111R, 139, 145P, 145R, 173, 177, 181, 183P, 183R, 211, 215, 217O, 217P, 217R, 225, 229P, 229R, 253, 253B, 259P, 259R, 281, 283, 285P, 285R, 285T, 315, 318, 321P, 321R, 330, 339, 339B, 343, 345P, 345R, 353, 357P, 357R, 379, 383P, 383R, 399, 403P, 403Rx **FCAT Test Prep:** 125-152
LA.3.1.7.8	use strategies to repair comprehension of grade-appropriate text when self-monitoring indicates confusion, including but not limited to rereading, checking context clues, predicting, summarizing, questioning, and clarifying by checking other sources.	**TE:** 3.1–3.3: 20, 22, 25, 48, 57, 59, 78, 92, 93, 94, 101, 103, 125, 128, 129, 130, 152R, 155A–155B, 156–169, 171, 177O, 177P, 177R, 181A–181B, 182–203, 211O, 211R, 216, 227A–227B, 228–247, 255O, 255R, 256I, 259, 262, 263, 266, 267, 291, 292, 297, 298, 299, 300, 301, 303, 324, 327, 328, 337, 365, 367, 368, 369, 374, 400, 401; 3.4–3.6: 13, 13A, 21, 25, 31, 39, 51, 58, 59, 60, 63, 64, 73, 81A, 81B, 82-85, 87, 89O, 89P, 89R, 89T, 93A–93B, 94–105, 107, 111O, 111P, 111R, 111T, 115A–115B, 116–137, 139, 145O, 145P, 145R, 145T, 156, 158, 159, 160, 163, 164, 174, 175, 179, 190, 201, 211, 213, 233B, 243, 244, 246, 253, 264, 267, 268, 270, 271, 273, 274, 278, 301, 302, 305, 306, 325A–325B, 326–337, 339, 345O, 345P, 345R, 345T, 361A–361B, 362–377, 383O, 383P, 383R, 383T, 387A–387B, 388–397, 403O, 403P, 403R, 403T
LITERARY ANALYSIS		**Macmillan/McGraw-Hill FLORIDA TREASURES**
Fiction: LA.3.2.1	**The student identifies, analyzes, and applies knowledge of the elements of a variety of fiction and literary texts to develop a thoughtful response to a literary selection.**	
LA.3.2.1.1	understand the distinguishing features among the common forms of literature (e.g., poetry, prose, fiction, drama);	**TE:** 3.1–3.3:11, 14, 18, 22, 32, 42, 46, 112, 115S, 122, 137, 156, 161, 163, 166, 169, 182, 184, 191, 193, 203, 204, 286, 304, 315, 320, 334, 336, 339P, 339S, 353, 356, 358, 373, 383R, 385, 417T, 421A, 3.4–3.6:13B, 14, 16, 21, 39B, 50, 70, 79, 91, 108, 109, 111S, 113, 116, 118, 151, 154, 157, 169, 175, 185, 219, 225, 231, 234, 241, 245, 253B, 264, 282, 294, 296, 297, 303, 312, 325B, 326, 331, 332, 337, 359, 377, 380, 381, 383S, 388, 400

Key 3.1 = Grade 3, Unit 1

LA.3.2.1.2	identify and explain the elements of story structure, including character/character development, setting, plot, and problem/resolution in a variety of fiction;	**TE:** 3.1–3.3, 13A, 13B, 14, 15, 16, 17, 18, 20, 21, 23, 24, 25, 27, 28, 29, 30, 33, 37O, 37P, 37R, 37T, 37V, 41A, 41B, 42, 45, 47, 50, 51, 53, 54, 55, 56, 59, 60, 61, 64, 65, 67, 73O, 73P, 73R, 73T, 73V, 116I, 119A, 119B, 120, 121, 123, 125, 126, 127, 129, 130, 132,134, 135, 138, 141, 147O, 147P, 147T, 147V, 160, 162, 163, 177V, 181A, 181B, 182, 185, 187, 188, 190, 192, 193, 194, 196, 199, 202, 204, 205, 277S, 285B, 288, 289, 295, 313P, 314I, 317A, 317B, 318, 321, 322, 323, 325, 326, 328, 332, 334, 335, 339O, 339R, 339T, 339V, 358, 360, 363, 367, 370, 371, 372, 379, 379B, 383T, 421A, 421C; 3.1: T1, T3; 3.2: T2; 3.4–3.6: 13A, 13B, 19, 22, 24, 25, 30, 33, 39, 45O, 49B, 50, 52, 55, 59, 61, 66, 69, 73B, 77V, 108, 113, 115B, 116, 119, 123, 125, 127, 131, 133, 134, 139, 139B, 145O, 145P, 145R, 157, 158, 163, 165, 173, 177B, 233A, 233B, 234, 238, 240, 243, 247, 249, 250, 253, 253B, 259O, 298, 300, 303, 304, 307, 309, 311, 315B, 321O, 321P, 321R, 321T, 322I, 325A, 325B, 326, 329, 330, 333, 337, 339, 339B, 345O, 345P, 345R, 345T, 404; 3.4: T1; 3.5: T4; 3.6: T2 **FCAT Test Prep:** 65-96
LA.3.2.1.3	identify and explain how language choice helps to develop mood and meaning in poetry (e.g., sensory and concrete words as well as figurative language);	**TE:** 3.1–3.3: 11, 112, 113, 115S, 136, 274, 277S, 336, 337, 341, 353, 372, 416, 417, 417A; 3.4–3.6: 108, 109, 113, 282, 283, 400, 401
LA.3.2.1.4	identify an author's theme, and use details from the text to explain how the author developed that theme;	**TE:** 3.1–3.3: 201, 219A, 304, 332; 3.4–3.6: 36, 70, 108, 109, 208, 293A, 293B, 294, 297, 305, 308, 311, 312, 315, 321O, 321P, 321R, 321T, 321V, 336, 380, 399B, 405, 406; 3.6: T1
LA.3.2.1.5	identify and explain an author's use of descriptive, idiomatic, and figurative language (e.g., personification, similes, metaphors, symbolism), and examine how it is used to describe people, feelings, and objects;	**TE:** 3.1–3.3: 11, 18, 24, 44, 64, 66, 98, 104, 110, 112, 113, 115S, 136, 140, 151A, 151D, 165, 176, 190, 244, 265, 272, 274, 277S, 293, 306, 332, 336, 339S, 341, 353, 355A, 361, 364, 365, 374, 378, 383F, 385, 416, 417, 417A; 3.4–3.6, 18, 33, 45D, 45O, 108, 109, 113, 125, 126, 138, 151, 162, 170, 176, 183F, 190, 210, 219, 233, 252, 259O, 259Q, 272, 282, 283, 285F, 304, 310, 314, 338, 378, 380, 381, 383S, 400, 401
LA.3.2.1.6	write a book report or review that identifies the main idea, character(s), setting, sequence of events, and problem/solution;	**TE:** 3.1–3.3: 109, 276, 277, 277A, 333; 3.4–3.6, 37, 45T, 71
LA.3.2.1.7	respond to, discuss, and reflect on various literary selections (e.g., poetry, prose, fiction, nonfiction), connecting text to self (personal connection), text to world (social connection), text to text (comparison among multiple texts); and	**TE:** 3.1–3.3: 11, 25, 31, 32, 33, 35, 37P, 37R, 37T, 39, 65, 66, 67, 71, 73P, 73R, 73T, 75, 81, 85P, 85R, 85T, 87, 109, 110, 111, 113, 115P, 115R, 115T, 117, 139, 140, 141, 145, 147P, 147R, 147T, 153, 169, 170, 171, 175, 177P, 177R, 177T, 179, 194, 203, 204, 205, 209, 211O, 211P, 211R, 211T, 213, 219, 221, 223P, 223R, 223T, 225, 247, 248, 249, 253, 255P, 255R, 255T, 257, 263, 271, 272, 273, 275, 277P, 277R, 277T, 283, 297, 303, 305, 306, 307, 311, 313P, 313R, 313T, 315, 323, 327, 333, 334, 335, 337, 339P, 339R, 339T, 341, 347, 349, 351P, 351R, 351T, 353, 367, 377, 378, 379, 381, 383P, 383R, 383T, 385, 394, 409, 410, 411, 415, 417P, 417R, 417T; 3.4–3.6, 11, 37, 43, 45P, 45R, 45T, 47, 71, 73, 77P, 77R, 77T, 79, 85, 89P, 89R, 89T, 89V, 91, 105, 107, 109, 111P, 111R, 111T, 113, 137, 139, 139B, 143, 145P, 145R, 145T, 151, 163, 173, 175, 177, 181, 183P, 183R, 183T, 185, 198, 201, 209, 211, 215, 217P, 217R, 217T, 219, 229P, 229R, 229T, 231, 243, 251, 253, 253B, 259P, 259R, 259T, 261, 279, 281, 285P, 285R, 285T, 291, 313, 315B, 319, 321P, 321R, 321T, 323, 337, 339, 343, 345P, 345R, 345T, 347, 353, 355, 357P, 357R, 357T, 359, 369, 377, 379, 381, 383P, 383R, 383T, 385, 397, 399, 401, 403P, 403R, 403T

FLORIDA Correlations

FLORIDA Correlations

LA.3.2.1.8	select a balance of age- and ability-appropriate fiction materials to read (e.g., chapter books, fairy tales, mythology, poetry), based on interest and teacher recommendations, to continue building a core foundation of knowledge.	**TE:** 3.1–3.3:10H, 10R, 37T, 38I, 73T, 116I, 147T, 169, 177T, 178I, 272, 299, 313T, 314I, 323, 339T, 352I, 378, 383T, 410; 3.4–3.6: 38, 39B, 45T, 46I, 73B, 77T, 89T, 112I, 145T, 173, 183T, 218I, 230I, 259T, 290R, 321T, 322I, 330, 345T
Non-Fiction: LA.3.2.2	**The student identifies, analyzes, and applies knowledge of the elements of a variety of non-fiction, informational, and expository texts to demonstrate an understanding of the information presented.**	
LA.3.2.2.1	identify and explain the purpose of text features (e.g., table of contents, glossary, headings, charts, graphs, diagrams, illustrations);	**TE:** 3.1–3.3: 34, 37S, 35, 68, 69, 71, 73S, 85R, 90, 95, 105, 106, 142, 143, 147S, 172, 174, 175, 177S, 206, 207, 209, 219B, 223P, 236, 238, 250, 282H, 308, 309, 311, 313S, 372, 383S, 393, 398, 410, 412, 413, 415, 417S; 3.4–3.6: 38, 40, 77S, 99, 142, 178, 180, 181, 203, 254, 257, 259S, 280, 290S, 316, 317, 340, 343, 345S, 398; 3.6 **T11** **TFK FCAT:** Issue 1, 2, 3, 4, 5, 6, 7, 8, 9, 10, 11, 12, 13, 14, 15 **FCAT Test Prep**:153-179
LA.3.2.2.2	use information from the text to answer questions related to explicitly stated main ideas or relevant details;	**TE:** 3.1–3.3: 70, 77B, 79, 81, 85T, 96, 101, 102, 104, 106, 107 108, 111, 175, 215B, 220, 221, 235, 249, 348, 349, 381, 392, 405, 411, 421K; 3.4–3.6: 41, 78, 85, 86, 87, 107, 140, 142, 143, 211, 269, 289, 289A, 317, 342, 352, 353, 388, 407A
LA.3.2.2.3	organize information to show an understanding of main ideas within a text through charting, mapping, or summarizing;	**TE:** 3.1–3.3: 77A, 77B, 78, 79, 80, 81, 85O, 85P, 85R, 85T, 86I, 89A, 89B, 90, 92, 93, 94, 97, 99, 101, 102, 104, 111, 115P, 115R, 115T, 217, 218, 219, 223O, 223R, 223T, 227B, 237, 245, 249, 255T, 256J, 259A, 268, 269, 270, 310, 313S, 347, 402, 411, 417S; 3.4–3.6: 45S, 45T, 45V, 84, 85, 183P, 183R, 183S, 183T, 202, 211B, 225, 225A, 257, 267, 285R, 285T, 321S, 353, 353A, 379, 399, 399B
LA.3.2.2.4	identify the characteristics of a variety of types of text (e.g., reference, children's newspapers, practical/functional texts); and	**TE:** 3.1–3.3: 34-35, 39, 68-71, 100, 142-145, 153, 172-175, 206-209, 250, 308-311, 380-381, 393, 412; 3.4–3.6: 40, 74-75,140-143, 178-181, 212-215, 254-257, 316-319 340-343, 396
LA.3.2.2.5	select a balance of age- and ability-appropriate non-fiction materials to read (e.g., biographies and topical areas, such as animals, science, history), based on interest and teacher recommendations, to continue building a core foundation of knowledge.	**TE:** 3.1–3.3:10H, 74I, 85T, 86I, 115T, 223T, 255T, 256I, 272, 277T, 351T, 410, 417T; 3.4–3.6: 38, 78I, 85A, 90I, 111T, 150R, 184I, 211B, 217T, 218I, 229T, 260I, 285T, 346I, 357T, 358I, 383T, 384I, 403T
WRITING PROCESS		**Macmillan/McGraw-Hill FLORIDA TREASURES**
Pre-Writing: LA.3.3.1	**The student will use prewriting strategies to generate ideas and formulate a plan.**	**TE:** 3.1–3.3: 37, 73, 85, 115, 147, 151B, 177, 211, 223, 255, 277, 281B, 313, 339, 351, 383, 417, 421B, 3.4–3.6: 45, 77, 89, 111, 145, 183A, 217, 229, 259, 285, 289, 321A, 345, 357, 383, 403, 407
LA.3.3.1.1	generating ideas from multiple sources (e.g., text, brainstorming, graphic organizer, drawing, writer's notebook, group discussion, printed material);	**TE:** 3.1–3.3:10H, 115, 147, 147A, 177, 282H, 313, 339, 415, 417; 3.4–3.6: 10H, 45, 77, 145, 289B **FCAT Test Prep:** 181-192, 193-204
LA.3.3.1.2	determining the purpose (e.g., to entertain, to inform, to communicate, to persuade) and the intended audience of a writing piece; and	**TE:** 3.1–3.3: 37, 73, 73B, 115, 147, 151B, 177, 177A, 211, 223, 255, 277, 281B, 313, 339, 339B, 350, 351, 383, 417, 421B; 3.4–3.6: 45, 77, 89, 111, 145, 149B, 183B, 228, 229, 285B, 289B, 289C, 321, 345, 356, 357, 383, 403, 407B **FCAT Test Prep:** 181-192, 193-204
LA.3.3.1.3	using organizational strategies (e.g., graphic organizer, KWL chart, log) to make a plan for writing that includes a main idea.	**TE:** 3.1–3.3: 37, 37A, 37B, 73, 73A, 85A, 115, 115B, 147, 151B, 151C, 152H, 177, 211, 223, 255, 277, 281B, 281C, 281K, 313, 339, 351, 351A, 351B, 383, 421B; 3.4–3.6: 45, 77, 89, 89B, 111, 145, 149B, 183A, 183B, 289B, 345, 357B, 399B, 403, 407B
Drafting: LA.3.3.2	**The student will write a draft appropriate to the topic, audience, and purpose.**	**TE:** 3.1–3.3:: 37, 73, 115, 147, 151C, 177, 211, 255, 277, 281C, 313, 339, 383, 417, 421C, 3.4–3.6: 45, 77, 111, 145, 183, 217A, 259, 285, 289, 321, 345, 383A, 403, 407

Key 3.1 = Grade 3, Unit 1

LA.3.3.2.1	using a pre-writing plan to develop the main idea with supporting details that describe or provide facts and/or opinions; and	**TE:** 3.1–3.3: 36, 37, 37A, 73A, 115, 115A, 147A, 147B, 151C, 177A, 254, 277, 277A, 281B, 281C, 338; 3.4–3.6: 89A, 110, 111A, 145, 145B, 149C, 182, 183, 183A, 258, 259A, 259B, 276, 277B, 281A, 289C, 321, 321B, 344, 345, 345B, 383, 383B, 407C **FCAT Test Prep:** 181-192, 193-204
LA.3.3.2.2	organizing information into a logical sequence through the use of time-order words and cause/effect transitions.	**TE:** 3.1–3.3: 73, 146, 151A, 151B, 151C, 151D, 177, 177B, 211, 211A, 281A, 312, 382, 383S, 417O; 3.4–3.6: 43, 44, 45, 76, 77, 89B, 107B, 144, 145, 145A, 145B, 149A, 149C, 176, 216, 217, 217A, 217B, 229F, 344, 345, 345A, 407A
Revising: LA.3.3.3	**The student will revise and refine the draft for clarity and effectiveness.**	**TE:** 3.1–3.3: : 37, 73, 115, 147, 151, 177B, 211, 255, 277, 281, 313B, 339, 383, 417, 421, 3.4–3.6: 45, 77B, 111, 145, 183, 217, 259, 285B, 289, 321, 345, 383, 403, 407D
LA.3.3.3.1	evaluating the draft for use of ideas and content, logical organization, voice (e.g., formal or informal), point of view, and word choice;	**TE:** 3.1–3.3: 36, 37, 115, 146, 147, 147A, 147B, 151D, 151F, 152H, 177, 211, 211B, 254, 255, 255A, 277, 277A, 277B, 281D, 281F, 281H, 312, 313, 313A, 313B, 339, 383, 383B, 417, 417A, 421B, 421C, 421D, 421F; 3.4–3.6: 44, 76, 77, 77A, 77B, 110, 111, 111A, 111B, 145A, 149D, 149F, 183, 217, 259, 259B, 285B, 289D, 289F, 320, 321, 321A, 321B, 382, 383, 383A, 402, 403, 403A, 403B, 407D, 407F **FCAT Test Prep:** 181-192, 205-216
LA.3.3.3.2	creating clarity by using a combination of sentence structures (i.e., simple, compound) to improve sentence fluency in the draft and by rearranging words, sentences, and paragraphs to clarify meaning;	**TE:** 3.1–3.3: 73B, 147B, 151D, 255, 255B, 281D, 313B, 339, 339B, 421D; 3.4–3.6: 44, 45, 45A, 77, 77B, 111B, 145, 145B, 149D, 183B, 217, 217B, 289D, 345, 345B, 383, 383B, 407D
LA.3.3.3.3	creating interest by adding supporting details (e.g., dialogue, similes) and modifying word choices using resources and reference materials (e.g., dictionary, thesaurus); and	**TE:** 3.1–3.3: 146, 147, 151D, 211, 211B, 254, 255A, 281K, 312, 313A, 338, 383A, 417A, 421C, 421D; 3.4–3.6: 44, 45, 45B, 77, 77A, 111, 111B, 144, 149A, 149K, 285B, 345B, 403A, 407D
LA.3.3.3.4	applying appropriate tools or strategies to refine the draft (e.g., peer review, checklists, rubrics).	**TE:** 3.1–3.3: 85, 147A, 147B, 151D, 151E, 151F, 151G, 151H, 211, 223, 255, 255A, 277, 281D, 281F, 281H, 313, 383, 417, 421D, 421F, 421G, 421H, 3.4–3.6: 45, 111, 111A, 145, 149D, 149F, 149G, 289D, 289E, 289F, 321, 345, 407D, 407F
Editing for Language Conventions: LA.3.3.4	**The student will edit and correct the draft for standard language conventions.**	
LA.3.3.4.1	spelling, using spelling patterns and generalizations (e.g., word families, diphthong, consonant digraphs, CVC words, CCVC words, CVCC words, affixes) and using a dictionary or other resources as necessary;	**TE:** 3.1–3.3: 37B, 37G, 37H, 38I, 73B, 73G, 73H, 85G, 85H, 115B, 115G, 115H, 147B, 147F, 147G, 147H, 147M, 151C, 151D, 151E, 177B, 177G, 177H, 211B, 211G, 211H, 212I, 223G, 223H, 223J, 255B, 255G, 255H, 277B, 277G, 277H, 281E, 313B, 313G, 313H, 339B, 339G, 339H, 351G, 351H, 383B, 383G, 383H, 417B, 417G, 417H; 3.4–3.6: 45B, 45G, 45H, 77B, 77G, 77H, 89G, 89H, 111B, 111G, 111H, 145B, 145G, 145H, 183B, 183G, 183H, 217B, 217G, 217H, 229G, 229H, 230I, 259B, 259G, 259H, 285B, 285G, 285H, 289E, 321B, 321G, 321H, 345B, 345G, 345H, 357G, 357H, 383B, 383G, 383H, 403B, 403G, 403H **FCAT Test Prep:** 181-192, 217-223, 224-230
LA.3.3.4.2	capitalization for proper nouns, including holidays, product names, titles used with someone's name, initials, and geographic locations;	**TE:** 3.1–3.3: 73B, 177B, 177I, 177J, 277J, 281E; 3.4–3.6: 183B, 183J, 321B, 321J, 407E **FCAT Test Prep**: 181-192, 217-223, 224-230
LA.3.3.4.3	punctuation, including end punctuation, apostrophes, commas, colons, quotation marks in dialogue, and apostrophes in singular possessives;	**TE:** 3.1–3.3: 37B, 37I, 37J, 73B, 147B, 151D, 211F, 255B, 255I, 255J, 277F, 281E, 313J, 351J, 383A, 383B, 383J, 417B, 417J, 421E; 3.4–3.6: 77B, 77J, 89D, 89J, 111G, 145B, 145I, 145J, 149E, 218I, 229O, 285B, 285I, 285J, 403B, 403J **FCAT Test Prep**: 181-192, 217-223, 224-230

FLORIDA Correlations

LA.3.3.4.4	present and past verb tense, noun-pronoun agreement, noun-verb agreement, subjective and objective pronouns, and plurals of irregular nouns;	**TE:** 3.1–3.3: 223I, 223J, 313B, 339, 339B, 339I, 339H, 351I, 351J, 417I; 3.4–3.6: 45B, 45I, 45J, 77B, 77I, 77J, 89I, 111B, 111I, 111J, 183I, 183J, 217J, 229J **FCAT Test Prep:** 181-192, 217-223, 224-230
LA.3.3.4.5	subject/verb and noun/pronoun agreement in simple and compound sentences;	**TE:** 3.1–3.3: 277I, 339, 339B, 339H, 383I, 417B, 417I, 421E; 3.4–3.6: 45A, 45B, 45J, 77B, 77I, 89I, 89J, 111B, 111I, 111J, 149E, 183B, 217B, 217I, 217J, 229I, 259B, 259I, 259J **FCAT Test Prep:** 181-192, 217-223, 224-230
LA.3.3.4.6	end punctuation for compound, declarative, interrogative, and exclamatory sentences;	**TE:** 3.1–3.3: 37B, 37I, 37J, 73I, 73J, 147J, 211J; 3.4–3.6: 149E, 407E
Publishing: LA.3.3.5	**The student will write a final product for the intended audience.**	
LA.3.3.5.1	prepare writing in a format appropriate to audience and purpose (e.g., manuscript, multimedia);	**TE:** 3.1–3.3: 223A; 3.4–3.6: 45A, 88, 289E, 345A, 407E **FCAT Test Prep:** 181-192, 217-223, 224-230
LA.3.3.5.2	add graphics where appropriate; and	**TE:** 3.1–3.3: 37A, 151E, 177A, 281E, 415; 3.4–3.6: 45A, 77A, 145A, 289K, 383A, 403A
LA.3.3.5.3	share the writing with the intended audience.	**TE:** 3.1–3.3: 37, 37A, 73, 74J, 85, 85F, 115, 147, 151E, 151F, 177, 211, 223, 255, 277, 281E, 281F, 313, 339, 351, 383, 417, 421B, 421E, 421F, 421G; 3.4–3.6: 45, 77, 89, 90J, 111, 145, 145A, 149E, 183B, 217, 229, 259, 285, 289, 321B, 345, 357, 383, 403, 407
WRITING APPLICATIONS		**Macmillan/McGraw-Hill FLORIDA TREASURES**
Creative: LA.3.4.1	**The student develops and demonstrates creative writing.**	
LA.3.4.1.1	write narratives based on real or imagined events or observations that include characters, setting, plot, sensory details, and a logical sequence of events; and	**TE:** 3.1–3.3: 36, 37, 37A, 37B, 73B, 115B, 116J, 147B, 151A-F, 151K, 176, 177, 177A, 177B, 210, 211, 211A, 211B, 212J, 223B, 248, 255B, 277B, 313B, 339B, 351B, 352J, 382, 383, 383A, 383B, 415, 416, 417, 417A, 417B, 421B, 421C; 3.4–3.6: 44, 45, 45A, 45B, 77B, 78J, 89, 89B, 111B, 145B, 150S, 183B, 184J, 216, 217, 217A, 217B, 218J, 229B, 229F, 230J, 252, 259B, 259F, 285B, 314, 321B, 344, 345, 345A, 345B, 345F, 345S, 346J, 357B, 358J, 383B, 383S, 402, 403, 403A, 403B
LA.3.4.1.2	write a variety of expressive forms (e.g., chapter books, short stories, poetry, skits, song lyrics) that may employ, but not be limited to, figurative language (e.g., simile, onomatopoeia), rhythm, dialogue, characterization, plot, and appropriate format.	**TE:** 3.1–3.3: 36, 37, 37A, 37B, 73B, 65, 86J, 110, 115S, 116J, 151A-F, 153, 176, 177, 177A, 178J, 202, 210,211, 211A, 211B, 212J,223C, 225, 255B, 256J, 274, 282S, 283, 305, 314J, 315, 338, 339, 339A, 341, 351C, 353, 352J, 382, 384J, 385, 416, 417, 417A, 417B, 421C; 3.4–3.6: 10S, 30, 33, 44, 45, 45A, 45B, 45S, 77B, 79, 90J, 91, 100, 113, 149E, 151, 185, 216, 217, 217B, 219, 229S, 231, 251, 260J, 261, 282, 284, 285A, 285S, 291, 323, 338, 344, 345A, 345B, 347, 357S, 359, 383F, 384J, 385, 402, 403, 403A, 403S, 403T
Informative: LA.3.4.2	**The student develops and demonstrates technical writing that provides information related to real-world tasks.**	
LA.3.4.2.1	write in a variety of informational/expository forms (e.g., rules, summaries, procedures, recipes, notes/messages, labels, instructions, graphs/tables, experiments, rubrics);	**TE:** 3.1–3.3: 37F, 38J, 74J, 86J, 103, 114, 15, 115A, 115F, 116J, 140, 146, 147, 147A, 152I, 152S, 167, 212J, 223, 223A, 223S, 247, 248, 254, 255, 255A, 276, 277, 277A, 282S, 283, 303, 306, 340J, 347, 351, 352J, 381, 410; 3.4–3.6: 10S, 46J, 76, 77, 77A, 112J, 144, 145, 145S, 167, 184J, 217F, 229A, 229B, 230J, 231, 260J, 261, 267, 280, 285F, 290S, 301, 310, 321F, 322J, 344, 345S, 347, 357S, 358J, 376, 378, 382, 383, 383A, 384J, 398, 399B

Key 3.1 = Grade 3, Unit 1

LA.3.4.2.2	record information (e.g., observations, notes, lists, charts, map labels, legends) related to a topic, including visual aids as appropriate;	**TE:** 3.1–3.3: 49, 85A, 85B, 178J, 212J, 223A, 223B, 224I, 224J, 277R, 281K, 282H, 282S, 340J, 351B, 351S, 352J, 352J, 394, 409; 3.4–3.6: 10H, 89B, 107B, 112J, 143, 149I, 149K, 174, 229A, 229B, 260I, 260J, 322J
LA.3.4.2.3	write informational/expository essays that contain at least three paragraphs and include a topic sentence, supporting details, and relevant information;	**TE:** 3.1–3.3: 85A, 85B, 170, 223A, 223B, 314J, 340J, 351A, 384J; 3.4–3.6: 69, 78J, 89A, 89B, 90J, 110, 111, 111A, 137, 182, 183, 183A, 184J, 230J, 258, 259, 259A, 319, 321S, 322J, 357, 357A, 357B, 358J, 377, 382, 397, 407A, 407C
LA.3.4.2.4	write a variety of communications (e.g., friendly letters, thank-you notes, formal letters, messages, invitations); and	**TE:** 3.1–3.3: 38J, 46, 72, 73, 73A, 73B, 139, 281B, 334, 378; 3.4–3.6: 38, 72, 105, 106, 209, 271, 279, 290S, 313, 320, 321, 321A, 321B, 397
LA.3.4.2.5	write simple directions to familiar locations using cardinal directions and landmarks, and create an accompanying map.	**TE:** 3.1–3.3: 352J, 376, 383S; 3.4–3.6: 144, 145, 145A, 169
Persuasive: LA.3.4.3	**The student develops and demonstrates persuasive writing that is used for the purpose of influencing the reader.**	
LA.3.4.3.1	The student will write persuasive text (e.g., advertisement, paragraph) that attempts to influence the reader.	**TE:** 3.1–3.3: 152S, 174J, 224J, 254–255B, 256J, 270, 276–277B, 281A–281H, 311, 338–339B, 340J, 3.4–3.6: 128, 184J, 215, 217S, 258
COMMUNICATIONS		**Macmillan/McGraw-Hill FLORIDA TREASURES**
Penmanship: LA.3.5.1	**The student engages in the writing process and writes to communicate ideas and experiences.**	
LA.3.5.1.1	The student will demonstrate beginning cursive writing skills.	**TE:** 3.1–3.3: 37A, 73A, 115A, 177A, 277A, 313A, 339A, 351A, 377, 383A, 394; 3.4–3.6: 210, 279, 321A, 345A
Listening and Speaking: LA.3.5.2	**The student effectively applies listening and speaking strategies.**	**TE:** 3.1–3.3: 10H, 10I, 10, 11, 37A, 38, 39, 73A, 74, 75, 85A, 86, 87, 115A, 116, 117, 147A, 151E, 151K, 151L, 152, 152H, 152I, 153, 175, 177A, 178, 179, 202, 211A, 212, 213, 223A, 224, 225, 255A, 256, 257, 277A, 281E, 281K, 281L, 282, 282H, 282I, 283, 313A, 314, 315, 339A, 340, 341, 351A, 352, 353, 373, 383A, 384, 385, 417A, 421E, 421K, 421L, 3.4–3.6: 10, 10H, 10I, 11, 45A, 46, 47, 77A, 78, 79, 89A, 90, 91, 111A, 112, 113, 128, 130, 132, 143, 145A, 149E, 149K, 149L, 150, 150H, 150I, 151, 183A, 184, 185, 217A, 217V, 218, 219, 229A, 229V, 230, 231, 259A, 259V, 260, 261, 285A, 285V, 289E, 289K, 289L, 290, 290H, 290I, 291, 321A, 322, 323, 345A, 346, 347, 357A, 358, 359, 383A, 384, 385, 403A, 407E, 407K, 407L
LA.3.5.2.1	recall, interpret, and summarize information presented orally; and	**TE:** 3.1–3.3: 71, 73A, 85A, 115A, 134, 147A, 151K, 177A, 211A, 223A, 255A, 277A, 281K, 339A, 421K; 3.4–3.6: 43, 45, 77A, 89A, 111A, 261, 321A
LA.3.5.2.2	plan, organize, and give an oral presentation and use appropriate voice, eye, and body movements for the topic, audience, and occasion.	**TE:** 3.1–3.3: 73A, 85A, 115A, 137, 145, 147A, 151E, 151I, 151K, 151L, 177A, 209, 211A, 223A, 255A, 274, 277A, 281E, 281K, 281L, 282I, 339A, 351A, 376, 421E, 421L; 3.4–3.6: 43, 45, 77A, 89A, 111A, 132, 143, 145A, 149K, 149L, 181, 208, 218J, 229A, 261, 289K, 290I, 321A, 357A, 383A, 407E
INFORMATION AND MEDIA LITERACY		**Macmillan/McGraw-Hill FLORIDA TREASURES**
Informational Text: LA.3.6.1	**The student comprehends the wide array of informational text that is part of our day to day experiences.**	

FLORIDA Correlations

LA.3.6.1.1	The student will read informational text (e.g., graphs, charts, manuals) and organize information for different purposes, including but not limited to being informed, following multi-step directions, making a report, conducting interviews, preparing to take a test, and performing a task.	**TE:** 3.1–3.3: 10H, 16, 34, 49, 71, 86I, 111, 116J, 134, 142, 151I, 151K, 152H, 172, 178J, 220, 223A, 224J, 223P, 223R, 223T, 224J, 239, 251, 256J, 281J, 282H, 282S, 348, 351A, 351T, 352J, 381, 384J, 398, 409, 410, 413; 3.4–3.6: 10H, 10I, 10S, 46J, 69, 76, 78J, 84, 85B, 86, 88, 89A, 89B, 90J, 112J, 140, 143, 144, 148, 149C, 149I, 150H, 150I, 150S, 174, 191, 208, 214, 218J, 225B, 226, 229A, 230J, 254, 256, 260J, 288, 290H, 307, 322J, 328, 340, 341, 345S, 346J, 353B, 354, 358J, 382, 383, 396, 406; 3.5: **T12**
Research Process: LA.3.6.2	**The student uses a systematic process for the collection, processing, and presentation of information.**	
LA.3.6.2.1	determine information needed for a search by narrowing or broadening a topic, identify key words;	**TE:** 3.1–3.3: 10H, 82, 83, 85A, 115, 115B, 152H, 219B, 223A, 281J, 282H, 347B, 349, 351B, 415, 417B; 3.4–3.6: 10H, 89A, 149B, 149K, 218J, 225B, 229A, 290H, 357A, 357B, 407K
LA.3.6.2.2	use predetermined evaluative criteria (e.g., readability, appropriateness, special features) to select appropriate reference materials, including multiple representations of information, such as maps, charts, and photos, to gather information;	**TE:** 3.1–3.3: 10H, 137, 145, 152H, 152S, 175, 219B, 223A, 247, 281C, 281J, 282H, 282S, 340I, 340J, 347B, 351A, 351B, 351S, 409, 413, 415; 3.4–3.6: 10H, 10S, 78J, 85B, 89A, 89B, 174, 181, 218J, 229B, 260J, 289C, 290H, 290S, 346J, 357A, 357B, 377, 384J, 407K
LA.3.6.2.3	communicate information in an informational report that includes main ideas and relevant details with visual support (e.g., text supported by poster, diagram, idea map); and	**TE:** 3.1–3.3: 49, 85A, 116J, 145, 175, 223A, 351A, 421K; 3.4–3.6: 10H, 10I, 46J, 69, 78J, 149K, 175, 191, 229B, 239, 328, 343, 345A, 357A, 377, 390
LA.3.6.2.4	record basic bibliographic data and recognize intellectual property rights (e.g., cites sources of ideas).	**TE:** 3.1–3.3: 151J, 152H, 281I, 282H, 347B, 351A, 351B; 3.4–3.6: 89A, 89B, 150H, 150I, 181, 229B, 290H, 357A, 357B, 407C
Media Literacy: LA.3.6.3	**The student develops and demonstrates an understanding of media literacy as a life skill that is integral to informed decision making.**	
LA.3.6.3.1	determine main content and supporting details, including distinguishing fact from opinion, in a print media message; and	**TE:** 3.1–3.3: 10I, 152I, 212I, 218, 311, 351A; 3.4–3.6: 102, 150I, 184J, 212, 214, 221A, 221B, 222, 224, 270, 353B, 373; 3.5: T3
LA.3.6.3.2	identify and explain different production elements used in media messages (e.g., color, sound effects, animation) and use the elements appropriately in a multimedia production.	**TE:** 3.1–3.3: 126, 151L, 152I, 415; 3.4–3.6: 168, 270, 343, 373, 407K
Technology: LA.3.6.4	**The student develops the essential technology skills for using and understanding conventional and current tools, materials and processes.**	
LA.3.6.4.1	use appropriate available technologies to enhance communication and achieve a purpose (e.g., video, websites); and	**TE:** 3.1–3.3: 10H, 10I, 10S, 15, 32, 66, 71, 74J, 110, 140, 151I, 151J, 151L, 152H, 152I, 170, 204, 209, 221, 248, 272, 281C, 281I, 281J, 281L, 282H, 282I, 306, 311, 334, 340J, 347B, 349, 351A, 378, 410, 415, 421I, 421J, 421K, 421L; 3.4–3.6: 10H, 10I, 38, 45F, 64, 72, 85B, 89A, 89S, 106, 138, 140, 142, 149I, 149J, 149L, 150H, 150I, 176, 181, 208, 210, 215, 229A, 252, 280, 283, 289I, 289J, 290H, 290I, 314, 322J, 338, 378, 384J, 398, 401, 407I, 407J; 3.4, T11
LA.3.6.4.2	use digital tools (e.g., word processing, multimedia authoring, web tools, graphic organizers) to present and publish in a variety of media formats.	**TE:** 3.1–3.3: 37B, 73B, 85A, 103, 115B, 177B, 211B, 253, 255B, 277B, 281J, 339B, 347B, 415, 417B, 421I, 421J, 421K; 3.4–3.6: 10I, 45B, 142, 145B, 149I, 149J, 183, 217B, 229A, 259B, 289J, 321B, 345B, 357A, 407I, 407K

Key 3.1 = Grade 3, Unit 1

Science
Sunshine State Standards Grade 3

Each standard is coded in the following manner

SC.	A.	1.	1.	1.	3.	1.
Subject	Strand	Standard	Level	Benchmark	Grade	Grade Level Expectation Number (GLE)

KEY	TE = Teacher's Edition	LR = Leveled Readers	TFK FCAT = Time for Kids FCAT Edition	FCAT Test Prep = FCAT Test Prep and Practice

STRAND A: THE NATURE OF MATTER		Macmillan/McGraw-Hill FLORIDA TREASURES
Standard 1: The student understands that all matter has observable, measurable properties.		
Benchmark SC.A.1.2.1	The student determines that the properties of materials (e.g., density and volume) can be compared and measured (e.g., using rulers, balances, and thermometers).	
GLE SC.A.1.2.1.3.1	determines the physical properties of matter using metric measurements that incorporate tools such as rulers, thermometers, balances.	**TE:** 3.4–3.6: 43, 140-142, 143, 150S **LR:** 3.4 Week 1: *Measurement*
Benchmark SC.A.1.2.2	The student knows that common materials (e.g., water) can be changed from one state to another by heating and cooling.	
GLE SC.A.1.2.2.3.1	understands that physical changes in the states of matter can be produced by heating and cooling.	**TE:** 3.1–3.3: 314J; 3.4–3.6: 10S, 40-43, 140-142, 143, 150S

STRAND B: ENERGY		Macmillan/McGraw-Hill FLORIDA TREASURES
Standard 1: The student recognizes that energy may be changed in form with varying efficiency.		
Benchmark SC.B.1.2.2	The student recognizes various forms of energy (e.g., heat, light, and electricity).	
GLE SC.B.1.2.2.3.1	knows objects that emit heat and light.	**TE:** 3.4–3.6: 230J
GLE SC.B.1.2.2.3.2	knows different forms of energy (for example, heat, light, sound).	**TE:** 3.4–3.6: 10S, 230J 254-257, 259P, 259R, 259T **LR:** 3.5 Week 4: *Energy*
Benchmark SC.B.1.2.3	The student knows that most things that emit light also emit heat.	
GLE SC.B.1.2.3.3.1	knows that the Sun provides energy for the Earth in the form of heat and light.	**TFK FCAT:** Issue 4, 5
Benchmark SC.B.1.2.4	The student knows the many ways in which energy can be transformed from one type to another.	
GLE SC.B.1.2.4.3.1	knows that heat can be produced by chemical reactions, electrical machines, and friction.	**TE:** 3.4–3.6: 230J, 259P, 259R, 259T
Benchmark SC.B.1.2.6	The student knows ways that heat can move from one object to another.	
GLE SC.B.1.2.6.3.1	knows that when a warmer object comes in contact with a cooler one, the warm object loses heat and the cool one gains it until they are both at the same temperature.	**TFK FCAT:** Issue 13
Standard 2: The student understands the interaction of matter and energy.		
Benchmark SC.B.2.2.2	The student recognizes the costs and risks to society and the environment posed by the use of nonrenewable energy.	

GLE SC.B.2.2.2.3.1	knows ways natural resources are important.	**TE:** 3.1–3.3: 340J, 344-347, 341A; 3.4–3.6: 78J, 86, 89A, 89P, 89R, 89T **LR:** 3.4 Week 3: *Resources All Around Us*
GLE SC.B.2.2.2.3.2	classifies resources as renewable or nonrenewable.	**TE:** 3.1–3.3: 340J, 344-347, 341A; 3.4–3.6: 78J, 86, 89A, 89P, 89R, 89T
Benchmark SC.B.2.2.3	The student knows that the limited supply of usable energy sources (e.g., fuels such as coal or oil) places great significance on the development of renewable energy sources.	
GLE SC.B.2.2.3.3.1	knows that alternate energy sources (for example, synthetic fuels, geothermal energy) are being explored using natural and mechanical processes.	**TFK FCAT:** Issue 4, 11
STRAND C: FORCE AND MOTION		**Macmillan/McGraw-Hill FLORIDA TREASURES**
Standard 1: The student understands that types of motion may be described, measured, and predicted.		
Benchmark SC.C.1.2.1	The student understands that the motion of an object can be described and measured.	**TFK FCAT:** Issue 6, 14
GLE SC.C.1.2.1.3.1	describes the motion of various objects (for example, forward, circular, wave).	**TE:** 3.4–3.6: 254-257; **TFK FCAT:** Issue 6, 14
Benchmark SC.C.1.2.2	The student knows that waves travel at different speeds through different materials.	**TFK FCAT:** Issue14
GLE SC.C.1.2.2.3.1	understands the characteristics of waves (for example, crest, trough, length).	**TE:** 3.4–3.6: 254-257; **TFK FCAT:** Issue 14
Standard 2: The student understands that the types of force that act on an object and the effect of that force can be described, measured, and predicted.		
Benchmark SC.C.2.2.1	The student recognizes that forces of gravity, magnetism, and electricity operate simple machines.	
GLE SC.C.2.2.1.3.1	knows the six types of simple machines (screw, inclined plane, wedge, pulley, lever, and wheel and axle).	**TE:** 3.4–3.6: 290S; **TFK FCAT:** Issue 14
Benchmark SC.C.2.2.4	The student knows that the motion of an object is determined by the overall effect of all of the forces acting on the object.	
GLE SC.C.2.2.2.3.1	knows that an object may move in a straight line at a constant speed, speed up, slow down, or change direction dependent on net force acting on the object.	**LR:** 3.4 Week 3: *Thrills and Chills;* **TFK FCAT:** Issue 14
STRAND D: PROCESSES THAT SHAPE THE EARTH		**Macmillan/McGraw-Hill FLORIDA TREASURES**
Standard 1: The student recognizes that processes in the lithosphere, atmosphere, hydrosphere, and biosphere interact to shape the Earth.		
Benchmark SC.D.1.2.3	The student knows that the water cycle is influenced by temperature, pressure, and the topography of the land.	
GLE SC.D.1.2.3.3.1	understands the stages of the water cycle (for example, evaporation, condensation, precipitation).	**TE:** 3.1–3.3: 90J, 256J, 314J
Benchmark SC.D.1.2.4	The student knows that the surface of the Earth is in a continuous state of change as waves, weather, and shifts of the land constantly change and produce many new features.	
GLE SC.D.1.2.4.3.1	understands the processes of weathering and erosion.	**TFK FCAT:** Issue 8, 13
Benchmark SC.D.1.2.5	The student knows that some changes in the Earth's surface are due to slow processes and some changes are due to rapid processes.	
GLE SC.D.1.2.5.3.1	knows that land forms change over time (for example, earthquakes, volcanoes).	**TFK FCAT:** Issue 3, 6, 8
Standard 2: The student understands the need for protection of the natural systems on Earth.		
Benchmark SC.D.2.2.1	The student knows that reusing, recycling, and reducing the use of natural resources improve and protect the quality of life.	
GLE SC.D.2.2.1.3.1	knows that reusing, recycling, and reducing the use of natural resources improve and protect the quality of life.	**TE:** 3.1–3.3: 51A, 340J, 344-347; 3.4–3.6: 86 **TFK FCAT:** Issue 4, 11
STRAND E: EARTH AND SPACE		**Macmillan/McGraw-Hill FLORIDA TREASURES**
Standard 1: The student understands the interaction and organization in the Solar System and the universe and how this affects life on Earth.		
Benchmark SC.E.1.2.4	The student knows that the planets differ in size, characteristics, and composition and that they orbit the Sun in our Solar System.	

Key 3.1 = Grade 3, Unit 1

GLE **SC.E.1.2.4.3.1**	knows characteristics of Mercury, Venus, Earth, and Mars.	**TE:** 3.1–3.3: 228-247; **TFK FCAT:** Issue 12
Benchmark **SC.E.1.2.5**	The student understands the arrangement of planets in our Solar System.	
GLE **SC.E.1.2.5.3.1**	knows the relative positions of all the planets	**TE:** 3.1–3.3: 228-247
Benchmark **SC.E.2.2.1**	The student knows that, in addition to the Sun, there are many other stars that are far away.	
GLE **SC.E.2.2.1.3.1**	knows that, in addition to the Sun, there are many other stars that are far away.	**TE:** 3.1–3.3: 224J; **TFK FCAT:** Issue 5
STRAND F: PROCESSES OF LIFE		**Macmillan/McGraw-Hill FLORIDA TREASURES**
Standard 1: The student describes patterns of structure and function in living things.		
Benchmark **SC.F.1.2.1**	The student knows that the human body is made of systems with structures and functions that are related.	**TE:** 3.1–3.3: 352J, 3.4–3.6: 257
Benchmark **SC.F.1.2.2**	The student knows how all animals depend on plants.	
GLE **SC.F.1.2.2.3.1**	understands the various ways that animals depend on plants for survival (for example, food, shelter, oxygen).	**TE:** 3.1–3.3: 116J, 134, 145; **TFK FCAT:** Issue 8, 11
Benchmark **SC.F.1.2.3**	The student knows that living things are different but share similar structures.	
GLE **SC.F.1.2.3.3.1**	knows the common and distinguishing characteristics of groups of vertebrate animals (mammals, birds, fish, reptiles, amphibians).	**TE:** 3.1–3.3: 86J, 116J, 145, 178J, 206-209, 340J, 3.4–3.6: 257, 358J, 384J; **TFK FCAT:** Issue 5, 6, 8, 11
GLE **SC.F.1.2.3.3.2**	understands similarities and differences among plants.	**TE:** 3.1–3.3: 10S, 49, 74J, 394; 3.4–3.6 43
GLE **SC.F.1.2.3.3.3**	understands that although plants and animals are different, they also share common characteristics (for example, they both have structures for reproduction, respiration, and growth).	**TE:** 3.1–3.3: 49, 74J, 134, 3.4–3.6: 382J
STRAND G: HOW LIVING THINGS INTERACT WITH THEIR ENVIRONMENT		**Macmillan/McGraw-Hill FLORIDA TREASURES**
Standard 1: The student understands the competitive, interdependent, cyclic nature of living things in the environment.		
Benchmark **SC.G.1.2.2**	The student knows that living things compete in a climatic region with other living things and that structural adaptations make them fit for an environment.	
GLE **SC.G.1.2.2.3.1**	knows how organisms with similar needs in a climatic region compete with one another for resources such as food, water, oxygen, or space.	**TE:** 3.1–3.3: 78-81, 88-89, 91-109, 116J; 3.4–3.6: 82-85, 262-263, 264-279 285P, 285R, 285T, 386-387; **LR:** 3.1 Week 4: *The Weddell Seals of Antarctica,* 3.3 Week 3: *Water in the Desert,* 3.5 Week 5: *Amazing Bird Builders*
GLE **SC.G.1.2.2.3.2**	knows behavioral and structural adaptations that allow plants and animals to survive in an environment.	**TE:** 3.1–3.3: 78-81, 88-89, 91-109, 116J, 209, 3.4–3.6: 262-263, 264-279 285P, 285R, 285T, 322J, 323, 383P, 383R, 383T, 386-387; **LR:** 3.1 Week 4: *The Weddell Seals of Antarctica,* 3.3 Week 3: *Water in the Desert,* ,3.5 Week 5: *Amazing Bird Builders*
Benchmark **SC.G.1.2.5**	The student knows that animals eat plants or other animals to acquire the energy they need for survival.	
GLE **SC.G.1.2.5.3.1**	understands that energy is transferred to living organisms through the food they eat.	**TE:** 3.1–3.3: 49 , 282S, 352J
Standard 2: The student understands the consequences of using limited natural resources.		
Benchmark **SC.G.2.2.1**	The student knows that all living things must compete for Earth's limited resources; organisms best adapted to compete for the available resources will be successful and pass their adaptations (traits) to their offspring.	
GLE **SC.G.2.2.1.3.1**	understands that plants and animals share and compete for limited resources such as oxygen, water, food, and space.	**TE:** 3.1–3.3: 49, 78-81, 91-109, 209; 3.4-3.6: 390, 397, 3.4–3.6: 390, 397 LR: 3.1 Week 3: *Saving the Rainforest,* 3.4 Week 3: *Resources All Around Us,* 3.6 Week 5: *Purple Loosestrife*; **TFK FCAT:** Issue 4, 5, 8, 9, 11
Benchmark **SC.G.2.2.2**	The student knows that the size of a population is dependent upon the available resources within its community.	
GLE **SC.G.2.2.2.3.1**	knows that the size of a population is dependent upon the available resources within its community.	**TE:** 3.1–3.3: 49, 78-81, 91-109, 340J; 3.4–3.6: 383P, 383R, 383T; **TFK FCAT:** Issue 4, 9

FLORIDA Correlations

Benchmark SC.G.2.2.3	The student understands that changes in the habitat of an organism may be beneficial or harmful.	**TE:** 3.1–3.3: 78-81, 91-109, 342-343, 348; 3.4–3.6: 78J, 82-85, 362-377
STRAND H: THE NATURE OF SCIENCE		**Macmillan/McGraw-Hill FLORIDA TREASURES**
Standard 1: The student uses the scientific processes and habits of mind to solve problems.		
Benchmark SC.H.1.2.2	The student knows that a successful method to explore the natural world is to observe and record, and then analyze and communicate the results.	**LR:** 3.6 **Week 4:** *Jane Goodall: Life Among the Chimpanzees*
GLE SC.H.1.2.2.3.1	plans and investigates an experiment that defines a problem, proposes a solution, identifies variables, collects and organizes data, interprets data in tables, charts and graphs, analyzes information, makes predictions, and presents and supports findings.	**TE:** 3.1–3.3: 152H, 224J
GLE SC.H.1.2.2.3.2	uses various kinds of instruments to collect and analyze information (for example, meter sticks, timing devices, graduated cylinders, force meters, pan balances, calipers, microscopes, cameras, sound recorders, hot plates, magnets, collecting nets).	**TE:** 3.4–3.6: 143
Benchmark SC.H.1.2.3	The student knows that to work collaboratively, all team members should be free to reach, explain, and justify their own individual conclusions.	
GLE SC.H.1.2.3.3.1	knows that to work collaboratively, all team members should be free to reach, explain, and justify their own individual conclusions.	**TE:** 3.1–3.3: 103, 209
Benchmark SC.H.1.2.4	The student knows that to compare and contrast observations and results is an essential skill in science.	
GLE SC.H.1.2.4.3.1	knows that to compare and contrast observations and results is an essential skill in science.	**TE:** 3.1–3.3: 35, 134, 145, 209, 224J, 394
Benchmark SC.H.1.2.5	The student knows that a model of something is different from the real thing, but can be used to learn something about the real thing.	
GLE SC.H.1.2.5.3.1	uses sketches, diagrams and models to understand scientific ideas.	**TE:** 3.1–3.3: 38J, 145, 224J, 340J, 352J, 394; 3.4–3.6: 46J, 112J
Standard 3: The student understands that science, technology, and society are interwoven and interdependent. TE: 3.4–3.6: 290I		
Benchmark SC.H.3.2.1	The student understands that people, alone or in groups, invent new tools to solve problems and do work that affects aspects of life outside of science.	**TFK FCAT:** Issue 7
GLE SC.H.3.2.1.3.1	understands the relationships between science concepts and the history of science and the contributions of scientists.	**TE:** 3.1–3.3: 214-215, 223A, 224J, 239; 3.4–3.6: 184J, 217P, 217R, 217T, 290H, 290I, 385; **TFK FCAT:** Issue 7
GLE SC.H.3.2.1.3.2	uses reference materials to obtain information related to science concepts.	**TE:** 3.1–3.3: 10S, 38J, 49, 74J, 86J, 103, 116J, 134, 152H, 152S, 178J, 209, 212J, 224J, 239, 253, 256J, 270, 282S, 352J; 3.4–3.6: 10I, 10S, 43, 46J, 78J, 89A, 90J, 112J, 150S, 184J, 218J, 230J, 257, 260J, 290I, 290S, 322J, 323, 343, 346J, 358J, 384J, 397
Benchmark SC.H.3.2.2	The student knows that data are collected and interpreted in order to explain an event or concept.	
GLE SC.H.3.2.2.3.1	knows that data are collected and interpreted in order to explain an event or concept.	**TE:** 3.1–3.3: 10S, 38J, 49, 74J, 86J, 103, 116J, 134, 152H, 209, 224J, 239, 253, 282S; 3.4–3.6: 10I, 10S, 43, 46J, 78J, 89A, 90J, 112J, 143, 150S, 184J, 218J, 290I, 322J, 343, 358J, 397
GLE SC.H.3.2.2.3.2	understands that scientific information can be presented in several ways (for example, using numbers and mathematics, drawings, words, graphs, tables).	**TE:** 3.1–3.3: 10S, 38J, 49, 74J, 86J, 103, 116J, 134, 152H, 209, 224J, 239, 253, 282S; 3.4–3.6: 10I, 10S, 43, 46J, 78J, 89A, 90J, 112J, 143, 150S, 184J, 218J, 290I, 322J, 343, 358J, 397
Benchmark SC.H.3.2.4	The student knows that, through the use of science processes and knowledge, people can solve problems, make decisions, and form new ideas.	
GLE SC.H.3.2.4.3.1	knows that, through the use of science processes and knowledge, people can solve problems, make decisions, and form new ideas.	**TE:** 3.1–3.3: 116J, 145, 152H, 216-219, 224J, 239, 253, 340J, 342-343, 344-347, 351A, 3.4–3.6: 10I, 43, 184J, 217P, 217R, 217T, 290H, 290I, 316-319 **TFK FCAT:** Issue 2, 3, 4, 7, 8

Key 3.1 = Grade 3, Unit 1

Social Studies
Sunshine State Standards Grade 3

Each standard is coded in the following manner

SS.	A.	1.	1.	1.	3.	1.
Subject	Strand	Standard	Level	Benchmark	Grade	Grade Level Expectation Number (GLE)

KEY	TE = Teacher's Edition	LR = Leveled Readers	TFK FCAT = Time for Kids FCAT Edition	FCAT Test Prep = FCAT Test Prep and Practice

STRAND A: TIME, CONTINUITY, AND CHANGE (HISTORY)		Macmillan/McGraw-Hill FLORIDA TREASURES
Standard 1: The student understands historical chronology and the historical perspective.		
Benchmark SS.A.1.2.1	The student understands how individuals, ideas, decisions, and events can influence history.	
GLE SS.A.1.2.1.3.1	understands ways selected individuals, ideas, and decisions influenced historical events (for example, in ancient times).	**TE:** 3.1–3.3: 282H, 350-353, 358J 3.4–3.6: 184J, 215, 230J, 346J **LR:** 3.5 Week 2: *Bright Ideas: Inventions That Changed History;* **TFK FCAT:** Issue 12
Benchmark SS.A.1.2.2	The student uses a variety of methods and sources to understand history (e.g., interpreting diaries, letters, newspapers; and reading maps and graphs) and knows the difference between primary and secondary sources.	**TE:** 3.1–3.3: 71, 85A, 152H, 224J, 282H, 282S, 3.4–3.6: 69, 175, 181, 191, 208, 215, 230J, 260J, 307, 322J, 328, 346J, 358J, 384J, 397
GLE SS.A.1.2.2.3.1	knows sources of information about ancient history (for example, books, magazines, documents at the school and community library, Internet sites about ancient history).	**TE:** 3.4–3.6: 175
Benchmark SS.A.1.2.3	The student understands broad categories of time in years, decades, and centuries.	
GLE SS.A.1.2.3.3.1	reads and interprets a single timeline identifying the order of events (for example, in ancient times).	**TE:** 3.1–3.3: 68, 69, 70, 71, 215, 239, 282I; 3.4–3.6: 148-149
Standard 2: The student understands the world from its beginnings to the time of the Renaissance.		
Benchmark SS.A.2.2.1	The student knows the significant scientific and technological achievements of various societies (e.g., the invention of paper in China, Mayan calendars, mummification and the use of cotton in Egypt, astronomical discoveries in the Muslim world, and the Arabic number system).	**TE:** 3.1–3.3: 282H, 381, 386, 417P, 417R, 417T **TFK FCAT:** Issue 3, 7, 12, 13
GLE SS.A.2.2.1.3.1	knows significant scientific and technological achievements of various societies (for example, bow and arrow, pottery, Egyptian pyramids).	**TFK FCAT:** Issue 2, 7, 12
Benchmark SS.A.2.2.2	The student understands developments in transportation and communication in various societies (e.g., the development of extensive road systems in various cultures, the difficulties of travel and communication encountered by people of various culture, the origins and changes in writing and how these changes made communication between people more effective).	**TFK FCAT:** Issue 12
GLE SS.A.2.2.2.3.2	understands the origins and changes in methods of writing prior to the Renaissance (for example, pictographs, cuneiform, hieroglyphics, alphabets).	**TE:** 3.1–3.3: 386, 417P, 417R, 417T
GLE SS.A.2.2.2.3.3	understands ways changes in transportation and communication affected the lives of people prior to the Renaissance.	**TE:** 3.1–3.3: 214-215, 386, 417P, 417R, 417T
Benchmark SS.A.2.2.3	The student understands various aspects of family life, structures, and roles in different cultures and in many eras (e.g., pastoral and agrarian families of early civilizations, families of ancient times, and medieval families).	
GLE SS.A.2.2.3.3.1	knows aspects of family life found in many eras (for example, in prehistory, ancient civilizations).	**TE:** 3.4–3.6: 66, 130
Benchmark SS.A.2.2.4	The student understands the emergence of different laws and systems of government (e.g., monarchy and republic).	
GLE SS.A.2.2.4.3.1	understands the emergence throughout history of different laws and systems of government (for example, monarchy, republic).	**TFK FCAT:** Issue 9
Benchmark SS.A.2.2.5	The student understands significant achievements in the humanities to the time of the Renaissance (e.g., Roman architecture and Greek art).	**TFK FCAT:** Issue 9

GLE SS.A.2.2.5.3.1	knows selected cultural and intellectual achievements of various early and ancient civilizations.	**TE:** 3.4–3.6: 66; **TFK FCAT:** Issue 10
Standard 3: The student understands Western and Eastern civilization since the Renaissance.		
Benchmark SS.A.3.2.1	The student knows significant people and their contributions in the field of communication and technology (e.g., inventors of various nonelectronic and electronic communication devices such as the steam engine and the television) and the impact of these devices on society.	
GLE SS.A.3.2.1.3.1	knows selected significant people and the impact of their achievements in world in the fields of communication and technology since the Renaissance.	**TE:** 3.1–3.3: 282H; **TFK FCAT:** Issue 1, 3, 7 **LR:** 3.2 Week 3: *Incredible Inventions: Everyday Wonders*
GLE SS.A.3.2.1.3.2	understands ways these devices impacted society.	**TFK FCAT:** Issue 1, 3, 7; **LR:** 3.2 Week 3: *Incredible Inventions: Everyday Wonders*
Benchmark SS.A.3.2.2	The student knows developments in the humanities since the Renaissance (e.g., Renaissance architecture, Japanese and Chinese influences on art, the impact of literary and theatrical development during the Renaissance, changes in music including opera and ballet, and major movements in the arts in 19th-century Europe).	
GLE SS.A.3.2.2.3.1	knows selected developments in the humanities since the Renaissance.	**LR:** 3.3 Week 5: *Old and New: Painting Through Time*
Standard 5: The student understands the United States history from 1880 to the present day.		
Benchmark SS.A.5.2.1	The student knows that after the Civil War, massive immigration, big business, and mechanized farming transformed American life.	**TE:** 3.4–3.6: 316-319
Benchmark SS.A.5.2.4	The student understands social and cultural transformations of the 1920s and 1930s.	**TE:** 3.1–3.3: 85A, 3.4–3.6: 148-149
Benchmark SS.A.5.2.7	The student knows the economic, political, and social transformations that have taken place in the United States since World War II.	**TE:** 3.1–3.3: 38J, 46, 82-83, 270
Standard 6: The student understands the history of Florida and its people.		
Benchmark SS.A.6.2.3	The student knows the significant individuals, events, and social, political, and economic characteristics of different periods in Florida's history.	**TE:** 3.4–3.6: 316-319
STRAND B: PEOPLE, PLACES, AND ENVIROMENTS (GEOGRAPHY)		**Macmillan/McGraw-Hill FLORIDA TREASURES**
Standard 1: The student understands the world in spatial terms.		
Benchmark SS.B.1.2.1	The students uses maps, globes, charts, graphs, and other geographic tools including map keys and symbols to gather and interpret data and to draw conclusions about physical patterns.	
GLE SS.B.1.2.1.3.1	uses maps and globes to locate and compare places and their environments (for example, oceans, river systems, continents, islands, mountains in or near areas where civilizations developed).	**TE:** 3.1–3.3: 352J; 3.4–3.6: 191
Benchmark SS.B.1.2.2	The student knows how regions are constructed according to physical criteria and human criteria.	
GLE SS.B.1.2.2.1	knows how regions around the world are constructed according to physical criteria and human criteria.	**TE:** 3.1–3.3: 77, 86J, 88-89, 91-109 3.4–3.6: 188-209, 212-215, 397; **TFK FCAT:** Issue 10
Benchmark SS.B.1.2.5	The student knows ways in which people view and relate to places and regions differently.	
GLE SS.B.1.2.5.3.1	knows different ways people view and relate to places and regions throughout the world.	**TE:** 3.1–3.3: 10S, 314J; 3.4–3.6: 188-209; **TFK FCAT:** Issue 1, 3
Standard 2: The student understands the interactions of people and the physical environment.		
Benchmark SS.B.2.2.3	The student understands how human activity affects the physical environment.	
GLE SS.B.2.2.3.1	understands ways human activity has affected the physical environment in various places and times throughout the world.	**TE:** 3.1–3.3: 340J, 342-343, 344-347, 348; 3.4–3.6: 78J, 80-81, 82-85, 86, 89A, 89P, 89R, 89T, 386-387, 388-396, 397, 403P, 403R, 403T TFK FCAT: Issue 1, 10
STRAND C: GOVERNMENT AND THE CITIZEN (CIVICS AND GOVERNMENT)		**Macmillan/McGraw-Hill FLORIDA TREASURES**
Standard 1: The student understands the structure, functions, and purposes of government and how the principles and values of American democracy are reflected in American constitutional government.		
Benchmark SS.C.1.2.4	The student knows possible consequences of the absence of government, rules, and laws.	
GLE SS.C.1.2.4.3.1	understands the benefits of the development of government (for example, in ancient civilizations).	**TFK FCAT:** Issue 9
Standard 2: The student understands the role of the citizen in American democracy.		

Key 3.1 = Grade 3, Unit 1

Benchmark SS.C.2.2.1	The student understands the importance of participation through community service, civic improvement, and political activities.	**TE:** 3.1–3.3: 74J; 3.4–3.6: 90J, 94-105, 290S, 291
Benchmark SS.C.2.2.2	The student understands why personal responsibility (e.g., taking advantage of the opportunity to be educated) and civic responsibility (e.g., obeying the law and respecting the rights of others) are important.	
GLE SS.C.2.2.2.3.1	understands ways personal responsibility (for example, taking advantage of the opportunity to be educated) and civic responsibility (for example, obeying the law and respecting the rights of others) are important.	**TE:** 3.1–3.3: 311; 3.4–3.6: 347, 347A, 348-349 **LR:** 3.4 Week 4: *On Patching a Playground;* 3.6 Week 3: *Getting Out the Vote* **TFK FCAT:** Issue 1, 3, 15

STRAND D: PRODUCTION, DISTRIBUTION, AND CONSUMPTION (ECONOMICS)		Macmillan/McGraw-Hill FLORIDA TREASURES
Standard 1: The student understands how scarcity requires individuals and institutions to make choices about how to use resources.		
Benchmark SS.D.1.2.1	The student understands that all decisions involve opportunity costs and that making effective decisions involves considering the costs and the benefits associated with alternative choices.	**TE:** 3.4–3.6: 181 **LR:** 3.5 Week 1: *Start Your Own Business!*
Benchmark SS.D.1.2.5	The student understands the concept of earning income and the basic concept of a budget.	**TE:** 3.4–3.6: 151S, 178-181, 182P 183R, 183T
Standard 2: The student understands the characteristics of different economic systems and institutions.		
Benchmark SS.D.2.2.2	The student understands the roles that money plays in a market economy.	
GLE SS.D.2.2.2.3.1	understands the role that money played in the development of ancient civilizations.	**TFK FCAT:** Issue 2

Mathematics
Sunshine State Standards Grade 3

Each standard is coded in the following manner

MA.	A.	1.	1.	1.	3.	1.
Subject	Strand	Standard	Level	Benchmark	Grade	Grade Level Expectation Number (GLE)

KEY	TE = Teacher's Edition	LR = Leveled Readers	TFK FCAT = Time for Kids FCAT Edition	FCAT Test Prep = FCAT Test Prep and Practice

STRAND A: NUMBER SENSE, CONCEPTS, AND OPERATIONS		Macmillan/McGraw-Hill FLORIDA TREASURES
Standard 1: The student understands the different ways numbers are represented and used in the real world.		
Benchmark MA.A.1.2.1	The student names whole numbers combining 3-digit numeration (hundreds, tens, ones) and the use of number periods, such as ones, thousands, and millions and associates verbal names, written word names, and standard numerals with whole numbers, commonly used fractions, decimals, and percents.	
GLE MA.A.3.2.2.3.2	uses problem-solving strategies to determine the operation needed to solve one-step problems involving addition, subtraction, multiplication, and division of whole numbers.	**TE:** 3.1–3.3: 152I, 167, 376
GLE MA.A.3.2.3.3.1	solves real-world problems involving addition, subtraction, multiplication, and division of whole numbers using an appropriate method (for example, mental math, paper and pencil, concrete materials, calculator).	**TE:** 3.1–3.3: 167, 239

STRAND B: MEASUREMENT		Macmillan/McGraw-Hill FLORIDA TREASURES
Standard 1: The student measures quantities in the real world and uses the measures to solve problems.		
Benchmark MA.B.1.2.1	The student uses concrete and graphic models to develop procedures for solving problems related to measurement including length, weight, time, temperature, perimeter, area, volume, and angle.	
GLE MA.A.1.2.1.3.3	knows about measurement of time including using A.M. and P.M., clocks and calendars.	**TE:** 3.1–3.3: 16, 31, 3.4–3.6: 178, 180, 181
Benchmark MA.B.1.2.2	The student solves real-world problems involving length, weight, perimeter, area, capacity, volume, time, temperature, and angles.	

GLE MA.A.1.2.2.3.3	uses schedules, calendars, and elapsed time in hour intervals to solve real-world problems.	TE: 3.1–3.3: 16, 3.4–3.6: 178, 180, 181
Standard 2: The student compares, contrasts, and converts within systems of measurement (both standard/nonstandard and metric/customary).		
Benchmark MA.B.2.2.1	The student uses direct (measured) and indirect (not measured) measures to calculate and compare measurable characteristics.	TE: 3.1–3.3: 303; TE: 3.4–3.6: 128
Standard 4: The student selects and uses appropriate units and instruments for measurement to achieve the degree of precision and accuracy required in real-world situations.		
Benchmark MA.B.4.2.1	The student determines which units of measurement, such as seconds, square inches, dollars per tankful, to use with answers to real-world problems.	
GLE MA.B.4.2.1.3.1	selects an appropriate measurement unit for labeling the solution to real-world problems.	TE: 3.1–3.3: 303
Benchmark MA.B.4.2.2	The student selects and uses appropriate instruments and technology, including scales, rulers, thermometers, measuring cups, protractors, and gauges, to measure in real-world situations.	
GLE MA.B.4.2.2.3.1	selects and uses the appropriate tool for situational measures (for example, measuring sticks, scales and balances, thermometers, measuring cups).	TE: 3.4–3.6: 25
STRAND C: GEOMETRY AND SPATIAL SENSE		**Macmillan/McGraw-Hill FLORIDA TREASURES**
Standard 1: The student describes, draws, identifies, and analyzes two- and three-dimensional shapes.		
Benchmark MA.C.1.2.1	The student given a verbal description, draws and/or models two- and three-dimensional shapes and uses appropriate geometric vocabulary to write a description of a figure or a picture composed of geometric figures.	
GLE MA.C.1.2.1.3.2	draws and classifies two-dimensional figures having up to six or more sides.	TE: 3.4–3.6: 64, 267
Standard 3: The student uses coordinate geometry to locate objects in both two and three dimensions and to describe objects algebraically.		
Benchmark MA.C.3.2.2	The student identifies and plots positive ordered pairs (whole numbers) in a rectangular coordinate system (graph).	
GLE MA.C.3.2.2.3.1	knows how to identify, locate, and plot ordered pairs of whole numbers on a graph.	TE: 3.1–3.3: 394
STRAND D: ALGEBRAIC THINKING		**Macmillan/McGraw-Hill FLORIDA TREASURES**
Standard 2: The student uses expressions, equations, inequalities, graphs, and formulas to represent and interpret situations.		
Benchmark MA.D.2.2.1	The student represents a given simple problem situation using diagrams, models, and symbolic expressions translated from verbal phrases, or verbal phrases translated from symbolic expressions, etc.	
GLE MA.D.2.2.1.3.2	creates a simple word problem for a given number sentence, diagram, or model.	TE: 3.1–3.3: 152I, 167, 239, 303, 3.4–3.6: 376
Benchmark MA.D.2.2.2	The student uses informal methods, such as physical models and graphs to solve real-world problems involving equations and inequalities.	
GLE MA.D.2.2.2.3.1	uses physical models and graphs (for example, cubes, number lines) to solve real-world equations and inequalities.	TE: 3.1–3.3: 68-69, 71, 83
GLE MA.D.2.2.2.3.2	uses information from physical models and graphs to solve problems.	TE: 3.1–3.3: 68-69, 71, 83
STRAND E: DATA ANALYSIS AND PROBABILITY		**Macmillan/McGraw-Hill FLORIDA TREASURES**
Standard 1: The student understands and uses the tools of data analysis for managing information.		
Benchmark MA.E.1.2.1	The student solves problems by generating, collecting, organizing, displaying, and analyzing data using histograms, bar graphs, circle graphs, line graphs, pictographs, and charts.	
GLE MA.E.1.2.1.3.1	identifies different parts of a graph (for example, titles, labels, key).	TE: 3.1–3.3: 34, 35
GLE MA.E.1.2.1.3.2	interprets and compares information from picto- and bar graphs including graphs from content-area materials and periodicals.	TE: 3.1–3.3: 34, 35
GLE MA.E.1.2.1.3.3	generates questions, collects responses, and displays data in a table, pictograph or bar graph.	TE: 3.1–3.3: 34, 35, 145
GLE MA.E.1.2.1.3.4	interprets and explains orally and in writing displays of data.	TE: 3.1–3.3: 34, 35

Key 3.1 = Grade 3, Unit 1